LEGAL SKILLS

LEGAL SKILLS

FIFTH EDITION

EMILY FINCH • STEFAN FAFINSKI

OXFORD

UNIVERSITY PRESS

OXFORD
UNIVERSITY PRESS

Great Clarendon Street, Oxford, OX2 6DP,
United Kingdom

Oxford University Press is a department of the University of Oxford.
It furthers the University's objective of excellence in research, scholarship,
and education by publishing worldwide. Oxford is a registered trade mark of
Oxford University Press in the UK and in certain other countries

Second edition 2009
Third edition 2011
Fourth edition 2013

Impression: 2

Published in the United States of America by Oxford University Press
198 Madison Avenue, New York, NY 10016, United States of America

British Library Cataloguing in Publication Data
Data available

Library of Congress Control Number: 2014954270

ISBN 978–0–19–871884–0

Printed in Great Britain by
Ashford Colour Press Ltd

For STG

Legal Skills includes a range of features to help support a practical approach to learning. This guided tour shows you how to fully utilize your textbook and get the most out of your study of legal skills.

LEARNING OUTCOMES

After studying this chapter, you will be able to:

- Explain the process by which Acts of Parliament come into being
- Describe various types of delegated legislation and their functio
- Understand the roles of the various institutions of the European
- Describe the process by which European Union legislation come

Learning outcomes

Each chapter begins with a bulleted outline of the main concepts and ideas you will encounter. These serve as a useful signpost to what you can expect to learn by reading the chapter.

1.1 Domestic legislation

Legislation is a broad term which covers *statutes* (**Acts of Parliament**) and o legislation, such as **delegated** (or **subordinate**) legislation and **European Un**

Definition boxes

Key terms are highlighted in colour when they first appear and are clearly, concisely explained in definition boxes. These terms are collected in a glossary which can be found on the Online Resource Centre that accompanies this book.

 Self-test questions

5. When did the Misrepresentation Act 1967 come into force?

 Answers to the self-test questions can be found on the Online

Self-test questions

Throughout each chapter self-test questions will help you assess your understanding of key skills, concepts, and your readiness to progress to the next topic. You will find answers to all self-test questions on the Online Resource Centre that accompanies the book.

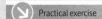 Practical exercise

Although this chapter will use a number of examples of variou which they can be used, these are no substitute for your own e and try to find as many of these example resources as you can. available in all law libraries. However, for those that are, you w layout and you will also know their location in the library whic future.

Practical exercises

When you feel confident you understand the principles underpinning each skill, it is important that you practise applying them. To help you foster a 'hands on' appreciation of legal skills practical exercises are provided throughout each chapter.

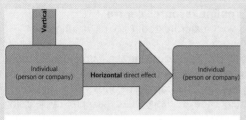

Figure 1.2 Horizontal and vertical direct effect

Diagrams and flowcharts
Numerous diagrams and flowcharts are used to provide a visual representation of concepts and processes.

Screen shots
Screen shots from important electronic databases such as LexisLibrary and Westlaw UK will help familiarize you with these vital online resources.

 CHAPTER SUMMARY

Statute law

- Public Bills are introduced by the Government as part of its programme of leg
- Private Bills are introduced for the benefit of particular individuals, groups of institutions, or a particular locality
- Hybrid Bills are a cross between Public and Private Bills
- Private Members' Bills are non-Government Bills that are introduced by priva Parliament
- Consolidating statutes re-enact a topic contained in several earlier statutes

Chapter summaries
The central points and concepts covered in each chapter are distilled into summaries providing a useful point for you to reinforce your understanding.

 FURTHER READING

- The law-making process is explained very clearly and wit parliament website at www.parliament.uk/about/how/l the reasons why new laws are needed and how they are different types of Bill, the passage of Bills through Parliar the role of secondary legislation, and the use of the Parlia

- This chapter gives a very brief overview of the EU institu come from Europe. It does not attempt to cover the subs

Further reading
Selected further reading is included at the end of chapters to provide a springboard for further study. This will help you to broaden your learning by guiding you to the key literature in the field.

online resource centre
www.oxfordtextbooks.co.uk/orc/finch5e/

The Online Resource Centre that accompanies this book provides students and lecturers with ready-to-use teaching and learning resources. They are free of charge and are designed to maximize the learning experience.

FOR STUDENTS

The following resources are accessible to all, with no registration or password required.

Web links

The UK **Statute Law Database** is the official revised edition of the primary legislation of the United Kingdom made available online
http://www.statutelaw.gov.uk

The **Office of Public Sector Information** site provides links to the full text of all UK Parliament Public General Acts (from 1988 onwards) and all Local Acts (from 1991 onwards)

Annotated web links allow you to easily research those topics that are of particular interest to you.

Glossary

BATNA (best alternative to a negotiated agreement) is an acronym used to describe the best possible outcome that will result for your client if you do not negotiate or if the negotiation fails. This will be explored in more detail in relation to negotiation strategy but needs to be taken into account at this stage because you need to know whether your case

A useful one-stop reference point for all the keywords and terms used within the text.

Answers to self-test questions
Self-test questions help you assess your own knowledge and understanding. Answers are provided, along with a commentary to help you understand how and why the correct answer was reached.

Essay writing
Advice on good essay writing practice to help you improve your writing skills in a legal context.

Problem solving
Samples of good and bad answers to problem questions are provided as marking exercises to help improve your ability to spot strengths and weaknesses in your own answers.

Exam strategy
Reference materials and practical exercises for improving your performance in exams. Answers written by students to the same question provide insight into the different approaches that can be taken to the same question; a commentary points out the strengths and weaknesses of each answer.

Mooting
Sample moots, including examples of mooting preparation plans and skeleton arguments, provide insight into the process of preparing for and participating in a moot.

Negotiation
Hints and tips for undertaking negotiation and examples of scenarios for you to practise your negotiation skills.

Presentations

A worked example of a presentation plan and examples of good practice in presentations.

Video clips

Video clips of students participating in a range of practical activities bring these skills to life and provide examples of good practice to emulate and bad practice to avoid. Clips featuring different individuals demonstrating their skills and talking about their experiences can be used to help students to overcome nerves, avoid common errors, and develop their own style.

Mooting

Watch mooting in action with clips of students at key moments of the moot demonstrating effective mooting strategies, illustrating core skills such as outlining their submissions, dealing with judicial interventions, and handling case law. The clips also give an engaging illustration of common mistakes with commentary on how to avoid them.

Presentations

Clips of student performances demonstrate the desirable and undesirable characteristics of presentations and are interspersed with comments from students on their own fears about delivering a presentation and their views on their own performances.

Negotiation

Video clips of a negotiation are interspersed with commentary on good and bad technique bringing this activity to life and providing an engaging demonstration of different negotiation styles. Comments from students about their own experiences provide helpful advice for inexperienced negotiators.

Lectures

Short lecture clips highlight the variety of ways that information can be recorded as part of an effective note-taking strategy.

FOR LECTURERS

Password protected to ensure only lecturers can access these resources.

Test bank

Which ONE of the following is the most valuable use of the *Chronological Table of the Statutes*?

- For keeping up to date with current legislation.
- For tracing the legislative history of older statutes.
- For a detailed commentary on the statutes.
- For looking at statutes on a particular topic.

1 out of 1
Correct. The *Chronological Table of the Statutes* provides historical, as well as current, information for all statutes since the Statute of Merton in 1235.
Page reference: 37

A fully customizable resource containing ready-made assessments with which to test students.

Diagrams

All of the diagrams in the textbook are available to download electronically and can be used in lectures to aid student understanding.

It's been eight years since we sat down with the metaphorical blank piece of paper—which was, in actual fact, two blank Word documents (one each)—to write *Legal Skills*. It was, oddly, a project that sort of happened by accident: a story with which we will bore you some other time. Anyway, we certainly never envisaged that we would, one day, sit down to write the preface to the fifth edition. At least we didn't have to start with two blank Word documents, but instead, the editable version of the fourth edition and an instruction to 'Track Changes'.[1] This has illustrated just how much the book has evolved and changed since the first edition published in 2007.[2] Much of this has, of course, resulted from amendments to the law, recognition of the ever-changing needs of students, and the way in which legal research is done in practice (with an inevitable shift towards online research and away from the traditional law libraries—certainly for 'mainstream' materials). However, the majority of enhancements have been direct responses to feedback from students and fellow lecturers together with the anonymous reviewers for each edition who always provide such constructive and useful feedback. As such, we would like to thank everyone who has commented on the first four editions—in whatever way. We hope that the changes that we have made for this new edition both reflect your comments and make the book better as a result. We really do rely on your thoughts and observations to keep the book useful and relevant, so do please contact us if you think that there are particular parts that are superfluous, missing, not to your liking, unclear, or (even) wrong. You can email us at hello@finchandfafinski.com, visit our website at www.finchandfafinski.com, or tweet at @FinchFafinski. Particular thanks for this edition to Jenna Jiggens, Law Librarian at St Mary's University College Twickenham for getting in touch and ultimately reviewing the bits concerning law librarians and why students really should befriend theirs as an often-untapped source of splendid information and advice, and to someone we only actually know by their Twitter handle of @marginview who pointed out quite a few points in the fourth edition which benefitted from a bit of clarification this time around. Whoever you are, well spotted and thanks for getting in touch.

One of the other things that have changed in this edition is the personnel involved. Not us, as authors, though. We're nowhere near rich and famous—or deceased—enough to have a ghost-writer doing this stuff. One day, but not right now. We mean, of course, our colleagues at OUP. We were supported throughout the third and fourth editions by Helen Davis who then worked in Central America for a bit and is now at the British Red Cross.[3] We really hope everything is going well for her. We worked on *Employability Skills for Law Students*[4] with Helen, who handed over to Joanna Williams for the later stages of that project. We were delighted to find out that Jo would be our editor for this fifth edition. As Jo is new to this title, she's brought a new perspective to everything and has really helped us to freshen up this latest edition. With Jo's help, the writing process

---

1. Word has a propensity to crash horribly and lose us some work if we try to change too much—even on a spanking new iMac with 32Gb of memory—but we've persevered. And got into the habit of saving very, very frequently indeed. Do the same with your coursework, just in case.
2. As well as the means of updating, which literally used to involve physical cutting and pasting and the liberal use of red pen.
3. Working with us and fleeing half way round the world were in no way related. We do, however, like to think that working with us gave Helen demonstrable skills in dealing with crisis situations which perhaps helped her get the job with the Red Cross.
4. A companion volume to this one, which deals with developing and demonstrating skills in an employment context (like Helen did). Have a look sometime. It's never too early to start.

for this edition has been pretty straightforward and, perhaps for the first time in our writing careers, we are handing the title over to production in time. Jo—don't get used to it.

Our thanks also to Hannah Marsden and Amar Pannu for managing the production process, Nick Wehmeier for keeping the ORC resources up together, Fiona Tatham our copy editor, and the ever-present and slightly mad John Martin, indexer.

We remain, as always, grateful to Professor Rosemary Pattenden who came up with the initial proposal for *Legal Skills*, Sarah Viner who commissioned the book and worked incredibly hard with us on the first and second editions, and to the many reviewers who were involved throughout all the stages of the first edition for their insightful and invaluable feedback:

> Nicola Aries, Kingston University
> Vanessa Bettinson, De Montfort University
> Jo Boylan-Kemp, Nottingham Trent University
> Tim Conner, Bradford University Law School
> Lynn Cousins, Leeds Law School, Leeds Metropolitan University
> Amy Croft, Kingston University
> Cath Crosby, University of Teesside
> Dr Haydn Davies, University of Central England
> Dennis Dowding, Bournemouth University
> Professor Kim Economides, University of Exeter
> Dr Martina Gillen, Oxford Brookes University
> Beverley Hopkins, University of Central England
> Matthew Humphreys, University of Surrey
> Nicola Isaacs, University of Plymouth
> Robert Jago, University of Surrey
> Neil Kibble, University of Wales, Aberystwyth
> Lesley Lomax, Sheffield Hallam University
> Dr Claire McGourlay, University of Sheffield
> Jeanette Porteous, University of Lincoln
> Dr Sue Prince, University of Exeter
> Stephanie Roberts, University of Westminster
> Dr Charlotte Smith, University of Reading
> Dr Rhiannon Talbot, Newcastle University
> Andy Vi-Ming Kok, Staffordshire University
> Roger Welch, University of Portsmouth
> Tony Wragg, University of Derby

Titles and affiliations are as they were at publication of the first edition.

Finally: Chris, Trish, Tom, Becky, Johnno, Jennifer, Alison, Philippa, Sue, Alan, Peter, Scrap and Fraggle.[5] Thank you.

Emily & Stef
September 2014

---

5. List of friends and creatures is non-exhaustive. If you know us and think you should have been thanked, sorry. Consider yourself included (and thanked).

- New section on improving your written work and moving marks across grade boundaries from 2:2 to a 2:1 and 2:1 to first class
- New section containing a structured approach to evaluating source material
- Expanded discussion of how to cite case law correctly
- New section on the use and application of Turnitin in the context of avoiding plagiarism
- Further clarification on citing statutory instruments
- Further emphasis and detail on online searching for legal resources
- Refreshed section on navigating an Act of Parliament with examples from the Anti-social Behaviour, Crime and Policing Act 2014
- Updated examples of possible dissertation topics and research questions
- References to EU Treaty Article numbers have been updated to take account of the renumbering effected by the Treaty of Lisbon
- References to the courts system and hierarchy now reflect the establishment of the new single County Court and single Family Court that came into effect on 22 April 2014
- Fully revised chapter on mooting with new problem

OUTLINE CONTENTS

DETAILED CONTENTS

Part III Practical legal skills

The cover of the first edition of *Legal Skills* featured armbands on a beach; the second edition continued the swimming theme with a rubber ring on the ocean; the third had a rescue buoy on a ship's rail and the fourth edition has a lifebelt being thrown to someone in distress. This fifth edition continues the lifebelt theme. Why do we have this strange obsession with floatation devices? Simply because the aim of *Legal Skills* is to provide you with the same sort of life-saving resource that will keep you afloat during your legal studies. The reason that we enjoy the images dates back to a question that was asked of one of us several years ago when we were putting together the very first edition: 'Why do you make such a fuss about skills? These students are at university. They ought to know how to study by now.' Our answer is that, yes, perhaps students *ought* to know how to write, reference, structure an argument, and do all the other things that are necessary to study the law effectively but if they don't know then it seems a bit unkind and unfair not to help them to develop the necessary skills. The swimming parallel that we make is that people *ought* to be able to swim but if they can't then it isn't really fair to push them overboard in the middle of the ocean. Why not? Because they are going to drown! Neither of us is willing to stand by and watch students drown in front of us simply because they have never been taught the skills that were once considered part of basic education and which are so necessary to engage in the study of the law. Of course this book covers a host of other skills as well.

The idea behind *Legal Skills* is that there should be a book that you can consult to find out how to do the things that you need to be able to do in order to study the law, to perform effectively in assessment, to complete your law degree successfully, and either to prepare you for the professional stages of legal education and a career in the legal profession or an alternative career which makes the very best of the portfolio of skills you have developed throughout your legal studies. The skills that we cover in the book are important because it is not enough for you just to know the content of the law: to succeed, you must be able to find the law, explain it using appropriate language, criticize it and, most importantly, *think* about it. You should be able to find out what the law once was and speculate about how it might develop in the future. If all that was required was knowledge of the law, you would probably be assessed exclusively by multiple choice questions or encouraged to write bullet point lists in answer to essay questions. The methods of assessment used in law—predominantly essays and problem questions—are selected because they can only be completed successfully if you both *know* the law and are able to *use* it: precisely what you will be required to do if you wish to go into practice.

The first part of *Legal Skills* covers sources of law. This section of the book will enable you to understand where the law comes from, how to find it (in print and online), how to understand it, and how to use it. This focus means that there is some overlap in terms of content with textbooks on the English Legal System. This overlap occurs because understanding matters such as hierarchy of the courts, the operation of precedent, and the way that judges interpret the law are essential both to learning about legal systems (hence their coverage in an English Legal System textbook) and also to studying the law (which is why we cover them in *Legal Skills*). Our coverage of these issues is slanted towards a practical purpose: you need to know where the law comes from and how it is applied and interpreted in order to incorporate it into your coursework and exam answers. It is also the case that you will be expected to know these things by the time you enter into legal practice. As such, although there is this clear crossover with the academic study of how the legal system works, the ability to find and understand the law is an essential practical legal skill.

In the second part of the book, the focus shifts to academic legal skills. As you will see, the bulk of the chapters relate to improving your performance in assessment. This section of the book starts, however, with a consideration of study skills so the aim here is to help you to strengthen the way that you go about the everyday business of learning the law. Even if you are confident that you have already developed an effective approach to studying, it will be worth looking through this chapter as you may find some tips that will help you to study in an even more effective manner. This chapter also contains a section on personal development planning. The chapter on writing skills is there since the ability to use language effectively is an essential skill for a lawyer. It is therefore of the utmost importance that you take time to learn how to construct a grammatical sentence now: not only will failure to use language correctly impact adversely on the marks that you receive in assessment, it is highly unlikely that prospective employers will bother to pursue an application that contains fundamental errors in the use of written language. There is a comprehensive chapter on referencing and avoiding plagiarism which reflects the concern that surrounds these issues: fear of being accused of plagiarism as a consequence of poor referencing is something that preoccupies many students. The chapter on legal reasoning is designed to help you engage with the law in more critical depth and to lead you to understand that judicial decision making is not just about the unthinking blind application of a set of rules. The essay-writing chapter contains much advice on structuring an essay and putting together effective introductions and conclusions; areas which students have told us they find particularly troubling. It also gives practical guidance on how to improve your performance and move your marks across grade boundaries. The chapter on problem solving aims to provide a step-by-step guide to this important activity. The chapter on dissertations acknowledges that the dissertation is more than a long essay: it is a challenging combination of research and writing skills that deserves separate focus over and above essay writing. The final chapter in the academic skills section of the book focuses on revision and exams. Our experience in working with students towards exams suggests that a great many students approach revision without a clear idea of what they are trying to achieve other than simply to 'pass the exam'. We have sought to make a range of practical suggestions that will introduce variety into the revision process whilst ensuring that you will emerge at the end with a store of knowledge and a clear insight into how you might use this knowledge once you get into the exam room.

The final section of the book deals with the use of the law in three practical situations: presentations, mooting, and negotiation. The predominant means of assessment used at university is in written form but these activities are focused on your ability to present an oral argument. Presentation skills are important for everyone. It does not matter whether or not you intend to practise the sort of law that will involve appearances in court or, indeed, whether you intend to practise law at all: in most professions, the ability to deliver a clear and coherent presentation or simply to speak with confidence in front of others is highly valued. Mooting is also an important activity. Not only will it enhance your ability to research and analyze the law as well as developing your skills of oral presentation, it is also something that prospective employers are keen to see and there is a strong expectation that you should find opportunities to moot during your undergraduate studies. Despite the importance with which mooting is viewed, not all institutions teach students how to moot so we have aimed to create a guide that will take you through each of the stages involved in preparing for a moot and delivering your submissions. Negotiation is a core legal skill due to the ever-increasing importance of alternative dispute resolution. Although we argue that we are all instinctive negotiators, there is still much that we can do to develop this natural skill so the advice in the final chapter of the book is aimed at helping you to become more proficient in seeking creative ways to reach a solution that keeps both parties to the dispute happy and out of the courtroom.

Throughout the book, we place a great deal of emphasis on practical activities. This is because we believe that people learn by doing things rather than by reading about doing things. After all, you wouldn't expect to be able to drive a car (safely) just because you had read a book that told you how to do it: you would expect to have to practise to build up the skills that you need. The same is true with your legal studies. The skills needed to find the law, extrapolate the key points, and craft them into a well-structured and focused essay or answer to a problem question are practical skills. The process of committing the law to memory, extracting it on demand, and using it to formulate a comprehensive and analytical essay under tight time constraints is a practical one. Most of the skills covered in this book are practical and require you to do something. For this reason, there is a range of practical activities for you to try out on the Online Resource Centre.

As a closing point, we want to emphasize that our aim when we set out to write *Legal Skills* was to produce the sort of book that we would have wanted when we were undergraduate law students. Our aim is to create a book that answers every question that a law student could possibly want to ask about the business of studying the law and so we have tried to ensure that we have addressed as many of the points that students have asked us to explain to them over the years as we can—and to each of them, we are very grateful.

Of course, even after five editions, it is inevitable that we will still have missed something, so if you have a question that is not answered by *Legal Skills*, think that there is something that could benefit from a bit more explanation, or something that you would really like to see (or not see) in a future edition, then get in touch and tell us. We always like to hear from our readers and always use the best suggestions. You can contact us by email at **hello@ finchandfafinski.com**—or just see what we're up to through our website (www.finchand-fafinski.com) or (succinctly) on Twitter (@FinchFafinski).

Emily Finch
Stefan Fafinski

PART I
Sources of law

This part of the book covers the skills that you will need to understand, use, and find various sources of law.

The first three chapters cover the skills required to understand *legislation* as a source of law. This will include UK Acts of Parliament and delegated legislation as well as legislation emanating from Europe. In the first chapter, the different types of legislation will be explained. This then leads on to chapter 2, in which you will learn the skills to find both the UK and European legislation discussed in the first chapter. Finally, chapter 3 will demonstrate how to use legislation, developing the skills you need to read and interpret legislation.

The next three chapters will take a similar approach to building the skills required to deal with *case law* as a further source of law. Chapter 4 will explain the role of the common law, equity, and custom as case-based sources of law, as well as explaining the different courts that are involved in deciding cases. This then leads on to chapter 5, in which you will learn the skills to find cases from the UK, the European Courts, and the European Court of Human Rights. Lastly, chapter 6 will give you the skills to use cases, describing how legal principles can be extracted from the case and the extent to which those principles are binding on other courts in the future.

Finally, in this part, chapter 7 will describe how *books, journals, and official publications* can be used as supplementary sources of law whilst chapter 8 will give you the skills you need to find these additional resources.

Legislation

1

INTRODUCTION

This chapter deals with the first primary source of law that you will need to be able to find, understand, and use as part of your legal skills portfolio: legislation. It will begin by looking at the process by which an Act of Parliament comes into existence before turning to consider delegated legislation—that is, law that is made by other bodies under Parliament's authority. It will then move on to consider European Union legislation, which has had an increasingly significant effect ever since the UK joined the European Economic Community in 1973. Although a large part of domestic law remains unaffected, certain high-profile areas are significantly affected; these include employment law, commercial and consumer law, environmental law, and the law relating to the free movement of goods and workers throughout Europe. This chapter will therefore discuss the various institutions of the European Union and their role in the law-making process before looking at the different types of EU legislation in detail and explaining the circumstances in which individuals may use them in domestic courts. Finally, the chapter will discuss the impact of the European Convention on Human Rights and the Human Rights Act 1998.

Understanding legislation as a source of law is a fundamentally important legal skill. Every legal topic that you study will generally involve a mixture of legislation, delegated legislation, case law, and equitable principles. Therefore, a thorough understanding of national legislation is key. Furthermore, you must also understand the operation of EU legislation as a source of law since it impacts many areas of domestic law. Without understanding the effects of the EU sources on our domestic law, you will not be able to see the 'whole picture' of a particular area of legal study—particularly in areas such as employment, commercial, environmental, and discrimination law.

LEARNING OUTCOMES

After studying this chapter, you will be able to:

- Explain the process by which Acts of Parliament come into being

- Describe various types of delegated legislation and their function

- Understand the roles of the various institutions of the European Union

- Describe the process by which European Union legislation comes into being

- Explain the differences between European Union Treaty Articles, Regulations, Directives, Decisions, Recommendations, and Opinions

- Distinguish between the concepts of direct *applicability* and direct *effect*

- Explain the principles underlying the supremacy of European Union law

- Discuss the effect of the European Convention on Human Rights and the Human Rights Act 1998

1.1 Domestic legislation

Legislation is a broad term which covers *statutes* (**Acts of Parliament**) and other types of legislation, such as **delegated** (or **subordinate**) legislation and **European Union** legislation.

1.1.1 Statute law

Parliament passes legislation in the form of statutes, or Acts of Parliament. On average, Parliament enacts around sixty or seventy statutes per session and, although this figure remains largely constant, the length of statutes seems to have expanded in recent years, hence increasing the overall volume of legislation.

An Act of Parliament will begin life as a Public Bill, Private Bill, or Hybrid Bill.

The procedure for enacting Private and Hybrid Bills is different to that for Public Bills. This chapter will concentrate on Public Bills and the resulting Public General Acts, although a brief overview of Private Bills, Hybrid Bills, and Private Members' Bills is included here for completeness.

1.1.1.1 Public Bills

Public Bills are introduced by the Government as part of its programme of legislation. Although many people think that most Public Bills arise from the commitments made by the Government as part of its election manifesto, in fact most Public Bills originate from Government departments, advisory committees or as a political reaction to unforeseen events of public concern (such as the Dangerous Dogs Act 1991 in response to public and media outcry over a number of attacks by pit-bull terriers in which some unfortunate individuals were severely or disfiguringly injured).

If enacted, most Public Bills result in Public General Acts which, as their name suggests, affect the general public as a whole.

1.1.1.2 Private Bills

Private Bills are introduced for the benefit of particular individuals, groups of people, institutions, or a particular locality. They are promoted by organizations outside the House to obtain powers for themselves in excess of, or in conflict with, the general law. They often fail to become law due to insufficient time in a particular Parliamentary session. For example, before divorce became generally available under the public law, it was granted by Private Act of Parliament. Nowadays, personal Private Bills are extremely rare. There are now only a few Private Bills in each session. Private Bills tend to deal with nationalized industries, local authorities, companies, and educational institutions.

If enacted, Private Bills generally result in Private Acts (for example, the George Donald Evans and Deborah Jane Evans (Marriage Enabling) Act 1987), unless (as with Public Bills) they deal with local authorities, in which case the resulting legislation is known as a Local Act (the most recent example being the St Austell Market Act 2008).

Take care not to confuse Private Bills with Private Members' Bills which are a type of Public Bill and are covered later in section 1.1.1.4.

1.1.1.3 Hybrid Bills

Hybrid Bills are a cross between Public Bills and Private Bills. According to the House of Commons Speaker, Hylton-Foster, they may be described as:

> A Public Bill which affects a particular private interest in a manner different from the private interests of other persons or bodies in the same category or class.

Bills which propose works of national importance that only affect a specific local area are generally Hybrid Bills. The most recent examples all deal with transport: the Channel Tunnel Bill of 1986–87, proposing the Channel Tunnel, the Crossrail Bill of 2005 which proposed the new east-to-west rail link throughout Central London, and the High Speed Rail (London – West Midlands) Bill 2013–14 to 2014–15 (dealing with the so-called HS2 rail link) which is still before Parliament at the time of writing. Each of these projects claim to benefit the country as a whole, although they clearly affect the private interests of those who are closest to the works more than those living a great distance from them.

1.1.1.4 Private Members' Bills

Private Members' Bills are non-Government Bills (Public, Private, or Hybrid) that are introduced by private Members of Parliament (MPs of any political party or members of the House of Lords who are not Government Ministers). They may be introduced in the Commons in a variety of ways: by ballot, under the 'ten minute rule', or by presentation. Private Members' Bills introduced in the House of Lords are treated in the same way as all other Public Bills. Relatively few Private Members' Bills end up as Acts of Parliament. Although they often deal with relatively narrow issues (such as mock auctions and drainage rates), they may also be used to draw attention to issues of concern that are not within the legislative agenda of Government. Significant pieces of legislation that have begun life as Private Members' Bills include the Abortion Act 1967 and the Hunting Act 2004.

Be careful not to confuse Private Members' Bills with Private Bills.

1.1.1.5 Consolidating and codifying statutes

Statutes may also be passed to consolidate or codify the law.

Consolidating statutes
....
A **consolidating statute** is one which re-enacts particular legal subject matter which was previously contained in several different statutes, which repeals obsolete law, or which gives effect to certain amendments.
....

According to the *Companion to the Standing Orders and guide to Proceedings of the House of Lords*, the following types of Bill are classified as consolidation Bills:

(a) consolidation Bills, whether public or private, which are limited to re-enacting existing law;

(b) Bills to consolidate any enactments with amendments to give effect to recommendations made by the Law Commissions;

(c) statute law repeals Bills, prepared by the Law Commissions to promote the reform of the statute law by the repeal of enactments which are no longer of practical utility;

(d) statute law revision Bills, which are limited to the repeal of obsolete, spent, unnecessary or superseded enactments;

(e) Bills prepared under the Consolidation of Enactments (Procedure) Act 1949, which include corrections and minor improvements to the existing law.

As Lord Simon stated in *Farrell v Alexander*:[1]

> All consolidation Acts are designed to bring together in a more convenient, lucid and economical form a number of enactments related in subject-matter [which were] previously scattered over the statute book.

Examples of such consolidation Acts include the Children Act 1989, the Limitation Act 1980, and the Companies Act 2006.

Codifying statutes

A **codifying statute** is one which restates legal subject matter previously contained in earlier statutes, the common law, and custom.

The meaning of 'common law' and 'custom' is considered in chapter 4.

Unlike consolidation, codification *may* change the law. An example of a codifying Act is the Theft Act 1968, which attempted to frame the law of theft in 'ordinary language'.

1.1.1.6 The domestic law-making process

White Papers and Green Papers

Before a Bill is introduced into Parliament, it may be preceded by a White Paper or a Green Paper.

White Papers set out Government proposals on topics of current concern. They signify the Government's intention to enact new legislation and may set up a consultative process to consider the finer details of the proposal.

Green Papers are issued less frequently. They are introductory higher-level Government reports on a particular area put forward as tentative proposals for discussion without any guarantee of legislative action or consideration of the legislative detail.

Drafting the Bill

Proposed Government legislation is passed to the Parliamentary draftsmen (officially the 'Parliamentary Counsel to the Treasury') who draft the Bill acting on the instructions of the Government department responsible for the proposal. Oddly, it is conventional practice that the Ministers responsible for the Bill do not usually see the instructions sent from their departments.

Procedure for Public Bills

Once drafted, the Parliamentary procedure for Bills introduced in the House of Commons can be depicted as shown in Figure 1.1.

---

1. [1977] AC 59 (HL) 82 (Lord Simon of Glaisdale).

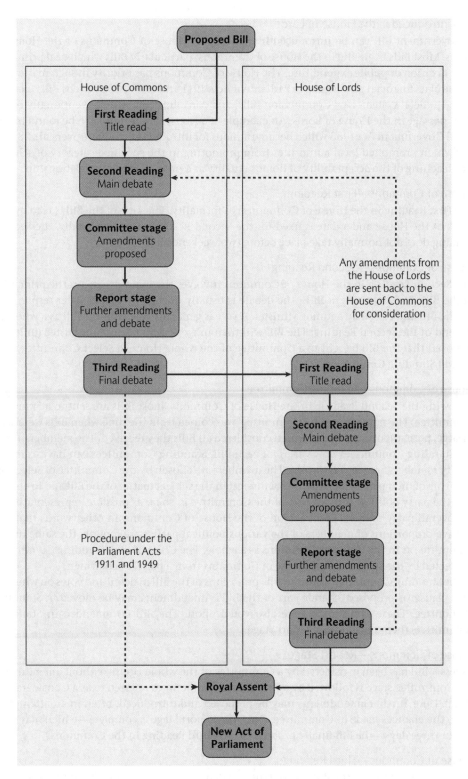

Figure 1.1 The Parliamentary procedure for Bills introduced in the House of Commons

Bills introduced in the House of Lords

A Government Bill can be introduced into either the House of Commons or the House of Lords. Most Bills begin life in the House of Commons; particularly Bills which deal primarily with taxation or public expenditure. The House of Commons has priority in such matters by virtue of its financial privileges (see Parliament Acts 1911 and 1949). Conversely, Bills relating to the judicial system, Law Commission Bills, and consolidation Bills conventionally begin their passage in the House of Lords. An example of a House of Lords Bill can be found in the Local Government Act 1988 which became famous for introducing the controversial s 28 into law which prohibited local authorities from promoting in the specified category of schools 'the teaching of the acceptability of homosexuality as a pretended family relationship'.

House of Commons—First Reading

The First Reading in the House of Commons is a formality. The Title of the Bill is read by the Clerk of the House and a date is fixed for the Second Reading. Conventionally, the Second Reading does not normally take place before two weekends have passed.

House of Commons—Second Reading

The Second Reading in the House of Commons involves the main debate on the principles of the Bill. For Government Bills, the debate is usually opened by the Minister responsible for the Bill and closed by a junior Minister. A vote is generally taken on the Bill as a whole at the end of the Second Reading. The Bill will then move to a Standing Committee (unless it is moved that the Bill be sent to a Committee of the whole House, a Select Committee, or a Special Standing Committee).

House of Commons—Standing Committee

Following the Second Reading in the House of Commons, most Bills are sent to a Standing Committee. The name 'Standing Committee' was coined from the time when Bills were sent to large, permanent committees which considered all Bills they received. The membership of the Standing Committees now varies for each Bill. Standing Committees can have as many as fifty members or as few as sixteen. The members are chosen by the Committee of Selection by virtue of their particular expertise or interest in the subject matter of the Bill and to ensure that the party political composition of the Committee is, so far as possible, representative of the overall party political composition of the House of Commons: in other words that the relative proportions of members of the various political parties are roughly the same in the Committee as in the House of Commons as a whole. The Chair of each Standing Committee is selected by the Speaker of the House of Commons from a panel of chairmen.

The Standing Committee examines the provisions of the Bill in detail and votes on whether each clause, as proposed, 'stands part of the Bill'. Amendments may be moved in Standing Committee. These amendments are also voted upon. The Bill (as amended in Standing Committee) then moves into a Report Stage.

House of Commons—Report Stage

Unless a Bill has been considered by a Committee of the whole House without amendment, the Committee stage is followed by a Report Stage (sometimes referred to as a Consideration Stage). Here, further amendments may be proposed and introduced, often in an attempt to undo the changes made in Committee. Once the Report Stage is complete—which may take two or three days—the Bill finally proceeds to its Third Reading in the Commons.

House of Commons—Third Reading

In the Third Reading of the Bill, its contents are debated for a final time. It is unusual for any further amendments to be made at this stage. Indeed, unless six members table a motion that 'the Question be not put forthwith', the Third Reading does not have to involve any debate at all.

Once the Third Reading is over, the Bill is then tied up with a green ribbon and taken to the House of Lords by the Clerk of the House of Commons with a message kindly requesting the Lords' agreement to its content.

Procedure in the House of Lords

The procedure in the House of Lords mirrors that in the House of Commons. Bills have a formal First Reading, are debated on a Second Reading, proceed to consideration in Committee (although, unlike in the House of Commons, the committee stage is almost invariably taken in the Committee of the whole House), are debated again on Report and then receive a final Third Reading. At the end of the Third Reading there is a formal motion 'that this Bill do now pass'.

Assuming that the Bill survives the motion at the end of the Third Reading in the House of Lords, it is returned to the House of Commons with the Lords' amendments which must be considered in the Commons. If the House of Commons does not agree with the Lords' amendments it can send it back with counter-amendments and its reasons for doing so. Therefore a Bill can go back and forth between the Houses several times until proceedings are terminated or the parliamentary session runs out of time. However, in practice, the House of Lords often accepts the second offering from the House of Commons.

The Parliament Acts 1911 and 1949

These Acts provide a means by which the House of Commons can under certain circumstances bypass the House of Lords to present a Bill for Royal Assent without it having been passed by the House of Lords. The procedure under the Parliament Acts has historically been used infrequently. The 1911 Act was used only three times: for the Welsh Church Act 1914, the Government of Ireland Act 1914, and the Parliament Act 1949, which amended the 1911 Act to reduce the power of the House of Lords further. The 1997 Labour Government used the Parliament Acts to force through three Acts: the European Parliamentary Elections Act 1999, the Sexual Offences (Amendment) Act 2000, and the Hunting Act 2004. Before 1997, the amended form of the 1911 Act had been used only once, in respect of the War Crimes Act 1991. The Parliament Acts do not apply to Bills which prolong the length of a Parliament beyond five years, Private Bills, Bills sent to the Lords less than a month before the end of the Parliamentary session, and Bills which are introduced in the Lords.

Royal Assent

Royal Assent is required before any Bill can become law. The Monarch is not required by the constitution to assent to any Act passed by Parliament. However, assent is conventionally given by the Monarch acting on ministerial advice. It has not been refused since Queen Anne refused to assent to the Scottish Militia Bill of 1707.

Indeed the Royal Assent Act 1967 has marginalized the personal involvement of the monarch to the extent that all that is now required for Royal Assent by Notification is a formal reading of the short title of the Act with a form of words signifying the fact of assent in both Houses of Parliament.

Without express provision to the contrary, an Act of Parliament is deemed to come into force on the day (and for the whole of the day)[2] that it receives Royal Assent. Otherwise it will

---

2. *Tomlinson v Bullock* (1879) 4 QBD 230 (DC).

come into force on a date specified within the Act itself, or via an 'appointed day' provision which allows the Act to be brought into force via a statutory instrument.

Statutory instruments are described in section 1.1.2.1.

Parts of the Act may be brought into force on different dates (for example, the provisions of the Anti-social Behaviour Act 2003 relating to high hedges did not come into force until June 2005).

For more information on the coming into force of statutes, see chapter 3.

Territorial extent

There is a presumption in the absence of proof to the contrary that Acts of the UK Parliament enacted after 1707 apply to the whole of the UK. If such an Act, or any part of it, does not apply to Scotland, this will usually be expressly stated within the Act itself. In modern practice, an 'extent' provision setting out any limitations on the geographical application of the Act is usually found in one of the final sections of the Act. Acts of the UK Parliament that apply only to Scotland are usually denoted by the inclusion of '(Scotland)' in the short title of the Act, e.g. the Solicitors (Scotland) Act 1980.

Following the passing of the Scotland Act 1998 and the creation of the Scottish Parliament in 1999, statutes can be enacted by the Scottish Parliament provided that the subject matter of the Act is within its legislative competence. These Acts are given Royal Assent under Letters Patent (a published written order issued by the Crown). The UK Parliament retains the power to legislate for Scotland on all matters, including those matters that are now within the legislative competence of the Scottish Parliament. However, a convention has developed (the Sewel Convention)[3] that the UK Government will not normally introduce legislation dealing with matters that have been devolved to the Scottish Parliament, or the other devolved legislatures within the UK, without the agreement of the devolved legislature.

In Wales, Measures of the National Assembly for Wales between 2006 and 2011 were given Royal Assent by means of an Order in Council. Following the extension of the Assembly's legislative powers after the 2011 referendum, Measures become known as Acts of the Assembly and are given Royal Assent via Letters Patent in the same way as Acts of the Scottish Parliament.

1.1.1.7 The impact of the Human Rights Act 1998

Section 19 of the Human Rights Act 1998 provides that the Minister in charge of each new Bill in either House of Parliament must, before the Second Reading of the Bill, either:

- make a statement of compatibility—that is, state that the provisions of the Bill are compatible with the European Convention on Human Rights; or

- make a statement acknowledging that it is not possible to make a statement of compatibility, but, despite this, the Government still wishes the House to proceed with the Bill.

The courts have no power to set aside any Act of Parliament that is incompatible with Convention rights; this is a function that is exercised by Parliament (which has a fast-track procedure under s 10 of the Act that it may use in such cases if it wishes to do so). The court may, however, make a 'statement of incompatibility' under s 4 of the Act if it is satisfied that the provision is incompatible with a Convention right. Such a statement does not affect the validity, continuing operation, or enforcement of the provision in respect of which it is given; and is not binding on the parties to the proceedings in which it is made.

3. House of Commons, 'The "Sewel Convention"' (Library Standard Note) (25 November 2005) SN/PC/2084.

1.1.2 Delegated legislation

Parliament has delegated legislative power to various other persons and bodies.

Delegated legislation is law made by persons or bodies with the delegated authority of Parliament. It is sometimes referred to as 'subordinate legislation'.

1.1.2.1 Statutory instruments

An Act of Parliament may grant the power to make statutory instruments, usually to a Minister of the Crown. The scope of this power can vary greatly, from the technical (for example, varying the dates on which different provisions of an Act will come into force or changing the levels of fines or penalties for offences) to much wider powers such as filling out the broad provisions in Acts. Often, Acts only contain a broad framework and statutory instruments are used to provide the necessary detail that would be considered too complex to include in the body of an Act. Statutory instruments can also be used to amend, update, or enforce existing primary legislation.

'Statutory instruments' is a general term that includes Regulations, Rules, and Orders. A very common form of statutory instrument is a commencement order which brings all, or part, of an Act into force.

For examples of commencement orders, see chapter 3.

The procedure for introducing a statutory instrument is usually laid down partly in the enabling (parent) Act and partly in the Statutory Instruments Act 1946. The use of statutory instruments is becoming increasingly widespread as a means of introducing some flexibility into the legislative process as well as helping to contain the ever-increasing length and complexity of statutes. For instance Parliament passed thirty-three Acts in 2013; 3,292 statutory instruments were made in the same year.

Procedures for creating statutory instruments

The procedure for creating a statutory instrument is laid down in the parent Act. These procedures can be categorized as:

- negative resolution;
- positive resolution;
- no approval by Parliament.

Approximately two-thirds of all statutory instruments are made under the negative resolution procedure. It is named as such since it does not require Parliament to act unless it disapproves of the statutory instrument. It takes one of two forms depending on the state of the statutory instrument at the time that it is presented to ('laid before') Parliament. In the first form, the statutory instrument is laid before Parliament in draft and cannot be made if Parliament votes its disapproval within forty days. In the second form, the statutory instrument is actually made and laid before Parliament. If Parliament votes its disapproval within forty days, then the statutory instrument cannot remain in force.

A further 10 per cent of statutory instruments require positive resolution—in other words they require positive Parliamentary approval. This procedure takes one of three forms. The first of these requires the draft statutory instrument to be laid before Parliament. It can only come into force if approved by resolution of the House or Houses specified in its parent Act. The second form is similar, except that the statutory instrument is made before being laid before Parliament. However, it cannot come into force until approved by resolution as before. The final situation occurs where the statutory instrument has been made, comes into immediate effect, and is then laid before Parliament. It cannot continue beyond the period specified in the parent Act without positive resolution.

The final two-fifths of statutory instruments require no approval by Parliament. This either means that they do not need to be laid before Parliament at all, or that they do, but do not require any subsequent form of approval.

1.1.2.2 By-laws

By-laws are laws which are made by a local authority and only apply within a specific geographical area. By-laws are usually only created when there is no general legislation that deals with particular matters of concern to local people, such as waste collection and public park opening hours. By-laws are made under the Local Government Act 1972. However, by-laws can only come into force once they have been affirmed by the relevant Minister. By-laws come into force one month after affirmation unless a specific date is specified within the by-law itself.

1.1.2.3 The Rule Committees

The Rule Committees have delegated power to make procedural rules for the courts. These consist of the Civil Procedure Rule Committee (who are responsible for the Civil Procedure Rules 1998 and their subsequent amendments), the Criminal Procedure Rule Committee, and the Family Procedure Rule Committee.

1.1.2.4 The Privy Council

The role of the Privy Council is described further in chapter 4.

The Privy Council may make Orders in Council, such as emergency regulations. These have the force of law. It may also implement resolutions of the United Nations Security Council.

1.1.2.5 Validity of delegated legislation

Unlike Acts of Parliament, delegated legislation may be challenged in the courts via the doctrine of *ultra vires*.

Ultra vires is a Latin term meaning 'outside (their) powers'.

If a body acts beyond the powers that are delegated to it by the parent Act, then the delegated legislation can be declared void by the court. The body is said to have acted *ultra vires* by exceeding its powers. The delegated legislation may also be referred to as being *ultra vires*.[4]

Delegated legislation is also *ultra vires* if it conflicts with an earlier Act of Parliament or, following s 2(4) of the European Communities Act 1972, European Union legislation.

Decisions which are made by the public bodies granted power by delegated legislation can also be challenged via judicial review. See section 4.3.4.2.

1.1.2.6 Advantages and disadvantages of delegated legislation

Advantages

The main advantage of delegated legislation is that detailed rules and regulations can be introduced relatively quickly without the need for full debate in Parliament that Acts would

---

4. For examples of the ways in which the courts have approached the issue of *ultra vires*, see *Commissioners of Customs & Excise v Cure & Deeley Ltd* [1962] 1 QB 340 (DC) and *R v Secretary of State for Social Security, ex p Joint Council for the Welfare of Immigrants* [1997] 1 WLR 275 (CA).

require. There is insufficient Parliamentary time available to debate all Bills in full and delegated legislation enables the most effective use of this limited time.

Moreover, Members of Parliament may not have the particular specialist knowledge to debate certain subject areas. It is therefore preferable to delegate authority to individuals or bodies with the requisite degree of specialist, technical, or local knowledge.

Disadvantages

Since delegated legislation is not debated before Parliament in the way that Acts are, the opportunity for public objection is minimized. Nor is delegated legislation publicized before and after implementation in the same way as some new Acts of Parliament. For instance, the Civil Partnership Act 2004 and the Identity Cards Act 2006 both received widespread media coverage, whereas a mass of delegated legislation was also introduced over the same period without any significant attention. While it could be argued that media attention derives from the very nature of primary legislation and its general public impact, it is also true that delegated legislation can have a significant public impact (for example, the majority of the Identity Cards Act 2006 would have been brought into force by delegated legislation).[5]

Finally, the proliferation of delegated legislation means that in researching any area of law, it is important to be sure that your research is up-to-date.

1.2 European legislation

An increasingly influential range of sources of law emanates from Europe. The majority of this arises by virtue of the UK's membership of the European Union.

With regard to human rights issues, individual citizens of the UK had the right to petition the European Court of Human Rights from 1966. Building on this, the Human Rights Act 1998 came into force in October 2000, allowing individuals to rely on (most) of the rights guaranteed by the European Convention on Human Rights directly in national courts as well as enabling courts to overrule earlier incompatible decisions. This section will consider European Union legislation in the form of Treaty Articles, Regulations, and Directives. It will also consider the European Convention on Human Rights as a further European source of law. However, it is important to remember throughout that the European Court of Human Rights is separate from the Court of Justice of the European Union.

1.2.1 European Union law

1.2.1.1 A brief history

The UK became a member of the European Communities on 1 January 1973 when the European Communities Act 1972 came into force.

At this time the 'European Communities' were the European Economic Community (the 'EEC'), established by the Treaty of Rome 1957, together with the European Coal and Steel Community,[6] and the European Atomic Energy Community ('Euratom'), with the EEC being the most significant.

---

5. Identity Cards Act 2006 s 44(3). The Identity Documents Act 2010 repealed the Identity Cards Act 2006 and requires the destruction of the information held on the National Identity Register.
6. Established by the Treaty of Paris 1951.

The 1992 Treaty on European Union (also known as the Maastricht Treaty or TEU) renamed the EEC as the European Community (EC) and the geographical entity formed by the Member States became the European Union (EU) when it came into force on 1 November 1993. As such, the EU has evolved from a trade body into an economic and political partnership.

The Maastricht Treaty is not the only Treaty that you will encounter. The Single European Act 1986 (which is actually a Treaty rather than an Act of Parliament—despite its name) initiated moves toward the harmonization of laws across the Member States. The 1997 Treaty of Amsterdam made further changes, not least of which was the renumbering of the pre-existing Treaty provisions.

The Maastricht Treaty established the three so-called 'pillars' of the European Union: the European Community, Common Foreign and Security Policy, and Police and Judicial Co-operation in Criminal Matters.

The 2001 Treaty of Nice effected further changes relating to the enlargement of the Community which allowed the addition of ten new Member States on 1 May 2004, and two more on 1 January 2007, increasing the membership from fifteen to twenty-eight by 1 July 2013. The expansion of the EU over time is illustrated in Table 1.1.

As the EU expanded to include more Member States, a new European Constitution was proposed which contained significant reforms to both the institutions of the EU and its operation. This proposed constitution was rejected by France and the Netherlands. Following this rejection, a new Reform Treaty was drawn up and was signed in Lisbon on 13 December 2007.[7] It was originally intended to have been ratified by all Member States by the end of 2008. However, following a referendum on 12 June 2008, the Irish electorate voted against its ratification by 53 to 47 per cent. This decision was reversed in a second referendum in 2009 after the Irish secured concessions on particular policies, including abortion, taxation, and military neutrality.

Table 1.1 The expansion of the European Union

Year	Countries	Membership
1957	Belgium, France, Germany, Italy, Luxembourg, Netherlands	6
1973	United Kingdom, Denmark, Ireland	9
1981	Greece	10
1986	Portugal, Spain	12
1995	Austria, Finland, Sweden	15
2004	Cyprus, Czech Republic, Estonia, Hungary, Latvia, Lithuania, Malta, Poland, Slovakia, Slovenia	25
2007	Bulgaria, Romania	27
2013	Croatia	28
Candidate countries	Montenegro, Serbia, former Yugoslav Republic of Macedonia, Turkey, Iceland	
Potential candidates	Albania, Bosnia and Herzegovina, Kosovo (in line with UN Security Council Resolution 1244/99 and the ICJ Opinion on the Kosovo declaration of independence)	

7.   Treaty of Lisbon amending the Treaty on European Union and the Treaty establishing the European Community (Treaty of Lisbon) [2007] OJ C306/1.

The Treaty of Lisbon was ratified by the UK on 19 June 2008 by the European Union (Amendment) Act 2008 and came into force on 1 December 2009.

The Treaty of Lisbon amended the Treaty on European Union and the Treaty establishing the European Community (Treaty of Rome)—which was also renamed the Treaty on the Functioning of the European Union). Its most significant changes include:

- the creation of a long-term President of the European Council;
- the elimination of the pillar system;
- the division of European policy areas into three categories: exclusive competence, shared competence (with the Member States), and supporting competence (where the EU supports, coordinates, or supplements the actions of the Member States);
- more qualified majority voting in the Council of Ministers;
- increased involvement of the European Parliament in the legislative process;
- the Charter of Fundamental Rights being given the status of a legally binding instrument.

Therefore, the two key treaties are the *Treaty on European Union* (TEU; Maastricht) and the *Treaty on the Functioning of the European Union* (TFEU; Treaty of Rome). The other treaties amended these as the scope of the EU changed over time.

1.2.1.2 The institutions of the European Union

It is important to be able to distinguish between the different institutions of the European Union and to understand their functions. These are set out in Article 13 TEU as:

- the European Commission;
- the Council of Ministers/European Council;
- the European Parliament;
- the Court of Justice of the European Union;
- the General Court;
- the European Central Bank;
- the Court of Auditors.

We will consider each of these in turn (with the exception of the European Central Bank and Court of Auditors which are less relevant to legal studies).

The European Commission

The **European Commission** represents the interests of the EU as a whole. It proposes new legislation to the European Parliament and the Council of the European Union, and it ensures that EU law is correctly applied by member countries.

The first main role of the European Commission lies in proposing new laws using its 'right of initiative' for the protection of the citizens and interests of the EU. It proposes such laws according to the principles of subsidiarity and proportionality: that is, it will only put forward proposals on issues that cannot be dealt with at national, regional, or local levels and then no more than necessary to achieve the agreed objectives. Legislative proposals are drafted by the Commission and, if approved by a minimum of fourteen of the (currently) twenty-eight Commissioners, are sent to the Council and the Parliament. Each EU Member State has one Commissioner, although the Commissioners are not representatives of their respective countries. Each Commissioner is responsible for one or more specific areas of policy. The appointments run for a term of five years and are subject to the approval of the European Parliament.

The second role of the Commission is in the enforcement of European law as 'guardian of the Treaties' together with the Court of Justice. It can take action, including the imposition of penalties, against an EU Member State that is allegedly in breach of its obligations under the Treaties (Article 258 TFEU) or for failure to implement a piece of EC legislation (Article 260 TFEU).

The Commission also has roles in managing the EU budget and allocating funding (with the Council and Parliament) and representing the EU on the world stage, negotiating agreements between the EU and other countries.

The Council of the European Union

The **Council of the European Union** represents the governments of the individual EU countries. It is one of the main law-making bodies of the EU, along with the European Parliament.

The Council of the European Union shares responsibility with the European Parliament for passing EU laws that are proposed by the Commission. It also coordinates the broad economic policies of the EU countries and develops the EU's foreign and defence policies. The Council also coordinates cooperation between the courts and police forces of EU countries to ensure equal access to justice for EU citizens throughout the Union and mutual recognition of court judgments. It is further concerned with policing the EU's borders and combating terrorism and organized crime. The EU budget is approved jointly between the Parliament and the Council. Finally, the Council can enter into international agreements on behalf of the EU on a range of diverse matters including: environment, trade, textiles, fisheries, science, technology, and transport.

The Council's members are politicians who are Ministers in their respective national Governments. Each Minister has the authority to commit its Government to a particular policy or decision. There are no fixed members: its membership fluctuates according to the subject matter under debate. For instance, if the debate concerns environmental issues, the UK would be represented by the Secretary of State for Environment, Food, and Rural Affairs. The presidency of the Council is held for six months by each EU Member State on a rotational basis.

The general voting method for the Council is qualified majority voting, except where the treaties require a different procedure (e.g. a unanimous vote). This means that the bigger the population of the EU Member State, the more votes it has (for example, Germany, France, Italy, and the UK have twenty-nine votes, while Malta has three). A qualified majority is reached when a majority of the EU countries are in favour and at least 260 of the possible 352 votes are cast.

In 2014, double majority voting will be introduced. Proposals will then require a majority not only of the EU countries (minimum of fifteen) but also of the total EU population (65 per cent). This has not been introduced at the time of writing, but should do so during the lifetime of this edition.

Take care not to confuse the Council of the European Union with the European Council or the Council of Europe. The Council of Europe is a separate body and has responsibility for the European Court of Human Rights.

The European Parliament

The **European Parliament** represents the people of the EU. It is one of the main EU law-making institutions, along with the Council of the European Union.

Members of the European Parliament (MEPs) are directly elected representatives of the people, with elections being held every five years. The first main role of the Parliament is debating and passing EU laws, together with the Council. The process by which this is done is known as the 'ordinary legislative procedure', set out by the Lisbon Treaty. In many areas (such as economic governance, immigration, energy, transport, consumer protection, and the environment) equal weight is given to the Parliament and the Council and most EU laws are adopted jointly between these two institutions. The steps in the ordinary legislative procedure are as follows:

- The Commission sends its proposal to Parliament and the Council.

- They consider it and discuss it on two successive occasions.

- After two readings, if they cannot agree, the proposal is brought before a Conciliation Committee made up of an equal number of representatives of the Council and Parliament.

- Representatives of the Commission also attend the meetings of the Conciliation Committee and contribute to the discussions.

- When the Committee has reached agreement, the agreed text is sent to Parliament and the Council for a third reading, so that they can finally adopt it as law. The final agreement of the two institutions is essential if the text is to be adopted as a law.

- Even if a joint text is agreed by the Conciliation Committee, Parliament can still reject the proposed law by a majority of the votes cast.

The number of MEPs for each EU Member State is broadly in proportion to its population, although, following the Lisbon Treaty, none may have fewer than six or more than ninety-six MEPs. The maximum number of members is set at 751.

The European Parliament also debates and adopts the EU budget with the Council. It also exercises democratic supervision of the other EU institutions: for instance, Parliament approves the nomination of the President of the Commission and the Commissioners (as a body)[8] and can censure the Commission, forcing its members to resign. It may also consider petitions from citizens and set up inquiry committees.

The Court of Justice of the European Union

The **Court of Justice of the European Union** (still often referred to by its former name as the **European Court of Justice** or **ECJ**) upholds the rule of EU law by ensuring consistency of application between EU countries, settling disputes between EU governments and institutions and hearing cases that are brought before it.

It is vitally important not to confuse the Court of Justice of the European Union (CJEU) (which sits in Luxembourg) with the European Court of Human Rights (which sits in Strasbourg). They are separate courts with separate jurisdictions.

The CJEU sits in Luxembourg and comprises one judge from each EU Member State. The judges sit in chambers of three or five as well as in plenary session (where all judges sit to hear a case). They are assisted by eight 'advocates-general' whose role is to submit reasoned, public, and impartial opinions to the Court on the cases brought before it. Each judge and advocate-general is appointed for a six-year term. The Court delivers a single judgment: separate concurring or dissenting judgments are not permitted.

The cases brought before the CJEU fall into certain types. The most common are:

- **Preliminary rulings.** National courts may make interim references directly to the Court if they need clarification on how a particular piece of European legislation should be

---

8.   Art 17(7) TEU.

interpreted. The need for such references will arise during the course of a national (domestic) action. In England and Wales this will typically occur in the Supreme Court (although it has been done directly from a magistrates' court).[9] In other words, if a national court cannot make a ruling because it is unsure how to interpret a piece of EU legislation, then it can effectively suspend the proceedings before it to ask the Court for its opinion. These references are made under Article 267 TFEU. The case will then proceed in the national court with the assistance of the European Court's ruling. It is the role of the national courts to give effect to and enforce the rulings of the CJEU.

- **Failure to fulfil an EU obligation.** The Court also hears actions for failure of an EU national government to fulfil its obligations under EU law. Proceedings before the CJEU are preceded by an investigation conducted by the Commission, which gives the defendant EU Member State the opportunity to reply to the complaints made against it. If that procedure does not result in remedy of the failure by the defendant EU Member State, an action for breach of EU law may be brought before the CJEU. That action may be brought by the Commission[10]—as is practically always the case—or by another EU Member State.[11] If the CJEU finds that an obligation has not been fulfilled, the EU Member State concerned must remedy the breach without delay. If the Court later finds that the breach has not been remedied, it may, upon request of the Commission, impose a financial penalty.[12]

- **Actions for annulment.** The CJEU may also hear applications seeking the annulment of a Regulation, Directive, or Decision. Such actions may be brought by a Member State, by the European Parliament, the Council of the European Union or the European Commission, or by individuals to whom a measure is addressed or which is of direct and individual concern to them.

- **Actions for failure to act.** The CJEU may also review the legality of a failure to act on the part of a EU institution. Where the failure to act is held to be unlawful, it is for the institution concerned to put an end to the failure by appropriate measures.

- **Direct actions**. Any legal person can bring an action directly before the CJEU if they have suffered loss or damage as a result of the acts or omissions of the EU's institutions or its staff.

- **Appeals from the General Court**. Appeals on points of law only may be brought before the CJEU against judgments given by the General Court. If the appeal is admissible and well founded, the CJEU may set aside the judgment of the General Court. The CJEU may decide this itself or may refer the case back to the General Court, which is bound by the decision of the CJEU given on appeal.

The General Court

The **General Court** has jurisdiction at first instance over all direct actions brought by individuals and EU countries, with the exception of those to be assigned to a 'judicial panel' and those reserved for the CJEU. It was formerly known (until 1 December 2010) as the **Court of First Instance**.

The Court of First Instance was established by the Single European Act of 1986 to ease some of the burden of cases on the Court of Justice. It was renamed as the General Court by the

---

9. Case C-145/88 *Torfaen Borough Council v B&Q plc* [1990] 2 QB 19 (CJEU) on application from Cwmbran Magistrates' Court regarding Sunday trading regulations.
10. Art 258 TFEU.
11. Art 259 TFEU.
12. Art 260 TFEU.

Treaty of Lisbon. It comprises at least one judge from each of the EU countries, but, unlike the CJEU, does not have permanent advocates general. Judges sit in chambers of three or five judges or, exceptionally, as a single judge. For complex or important cases it may sit as a Grand Chamber of thirteen or as a full court. However, around 80 per cent of cases are heard by a chamber of three. It deals with:

- direct actions against the institutions, bodies, offices or agencies of the European Union;
- actions brought by the Member States against the Commission;
- actions brought by the Member States against the Council relating to acts adopted in the field of State aid, 'dumping' and acts by which it exercises implementing powers;
- actions seeking compensation for damage caused by the institutions of the European Union or their staff;
- actions based on contracts made by the European Union that expressly give jurisdiction to the General Court;
- actions relating to Community trade marks;
- appeals, limited to points of law, against the decisions of the European Union Civil Service Tribunal;
- actions brought against decisions of the Community Plant Variety Office or of the European Chemicals Agency.

There is a route of appeal to the CJEU within two months on points of law only.

As previously stated, it is vitally important not to confuse the Court of Justice of the European Union (CJEU) (which sits in Luxembourg) with the European Court of Human Rights (which sits in Strasbourg). They are separate courts with separate jurisdictions.

The European Council

The **European Council** is composed of the Heads of State or Government of the EU countries together with its President and the President of the Commission. It defines general political directions and priorities of the Union. It does not have any law-making function.

The European Council was introduced in 1974 in an attempt to deal with policy matters at the highest level, comprising the individual Heads of State or Governments of each of the Member States. It acquired a formal status in the Maastricht Treaty and became a formal institution of the Union following the Treaty of Lisbon.

The European Council defines the general political direction and priorities of the European Union, but does not exercise any legislative function. It meets twice every six months, convened by its President, but may convene specially if a specific situation requires it to do so. Decisions of the European Council are taken by consensus unless the Treaties require unanimity or qualified majority voting. The European Council elects its President by qualified majority. The President's term of office is two and a half years, renewable once.

Take care not to confuse the European Council with the Council of the European Union or the Council of Europe.

1.2.1.3 Sources of EU law

There are three sources of EU law:

- **Primary sources.** A number of primary sources of European law have already been mentioned. These are the founding Treaties: the Treaty on European Union and the Treaty on the Functioning of the EU. These Treaties provide the framework of competencies between the EU as a body and its member countries. They also set out the powers of the EU institutions. Therefore, they set out a broad legal framework within which the institutions implement EU policy. Other primary sources include the amending EU Treaties, the annexed protocols, and the accession Treaties for new EU countries.

- **Secondary sources.** Secondary sources supplement the primary sources by providing a more detailed treatment of the law in a given area and establishing how the principles and objectives identified in the primary sources are to be achieved. The secondary sources of European law comprise **unilateral acts** (regulations and directives, decisions, opinions, and recommendations) and **conventions and agreements** (international agreements between the EU and an external country or body and agreements between EU countries and between EU institutions).

- **Supplementary law.** This covers the case law of the CJEU, relevant international law, custom and usage, and general unwritten principles of law and justice.

The sources of EU law can be summarized as shown in Table 1.2.

The interrelationship between EU law and domestic law

The body of EU law became part of domestic law by virtue of the European Communities Act 1972. Section 2(1) of the Act provides that:

> All such rights, powers, liabilities, obligations and restrictions from time to time created or arising by or under the Treaties, and all such remedies and procedures from time to time provided for by or under the Treaties, as in accordance with the Treaties are without further enactment to be given legal effect or used in the United Kingdom shall be recognised and available in law, and be enforced, allowed and followed accordingly; and the expression 'enforceable Community right' and similar expressions shall be read as referring to one to which this subsection applies.

This meant that all directly applicable EU law, regardless of whether it has already been made or is to be made in the future, became part of national law.

Before proceeding much further, we must cover some important terminology.

Direct *applicability* and direct *effect*

It is important that you understand the distinction between provisions of EU law which are directly applicable and provisions that are directly effective.

Table 1.2 Sources of EU Law

Primary sources of EU law	Secondary sources of EU law	Supplementary law
Treaty of Rome 1957	Regulations	Case law of the CJEU
Single European Act 1985	Directives	Principles of international law
Treaty on European Union (Maastricht Treaty) 1992	Decisions issued by the Commission	Unwritten principles of law and justice
Treaty of Amsterdam 1996	Opinions	
Treaty of Nice 2001	Recommendations	
Treaty of Lisbon 2009	Conventions and agreements	

A provision of EU law is **directly applicable** if it automatically becomes part of the law of an EU Member State without the need for that EU Member State to enact any further legislation.

A provision of EU law is **directly effective** if (and only if) it creates rights upon which individuals may rely in their national courts and which are enforceable by those courts.

Thus, direct *applicability* is concerned with the incorporation of EU law into the legal system of an EU Member State, whereas direct *effect* is concerned with its enforceability.

Before considering which of the different types of EU law have direct effect (that is, can be relied upon by individuals in national courts and are enforceable by those courts) it is necessary to understand the distinction between vertical direct effect and horizontal direct effect as illustrated in Figure 1.2.

A provision of EU law has **vertical direct effect** if it can be enforced against an EU Member State in its own courts.

A provision of EU law has **horizontal direct effect** if it can be enforced against another individual in the courts of an EU Member State.

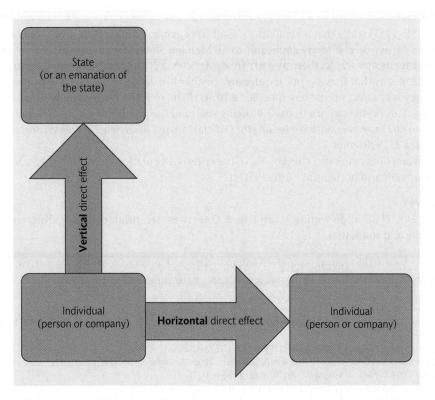

Figure 1.2 Horizontal and vertical direct effect

Therefore, provisions of EU law with vertical direct effect can be enforced against the UK (or indeed, any other EU Member State) itself. Vertically directly effective provisions may also be enforced against emanations of the state, such as local authorities and health authorities[13] and nationalized industries.[14]

You should take care when reading cases which consider the distinction between direct applicability and direct effect since the CJEU does not always distinguish between its use of the two terms.

We have looked at the different sources of EU law and the rules of direct applicability and direct effect which determine how those provisions operate within domestic law. To complete the puzzle, we finally have to establish the applicability and effect of each type of provision.

Treaty Articles

Although it is for the CJEU to determine, Treaty Articles are normally held to be directly applicable. Therefore, following s 2(1) of the European Communities Act 1972, they require no further legislative action by the UK to take effect as law.

A Treaty Article will have vertical direct effect (it will create individual enforceable rights against the state) if its terms are 'clear, precise and unconditional' and its implementation required no further legislation in EU member countries (i.e. it was directly applicable).[15] These are often referred to as the *Van Gend* criteria from the case in which the matter was first considered. In other words, an Article has vertical direct effect if the EU countries had no discretion in the means of its implementation.

Treaty Articles may also have horizontal direct effect.[16] Therefore, provided that the *Van Gend* criteria are satisfied, Treaty Articles can be enforced directly in UK courts, regardless of any other domestic legislation.

Regulations

Article 288 TFEU states that a Regulation 'shall have general application' and 'shall be binding in its entirety and directly applicable in all Member States'. Since Regulations are immediately directly applicable, then, as with Treaty Articles, s 2(1) of the European Communities Act 1972 means that they do not require any further legislative work for their implementation. They take effect on the day specified within them, or if the Regulation is silent as to its effective date, on the twentieth day following their publication in the *Official Journal*.[17]

You can find more information regarding the Official Journal *in section 2.2.1 which demonstrates how to find EC legislation.*

Therefore, subject to satisfying the *Van Gend* criteria, Regulations, like Treaty Articles, have both vertical[18] and horizontal[19] direct effect.

Directives

Article 288 TFEU shows quite clearly that Directives are fundamentally different from Regulations. It states that:

> A directive shall be binding, as to the result to be achieved, upon each Member State to which it is addressed, but shall leave to the national authority the choice of form and methods.

---

13.   Case C-271/91 *Marshall v Southampton and South West Hampshire Area Health Authority (No 2)* [1993] ECR I-4367 (CJEU).

14.   Case C-188/89 *Foster v British Gas plc* [1990] ECR I-3133 (CJEU).

15.   Case 26/62 *Van Gend en Loos v Nederlandse Administratie der Belastingen* [1963] ECR 1 (CJEU).

16.   Case 43/75 *Defrenne v Sabena (No 2)* [1976] ECR 455 (CJEU).

17.   Case 39/72 *Commission v Italy* [1973] ECR 101 (CJEU).

18.   Case 93/71 *Leonesio v Italian Ministry of Agriculture* [1972] ECR 287 (CJEU).

19.   Case C-253/00 *Antonio Munoz Cia SA v Frumar Ltd* [2002] ECR I-7289 (CJEU).

In other words, Directives tell the Member States of the EU what needs to be done, but leave each of the States to decide what provisions of domestic law to enact in order to implement that Directive. There is always a specified period of time for the EU Member States to implement any given Directive.

Directives often provide the fine detail on a given area; here, the EU recognizes that individual EU Member States may need to implement them in slightly different ways, to reflect their own national cultures or customs. Therefore, as long as the objective of the Directive is met, the EU gives each EU Member State a measure of discretion as to its precise method of implementation in its domestic law. Many pieces of important and influential UK legislation have arisen from the implementation of EU Directives, such as the Equal Pay Act 1970 and the Sex Discrimination Act 1975.

Since Directives require domestic legislation for their implementation, they are not directly applicable forms of EU law. Moreover, if the Directive has been properly implemented, an individual who wishes to bring an action based on that Directive will use the national law rather than relying on the Directive itself; therefore, in general, Directives do not have horizontal direct effect.[20]

However, a Directive will have vertical direct effect if it satisfies the *Van Gend* criteria and the time for implementation specified in the Directive has passed.[21]

Directives may also be said to have indirect effect, since the CJEU also requires national law to be interpreted in accordance with Directives.[22]

Finally, an EU Member State that has failed to implement a Directive may be liable to compensate individuals who have suffered as a result.[23] In other words, if an individual has lost out because of defective implementation of a Directive by an EU Member State, they may be able to sue that state for their losses provided that the breach was sufficiently serious (which will be so if the Member State 'manifestly and gravely disregard[ed]' its obligations).[24]

Decisions

The final secondary sources of European law are decisions. Article 288 TFEU provides that a decision 'shall be binding in its entirety upon those to whom it is addressed'. The addressees may be individuals, companies, or EU Member States. Thus, they are not directly applicable, but may be capable of having direct effect.

1.2.1.4 'Soft law'—Recommendations and opinions

Recommendations

Recommendations are not legally binding. However, courts of EU Member States are required to interpret their own law in the light of recommendations.[25]

Opinions

In common with recommendations, opinions also have no legal authority. However, the opinion of the Commission may be a precursor to legal proceedings. If the Commission

---

20. However, see Case C-1994/94 *CIA Security International SA v Signalson SA and Securitel SPRL* [1996] ECR I-2201 (CJEU) and Case C-443/98 *Unilever Italia v Central Food* [2000] ECR I-7535 (CJEU) where it appears that, in some instances, Directives may be pleaded against an individual or non-state body.

21. Case 148/78 *Pubblico Ministero v Ratti* [1979] ECR 1629 (CJEU).

22. Case 14/83 *Von Colson and Kamann v Land Nordheim-Westfalen* [1984] ECR 1891 (CJEU); Case C-106/89 *Marleasing SA v La Commercial Internacionale de Alimentacion SA* [1990] ECR I-4135 (CJEU).

23. Cases C-6/90 and C-9/90 *Francovich and Bonifaci v Italian Republic* [1991] ECR I-5357 (CJEU).

24. Cases C-178/94, etc. *Dillenkofer and Others v Germany* [1996] ECR I-4845 (CJEU).

25. Case 322/88 *Grimaldi v Fonds des Maladies Professionelles* [1989] ECR 4407 (CJEU).

states an opinion that a Member State is in breach of an obligation, then it would be fool-hardy for a Member State to ignore it.

Despite their evidently persuasive nature, Article 288 TFEU states that 'Recommendations and opinions shall have no binding force'.

1.2.1.5 The supremacy of EU law

From the point of view of the EU, where there is a conflict between EU law and the law of EU Member States, EU law prevails. This has been clear since *Van Gend en Loos* in 1963 where the European Court of Justice (as it then was) clearly stated that 'the Community constitutes a new legal order . . . for whose benefit the states have limited their sovereign rights'.[26]

In *Costa v ENEL*[27] the following year, the European Court of Justice made two impor-tant observations regarding the relationship between Community law (as it then was) and national law; first, that the Member States have definitively transferred sovereign rights to a Community created by them. They cannot reverse this process by means of subsequent uni-lateral measures which are inconsistent with the concept of the Community. In other words, the autonomy of the Member States to act as they wish has been limited by virtue of their membership of the Community.

Moreover, it is a principle of the founding Treaties that no Member State may call into question the status of Community law as a system uniformly and generally applicable throughout the Community. Therefore, it follows that Community law, which was enacted in accordance with the Treaties, has priority over any conflicting law of the Member States. Therefore, in *Costa v ENEL* the European Court of Justice emphatically established the pri-macy of Community law over national law. In *Simmenthal*, the Court further held that the principle of supremacy does not invalidate conflicting national law, rather that the national law was of no effect to the extent of the conflict. Moreover, the national court should apply European law in the case of a conflict without waiting for the setting aside of the offending national provision.[28]

This implies that the enactment of the European Communities Act 1972 prevents Parliament from introducing new statutes which conflict with European law. This impacts upon the constitutional principle of Parliamentary sovereignty which, in essence, requires that Parliament has unlimited legislative competence (that is, it may enact any law that it wishes) and that there is no competing legislative body (that is, no body may challenge the validity of a properly-enacted Act of Parliament). Initially, the courts viewed that national law remained supreme. In *Felixstowe Dock & Railway Co v British Transport Docks Board*[29] Lord Denning stated *obiter* that:

> It seems to me that once the Bill is passed by Parliament and becomes a statute that will dispose of all discussion about the Treaty. These courts will have to abide by the Statute without regard to the Treaty.

However, in *Macarthys v Smith*[30] the courts considered that national law *was* subservient to Europe, although Lord Denning again considered that if Parliament deliberately and

---

26. Case 26/62 *Van Gend en Loos v Nederlandse Administratie der Belastingen* [1963] ECR 1 (CJEU).
27. Case 6/64 *Costa v ENEL* [1964] ECR 585 (CJEU).
28. Case 106/77 *Amministrazione delle Finanze Dello Stato v Simmenthal* [1978] ECR 629 (CJEU).
29. [1976] 2 CMLR 655 (CA) 664 (Denning MR).
30. [1979] ICR 785 (CA) 789 (Denning MR).

consistently breached European law, 'it would be the duty of our courts to follow the statute of our Parliament'.[31]

This situation was not tested in the domestic courts for some years. It was eventually considered in the *Factortame* cases.[32] Here, a conflict arose between certain provisions of the EC Treaty (as it was then) which prevented discrimination on the grounds of nationality and Part II of the Merchant Shipping Act 1988 which provided that fishing boats registered in the UK which were fishing for the quotas allocated to the UK by the EC must be owned and managed by UK citizens.

The House of Lords upheld the opinion of the European Court of Justice that it could grant an interim injunction against the Crown to prevent it enforcing an Act which contravened European law. The act of binding the Crown was previously constitutionally impossible. The House of Lords later held that parts of the Merchant Shipping Act 1988 were incompatible with the relevant provisions of the EC Treaty. This conundrum was cleverly and carefully reconciled by Lord Bridge who firstly considered s 2(4) of the European Communities Act 1972 which provided that:

> Any enactment passed or to be passed . . . shall be construed and have effect subject to the foregoing provisions of this section.

In other words, any legislation passed or to be passed in the UK must be interpreted with applicable European law in mind.

Lord Bridge argued that, since s 2(4) of the European Communities Act 1972 states that any enactment must have regard to Community obligations, this effectively meant that Parliament's intention was that *all* future legislation would be EC-compliant and would contain a fictional 'invisible clause' to this effect, unless the incompatibility was so important, in which case it could be explicitly excluded in the new legislation. Lord Bridge stated that:

> Whatever limitation of its sovereignty Parliament accepted when it enacted the European Communities Act 1972 it was entirely voluntary . . . when decisions of the Court of Justice have exposed areas of United Kingdom law which failed to implement Council Directives, Parliament has always loyally accepted the obligation to make appropriate and prompt amendments. Thus there is nothing in any way novel in according supremacy to rules of Community law.

Therefore the relevant provisions of the Merchant Shipping Act 1988 took effect subject to directly enforceable Community rights. In doing so, the House of Lords affirmed that, for all future cases, where a statute is silent on a matter covered by European law, it is presumed that it is intended to comply with European law.

The *Conservative – Liberal Democrat Coalition Agreement* published following the 2010 general election contained a promise to 'ensure that there is no further transfer of sovereignty or powers [to the EU] over the course of the next Parliament'; to 'amend the 1972 European Communities Act so that any proposed future treaty that transferred areas of power, or competences, would be subject to a referendum on that treaty'; and to 'examine the case for a United Kingdom Sovereignty Bill to make it clear that ultimate authority remains with Parliament'. The ensuing European Union Act 2011 contains a sovereignty clause in s 18 as follows:

> Directly applicable or directly effective EU law (that is, the rights, powers, liabilities, obligations, restrictions, remedies and procedures referred to in section 2(1) of the European

---

31. [1979] ICR 785 (CA) 789 (Denning MR).
32. *R v Secretary of State for Transport, ex p Factortame Ltd (No 2)* [1990] 2 AC 85 (HL).

> Communities Act 1972) falls to be recognised and available in law in the United Kingdom only by virtue of that Act or where it is required to be recognised and available in law by virtue of any other Act.

Thus, s 18 demonstrates the clear intention of Parliament that if UK law clearly, deliberately, and explicitly states that EU law is not to be followed then the courts should apply the domestic UK law. The associated Explanatory Note states that s 18 is 'declaratory' of the current position:

> This declaratory provision was included in the Act in order to address concerns that the doctrine of parliamentary sovereignty may in the future be eroded by decisions of the courts. By providing in statute that directly effective and directly applicable EU law only takes effect in the UK legal order through the will of Parliament and by virtue of the European Communities Act 1972 or where it is required to be recognised and available in law by virtue of any other Act, this will provide clear authority which can be relied upon to counter arguments that EU law constitutes a new higher autonomous legal order derived from the EU Treaties or international law and principles which has become an integral part of the UK's legal system independent of statute.

1.2.2 The European Convention on Human Rights

1.2.2.1 A brief history

The European Convention on Human Rights and Freedoms is a creation of the Council of Europe although it is, at least in part, based upon the 1948 United Nations Declaration of Human Rights. The Council of Europe was formed in 1949, shortly after the end of the Second World War, with the aim of international cooperation and the prevention of the kinds of widespread atrocious violations of human rights which had occurred during the war. The European Convention on Human Rights was signed in Rome in 1950, ratified by the UK a year later and came into force in 1953.

1.2.2.2 Convention Rights

The European Convention on Human Rights establishes a number of fundamental rights and freedoms (see Table 1.3).

1.2.2.3 The European Court of Human Rights

The European Court of Human Rights was established in 1959 as a final avenue of complaint for claimants who had exhausted the remedies available to them in their domestic courts for alleged breaches of Convention rights. At the same time, the European Commission of Human Rights was also established. The Commission's role was to decrease the caseload of the European Court of Human Rights by filtering out some cases and attempting to resolve others by conciliation. The individual's right to petition the European Court of Human Rights became available to UK citizens in 1966.

The European Court of Human Rights and the European Commission of Human Rights were abolished on 31 October 1998 and replaced by a single Court of Human Rights. Questions of admissibility (formerly dealt with by the Commission) are now dealt with by its judges sitting in committee.

It is worth repeating the point that it is vitally important not to confuse the European Court of Human Rights (which sits in Strasbourg) with the Court of Justice of the European Union (which sits in Luxembourg). They are separate courts with separate jurisdictions.

Table 1.3 Convention rights by Article number

Article	Convention right
1	Obligation to respect human rights
2	Right to life
3	Prohibition of torture
4	Prohibition of slavery and forced labour
5	Right to liberty and security
6	Right to a fair trial
7	No punishment without law
8	Right to respect for private and family life
9	Freedom of thought, conscience, and religion
10	Freedom of expression
11	Freedom of assembly and association
12	Right to marry and found a family
13	Right to an effective remedy
14	Prohibition of discrimination

CHAPTER SUMMARY

Statute law

- Public Bills are introduced by the Government as part of its programme of legislation

- Private Bills are introduced for the benefit of particular individuals, groups of people, institutions, or a particular locality

- Hybrid Bills are a cross between Public and Private Bills

- Private Members' Bills are non-Government Bills that are introduced by private Members of Parliament

- Consolidating statutes re-enact a topic contained in several earlier statutes

- Codifying statutes restate a topic previously contained in statute, common law, and custom

- Government Bills can be introduced in the House of Commons or House of Lords

- The Parliament Acts 1911 and 1949 provide a means by which the House of Commons can (under certain circumstances) bypass the House of Lords to present a Bill for Royal Assent without it having been passed by the House of Lords

- Royal Assent is required before any Bill can become law; it is customarily given

- The Human Rights Act 1998 requires that new Bills must be accompanied by a statement of compatibility (or a declaration that a statement of compatibility is not possible)

- The courts may make a declaration of incompatibility for Acts of Parliament which are incompatible with the European Convention on Human Rights; this does not affect the validity of the Act

- Delegated legislation is made under powers delegated by Parliament

- Delegated legislation includes statutory instruments (Rules, Regulations, and Orders) and by-laws

European institutions

- The European Commission represents the interests of the Union as a whole

- The Council of the European Union represents the governments of the individual member countries

- The European Parliament is directly elected by the citizens of the EU, which it represents

- The Court of Justice of the European Union (CJEU) interprets EU law to ensure uniform application and settles disputes

- The CJEU and the European Court of Human Rights are different

- The General Court deals with most European cases at first instance

- The European Council is composed of the Heads of State or Government of the EU Member States

Interrelationship between EU law and domestic law

- A provision of EU law is directly applicable if it becomes part of the law of a Member State without need for further legislation

- A provision of EU law is directly effective if it creates rights upon which individuals may rely in their national courts (and which are enforceable by those courts)

- A provision of EU law has vertical direct effect if it can be enforced against a Member State in its own courts

- A provision of EU law has horizontal direct effect if it can be enforced against another individual in the courts of a Member State

- Treaty Articles and Regulations have both vertical and horizontal direct effect if they satisfy the *Van Gend* criteria: that its terms are 'clear, precise and unconditional' and its implementation required no further legislation in Member States

- Directives do not have horizontal direct effect

- Directives may have vertical direct effect if they satisfy the *Van Gend* criteria and the time limit for their implementation has expired

- Where a statute is silent on a matter covered by EU law, it is presumed that it is intended to comply with European law—the UK's position is declared in s 18 of the European Union Act 2011.

European Convention on Human Rights

- The European Convention on Human Rights establishes a number of fundamental rights and freedoms

- The European Court of Human Rights is a final avenue of complaint for individuals who have exhausted national remedies available for alleged breaches of Convention Rights

- The European Court of Human Rights is not the same as the Court of Justice of the European Union

 FURTHER READING

- The law-making process is explained very clearly and with a good level of detail on the UK parliament website at www.parliament.uk/about/how/laws/. In particular the site covers the reasons why new laws are needed and how they are developed, the use of draft Bills, the different types of Bill, the passage of Bills through Parliament, the nature of Acts of Parliament, the role of secondary legislation, and the use of the Parliament Acts.

- This chapter gives a very brief overview of the EU institutions and the sources of law which come from Europe. It does not attempt to cover the substantive EU law. EU law is a huge subject area in its own right. For further detail, see S Weatherill, *Cases and Materials on EU Law* (11th edn, OUP 2014); N Foster, *Blackstone's EU Treaties and Legislation 2014–15* (25th edn, OUP 2013); and P Craig and G de Burca, *EU Law: Text, Cases and Materials* (6th edn, OUP 2015).

2 Finding legislation

INTRODUCTION

The first chapter of this book described the various sources of legislation. This chapter will show you how to locate statutes, statutory instruments, and EU legislation. The methods you will use to search will depend on whether you know the name of the particular piece of legislation in question or whether you are looking for any legislation which covers a certain subject area. The chapter will then close by showing you where to find the European Convention on Human Rights.

The ability to find legislation is an important legal skill. Legislation is a primary source of law affecting virtually every area of legal study. Clearly, you will not be able to read, understand, and use legislation without being able to find it first.

LEARNING OUTCOMES

After studying this chapter, you will be able to:

- Find Acts of Parliament and statutory instruments online

- Determine whether there is any statute law on a particular topic

- Work out whether a piece of legislation is in force

- Locate the official texts of EU Treaty Articles, Regulations, and Directives

- Source the official current text of the European Convention on Human Rights

 Practical exercise

Although this chapter will use a number of examples of various materials to demonstrate the ways in which they can be used, these are no substitute for your own experience and practice. Go to a law library and try to find as many of these example resources as you can. Bear in mind that not all resources will be available in all law libraries. However, for those that are, you will become familiar with their contents and layout and you will also know their location in the library which could save a lot of searching time in the future.

2.1 Finding domestic legislation

This section will describe the various ways in which statutes and statutory instruments can be located, both online and in a library. By way of example, we will use the Anti-social Behaviour, Crime and Policing Act 2014, an Act which made a large number of changes to the law relating to many areas of anti-social behaviour, crime, and disorder. Throughout this section we will refer to s 121 of that Act: a new provision which created an offence of forced marriage.

2.1.1 Online

2.1.1.1 Legislation.gov.uk

UK legislation is published on the official legislation.gov.uk website, managed by the National Archives on behalf of the Government. It contains most types of UK legislation, from the Statute of Marlborough 1267, to the most recent (at the time of writing) Data Retention and Investigatory Powers Act 2014. It also carries draft legislation and UK impact assessments for all new legislation since 2008.

You can simply browse the legislation on the database, or search by title or keywords. Some revised legislation may also be viewed as a snapshot at a particular point in time. These options are found on the 'Advanced Search' page.

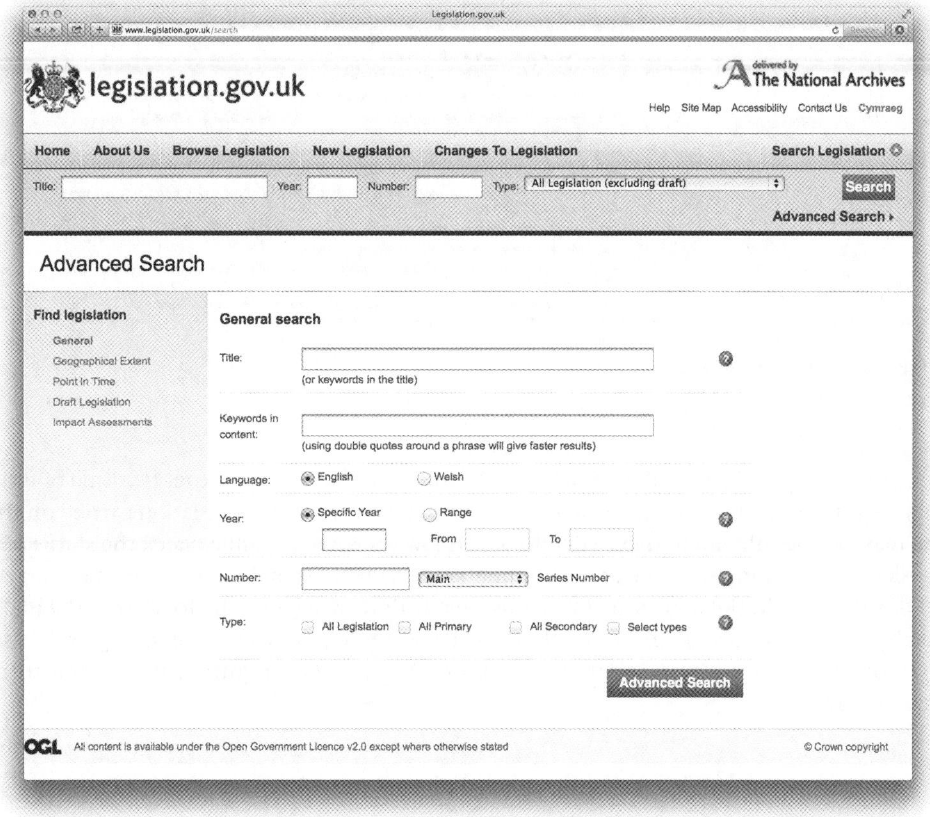

Figure 2.1 Legislation.gov.uk screenshot

So, if you wanted to find the text of s 121 of the Anti-social Behaviour, Crime and Policing Act 2014, you could simply enter the name of the Act in the search box, and browse to s 121.

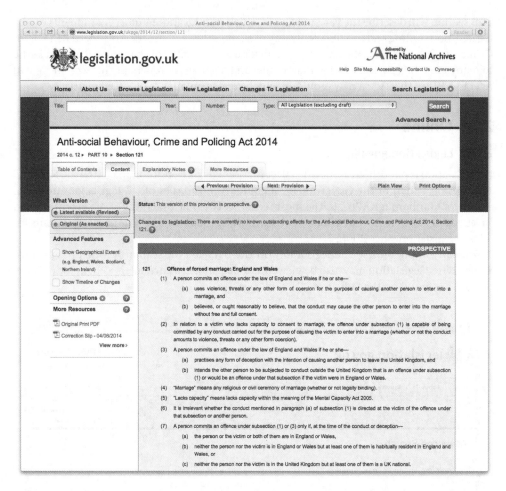

Figure 2.2 Anti-social Behaviour, Crime and Policing Act 2014

You will see that this section is showing as 'Prospective' on the website (at the time of writing). This may lead you to think that it is not yet in force. However, legislation carried on the site may not be fully up to date. Therefore, it is always wise to double check the status of a legislative provision using one of the commercially-available databases—which also carry a lot of valuable additional information. Most institutions will subscribe to most of the main databases that are covered in this book. These typically require you to log in to gain access, so if you do not have a login and password, a good first point of enquiry will be your institution's library.

2.1.1.2 Westlaw UK

Westlaw UK provides a range of browsing and searching facilities which can be used to find both Acts of Parliament and statutory instruments. It also contains a useful search facility to find historic law at a particular point in time (from 1991 for Acts, and 1948 for statutory instruments).

Figure 2.3 Westlaw UK screenshot

So, if you use Westlaw's browse or search facility to find s 121 (again, as shown at the time of writing) you should also find some extra useful material.

First of all, you will see at the top of the provision that it has the status of 'Law In Force'. This differs from that shown on legislation.gov.uk and should illustrate the point that it should be used with caution. In addition to the fact that s 121 is in force, you should also see the date on which it came into force, namely 16 June 2014. Westlaw UK also provides a 'Legislation Analysis' which gives you the actual statutory instrument that brought the provision into force—in this case SI 2014/949 art 5(b)—with a link to the full Anti-social Behaviour, Crime and Policing Act 2014 (Commencement No. 2, Transitional and Transitory Provisions) Order. It further provides details of geographical extent (England and Wales) and details of any historical amendments.

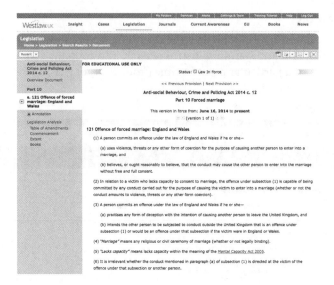

Figure 2.4 Westlaw UK: Anti-social Behaviour, Crime and Policing Act 2014

2.1.1.3 LexisLibrary

LexisLibrary provides searchable legislation and statutory instrument databases as well as cross-references to *Halsbury's Laws of England*. It has various online interactive tutorials.

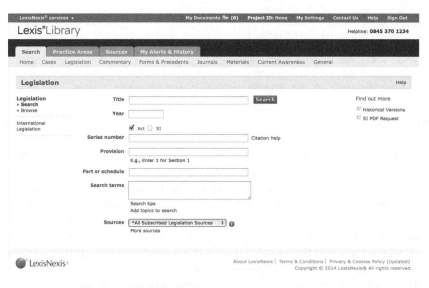

Figure 2.5 LexisLibrary screenshot
Reproduced with the kind permission of LexisNexis®

As with Westlaw UK, LexisLibrary also offers browse and search facilities, as well as the ability to look for historic versions of legislation. Section 121 of the Act looks like this:

Figure 2.6 Lexislibrary: Anti-social Behaviour, Crime and Policing Act 2014
Reproduced with the kind permission of LexisNexis®

As you will see, LexisLibrary also shows that the section is in force (by the green tick at the top of the page). In the notes found by scrolling down to the bottom of the page, it also gives details of the section coming into force, the SI that brought it into force, and its geographical extent.

In addition, though, LexisLibrary also offers links (within the 'Find out more' box on the right hand side of the page) to a number of other useful pieces of information. First, the 'Status Snapshot' which gives details of the Part of the Act in which s 121 is found (Part 10), the date of Royal Assent of the Act as a whole (13 March 2014), the commencement date and SI which brought s 121 into force (16 June 2014; SI 2014/949) and any subsequent amendments (none at the time of writing).

LexisLibrary also offers (exclusively) links to various parts of the *Halsbury* series of legal information, which are extremely useful:

- **Halsbury's annotations.** This may be accessed via the link within 'Find out more' or simply by clicking the speech bubble next to the provision itself. *Halsbury's annotations* are derived from the notes that appear in the volumes of *Halsbury's Statutes of England and Wales*. These notes provide precise information relating to:

  - Commencement

  - Parliamentary debates and, where appropriate, the background to legislation

  - Words and phrases defined statutorily

  - Judicial interpretation of statutes, whether of individual words and phrases, or sections as a whole

- Cross-references to other provisions of the Act and to other relevant legislation
- Subordinate legislation
- The origin of consolidating legislation.

The annotations are updated weekly to reflect changes brought about by new cases and new legislation.

- *Halsbury's Statutes Citator.* This gives details of any amendments to the provision. *Halsbury's Statutes Citator* provides a comprehensive list of amendments to all statutes which have been considered in *Halsbury's Statutes* since 1929. Amendments are noted to provision level, with any general notes relating to the Act as a whole appearing as the first note.
- *Halsbury's Is it in Force?* This provides the information you need to establish the exact commencement dates of Acts passed since 1960. The short title and chapter number of every Public General Act is given, and the following details are generally provided:
  - the date on which the Act received Royal Assent
  - a list of provisions which deal with the commencement of the Act or any part thereof (including any commencement orders which have been made)
  - any date or dates which have been appointed for the provisions of the Act to come into force
  - an indication where any provision is not in force.

?   Self-test questions

1. Which pieces of legislation amended s 39 of the Terrorism Act 2000 in 2007?
2. Which section was added to the Terrorism Act 2000 by s 117(2) of the Anti-terrorism, Crime and Security Act 2001?

ω   *Answers to the self-test questions can be found on the Online Resource Centre.*

2.1.2 In a library

Although much legal research is now done online, the ability to use a law library is still a very useful legal skill. There are some suggestions for further reading which goes into much greater depth than is possible in this book at the end of the chapter. More practically speaking, though, should you ever need to find legislation in the library (remember that online services can go down), then you should first seek out your law librarian who will be able to assist.

Legislation is published in a range of print publications:

- *Public General Acts and Measures.* At the end of each year, the Public General Acts which have been enacted during the year are published together in the official series *Public General Acts and Measures.* This series includes an index to all Acts passed during the year in alphabetical order; a chronological index to all Acts passed during the year (by chapter number); the full text of all Public General Acts enacted during the year in chapter number (chronological) order; the full text of all the General Synod Measures of the Church of England passed in the year, and; a list (but not the full text) of Local and Personal Acts enacted during the year.

- *Chronological Table of the Statutes.* The *Chronological Table of the Statutes* provides historical as well as current information. As its name suggests it lists all statutes enacted since 1235 (the Statute of Merton). It then shows, for each, whether it has been repealed or amended. The statutes are listed in year and chapter order.

- *Current Law Legislation Citator.* Since 1972 the *Current Law Legislation Citators* have provided an alphabetical list of statutes at the start of each volume. This can be useful if you know the name of the Act but are unsure of its year or chapter number.

- *Current Law Statutes Annotated.* *Current Law Statutes Annotated* provides the full text of all Public General Acts shortly after the official Act is published by the Queen's Printer (and will ultimately be bound into *Public General Acts and Measures*). They are supplied as individual booklets and filed in a loose-leaf service binder in chapter number order. The annotations generally provide a detailed account of the legislative history of the Act including references to the key debates in *Hansard*, provision by provision. Although these annotations carry no legal authority, they are extremely useful.

- *Halsbury's Statutes.* *Halsbury's Statutes of England* aims to provide current versions of all Public General Acts in force in England and Wales. As you would probably imagine, it is a mammoth undertaking which comprises a number of different volumes, all of which work together to keep the publication overall as up-to-date as possible. The information listed in the main volumes is brought up-to-date annually via the *Cumulative Supplement* with more recent (i.e. this year's) developments being available via the *Noter-Up Service*.

- *Halsbury's Is it in Force?* The quickest way to determine whether a particular statutory provision is in force is to use *Is it in Force?* which is part of the *Halsbury's Statutes* suite. However, it only covers statutes enacted since 1961. For older statutes, you should use the *Chronological Table of the Statutes*.

As you have already seen, the suite of *Halsbury* publications is available via LexisLibrary, where it is kept up-to-date.

2.2 Finding EU legislation

2.2.1 The *Official Journal of the European Union*

The *Official Journal of the European Union* (generally referred to as the *Official Journal* or just the *OJ*) is the only official source of the officially adopted texts of the EU.

The *Official Journal* is published almost daily (usually around six times a week). It is vast—running to over 30,000 pages annually![1] It comprises several parts, as listed in Table 2.1.

Table 2.1 Parts of the *Official Journal*

Part	Contents
L series (Legislation)	The *L series* contains all EU legislation including: • regulations • directives • decisions • recommendations • opinions The *Directory of Community legislation in force* is published as part of the *L series*. This lists references to the initial texts and to any subsequent amendments. It also includes references to agreements made and conventions signed by the European Union in the framework of external relations, binding acts under the EU Treaties, complementary acts, such as those of the Council of Ministers and Heads of State or Government, and other non-binding acts which are relevant for the institutions.
C series (Information and Notices)	The *C series* contains EU information and notices and includes: • summaries of judgments of the Court of Justice and the General Court; • minutes of parliamentary meetings; • reports of the Court of Auditors; • parliamentary written questions and answers from the Council or Commission; • statements from the European Economic and Social Committee and the Committee of the Regions; • competition notices for recruitment by the EU institutions (if you are interested only in these notices, there is a special subscription—see price list); • calls for expressions of interest for EU programmes and projects; • other documents published pursuant to EU legislation; • public contracts for food aid; • the table of contents of the OJ CE series.

(Continued)

1.   The figure of 30,000 pages only refers to the *L series* and the *C series*. Adding the material that is only available electronically clearly expands the mass of information in the *Official Journal* even more.

Table 2.1 *(Cont.)*

Part	Contents
CE series	The *CE series* contains preparatory acts in the legislative process.
S series (Supplemental)	The *S series* publishes details of public contracts which are open to competitive tender
Annex	Contains full text transcripts of debates in the European Parliament
Special Edition	Contains official English translations of all EC legislation in force as at 1 January 1973 when the UK joined the European Communities.

Note that the *S series*[2] and the *Annex*[3] are only available electronically. The *S series* can be found as Tenders Electronic Daily (TED) at www.ted.europa.eu.

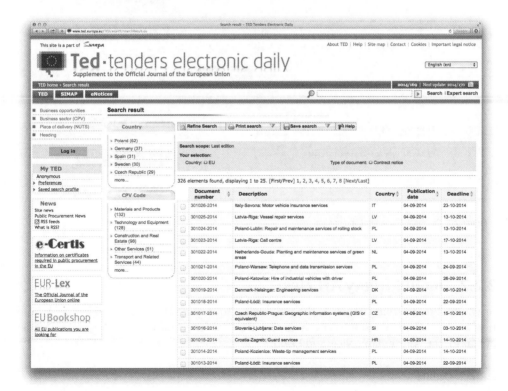

Figure 2.7 TED screenshot
© European Union, 1995–2013

2. Since 1997.
3. Since 2000.

Debates of the Parliament can be found at www.europarl.europa.eu.

Figure 2.8 European Parliament screenshot

2.2.2 Finding Treaty Articles

As you will recall from chapter 1, the underlying source of EU law is found in the various treaties. The EU Treaty itself has been amended by the Single European Act and the Treaties of Maastricht, Amsterdam, Nice, and Lisbon.

2.2.2.1 Online

EU website

The text of the Treaties can be found online on the EU website at http://europa.eu/eu-law/decision-making/treaties/index_en.htm

Figure 2.9 Europa screenshot: EU Treaties

2.2.2.2 In a library

The authoritative text for all EU legislation is the *Official Journal*.[4]

An unofficial, but nonetheless very useful, compilation of the unannotated texts of the main treaties can be found in N Foster, *Blackstone's EU Treaties and Legislation*, published and updated regularly by Oxford University Press.

2.2.3 Finding EU secondary legislation

2.2.3.1 Online

EUROPA (www.europa.eu)

EUROPA is the main website of the European Union. It contains over 1.5 million pages and contains a free searchable database of EU legislation and case law at http://europa.eu/eu-law/index_en.htm.

---

4.   For instance, the text of the Treaty of Nice was found in the *Official Journal C series* on 10 March 2001.

Other databases

LexisLibrary and Westlaw UK also provide search facilities for EU legislation.

2.2.3.2 In a library

The *Official Journal Index*

Despite its helpful sounding name, the *Official Journal Index* does not greatly assist in navigating the vast expanse of material that is the *Official Journal*. For instance, it only indexes the *L series* (of enacted legislation) and the case lists and summaries (from the Court of Justice and General Court) from the *C series*.

It is published monthly, with a cumulative index only being published annually. This means that you may have to search through a number of monthly copies of the *Index*.

It is, therefore, much easier to search for EU materials via one or more of the electronic sources available.

2.3 European Convention on Human Rights

The official text of the European Convention on Human Rights and the various protocols which amend it can be found online at the Council of Europe's official treaty website (www. conventions.coe.int/Treaty/en/Treaties/Html/005.htm).

Individual copies of the Convention on Human Rights are also published by the Council of Europe.

?   Self-test questions

Having completed this chapter, use your research skills to attempt the following more challenging research questions involving legislation.

1. What is the *OJ* reference of the Preamble to the Accession Treaty of Austria, Finland, and Sweden to the European Union?

2. Which primary statutory provision concerns the use of poison against grey squirrels and coypus and what secondary legislation was made under it?

3. What legislation excepted the Brazilian wolf spider from the provisions of the Dangerous Wild Animals Act 1976?

4. Which private Act ensures that the flood arches at each end of Gunthorpe bridge are at all times kept open and free for the passage of water?

5. What was the wording of s 15A of the Theft Act 1968 as at 20 January 1995?

@   *Answers to the self-test questions can be found on the Online Resource Centre.*

CHAPTER SUMMARY

Domestic statutes

- The legislation.gov.uk website provides free links to the full text of all Public General Acts from 1988 and Local Acts from 1991

- Westlaw UK and LexisLibrary all provide commercially-available legislation search engines which are kept up-to-date and provide much additional valuable information

- *Halsbury's Statutes of England* provides current volumes of all Public General Acts, arranged by subject matter. It also contains a very useful *Is It In Force?* service

- *Public General Acts and Measures* contains the full text of all statutes

- The *Chronological Table of the Statutes* is useful for tracing very old statutes, but is of less use for modern statutes as it is often two or three years out of date

- The *Current Law Legislation Citator* lists all statutes and provides information as to where and how that legislation has been used

- *Current Law Statutes Annotated* provides the full text of all Public General Acts annotated with a detailed account of the history of the Act (including Parliamentary debate) and other useful notes and cross-references

EU law

- The *Official Journal of the European Union (OJ)* is the only official source of the officially adopted texts of the EU

- The *OJ* is vast and easier to navigate electronically

- The *CE series, S series,* and *Annex* to the *OJ* are only available electronically

- Compilations of EU legislation are widely available in student statute texts

- EU legislation can be found online for free via EUROPA

- Westlaw UK and LexisLibrary all provide commercially-available EU legislation search engines which are generally easier to use than EUROPA

- The European Convention on Human Rights and various protocols which amend it can be found on the Council of Europe official website

 FURTHER READING

- Although much legal research is now done online, the ability to use a law library is still a very useful legal skill. Two books that go into greater depth than has been possible in this chapter are P Clinch, *Using a Law Library* (2nd edn, Blackstone Press 2001), and PA Thomas and J Knowles, *Dane and Thomas: How to Use a Law Library* (2nd edn, Sweet & Maxwell 2001). Despite being over ten years old, the principles of library research remain the same, and these books will assist you in finding your way around the library at your own university.

3 Using legislation

INTRODUCTION

The place of legislation within the range of sources of law was covered in chapter 1 while various means of finding legislation were considered in chapter 2. Having learnt where legislation fits into the structure of the legal system and how it can be found, this chapter will discuss how to use legislation. It will firstly look at the 'anatomy' of an Act of Parliament and describe each of its composite parts. It will then move on to consider the various means by which the courts can interpret the wording of statutory provisions, including a discussion of the impact of the European Communities Act 1972 and the Human Rights Act 1998.

Using legislation is an important legal skill. Legislation is a primary source of law and represents the will of Parliament as the legislature. Therefore it is essential that you are able to negotiate your way around a piece of legislation and understand how it all fits together. You will also need to be able to interpret potentially ambiguous legislative provisions to determine whether they will support your argument or whether an interpretation could be found that might go against your argument. Most importantly, using and understanding legislation is vital to the study of every area of law.

LEARNING OUTCOMES

After studying this chapter, you will be able to:

- Navigate an Act of Parliament and a statutory instrument and distinguish its component parts

- Interpret the possible meanings of a legislative provision in the case of ambiguity

- Describe the impact that the European Communities Act 1972 and the Human Rights Act 1998 have had on the interpretation of legislation

3.1 Anatomy of an Act of Parliament

In order to make any sense at all of a statute, you will need first to understand the way in which it is structured. We will use the Anti-social Behaviour, Crime and Policing Act 2014 as an example. Look at the extracts from the statute provided. You will see that a number of areas of the statute have been highlighted. These will be covered in turn (see Figure 3.1 and Figure 3.2).

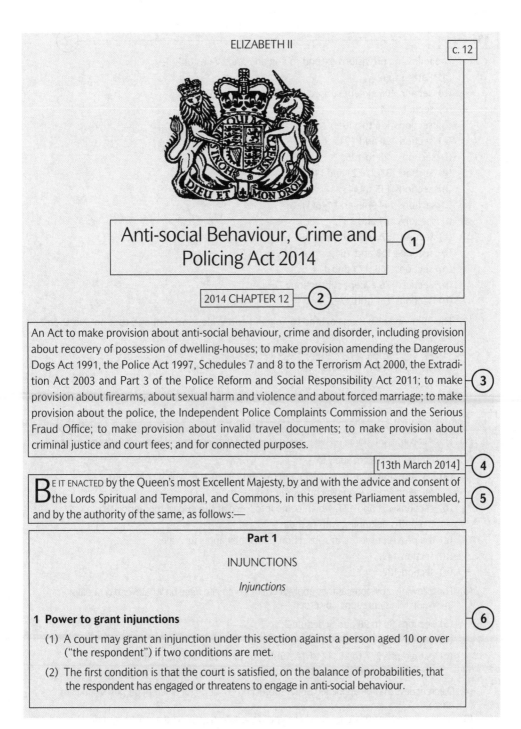

ELIZABETH II

c. 12

Anti-social Behaviour, Crime and Policing Act 2014 ①

2014 CHAPTER 12 ②

An Act to make provision about anti-social behaviour, crime and disorder, including provision about recovery of possession of dwelling-houses; to make provision amending the Dangerous Dogs Act 1991, the Police Act 1997, Schedules 7 and 8 to the Terrorism Act 2000, the Extradition Act 2003 and Part 3 of the Police Reform and Social Responsibility Act 2011; to make provision about firearms, about sexual harm and violence and about forced marriage; to make provision about the police, the Independent Police Complaints Commission and the Serious Fraud Office; to make provision about invalid travel documents; to make provision about criminal justice and court fees; and for connected purposes. ③

[13th March 2014] ④

BE IT ENACTED by the Queen's most Excellent Majesty, by and with the advice and consent of the Lords Spiritual and Temporal, and Commons, in this present Parliament assembled, and by the authority of the same, as follows:— ⑤

Part 1

INJUNCTIONS

Injunctions

1 Power to grant injunctions ⑥

(1) A court may grant an injunction under this section against a person aged 10 or over ("the respondent") if two conditions are met.

(2) The first condition is that the court is satisfied, on the balance of probabilities, that the respondent has engaged or threatens to engage in anti-social behaviour.

Figure 3.1 Anti-social Behaviour, Crime and Policing Act 2014

184 Extent ── (7)

(1) The following provisions extend to England and Wales only —

(a) Parts 1 to 6;

(b) section 106 except subsections (2)(a)(ii) and (6);

(c) section 114;

(d) sections 116 to 119;

(e) section 120 and 121;

(f) sections 123 to 130;

(g) section 133(1), (2) and (4)

(h) sections 135 to 143;

(i) sections 144, 145 and 146(1);

(j) sections 149 and 151;

(k) section 152 and Schedule 10;

(l) sections 153 and 154;

(m) sections 166, 171 and 174;

(n) section 176 except subsection (7);

(o) sections 177 and 179.

(2) The following provisions extend to England and Wales and Scotland (but not Northern Ireland)—

(a) sections 106(2)(a)(ii) and (6) and 107;

(b) sections 108 to 110 and 112;

(c) section 133(3);

(d) section 178.

185 Commencement ────────────────────────────── (8)

(1) This Act comes into force on whatever day or days the Secretary of State appoints by order.

(2) Subsection (1) does not apply to —

(a) sections 150, 175, 180, 181(2) and (4) and 182 to 186, which come into force on the day on which this Act is passed;

(b) sections 151 and 177, which come into force at the end of the period of 2 months beginning with that day;

(c) the provisions listed in subsection (3) as they apply in Wales;

(d) section 149;

(e) section 122.

(3) The following provisions, as they apply in Wales, come into force on whatever day or days the Welsh Ministers appoint by order —

(a) sections 94 to 98 and Schedule 3;

(b) section 100;

(c) paragraphs 2, 7 to 10, 12 to 14, 15(4), 16, 18 to 20, 47(4) and 48 of Schedule 11 (and section 181(1) sor far as it relates to those paragraphs).

(4) Different days may be appointed under subsection (1) or (3) for different purposes or different areas.

(5) Section 149 comes into force on whatever day the Attorney General appoints by order.

Figure 3.2 Anti-social Behaviour, Crime and Policing Act 2014 ss 184 and 185

3.1.1 Short title ①

The short title of this Act is the 'Anti-social Behaviour, Crime and Policing Act 2014'. The short title is the normal way in which to refer to a statute. In this example the Act provides its own short title in s 186 (Figure 3.3).

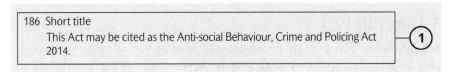

186 Short title
   This Act may be cited as the Anti-social Behaviour, Crime and Policing Act 2014.

Figure 3.3 Anti-social Behaviour, Crime and Policing Act 2014 s 186

Sometimes, the short title might actually be quite long—as is the case with this statute. If the Act is referred to constantly then the short title may be informally abbreviated further. For instance, the Anti-social Behaviour, Crime and Policing Act 2014 might be referred to as the 'ASBO Act'; however, this would not be the official short title which remains as the Anti-social Behaviour, Crime and Policing Act 2014.

More extreme examples of short-title abbreviation can be found with the Police and Criminal Evidence Act 1984 and the Trusts of Land and Appointment of Trustees Act 1996 which for reasons of manageability are almost universally referred to as PACE and TOLATA respectively.

3.1.2 Citation ②

The official citation for this statute is '2014 Chapter 12'. Each Act passed in any calendar year is given its own number, known as the chapter number. The official citations—comprising year and chapter number—are therefore unique. In this case, the Anti-social Behaviour, Crime and Policing Act 2014 was the twelfth statute passed in 2014. The word 'chapter' can be abbreviated to 'c.'—an example of this can be seen in the top right-hand corner of the page. The official citation is not usually used in referencing, although some international journals (particularly American journals) do require full citations to be used, often in connection with the short title; for example, the Anti-social Behaviour, Crime and Policing Act 2014 (c. 12).

This system has been used for Acts passed since 1 January 1963 when the Acts of Parliament Numbering and Citation Act 1962 came into force. Prior to that a more complex system involving regnal years was used. This is derived from the year of the sovereign's reign corresponding to the Parliamentary session in which the Act was passed. It was common for Parliamentary sessions to span more than one year, in which case all are shown. Look at the example in Figure 3.4.

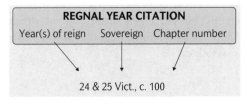

Figure 3.4 Regnal year citation

This is the citation for the 100th Act that was passed in the session beginning the 24th year of Queen Victoria's reign and which ended in the 25th year. It is more commonly (and conveniently) known as the Offences against the Person Act 1861.

There is a very useful calendar year to regnal year conversion table covering 1235–1862 available on the JustCite website at www.justcite.com/kb/search-technology/regnal-years/.

3.1.3 Long title ③

The long title of this statute is 'An Act to make provision about anti-social behaviour, crime and disorder, including provision about recovery of possession of dwelling-houses; to make provision amending the Dangerous Dogs Act 1991, the Police Act 1997, Schedules 7 and 8 to the Terrorism Act 2000, the Extradition Act 2003 and Part 3 of the Police Reform and Social Responsibility Act 2011; to make provision about firearms, about sexual harm and violence and about forced marriage; to make provision about the police, the Independent Police Complaints Commission and the Serious Fraud Office; to make provision about invalid travel documents; to make provision about criminal justice and court fees; and for connected purposes'. Generally speaking, the long title of an Act gives an indication as to its purpose and content.

3.1.4 Date of Royal Assent ④

This Act received the Royal Assent on 13 March 2014. This is the date upon which the preceding Bill became law. The provisions of the Act come into force on the date of Royal Assent unless the Act itself states otherwise. For example, the Act, or various parts of it, may come into force by order of a Government Minister. This will be provided for within the Act itself and will involve the passing of a commencement order (which is a statutory instrument).

In section 3.2, you will see how the Sustainable and Secure Buildings Act 2004 (Commencement No 1) Order 2006 brings part of the Sustainable and Secure Buildings Act 2004 into force.

The date of the Act in its short title can sometimes be misleading. For example, the European Communities Act 1972 actually came into force on 1 January 1973. An Act or provision of an Act comes into force at the beginning of the day where provision is made for it to come into force on that day, or if not, at the beginning of the day on which the Act receives the Royal Assent[1] (see section 3.1.7 on 'Commencement').

3.1.5 Enacting formula ⑤

The enacting formula introduces the main provisions of the statute. It declares that the law derives its authority from having been properly passed by the legislature. The enacting formula is generally the same, namely:

> BE IT ENACTED by the Queen's most Excellent Majesty, by and with the advice and consent of the Lords Spiritual and Temporal, and Commons, in this present Parliament assembled, and by the authority of the same, as follows:

---

1. Interpretation Act 1978 s 4.

However, if the Parliament Acts 1911 and 1949 have been used to force legislation through Parliament against the wishes of the House of Lords, the enacting formula used is different:

> BE IT ENACTED by the Queen's most Excellent Majesty, by and with the advice and consent of the Commons in this present Parliament assembled, in accordance with the provisions of the Parliament Acts 1911 and 1949, and by the authority of the same, as follows:

This formula removes references to the 'advice and consent of the Lords Spiritual and Temporal'.

See chapter 1, section 1.1.1.6 for more information on the use of the Parliament Acts.

3.1.6 Main body ⑥

The main body of the Act is divided into sections, subsections, paragraphs, and subparagraphs. When referencing particular parts of an Act, it is important to be precise. You should identify exactly where the wording of the law can be found.

In this Act, s 1 deals with the power to grant injunctions. Figure 3.5 shows an extract from s 13 which concerns the power to exclude a person from their home in cases of violence or where there is a risk of harm. Section 13 is divided into subsections. Subsection 13(1) sets out the conditions under which an injunction granted under s 1 will exclude the respondent from their home. The first of these is in para. 13(1)(a), namely that the respondent is aged 18 or over. The second condition is in para. 13(1)(b), which states that the injunction must be granted on the application of one of three particular bodies or individuals. This paragraph is further divided into subparagraphs—one per body. This is often the case in complex statutory provisions where, in order to aid clarity, an additional level of subdivision is required. This is also useful for ease of referencing very specific parts of an overall provision. So subpara. 13(1)(b)(iii), highlighted in the extract from the Act refers to a housing provider (see Figure 3.5).

'Section' is commonly abbreviated to 's'[2]—the examples highlighted above could therefore be referred to as s 13, s 13(1), s 13(1)(a), s 13(1)(b), and 13(1)(b)(iii). However, you should avoid

13 Power to exclude person from home in cases of violence or risk of harm

(1) An injunction under section 1 may have the effect of excluding the respondent from the place where he or she normally lives ("the premises") only if —
  (a) the respondent is aged 18 or over,
  (b) the injunction is granted on the application of —
    (i) a local authority,
    (ii) the chief officer of police for the police area that the premises are in, or
    (iii) if the premises are owned or managed by a housing provider, that housing provider, and ⑥
  (c) the court thinks that—
    (i) the anti-social behaviour in which the respondent has engaged or threatens to engage consists of or includes the use or threatened use of violence against other persons, or
    (ii) there is a significant risk of harm to other persons from the respondent.

Figure 3.5 Anti-social Behaviour, Crime and Policing Act 2014, subparagraph 13(1)(b)(iii)

2. Even though it might look unusual, OSCOLA referencing (see chapter 12) does not use a full stop after the 's' for 'section'.

using the abbreviated form at the beginning of a sentence. Therefore, it is preferable to start a sentence with, for example, 'Section 3 of the Human Rights Act 1998 . . .' than with 'S 3 of the Human Rights Act 1998 . . .'.

See chapter 10 for more discussion on written style.

3.1.6.1 Headings

Each section in this particular Act has a heading. For example the heading to section 184 (Figure 3.2) is 'Extent'. The headings give some indication of the content of the particular section, but are not especially helpful in resolving matters of interpretation.

Many older statutes have marginal notes instead of headings. Look at the extract from the Misrepresentation Act 1967 in Figure 3.6. You will see an example of a marginal note highlighted.

However, there is one key difference between marginal notes and headings. The headings are part of the Act (they are debated during the passage of the legislation) and marginal notes are not. This means that marginal notes have no direct legal effect. Despite this distinction, both marginal notes and headings are of limited use beyond being a useful means of navigating around the Act.

Misrepresentation Act 1967

1967 CHAPTER 7

An Act to amend the law relating to innocent misrepresentation and to amend sections 11 and 35 of the Sale of Goods Act 1893.   [22nd March 1967]

BE IT ENACTED by the Queen's most Excellent Majesty, by and with the advice and consent of the Lords Spiritual and Temporal, and Commons, in this present Parliament assembled, and by the authority of the same, as follows:—

1. Where a person has entered into a contract after a misrepresentation has been made to him, and—

    (*a*) the misrepresentation has become a term of the contract;

      or

    (*b*) the contract has been performed;

or both, then, if otherwise he would be entitled to rescind the contract without alleging fraud, he shall be so entitled, subject to the provisions of this Act, notwithstanding the matters mentioned in paragraphs (*a*) and (*b*) of this section.

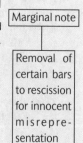

Marginal note

Removal of certain bars to rescission for innocent misrepresentation

Figure 3.6 Misrepresentation Act 1967, marginal note

Self-test questions

1. When did the Misrepresentation Act 1967 receive Royal Assent?

2. What is its long title?

3. What is its citation?

4. What does '1967 Chapter 7' signify?

Answers to the self-test questions can be found on the Online Resource Centre.

3.1.7 Extent and commencement (7) and (8)

As we have found, the provisions of the Act come into force on the date of Royal Assent unless the Act itself states otherwise. The commencement provisions are normally found towards the end of the Act. In this example, the commencement provisions are found in s 185. You will see that s 185(1) sets out a default position that the Act only comes into force as appointed by order of the Secretary of State. Therefore, the Secretary of State has the power to decide when certain parts of the Act become law. Those parts of the Act will be brought into effect by a statutory instrument known as a commencement order. This means that certain statutory provisions might *never* come into force at all. For example, the Family Law Act 1996 was intended to revolutionize the divorce process. It received Royal Assent on 4 July 1996 but at the time it was not expected to be brought into effect until 2000. Unfortunately, the results from a pilot study established that the amendments that it brought into the divorce process were ineffective. This led to the Government abandoning the reforms altogether and consequently Part 2 of the Act will never be brought into force.

Later subsections of s 185 provide exceptions to the default 'by order of the Secretary of State' commencement position. For example s 185(2)(a) provides that ss 150, 175, 180, 181(2), 181(4), and 182 to 186 come into force on Royal Assent—that is, 13 March 2014. Similarly, s 185(5) provides a further exception that s 149 comes into force when appointed by order of the Attorney General (and not the Secretary of State) and s 185(3) grants commencement powers for certain provisions to the Welsh Ministers.

An Act might specify that certain provisions come into force on a fixed date, or a date relative to its receiving Royal Assent. Look at s 185(2)(b) which brings ss 151 and 177 into force two months from Royal Assent.

Acts do not take effect retrospectively unless expressly provided for within the Act. Examples of retrospective legislation are rare, but one example can be found in s 1 of the War Crimes Act 1991; an Act which confers jurisdiction on UK courts in respect of certain grave violations of the laws and customs of war committed in German-held territory during the Second World War.

An 'extent' provision in the Act (or in a later commencement order made under the Act) might specify that certain provisions only come into force in particular areas. In this example, s 184(1) sets out provisions of the Act that only apply to England and Wales and s 184(2) those applying to England, Wales, and Scotland (but not Northern Ireland).

Self-test questions

5. When did the Misrepresentation Act 1967 come into force?

Answers to the self-test questions can be found on the Online Resource Centre.

3.1.8 Schedules (9)

Some statutes have one or more schedules at the end (see Figure 3.7). These may contain a number of different things, such as:

- Definitions of terms used in the Act (e.g. Schedule 1, Interpretation Act 1978)
- Detailed provisions which are referred to in the main Act (e.g. Schedule 1, Football (Disorder) Act 2000)
- Details of minor and consequential amendments to other legislation (e.g. Schedule 2, Football (Disorder) Act 2000)
- Repeals of pre-existing legislation (e.g. Schedule 3, Football (Disorder) Act 2000)

In this example, Schedule 1 refers to 'Remands under sections 9 and 10' which are set out in the main Act. The schedule provides more details as to the operation of remands. It is split out into a schedule to enable easier navigation around the main body of the Act.

Schedules are divided into paragraphs and subparagraphs. In this example, Schedule 1, paragraph 1, subparagraph 2 provides that 'A reference in the following paragraphs of this Schedule to a judge is to be read as including a justice of the peace'. 'Schedule' is often abbreviated to 'sch' and paragraph to 'para'. It is an incorrect use of terminology to refer to the divisions and subdivisions of a schedule as sections and subsections.

3.1.9 Preambles

Older statutes contain preambles, which describe the purpose of the Act in more detail than the long title. For example, the preamble to the Statute of Charitable Uses 1601 sets out a list of charitable purposes or activities.

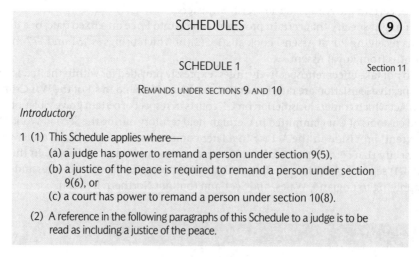

Figure 3.7 Schedule 1—Remands under sections 9 and 10

The Statute of Charitable Uses (1601), 43 Elizabeth I c. 4

An Acte to redresse the Misemployment of Landes Goodes and Stockes of Money heretofore given to Charitable Uses

Whereas Landes Tenementes Rentes Annuities Profittes Hereditamentes, Goodes Chattels Money and Stockes of Money, have bene heretofore given limitted appointed and assigned, as well by the Queenes most excellent Majestie and her moste noble Progenitors, as by sondrie other well disposed persons, some for Releife of aged impotent and poore people, some for Maintenance of sicke and maymed Souldiers and Marriners, Schooles of Learninge, Free Schooles and Schollers in Universities, some for Repaire of Bridges Portes Havens Causwaies Churches Seabankes and Highwaies, some for Educacion and prefermente of Orphans, some for or towardes Reliefe Stocke or Maintenance of Howses of Correccion, some for Mariages of poore Maides, some for Supportacion Ayde and Helpe of younge tradesmen Handicraftesmen and persons decayed, and others for reliefe or redemption of Prisoners or Captives, and for aide or ease of any poore Inhabitantes concerninge payment of Fifteenes, setting out of Souldiers and other Taxes; Whiche Landes Tenementes Rents Annuities Profitts Hereditaments Goodes Chattells Money and Stockes of Money nevertheles have not byn imployed according to the charitable intente of the givers and founders thereof, by reason of Fraudes breaches of Truste and Negligence in those that shoulde pay delyver and imploy the same . . .

However, since the list was in the preamble, rather than in the main body of the Act, it did not form part of the statute. However, the list in the preamble to the 1601 statute has nevertheless formed the foundation of the modern definition of charitable purposes which can be found in s 2(1) of the Charities Act 2011: this requires a purpose which falls within the list of charitable purposes set out in s 3(1) and which is for the public benefit (s 4).

Preambles in older statutes are also useful if you need to evaluate whether an old piece of legislation has actually achieved what it set out to achieve. The purposes set out in the preamble can then be compared to the effect of the Act's application by the courts.

3.1.10 Explanatory Notes

Most recent Acts will carry accompanying Explanatory Notes. These are useful information but are not legally binding. The Office of Public Sector Information describes Explanatory Notes as follows:

The purpose of these Explanatory Notes is to make the Act of Parliament accessible to readers who are not legally qualified and who have no specialised knowledge of the matters dealt with. They are intended to allow the reader to grasp what the Act sets out to achieve and place its effect in context.

The Explanatory Notes can give an indication of the purpose of a particular statute which might be useful background when trying to establish the meaning behind any seemingly ambiguous provision.

See section 3.3 for a discussion of statutory interpretation.

3.2 Anatomy of a statutory instrument

Chapter 1 describes statutory instruments as sources of law.

Statutory instruments are also built up from a number of standard components. Look at the Pensions Act 2011 (Commencement No. 5) Order 2014. As before, a number of the parts of the statutory instrument have been highlighted (see Figure 3.8).

3.2.1 Citation ①

The citation for this example is '2014 No 1683 (C. 71)' This means that it is the 1683rd statutory instrument of 2014.

Some (but not all) statutory instruments have letters and a number in brackets after the sequence number:

- C stands for commencement order
- L relates to fees and procedures in courts
- S relates to Scotland only

The number that follows is a sequence number relating to the type of statutory instrument in question. In this example, we see 'C.71' which indicates that this is the 71st commencement order of 2014.

3.2.2 Subject matter ②

The subject matter of the statutory instrument in this case is pensions.

3.2.3 Title ③

The title of the statutory instrument is The Pensions Act 2011 (Commencement No. 5) Order 2014. This refers to its parent Act, namely the Pensions Act 2011 and to its purpose as a commencement order. The 'No 5' refers to it being the fifth commencement order made under the parent Act.

3.2.4 Date made ④

The date shown in the statutory instrument (30 June 2014) is that on which it was made (or in the case of instruments that are required to be laid before Parliament, the date on which it was laid before Parliament). If the statutory instrument comes into force after the date of the order, then it will give the commencement date.

3.2.5 Authority ⑤

This section of the statutory instrument shows the authority by which it is made. In this case, the order was made under the power delegated to the Secretary of State for Work and Pensions by s 38(4) of Pensions Act 2011. There is a footnote reference (a) to the official citation (see section 3.1.2) of the parent Act—2011 c. 19—so in this example it shows that the Pensions Act 2011 was the 19th Act of 2011.

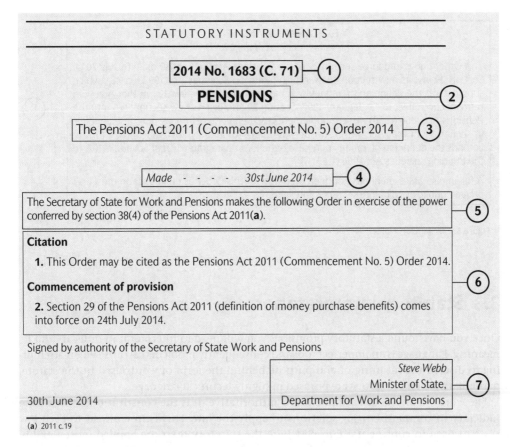

STATUTORY INSTRUMENTS

2014 No. 1683 (C. 71) — (1)

PENSIONS — (2)

The Pensions Act 2011 (Commencement No. 5) Order 2014 — (3)

Made - - - - 30st June 2014 — (4)

The Secretary of State for Work and Pensions makes the following Order in exercise of the power conferred by section 38(4) of the Pensions Act 2011(**a**). — (5)

Citation

1. This Order may be cited as the Pensions Act 2011 (Commencement No. 5) Order 2014.

Commencement of provision

2. Section 29 of the Pensions Act 2011 (definition of money purchase benefits) comes into force on 24th July 2014. — (6)

Signed by authority of the Secretary of State Work and Pensions

Steve Webb
Minister of State,
Department for Work and Pensions — (7)

30th June 2014

(**a**) 2011 c.19

Figure 3.8 The Pensions Act 2011 (Commencement No. 5) Order 2014

3.2.6 Main body (6)

The main body of the statutory instrument contains paragraphs or articles if it is an order (as here), regulations if it is a regulation, or rules if it is a set of rules. Regulations are often abbreviated to 'reg' and rules to 'r'. In this case, the order brings s 29 of the Pensions Act 2011 into force on 24 July 2014.

3.2.7 Minister (7)

This is the name of the Minister signing the order. In this case, Steve Webb.

3.2.8 Explanatory Note (8)

As with statutes, the Explanatory Note is not part of the order (see Figure 3.9). It generally either:

- explains the purpose of the statutory instrument;
- details amendments or revocations of previous statutory instruments; and/or
- notes implementation of European legislation.

EXPLANATORY NOTE
(This note is not part of the Order)

This Order brings into force section 29 of the Pensions Act 2011 (c.19) on 24th July 2014. Section 29 inserts new section 181B into the Pension Schemes Act 1993. (c. 48), which supplements the definition of 'money purchase benefits' in section 181 of that Act, with retrospective effect to 1st January 1997. Section 29 also inserts new section 99A into the Pensions Act 2008 (c. 30), which supplements the definition of 'money purchase benefits' in section 99 of that Act, with retrospective effect to 5th July 2010. Section 29 further amends the definition of 'money purchase benefits' in paragraph 1(2) of Schedule 10A to the Building Societies Act 1986 (c.53).

A full impact assessment has not been prepared for this Order as no impact on the private, public or voluntary sectors is foreseen.

(8)

Figure 3.9 Explanatory Note

3.3 Statutory interpretation

Once you have found a statutory provision, you will need to interpret it in order to find its meaning. Language is an imperfect tool and consequently problems can arise when attempting to discern the meaning of and purpose behind the form of words used in the statute, particularly when provisions are phrased in highly technical language.

The words of an Act of Parliament are authoritative. It is the constitutional role of the judiciary in common-law jurisdictions to apply the law. This is in contrast to civil law systems used in continental Europe where the statutory texts are applied more flexibly by the courts which may declare what the law should mean in a particular set of circumstances. In this sense, it is often said that the role of our courts in statutory interpretation is to discern Parliament's intention from the words of the statute. However, it may be that the particular set of circumstances before the court were never actually foreseen or considered by Parliament (or indeed considered and left out), and therefore Parliament's intention could *never* be ascertained. In this case, it can be argued that the courts are trying to guess what Parliament *would have* meant had it directed its mind to the circumstances in question.[3]

The situation in which Parliament (the legislature) creates the law, Government (the Executive) implements the law, and the courts (the judiciary) interpret the law gives rise to an overlap and hence competing tensions between the three 'organs' of state. Most law is initiated by the Executive but can be checked by the judiciary in its application, as the judiciary will seek the most just outcome, often in spite of the will of Parliament.

Whatever the reasons for interpretation, the situation is straightforward. If the wording of the legislation is ambiguous or unclear, then its meaning will need to be interpreted. While the ordinary meaning of a word in the English language is a matter of fact, its legal meaning is, self-evidently, a matter of law. This can prove to be a great source of legal argument.

---

3. *Farrell v Alexander* [1977] AC 59 (HL) 95B (Lord Edmund-Davies).

For that reason, an understanding of the approaches that can be used to interpret a statutory provision is vital. As Lord Steyn commented: 'The preponderance of enacted law over common law is increasing year by year . . . and the subject of interpretation has moved to the centre of the legal stage'.[4] In other words, the sheer volume of legislation and the pace with which it is introduced provides more opportunities for creative arguments before the courts. Knowledge of how to interpret a statutory provision in your favour—or know how it might be used against you—is therefore of paramount importance.

3.3.1 How to interpret a statutory provision

Judges use a variety of different approaches when faced with an issue of statutory interpretation. These are commonly referred to as the 'rules' of interpretation, although they are not strict rules. They are sometimes referred to as the 'rules of construction'. This is derived from the verb 'to construe', meaning 'to interpret'.

Judges are not bound to follow one, or indeed any, of them and do not have to state which 'rule' they have used. It is perhaps better, then, to think of them as *approaches* to interpretation, rather than as hard-and-fast rules. The 'rules' in question are:

- the literal rule
- the golden rule
- the mischief rule

In addition to these rules, the purposive approach considers the wider purpose of the legislation and the teleological approach is particularly important in the interpretation of European law. There are also various rules of language, presumptions and extrinsic aids that can be used to help.

3.3.1.1 The literal rule

The **literal rule** provides that words must be given their plain, ordinary, and literal meaning.

The rationale behind the use of the literal rule is that if the words of the statute are clear they must be applied as they represent the intention of Parliament as expressed in the words used.

This is so even if the outcome is harsh or undesirable. This was made clear in the *Sussex Peerage Case*:[5]

> The only rule for construction of Acts of Parliament is that they should be construed according to the intent of the Parliament which passed the Act. If the words . . . are themselves precise and unambiguous, then no more can be necessary than to expound those words in that natural and ordinary sense.

An example of the use of the literal rule can be found in *Cutter v Eagle Star Insurance Co Ltd*.[6] The claimant was sitting in his friend's car in a car park and was injured when a can of lighter fuel exploded. The driver was insured as required by the Road Traffic Act 1988, for injury caused while on a 'road'. Here the House of Lords ruled that a car park is not a 'road' for the

---

4. Lord Steyn, '*Pepper v Hart*: a Re-examination' (2001) 21 OJLS 59.
5. (1844) 1 Cl & Fin 85.
6. [1998] 1 WLR 1647 (HL).

purposes of the Road Traffic Act 1988, since the purpose of a road is a means for cars to move along it to a destination and the purpose of a car park is for cars to stand still. Parking a car on a road does not make it a car park. Driving a car across a car park does not make it a road as it is incidental to its main function.

In *Whiteley v Chappell*[7] the defendant had impersonated a dead person and voted in an election in his name. The relevant statute provided that it was an offence to impersonate 'any person entitled to vote' at an election. Since the person impersonated was dead he was not entitled to vote, and thus Whiteley could not be convicted. Of course, this application of the literal rule went *against* Parliament's intention, which was to ensure that only those entitled to vote were able to do so, and then only to do so once at each election.

Although use of the literal rule gives utmost primacy to the precise words used by Parliament, emphasizing the literal meaning of statutory provisions can lead to 'unthinking' decisions where the meaning in the wider context is ignored or lost. It assumes perfection in parliamentary draftsmen and ignores the natural limitations of language. However, there is still scope for judicial intervention: in deciding on the literal meaning of a word, the court may still refer to its own interpretation of the meaning of that word, or have recourse to an extrinsic aid such as a dictionary to assist them in suggesting what the literal meaning of the particular word actually is.

3.3.1.2 The golden rule

The **golden rule** provides that words must be given their plain, ordinary, and literal meaning as far as possible but only to the extent that they do not produce absurdity (the 'narrow golden rule' approach) or an affront to public policy (the 'wide golden rule' approach).

In terms of the relationship between the legislature and the judiciary, the golden rule may be used by the judiciary where the literal rule would produce a result that was actually contrary to the intention of Parliament. There is, however, a presumption that the literal rule should be used—in other words, that Parliament would not normally intend to legislate to produce absurdity or an affront to public policy. The failure of Parliament to consider a particular situation does not permit the courts to depart from the literal rule if the words of the statute are clear and there is no absurdity created. In such an event, the court is limited to drawing the matter to Parliament's attention and urging the enactment of remedial legislation.

The rationale behind the golden rule is that it mitigates some of the potential harshness arising from use of the literal rule. An early reference to it can be found in *Grey v Pearson*:[8]

> The grammatical and ordinary sense of the words is to be adhered to unless that would lead to some absurdity or inconsistency with the rest of the instrument, in which case the grammatical and ordinary sense of the words may be modified so as to avoid that absurdity or inconsistency, but not farther.

Absurdity

R v Allen[9] concerned the application of s 57 of the Offences against the Person Act 1861. This provided that 'whosoever being married shall marry any other person during the lifetime of his spouse' shall commit bigamy. If 'marry' had been interpreted literally the offence could

---

7.   (1868) LR 4 QB 147.
8.   (1857) 6 HL Cas 61.
9.   (1872) LR 1 CCR 367.

never have been committed, since no one married could ever marry another. The court interpreted the words 'shall marry' as if they said 'shall go through the ceremony of marriage'.

Affront to public policy

A more unpleasant example is found in *Re Sigsworth*.[10] Under the Administration of Estates Act 1925 the estate of a person dying without leaving a will was to be divided among the 'issue'. Mrs Sigsworth was murdered by her son who stood to inherit her estate. Even though there was only one possible interpretation of the word 'issue' the court held that the son could not inherit the estate as it would be contrary to the public policy principle that a murderer should not benefit from his crime. Here the golden rule was applied in preference to the literal rule.

3.3.1.3 The mischief rule

The **mischief rule** (or the rule in *Heydon's Case*)[11] involves an examination of the former law in an attempt to deduce Parliament's intention ('mischief' here means 'wrong' or 'harm').

The mischief rule differs from the literal rule and the golden rule in that it places less emphasis on the words of the statute themselves, but instead seeks the reason for Parliament legislating in the first place.

The mischief rule asks four questions, the answers to which provide some sort of structured evaluation of Parliament's intention in passing the Act in question:

1. What was the common law before the making of the Act?
2. What was the mischief and defect for which the common law did not provide?
3. What was the remedy proposed by Parliament to rectify the situation?
4. What was the true reason for that remedy?

The rule itself dates from a time when the law was primarily common (case) law and there was a relatively limited amount of statute. Statutes were historically only enacted when Parliament wished to remedy what it considered to be a defect in the common law.

The rule was restated by Lord Diplock in *Jones v Wrotham Park Settled Estates*[12] where he identified three necessary conditions:

- It must be possible to determine precisely the mischief that the Act was drafted to remedy.
- It must be apparent that Parliament had failed to deal with the mischief.
- It must be possible to state the additional words that would have been inserted had the omission been drawn to Parliament's attention.

Corkery v Carpenter[13] concerned the interpretation of s 12 of the Licensing Act 1872. This provided that a person drunk in charge of a 'carriage' on the highway could be arrested without a warrant. The defendant was found drunk in charge of a bicycle. Although it was argued that a bicycle is not a carriage in the normal meaning of the word (the term generally refers to a vehicle of some kind), the Divisional Court held that a bicycle was a carriage for the purposes of the Act. The mischief here was the prevention of drunken persons from being on

---

10. [1935] Ch 89 (DC).
11. (1584) 3 Co Rep 7a.
12. [1980] AC 74 (HL).
13. [1951] 1 KB 102 (DC).

the highway in charge of some form of transportation and was addressed by the Act for the purposes of public order and safety.

Royal College of Nursing v DHSS[14] involved the wording of the Abortion Act 1963. This allows abortions by 'a registered medical practitioner'. The first part of the procedure was carried out by a doctor. The second part was performed by nurses but without a doctor being present. The House of Lords held by a 3–2 majority that this procedure *was* lawful because the mischief Parliament was trying to remedy was back street abortions performed by unqualified people.

In *Manchester City Council v McCann*,[15] the defendant had threatened a witness who had given evidence against his wife on his return home from court. Section 118(1)(a) of the County Courts Act 1984 provides that county courts may deal with anyone who 'wilfully insults the judge . . . or any juror or witness, or any officer of the court'. The Court of Appeal held that a threat was an insult for the purposes of the Act. The mischief here was protection of various participants in the civil process. Even though a threat is not necessarily an insult using the normal meanings of the words, the ability for the court to deal with insults but not threats was contrary to Parliament's intention. Of course, an Act may have more than one mischief, and this may affect the interpretation as a whole.[16]

3.3.1.4 The purposive approach

....

The **purposive approach** involves seeking an interpretation of the law which gives effect to its general purpose. It is based upon the mischief rule.

....

The purposive approach is based upon the mischief rule and allows the courts to look beyond the wording of the legislation to find an interpretation which furthers its general purpose. In *Bulmer v Bollinger*,[17] Lord Denning stated:

> What are the English Courts to do when they are faced with a problem of interpretation? . . . No longer must they examine the words in meticulous detail. No longer must they argue about the precise grammatical sense. They must look to the purpose or intent.. . .They must not confine themselves to the English text. . . .. If they find a gap, they must fill it as best they can. They must do what the framers of the instrument would have done if they had thought about it. So we must do the same.

In that sense it is similar to the mischief rule, which attempts to deduce Parliament's intention (or purpose) in enacting a particular provision. It assumes that Parliament legislated intending to remedy some defect in the law and therefore that the courts should seek an interpretation of the legislation which gives effect to the purpose of legislating (which was to correct the defect).

The shift towards the use of the purposive approach was recognized by the House of Lords in *R (Quintavalle) v Secretary of State for Health*.[18] Here, the House of Lords endorsed the decision of the Court of Appeal who adopted a purposive approach to the

....

14. [1981] AC 800 (HL).
15. [1999] 2 QB 1214 (CA).
16. *R (Spath Holme Ltd) v Secretary of State for the Environment, Transport and the Regions* [2001] 2 AC 249 (HL).
17. [1974] Ch 401 (CA).
18. [2003] 2 AC 687 (HL).

interpretation of s 1(1) of the Human Fertilisation and Embryology Act 1990. Lord Steyn explained that:

> ... the adoption of a purposive approach to construction of statutes generally, and the 1990 Act in particular, is amply justified on wider grounds. In *Cabell v Markham* (1945) 148 F 2d 737 Justice Learned Hand explained the merits of purposive interpretation, at p. 739:
>
> > Of course it is true that the words used, even in their literal sense, are the primary, and ordinarily the most reliable, source of interpreting the meaning of any writing: be it a statute, a contract, or anything else. But it is one of the surest indexes of a mature developed jurisprudence not to make a fortress out of the dictionary; but to remember that statutes always have some purpose or object to accomplish, whose sympathetic and imaginative discovery is the surest guide to their meaning.
>
> > The pendulum has swung towards purposive methods of construction. This change was not initiated by the teleological approach of European Community jurisprudence, and the influence of European legal culture generally, but it has been accelerated by European ideas ... In any event, nowadays the shift towards purposive interpretation is not in doubt. The qualification is that the degree of liberality permitted is influenced by the context, e.g. social welfare legislation and tax statutes may have to be approached somewhat differently.

A further example can be found in *Jones v Tower Boot Co Ltd*[19] which concerned a 16-year-old of mixed ethnic parentage who worked at a shoe factory. During his employment he was subjected to physical and verbal racial abuse from his work colleagues (including burning his arm with a hot screwdriver, throwing metal bolts at his head, and calling him racially abusive names including 'chimp', 'monkey', and 'baboon'). Jones sued the company for damages under s 32 of the Race Relations Act 1976 which said the employer shall be held liable for racial discrimination of its employees 'in the course of employment'. The company argued that the racial harassment was not done 'in the course of employment' because, under common law, employees' conduct is only considered to be in the course of employment if it was directly authorized by the employer or closely connected to the job they were hired to do.

The Court of Appeal held that interpretation of the terms should not be restricted by the common law principles and that a broad interpretation has to be adopted. The court then looked at the purpose of the Act and held the company was liable even though it had never authorized the racial abuse and the abuse had nothing to do with the abusers' job:

> A purposive construction accordingly requires section 32 of the Race Relations Act 1976 and the corresponding section 41 of the Sex Discrimination Act 1975 to be given a broad interpretation. It would be inconsistent with that requirement to allow the notion of the 'course of employment' to be construed in any sense more limited than the natural meaning of those everyday words would allow.

3.3.1.5 The teleological approach

The **teleological approach** requires that the spirit of the legislation, rather than merely its purpose, is considered. It is therefore much broader than the purposive approach.

The teleological approach is particularly important when considering EU law, since EU law is often drafted in terms of wide general principles and not in the detailed manner found in domestic legislation. It is the predominant approach used in civil law systems which tend

---

19. [1997] 2 All ER 406 (CA).

to favour simplified drafting and a high degree of abstraction. It is also used by the Court of Justice of the European Union and the UK courts in interpreting EU law.

You may wish to refer back to chapter 1 which considered the various types of EU legislation.

Section 2(4) of the European Communities Act 1972 provides that:

> . . . any enactment passed or to be passed. . . shall be construed and have effect subject to the foregoing provisions of this section.

The primary foregoing provision is s 2(1) of the Act which effectively incorporates all directly applicable European law into the legal system.

> . . . all rights, powers, liabilities, obligations and restrictions from time to time created or arising by or under the Treaties, and all such remedies and procedures from time to time provided for by or under the Treaties, as in accordance with the Treaties are without further enactment to be given legal effect or used in the United Kingdom shall be recognised and available in law, and be enforced, allowed and followed accordingly.

In other words, when interpreting legislation which implements EU law, the courts should give preference to an interpretation which gives effect to the general spirit of the legislation. This necessarily means that questions of wide economic or social policy are often considered by the courts.

In some circumstances this approach involves the courts reading certain words into legislation. This is a clear departure from using the literal words as chosen by Parliament. In *Pickstone v Freemans plc*,[20] the House of Lords held that it was proper to give a broad construction to the Equal Pay Act 1970, as amended by the Sex Discrimination Act 1975, so as to arrive at a result consistent with the UK's obligations under European law.

A further example is provided by *Litster v Forth Dry Dock and Engineering Co Ltd*.[21] Here, employees were dismissed one hour before a business was transferred to a new owner. The employees claimed they were unfairly dismissed. The Transfer of Undertakings (Protection of Employment) Regulations 1981[22] ('TUPE') implement a European Directive to protect employees who are employed during the transfer of a business. However, taking a literal approach, the employees here were not actually employed at the moment of transfer, having been dismissed an hour previously and therefore their situation seemed to fall outside the protection offered by TUPE. However, the House of Lords read in additional words such that the regulations covered an individual who was employed 'or would have been so employed if he had not been unfairly dismissed as a reason connected with the transfer before the transfer'. In doing so, the spirit of the Directive, to protect the employees on the transfer of a business, was upheld.

3.3.1.6 Rules of language

In addition to the rules of construction, there are also rules of language which the courts may use. They are known by the following Latin terms:

- *Ejusdem generis*
- *Noscitur a sociis*
- *Expressio unius est exclusio alterius*

---

20.   [1989] AC 66 (HL).
21.   [1990] 1 AC 546 (HL).
22.   SI 1981/1794.

Ejusdem generis

Ejusdem generis means 'of the same type'.

In other words, if a word with general meaning follows a list of specific words, then the general word only applies to things of the same type as the specific words. The general words are interpreted as a continuation of the list of specific words. All the words must constitute the same 'type' of thing and that type must be construed as narrowly as possible. For example, a list stating 'hats, coats, scarves, gloves, and other articles' would imply that the list contained items of outdoor clothing and not all clothing.

In *Powell v Kempton Park Racecourse*,[23] the defendant was operating an outdoor betting ring. It was an offence to use a 'house, office, room or other place for betting'. The court held that since the specific places listed are all indoors, an outdoor betting ring was not covered within the statute and the defendant was found not guilty.

Wood v Commissioner of Police of the Metropolis[24] considered whether a piece of (accidentally broken) glass was covered by 'any gun, pistol, hangar, cutlass, bludgeon or other offensive weapon'. It was held that the list contains items made or adapted for the purposes of causing harm. Therefore a piece of accidentally broken glass was not included, although presumably it would have been if it had been smashed in order for it to be used as a weapon.

Noscitur a sociis

Noscitur a sociis means that a word is 'known by the company it keeps'.

Words in a statute derive meaning from the words surrounding them. That is to say that a statutory provision should be read in the context of its neighbouring provisions. It is presumed that words have the same meaning throughout an Act—although this is not always the case. For instance, the word 'sexual' has a different meaning in s 71 of the Sexual Offences Act 2003 (sexual activity in a public lavatory) to that which it has in the rest of the Act. There is also a presumption that words in a list have related meanings and are to be interpreted in relation to each other.

In *Pengelley v Bell Punch Co Ltd*[25] it was held that the word 'floors' in a statute requiring 'floors, steps, stairs, passages and gangways' to be kept clear did not include part of a factory floor used for storage, since the words listed related to passageways and not static storage.

Muir v Keay[26] concerned a café owner. All houses kept open at night for 'public refreshment, resort and entertainment' had to be licensed. The defendant argued that his café did not need a licence because he did not provide entertainment. The court held that 'entertainment' did not mean musical entertainment but the reception and accommodation of people. Therefore the owner was required to have a licence by law.

Expressio unius est exclusio alterius

Expressio unius est exclusio alterius means that to 'express one thing is to exclude others'.

In other words, a list of a number of specific things may be interpreted as impliedly excluding others of the same type. If there are no general words, then the list is considered to be

---

23. [1899] AC 143 (HL).
24. [1986] 1 WLR 796 (DC).
25. [1964] 1 WLR 1055 (CA).
26. (1875) LR 10 QB 594.

exhaustive. For example, in *R v Inhabitants of Sedgley*[27] it was held that the poor rate levied on owners of 'lands, houses, tithes and coal mines' could not be levied on owners of limestone mines, as these were impliedly excluded by the specific mention of coal mines.

3.3.1.7 Presumptions

....

A legal **presumption** is an inference established by the law as universally applicable to certain circumstances.

....

In addition to the rules of construction and rules of language, there are also a number of presumptions which are made when interpreting legislation. These are generally expected to be taken 'as read' without the need for Parliament specifically to address them in the wording of a statute, since they deal with traditional ideas of natural justice and fairness or matters so uncontroversial that they would almost certainly represent the intention of Parliament. A number of these presumptions are as follows:

Against alteration of the common law
Although Parliament can change the existing common law, such an intention cannot be implied (e.g. *Beswick v Beswick*).[28]

Against retrospective operation of statute
It is presumed that statutes do not operate retrospectively (this is particularly important in Acts which criminalize, since it could lead to criminal liability arising for acts which were lawful at the time they were committed). This presumption can, however, be rebutted by express words by Parliament (e.g. War Crimes Act 1991; War Damage Act 1965 overruling the House of Lords' decision in *Burmah Oil Co Ltd v Lord Advocate*).[29]

Against deprivation of liberty
Parliament is presumed not to intend to deprive a person of his liberty; if it does, clear words must be used and will be construed so as to interfere with the subject's liberty as little as possible (e.g. *R (H) v London North and East Region Mental Health Review Tribunal*).[30]

Against deprivation of property and against interference with private rights
Parliament is presumed not to wish to interfere with a person's private rights or deprive him of his property without compensation (e.g. *Glassbrook Bros v Leyson*;[31] *Bowles v Bank of England*).[32]

Against binding the Crown
Parliament is presumed not to bind the Crown except expressly or by necessary implication of the statute (e.g. Equal Pay Act 1970; Sex Discrimination Act 1975).

Against ousting the jurisdiction of the courts
Even where clear ouster clauses have been used, the courts will try to construe them in a way which permits judicial review (e.g. *Anisminic Ltd v Foreign Compensation Commission*).[33]

....

27. (1831) 2 B & Ald 65.
28. [1968] AC 58 (HL).
29. [1965] AC 75 (HL).
30. [2001] 3 WLR 512 (CA).
31. [1933] 2 KB 91 (CA).
32. [1913] 1 Ch 57 (DC).
33. [1969] 2 AC 147 (CA).

Against criminal liability without *mens rea* (a guilty mind)

There is a presumption that, for statutory criminal offences, Parliament intended no liability without proof of *mens rea* (e.g. *R v K*).[34] This can be rebutted by express words or by implication in offences of strict liability.

3.3.1.8 Intrinsic aids to interpretation

Intrinsic aids to interpretation are found within the statute itself.

Any statute must be read as a whole. That is to say that before looking outside the statute to seek its meaning, every word within the statute should be considered in the search for meaning. There are a number of areas within the statute which could potentially be used as an intrinsic aid to construction.

Look back at section 3.1 which describes the anatomy of an Act of Parliament.

Short title

This is usually descriptive only and therefore of limited value.

Long title

The long title may be considered but only where there is ambiguity within the body of the Act (e.g. *R (Quintavalle) v Secretary of State for Health*).[35]

Preamble

Preambles tend not to be found in recent statutes. Where preambles do exist, they may be considered for guidance purposes in cases of ambiguity.

Marginal notes

These are not debated in Parliament and are not normally used in determining the precise scope of a provision (*DPP v Schildkamp*);[36] they can however give some general indication of the provision's purpose (*DPP v Johnson*).[37] They were, however, used quite recently in *R v Montilla*.[38]

Punctuation

Old statutes did not use punctuation at all. Punctuation may be used as an aid to interpretation where there is ambiguity (*DPP v Schildkamp*).[39]

See chapter 10 for more information on punctuation.

Examples

Statutes may provide examples to illustrate how the Act might work or how terminology within it might be used. These are part of the statute and carry great persuasive authority (examples include s 44(6) of the Criminal Justice Act 2003; Consumer Credit Act 1974; Law of Property Act 1925).

34. [2001] 3 WLR 471 (HL).
35. [2003] 2 AC 687 (HL).
36. [1971] AC 1 (HL).
37. [1995] 4 All ER 53 (DC).
38. [2004] UKHL 50; [2004] 1 WLR 3141.
39. [1971] AC 1 (HL).

Schedules

Some statutes may contain a Schedule which includes an interpretation and definition section of terms used in the Act (e.g. Schedule 1, Interpretation Act 1978). These definitions are part of the statute and are strongly persuasive.

3.3.1.9 Extrinsic aids to interpretation

....

Extrinsic aids to interpretation are found outside the statute.

....

The Interpretation Act 1978 defines words that are commonly used within legislation. For example:

- In any Act, unless the contrary intention appears, words importing the masculine gender include the feminine and vice versa (section 6)
- 'Land' includes buildings and other structures, land covered with water, and any estate, interest, easement, servitude or right in or over land (Schedule 1)
- 'Writing' includes typing, printing, lithography, photography and other modes of representing or reproducing words in a visible form, and expressions referring to writing are construed accordingly (Schedule 1)

Where a word has no specific legal meaning, dictionaries may also be used.[40] Courts may also consider the interpretation of the same words used in earlier or related statutes.

Historically, since the court was only allowed to interpret the words used, reference to preparatory works (*travaux préparatoires*) was not permitted. Article 9 of the Bill of Rights 1689 provides:

> That the freedom of speech and debates or proceedings in Parliament ought not to be impeached or questioned in any court or place out of Parliament.

Therefore, members of the Houses of Parliament had the right to say whatever they wished and to discuss whatever they wished. Until 1993, the protection given by Article 9 was held to prevent the courts from using statements made in Parliament concerning the purpose of Bills as a guide to the interpretation of ambiguous statutory provisions. This meant that courts could not refer to records of Parliamentary debate on the statute in *Hansard*.

However, this rule was relaxed in 1993 following the ruling of the House of Lords in *Pepper v Hart*.[41] Here the House of Lords held that the rule against the use of *Hansard* as an extrinsic aid to interpretation would be relaxed to permit reference to Parliamentary materials where:

(a) the legislation is ambiguous or obscure, or its literal meaning leads to an absurdity;

(b) the material relied on consists of statements by a Minister or other promoter of the Bill together with such other Parliamentary material as is necessary to understand such statements and their effect; and

(c) the statements relied upon are clear.

The House of Lords held such use of statements did not infringe Article 9 because it did not amount to questioning a proceeding in Parliament. Indeed, they considered that far from

....

40.   See, e.g., *Cheeseman v DPP* [1992] QB 83 (DC) which concerned the interpretation of the word 'passengers' in relation to the users of a public lavatory.

41.   [1993] AC 593 (HL).

questioning the independence of Parliament and its debates, the use of *Hansard* would allow the courts to give effect to what was said and done there.

Note that the use of *Hansard* is only permitted under the circumstances outlined in *Pepper v Hart*. It is a common mistake to state that reference to *Hansard* may always be made.

Although *Pepper v Hart* concerned the use of *Hansard*, its principles extend to the reports of recommendations made by the Law Commission and government departmental committees. For example, in *R v Allen*,[42] the House of Lords considered the report of the Criminal Law Revision Committee when considering the meaning of s 3 of the Theft Act 1978. The Act was silent on the point in question—specifically, whether intent never to pay had to be proved as an element of the offence of making off without payment—but the committee report made it clear that such intention *did* have to be proved.

In practice, however, courts have demonstrated some reluctance to allow reference to *Hansard*.[43] In *Wilson v First County Trust Limited (No 2)*,[44] the House of Lords commented that:

> What is important is to recognise there are occasions when courts may properly have regard to ministerial and other statements made in Parliament without in any way 'questioning' what has been said in Parliament, without giving rise to difficulties inherent in treating such statements as indicative of the will of Parliament, and without in any other way encroaching upon parliamentary privilege by interfering in matters properly for consideration and regulation by Parliament alone. The use by courts of ministerial and other promoters' statements as part of the background of legislation, pursuant to *Pepper v Hart*, is one instance.[45]

In other words, the statement of a Minister does not necessarily reflect the intentions of Parliament as a whole. More recently, the House of Lords considered the use of *Pepper v Hart* in *R (Jackson) v Attorney General*,[46] in which Lord Nicholls of Birkenhead stated that it would be 'unfortunate' if the rule were sidelined. Lord Steyn, however, considered that 'trying to discover the intentions of the Government from Ministerial statements in Parliament is unacceptable'.[47]

The use of *Pepper v Hart* therefore remains the subject of judicial debate.

The courts may also refer to the Explanatory Notes which have accompanied all Acts since 1999. They do not form part of the Act and have not been debated by Parliament. They are there to assist in discerning Parliament's intention and have been referred to by the courts,[48] although it could be argued that the courts are giving them a status that they should not carry particularly since they have been drafted by the Executive (the Government department supporting the original Bill) and not the legislature.

The courts may also sometimes refer to academic writing. For example, the court in *R v Dooley*[49] referred to *Smith and Hogan's Criminal Law*.

42. [1985] AC 1029 (HL).
43. See, e.g., *Zafar v DPP* [2004] EWHC 2468 (Admin); *Hone v Going Places Travel Ltd* [2001] EWCA Civ 947; *Thet v DPP* [2001] 1 WLR 2022 (DC).
44. [2004] 1 AC 816 (HL).
45. [2004] 1 AC 841 (Lord Nicholls of Birkenhead).
46. [2006] 1 AC 262 (HL).
47. [2006] 1 AC 262 (HL), [97] (Lord Steyn).
48. *Attorney General's Reference (No 5 of 2002)* [2005] 1 AC 167 (HL).
49. [2005] EWCA Crim 3093.

3.3.2 Interpretation and the European Communities Act 1972

Section 2(4) of the European Communities Act 1972 provides that:

> Any enactment passed or to be passed. . . shall be construed and have effect subject to the forego-ing provisions of this section.

In other words, any legislation passed or to be passed in the United Kingdom must be inter-preted with applicable EU law in mind. There is therefore a strong presumption of compli-ance with EU law.

In *Garland v British Rail Engineering*,[50] Lord Diplock suggested that where words of domestic law were incompatible with the Community law in question, they should be construed so as to comply with it. This creative approach—not applying the plain meaning of words in a statute, if that meaning will conflict with EU law—was also taken by the House of Lords in *Pickstone v Freemans plc*.[51] The Court of Appeal had declared that the Equal Pay (Amendment) Regulations 1983 were inconsistent with Article 141 (ex 119) of the EC Treaty. However, the House of Lords ruled that the Regulations should in fact be interpreted in a manner compat-ible with the provisions of the Treaty.

The supremacy of EU law is considered in general in chapter 1.

3.3.3 Interpretation and the Human Rights Act 1998

The Human Rights Act 1998 has had an effect on the traditional role of the courts in the interpretation of statutes.

Section 3 of the Act provides that:

(1) So far as it is possible to do so, primary legislation and subordinate legislation must be read and given effect in a way which is compatible with the Convention rights.

(2) This section—

   (a) applies to primary legislation and subordinate legislation whenever enacted;

   (b) does not affect the validity, continuing operation or enforcement of any incompat-ible primary legislation; and

   (c) does not affect the validity, continuing operation or enforcement of any incompat-ible subordinate legislation if (disregarding any possibility of revocation) primary legislation prevents removal of the incompatibility.

Section 3(1) imposes a duty upon the courts to try and discern a meaning *so far as it is possible to do so* with Convention rights. This is a weaker presumption of compliance than that concerning European law; s 2(4) of the European Communities Act 1972 uses the imperative 'shall' rather than 'so far as it is possible'. If the courts are unable to find a compatible interpretation, then they may make a 'declaration of incompatibil-ity' under s 4. The effect of such a declaration is that the law must then be changed to

---

50.   [1983] 2 AC 751 (HL).
51.   [1989] AC 66 (HL).

remove the incompatibility. Section 10(2) provides a fast-track route by which this may be done:

> If a Minister of the Crown considers that there are compelling reasons. . . he may by order make such amendments to the legislation as he considers necessary to remove the incompatibility.

The s 3 power has been considered in a number of cases since the provision came into force on 2 October 2000.

R v A[52] concerned the interpretation of s 41 of the Youth Justice and Criminal Evidence Act 1999 which placed the court under a restriction that seriously limited the evidence that could be raised in cross-examination of a sexual relationship between an alleged rape victim and the accused. Section 41(1) provided that:

If, at a trial, a person is charged with a sexual offence, then, except with the leave of the court—

(a) no evidence may be adduced, and

(b) no question may be asked in cross-examination, by or on behalf of any accused at the trial, about any sexual behaviour of the complainant.

This remained so even in a case where the defendant claimed that the complainant had consented. *A* argued that s 41 of the Act was incompatible with Article 6 of the Convention to the extent that it prevented him from putting forward a full and complete defence. The House of Lords held that s 3 required them to consider Article 6 and its concomitant right to a fair trial. This allowed them to read s 41 as permitting the admission of evidence or questioning relating to a relevant issue in the case where it was considered necessary by the trial judge to make the trial fair.

In reaching its decision, the House of Lords was well aware that its interpretation of s 41 went against its actual meaning, but it nonetheless (by a majority) felt it within its power to do so. As Lord Steyn stated:

> In my view s 3 of the 1998 Act requires the court to subordinate the niceties of the language of s 41(3)(c) of the 1999 Act, and in particular the touchstone of coincidence, to broader considerations of relevance judged by logical and commonsense criteria of time and circumstances. After all, it is realistic to proceed on the basis that the legislature would not, if alerted to the problem, have wished to deny the right to an accused to put forward a full and complete defence by advancing truly probative material. It is therefore possible under s 3 of the 1998 Act to read s 41 of the 1999 Act, and in particular s 41(3)(c), as subject to the implied provision that evidence or questioning which is required to ensure a fair trial under Art 6 of the convention should not be treated as inadmissible.[53]

Lord Hope (dissenting) felt that the courts were going too far towards legislating:

> The rule of construction which s 3 lays down is quite unlike any previous rule of statutory interpretation. There is no need to identify an ambiguity or absurdity. Compatibility with convention rights is the sole guiding principle. That is the paramount object which the rule seeks to achieve. But the rule is only a rule of interpretation. It does not entitle the judges to act as legislators.[54]

---

52. [2002] 1 AC 45 (HL).
53. [2002] 1 AC 68 (HL).
54. [2002] 1 AC 87 (HL).

However, Parliament *did* seek to limit the rights of the defence to question alleged victims of rape. *R v A* could therefore be considered to be an act of quasi-legislation by the House of Lords.

In *Re S (Care Order: Implementation of Care Plan)*[55] Lord Nicholls explained the operation of s 3 as follows:

> The Human Rights Act reserves the amendment of primary legislation to Parliament. By this means the Act seeks to preserve parliamentary sovereignty. The Act maintains the constitutional boundary. Interpretation of statutes is a matter for the courts; the enactment of statutes, are matters for Parliament.

In *Ghaidan v Godin-Mendoza*[56] the House of Lords significantly clarified the force to be given when construing legislation under s 3. Lord Nicholls stressed that the intention of Parliament in enacting s 3 was, to the extent bounded only by what is 'possible', to allow the court to modify the meaning and hence the effect of primary and secondary legislation,[57] pointing out that s 3 is the principal remedial measure and that declarations of incompatibility were a measure of last resort.[58]

He also rejected the literal approach to interpretation, emphasizing a broad approach, concentrating, amongst other things, in a purposive way on the importance of the fundamental right involved.[59] The practical effect of *Mendoza* is to establish a strong, but rebuttable, presumption in favour of an interpretation consistent with Convention rights.[60]

CHAPTER SUMMARY

Anatomy of an Act of Parliament

- The short title is the normal way in which to refer to a statute

- The chapter number of an Act (since 1963) is the sequence number of the Act in the particular calendar year

- The long title of an Act gives an indication of its purpose and content

- Royal Assent is needed before an Act can come into force

- The enacting formula declares that the law derives its authority from being properly passed by the legislature

- The main body of an Act is divided into sections, subsections, paragraphs, and subparagraphs

- Any commencement provisions are normally found towards the end of an Act

- Schedules may contain further information such as definitions, further detail, minor and consequential amendments to other legislation or repeals of pre-existing legislation

---

55. [2002] UKHL 10, [2002] 2 AC 291.
56. [2004] UKHL 30, [2004] 2 AC 557.
57. [2004] UKHL 30, [2004] 2 AC 557, [33].
58. [2004] UKHL 30, [2004] 2 AC 557, [39].
59. [2004] UKHL 30, [2004] 2 AC 557, [42].
60. [2004] UKHL 30, [2004] 2 AC 557, [50].

- Older statutes may contain preambles which describe the purpose of the Act in more detail than the long title; these are not part of the Act itself

- Most recent Acts will carry accompanying Explanatory Notes which contain useful information but are not legally binding

Anatomy of a statutory instrument

- Statutory instruments show the authority by which they are made

- Orders are divided into paragraphs or articles

Statutory interpretation

- The literal rule provides that words must be given their plain, ordinary, and literal meaning

- The golden rule provides that words must be given their plain, ordinary, and literal meaning as far as possible but only to the extent that they do not produce absurdity (narrow approach) or an affront to public policy (wide approach)

- The mischief rule (or the rule in *Heydon's Case*) involves an examination of the former law in an attempt to deduce Parliament's intention

- The purposive approach involves seeking an interpretation of the law which gives effect to its general purpose. It is based upon the mischief rule

- The teleological approach requires that the spirit of the legislation, rather than merely its purpose, is considered. It is therefore much broader than the purposive approach

- *Ejusdem generis* is a rule of language meaning 'of the same type'

- *Noscitur a sociis* is a rule of language meaning that a word is 'known by the company it keeps'

- *Expressio unius est exclusion alterius* is a rule of language meaning that to 'express one thing is to exclude others'

- A legal presumption is an inference established by the law as universally applicable to certain circumstances

- Intrinsic aids to interpretation are found within the statute itself

- Extrinsic aids to interpretation are found outside the statute

- *Pepper v Hart* allows courts to refer to clear statements made by a Minister or other promoter of a Bill in *Hansard* where the legislation is ambiguous or obscure or its literal meaning leads to absurdity

- Section 2(4) of the European Communities Act 1972 requires that legislation must be interpreted with applicable EU law in mind. There is a strong presumption of compliance with EU law

- Section 3(1) of the Human Rights Act 1998 requires that legislation must be interpreted *so far as it is possible to do so* in a way that is compatible with Convention rights. There is a rebuttable presumption of compliance with the European Convention on Human Rights

FURTHER READING

- An interesting article which considers the 'radical' approach to interpretation of s 41 of the Youth Justice and Criminal Evidence Act 1999 by the House of Lords in the light of s 3(1) of the Human Rights Act 1999 in *R v A (No. 2)* [2002] 1 AC 45 is A Kavanagh, 'Unlocking the Human Rights Act: the Radical Approach to Section 3(1) Revisited' [2005] 3 EHRLR 259.

- A further discussion of the interpretative obligation arising from s 3(1) of the Human Rights Act 1999 and its impact on discerning the will of Parliament can be found in G Marshall, 'The Lynchpin of Parliamentary Intention: Lost, Stolen or Strained' [2003] Public Law 236.

- The use of the principle from *Pepper v Hart* is evaluated in A Kavanagh, '*Pepper v Hart* and Matters of Constitutional Principle' (2005) 121 LQR 98 and S Vogenaver, 'A retreat from *Pepper v Hart*? A reply to Lord Steyn' (2005) 25 OJLS 629.

- The use of dictionaries in legal cases and the problems that can arise from disputes over dictionary definitions is discussed in R Munday, 'The Bridge that Choked a Watercourse or Repetitive Dictionary Disorder' (2008) 1 Statute Law Review 26.

Case law

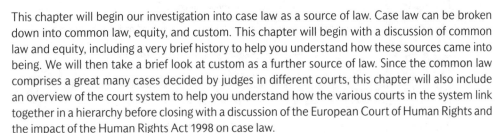

4

INTRODUCTION

This chapter will begin our investigation into case law as a source of law. Case law can be broken down into common law, equity, and custom. This chapter will begin with a discussion of common law and equity, including a very brief history to help you understand how these sources came into being. We will then take a brief look at custom as a further source of law. Since the common law comprises a great many cases decided by judges in different courts, this chapter will also include an overview of the court system to help you understand how the various courts in the system link together in a hierarchy before closing with a discussion of the European Court of Human Rights and the impact of the Human Rights Act 1998 on case law.

Understanding the sources of case law is as fundamental a legal skill as understanding the role of legislation. Since all legal topics will generally include some case law, equitable principles or both, you would not otherwise be able to understand how the particular area of law you are studying came into existence or has evolved over time. The law is a constantly changing creature which takes its shape from a whole range of sources. You must therefore understand these sources if you wish properly to understand the law and its development.

LEARNING OUTCOMES

After studying this chapter, you will be able to:

- Distinguish between the common law and equity as sources of law

- Chart the historical development of the common law and equity

- Appreciate the role of custom as a further source of law

- State the hierarchy of the courts and the types of case heard in the various courts

- Discuss the effect of the European Convention on Human Rights and the Human Rights Act 1998 on case law

4.1 Common law and equity

Having considered the role of legislation as a source of law in the last three chapters the next sources of law to consider are the common law and equity. However, before looking at them in detail, it will be useful to provide a very brief legal history. This will help you to understand the development of the common law and equity as two key sources of law and their interrelationship today. It will also greatly assist us later in dealing with some terminology.

4.1.1 A brief legal history

A timeline to give you an overview of the history that we are about to cover is provided in Figure 4.1.

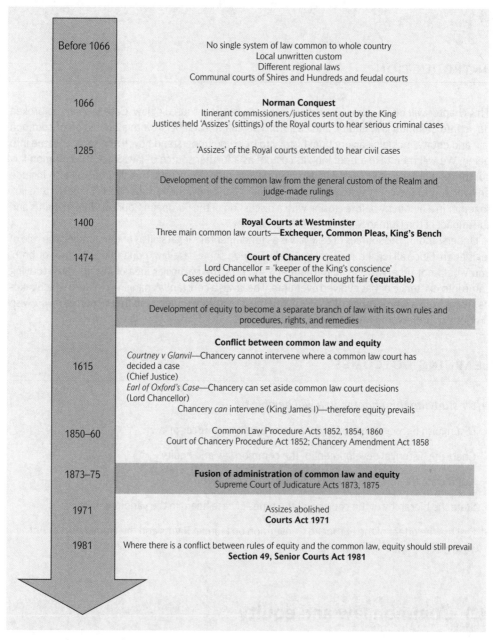

Before 1066	No single system of law common to whole country Local unwritten custom Different regional laws Communal courts of Shires and Hundreds and feudal courts
1066	**Norman Conquest** Itinerant commissioners/justices sent out by the King Justices held 'Assizes' (sittings) of the Royal courts to hear serious criminal cases
1285	'Assizes' of the Royal courts extended to hear civil cases
	Development of the common law from the general custom of the Realm and judge-made rulings
1400	**Royal Courts at Westminster** Three main common law courts—**Exchequer, Common Pleas, King's Bench**
1474	**Court of Chancery** created Lord Chancellor = 'keeper of the King's conscience' Cases decided on what the Chancellor thought fair **(equitable)**
	Development of equity to become a separate branch of law with its own rules and procedures, rights, and remedies
1615	**Conflict between common law and equity** *Courtney v Glanvil*—Chancery cannot intervene where a common law court has decided a case (Chief Justice) *Earl of Oxford's Case*—Chancery can set aside common law court decisions (Lord Chancellor) Chancery *can* intervene (King James I)—therefore equity prevails
1850–60	Common Law Procedure Acts 1852, 1854, 1860 Court of Chancery Procedure Act 1852; Chancery Amendment Act 1858
1873–75	**Fusion of administration of common law and equity** Supreme Court of Judicature Acts 1873, 1875
1971	Assizes abolished **Courts Act 1971**
1981	Where there is a conflict between rules of equity and the common law, equity should still prevail **Section 49, Senior Courts Act 1981**

Figure 4.1 Timeline of legal developments

4.1.1.1 The emergence of the common law

Before the Norman Conquest in 1066 there was no single system of law common to the whole country. There was a range of local customs which were unwritten and varied throughout the country, although the general effect of the local laws was similar in practice.

The use of custom as a source of law today is covered later in section 4.2.

Disputes according to these laws were judged by the local sheriffs sitting in the courts of the Shires and Hundreds (subdivisions of the Shires) and feudal courts held by landowners. In an attempt to create some level of uniformity and consistency in the law, the King sent itinerant commissioners into the country to perform various tasks on his behalf, such as checking on local administration and tax collection and hearing cases. The judicial functions of the itinerant commissioners increased, evolving a system of itinerant justices who held Assizes (or sittings) of the Royal courts in each county, three or four times a year, to hear serious criminal cases. Less serious cases were still dealt with by the local sheriff.

This system was extended to hear civil cases in 1285. Over time the judges began to establish a system of law common to the whole country—the common law—by the universal application of the best local customs (from outside the county if necessary) and rules derived from the judges' own decisions in cases. Therefore the common law emerged from a combination of local custom and case law.

The Royal Courts at Westminster comprised three main common law courts. By 1400 they were staffed by professional judges. The three courts were:

- The Court of Common Pleas dealing with disputes between the King's subjects
- The Court of Exchequer dealing primarily with matters concerning taxes but also later dealing with some common law matters
- The Court of King's Bench dealing with cases of particular concern to the King

The common law developed as a system because the judges tended to follow the decisions of earlier judges in similar cases. Over time, and in certain circumstances, judicial precedents became binding rather than merely being useful persuasive guidance.

The operation of the doctrine of judicial precedent is covered in detail in section 6.3.

4.1.1.2 Problems with the common law

An action could only be started in the Royal courts by a writ purchased from the office of the Chancellor. Since the existence of a common law right depended on there being a procedure for enforcing that right, an action could only be brought if an appropriate writ already existed which covered the facts of the case. As a result, the number of writs grew to many hundreds.

Moreover, the procedure for bringing an action before the courts was very formal and inflexible, leading to delay and expense. The only remedy generally available to a successful claimant was monetary damages—which was not always adequate. For instance, the courts could not compel individuals to do (or stop doing) something; not even to return personal property.[1]

Finally, the common law did not recognize certain rights, such as trusts or the borrower's rights under a mortgage. At common law, once the date for repayment of a mortgage had passed, the lender regained ownership of the land. This was so even if the borrower was able to pay back the loan. The repayment had to be counted by sunset on the repayment day for

---

1. Although actions for recovery of land, known as 'real actions', did enable successful claimants to recover their land at common law.

it to be effective and prevent the lender from reclaiming the land. Many unscrupulous lenders mysteriously vanished on the repayment day, meaning that the borrowers lost the land.

4.1.1.3 The emergence of equity

The rigid nature of the common law, together with its associated expense and delay, led to an increasing number of unhappy citizens petitioning the King directly to exercise his Royal prerogative as the 'fountain of justice'. The King (in Council) originally heard these petitions, but as their number increased, this duty was delegated by the King to the Lord Chancellor, who, as a result, was known as the 'Keeper of the King's Conscience'.

In 1474, the Court of Chancery was established, entirely separate from the King's common law courts. Proceedings in the Court of Chancery did not require a writ, and the Chancellor decided cases according to the rules of fairness and natural justice. In other words, he sought to achieve equity. He was able to develop new equitable rights and equitable remedies to mitigate the harshness of the common law and was not bound by the excessive procedural burden of the common law courts.

Although the Chancery was more concerned with equity in individual cases, general equitable maxims developed along with a set of rules and procedures for their application.

Equitable maxims, rights, and remedies are covered later in section 4.1.3.

4.1.1.4 The conflict between common law and equity

In certain situations the common law was directly challenged by equity. For instance, in the example given earlier regarding mortgages, equity deemed that it was unfair to the borrower to lose the right to redeem the mortgage even though the redemption date had passed. Therefore at common law, the borrower could not repay the mortgage after the redemption date, but in equity, this was permissible. This is known as the equity of redemption.

In 1615 the Chief Justice held that the Court of Chancery (i.e. equity) had no power to intervene where a common law court had decided a case[2] whereas the Lord Chancellor stated that the Court of Chancery could set aside the decision of the common law courts.[3] The matter was referred to King James I, who decreed that, even where a case had been decided at common law, the Court of Chancery could intervene. Therefore equity prevailed over the common law.

4.1.1.5 Reform and the present day

Over time, equity developed further and became more systematic. This led to a legal system with too many courts and too much jurisdictional overlap. As a result it was time-consuming, expensive, and difficult to resolve cases. Moreover, the disparate remedies meant that, in certain cases, a claimant would have to bring two actions arising from the same dispute: one in the common law courts for monetary damages and the other in the Court of Chancery for an equitable remedy.

Bleak House by Charles Dickens[4] illustrates the problems that could be caused by long drawn-out suits in the Courts of Chancery. Dickens had observed the inner workings of the courts as a reporter in his youth and observed that the 'one great principle of the English law is to make business for itself'.

---

2. *Courtney v Glanvil* (1615) Croke Jac 343, 79 ER 294.
3. *Earl of Oxford's Case* (1615) 1 Rep Ch 1.
4. Published in monthly parts between March 1852 and September 1853.

The overhaul of this unsatisfactory system began in the 1850s with the Common Law Procedure Acts 1852, 1854, and 1860, the Court of Chancery Procedure Act 1852, and the Chancery Amendment Act 1858. This enabled equitable remedies and defences to be available in the common law courts and allowed the Court of Chancery to make monetary awards of damages.

The Supreme Court of Judicature Acts 1873 and 1875 fused the administration of law and equity into a single court structure regulated by a single set of procedures. However, in cases of conflict (which are rare since equity evolved to supplement the common law), equitable principles still prevail.[5] In 1981, the Supreme Court of Judicature was renamed the Supreme Court of England and Wales.[6] The Constitutional Reform Act 2005 established a new Supreme Court of the United Kingdom from 1 October 2009. To avoid confusion, the Supreme Court Act 1981 was renamed the Senior Courts Act 1981, and all statutory references to the Supreme Court of England and Wales have been amended to refer to the Senior Courts of England and Wales: the Court of Appeal, the High Court, and the Crown Court.

An overview of the court structure and the jurisdictions and personnel of the courts is given in section 4.3.

4.1.2 The common law

With the brief history of the law in mind, you will have seen that, originally, the common law was the law that was common to the whole of England. Although this is true, it is not nowadays the usual meaning of the phrase.

'The common law' is usually taken to mean the law that is not the result of legislation; in other words the law which derives from cases decided by judges and the value of the judicial precedents that these decisions set. Case law is a major source of domestic law, since a great deal of law has not been enacted as legislation, and is therefore found in the results of decided cases.

The operation of the doctrine of judicial precedent is explained in section 6.3.

4.1.3 Equity

Equity is a source of law. You may hear, or read, of the contrast between 'law' and 'equity'. However, in this case 'law' is an abbreviation for 'the common law'. Therefore equity *is* law in that it is part of the law of England and Wales. However, it is *not* part of the common law. Although the *administration* of common law and equity has been fused into the Senior Courts of England and Wales, the distinction between common law principles and equitable principles is still important. For instance, common law remedies are granted as of *right* whereas equitable remedies remain within the *discretion* of the court and are subject to equitable principles.

The brief history provided earlier referred to equitable maxims, rights, and remedies. These will be explained here in more detail.

---

5.   Senior Courts Act 1981 s 49.
6.   Supreme Court Act 1981 s 1(1) (as it was at the time; now the Senior Courts Act 1981).

4.1.3.1 Equitable maxims

....

Equitable maxims are sometimes referred to as 'equitable doctrines'.

....

There are a number of equitable maxims that have developed over the years. Table 4.1 sets out some of the more commonly encountered.

4.1.3.2 Equitable rights

Equity also evolved to recognize new rights that were not within the scope of the common law. These include the equity of redemption discussed earlier, which protects the rights of borrowers under a mortgage. A further example is that of the equitable rights of beneficiaries

Table 4.1 Some equitable maxims

Maxim	Meaning
He who comes to equity must come with clean hands	Equity will not be available to a party that has behaved unreasonably in relation to the disputed matter
Equity looks on that as done which ought to be done. Equity looks to intent rather than to form	Equity will enforce the intentions of the parties rather than enforcing the position reached by inflexible adherence to the common law
Delay defeats equity	Equity will not be available to someone who seeks it after an unreasonable delay
Equity is a shield not a sword	A party cannot bring a claim in equity (sword) but may rely on equity to protect their own position (shield)
Equity will not suffer a wrong to be without a remedy	Equity will allow a party that has been wronged the capacity to ask for a remedy
Equity follows the law	Equity will not allow a remedy that is contrary to law
Where there is equal equity, the law will prevail	Equity will not provide a remedy where the parties are equal, or where neither has been wronged
Equity will not assist a volunteer	Equity will not assist someone who has given no consideration for a promise
Equity will not allow a statute to be used as an instrument of fraud	Equity will not allow someone to rely upon an absence of a statutory formality if to do so would be unconscionable and unfair
Equity will not perfect an imperfect gift	In general, equity will not complete a gift where the formalities required at common law have not been effected (similar to *equity will not assist a volunteer*). However there is an exception in *Strong v Bird*:[7] where the donor appoints the intended donee as executor of their will, and the donor subsequently dies, equity *will* perfect the imperfect gift
Equity will not allow a trust to fail for want of a trustee	Where there is no trustee, whoever has title to the trust property will be considered the trustee, or the court may appoint a trustee
Equality is equity	If a trust does not specify how property is to be divided, then there is a presumption of equal shares

....

7.   (1874) LR 18 Eq 315.

under a trust. Although the law of trusts (or, at the time, 'uses') developed in the 1200s as a means of protecting the land of crusaders and land held for the benefit of religious orders, it is still relevant today in matters of, for example, co-ownership of property, wills, charity, pension funds, and taxation.

4.1.3.3 Equitable remedies

As mentioned in the brief history, the Court of Chancery developed a range of new equitable remedies. These still exist, but remember that they are only available at the discretion of the court. The most common equitable remedies sought are injunction, specific performance, and rescission.

Injunction

An **injunction** is a court order which compels a person or body to perform some action or to cease some action.

There are different types of injunction. Examples include:

- Mandatory injunctions compelling someone to perform an act
- Prohibitory injunctions restraining someone from committing some act
- Interim injunctions granted before trial to preserve the status quo until the case is decided

Specific performance

An order of **specific performance** compels a person or body to perform their obligations under a contract or trust.

Specific performance is not generally available where damages (i.e. the common law remedy as of right) would provide an adequate remedy. It is therefore usually only relevant to special situations (such as a contract for the sale of land).

Rescission

An order of **rescission** sets aside a contract.

As well as being subject to the usual equitable principles, rescission is only generally available where it is possible to restore the parties to the contract to the positions that they were in before entering into the contract.

4.2 Custom

In order to enforce a local custom as an exception to the common law, it is necessary to show that the custom meets seven main tests. These were introduced by judges as a means of giving them the power to disregard any local custom which they considered unsuitable for recognition as a legal right. As you will see, the tests are very difficult to establish:

- The custom must have existed from time immemorial. This was arbitrarily defined as meaning the year 1189 (or the start of the reign of Richard I). If it can be proved that the custom did not exist in 1189, then it will fail

- It must have existed without interruption since 1189
- It must have been enjoyed without force, stealth, or permission
- It must have been observed because people felt that it was obligatory
- It must be capable of being precisely defined
- It must be reasonable. It must also have been reasonable throughout its entire period of use
- It must be consistent with other local customs

In practice, if the custom has been observed 'in living memory', this raises a presumption that it has been observed since 'time immemorial' unless evidence can be provided to rebut this presumption.

Custom is typically used in connection with land disputes, such as rights of way or access. However, as you might imagine, the difficulties involved in passing these tests mean that claims to local custom are nowadays extremely rare and success is rarer still. For instance in *Beckett Ltd v Lyons*[8] the claimant company sued in trespass to land after the defendant had been removing sea coal from a shore over which the company held the right to do so. The defendants attempted to rely on lawful custom, claiming that the inhabitants of County Durham had a customary right to take the sea coal. They introduced witnesses who had lived locally since 1886 who confirmed their story. However, the Court of Appeal held that the practice could also be considered to have been mere tolerance on the part of the landowner in earlier times, when the collection of the coal was not a business enterprise. Moreover, the evidence put forward by the witnesses related to the removal of the coal by means of buckets and wheelbarrows, as opposed to the more recent removal by the defendants in lorries!

Despite the inherent difficulties in proving local custom, examples of successful claims include *Egerton v Harding*[9] involving a customary duty to erect a fence to prevent cattle straying from the common, and *New Windsor Corporation v Mellor*,[10] in which the customary right of the mayor, bailiff, burgess, and others to indulge in lawful sports (including shooting) on land in a local borough was upheld.

4.3 The courts, their personnel, and their jurisdictions

Without a set of institutions to enforce legal rules, there would be no legal system. A set of rules cannot usefully exist in isolation. There needs to be a system of courts to hear cases at first instance, as well as higher courts which offer the mechanism for individuals to bring appeals arising from the outcome of cases in lower courts.

As you will see when looking at the doctrine of judicial precedent in section 6.3, there are rules which determine whether or not a particular court will be bound by a decision of a higher court—generally meaning that it will have to follow the particular legal reasoning of that higher court.

---

8. [1967] Ch 449 (CA).
9. [1975] QB 62 (CA).
10. [1974] 1 WLR 1504 (DC).

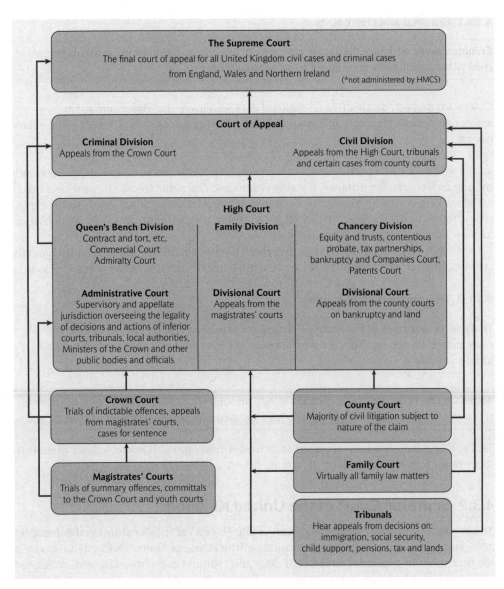

Figure 4.2 The courts

Therefore, a thorough understanding of the institutions of the modern court system is vital to your study of law. This section will provide an overview of the various courts, the types of case which they hear and the personnel who hear and decide those cases.

The domestic courts can be depicted as shown in Figure 4.2.

4.3.1 Classification of the courts

Courts may be classified in two different ways:

- Criminal and civil courts
- Trial and appellate courts

4.3.1.1 Criminal and civil courts

Criminal courts determine the guilt or innocence of defendants according to the parameters of the criminal law and dispense punishment to convicted offenders.

Civil courts primarily deal with the resolution of disputes between individuals and award appropriate remedies to successful claimants. These remedies are normally in the form of monetary damages.

You should note that a particular set of facts can give rise to proceedings in both the criminal and civil courts. For instance, if you were knocked down and injured by a reckless driver while walking down the street, this could lead to a case in the criminal courts (for, say, possible offences under the Road Traffic Act 1988) and in the civil courts (to seek compensation for your injuries in the tort of negligence).

The Crown Court deals almost exclusively with criminal matters. The county court has only civil jurisdiction. However, all the other courts have both criminal and civil jurisdictions.

4.3.1.2 Trial and appellate courts

Trial courts hear cases 'at first instance'. This refers to the first time that a case is heard in court, before any appeals. They consider the matters of fact and law in the case and make an appropriate ruling.

Appellate courts consider the application of legal principles to a case that has already been heard at first instance. Some appellate courts also have jurisdiction to reconsider disputed issues of fact.

Trial and appellate functions are often combined within one court as you will see when considering the functions of each court in more detail.

4.3.2 Supreme Court of the United Kingdom

The Supreme Court was created on 1 October 2009 by s 23 of the Constitutional Reform Act 2005 and replaced the Appellate Committee of the House of Lords. The Supreme Court is the final court of appeal for all UK civil cases and criminal cases from England, Wales and Northern Ireland and the Inner House of the Court of Session in Scotland.

The Supreme Court consists of twelve judges with a President and a Deputy President. The judges (other than the President and Deputy President) are styled 'Justices of the Supreme Court'. The Lords of Appeal in Ordinary became Justices of the Supreme Court; the senior Lord of Appeal in Ordinary became the President of the Court, and the second senior Lord of Appeal in Ordinary became the Deputy President of the Court.

The Supreme Court does not hear evidence from witnesses but instead considers legal argument and documentary evidence. It is located in Middlesex Guildhall on Parliament Square opposite the Houses of Parliament.

4.3.3 Court of Appeal

The Court of Appeal is the highest of the senior courts (which includes the High Court and the Crown Court). It is a single court which is split into two divisions—the Civil Division and the Criminal Division. The Court of Appeal does not hear witnesses but instead considers legal argument and documentary evidence. The majority decision will prevail, so, in practice, an odd number of judges—usually three—sit. In certain cases of major public importance, sometimes five or even seven Lord Justices of Appeal will sit. Note that, although unlikely in practice, the court is properly constituted even if only one judge sits.

4.3.3.1 Court of Appeal (Criminal Division)

The Court of Appeal (Criminal Division), as its name suggests, has an entirely appellate jurisdiction. It mainly deals with appeals from the Crown Court against conviction, sentence, or a finding of fact; references made by the Attorney-General following an acquittal on indictment under s 36 of the Criminal Justice Act 1972 on a point of law (this is not an appeal by the prosecution as the Court of Appeal's findings will have no effect on the defendant who will remain acquitted whatever happens); references made by the Attorney-General under s 36 of the Criminal Justice Act 1988 against an unduly lenient sentence; cases referred by the Criminal Cases Review Commission under s 9 of the Criminal Appeal Act 1995 where there has been a possible miscarriage of justice; and applications for leave (permission) to appeal to the Supreme Court.

It is comprised of Lord and Lady Justices of Appeal. Its head is the Lord Chief Justice.

4.3.3.2 Court of Appeal (Civil Division)

The Court of Appeal (Civil Division) deals with appeals from the three divisions of the High Court, county courts, and certain tribunals (for example, the Upper Tribunal, and the Employment Appeal Tribunal).

It is also comprised of Lord and Lady Justices of Appeal. Its head is the Master of the Rolls.

4.3.4 High Court

The High Court is one court. However, it is divided into three 'divisions' for administrative purposes. These are the Queen's Bench Division, Chancery Division, and Family Division.

It is staffed by High Court judges (also known as *puisne* judges—from the Old French, pronounced 'puny' and meaning 'inferior in rank'). The head of the Queen's Bench Division is the Lord Chief Justice. The nominal head of the Chancery Division is the Lord Chancellor (who never actually sits in the Chancery Division); in effect it is headed by the Vice-Chancellor. The Family Division is headed by the President of the Family Division.

None of the Divisions has any practically significant criminal jurisdiction at first instance.

4.3.4.1 Queen's Bench Division

The Queen's Bench Division hears criminal appeals from magistrates' courts by way of case stated and from the Crown Court sitting without a jury (for example, a Crown Court hearing an appeal from the magistrates' court). Its civil jurisdiction includes contractual disputes and actions in tort (with no upper limit on value) at first instance and appeals from the county court. It also has notable specialist subdivisions: the Administrative Court (which deals with applications for judicial review), the Admiralty Court (dealing with shipping and aircraft), the Technology and Construction Court (which also deals with certain other types of complex civil litigation), the Election Court (which deals with disputed elections), and the Commercial Court (covering banking, insurance, and finance).

4.3.4.2 Judicial review

Judicial review is a procedure by which, on the application of an individual, the courts may determine whether a public body (or a private body exercising a public function) has acted lawfully. It is available to applicants with 'sufficient interest' in the matter to which the application relates.[11]

The most common classification of grounds of challenge in judicial review is that of Lord Diplock who defined three broad (and arbitrary) headings: illegality, irrationality, and procedural impropriety.[12] Illegality was defined as failure to recognize and give effect to the law which regulates a decision-making power: to determine whether a public body has acted *ultra vires*. Irrationality was described as a decision that was so outrageous in its defiance of logic or accepted moral standards that no reasonable decision maker could have arrived at it. Procedural impropriety covers both any statutory procedural requirements and the common law rules of natural justice, namely bias and failure to give a fair hearing.

It is also unlawful for a public body to act in a way which is incompatible with the European Convention on Human Rights.[13] The victim of the breach of Convention rights relating to the actions of a public body (or a private body exercising a public function) may also challenge by judicial review. In reaching its decision, the court will consider:

- What Article was breached? How was it breached?
- Was the interference with the right prescribed by law?
- Was the interference necessary in a democratic society or in pursuit of a legitimate aim?
- Was the interference proportional?

4.3.4.3 Chancery Division

The Chancery Division deals with business and property related disputes, competition, general Chancery Claims, patents claims, intellectual property claims (patents, trademarks, and copyright), company law claims, insolvency claims, trust claims, probate claims, and appeals from the county courts on matters such as bankruptcy. It includes Chancery Chambers, the Bankruptcy and Companies Court, and the Patents Court.

4.3.4.4 Family Division

The Family Division has the inherent jurisdiction to deal with cases of defended divorce, adoption, and wardship.[14] It also considers certain wills and probate cases along with matters relating to family homes and domestic violence, and declarations in medical treatment cases.

4.3.5 Crown Court

The Crown Court deals with trials on indictment (by jury); cases where the magistrates have declined jurisdiction before trial; offences triable either-way where the defendant has elected for trial by jury in the Crown Court; and referrals for sentence from the magistrates' court

---

11.   Senior Courts Act 1981 s 31(3).
12.   *Council for Civil Service Unions v Minister for Civil Service* [1985] 1 AC 374 (HL).
13.   Human Rights Act 1998 s 6.
14.   Any person may, by issuing proceedings, make the High Court guardian of any child within its jurisdiction as a 'ward of court' (Family Proceedings Rules 1991, SI 1991/1247, Part V). No important decision concerning the child's life (such as, say, transfer to a different school or medical treatment) can then be taken without the court's permission.

where the magistrates consider that their sentencing powers are inadequate for the case in question (by virtue of the statutory limit on sentences in magistrates' courts which are currently six months' imprisonment and/or a £5,000 fine).

The Crown Court hears appeals from defendants against conviction or sentence or both in the magistrates' court.

Its first instance civil jurisdiction is limited so much as to be practically insignificant (for example, it hears certain disputes as to whether particular highways are in disrepair!)

It is staffed by High Court judges, circuit judges, deputy circuit judges (part-time), recorders (part-time), assistant recorders (part-time), and a jury (for trials).

4.3.6 County Court

The County Court deals with all but the most complicated civil law matters, such as:

- Claims for repayment of debt
- Claims for compensation in personal injury cases
- Cases involving breach of contract concerning goods or property
- Administration of wills
- Bankruptcy proceedings
- Housing disputes, including mortgage and council rent arrears and re-possessions.

Section 17(1) of the Crime and Courts Act 2013 removed the former geographical jurisdictional boundaries of county courts and established 'the County Court' with effect from 22 April 2014. The single County Court consists of an entirely civil jurisdiction: unlike its predecessor it does not have a family jurisdiction. Family proceedings are heard in the new Family Court, established by s 17(2) of the 2013 Act. The County Court has a national jurisdiction with unlimited financial jurisdiction and its business takes place at County Court hearing centres. These hearing centres correspond to the locations of the former 200+ county courts.

County Court proceedings can be submitted to the court in person, by post, or online (for some matters) through the County Court Bulk Centre. Cases are normally heard at the centre having jurisdiction over the area where the defendant lives.

The County Court Money Claims Centre (CCMCC) deals with claims for money only. If at any stage an oral hearing is required the claim will be sent to a local County Court hearing centre.

There are three 'tracks' which a case may take through the County Court. The small claims track (often referred to incorrectly as the 'small claims court') hears any claim which has a financial value of not more than £10,000 (except personal injury claims over £1,000, claims by residential tenants against landlords requiring repairs or other work with an estimated cost of over £1,000, or claims for a remedy for harassment or unlawful eviction relating to residential premises). The fast track hears claims which fall outside the scope of the small claims track, have a financial value of not more than £25,000 and which are likely to be tried in one day. Claims in the fast track also limit oral evidence at trial to two expert fields, with one expert per party in relation to each field. Finally, the multi-track hears any claim which falls outside the small claims track or the fast track. Therefore, the multi-track is generally used for higher value, more complex claims (with a value of over £25,000). Most commercial cases fall within the multi-track. The equitable jurisdiction of the court under s 23 of the County Court Act 1984 was increased from £30,000 to £350,000.

County Court staff comprise circuit judges, deputy circuit judges, district judges (formerly known as registrars), and deputy district judges (part-time).

4.3.7 Family Court

The new single Family Court came into existence on 22 April 2014, created by s 17(2) of the Crime and Courts Act 2013. The Family Court has jurisdiction in all family proceedings (with some exceptions) and so there is no longer a separate family jurisdiction in the magistrates' courts or the County Court. The Family Court is a national court and can sit anywhere. In practice it generally sits at the County Court hearing centres and magistrates' courts where family cases were formally heard.

4.3.8 Magistrates' court

All criminal proceedings begin in the magistrates' courts and well over 90 per cent end there. The main types of hearing are the trial of summary offences; applications for bail; issue of summonses and warrants for arrest or search; Youth Courts for defendants under the age of 18; plea before venue hearings; committal proceedings for Crown Court trial or sentence.

Magistrates' courts also have an extensive civil jurisdiction, much of which concerns local government matters. The main categories of civil hearing include: highways, public health, licensing, and recovery of civil debts such as national insurance contributions and income tax.

Magistrates' court proceedings are either heard by Justices of the Peace (lay magistrates), usually sitting as a bench of three, or a single district judge (magistrates' courts) working on a full-time salaried basis.

4.3.9 The Judicial Committee of the Privy Council

The Judicial Committee of the Privy Council is the court of final appeal for UK overseas territories and Crown dependencies, and for Commonwealth countries that have retained the appeal to the Queen in Council or, in the case of Republics, to the Judicial Committee.

When we consider the doctrine of judicial precedent in section 6.3, you will see that decisions of the Privy Council are not binding on any domestic court, but are highly persuasive. This is a result of the high judicial standing of its members.

It comprises at least three, and usually five, of the following:

- Justices of the UK Supreme Court
- other former Lords of Appeal in Ordinary (members of the former judicial committee of the House of Lords)
- Privy Councillors who are or were judges of the Court of Appeal
- Privy Councillors who are judges of certain superior courts in Commonwealth nations

The Judicial Committee of the Privy Council hears appeals from many current and former Commonwealth countries, as well as the UK's overseas territories, Crown dependencies, and military sovereign base areas. It also hears very occasional appeals from a number of ancient and ecclesiastical courts. These include the Church Commissioners, the Arches Court of Canterbury, the Chancery Court of York, prize courts, and the Court of Admiralty of the Cinque Ports.

4.3.10 Tribunals

It is usual to think of legal disputes being settled in the courts. However, there are other mechanisms for resolution, including tribunals. These are an alternative to using the 'traditional' courts and their use is, in fact, mandatory in certain types of dispute. Many disputes are dealt with in the network of administrative tribunals that has evolved throughout the twentieth century. Each tribunal dealt with a particular area of specialism such as employment, rent, immigration, and mental health.

Tribunals were seen as a more effective way of dealing with specialist disputes in such areas as they had particular expertise to deal with the intricacies of the law and a better understanding of the types of disputes that would come before them. They adopted less formal procedures to hear and decide cases more quickly: this, in turn, helped to minimize costs. The lack of formality also meant that, in theory at least, there would be less need for legal representation.

The function of tribunals was first reviewed in depth by the Franks Committee in 1957. It described them as:

> [Not] ordinary courts, but neither . . . appendages of Government Departments . . . Tribunals should properly be regarded as machinery provided by Parliament for adjudication rather than as part of the machinery of administration.

The Franks Report made a number of recommendations for the reform of the tribunal system that would ensure that it had three key characteristics:

- Fairness

- Openness

- Impartiality

It also listed the strengths of the tribunal system as cheapness, accessibility, freedom from technicality, expedition (being able to deal with cases relatively quickly; at least compared to the court system), and expert knowledge of their own area of jurisdiction.

Its recommendations were implemented by the Tribunals and Inquiries Act 1958. Later changes were also introduced by the Tribunals and Inquiries Act 1992.

The number of tribunals grew as new tribunals were introduced by legislation to deal with particular disputes. For example, the Mental Health Act 1983 created the Mental Health Review Tribunal, with responsibility for hearing applications from people who had been detained under the Act against their wishes. Each tribunal was operating under the rules stipulated by the particular piece of legislation that created it. For example, there were no uniform rules concerning the availability of appeals against tribunal decisions or the procedures by which an appeal could be brought.

These concerns of lack of consistency were addressed by Sir Andrew Leggatt who headed a review of the tribunal system. The brief of this review was to recommend a system that was 'coherent, professional, cost effective and user-friendly' and which would also be compatible with the Convention right to a fair trial under Article 6 ECHR. The resulting report *Tribunals for Users: One System, One Service*[15] recommended that the tribunal system should be unified into a single administrative body.

The recommendations of the Leggatt Report were enacted by the Tribunals, Courts and Enforcement Act 2007.

The functions of the majority of existing tribunals have been transferred to the new First-tier Tribunal created by s 3 of the Act. This First-tier Tribunal is divided into a number of chambers, each of which has its own area of specialism as shown in Table 4.2.

---

15. Available online at <http://www.tribunals-review.org.uk>.

Table 4.2 The Chambers of the First-tier Tribunal

General Regulatory Chamber	Alternative business structures
	Charity
	Claims management services
	Consumer credit
	Environment
	Estate agents
	Gambling appeals
	Immigration services
	Information rights
	Local Government standards in England
	Transport
Social Entitlement Chamber	Asylum support
	Criminal injuries compensation
	Social security and child support
Health, Education, and Social Care Chamber	Care standards
	Mental health
	Special educational needs and disability
	Primary health lists
War Pensions and Armed Forces Compensation Chamber	War pensions and armed forces compensation
Tax Chamber	Tax
	MP expenses
Immigration and Asylum Chamber	Immigration
	Asylum

It is envisaged that further tribunals will be added to the new structure as part of a phased implementation programme.

Section 11 of the Act creates an Upper Tribunal, which provides the normal route of appeal from decisions made by the First-tier Tribunal on a point of law. However, some decisions (such as decisions relating to asylum support and criminal injuries compensation) do not carry a right to appeal and can therefore only be challenged via judicial review. Some cases will commence directly in the Upper Tribunal.

The Upper Tribunal is divided into four chambers:

- Administrative Appeals Chamber
- Tax and Chancery Chamber
- Lands Chamber
- Immigration and Asylum Chamber

Section 13 of the Act provides that a route of appeal lies from decisions of the Chambers of the Upper Tribunal to the Court of Appeal (Civil Division) on a point of law. See Figure 4.3 for an overview of the general structure.

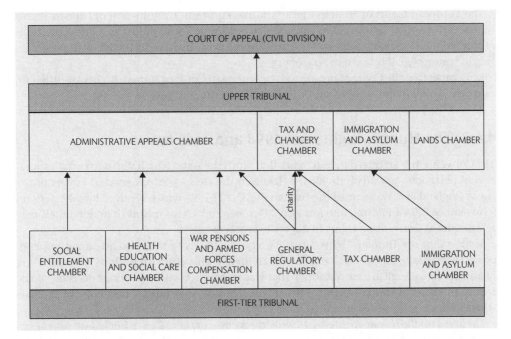

Figure 4.3 The structure of the tribunal system

Section 44 of the Tribunals, Courts and Enforcement Act 2007 creates the Administrative Justice and Tribunals Council. This is a public body with responsibility for supervising and regulating the administrative justice system. In relation to the new tribunal system, the Council must review and report on the operation of the tribunals under its supervision and scrutinize legislation relating to tribunals.

4.4 The European Court of Human Rights

4.4.1 A brief history

The European Convention on Human Rights and Freedoms is a creation of the Council of Europe although it is, at least in part, based upon the 1948 United Nations Declaration of Human Rights. The Council of Europe was formed in 1949, shortly after the end of the Second World War, with its aim of international cooperation and the prevention of the kinds of widespread atrocious violations of human rights which had occurred during the war. The European Convention on Human Rights was signed in Rome in 1950, ratified by the UK a year later and came into force in 1953.

The European Court of Human Rights was established in 1959 as a final avenue of complaint for claimants who had exhausted the remedies available to them in their domestic courts for alleged breaches of Convention rights. At the same time, the European Commission of Human Rights was also established. The Commission's role was to decrease the caseload of the European Court of Human Rights by filtering out some cases and attempting to resolve others by conciliation. The individual's right to petition the European Court of Human Rights became available to UK citizens in 1966.

The European Court of Human Rights and the European Commission of Human Rights were abolished on 31 October 1998 and replaced by a single Court of Human Rights. Questions of admissibility (formerly dealt with by the Commission) are now dealt with by its judges sitting in committee. It is based in Strasbourg.

Remember that the Court of Justice and the European Court of Human Rights are different, as are the Council of the European Union and the Council of Europe.

4.4.2 The Human Rights Act 1998 and case law

The Convention is an international treaty that binds the states which sign it to certain standards of behaviour towards individuals. However, the treaty was not enacted as part of the law of England and Wales until the Human Rights Act 1998 which received Royal Assent on 9 November 1998 and came into force on 2 October 2000. This means that individuals may rely on (most) Convention rights in domestic proceedings.

Section 2 of the Human Rights Act 1998 requires courts to take into account any previous decision of the European Court of Human Rights. This effectively allows the overruling of any previous English case authority that was in conflict with a previous decision of the European Court of Human Rights. This enables the courts to build a new body of case law where human rights issues are raised.

The impact of the Human Rights Act 1998 on the doctrine of judicial precedent is dealt with in section 6.4. Section 5.4 describes how to find decisions of the European Court of Human Rights.

 CHAPTER SUMMARY

Common law and equity

- The common law evolved following the Norman Conquest in 1066

- It emerged from a combination of local custom and case law

- The common law became very bureaucratic in operation, costly, and time-consuming

- The common law did not recognize certain rights

- Equitable rights and remedies became available from the Court of Chancery

- Where there was conflict between law and equity, equity prevailed

- The administration of common law and equity was fused by the Supreme Court of Judicature Acts 1873 and 1875

- Equity has its own system of equitable maxims (doctrines), rights and remedies including injunctions, specific performance, and rescission

Custom

- Local customs can be enforced as exceptions to the common law

- In order to enforce a custom, it is necessary to show that it meets a very stringent set of conditions

- Custom is consequently very difficult to prove

- Custom is typically used in connection with disputes over land

The courts and their jurisdictions

- Criminal courts determine guilt or innocence of defendants and dispense punishment to convicted offenders

- Civil courts primarily deal with the resolution of disputes between individuals

- Trial courts hear cases at first instance—before any appeals

- Appellate courts consider the application of legal principles to cases that have already been heard at first instance

- The Supreme Court of the United Kingdom is the final court of appeal for all UK civil cases and criminal cases from England, Wales, and Northern Ireland

- The Court of Appeal is divided into Civil and Criminal Divisions

- The High Court is divided into three divisions for administrative purposes—the Queen's Bench, Family, and Chancery Divisions

- The Crown Court primarily deals with trial by jury in criminal cases

- The County Court deals with all but the most complicated civil law matters

- The Family Court deals with almost all family matters

- All criminal proceedings begin in the magistrates' court

- The Privy Council hears appeals from certain Commonwealth countries and UK overseas territories, appeals in professional disciplinary cases, and ecclesiastical appeals

- Tribunals are specialist bodies established with the aim of providing quicker, cheaper, and more accessible routes to justice

The European Court of Human Rights

- Not to be confused with the European Court of Justice

- The European Court of Human Rights is based in Strasbourg

- The European Convention on Human Rights was signed in Rome in 1950, ratified by the UK in 1951 and came into force in 1953

- The individual's right to petition the European Court of Human Rights became available to UK citizens in 1966

- The Human Rights Act 1998 came into force on 2 October 2000. This means that individuals may rely on (most) Convention rights in domestic proceedings

- Section 2 of the Human Rights Act 1998 requires courts to take into account any previous decision of the European Court of Human Rights

- This enables the courts to build a new body of case law where human rights issues are raised

FURTHER READING

- You can find a consideration of the creation of the UK Supreme Court in J Lennan, 'A Supreme Court for the United Kingdom: a note on early days' (2010) 29(2) Civil Justice Quarterly 139.

- A brief discussion of the new single Family Court can be found in H Johns, 'The new Family Court' (2014) Family Law 110.

- The discussion of custom as a source of law is covered briefly in this chapter. If you would like to know more, then see EK Braybrooke, 'Custom as a Source of English Law' (1951) 50 Michigan Law Review 70.

Finding cases

5

INTRODUCTION

The previous chapter explained the role of case law as a source of law. This chapter will give you the skills to find cases. It will start by explaining the meanings of case citations before moving on to discuss how to locate domestic cases both in a law library and electronically via a number of the online databases which are currently available. It will then explain how to find decisions of the Court of Justice of the European Union, the General Court, and the European Court of Human Rights.

The ability to locate case law is as important as finding legislation. Without being able to find the primary sources of law you will struggle in every area of your legal study. You will need to be able to find the cases that you encounter during your studies in order to read and understand them. This is important both in terms of analyzing the operation of particular areas of the law as well as more practically in constructing legal arguments based on the outcomes of previous cases.

LEARNING OUTCOMES

After studying this chapter, you will be able to:

- Understand the meaning of case citations

- Explain the use of the neutral citation system

- Distinguish between reported and unreported cases

- Find domestic and European cases in a law library and online

5.1 Law reporting

Unless you are actually present in court at the time that the judgment in a particular case is made, you will have to rely on a report of the case to find out what happened. Clearly, then, accurate law reporting is extremely important and citations are your means of finding those reports.

5.1.1 Making sense of case citations

Case citations are an abbreviated form of reference to a particular report of a case. This section deals with the main citations for cases heard in England and Wales. For an explanation of citations used for EU cases, see 'Finding EU case law' in section 5.3. By way of example, we will look at the case of *R v Mirza* which dealt with misconduct in the jury room during a criminal trial.

The citation for *R v Mirza* is [2004] UKHL 2; [2004] 1 AC 1118 and indicates where this particular reported case can be found. You will notice that this particular case has two citations: one *neutral citation* and one *law report citation* (see Figure 5.1).

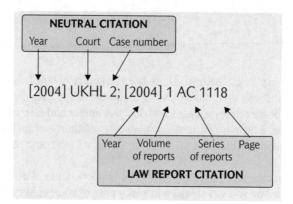

Figure 5.1 Case citations

5.1.1.1 Neutral citations

The neutral citation system was introduced to the Court of Appeal and the Administrative Court in 2001 and extended to all divisions of the High Court in 2002.

The main reason for the introduction of the neutral citation system was to facilitate the publication of judgments online and the access of judgments stored on electronic databases.

First, the **year** of the judgment is given in square brackets. This is followed by an **abbreviation for the court**, preceded by UK (for 'United Kingdom' in relation to the jurisdiction of the Supreme Court and its predecessor, the House of Lords) or EW (for 'England and Wales' in relation to the jurisdiction of the other courts). The abbreviations used for each of the courts that use the neutral citation system are set out in Table 5.1:

Table 5.1 Abbreviations used in the neutral citation system

Court	Abbreviation
Supreme Court	UKSC
House of Lords	UKHL
Privy Council	UKPC
Court of Appeal (Criminal Division)	EWCA Crim
Court of Appeal (Civil Division)	EWCA Civ
Family Court	EWFC
Court of Protection	EWCOP
High Court (Administrative Court)	EWHC (Admin)

(Continued)

Table 5.1 *(Cont.)*

Court	Abbreviation
Chancery Division	EWHC (Ch)
Patents Court	EWHC (Pat)
Queen's Bench Division	EWHC (QB)
Commercial Court	EWHC (Comm)
Admiralty Court	EWHC (Admlty)
Technology and Construction Court	EWHC (TCC)
Family Division	EWHC (Fam)

Finally, a unique **serial number** is given to each approved judgment issued by the Supreme Court, Court of Appeal and High Court and is appended to the end of the citation.

Therefore, *R v Mirza* was the second reported judgment of the House of Lords in the United Kingdom in 2004.

The neutral citation *precedes* the citation for any law report in which the case has been published. If the report has not been published then the neutral citation stands alone. In summary:

- Pre-2001 cases give a law report citation only

- Post-2001 cases give the neutral citation *followed by* the law report citation if there is one available.

You may see cases given with a neutral citation which pre-dates 2001, particularly those retrieved from the BAILII database (see section 5.2.1.8). For example, *R v Chandler* [1964] 2 QB 322 is shown on BAILII as [1964] EWCA Crim 1. These neutral citations are *not* official and should not be used. As BAILII states:

> All other vendor neutral citations [that is, those not provided by the courts themselves] and paragraph numbering may have been added by BAILII and should be considered unofficial, but are nevertheless useful for referring to cases on BAILII.[1]

5.1.1.2 Law report citations

The judgments of cases are also published in various series of law reports, the most authoritative of which are published by the Incorporated Council for Law Reporting. References to law reports follow a different convention to that used for neutral citations.

The first element of the citation is a *year*. This will almost always refer to the year in which the case was reported or, very infrequently, to the year in which the judgment was given. In actual fact, these years are usually the same, since cases are most commonly reported in the same year as the judgment is given. There can, however, be situations where the reports are published in a different year:

- **If the case was heard late in one year, but reported early in the next year.** An example of this can be found in *Wilkey and another v British Broadcasting Corporation and another* [2002] EWCA Civ 1561; [2003] 1 WLR 1. This case was heard on 21 and 22 October 2002 but reported in the first issue of the Weekly Law Reports of 2003.

---

1. BAILII, 'Citations' <http://www.bailii.org/bailii/citation.html> accessed 21 August 2014.

- **If the importance of the case was not appreciated at the time of the judgment.** For example, the judgment in *Mesher v Mesher* [1980] 1 All ER 126 which deals with the division of marital property on divorce, was reported in 1980 but delivered on 13 February 1973, some seven years previously.

To complicate matters further, there is a convention surrounding the use of round or square brackets around the year of the report.

For cases heard prior to 1890, the year does not form part of the citation; in other words, it is not necessary to know the year of the report in order to find the case report itself. However, the year is now conventionally inserted for ease of reference, but is shown in *round* brackets to indicate that it is for information only. An example of this can be found in *R v Dudley and Stephens* (1884) 14 QBD 273, which considered the defence of necessity in relation to murder: specifically the killing and cannibalization of a crewmember following a shipwreck.

From 1890 to the present day, the year of the case *does* form part of the citation, so it must always be provided. Whether it is put in (round) or [square] brackets depends on the way in which the individual report series is numbered.

In order to illustrate this, we will first look at a report in the European Human Rights Reports (EHRR). Volume 1 of the EHRR was published in 1979 and the most recent volume at the time of writing, covering 2014, is volume 59. You will notice that there are more volumes than there are years between 1979 and 2012: this is because the reports for a single year often span more than one volume. Look at Figure 5.2 which shows how some of the reports might look on the library shelf.

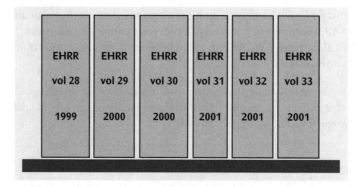

Figure 5.2 European Human Rights Reports (sequential volume numbers)

You should be able to see that the volume number alone is enough to locate a particular report. For example, the case of *Riera Blume v Spain* is reported on page 632 of volume 30. You would not need to know the year to find the case since the volume numbers run sequentially. Therefore a citation of *Riera Blume v Spain* 30 EHRR 632 would be sufficient. However, it is very useful to know the year of the report as well, which, as you will see from Figure 5.2 is 2000. This is conventionally provided with the citation as well, but since it is not required uniquely to identify the report it is given in round brackets. The full citation of the case is therefore *Riera Blume v Spain* (2000) 30 EHRR 632. Note here, that the judgment in this case was given on 14 October 1999, so the year in the citation refers to the year of the report and not the year of the judgment.

The year of the report is put in [square] brackets when the volume of the report series in question is identified by the year itself. For example, the Appeal Cases reports do not have sequential volume numbers starting from 1. The reports are bound by year (and sometimes with multiple volumes within each year). Take a look at Figure 5.3 which shows some volumes of the Appeal Cases on our hypothetical library shelf.

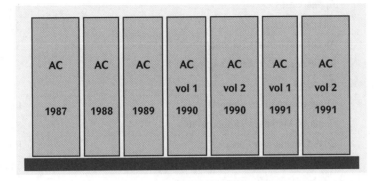

Figure 5.3 Appeal Cases Reports (non-sequential volume numbers)

In a series presented like the Appeal Cases, a volume number on its own is pretty useless. If you were told that *R v Secretary of State for Transport, ex parte Factortame (No. 2)* was reported on page 603 of volume 1 of the Appeal Cases Reports, you still would not have enough information to know which book to take off the shelf in order to find the case report. You would need to know the year of the report as well which, in this example, was 1991.

Since the year of the case is required in order to find it, it is conventionally given in square brackets in the citation. The correct citation of this case is therefore *R v Secretary of State for Transport, ex parte Factortame (No. 2)* [1991] 1 AC 603.

Note again, that the judgment in this case was given in October 1990, so the year in the citation again refers to the year of the report and not the year of the judgment. Also, where there is only one volume for a year, as was the case in 1987, 1998, and 1989 for instance, the volume number is omitted from the citation: so *R v Gold* [1988] AC 1063 is correct (and *not R v Gold* [1988] 1 AC 1063).

Students are frequently confused on the conventional use of brackets and so this is an area of referencing that is frequently done badly. Practically speaking, you should just remember that the correct use of round and square brackets is important: all the legal databases give correct citations, and you should take care to be accurate when you are copying citations from materials that you find. If you are in any further doubt, Table 5.2 should guide you on the use of the convention for the most commonly encountered series of law reports.

As already mentioned in the examples so far, the **volume number** of the law report series is given after the year, if the volume numbers run sequentially (as with the European Human Rights Reports), or if there is more than one volume of the reports for a particular year (as with the Appeal Cases Reports for 1990 and 1991). If neither of these situations apply, then no volume number is given.

Next comes an abbreviation for the **series of law reports** in which the case was reported. Some common series of law reports are listed in Table 5.2.

The final part of the citation is the **page number** on which the report begins.

If there is no neutral citation, an abbreviation for the court in which the case was heard should follow the case citation in brackets: for example, *R v R* [1992] 1 AC 599 (HL) was heard in the House of Lords (and can be found on page 599 of volume 1 of the Appeal Cases Reports for 1992). You may see HL for House of Lords, CA for Court of Appeal, DC for Divisional Court, or PC for Privy Council. This abbreviation is not required where the law report citation

Table 5.2 Some common law report series

Abbreviation	Law report series	Year brackets
AC	Appeal Cases	Square
All ER	All England Law Reports	Square
All ER (EC)	All England Reports European Cases 1995–	Square
BCLC	Butterworths Company Law Reports 1983–	Square
Ch	Chancery	Square
CLR	Commonwealth Law Reports	Round
CMLR	Common Market Law Reports 1962–	Square
Cox CC	Cox's Criminal Law Cases	Round
Cr App R	Criminal Appeal Reports	Square
Cr App R (S)	Criminal Appeal Reports Sentencing	Square
Crim LR	Criminal Law Review	Square
ECHR	European Commission of Human Rights Decisions and Reports 1976–98	Square
ECR	European Court Reports 1954 (Court of Justice of the European Community)	Square
ECR I-	European Court of First Instance/General Court	Square
EHRR	European Human Rights Reports 1993–	Round
Fam	Family	Square
KB	King's Bench	Square
QB	Queen's Bench	Square
WLR	Weekly Law Reports 1957–	Square

follows a neutral citation, since the court in which the case was heard is made clear within the neutral citation itself.

5.1.1.3 Which citation?

The 2012 Practice Direction: Citation of Authorities clarified the practice and procedure governing the citation of authorities and applies throughout the Senior Courts of England and Wales, including the Crown Court, in county courts, and in magistrates' courts. In summary:

- Where a judgment is reported in the official reports (AC, QB, Ch, Fam) it must be cited
- If a judgment is not (or not yet) reported in the official reports, but is reported in the WLR or the All ER, then that should be cited. If it is reported in both the WLR or the All ER then either may be used
- If a judgment is not in the official reports, the WLR or the All ER, but is reported in any specialist reports which contain a headnote and are made by qualified practitioners in the senior courts, then the specialist reports may be cited
- Failing all of the above, any other reports may be cited

- For unreported cases, the official transcript may be used (available from BAILII): [2] however, unreported cases should not normally be used unless they contain a relevant statement of legal principle not found in reported authority

This hierarchy of court reports is also important in mooting; see chapter 18.

5.1.2 Reported and unreported cases

Since only a relatively small proportion of cases end up being reported, it follows that there are a vast number of 'unreported' cases each year. There are an increasing number of these unreported cases available online. Since 1996, various unreported judgments have been freely available as courts have published verbatim transcripts online.

 Practical exercise

Visit the free databases listed in this section. Have a look around each to get used to their layout and content. If you are using your own computer, bookmark the sites for quick access later.

5.1.3 Case summaries

In addition to the full reports, there are a number of sources of case summaries and commentaries. For instance, the Criminal Law Review and the Journal of Criminal Law contain brief summaries of pertinent criminal cases. There are similar journals and digests for other areas of the law. The summaries tend to comprise a brief summary of the facts and the judgment accompanied by a pithy commentary.

However, you should remember that these summaries only provide indications of the law and pointers to the actual cases themselves. You should therefore use case summaries with caution—if you wish to rely on the opinion in a case summary, it would be prudent to seek out the full transcript of the case to try and understand for yourself the reasoning used by the author of the summary.

5.2 Finding case law

5.2.1 Online

There are a number of freely available online resources for finding case law, as well as the subscription only services which may or may not be available for you to use at your institution. The subscription services usually offer a selection of 'value-added' features that the free resources do not: these will be pointed out in the discussions of each. Remember that most institutions will provide a guide, or offer training (or both) to using each of the main databases and you should check with your law librarian for details. It may even be the case that you are required to do database training as part of your university induction, or as a component of a legal skills or legal systems module. LexisLibrary and Westlaw UK often have student representatives at institutions who are another useful source of information. In any event, you will need to spend time finding

---

2. Note however the comment on BAILII's use of 'unofficial' neutral citations at the end of section 5.1.1.1.

cases throughout your studies, and there is no substitute for practical experience. You should therefore try to get familiar with the various searching tools at your disposal as soon as you can.

Practical exercise

Visit as many of the legal databases from this section as you can. Make a list of those to which you are allowed access. Take some time to click around them and perform a few practice searches.

5.2.1.1 Where to start?

So. Let's imagine that you need to find the case report for *Donoghue v Stevenson*.[3] You could simply start by doing a Google search[4] which would turn up something like this:

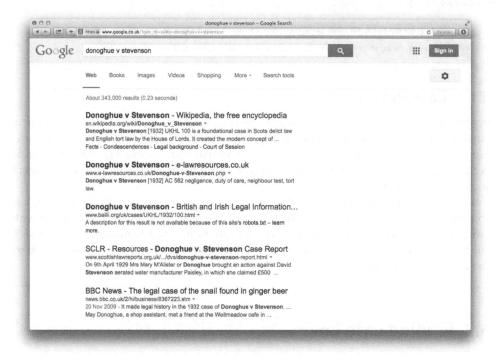

Figure 5.4 Google screenshot

The first five matches (of about 343,000!) are shown. The first of these is Wikipedia.[5]

---

3. This is a famous case from the 1930s which became the basis for the modern law of negligence today. If you have not come across it before, you will undoubtedly do so quite soon.
4. Other search engines are available.
5. See section 13.3.4.5 on the general perils of using Wikipedia for legal research.

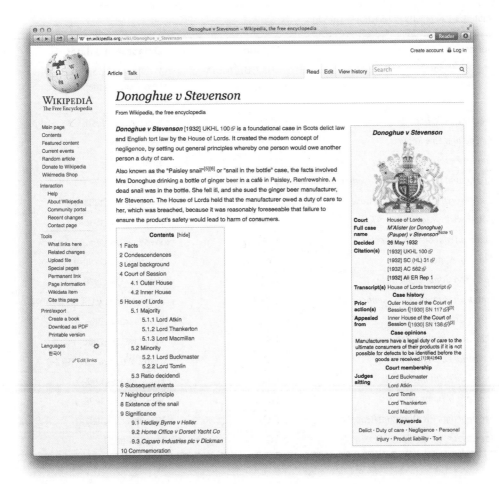

Figure 5.5 Wikipedia screenshot

You will see that this gives a summary of the case, some of the case history, citations, key dates, and quite a lot of commentary. However, some initial points to note:

- The first citation given [1932] UKHL 100 is the unofficial neutral citation from BAILII which should not be used

- The Wikipedia page does not contain the actual case report itself. If you want to read the case report itself, you can link to BAILII (an unofficial site), or UK Law Online (an unofficial site hosted by the University of Leeds), or the Scottish Council for Law Reporting (via a Scottish citation which does give an authoritative transcript)

The second match is e-lawresources.co.uk.

This is a private site with some resources relating to some areas of law. The discussion here is more of a case synopsis, rather than the official report. There are no links to actual reports, although the citation given is correct. The site also has a number of banner ads.

The third match goes straight to the BAILII report. This was also referenced from Wikipedia and has the benefit of being an accurate transcript of the judgment itself. It does, however, suffer from the use of the unofficial neutral citation already mentioned in the discussion on Wikipedia. The fourth match goes to the Scottish Council for Law Reporting site, also linked

Table 5.3 Law reports and electronic databases

Series	Citation	Database and dates
The Law Reports	AC, QB, Ch, Fam	Westlaw UK (1865–)
		LexisLibrary (1865–)
		Justis
Weekly Law Reports	WLR	Westlaw UK Justis
All England Law Reports	All ER	LexisLibrary
English Reports	ER	Justis
All England Law Reports European Cases	All ER (EC)	LexisLibrary (1995–)
Butterworths Company Law Cases	BCLC	LexisLibrary (1983–)
Butterworths Medico-Legal Reports	BMLR	LexisLibrary (1986–)
Common Market Law Reports	CMLR	Westlaw UK (1962–)
Criminal Appeal Reports	Cr App R	Westlaw UK (1990–)
European Commercial Cases	ECC	Westlaw UK (1978–)
European Human Rights Reports	EHRR	Justis, Westlaw UK (1979/80–)
Family Court Reporter	FCR	LexisLibrary (1998–)
Human Rights Law Reports	HRLR	Westlaw UK (2000–)
Industrial Cases Reports	ICR	Justis, Westlaw UK (1972–)
Industrial Relations Law Reports	IRLR	LexisLibrary (1972–)
Landlord & Tenant Reports	L&TR	Westlaw UK (1998–)
Personal Injury & Quantum Reports	PIQR	Westlaw UK (1992–)
Tax Cases	TC	LexisLibrary

to from Wikipedia. The fifth match is a BBC News story about the circumstances of the case and an associated Radio 4 documentary from 2010.

As you can see, there is a wide variety of different sources available via a simple web search. For that reason, it is preferable to use one (or more) of the recognized legal databases, all of which offer greater features and functionality than a general web search. The question 'where to start?' then becomes 'which database to use?'

However, although there are a number of different legal databases available online, not all databases contain all reports. Table 5.3 provides a summary of some of the more common report series and the database (or databases) in which they are covered.

5.2.1.2 How do the databases work?

A detailed description of the operation of each of the various databases is beyond the scope of this book.

In general terms, the databases allow you to search by a name, citation or keywords, or any combination of the above. The best strategy with all database searches is to try and keep it as simple as possible. For instance if you are searching for a case called *DPP v Majewski* it would be simple to put in the appellant's name. It is an uncommon name so you would therefore not expect there to be too many cases involving a party called Majewski.

However, if the case was *R v Smith* and you did not know the year, you would need to try to find some appropriate subject matter keywords to narrow your search results; otherwise you would very likely end up with an unmanageable number of potential cases. The pictures that follow in this chapter show the options available on the main search screen of a range of different online resources.

5.2.1.3 Westlaw UK

Westlaw UK allows searching for cases by party name, citation, or keyword. Even if the case is not available on full text in Westlaw UK, links will be given to the location of the report or transcript (if available). Westlaw UK also contains transcripts of recent cases. However, Westlaw UK does not contain all series of reports (see Table 5.3) and for this reason it is often best used together with another broad database such as LexisLibrary.

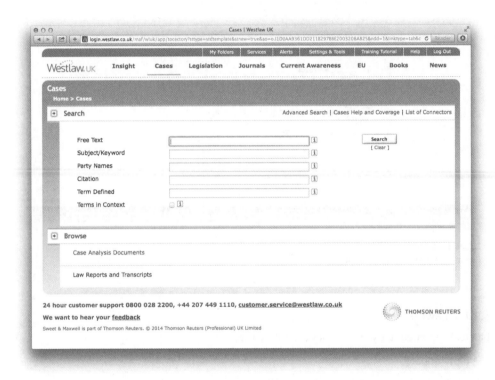

Figure 5.6 Westlaw UK screenshot

5.2.1.4 LexisLibrary

Like Westlaw UK, LexisLibrary is also a subscription service which contains a very broad selection of reports. As well as the standard search criteria it also allows searches by the judge (or judges) or searches for cases which refer to a particular statutory provision. This can be useful if you need to research how a particular piece of legislation has been applied by the courts.

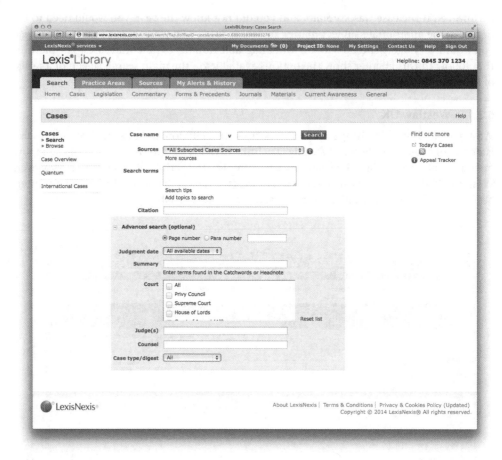

Figure 5.7 LexisLibrary screenshot
Reproduced with the kind permission of LexisNexis®

5.2.1.5 Lawtel

Lawtel is updated daily. It includes the following:

- A daily update
- Summaries of cases 1980–, with some links to full text from 1993–
- Personal injury quantum reports
- Practice directions 1980–

It contains summaries and transcripts only. The summaries provide links to full reports. Lawtel covers an immense range of cases and often carries judgments which are not included in the other databases.

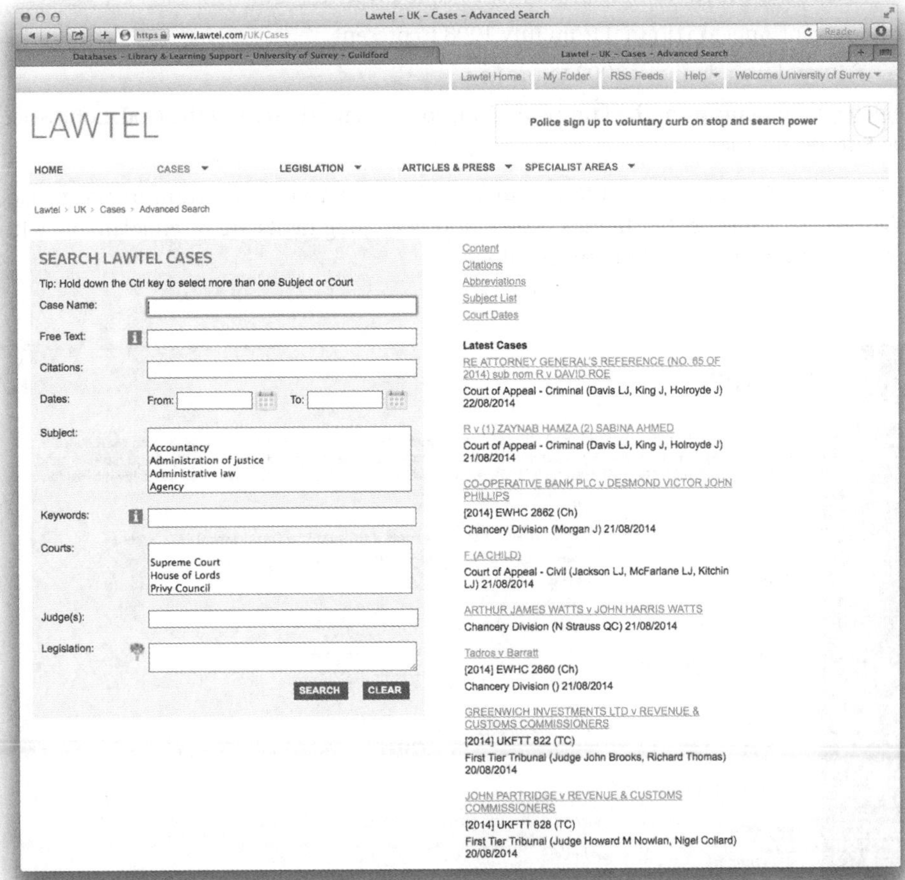

Figure 5.8 Lawtel screenshot

5.2.1.6 Justis

Justis contains the *Law Reports, English Reports, Industrial Cases Reports*, and *Family Law Reports*. It also contains the *Weekly Law Reports*. It is a full text online legal library of UK, Irish, and EU case law dating back to 1163 and legislation from 1235 and includes exact replica PDF files of reported cases.

5.2.1.7 Casetrack

Casetrack is a subscription service provided by Merrill Legal Solutions. It contains judgments as follows:

- Court of Appeal (Criminal and Civil Divisions) from April 1996 to present
- Administrative Court from April 1996 to present

- All divisions of the High Court from July 1998 to present
- Employment Appeal Tribunal from July 1998 to present
- VAT Tribunal from January 2002 to present
- Selected judgments from the European Court of Human Rights and the Court of Justice of the European Union

Merrill Legal Solutions is the official source of Court of Appeal and Administrative Court transcripts. This means that handed-down approved judgments are often available within hours (and in one instance, twenty-six minutes).

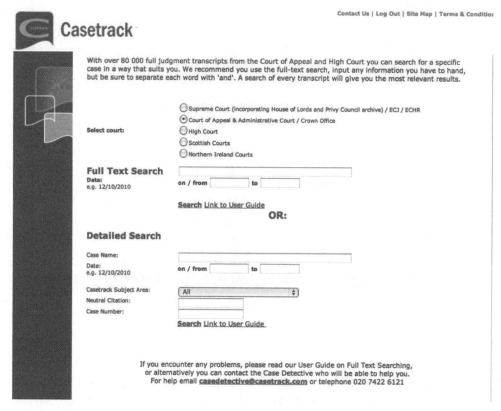

Figure 5.9 Casetrack screenshot

5.2.1.8 Bailii

BAILII is a free service which contains judgments from a wide range of sources. It has an extremely comprehensive coverage of case law. BAILII's coverage extends beyond England and Wales to Scotland, Northern Ireland, and the European Union. It can be found at www.bailii.org. It allows searching by keyword and first named party.

See the note on BAILII's use of unofficial neutral citations in section 5.1.1.1.

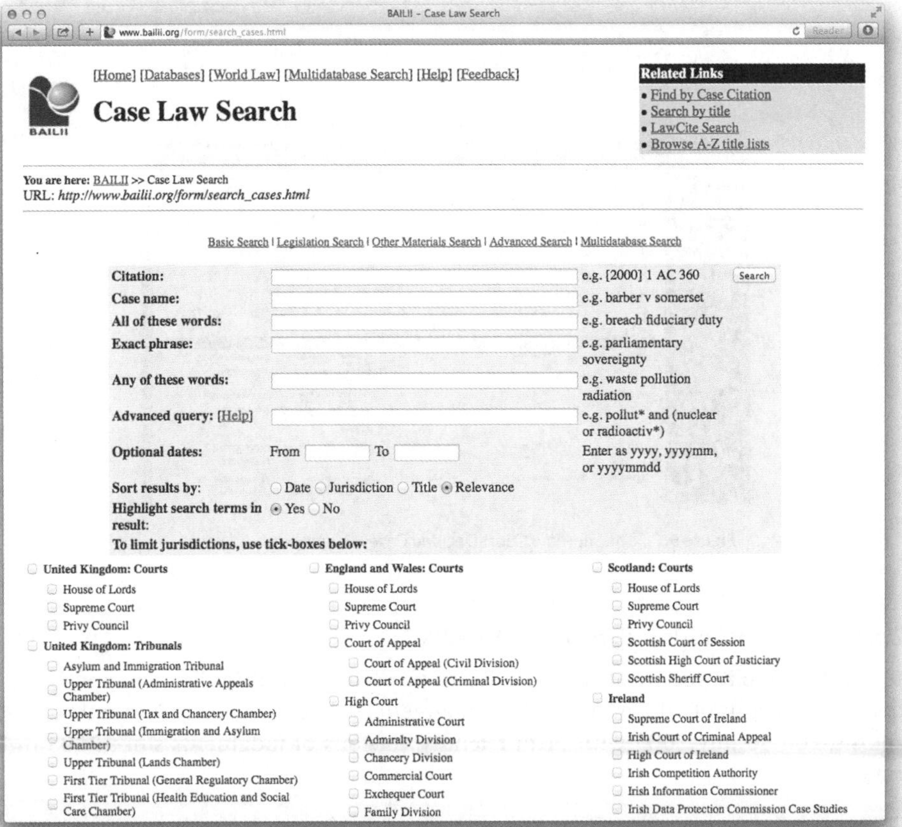

Figure 5.10 BAILII screenshot
http://www.bailii.org/

5.2.1.9 Supreme Court judgments

Decided cases from the Supreme Court are published on its website at http://www.supremecourt.uk/decided-cases/index.shtml. It has fairly rudimentary search facilities, but if you know the neutral citation it is easy to use. Each case also has a Press Summary which gives an outline of the case and the judgment. Be careful, though, to note the disclaimer on each:

> This summary is provided to assist in understanding the Court's decision. It does not form part of the reasons for the decision. The full judgment of the Court is the only authoritative document.

Therefore, when using extracts from the cases, ensure that you are looking at the full judgment and not the Press Summary (although the summaries are extremely useful to get a quick overview of the facts, the legal issue, and a basic understanding of the court's decision).

Figure 5.11 The Supreme Court Decided Cases screenshot

5.2.1.10 House of Lords judgments (1996–2009)

The UK Parliament website at www.publications.parliament.uk/pa/ld/ldjudgmt.htm contains html versions of all House of Lords judgments delivered from 14 November 1996 to its closure on 30 July 2009 with print-friendly versions of judgments since 2005 in PDF format.

Figure 5.12 Parliament.co.uk screenshot

5.2.1.11 Courts and tribunals judiciary

The Courts and tribunals judiciary website at http://www.judiciary.gov.uk/judgments/ carries certain judgments from 2012 from the Court of Appeal, High Court, Family Court, Crown Court, County Court, Magistrates' Court, Court of Protection, Military Court and Tribunals. It allows free text searches and filtering by court and/or jurisdiction, and date range.

Judgments from 2009 are available via a link to the National Archives.

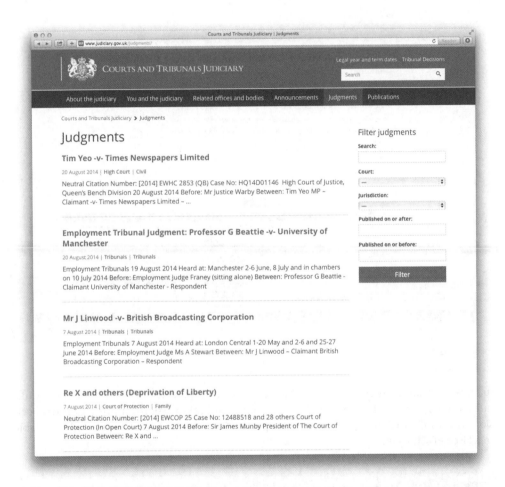

Figure 5.13 Courts and Tribunals screenshot

5.2.1.12 Privy Council

Judgments of the Privy Council made after August 2009 are available on the Judicial Committee website at www.jcpc.gov.uk/decided-cases/index.html

Figure 5.14 Privy Council screenshot

Judgments prior to August 2009 can be found at http://privycouncil.independent.gov.uk/judicial-committee/judgments/. This site contains full-text versions of Privy Council decisions from 1999 to 2009 and a selection of pre-1999 decisions. These are generally available in RTF or PDF format.

Practical exercise

Try to find the following cases using each of the databases from their names alone:

- *R v Dudley and Stephens*
- *Eves v Eves*
- *Nettleship v Weston*
- *Pennington v Waine*
- *R v Gold; R v Schifreen*
- *R v Mirza*

5.2.2 In a library

As you have seen from the previous section, there is a wealth of authoritative online resources available for finding case law. The continuing increase in the availability of case law online and the power of electronic searches has, of course, impacted on the traditional methods of case law searching in a law library. Of course, there are a range of different paper resources that you can use to find case law in a library. It may also be the case that your institution requires you to demonstrate proficiency in library use. Even if it does not, you would be well advised to learn how to use paper resources. Electronic databases can (and do!) go down at the most inopportune times, so being able to use the library as a back up is essential. Some texts, statues, and cases are still only available in print form and many law firms still rely heavily on books. That said, most case law research is now done online, and you should find that virtually all the cases you will need as an undergraduate exist on at least one of the databases somewhere. However, do not overlook the law librarian if you are stuck. Not only should they be able to help you with the legal databases, but also in the use of paper resources for any case rarities. Many libraries also offer 'Book a Librarian' service where students can book individual or group sessions with the librarian and get assistance with searching and locating resources, legal database training, search strategies, and referencing help. Some librarians are also involved in teaching legal research as part of the law programme but of course this varies between institutions. Many librarians create subject guides and online links to other resources that can support you in your studies. Your librarian is a very useful and skilled resource who often gets overlooked—remember that they are there to help. You will almost certainly meet your law librarian very early on in your time at university since most students attend a presentation given by their librarian and/or tour the law library in their first week.

5.3 Finding European case law

Decisions of the European Court of Justice and the General Court/Court of First Instance also have a bearing on the law of England and Wales. It follows that you will need to know how to find EU case law.

For a reminder of the operation of the European Institutions and Courts, see section 4.4. The effect of European cases on the doctrine of judicial precedent is covered in section 6.5.

5.3.1 Making sense of European case citations

The official reports of cases are found in the *Reports of Cases before the Court*. These are more commonly referred to as the *European Court Reports*, abbreviated to ECR. The reports are structured differently from those of England and Wales. Their component parts are as shown in Table 5.4.

Table 5.4 Components of the *European Court Reports*

Reports before 1994	Reports since 1994
Report for the hearing	
Advocate General's opinion	Advocate General's opinion
Judgment of the court	Judgment of the court

The report for the hearing was included in reports before 1994. This is a summary of the facts and legal arguments prepared for the court by a 'reporting judge'. The Advocate General's opinion is precisely that—an opinion. Therefore, it is not binding (although in practice it is usually followed). It contains a detailed analysis of the facts and legal arguments. The judgment of the court is a single judgment, even though there are always at least three judges hearing the case. Unlike the courts of England and Wales, separate concurring or dissenting judgments are not permitted.

Since 1990 the *Reports* have been split into two parts. Part I covers reports of cases from the European Court of Justice and Part II contains cases from the Court of First Instance.

The main problem with the *European Court Reports* is the delay in publication. The courts can hear cases in any of the eleven official languages of the European Union, although they work in French. Judgments have to be translated into each of the official languages. This can take up to two years since the translations must be accurate and precise in each of the languages. Therefore, because of this delay, it is very difficult to use the *Reports* for relatively recent cases.

European cases are cited differently from those in England and Wales. We will use the following two cases by way of example.

- Case C-260/09 *Blizzard Germany GmbH v European Commission* [2011] ECR I-419
- Case T-465/08 *Czech Republic v European Commission* [2011] ECR II-1941

The elements of the citations are broken down in Figure 5.15

Looking at the elements of the citation, we can see that *Blizzard Germany GmbH v European Commission* was the 260th case (serial number) reported to the Court of Justice (serial number is prefixed by C and the report appears in Part I of the ECR) in 2009 (the year of application or reference is '09'). It was reported in Part I of the ECR for 2011 at page 419.

Figure 5.15 Citing European cases

Similarly, you should be able to tell that *Czech Republic v European Commission* was heard in the General Court, since the case reference is prefixed by T (from the French *Tribunal*) and it is reported in Part II of the ECR for 2011 at page 1941. It was the 465th case heard by the General Court in 2008.

You will notice from both these examples that there is a lapse of time between the hearings (2009 and 2008 respectively) and the official reports (2011). This illustrates the delay in publication. Alternative (unofficial) reports of selected cases include the weekly *Common Market Law Reports* and the *All England Law Reports (European Cases)* published ten times a year.

5.3.2 Online

There are various online resources for EU case law.

5.3.2.1 EUROPA/EUR-Lex

EUROPA is the main website of the European Union. It contains over 1.5 million pages and links to the European legal portal, EUR-Lex (eur-lex.europa.eu/homepage.html). This includes coverage of the judgments of the European Court of Justice and the General Court. It also includes opinions of the Advocates General as published in the *European Court Reports*. It is updated daily.

Figure 5.16 EUR-Lex screenshot
© European Union, 1995–2013

5.3.2.2 Celex

CELEX is the official multilingual legal database of the European Union. It contains the full text of the *European Court Reports*. It is available as a subscription service via EUROPA, or commercially via a number of commercial publishers such as Justis, CELEX, and Eurolaw. The commercial variants offer a broader range of search facilities.

5.3.2.3 Other databases

LexisLibrary, Lawtel, and Westlaw UK also provide search facilities for European cases (see section 5.2 for details).

 Practical exercise

Access the European databases listed in this section. Try to find *Blizzard Germany GmbH v European Commission* and *Czech Republic v European Commission* in each of them.

5.4 Finding decisions of the European Court of Human Rights

The final cases that you will need to find are those decided in the European Court of Human Rights.

The operation of the European Court of Human Rights was dealt with in section 4.4.

5.4.1 Making sense of ECHR case citations

The first series of official reports were published in *Publications of the European Court of Human Rights, Series A: Judgments and Decisions*. Series B contained pleadings, oral arguments, and other supporting documentation. These reports cover the period up until the end of 1995.

From 1996 onwards, the official reports were published in *Reports of Judgments and Decisions*, but from 2006 onwards only selected cases were reported. In any event, there is usually a delay of around a year from the date of the judgment before a case report is published.

European Court of Human Rights cases are cited differently from those in England and Wales and differently from those in the European Court of Justice and General Court.

For cases reported in *Publications of the European Court of Human Rights, Series A: Judgments and Decisions* (i.e. those reported before 1996) the correct form of citation is, for example:

> *Golder v United Kingdom* (1975) Series A, no 18

For cases reported from 1996 in *Judgments and Decisions*, the citations take the following form:

> *Robins v United Kingdom* [1997] ECHR 72

References to unreported judgments should give the application number, and then the abbreviated reference to the court (ECtHR) and the date of the judgment in brackets.

> *Goloshvili v Georgia* App no 45566/08 (ECtHR, 20 November 2012)

5.4.2 European Commission of Human Rights

The European Commission of Human Rights, which was abolished on 31 October 1998, published its decisions in the following reports:

Table 5.5 Reports of the European Commission of Human Rights

1955–73	*Collection of Decisions of the European Commission of Human Rights* (vols 1–46)—cited as CD
1974–98	*Decisions and Reports* (vol. 46 onwards)—cited as DR

These reports are cited following the usual citation system for law reports outlined in section 5.1. For example:

X v UK (1967) 25 CD 76
S v UK (1986) 47 DR 274

The Commission's role was to decrease the caseload of the European Court of Human Rights by filtering out some cases and attempting to resolve others by conciliation. Questions of admissibility are now dealt with by judges of the European Court of Human Rights sitting in committee.

5.4.3 European Human Rights Reports

The *European Human Rights Reports* are a commercially available series of reports, published monthly by Sweet & Maxwell. They contain the full judgments of all decisions of the European Court of Human Rights. They are commonly cited in courts in England and Wales and follow the normal citation system for law reports outlined in section 5.1, except that, from 2001, case numbers replaced page numbers.

You should cite either the official reports, that is the Reports of Judgments and Decisions or the European Human Rights Reports (EHRR), but be consistent in your practice.

For example:

Austin v United Kingdom (2012) 55 EHRR 32
Shannon v Latvia (2012) 55 EHRR 29

5.4.4 Online

5.4.4.1 HUDOC (www.echr.coe.int)

HUDOC is the official database of the European Court of Human Rights and contains all judgments.

Figure 5.17 HUDOC screenshot
© European Court of Human Rights. http://hudoc.echr.coe.int/

5.4.4.2 Other databases

Lawtel, Westlaw UK, Justis, and Casetrack also provide search facilities for cases decided in the European Court of Human Rights.

 Self-test questions

Having completed this chapter, use your research skills to attempt the following more challenging research questions involving case law.

1. The Court of Appeal (Civil Division) heard a case in which a number 12 Routemaster bus had seriously injured an 11-year-old boy. What was the name of the boy's litigation friend and their relationship to him?

2. Give the citation of a case in the House of Lords that involved a finger being mistaken for an imitation firearm.

3. Who represented the claimant found working in a halal butcher's shop in a 2010 judicial review case that considered the operation of s 94 of the Nationality, Immigration and Asylum Act 2000?

4. Give the citation of a negligence case involving bacon, eggs, and sherry.

5. Which judges considered the appeal in a case involving covert police observation of indecent behaviour in a churchyard on 15 September 1989?

Answers to the self-test questions can be found on the Online Resource Centre.

CHAPTER SUMMARY

Finding case law

- Common case databases include Westlaw UK, LexisLibrary, Lawtel, Justis, Casetrack, BAILII, and JustCite

Finding European case law

- The official reports are found in the *European Court Reports*

- The *Common Market Law Reports* cover significant European cases from 1962

- The *All England Law Reports (European Cases)* have been published since 1995

- European cases may be found online via EUROPA, EUR-Lex, and CELEX as well as via LexisLibrary, Lawtel, and Westlaw UK

Finding decisions of the European Court of Human Rights

- The official reports are published in the *Reports of Judgments and Decisions* although there is often a delay of up to a year before publication

- The *European Human Rights Reports* contain full judgments of all decisions of the European Court of Human Rights and are published monthly

- European Court of Human Rights cases may also be found online via HUDOC as well as via Lawtel, Westlaw UK, Justis, and Casetrack

FURTHER READING

- You can find out more about the Incorporated Council of Law Reporting and the 2012 Practice Direction: Citation of Authorities at www.iclr.co.uk/news-and-events/about-us.

- The Cardiff Index to Legal Abbreviations is an excellent free online resource which allows you to search for the meaning of a multitude of abbreviations for legal publications from over 295 jurisdictions. You can find it at www.legalabbrevs.cardiff.ac.uk/.

6

Using cases

INTRODUCTION

The two previous chapters described why case law is an important source of law and gave you the skills necessary to find it. This chapter will build on these skills by discussing how to use cases. It will firstly look at the 'anatomy' of a law report, before considering the means by which the key legal principles can be extracted from the case. Once the legal principles are known we will then consider the extent to which those principles are binding on other courts via the doctrine of judicial precedent. Finally, the chapter will consider the impact of both the Human Rights Act 1998 and EU law on the operation of precedent.

The ability to use cases is a vital legal skill. You will come across a multitude of cases throughout your legal career, so you must be able to work with them effectively. Knowledge of the operation of precedent is also vital, since you will need to know whether the case which you hope to rely upon will have any legal force in the court where your case is being heard. Equally, when you chart the development of particular areas of law you must understand how the decisions given in cases change the law over time depending on the court in which they are heard. Therefore understanding cases is key to each and every area of law.

LEARNING OUTCOMES

After studying this chapter, you will be able to:

- Navigate a law report and identify its component parts

- Understand the meaning of case citations

- Explain the use of the neutral citation system

- Outline the operation of the doctrine of judicial precedent and explain whether a particular court will be bound by a particular decision

- Determine the *ratio decidendi* of a case and distinguish it from the *obiter dicta*

- Demonstrate how courts can avoid being bound by 'difficult' precedents

- Assess the impact of European law and the Human Rights Act 1998 on the system of precedent

6.1 Reading UK cases

Before you can start making effective use of cases, you will need to understand the layout of a reported case and the information that the reports provide. You will then be able to move onto analyzing the information that you have been able to glean from the case before you.

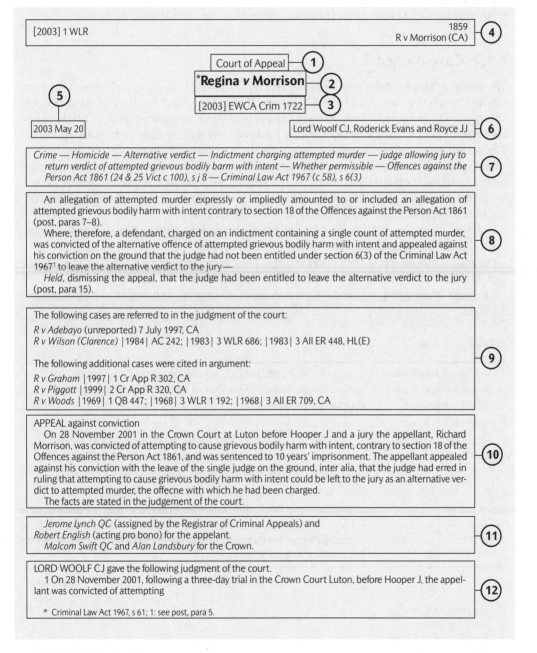

Figure 6.1 *R v Morrison:* First page

We will use a real example: *R v Morrison*.[1] Part of this case is provided in Figure 6.1. Each of the highlighted areas of the report will be covered in turn.

6.1.1 Court ①

The court is the court in which the case was heard; in this case, the Court of Appeal. It is important to know which court heard the case because of the doctrine of judicial precedent: generally speaking, the more senior the court, the more binding the legal principle.

6.1.2 Case name ②

The name of this case is *Regina v Morrison*. This is a criminal case and, as such, one of the parties involved is the Crown, indicated by *Regina*. If the Monarch at the time of the case were a King then the masculine form *Rex* would be used instead of *Regina*. *Regina* (or *Rex*) is often abbreviated to *R*, so the parties to this case could equally well be referred to as *R v Morrison*. The person against whom a criminal case is brought is referred to as the 'defendant'.

In civil cases, the names of the two parties are used. The first party is the claimant (the person bringing the claim) and the second party is the respondent (the person against whom the claim is brought). For example, in the well-known case of *Donoghue v Stevenson*,[2] the parties were Mrs Donoghue (claimant) and Stevenson (respondent).

You may also encounter the word 'plaintiff' which was formerly used in civil proceedings instead of 'claimant', but 'claimant' is now the correct term.

On appeal, the names of the parties change. The person bringing an appeal is the 'appellant' and the person against whom the appeal is brought is known as the 'respondent'.

There are other commonly encountered forms of case name as shown by the examples in Table 6.1:

Table 6.1 Case citations

R v Secretary of State for Foreign and Commonwealth Affairs, ex p World Development Movement Ltd[3]	Judicial review cases prior to 2001 are cited as the Crown against a particular public body *ex parte* (often abbreviated to ex p, meaning on behalf of) an applicant.
R (Quintavalle) v Secretary of State for Health[4]	Judicial review cases after 2001 are cited with the applicant's name in brackets after the '*R*'. Such cases are spoken as 'the Crown *on the application of* Quintavalle against the Secretary of State for Health'
R v R[5]	Family cases are usually kept anonymous. There is some scope for confusion here if one of the party's names begins with 'R'. It would not then be immediately apparent whether the case in question was a criminal matter or a civil matter. However, the facts of the particular case should make this clear very quickly.

(Continued)

1. [2003] 1 WLR 1859 (CA).
2. [1932] AC 562 (HL).
3. [1995] 1 WLR 386 (DC).
4. [2003] 2 AC 687 (HL).
5. [1992] 1 AC 599 (HL).

Table 6.1 *(Cont.)*

Re W; Re: A; Re: B (Change of name)[6]	Cases in the family courts often have some explanatory subject-matter text associated with them in order to aid identification and differentiation.
In re Jones[7] (or *Re Jones*)	'In the matter of' Jones. This citation is often used in cases involving wills or probate.
Liesbosch Dredger[8]	Shipping cases are conventionally referred to by the name of the vessel involved.

6.1.3 Neutral citation ③

The neutral citation of this case is '[2003] EWCA Crim 1722'.
  For information on the operation of the neutral citation system, see section 5.1.1.1.

6.1.4 Case citation—law report ④

The citation for this particular reported case is '[2003] 1 WLR 1859'.
  For a detailed description of case citations, see chapter 5.

6.1.5 Date of the hearing and judgment ⑤

This case was heard and the judgment was given on 20 May 2003. Remember that the year of the judgment might be different from the year of the report.

  In a *reserved judgment*, the judges take time after the hearing to consider the issues and provide a written judgment at a later date. The date of the written judgment will be given before the judgment after the words *cur adv vult*. This is short for *curia advisari vult* (literally 'the court wishes to be advised').

6.1.6 Judges ⑥

In this case the Court of Appeal comprised Lord Chief Justice Woolf, Mr Justice Roderick Evans, and Mr Justice Royce. It is sometimes useful to know the seniority or reputation of the judges involved in making a particular decision since this may affect the extent to which the judgment may be persuasive (if it is not automatically binding).

6.1.7 Subject matter ⑦

This section contains a series of catchwords which are provided by the editors of the law report. It provides a very brief list of the subject matter and key legal points of the case as well as any references to particular statutory provisions which the case considers (in this case, s 18 of the Offences against the Person Act 1861 and s 6(3) of the Criminal Law Act 1967). These points are also repeated in the summaries at the start of each volume of the reports.

6. [2001] Fam 1 (CA).
7. [1931] 1 Ch 375 (DC).
8. [1933] AC 449 (HL).

6.1.8 Headnote (8)

The headnote contains a summary of the case. However, the headnote carries no legal authority. It is prepared by the reporter and not by the judges. Although it usually carries an accurate summary of the case, it sometimes does not. For instance in *Young v Bristol Aeroplane Co.*[9]—a case which we will return to later in this chapter when we consider the doctrine of judicial precedent—the headnote states that:

> (b) [The Court of Appeal] must refuse to follow a decision of its own which, though not expressly overruled, is inconsistent with a decision of the House of Lords

whereas the actual text of the judgment says that:

> The third is where this court comes to the conclusion that a previous decision, although not expressly overruled, cannot stand with a *subsequent* [emphasis added] decision of the House of Lords.

Therefore the headnote of the case should always be used with some caution and you should read the whole report.

The headnote may also usefully summarize the effect of the case on the existing case law, using the terms in Table 6.2.

The effect on the existing case law is explained in detail in section 6.6.

Table 6.2 Headnote terminology

Affirmed	The court in the present case agreed with the decision of a lower court on the same case
Applied	The court in this case considered itself to be bound by the precedent set by an earlier (and different) case and has therefore used the same legal reasoning in the present case
Approved	The court in the present case agreed with the decision of a lower court in a different case
Considered	The court discussed a different case. This is often a case that has been decided by a court at the same level in the hierarchy
Distinguished	The court in the present case does not wish to (or cannot) overrule a previous decision and also does not wish to apply it. It has found sufficient differences between the cases to avoid being bound by the earlier case
Overruled	The court in the present case has overturned a decision in a different case, usually made in a lower court (although occasionally in a court of equal status)
Reversed	The court in the present case on appeal overturned the decision of a lower court in the same case
Semble	(literally 'it appears') The court gives an opinion on a point that is not directly at issue in this case. (This is *obiter dictum*)

6.1.9 List of cases (9)

The report provides a list of cases in two sections. The first section contains two cases (*Adebayo* and *Wilson* (*Clarence*)) which were referred to by the judges in their judgment. The second section contains a list of cases (*Graham*, *Piggott*, and *Woods*) which counsel also raised in

9.   [1944] KB 718 (CA).

argument but which were not referred to by the judges. These cases are of less importance than those referred to directly by the judges.

6.1.10 Details of the action ⑩

This section of the report provides a brief history of the case proceeding to date. In this case, the Court of Appeal (Criminal Division) is considering an appeal against a ten-year conviction for causing grievous bodily harm with intent. Any relevant statute law is usually stated in this section (as well as in the catchwords).

6.1.11 Counsel ⑪

The names of counsel who appeared for each party in the case are listed. These may be barristers or solicitor advocates. Senior barristers are known as 'Queen's Counsel' and designated by the letters QC. The names of the barristers are particularly useful to solicitors. If a similar case comes up again, then solicitors may choose to instruct barristers who have success or experience in similar cases.

This section also informs us that Robert English was acting '*pro bono*'—that is, without charge.

6.1.12 Judgment ⑫

The judgment is the most important part of the report. Where there is more than one judge hearing a particular case, each judge may deliver his own judgment. Typically one judge—usually, but not always, the most senior—delivers the first judgment. The other judges may then give their own judgments. These may be as brief as 'I agree' or given at length and dissenting (i.e. disagreeing with) from one or more of the other judgments.

Judgments often (but not always) are broken down as follows:

- Summary of the material facts of the case
- Statement of the applicable law
- Legal reasoning
- Decision

Some reports also contain a summary of the arguments presented by counsel for each side. An example of such a report can be found in *R (Holding & Barnes plc) v Secretary of State for the Environment, Transport and the Regions.*[10]

Practical exercise

Look up the *Holding & Barnes plc* case referred to here and find the summary of counsels' arguments.

The judgment in *R v Morrison* is divided up into numbered paragraphs. The report also contains marginal letters for ease of reference. Pinpoint referencing provides a useful way of referencing particular quotations from a judgment in a piece of legal writing or to support an argument put forward in a moot. The reader (or judge) may then direct their attention easily to the precise wording to which you wish to draw reference.

For more information on pinpoint referencing, see chapter 12.

---

10. [2003] 2 AC 295 (HL).

6.1.13 Solicitors and reporter (13)

The end of the report shown in Figure 6.2 gives details of the solicitors who represented each party and instructed counsel on their behalf. Finally, the name or initials of the reporter are provided.

C argument does not succeed.

   14 There is one further matter to which we should refer. In his helprun skeleton argument, Mr Swift on behalf of the Crown tried to envisage a case where it was possible for a person to attempt to murder his victim, demonstrating the necessary intention to kill, but without attempting to cause grievous harm and without demonstrating an intention to cause grievous bodily harm. Although

D in his skeleton argument Mr Swift made that attempt, on further reflection he acknowledges that it is impossible to envisage a case where it is conceivable that there is an intention to kill without also there being an intention to inflict grievous bodily harm.

   15 The appeal against conviction is therefore dismissed.

Appeal dismissed.

E Solicitors: *Crown Prosecution Service, Luton*.

JBS — (13)

F

Figure 6.2 *R v Morrison*: final page
Reproduced by permission of the Incorporated Council of Law Reporting for England and Wales

6.1.14 Electronic reports

As well as paper law reports, most case reports are also available electronically. This section briefly considers the electronic versions of *R v Morrison* that are available online via LexisLibrary and Westlaw UK which have been chosen to illustrate some of the distinctions between the electronic and paper presentations of the cases.

Practical exercise

Look up *R v Morrison* on LexisLibrary and Westlaw UK. Compare the electronic versions with the printed extract from the Weekly Law Reports.

6.1.14.1 Citations

You will see that although the LexisLibrary report gives the citation of [2003] 1 WLR 1859, it does not allow you to click through to access that version of the report. This is because the *Weekly Law Reports* (WLR) are not part of the LexisLibrary database. However, alternative reports are cited as [2003] 2 Cr App Rep 563 and [2003] Crim LR 801.

On the other hand, Westlaw UK *does* permit access to the version from the *Weekly Law Reports*.

Self-test questions

1. What does [2003] 2 Cr App Rep 563 mean?

2. What does [2003] Crim LR 801 mean? Why is 2003 in square brackets?

3. What does (2003) 147 SJLB 626 mean? Why is 2003 in round brackets?

Answers to the self-test questions can be found on the Online Resource Centre.

6.1.14.2 Content

You will see that the catchwords on the LexisLibrary report are different from that on the printed law report and that there is no headnote at all. There is, however, a digest of the case. There is no list of the cases considered or used in argument, or any summary of the history of the case. The Westlaw UK report is identical in content to that in the paper version of the *Weekly Law Reports*. Westlaw UK also allows users to download a PDF version of the case report that is identical in every respect to that which would be found in a law library.

Both reports contain paragraph numbers. The Westlaw UK report also shows the corresponding page numbers from the bound version of the *Weekly Law Reports*. You will see *1859 at the very start of the report. This denotes the start of page 1859 in the bound version.

Follow paragraph 1 in the bound version and the Westlaw UK report. You will see that there is a page break after the words 'On 28 November 2001, following a three-day trial in the Crown Court at Luton, before Hooper J, the appellant was convicted of attempting' in the bound version. In the Westlaw UK transcript the words 'convicted of attempting' are followed by *1860. This denotes the start of page 1860.

Therefore, if you need to refer to the page number of a particular part of an electronic transcript, you must work backwards until you reach a page number mark. The material you want to reference is on that page.

However, the electronic versions do allow direct links to academic and professional commentary on the case, as well as to cases which are referred to in the judgment so despite some key differences from the paper reports, they can in many respects be considered to be a richer resource than the paper report in isolation.

6.2 Reading European cases

There are some differences in the ways that cases are presented in the official European Court reports, as you will see from Figure 6.3, which shows the start of the report of *Commission v Spain*.[11]

CASE C-136/07

Commission of the European Communities v Kingdom of Spain
(Failure of a Member State to fulfil obligations – Directives 89/48/EEC and 92/51/EEC – Recognition of diplomas and professional education and training – Profession of air traffic controller)

Summary of the Judgment

Where a Member State does not adopt a system for the recognition of the profession of air traffic controller, it fails to fulfil its obligations pursuant to Directive 89/48 on a general system for the recognition of higher-education diplomas awarded on completion of professional education and training of at least three years' duration and Directive 92/51 on a second general system for the recognition of professional education and training to supplement Directive 89/48.

Such a profession must be classified as a regulated profession within the meaning of those directives and thus falls within their scope where the pursuit of the activity of air traffic controller is effectively

---

Figure 6.3 European Court Report

11. Case C-136/07 *Commission v Spain* [2008] ECR I-7793.

governed by legislative provisions creating a system under which that professional activity is expressly reserved to those who fulfil certain conditions and access to it is prohibited to those who do not fulfil them. That conclusion cannot be called into question by the fact that there is no training leading to a single diploma which gives the right to pursue the profession in question. As access to the profession of air traffic controller is subject to possession of a 'diploma' as defined by Directive 89/48, it follows that the Member State concerned must ensure provision for the recognition of diplomas which fall either within the definition contained in Directive 89/48, or within that contained in Directive 92/51.

As the directives do not establish a system of automatic recognition, the specific or local character of certain ratings which a person wishing to pursue the profession of air traffic controller in the host Member State is required to have does not preclude the comparison of, first, the skills attested to by the diplomas or the professional education and training acquired in a Member State other than the host Member State with the objective of pursuing that profession and, second, the knowledge and the ratings required for the pursuit of that profession in the Kingdom of Spain.

(see paras 38-40, 45, 47, 53, 55, 57, operative part)

JUDGMENT OF THE COURT (Second Chamber)
16 October 2008

In Case C-136/07,

ACTION under Article 226 EC for failure to fulfil obligations, brought on 7 March 2007,

Commission of the European Communities, represented by H. Støvlbæk and R. Vidal Puig, acting as Agents, with an address for service in Luxembourg,

applicant,

v

Kingdom of Spain, represented by M. Muñoz Pérez, acting as Agent, with an address for service in Luxembourg,

defendant,

HE COURT (Second Chamber),

composed of C.W.A. Timmermans, President of the Chamber, L. Bay Larsen, K. Schiemann (Rapporteur), P. Kūris and J.-C. Bonichot, Judges,

Advocate General: Y. Bot,

Registrar: R. Grass,

having regard to the written procedure,

having decided, after hearing the Advocate General, to proceed to judgment without an Opinion,

gives the following

Judgment

1 By its action, the Commission of the European Communities asks the Court to find that, in failing to adopt, in connection with the profession of air traffic controller, the laws, regulations and administrative provisions necessary to comply with Council Directive 89/48/EEC . . .

Figure 6.3 *(Continued)*

You will notice the following differences from a UK court report:

- **The court and chamber.** The report contains the name of the court and the chamber in which it was held. In this context, 'chamber' refers to a particular group of judges who are listed within the report. Here, the case was heard by the Court of Justice of the European Communities (now the CJEU) with the court comprising C.W.A. Timmermans, L. Bay Larsen, K. Schiemann, P. Kūris, and J.–C. Bonichot.

- **President, Rapporteur, Advocate General and Registrar.** Each chamber has a president elected annually. In effect, each judge takes the presidency by rotation. Each case also has a rapporteur, who undertakes preparatory enquiries after an application has been received by the court. The rapporteur puts together a report for the court to decide on the procedure by which the case will be heard (including witnesses to be called and the number of judges that should sit). The Advocate General advises the court and gives a reasoned opinion to the court on the decision that, in their opinion, the court should reach. In this particular case, the court decided to proceed to give its judgment without the opinion of the Advocate General. The Registrar deals with procedural points and administration of the court itself.

- **Headnote.** Here the headnote gives only a few short phrases on the key points within the case itself.

- **Summary of the judgment.** Before the judgment is given in detail it is fully summarized as part of the official report.

- **Advocates.** Each party to the proceedings must usually be represented by an advocate.

- **Judgment.** Finally comes the judgment itself, which is given as a collegiate decision of the court as a whole. There are no opinions of individual judges, nor any dissenting judgments. Similarly, the language used may be more bland than the more creative and florid language often used by judges in England and Wales. The courts are also less inclined to speculate on alternative circumstances and this leads to judgments which are very focused on the particular matter in hand, but do not often consider the wider implications of the final ruling.

As you have seen in this case, the court decided to give its judgment without requiring an Advocate General's opinion. This is not always the case, and Advocate General's opinions may also be found, where available, via Eur-Lex. These look very similar to judgments of the CJEU themselves, and give a legally reasoned conclusion to the matter before the court, as you will see from the extract of the start and end of the Opinion in Extract 6.1.

OPINION OF ADVOCATE GENERAL

BOT

delivered on 6 September 2012

Case C-456/11

Gothaer Allgemeine Versicherung AG,

ERGO Versicherung AG,

Versicherungskammer Bayern-Versicherungsanstalt des öffentlichen Rechts,

Nürnberger Allgemeine Versicherungs AG,

Krones AG

v

Samskip GmbH

(Reference for a preliminary ruling from the Landgericht Bremen (Germany))

(Judicial cooperation in civil matters – Recognition and enforcement of judgments – Regulation (EC) No 44/2001 – Concept of 'judgment' – Judgment of a court of a Member State declining jurisdiction – Judgment based on a finding as to the validity and scope of a term conferring jurisdiction on the Icelandic courts – Effect – Scope)

1. Does a judgment of a court of a Member State declaring, in the operative part, that it 'has no authority to hear and decide the case' after accepting, in the grounds of the judgment, the validity of a term conferring jurisdiction on the courts of a third State oblige the court of another Member State before which the same claim is brought also to decline jurisdiction?

2. That is in essence the question put by the Landgericht Bremen (Regional Court, Bremen, Germany) in connection with an action brought by Krones AG and its insurers against Samskip GmbH for compensation for damage allegedly caused during the transport of goods.

3. By that question the Court is asked to interpret Articles 32 and 33 of Council Regulation (EC) No 44/2001 of 22 December 2000 on jurisdiction and the recognition and enforcement of judgments in civil and commercial matters, (2) which deal respectively with the definition of the term 'judgment' within the meaning of Regulation No 44/2001 and the principle of automatic recognition of any 'judgment' given in a Member State.

    . . .

99. In the light of the foregoing, I propose the following answer to the questions referred for a preliminary ruling by the Landgericht Bremen:

Articles 32 and 33 of Council Regulation (EC) No 44/2001 of 22 December 2000 on jurisdiction and the recognition and enforcement of judgments in civil and commercial matters must be interpreted as meaning that:

> a judgment by which a court of a Member State rules on its international jurisdiction, whether it accepts or declines jurisdiction, falls within the concept of 'judgment' within the meaning of Regulation No 44/2001, regardless of the fact that the judgment is classified as a 'procedural judgment' by the law of the Member State addressed; and

> where the court of the Member State of origin has declined jurisdiction after first ruling, in the grounds of its decision, on the validity and scope of an agreement on jurisdiction, the court of the Member State addressed is bound by that finding, regardless of whether it is regarded as *res judicata* by the law of the Member State of origin or the Member State addressed, except in the cases in which Article 35(3) of Regulation No 44/2001 authorises that court to review the jurisdiction of the court of the Member State of origin.

Extract 6.1 *Opinion of Advocate General Bot Case C-456/11*

6.3 Judicial precedent

Having worked out how to navigate a law report, we must move on to consider how legal rules arise from these cases and how they might then be applied in later cases. In this section 'judicial precedent' refers to the process by which judges follow previously decided cases.

Before considering the doctrine of judicial precedent in more detail, it is important to recap on the way in which the courts are arranged in a hierarchy and to demonstrate the importance of the status of the courts in relation to the operation of judicial precedent.

6.3.1 Precedent and the hierarchy of the courts

The courts of the English legal system are arranged in a hierarchy which can be depicted as shown in Figure 6.4.

Since the courts at the top of the hierarchy are more 'important' than lower courts, their decisions carry a greater legal 'value' than the decisions of lower courts. It is the doctrine of judicial precedent, or *stare decisis*, that explains the way in which these decisions relate to each other.

....

Stare decisis is a Latin phrase which means 'let the decision stand'.

....

The doctrine of precedent is based on the principle that *like cases should be treated alike*. This means that once a decision has been reached in a particular case, it stands as good law and

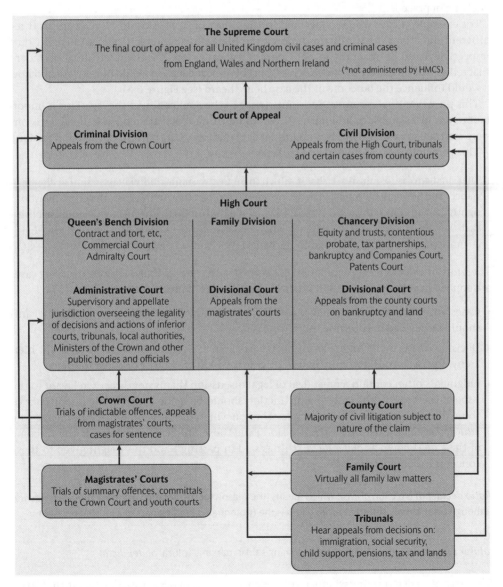

Figure 6.4 The hierarchy of the courts

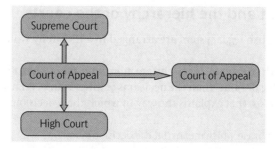

Figure 6.5 Possible directions in which a Court of Appeal case could be relevant

should be relied upon in other cases as an accurate statement of law. This is the essence of the doctrine of precedent.

For example, a case which is decided in the Court of Appeal could be relevant in three different directions: vertically up or down the hierarchy (Supreme Court and High Court respectively) and horizontally (other Court of Appeal cases). It is the doctrine of precedent that tells us in which of the courts such a Court of Appeal decision would be relevant and how it would influence the outcome of the case being heard (see Figure 6.5).

This preserves legal certainty and consistency in the application of the law. This is important to our ideas of justice and fairness. We would think it questionable if judicial decisions were contradictory or if there was no logical explanation to the pattern of their application.

This principle is encapsulated by Frankena:

> The paradigm case of injustice is that in which there are two similar individuals in similar circumstances and one of them is treated better or worse than the other. In this case, the cry of injustice rightly goes up against the responsible agent or group; and unless that agent or group can establish that there is some relevant dissimilarity after all between the individuals concerned and their circumstances, he or they will be guilty as charged (WK Frankena, Ethics (Prentice-Hall 1973) 49).

Therefore, the doctrine of precedent is concerned with the way that decisions in earlier cases are applied in subsequent cases. It is based upon a series of presumptions:

- Cases with the same or similar material facts (that is, facts which are legally relevant) should be decided in the same way

- Decisions made in the higher level courts carry greater weight than those lower in the hierarchy, thus a court is normally bound by courts which are higher or equal to them

- Judgments often contain a great deal of legal discussion that is not directly relevant to the issue at the heart of the case so a distinction should be made between the importance of those things that address the principle of law on which the decision is based (known as the *ratio decidendi*, 'the reason for the decision') and those which are peripheral to the outcome of the case (known as *obiter dicta*, 'things said in passing') and the weight given to these concepts in subsequent cases

....

Ratio decidendi is a Latin phrase which means 'the reason for the decision' (plural *rationes decidendi*, although often simply stated as *ratios*). This is the (potentially) binding part of a judicial decision.

....

....

Obiter dictum is a Latin phrase meaning 'thing said in passing' (plural *obiter dicta*).

....

The first step in determining whether a precedent is binding or persuasive is to isolate the legally relevant facts and use them to distinguish between the *ratio* of the judgment and the *obiter dicta*

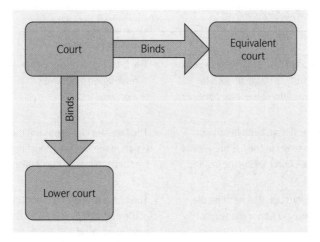

Figure 6.6 Courts binding equivalent and lower courts

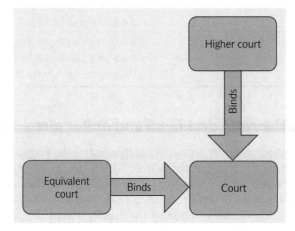

Figure 6.7 Courts being bound by equivalent and higher courts

as outlined earlier. Just because a statement is the *ratio* of an earlier case does not mean it is automatically binding in subsequent cases just as the fact that a statement is *obiter* does not mean that it has no precedent value—it all depends on the relationship between the court in which the original decision was made and the case in which the precedent is to be applied.

The general rule is that each court is bound by the decisions of those that are higher and of equivalent level in the hierarchy of the courts. For example, the Court of Appeal is normally bound by decisions of the Supreme Court (higher) and other Court of Appeal decisions (equivalent) (see Figures 6.6 and 6.7).

6.3.2 Binding and persuasive precedents

A binding precedent is a decided case that *must* be applied in a later case—even if it is considered to have been wrongly decided. It exists when the material facts of a case are similar to those of an earlier decision in a higher or equivalent court in which the applicable statement of law was part of the *ratio* of the earlier decision.

A persuasive precedent is one which *may* be followed by a court (provided no binding precedent exists) but there is no compulsion on the courts to do so. See Table 6.3.

Table 6.3 Binding and persuasive precedents

Binding precedent	Persuasive precedent
• The facts in the decided case and the case before the courts must be sufficiently analogous to justify the imposition of the same legal principle/rule. AND	• The facts in the decided case and the case under consideration may have similar, but not directly analogous, facts. OR
• The decided case must have been heard in a court which is more senior in the hierarchy or at the same level as the court making the instant decision. AND	• The facts are analogous but the relevant legal rule is part of the *ratio* of a court that is lower in the hierarchy than the court making the decision. OR
• The part of the previous decision must be the *ratio decidendi* of the case rather than *obiter dicta*.	• The facts are analogous but the legal rule was part of the *obiter dicta* of a case heard in a higher or equivalent court. OR
	• The facts are analogous but the legal rule is part of the dissenting judgment of a case heard in a higher or equivalent court. OR
	• The facts are analogous but the legal rule is part of a judgment of a court outside of England and Wales. This includes decisions of the Privy Council.

6.3.3 Finding the *ratio decidendi* and *obiter dicta*

The judgment in a case generally contains a statement of the facts and the relevant law and an explanation by the judge of the way in which the law applies to the particular situation before him and his conclusion as to the outcome of the case. The *ratio* of the case is the legal rule and associated reasoning that is essential to the resolution of the case. It is the conclusion that is reached by the application of the relevant legal rule to the material facts.

This was summed up by Buxton LJ in *R (Kadhim) v Brent London Borough Council Housing Benefit Review Board*:[12]

> Cases as such do not bind: their rationes decidendi do. While there has been much academic discussion of the proper way of determining the ratio of a case, we find the clearest and most persuasive guidance . . . to be . . . the ratio decidendi of a case is any rule of law, expressly or impliedly treated by the judge as a necessary step in reaching his conclusion, having regard to the line of reasoning adopted by him.

Therefore, in order to identify the *ratio* of a case, you must first isolate the material, or legally relevant, facts. Most judgments contain a wide general statement of the facts to establish the context in which the events occurred that gave rise to the case before the court. Many of these facts are not legally relevant—the outcome in the case would be the same even if these facts were different as they were not material to the legal question at the heart of the case.

12.   [2001] QB 955 (CA).

In addition to isolating the material facts and determining what aspects of the reasoning are relevant to making a decision on the outcome of the case in order to identify the *ratio* of a judgment, the following are useful ways to identify *obiter*:

- The discussion, explanation or reasoning of the judge is wider than that which is necessary to reach a decision on the facts of the case

- The judge hypothesizes about the decision that he would have reached if the facts had been different

- The judge explains what his decision would have been in this case if he had not been compelled to reach a different decision due to binding precedent

- It is something said by a dissenting judge

Identifying the *ratio* is often difficult as it can be difficult to separate it from the *obiter*. Judges do not specifically state the *ratio* of the case in their judgment and there is no straightforward set of rules to apply to a judgment to discern the *ratio* of that judgment.

This can be illustrated by way of example.

In *Donoghue v Stevenson*,[13] the claimant's friend purchased a bottle of ginger beer which was served in an opaque bottle. After drinking some of the ginger beer, the claimant discovered that the bottle contained the decomposing remains of a snail. The claimant was distressed as a result and suffered a period of gastric illness. There was no basis for a contractual claim as the claimant did not purchase the ginger beer and the friend could not claim as it was the claimant that suffered harm. The House of Lords held that the claimant could recover damages from the manufacturer due to their negligence, Lord Atkin stating that:

> . . . a manufacturer of products, which he sells in such a form as to show that he intends them to reach the ultimate consumer in the form in which they left him with no reasonable possibility of intermediate examination and with the knowledge that the absence of reasonable care in the preparation or putting up of the products will result in an injury to the consumer's life or property, owes a duty to the consumer to take that reasonable care.[14]

This case became the cornerstone of the duty of care in negligence and therefore guides the availability and operation of this tort. Each of the following could have been the *ratio* of this case:

- The manufacturer owes a duty to take reasonable care that the consumer is not injured as a result of a snail in a bottle of ginger beer

- The manufacturer owes a duty to take reasonable care that the consumer is not injured by a foreign body in a container

- The manufacturer owes a duty to take reasonable care that the consumer is not injured by defective products

- A person owes a duty to take reasonable care that he does not commit any act which he could reasonably foresee as injuring another person

The first option is too specific to the facts and would create an unrealistically narrow *ratio* that would be unlikely ever to be raised in later cases. The fact that it is a snail and a bottle of ginger beer is not material—the decision would have been no different if it had been a

---

13. [1932] AC 562 (HL).
14. [1932] AC 562 (HL) 599 (Lord Atkin).

decomposed stag beetle and a pork pie, for example. The second option is wider but it could still be questioned whether a *ratio* that limits the value of a case to foreign bodies in containers is desirable; would it really be sufficiently distinct if the snail had been in a sandwich? The third option seems reasonable; it is sufficiently general to create a legal principle that can be used in a range of situations thus not creating an undue restriction on its use in future cases. The fourth option may seem too wide; it moves beyond the particular relationship (manufacturers and consumers) and the particular negligent behaviour (failing to check the quality of products). However, it was this wide *ratio* that was followed in later cases and which is the basis for the law of negligence as it exists today. This *ratio* is so wide that it has been suggested that it was actually the third option that was the *ratio* and that the wider principle was merely *obiter* but obtained the status of binding precedent by its use in later cases. The *ratio* from *Donoghue v Stevenson* has been applied to products including lifts, chemicals, and motor cars, and manufacturers' liability extended to repairers and assemblers. Therefore it is perhaps more accurate to say that the *ratio decidendi* of a case is ultimately determined by its application by a court in a later case. The courts only need to interpret and determine the *ratio* of an earlier case when considering whether it applies to a new set of facts before them.

Isolating the material facts is not always straightforward. One test in deciding whether or not you think a particular fact is material to the outcome of the case is to ask yourself 'so what?' in relation to each one. If you think that changing a certain fact would have altered the legal reasoning such that the ultimate judgment was different, then it is likely that the particular fact was material to the case. If changing a fact would most likely have made no difference at all, then you should question whether it was a material fact.

6.3.4 The operation of judicial precedent in the courts

6.3.4.1 Court of Justice of the European Union

The CJEU is not bound by its own previous decisions, as it does not formally have the concept of *stare decisis*. This allows it to take future changes in European policy into account. However, it is strongly persuaded by its own previous decisions and rarely departs from them in practice in the interests of legal certainty. All UK courts are bound by the CJEU on matters of interpretation of EU Treaties themselves and on the interpretation and validity of EU Regulations and Directives.[15]

6.3.4.2 The Supreme Court

For practical purposes, at present, it is safe to assume that whatever had been written about the operation of the doctrine of precedent in the House of Lords applies equally to the Supreme Court. Since the Supreme Court was established there has been nothing to suggest that precedent operates any differently to the way that it did in its predecessor.

Until 1966 the House of Lords was bound by its own previous decisions. This was established in the mid-nineteenth century and became known as the *London Tramways* rule after the House of Lords affirmed the position in the 1898 case of *London Tramways Co Ltd v London County Council*.[16] Since the House of Lords was the highest appeal court in the hierarchy of the courts, it was considered to be in the public interest for its decisions to be final. The rule was intended to provide absolute certainty in the law and to cut down on cases from being brought to court.

---

15. European Communities Act 1972 s 3(1).
16. [1898] AC 375 (HL).

The rigidity of this rule was increasingly criticized throughout the twentieth century,[17] and the *London Tramways* rule was eventually abolished by the 1966 *Practice Statement (Judicial Precedent)*[18] made on behalf of himself and of the House of Lords by Lord Gardiner LC who stated:

> Their Lordships regard the use of precedent as an indispensable foundation upon which to decide what is the law and its application to individual cases. It provides at least some degree of certainty on which individuals can rely in the conduct of their affairs, as well as a basis for orderly development of legal rules.
>
> Their Lordships nevertheless recognise that too rigid adherence to precedent may lead to injustice in a particular case and unduly restrict the proper development of the law. They propose, therefore, to modify their present practice and *while treating former decisions of this House as normally binding, to depart from a previous decision where it appears right to do so.* [emphasis added]
>
> In this connection they will bear in mind the danger of disturbing retrospectively the basis upon which contracts, settlements of property and fiscal arrangements have been entered into and also the especial need for certainty in the criminal law.
>
> This announcement is not intended to affect the use of precedent elsewhere than in this House.

The impact of the *Practice Statement* gave the House of Lords sufficient flexibility to deal with novel situations and to ensure justice in each particular case. This flexibility meant that the law could develop in line with the changes in society and that judicial decisions would be in line with the morals and expectations of the community. While the *Practice Statement* was generally well received at the time, some considered that such a significant change in the judicial process should have been brought about via legislation rather than a 'mere' Practice Statement in which the House of Lords used its inherent jurisdiction to change its own practices. If an appellant or respondent in an appeal to the House of Lords intended to ask the House to depart from a previous decision it had to draw specific attention to this in the appeal paperwork.[19]

When will the House of Lords depart from its own previous decisions?

The *Practice Statement* 'does not mean that whenever . . . a previous decision was wrong, we should reverse it' (*Miliangos v George Frank (Textiles) Ltd*).[20] This point of view might seem to contradict the *Practice Statement*; in fact it shows that the House of Lords was extremely reluctant to use it, as it was acutely aware of the need for certainty and the dangers attached to departing from its previous decisions (as stated in the *Practice Statement*). Thus, it required more than just a previous decision to be wrong; it would only be used where a previous decision caused injustice, uncertainty, or hindered the development of the law. It was not enough that the earlier decision caused grave concern or was passed by a narrow majority. Even if the *Practice Statement* might have applied, the House of Lords still considered whether legislation might provide a better solution than departing from its previous decisions.

In *R v Secretary of State for the Home Department ex p Khawaja*,[21] it was held that, before departing from its own decisions, the House of Lords should be sure that continued adherence to precedent involves the risk of injustice and would obstruct the proper development

---

17. See, e.g. *Midlands Silicones Ltd v Scruttons Ltd* [1962] AC 446 (HL) 475 (Lord Reid).
18. [1966] 1 WLR 1234 (HL).
19. *Practice Direction (House of Lords: Preparation of Case)* [1971] 1 WLR 534 (HL).
20. [1976] AC 433 (HL) 496 (Lord Cross).
21. [1984] AC 74 (HL).

of the law and departure from the precedent is the safe and appropriate way of remedying the injustice and developing the law.

Further evidence in support of the reluctance of the House of Lords to exercise its powers to bring about change to well-established law could be seen in the approach taken in *C v Director of Public Prosecutions*.[22] Here the House of Lords refused to abolish the presumption of *doli incapax* (the presumption that children under the age of 14 were incapable of criminal wrong-doing) despite finding it to be anomalous and absurd, preferring to call upon Parliament to remedy the situation. Lord Lowry stated the guidelines for judicial law-making as follows:

(a) judges should exercise caution before imposing a remedy where the solution to the problem is doubtful;

(b) they should be cautious about making changes if Parliament had rejected opportunities of dealing with a known problem or had legislated whilst leaving the problem untouched;

(c) they are more suited to dealing with purely legal problems than disputed matters of social policy;

(d) fundamental legal doctrines should not be lightly set aside; and,

(e) judges should not change the law unless they can achieve finality and certainty.

Therefore, despite the freedom conferred by the *Practice Statement* to set aside its own decisions and exercise greater freedom in the development of the law, it is clear that the House of Lords was reluctant to exercise these powers.

However, there are examples of cases in which the House of Lords *did* depart from its previous decisions. The first example of this was in *Conway v Rimmer*,[23] where the House of Lords unanimously overruled its previous decision (made in wartime) in *Duncan v Cammel, Laird & Co.*[24] In *R v Shivpuri*,[25] the House of Lords overruled its decision in *Anderton v Ryan*[26] which it had made only one year previously, effectively admitting its error in the earlier case. As Lord Bridge commented: 'the Practice Statement is an effective abandonment of our pretension to infallibility'.[27]

In *R v Howe*[28] the House of Lords took public and social policy factors into account in overruling its previous decision in *Director of Public Prosecutions for Northern Ireland v Lynch*[29] which involved the availability of the defence of duress to a person facing criminal liability for murder. More recently, in *Lagden v O'Connor*,[30] the House of Lords overruled its long-standing decision concerning the position of impecunious defendants in tort from the *Liesbosch Dredger*.[31]

6.3.4.3 The Court of Appeal

Civil Division

In *Young v Bristol Aeroplane Co. Ltd*[32] the Court of Appeal considered whether it is bound by its own decisions. It was held that it is normally bound, subject to three exceptions:

22. [1996] AC 1 (HL).
23. [1968] AC 910 (HL).
24. [1942] AC 624 (HL).
25. [1987] AC 1 (HL).
26. [1985] AC 560 (HL).
27. [1987] AC 1 (HL) 23 (Lord Bridge).
28. [1987] 2 WLR 568 (HL).
29. [1975] AC 653 (HL).
30. [2003] 3 WLR 1571 (HL).
31. [1933] AC 449 (HL).
32. [1944] KB 718 (CA).

1. **Where its own previous decisions conflict**

   This may arise if the court in the later case was unaware of the decision of the earlier case; for instance, if the earlier case was very recent or unreported, or the second case might have distinguished the first, or one of the cases had been decided *per incuriam* (see definition later in this section). In such situations, the Court of Appeal must decide which of its previous decisions to follow and which to reject. Whilst this has obvious implications for the future precedent value of the decision which is not followed, its status is not technically affected by the fact that it has not been followed; it could still be adopted in subsequent cases. For example, in *National Westminster Bank plc v Powney*[33] the Court of Appeal had to choose between its own previous judgments in *WT Lamb & Sons v Rider*[34] and *Lougher v Donovan*[35] which were irreconcilable.

2. **Where its previous decision had been implicitly overruled by the House of Lords**

   This occurs when a previous Court of Appeal decision is inconsistent with a later decision of the House of Lords (and, now, a later decision of the Supreme Court). Therefore the Court of Appeal must refuse to follow a decision of its own which cannot stand with a decision of the House of Lords or the Supreme Court. For example in *Family Housing Association v Jones*[36] the Court of Appeal refused to follow its own recent decisions which were inconsistent with the House of Lords decision in *AG Securities Ltd v Vaughan*[37] and *Street v Mountford*,[38] even though the decisions of the Court of Appeal had not been expressly overruled by the House of Lords at that time.

   This situation does not apply where a Court of Appeal decision has been disapproved by the Privy Council. The Court of Appeal held this itself in *In Re Spectrum Plus*.[39] The House of Lords later agreed with this approach, although Baroness Hale considered that the question was open and that there was a possibility that an exception might be developed such that the Court of Appeal should refuse to follow a decision disapproved by the Privy Council.[40]

   An inconsistency can also arise where an appeal case has bypassed the Court of Appeal and gone straight to the Supreme Court via the so-called 'leapfrog' procedure.[41] Appeals direct from the High Court to the Supreme Court are very rare. An example can however be found in *Kleinwort Benson Ltd v Lincoln City Council*.[42]

3. **Where its previous decision was made *per incuriam***

   Per incuriam is a Latin phrase meaning 'through carelessness'.

A decision made *per incuriam* is one made 'through carelessness' or without due regard to the relevant law. It should not be confused with *per curiam* which is a part of a judgment upon which all the judges are agreed.

---

33. [1991] Ch 339 (CA).
34. [1948] 2 KB 331 (CA).
35. [1948] 2 All ER 11 (CA).
36. [1990] 1 WLR 779 (CA).
37. [1990] AC 417 (HL).
38. [1985] AC 809 (HL).
39. [2004] 3 WLR 503 (CA).
40. [2005] 3 WLR 58 (HL).
41. Administration of Justice Act 1969 ss 12–15.
42. [1999] AC 358 (HL).

Examples of cases in which *per incuriam* decisions have been considered include *Morelle v Wakeling*[43] which provided a definition of *per incuriam* as 'decisions given in ignorance or forgetfulness of some inconsistent statutory provision or of some authority binding on the court concerned . . . '. In other words, where the decision was reached without due regard for the correct law. In *Duke v Reliance Systems Ltd*,[44] it was held that 'if the court has failed to consider the relevant law, the decision will be *per incuriam* if the court *must* inevitably have reached a different decision had it considered the correct law; it will not suffice that the court might have reached a different decision had it considered the correct law'. In *Williams v Fawcett*[45] the Court of Appeal declared several of its previous decisions *per incuriam* which had held that a person could not be committed to prison for breach of a non-molestation order unless the notice had been signed by the 'proper officer' of the court. Since this was not a requirement of the statute or of the procedural rules the decisions lacked a rational legal basis.

In *Cave v Robinson Jarvis & Rolf*[46] the Court of Appeal stated that any departure from a previous decision is 'highly undesirable' and that the decision in question had to be 'manifestly' or 'incontestably' wrong before it could be declared *per incuriam*.

Criminal Division

All the exceptions from *Young v Bristol Aeroplane* that apply in the Civil Division also apply to the Criminal Division.[47] However, in practice, the Court of Appeal gives itself a wider discretion in criminal cases where the liberty of the individual is at stake. In *R v Gould*,[48] Lord Diplock stated:

> if upon due consideration we were to be of the opinion that the law had been either misapplied or misunderstood in an earlier decision . . . we should be entitled to depart from the view as to the law expressed in the earlier decision notwithstanding that the case could not be brought within any of the exceptions laid down in *Young v Bristol Aeroplane Co. Ltd*.

There has been no ruling on whether the Civil and Criminal Divisions are bound by each other. However, their predecessors (the Court of Appeal and the Court of Criminal Appeal) were not. It is also accepted that, when dealing with criminal appeals, a 'full' Court of Appeal (five judges) can depart from decisions made by three judges.[49] The rule in *Young v Bristol Aeroplane* gives the Court of Appeal some capacity to depart from its own decisions but only in narrowly defined circumstances. The Supreme Court has broad discretion to depart from its own decisions where it appears right to do so, but, in practice, this discretion is exercised sparingly.

6.3.4.4 The Divisional Courts and the High Court

The Divisional Courts (i.e. the Divisional Court of the appropriate division of the High Court for the particular matter) are bound by their own decisions subject to the same exceptions as the Civil Division of the Court of Appeal, and, arguably, the Criminal Division (following

---

43. [1955] 2 QB 379 (CA).
44. [1988] QB 108 (CA).
45. [1986] QB 604 (CA).
46. [2001] EWCA Civ 245.
47. *R v Spencer* [1985] 1 All ER 673 (CA).
48. [1968] 2 QB 65 (CA) 69 (Lord Diplock).
49. See, e.g., *R v Simpson* [2003] 3 WLR 337 (CA).

the decision in *R v Greater Manchester Coroner, ex p Tal*).[50] Decisions of the Divisional Courts are binding on the High Court for that particular Division.

High Court decisions are not binding on the Divisional Courts (since the Divisional Courts operate at a higher level than the High Court by virtue of the nature of their jurisdiction, which is mostly appellate).

Decisions of individual High Court judges are binding on lower courts but not on other High Court judges. However, they are of strongly persuasive authority in the High Court and are usually followed in practice. If they are not followed, then they are 'disapproved' rather than being formally overruled.

The structure of the High Court is complicated. You may wish to review the explanation of its organization which is provided in section 4.3.

6.3.4.5 The Crown Court, County Court, Family Court, and magistrates' courts

The Crown Court is not bound by its previous decisions but, in order to promote certainty in the criminal law, is strongly persuaded by them. Inconsistent Crown Court decisions are generally resolved by a higher appellate court as quickly as possible.

The County Court, Family Court, and the magistrates' courts are not bound by their own decisions and bind no other courts. The decisions made on points of law at this level are rarely of legal importance and are hardly ever formally reported in the law reports. However, their decisions can, of course, be considered on appeal in the higher courts in which case they will be reported, albeit indirectly.

In summary, the question 'who is bound by whom?' can be shown in a diagram as shown in Figure 6.8.

6.4 Precedent and the Human Rights Act 1998

Section 6(1) of the Human Rights Act 1998 provides that:

> 6.–(1) It is unlawful for a public authority to act in a way which is incompatible with a Convention right.

Section 6(3) of the Act makes it clear that 'public authority' includes a court or a tribunal. Therefore it is unlawful for courts to deliver a judgment which is incompatible with Convention rights.

Moreover, s 2(1) of the Human Rights Act 1998 provides that:

> 2.–(1) A court or tribunal determining a question which has arisen in connection with a Convention right must take into account any
> **(a)** judgment, decision, declaration or advisory opinion of the European Court of Human Rights,
> **(b)** opinion of the Commission given in a report adopted under Article 31 of the Convention,
> **(c)** decision of the Commission in connection with Article 26 or 27(2) of the Convention, or
> **(d)** decision of the Committee of Ministers taken under Article 46 of the Convention,
>
> whenever made or given, so far as, in the opinion of the court or tribunal, it is relevant to the proceedings in which that question has arisen.

---

50. [1985] QB 67 (DC).

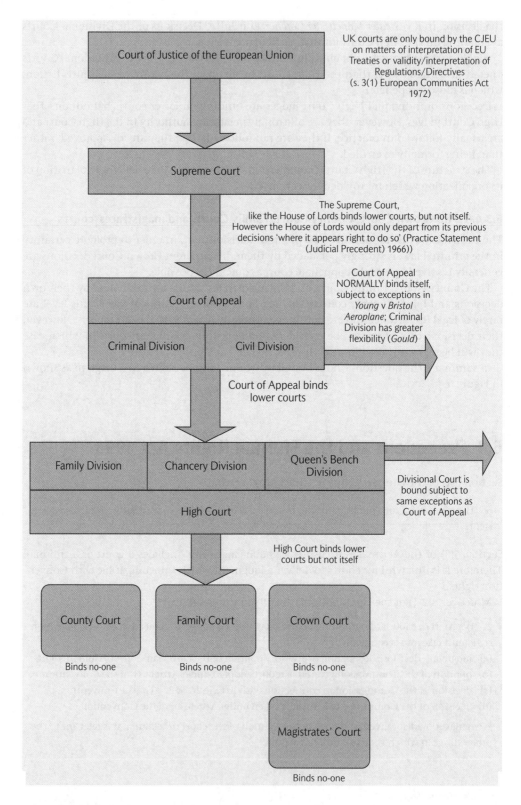

Figure 6.8 A summary of the operation of judicial precedent

The courts are only required to take such decisions 'into account'. They are not compelled to follow them and they are not bound by those decisions. As Lord Hoffmann stated in *In Re McKerr*:[51]

> **63** It should no longer be necessary to cite authority for the proposition that the Convention, as an international treaty, is not part of English domestic law . . . Although people sometimes speak of the Convention having been incorporated into domestic law, that is a misleading metaphor. What the Act has done is to create domestic rights expressed in the same terms as those contained in the Convention. But they are domestic rights, not international rights. Their source is the statute, not the Convention. They are available against specific public authorities, not the United Kingdom as a state. And their meaning and application is a matter for domestic courts, not the court in Strasbourg.
>
> **64** This last point is demonstrated by the provision in section 2(1) that a court determining a question which has arisen in connection with a Convention right must 'take into account' any judgment of the Strasbourg court. Under the Convention, the United Kingdom is bound to accept a judgment of the Strasbourg court as binding: article 46(1). But a court adjudicating in litigation in the United Kingdom about a domestic 'Convention right' is not bound by a decision of the Strasbourg court. It must take it into account.

It is clear then, that the House of Lords did not consider itself bound by the judgments, decisions, declarations, or opinions listed in the Human Rights Act 1998—it merely acknowledged the position that it had to 'take them into account'.

Having said that, the courts have tended thus far to act as if they were generally bound to follow the interpretation of the European Court of Human Rights. In *R v Secretary of State for the Environment, Transport and the Regions ex p Alconbury Developments Ltd*,[52] Lord Slynn stated that:

> In the absence of some special circumstances it seems to me that the court should follow any clear and constant jurisprudence of the European Court of Human Rights. If it does not do so there is at least a possibility that the case will go to that court which is likely in the ordinary case to follow its own constant jurisprudence.[53]

If a court decides that a previous decision by which it would otherwise be bound is incompatible with Convention rights (as determined by, for instance, a decision of the European Court of Human Rights) it is required by virtue of s 6(1) to give effect to any Convention-compatible decision from the European Court of Human Rights rather than the otherwise binding decision of the higher UK court. An example of this can be seen in *In Re Medicaments and Related Classes of Goods (No 2)*[54] where the Court of Appeal made a 'modest adjustment' to the House of Lords' decision in *R v Gough*[55] to make it compatible with the view of the European Court of Human Rights: although this 'modest adjustment' involved substituting an objective test to determine whether or not a tribunal was biased for the earlier subjective test. This fundamentally changed the decision of the House of Lords in *Gough*.[56]

---

51. [2004] 1 WLR 807 (HL) 825.
52. [2001] UKHL 23, [2003] 2 AC 295.
53. [2001] UKHL 23 [26] (Lord Slynn)
54. [2001] 1 WLR 700 (CA).
55. [1993] AC 646 (HL).
56. See also, e.g., *Price v Leeds City Council* [2005] EWCA Civ 289; [2005] 1 WLR 1825.

6.5 Precedent and EU law

Section 3(1) of the European Communities Act 1972 (as amended by s 2 of the European Communities (Amendment) Act 1986) provides that:

> 3.–(1) For the purposes of all legal proceedings any question as to the meaning or effect of any of the Treaties, or as to the validity, meaning or effect of any Community instrument, shall be treated as a question of law and, if not referred to the European Court, be for determination as such in accordance with the principles laid down by and any relevant decision of the European Court or any court attached thereto.
>
> (2) Judicial notice shall be taken of the Treaties, of the Official Journal of the European Communities and of any decision of, or expression or opinion by, the European Court or any court attached thereto, on any such question as aforesaid.

Under Article 267 TFEU, courts may if necessary (or in the case of the Supreme Court, must) refer any question regarding the interpretation of EU legislation to the CJEU for a ruling:

> The Court of Justice shall have jurisdiction to give preliminary rulings concerning:
>
> **(a)** the interpretation of this Treaty;
> **(b)** the validity and interpretation of acts of the institutions of the Community and of the ECB;
> **(c)** the interpretation of the statutes of bodies established by an act of the Council, where those statutes so provide.
>
> Where such a question is raised before any court or tribunal of a Member State, that court or tribunal may, if it considers that a decision on the question is necessary to enable it to give judgment, request the Court of Justice to give a ruling thereon.
>
> Where any such question is raised in a case pending before a court or tribunal of a Member State against whose decisions there is no judicial remedy under national law, that court or tribunal shall bring the matter before the Court of Justice.

In *CILFIT Srl v Ministero della Sanita*[57] the Court of Justice held that a reference is not necessary if:

> **(a)** the question of Community law is irrelevant; or
> **(b)** the provision has already been interpreted by the Court of Justice; or
> **(c)** the correct application is obvious.

These are commonly referred to as the 'CILFIT criteria'.

The ruling of the CJEU given in response to an Article 234 reference is then binding in that particular case. This means that domestic courts must follow decisions on European law made by the European Court of Justice in particular cases.[58]

However, such decisions are not binding on the UK courts in the future. Since the CJEU is not bound by its previous decisions, the Supreme Court can refer the same point of law to the CJEU again in a later case if it considers that the earlier decision of the CJEU (by which the Supreme Court would have been bound in the particular case) was wrong, or merely if the Supreme Court considered it to be unsatisfactory.

---

57.   [1983] ECR 3415 (CJEU).
58.   See, e.g., *Sharp v Caledonia Group Services Ltd* [2005] All ER (D) 09 (Nov) (EAT).

6.6 Avoiding difficult precedents: distinguishing, reversing, and overruling

The 1966 *Practice Statement* and the rule in *Young v Bristol Aeroplane* give the Supreme Court (and its predecessor) and Court of Appeal respectively the ability to avoid previous decisions of courts at the same level. In the case of the Court of Appeal, the circumstances in which the previous decisions of the Court of Appeal can be avoided are narrowly defined whereas the House of Lords exercised its power with caution because of the wider implications of departing from its own decisions in terms of the legal principles that resulted.

Other than by the operation of these particular rules, there are several methods that a court (at any level) can use to avoid an otherwise binding precedent. The approach taken depends upon whether the court which is confronted with the precedent wishes merely to avoid the precedent but to allow it to continue to exist as legal authority or whether the court wishes to deprive the precedent of any future legal effect.

6.6.1 Distinguishing

As you have already seen, it is the *ratio decidendi* of a case that forms the binding part of the judgment and that this *ratio decidendi* only applies to cases where the material facts are the same. In distinguishing a case, the court can decide that the case before it is materially different on the facts. By distinguishing in this way, the court is saying it will not be applying the *ratio* of the earlier case because it is not sufficiently similar to the case before it and that different reasoning must be used to reach its decision.

The courts will normally explain why an earlier case is being distinguished: of course, this new reasoning could be re-examined by a higher court in the event of an appeal. The appellate court could decide not to distinguish the case, reverse the decision of the court, and reapply the *ratio* of the case that the court sought to distinguish.

It has also been argued that distinguishing could be taken further to include not just material factual differences but also social changes that have taken place since the original precedent was decided. In this way, the courts would be free to develop the law in such a way that they could avoid being bound by precedents reflecting historic or outdated societal norms.

It could be said that the *ratio* of a case remains unclear until it is identified and applied by a later court. Accordingly, the operation of the doctrine of precedent is contingent not on the judgment at the time it is given but the way in which a case is used by later courts; a case does not necessarily have precedent value until it acquires precedent value by usage. Therefore, the decision as to whether a case has a wide or narrow *ratio* is one for the later courts. The court may also decide that an earlier case has no clear *ratio* at all and therefore cannot be binding. An example of such a case can be found in *Esso v Commissioners of Customs and Excise*[59] which has judicial conclusions on differing points of law, many *obiter* statements, and a dissenting judgment.

---

59. [1976] 1 WLR 1 (HL).

6.6.2 Overruling and reversing

Overruling occurs when a court higher in the hierarchy overturns the decision of a lower court in a different case. This not only means that the higher court is not bound to follow the earlier decision but that it is negated of any legal force; indeed, it is regarded as never having been the law.

This is to be distinguished from reversing a decision whereby a court higher in the hierarchy overturns the decision (or part of the decision) of a lower court in the same case. For example, the House of Lords in *R v Woollin*[60] refused to follow the approach taken by the Court of Appeal in relation to oblique intention in the same case, upholding the defendant's appeal against his conviction for murder and reversing the decision of the Court of Appeal.

In both of these situations, the earlier decision (or part of it) is negated by the later decision of the higher court.

CHAPTER SUMMARY

Reading cases

- The party against whom a criminal case is brought is called the defendant

- The party bringing a civil claim is called the claimant

- The party against whom a civil claim is brought is called the respondent

- The party bringing an appeal is called the appellant

- The party against whom an appeal is brought is called the respondent

- The headnote of a case report is not part of the judgment

- The headnote may summarize the effect of the judgment on the existing case law

- Electronic reports may not contain all the information in a printed report, but often provide links to useful academic and professional commentary on the case

Judicial precedent

- *Stare decisis* is a Latin phrase meaning 'let the decision stand'

- *Ratio decidendi* is a Latin phrase which means the 'reason for the decision'. This is the (potentially) binding part of a judicial decision

- *Obiter dicta* is a Latin phrase meaning 'things said in passing'

- Binding precedents must be applied in a later case

- Persuasive precedents may be followed in later cases, but there is no compulsion on the courts to do so

- The CJEU is not bound by its previous decisions

---

60.   [1999] AC 82 (HL).

- All UK courts are bound by the CJEU on matters of interpretation of EU Treaties and the interpretation and validity of Regulations and Directives

- The House of Lords was permitted to depart from its previous decisions where it appeared right to do so (*Practice Statement 1966*) although it was often reluctant to do so; it is likely that the Supreme Court will behave in the same way

- The Court of Appeal (Civil Division) is normally bound by its previous decisions unless they conflict; its previous decision has been implicitly overruled by the House of Lords, or; its previous decision was made *per incuriam* (*Young v Bristol Aeroplane*)

- *Per incuriam* is a Latin phrase meaning 'through carelessness'

- The Court of Appeal (Criminal Division) is also subject to the *Young v Bristol Aeroplane* exceptions, but does have greater discretion where the liberty of the individual is at stake (*Gould*)

- The Divisional Courts are bound by their own decisions subject to the *Young v Bristol Aeroplane* exceptions

- The High Court is bound by decisions of the Divisional Court

- Decisions of individual High Court judges are binding on lower courts, but not on individual High Court judges

- The Crown Court is strongly persuaded by its previous decisions

- The County Court, Family Court, and magistrates' courts do not bind themselves and bind no other courts

- The Supreme Court must take decisions of the European Court of Human Rights into account but is not bound by them (Human Rights Act 1998 s 2)

- However, courts must act in a way compatible with Convention rights (Human Rights Act 1998 s 6)

- Domestic courts must follow decisions of the CJEU in matters of EU law in particular cases

- Difficult precedents may be avoided by distinguishing, reversing, or overruling

- Cases may be distinguished from one another if the material facts of the two cases are different

- Reversing occurs when a court higher in the hierarchy overturns the decision of a lower court in the same case

- Overruling occurs when a court higher in the hierarchy overturns the decision of a lower court in a different case

FURTHER READING

- Some of the issues that arise from using case law as a means of law-making are discussed in R Buxton, 'How the Common Law Gets Made' (2009) 125 LQR 60.

- A very comprehensive treatment of the use of precedent in English law set against the wider context of judicial reasoning and legal theory is provided in R Cross, *Precedent in English Law* (Clarendon Press 1991).

- The role of the courts of final appeal in doing justice in the particular appeal and in the setting of an improved precedent is discussed in BV Harris, 'Final appellate courts overruling their own "wrong" precedents: the ongoing search for principle' (2002) 118 LQR 408.

- Two contrasting articles on the meaning of *ratio decidendi* which illustrate the difficulties in defining it are JL Montrose, 'The *Ratio Decidendi* of a Case' (1957) 20 MLR 587, AWB Simpson, 'The *Ratio Decidendi* of a Case' (1957) 20 MLR 413.

- The use of precedent in criminal appeal cases is considered in R Pattenden, 'The Power of the Criminal Division of the Court of Appeal to Depart from its own Precedents' [1984] Crim LR 592.

Books, journals, and official publications

7

INTRODUCTION

The earlier chapters in this part of the book have explored the primary domestic and European sources of law. As you will have seen, these sources derive either from legislation (an Act of Parliament, statutory instrument, EU Treaty Article, Regulation, or Directive) or from cases decided before the courts (common law, equity, custom, or decision of the CJEU). However, in addition to these sources, there is a wide range of secondary sources of law. This chapter will complete your appreciation of the spectrum of legal sources by describing the role of books, journals, and official publications among the secondary sources that you might encounter during your legal studies.

Without a good grasp of secondary sources of law you will miss out on an entire range of legal knowledge and comment. Speaking more pragmatically, you will have to engage with secondary sources if you want to achieve higher marks: secondary sources are a vital resource for a fully-rounded legal knowledge and will give you the means to start critically analyzing the law as well as just reading and describing it. Successful essays and dissertations will require you to demonstrate understanding, analysis, and synthesis skills as well as merely demonstrating simple knowledge of a particular area of law: an appreciation of the range of sources which will help you to develop and demonstrate these skills is therefore essential.

LEARNING OUTCOMES

After studying this chapter, you will be able to:

- Distinguish between textbooks, monographs, and practitioners' books

- Understand the role of legal encyclopedias and digests

- Appreciate the distinction between standard dictionaries, legal dictionaries, and specialist dictionaries

- Choose and use revision guides appropriately

- Understand the use of journals as important sources of information

- Describe the origins and sources of various official publications

- Express an awareness of newspapers, other reports, websites, and 'soft law' as other potential sources of law

7.1 Books

7.1.1 Student textbooks

Student textbooks collect together, analyze, and criticize the law in particular areas. They traditionally deal with an individual area of legal study. There is a wide range of textbooks within each of the core subject areas:

- Constitutional and administrative law (or Public law)
- Contract law
- Criminal law
- EU law
- English legal systems
- Equity and trusts
- Land law (or Property law)
- Tort law

as well as most of the popular optional subject areas such as family law, medical law, employment law, intellectual property law, and company law.

There are usually several textbooks available for each topic. You should be given guidance as to the preferred textbook for your particular course. However, textbooks are written in different styles and have widely varying degrees of difficulty. If you find that you are not getting on with your set text, you should ask your course leader whether there is a different text that might suit you better. For instance, if you find the set text hard to follow, then you might need a more basic book to give you a lower-level grounding in the material before building upon that with the set text. Equally, if you are fortunate enough to think that your textbook is too simple, then a higher-level text will allow you to deepen your understanding and build upon your skills of analysis and critical evaluation.

Textbooks do not generally carry any great legal authority although some established texts are occasionally cited in court. These include *Smith & Hogan: Criminal Law, Winfield and Jolowicz on Tort, Megarry & Wade: The Law of Real Property*, and *Treitel: The Law of Contract.*

Student textbooks undergo frequent revision to ensure that they stay current and relevant. You should always make sure that you are using the most recent edition of your particular textbook. For that reason, buying second-hand textbooks in student shops or online should be done with care, as you would not want to be working from a book which did not cover or explain more recent developments—unless you wanted to use one to research the state of the law at a particular point in time for some sort of comparative exercise. Generally speaking, though, if you use an old textbook, you run the risk of inaccuracy in your research for essays and problem answers. Even so, the lapse of time between manuscript submission and publication can mean that even new books can be out of date. Moreover, each new edition has a lifespan of a few years: therefore, you should always supplement your reading with online research to look out for any contemporary developments during the text's lifetime.

7.1.2 Cases and materials books

Cases and materials books contain a collection of key cases, statutes, reports, articles, and book extracts arranged by topic area within a subject. These are sometimes stand-alone publications, although an increasing number of textbooks have accompanying books of cases and materials.

These are an extremely useful way of gathering together all the supplementary materials you need to support your studies. However, they should be used with caution since they contain only extracts from the materials and those materials that the editor has considered appropriate. They are not a substitute for finding and reading the original and complete statutes, cases, and articles. Therefore, while very valuable as a starting point for research, a reliance upon cases and materials books alone can lead to lazy or unthinking research and, at worst, a blinkered view of the subject area.

7.1.3 Monographs

Monographs are a detailed written study of a single specialized topic. They are usually more expensive than student textbooks and cover particular narrow subject areas in much greater depth (often considerably greater than that required for a first degree in law). For example, while you might think that your set criminal law textbook goes into more than enough detail, there are a large number of books which take particular topics and analyze them in very fine detail, such as:

- M Innes, *Investigating Murder* (OUP 2003)
- JC Smith, *The Law of Theft* (8th edn, Butterworths 1997)
- I Kugler, *Direct and Oblique Intention in the Criminal Law* (Ashgate 2002)
- R Stone, *Offences Against the Person* (Cavendish 1999)

When you consider that many of these books are similar in size to an introductory-level student textbook designed to cover the whole of the criminal law, you should begin to appreciate the distinction between textbooks and monographs.

7.1.4 Practitioners' books

As distinct from textbooks, which are usually written by law lecturers for student use, practitioners' books are usually written by practising lawyers for practising lawyers (although some practitioners write student texts and academics sometimes write for the practitioner market). These are primarily reference works and often span several volumes. As a result new editions appear much less frequently than for student textbooks and updates may be issued in the form of cumulative supplements. Some practitioner works are entirely loose-leaf, such as:

- *Chitty on Contracts*
- *Clerk and Lindsell on Torts*
- *Palmer's Company Law*
- *Woodfall: Landlord and Tenant*

- *Emmet & Farrand on Title*
- *Kemp & Kemp Personal Injury Law, Practice and Procedure*

They are also generally very expensive—the titles listed above range in price from around £200 to over £850. However, some of these (including *Chitty* and *Clerk and Lindsell*) are available online within the Common Law Library section on Westlaw UK.

7.1.5 Legal encyclopedias and digests

There are various legal encyclopedias and digests which are extremely useful research tools.

7.1.5.1 *Halsbury's Laws of England*

Halsbury's Laws of England aims to provide a complete statement of English law, derived from all sources. As you can imagine, this is a massive work. It comprises sixty volumes in several parts. Using *Halsbury* in the library is quite an involved process. Should you wish to do so, then you should consult the law librarian at your institution. However, *Halsbury* is much easier to use in its online form available via LexisLibrary as a source under the 'Commentary' tab.

7.1.5.2 *Halsbury's Statutes of England and Wales*

Halsbury's Statutes of England and Wales aims to provide current versions of all Public General Acts in force in England and Wales. As with *Halsbury's Laws of England* these are arranged by subject area.

Each Act is fully annotated to provide precise information relating to Parliamentary debates, amendments and repeals, derivation notes in the case of consolidating legislation, commencement, cross-references to other provisions of the Act and to other relevant provisions in Halsbury's Statutes, cases, subordinate legislation and references to words specifically defined in the Act.

7.1.5.3 *Halsbury's Statutory Instruments*

Halsbury's Statutory Instruments provides current information on all statutory instruments of general application to the whole of the England and Wales which are in force. Once again, these are arranged by topic.

7.1.5.4 *The Digest*

The Digest provides, in digested form, the whole case law of England and Wales, together with a considerable body of cases from the courts of Scotland, Ireland, Canada, Australia, New Zealand, and other countries of the Commonwealth. Cases dealing with EU law are also included. The case digests are printed with annotations listing the subsequent cases in which judicial opinions have been expressed in the English courts. *The Digest* contains summaries of hundreds of thousands of cases drawn from over a thousand different series of law reports.

7.1.5.5 *Current Law*

Current Law is published in several parts:

- *Current Law Yearbook*
- *Current Law Statutes Annotated*
- *Current Law Case Citator* 1947–76, 1977–88, and 1989–2002

- *Current Law Statute Citator* 1947–71

- *Current Law Legislation Citator* 1972–88; 1989–2002

Its component parts provide access to both legislation and case law along with commentary.

7.1.6 Dictionaries

7.1.6.1 Conventional and legal dictionaries

The *Shorter Oxford English Dictionary* is the conventional dictionary which is most frequently cited in court, followed by the *Oxford English Dictionary*.[1]

The *Oxford English Dictionary* is also available online at www.oed.com. This is not a publically available resource, but many universities will have online access either direct or through a library portal.

As well as conventional dictionaries, there is a range of legal dictionaries available. If your course does not recommend a particular dictionary, it is a good idea to browse a few in the bookshop or the library. Legal dictionaries are very useful as a quick means of checking whether a word has a specific legal meaning as well as an everyday meaning. They can also be used when you encounter an unfamiliar term—which is likely, particularly if it is in Latin or Law French. Examples of legal dictionaries include:

- E Martin and J Law (eds), *A Dictionary of Law* (7th edn, OUP 2013)

- M Woodley (ed), *Osborn's Concise Law Dictionary* (12th edn, Sweet & Maxwell 2013)

- L Curzon and P Richards, *The Longman Dictionary of Law* (8th edn, Longman 2011)

Finally, there are also a range of specialist dictionaries which cover definitions that are restricted to certain topics including Employment Law, Company Law, and Commercial Law. These will possibly be too detailed for the purposes of your course of study; therefore, one of the general legal dictionaries will probably be the more appropriate resource.

7.1.6.2 Judicial dictionaries

Judicial dictionaries contain details of the ways in which judges have interpreted particular words or phrases as well as definitions contained in statute. They are very expensive, so are best used as a library resource or online, where available.

Stroud's Judicial Dictionary of Words and Phrases includes definitions from English, Scottish, and Commonwealth sources. Judicial interpretations of words and phrases used in statutes which have been repealed or amended have been retained. It comprises six volumes and is updated annually.

Words and Phrases Legally Defined is similar to *Stroud's Judicial Dictionary* and is also updated via annual cumulative supplements.

Finally, *Halsbury's Laws of England* may also be used to find definitions of words and phrases via the index to the main volumes.

7.1.7 Revision guides

Many students rely upon revision guides as a safety net. Revision guides do exactly what their name suggests—they are guides to revision. They are not a substitute for attendance at

---

1. P Clinch, 'Systems of Reporting Judicial Decision Making' (PhD thesis, University of Sheffield 1989) 481.

lectures and seminars. Moreover, they do not provide an excuse not to read and follow your own course materials and textbooks and should not cut down on the amount of reading and thinking that you have to do.

If you compare the size of most revision guides to that of your recommended textbook, it follows that a revision guide could never be expected to cover the subject in the depth required to succeed in coursework or examinations. However, they can serve a useful purpose in providing a concise overview of the key areas for revision—reminding you of the headline points to enable you to focus your revision and identify the key points you need to know. Some students also like to use revision guides at the start of a module to gain a quick overview of the subject.

7.2 Journals

Journals are also referred to as periodicals.

Journals are an important resource which can be used to keep up-to-date with latest developments in the law. They are also a key source of academic criticism and commentary upon the law which should be used in addition to textbooks, particularly when researching for a piece of written work, a seminar, or a moot. Books are always out of date to a greater or lesser extent. Even with a new book there is usually a delay of some months between the submission of the final manuscript by the author(s) and the book finally appearing on the shelves. New editions rarely come out more frequently than once every two years.

Journals contain a mixture of articles, news, notes, reviews, and digests. They are usually published as individual issues, which combine to make up volumes.

7.2.1 General journals

General journals tend to contain lengthy articles based on extensive academic research. Most include notes of recent cases, news of legal developments, and book reviews. The general journals most frequently encountered are the *Law Quarterly Review*, *Legal Studies*, the *Cambridge Law Journal*, the *Oxford Journal of Legal Studies*, and the *Modern Law Review*. They are published relatively infrequently; typically with four or six issues per year.

7.2.2 Specialist journals

Specialist journals are similar to the general journals in that they primarily provide academic commentary and news on the law. However, they focus on particular aspects of the law. Examples of these include the *Criminal Law Review*, *Family Law*, *Civil Justice Quarterly*, and the *Journal of Business Law*.

There are also shorter specialist bulletins and newsletters which are focused on the needs of practitioners, such as *Simon's Tax Intelligence*, *Property Law Bulletin*, and *Business Law Brief*. These are of less immediate importance to your core studies, although you should at least be aware of their existence.

7.2.3 Practitioner journals

Practitioner journals are usually published weekly or bi-weekly. These tend to contain shorter articles on a wide range of topics of interest to lawyers in practice as well as case notes, digests, and practice notes. The articles are not usually covered in as great a depth as the general or specialist journals and are often written by other practitioners rather than by academic lawyers. They still provide useful information and should not be overlooked, although they do carry less academic weight than the general and specialist academic journals. The journals in this category that you are most likely to encounter include the *New Law Journal*, *Solicitors' Journal*, the *Law Society Gazette*, *Counsel*, and *Justice of the Peace*.

7.2.4 Foreign journals

English-language journals, in particular those from other common law jurisdictions such as the United States, Canada, Australia, and New Zealand, can be useful when undertaking comparisons with the UK. Most libraries will carry a selection of foreign journals, such as the *Harvard Law Review*, the *Australian Law Journal*, and the *Canadian Bar Review*.

7.2.5 Some guidance on using journals

It is important to remember that academic journal articles are explanations, commentaries, criticisms, and analysis of specific aspects of the law and the significance or implications of the law—they are *not* the law itself. They are an opinion on the law and are therefore a useful *secondary* source which can be used in conjunction with *primary* legal sources (cases and legislation) to supplement the arguments which you are making. If you are talking about primary sources, you must reference them and not the article which you have read about them.

While journal articles can certainly provide evidence of further research and reading, particularly in essay questions (see chapter 13) and dissertations (see chapter 14), you must still take care in selecting and using them. Ensure that the journals that you are using are appropriate. Academic journals are usually regarded as more authoritative than practitioner (or trade) journals. Although practitioner journals are useful for keeping you up-to-date with developments in the law since they are often published more frequently than the 'heavyweight' journals, you should try to avoid using them as serious academic authority. If you find an interesting article or case note in a practitioner journal, you should always try to see if you can find material on the same (or a similar) topic in a journal which carries greater academic authority. That is not to say that practitioner journals have no merit. They may carry the only commentary on a new development and, as such, can be used together with other journal articles within your essay. As long as you strike an appropriate balance between the two types of journal, you will demonstrate your ability to select and present commentary on the law.

You should also be careful to make sure that you understand the point which the article you wish to use is trying to make. Do not fall into the trap of using a quotation from an article 'just because it sounded clever' if you fail to realize the point that the author is trying to make. Your lecturer will understand the quotation and will also spot if you are misusing or misinterpreting it.

Ensure that you explain why the views you are including from journals are relevant to your essay and significant in terms of the argument you are putting forward. Well-used academic commentary should help you to support the points you are making. You can then give your own comment on the journal's perspective: do you agree or disagree with it? Explain why. This will demonstrate your ability to synthesize and analyze multiple sources.

Finally, be careful with articles which put forward extreme or sensationalist views. These will typically represent one side of an argument, and it is important to put forward a balanced view which evaluates and considers both sides.

7.3 Official publications

7.3.1 Command Papers

Command Papers derive their name from the fact that they are presented to Parliament 'by Command of Her Majesty'. In fact, they are generally presented by a Government Minister. Command Papers are papers of interest to Parliament where presentation to Parliament is not required by statute. The subjects may include:

- Major policy proposals (White Papers)
- Consultation documents (Green Papers)
- Diplomatic documents such as treaties
- Government responses to Select Committee reports
- Reports of major committees of inquiry
- Certain departmental reports or reviews.

7.3.2 Bills

As you will recall from section 1.1.1, Bills are draft Acts of Parliament, put forward for debate. They are particularly useful when used in conjunction with the reports of Parliamentary debate, as you will be able to follow the various amendments made between versions of the Bill and the final Act of Parliament alongside the debate in Parliament that drove those amendments.

7.3.3 Parliamentary papers

The papers of the House of Commons originate inside the House and are 'Ordered by the House of Commons to be printed . . .'. They comprise the reports and evidence of Select Committees or the proceedings of Standing Committees considering legislation. Other House of Commons papers include:

- Reports of investigations of the National Audit Office
- Financial papers
- Annual reports of official bodies
- Accounts of official bodies
- Various administrative reports

The House of Lords publishes substantially fewer papers than the Commons. Until the 1986/87 session both Bills and papers were numbered in one single sequence. From 1987/88 House of Lords papers and Bills were split into two separately numbered sequences.

7.3.4 Parliamentary debates (*Hansard* or the Official Report)

Parliament once prohibited all reporting and publishing of its proceedings, believing that it should deliberate in private. Indeed, it regarded any attempt to publicize its proceedings as a serious punishable offence. However, by the late 1700s, dissent both from the public and within Parliament persuaded Parliament to relax its stance. In 1803 the House of Commons allowed the press to enter the public gallery and William Cobbett, publisher of *Cobbett's Weekly Political Register* added reprints of reports of speeches taken from other newspapers in a new supplement. In 1812 publication was taken over by Cobbett's assistant, Thomas Hansard, who in 1829 changed the title of the reports to *Hansard's Parliamentary Debates*.

By 1878 dissatisfaction with the accuracy of the report was being expressed, and Hansard received a special subsidy conditional upon his employing special Parliamentary reporters. In 1888 a Parliamentary Select Committee recommended that rather than let Hansard publish the debates an authorized version ought to be published. This version was published without using the name *Hansard*.

This authorized version was officially adopted by Parliament in 1907 as a 'full report, in the first person, of all speakers alike', with a full report being defined as:

one which, though not strictly verbatim, is substantially the verbatim report, with repetitions and redundancies omitted and with obvious mistakes corrected, but which on the other hand leaves out nothing that adds to the meaning of the speech or illustrates the argument.

In 1943 it was decided to reintroduce the name *Hansard* because of its popular usage.

Therefore *Hansard* (the *Official Report*) is the edited verbatim report of proceedings in both the House of Commons and the House of Lords. Commons *Hansard* covers proceedings in the Commons Chamber, Westminster Hall, and Standing Committees. Lords *Hansard* covers proceedings in the Lords Chamber and its Grand Committees. Both contain Written Ministerial Statements and Written Answers.

7.3.5 Law Commission reports

The Law Commission was set up by the Law Commissions Act 1965 for the purpose of promoting reform of the law. Its key aims are:

- to ensure that the law is as fair, modern, simple, and as cost-effective as possible;
- to conduct research and consultations in order to make systematic recommendations for consideration by Parliament;
- to codify the law, eliminate anomalies, repeal obsolete and unnecessary enactments and reduce the number of separate statutes.

Law Commission reports provide a useful insight into reasons behind law reforms and more than two-thirds of the Commission's law reform recommendations have been implemented. There are also recommendations that are waiting for the Government's decision, or Parliamentary time for debate. Recent examples of legislation that have followed, in whole or in part, from Commission reports include the Inheritance and Trustees' Powers Act 2014, the Care Act 2014, the Social Services and Well-being (Wales) Act 2014, and the Co-operative and Community Benefit Societies Act 2014. Even recommendations that have not been implemented will give an overview of the problems that were perceived in the law and may prove useful in essays that require a critical discussion of the topic.

The Law Commission Act 2009 was implemented to improve the rate at which the Commission's recommendations for reform of the law are implemented by Government. It requires the Lord Chancellor to report annually to Parliament on the extent to which Government has implemented Law Commission recommendations.

Many Law Commission reports are published as Command Papers or Parliamentary Papers.

7.4 Other secondary sources

7.4.1 Websites

Although there is a vast amount of material available online, you need to exercise care to ensure that material you find is reliable, valuable, and credible. This can be a difficult task, although the following pointers should be borne in mind:

- Does the material give an author's name? If so, is the author a reputable academic or practitioner? Can you find any biographical information which will enable you to determine the academic value of the material?

- Is the information in a reputable online publication?

- Does the article carry a bibliography? Is it adequately referenced (either using footnotes, endnotes, or Harvard referencing)?

- Is the material on an official website or a personal website? The latter should be used with caution since anyone can set up a personal site.

- Has the material been evaluated independently before publication?

7.4.2 Newspapers

In addition to law reports, newspapers often contain comment and analysis on recent legal developments and interesting background material on topical issues. *The Times* in particular carries a law supplement on Tuesdays.

7.4.3 Think-tanks

Think-tanks are typically research institutes or other organizations who provide specialist advice and ideas on national problems, such as the Centre for Policy Studies, the Commonwealth Policy Studies Institute, or the Institute for Public Policy Research. While their reports are not official, they can sometimes be influential in driving legislative policy.

7.4.4 'Soft law'

....

Soft law is sometimes referred to as *quasi-legislation*—or 'law-which-is-not-law'.

....

There are a number of sources of 'soft law'. Soft law is typically administrative in nature and is probably best explained by way of examples (see Table 7.1).

Table 7.1 Some examples of 'Soft law'

Category	Examples
Prescriptive rules	• Codes of Practice issued under the Police and Criminal Evidence Act 1984 • Highway Code • ACAS (Advisory Conciliation and Arbitration Service) codes relating to employment disputes
Procedural rules	• Practice Directions • Prison rules • Gaming Board rules for application for gaming licences • Codes of Practice issued under the Police and Criminal Evidence Act 1984
Instructions	• Home Office Circulars to magistrates' courts • Home Office Circulars to Chief Constables • Prison Department Circulars, Orders, and Regulations
Guides to interpretation	• Official statements explaining how terms or rules will be interpreted
Recommendations	• Specimen directions to juries formulated by the Judicial Studies Board • Guidance notes issued by the Health and Safety Executive
Rules of practice	• Tax concessions made by the Commissioners for the Inland Revenue outside those permitted by statute
Voluntary codes	• Broadcasting Complaints Authority • Press Complaints Commission • City Code on takeovers and mergers

The legal effect of these various sources is not certain until they have been tested in court. Sometimes they are given legal effect, sometimes not, and in some instances, inconsistently. The House of Lords[2] has expressed concern regarding the uncertain legal consequences of non-compliance and the Cabinet Office has provided some 'Guidance on Codes of Practice and Legislation' in its *Guide to Making Legislation*.[3]

 CHAPTER SUMMARY

Books

- Student textbooks collect together, analyze, and criticize the law in particular areas

- They do not generally carry any great authority

- Cases and materials books provide a useful starting point for research, but are not a substitute for finding and reading original materials

- Monographs are a detailed written study of a single specialized topic. They cover particular narrow subject areas in much greater depth than student textbooks

---

2. *Hansard* HL vol 469 cols 1075–1105 (15 January 1986).
3. Cabinet Office, *Guide to Making Legislation* (July 2014) Appendix D. <https://www.gov.uk/government/uploads/system/uploads/attachment_data/file/328408/Guide_to_Making_Legislation_July_2014.pdf>.

- Practitioners' books are primarily reference works for practising lawyers

- Legal encyclopedias and digests such as *Halsbury's Laws of England, Halsbury's Statutes*, and *The Digest* are extremely useful and comprehensive research tools

- Legal dictionaries exist alongside conventional dictionaries; some specialize in a particular topic

- Judicial dictionaries are large reference works which provide detailed commentary on judicial interpretation of words and phrases

- Revision guides can serve a useful purpose, but are not a substitute for attendance at lectures or seminars or a short cut for reading and thinking

Journals

- Journals are an important resource which can be used to keep up-to-date with latest developments in the law

- General journals contain articles based on extensive academic research

- Specialist journals also contain academic articles but with a focus on a particular area of the law

- Practitioner journals carry less academic weight but are published more frequently. They tend to contain shorter articles

- Foreign journals from other common law jurisdictions can be a useful resource when undertaking comparative research

Official publications

- Command Papers contain matters of interest to Parliament

- Bills are draft Acts of Parliament put forward for debate

- Papers of the House of Commons primarily comprise reports and evidence of select committees or the proceedings of standing committees

- The House of Lords publishes substantially fewer papers than the Commons

- *Hansard* (the *Official Report*) is the edited verbatim report of proceedings in both the House of Commons and the House of Lords

- Law Commission reports give insight into areas of the law requiring reform. Over two-thirds of its recommendations are implemented

Other secondary sources

- Online material can be useful but should be used with caution

- Newspapers often contain comment and analysis on recent legal developments

- Think-tank reports can be influential in driving legislative policy

- 'Soft law' comprises rules, guidelines, codes, and recommendations which may be given legal effect when tested in court

FURTHER READING

- An interesting historical legal perspective on the emergence of quasi-legislation is given in RE Megarry, 'Administrative Quasi-legislation' (1944) 60 LQR 125.

- The varieties of quasi-legislative rule, the means by which the courts have dealt with them, and how they may best be accommodated within the UK constitutional framework is discussed in R Baldwin and J Houghton, 'Circular Arguments: The Status and Legitimacy of Administrative Rules' [1986] PL 239.

8

Finding books, journals, and official publications

INTRODUCTION

Chapters 2 and 5 covered the ways in which you can locate legislation and case law. However, as you will appreciate from the explanation provided in chapter 7, there are a range of important sources of law beyond legislation and case law. These are materials that provide information on the content, meaning, and operation of the law and which will assist you in your quest to understand the law. This chapter will complete your portfolio of 'finding' skills by explaining how to find these important supplementary resources, both in the library and online. It will cover books, journals, official publications, Bills and *Hansard*.

The ability to find supplementary legal resources will give you a fully-rounded set of skills by which you can find the most useful sources of law. The use of supplementary resources will give you a much greater depth of knowledge than can easily be acquired from statutes and cases alone. There is a wealth of legal literature available, so without the ability to find it you will find yourself unable to benefit from the learned commentary of others—all of whom will (usually) have much more legal experience than you.

LEARNING OUTCOMES

After studying this chapter, you will be able to:

- Use online library catalogues and legal bibliographies to find books on a particular topic

- Understand journal citations

- Recognize the more common journal abbreviations

- Find journals in a library and online

- Distinguish between the various series of Command Papers

- Locate official publications in both paper and electronic form

- Find Parliamentary Bills

- Use *Hansard* to find and follow debates in the House of Commons and House of Lords

8.1 Finding books

The ability to find books, either a specific title or a range of books on a particular topic, is important. Even if you purchase the set textbook for each of your subjects, there will still come a time when you need to find out what other books are available. You might, for instance, find that the set text is too complex, in which case you will want to find a more straightforward alternative. Conversely, if you are researching for a tutorial, a moot, or a piece of coursework, you may want to find books that go into more detail than the textbook that you have purchased.

8.1.1 Library catalogues

The first place to start looking for books on a particular topic is in your own library's catalogue as this will enable you to find which books are held at your own institution. However, there are also catalogues that provide information about the holdings of other libraries. This will be useful information if you want to know whether the university near your home town has sufficient books for your purposes during the vacation, for example, or it can enable you to locate a particular book that you need and order it from another library.

Most libraries provide an electronic facility by which you can search by author, title, or subject area.

It is clearly impossible to provide details of how the catalogue works at every library. You should take time to familiarize yourself with the catalogue at your own institution. Your library will have instructions on how to use its catalogue. However, the experience of trial and error is also useful. Pick an area of law and try a few searches.

8.1.1.1 Copac (copac.ac.uk)

The Copac library catalogue gives free access to the merged online catalogues of major University, Specialist, and National Libraries in the UK and Ireland, including the British Library.

Copac is a great way of tracking down less common materials, such as specialist monographs or theses, that may not be available in your local library. It can also be used for searching across a subject, checking document details, and downloading records to create a bibliography.

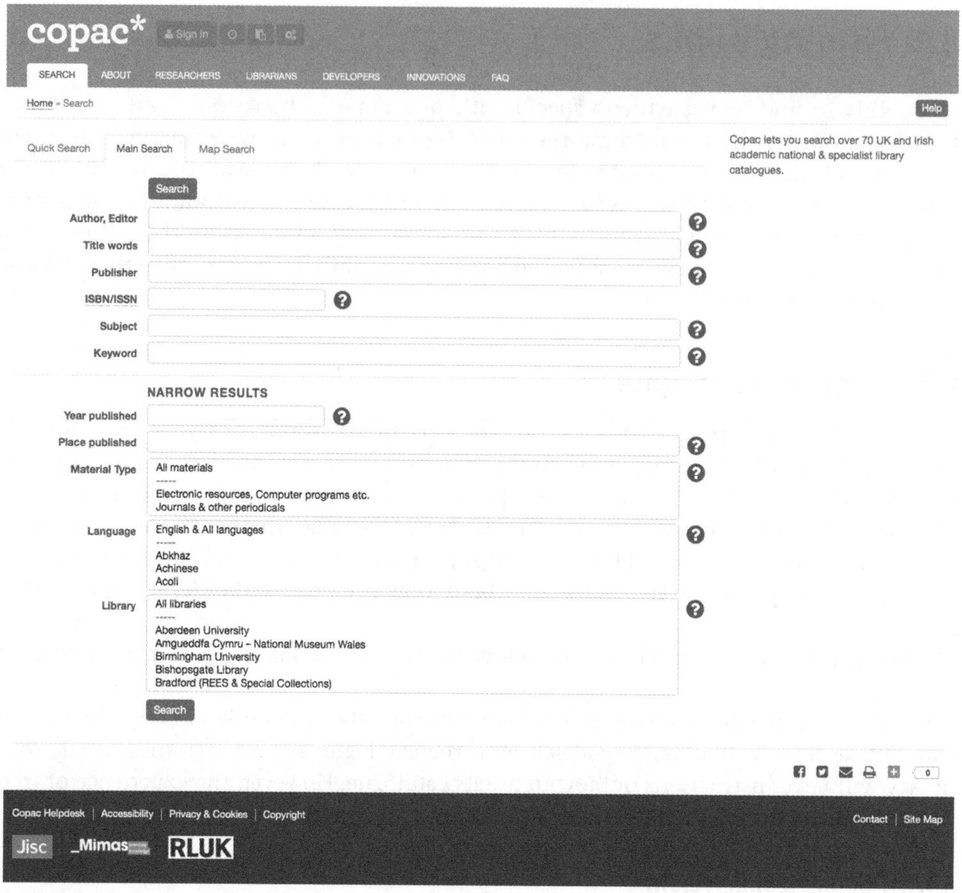

Figure 8.1 Copac

8.1.2 Legal bibliographies

Whilst the ability to locate books using the library catalogue and the Internet are useful skills, you should not overlook the importance of 'paper-based' research skills. It may be, for example, that you are using a library that does not have computer terminals in the area that you are using and you want to be able to locate material without constantly trotting backwards and forwards between the library catalogue and the area where the books are shelved. Equally, it can be very frustrating to have to wait in a queue to use a catalogue or online search facility when you are in a hurry and want to find a book. At such times, the ability to locate materials using an alternative method may be invaluable.

8.1.2.1 *Current Law Monthly Digest*

The *Current Law Monthly Digest* contains a list of new books published during the month. At the end of the year these lists are reprinted in the *Current Law Year Book*.

This is useful to check for current books which might have been published in a particular area very recently, although it can be cumbersome to use when looking for books over more than one or two years, since the list is not cumulative and the subject headings used are quite broad.

8.1.2.2 Specialist legal bibliographies

As well as *Current Law* there are a number of other legal bibliographies which provide listings of books for particular areas of law. These are too numerous to list here; you should check with your law librarian which ones are available.

8.1.2.3 References in textbooks

Never underestimate the value of simple strategies for locating secondary sources. All good-quality textbooks contain references to further secondary sources such as books and articles, either in the footnotes, additional reading sections, or in the bibliography. Not only do these provide the bibliographic details of books but also may give you an indication of *why* they are valuable sources. For example, if your textbook touches on a particular topic but not in any great detail—perhaps the point is too marginal for any great coverage in a textbook—it may provide a pointer to the leading work(s) on that topic.

8.2 Finding journals

It is inevitable that you will need to locate journal articles at some point during your studies. Your tutorial reading is likely to contain references to publications in journals and, of course, you will want to demonstrate your research skills in your coursework essays by making reference to relevant journal articles.

See chapter 10 (writing skills) and chapter 13 (essay writing) for a more detailed discussion of the value of journal articles in coursework.

The approach that is needed to locate journal articles will depend upon whether you are looking for a particular article that you know exists or whether you are having a speculative search to determine whether there are any articles on a particular topic.

8.2.1 Making sense of journal references

Journal references are used as a convenient shorthand means of pinpointing the location of a particular article. In other words, if you want to find a particular journal, its reference is the 'address' you need to track it down.

Journal references are covered in section 12.3.6.1.

For example, if you wish to find the article cited as:

J Murphy, 'Understanding Intimidation' (2014) 77 MLR 33.

you need to extract the key elements from the citation, so that you may find it easily in a library or online (see Figure 8.2).

The year of publication and first page number are self-explanatory. However, unlike the various series of law reports, there is unfortunately no single standard way of abbreviating journal titles. There are sometimes a couple of options for each journal.

Sometimes journal titles are written out in full rather than being abbreviated which makes the task of finding them much easier.

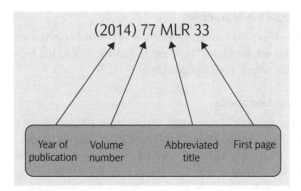

Figure 8.2 Journal citation

A useful free electronic guide to deciphering the multitude of journal (and law report) abbreviations is the *Cardiff Index to Legal Abbreviations* available online at www.legalabbrevs. cardiff.ac.uk. It can be searched either from abbreviation to title or from title to abbreviation. It is also possible to search from abbreviation to title using only a part of an abbreviation, and from title to abbreviation using any words (not just the first word) which appear in the title.

There may or may not be a volume number. Some journal series are just referenced by their year of publication (and do not have consecutive volume numbers). Other references might provide an issue number as well as a volume number, given in brackets after the volume number.

Breaking down the elements of the citation, you should see that it refers to:

- An article by J Murphy
- In volume 77
- Of the *Modern Law Review*
- Which was published in 2014
- Called 'Understanding Intimidation'
- Starting on page 33

This should be all the information you need to find the article, either online or in the library.

8.2.2 Online

There are a number of online databases devoted to legal publications that you will find useful when searching for journal articles. You should, however, be aware that each database will only list articles in journals that are published by an organization that subscribes to that particular database. This means that you may find that the results of your search in any one database will not necessarily give you information about all the articles that have been published on a particular topic, only the articles that have been published in journals that have paid to be listed in that database. Therefore, you may need to make reference to more than one database in order to find the article that you want or to obtain a complete list of all available articles.

For example, using criminal law as an example, Westlaw UK lists articles published in the *Criminal Law Review* whilst LexisLibrary publishes articles published in the *Journal of Criminal Law*.

Table 8.1 Journals, abbreviations, and databases

Journal	Abbreviation	Database
British Journal of Criminology	BJ Crim	Westlaw UK
Cambridge Law Journal	CLJ	HeinOnline
Child and Family Law Quarterly	CFLQ	LexisLibrary
Civil Justice Quarterly	CJQ	Westlaw UK
Computer & Telecommunications Law Review	CTLR	Westlaw UK
Conveyancer and Property Lawyer	Conv	Lawtel
Counsel	*Counsel*	Lawtel
Criminal Law Review	Crim LR	Westlaw UK, Lawtel
Employment Law Bulletin	ELB	Westlaw UK
Employment Law Journal	ELJ	Lawtel
Estates Gazette	EG	Lawtel, LexisLibrary
European Human Rights Law Review	EHRLR	Westlaw UK
Family Law	Fam Law	Lawtel, LexisLibrary
Human Rights Law Review	HRLR	Westlaw UK
Industrial Law Journal	ILJ	Westlaw UK, LexisLibrary
International and Comparative Law Quarterly	ICLQ	Westlaw UK
International Journal of Law and Information Technology	IJLT	LexisLibrary
IT & Communications Law Journal	ITC	Lawtel
Journal of Business Law	JBL	
Journal of Criminal Law	JCL	LexisLibrary
Journal of Environmental Law	JEnvL	Westlaw UK, LexisLibrary
Journal of Information, Law & Technology	JILT	Lawtel
Journal of Law and Society	JLS	
Journal of Planning and Environment Law	JPL	
Justice of the Peace	JP	
Landlord and Tenant Review	LTR	Lawtel, Westlaw UK
Law Quarterly Review	LQR	Westlaw UK, HeinOnline
Law Society's Gazette	*Gazette*	Lawtel, LexisLibrary
Legal Studies	LS	HeinOnline
Litigation	*Litigation*	Lawtel
Medical Law Review	Med LR	Westlaw UK, LexisLibrary
Modern Law Review	MLR	Lawtel, HeinOnline
New Law Journal	NLJ	Lawtel, LexisLibrary
Oxford Journal of Legal Studies	OJLS	Westlaw UK, LexisLibrary
Police Journal	Police J	LexisLibrary

(Continued)

Table 8.1 *(Cont.)*

Property Law Journal	PLJ	Lawtel
Public Law	PL	Westlaw UK, Lawtel
Solicitors Journal	SJ	Lawtel
Statute Law Review	SLR	Westlaw UK
The Guardian (Legal Section)	*Guardian*	Lawtel
The Independent (Legal Section)	*Independent*	Lawtel
The Times (Legal Section)	*Times*	Lawtel
Web Journal of Current Legal Issues	WebJCLI	Lawtel

As the two main UK journals on criminal law are covered by different databases, you would need to use both to ensure that you had been thorough in your search for articles on a topic in criminal law. By way of example, a search for articles using the search term 'intoxicated consent in rape' conducted in 2014 found fifty-one relevant articles in Westlaw UK, four in Lawtel, and three in LexisLibrary.

8.2.2.1 Which database?

You may find Table 8.1 useful if you wish to search for a particular journal online. Where no database is shown, this indicates that the journal is not available through the common online databases. You will either have to see if your library or institution provides alternative online means of access (such as a direct subscription to the electronic form of the journal) or whether the library carries the paper journal.

8.2.2.2 Westlaw UK

Westlaw UK lists all articles that appear in its publisher's own journals as well as a selection of those owned by other publishers such as Oxford University Press. It is a well-maintained database that is updated on a daily basis, so it is a good way of locating articles that have just been published. It has the advantage of being a full-text database in relation to approximately sixty of its journals which means that it not only finds the article but also provides it in full for you to read on screen or print out. This can be a real asset if the article that you want is in a journal that is not held in your own library.

Westlaw UK has a 'quick search' page which enables you to get straight on with a search of journals, case law, or legislation as well as more detailed search facilities.

The Legal Journals Index database is also available via Westlaw UK. This provides an up-to-date list of legal journals which may be searched by:

- General terms, subject area, or keyword
- Legislation cited (all articles which refer to a particular section of an Act)
- Case cited (all articles which refer to a particular case)
- Journal or article title
- Name of the author(s)

If you are looking for an article that you know exists, it is likely that you will have sufficient information to find it without a great deal of difficulty by using the title of the article or the name of the author in combination with a keyword as the basis of the search.

However, it will often be the case that you are looking for articles on a topic and are not sure whether any have been written. Here, you will need to use keyword searching and it may take a fair amount of experimentation with search terms to find material that is useful to you.

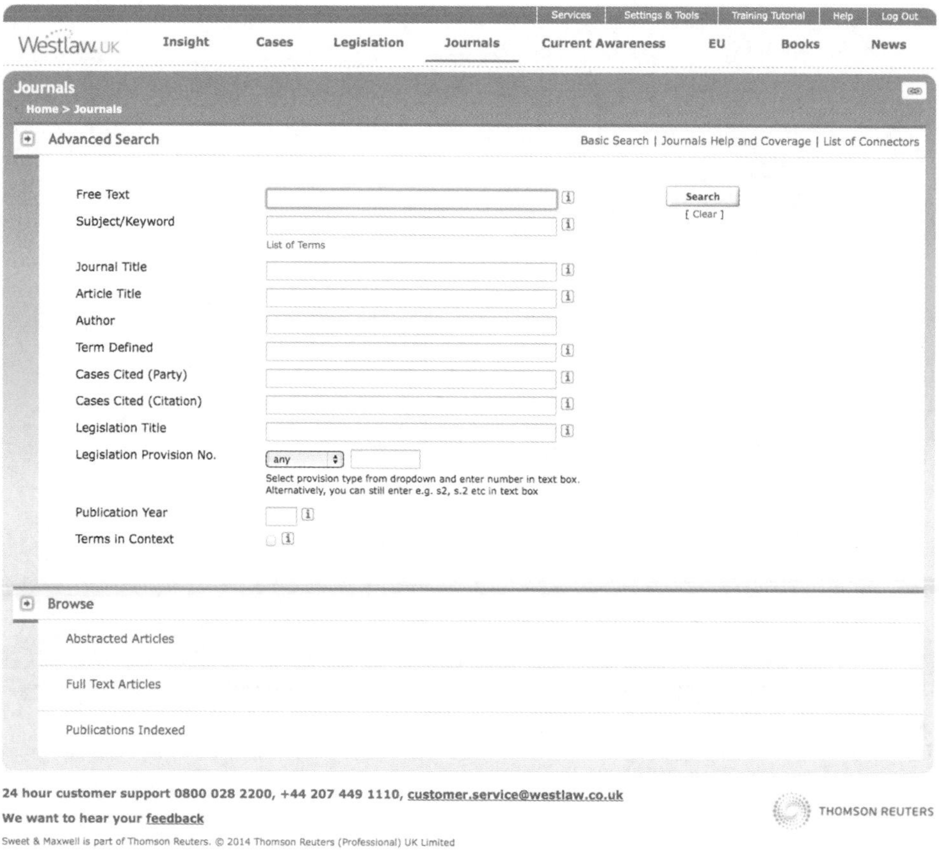

Figure 8.3 Westlaw UK

8.2.2.3 Lawtel

Lawtel provides a search facility for many different UK legal publications. It is also owned by Sweet & Maxwell so you may find that there is a fair degree of overlap with Westlaw UK in terms of its coverage. Lawtel also includes a number of practitioner-focused journals such as the *Solicitors Journal* and *Counsel* as well as more academic titles. Practitioner journals can be particularly useful as they are published far more frequently than academic journals—the *Solicitors Journal*, for example, is a weekly publication—so it often has comment on recent cases and events. Lawtel also provides access to newspaper law reports from *The Times, The Independent*, and *The Guardian*.

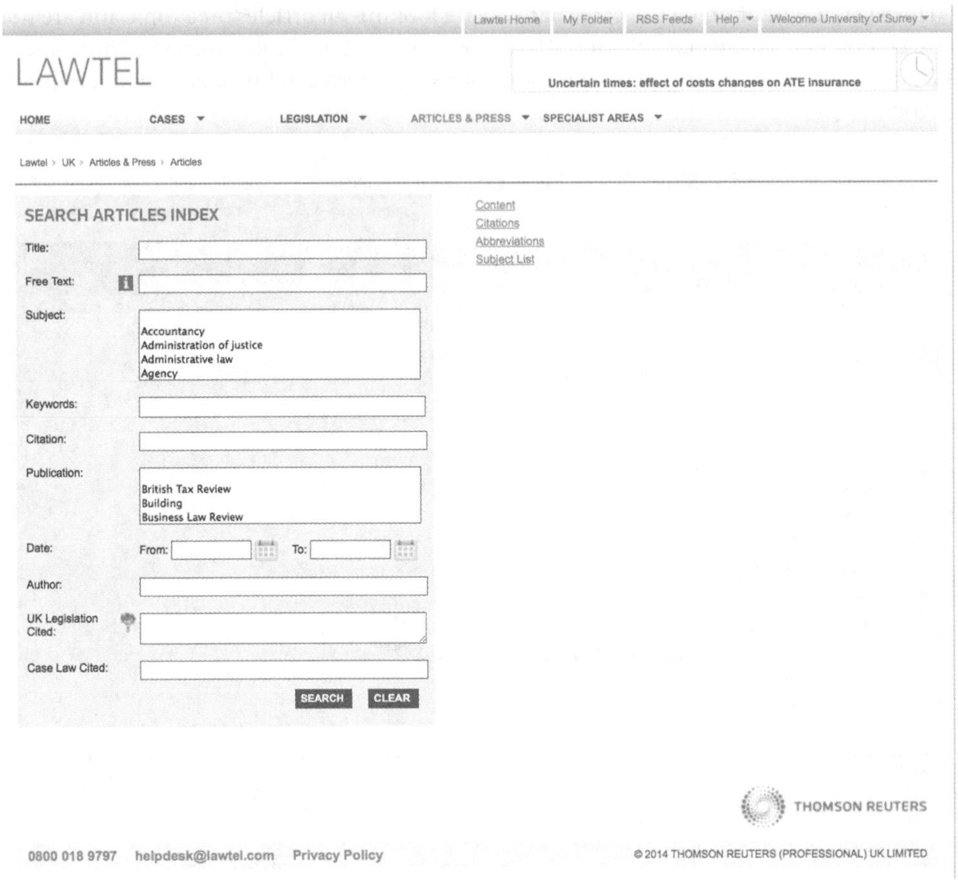

Figure 8.4 Lawtel

8.2.2.4 LexisLibrary

LexisLibrary contains the full text of articles published in around eighty-five journals and summaries of the articles found in many more journals. It is also updated regularly. In addition to academic journals, LexisLibrary covers a range of practitioner titles such as the *New Law Journal*.

As with Westlaw UK and Lawtel, it provides the ability to search by title, author, or general search terms but it has the additional benefit of providing a drop-down list of the journals covered which can facilitate a more focused search of a particular publication. For example, if you were looking for articles on a topic within criminal law and did not want to trawl through a long list of results, you could search exclusively within the *Journal of Criminal Law*. This can be useful in speeding up your search and eliminating unwanted materials from the outset. You should be wary, however, of being overly selective in your searching as general journals, such as the *Oxford Journal of Legal Studies*, cover articles on any topic within the law, so searching in a particular specialist journal would automatically exclude relevant articles published in general journals.

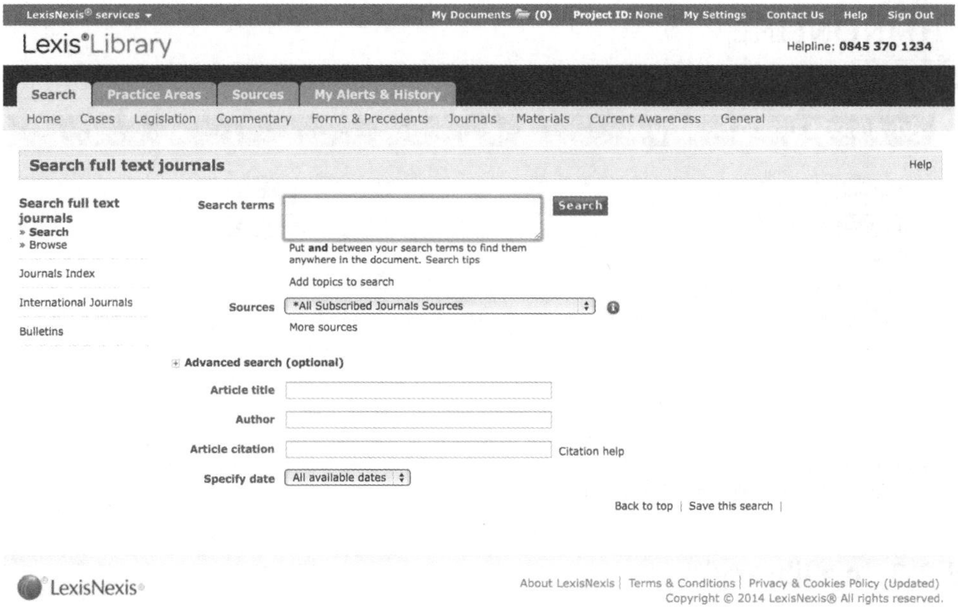

Figure 8.5 Lexislibrary
Reproduced with the kind permission of LexisNexis®

8.2.2.5 HeinOnline

HeinOnline was introduced in 2000 by William S Hein & Co, an American legal publisher. It contains full text resources from a large number of journals. However, unlike the other full-text services, it provides exact page images. This means that you can see all the pages as they originally appeared in print. It is the world's largest image-based legal research database. However, as you might expect from an American service, the journal coverage is predominantly American, although it does cover certain volumes of a number of the major UK journals including:

- *Modern Law Review* (1937–2001)
- *Law Quarterly Review* (1885–1925)
- *Cambridge Law Journal* (1921–2001)
- *Legal Studies* (1981–2004)

It also carries *Statutes of the Realm* (1235–1713) and a full reprint of volumes 1–176 of the *English Reports* (1694–1867).

Figure 8.6 HeinOnline
Used with permission of William S. Hein & Co, Inc.

8.2.3 In a library

If you have the citation of the article, it should be a relatively straightforward task to find it in your library. Check the library catalogue or ask your librarian to make sure that the library carries the particular series of journals covering the date and/or volume that you need. Not all libraries carry all journals. To make matters even more complicated, even if your library *does* carry the series you need, there is no guarantee that it will have the particular volume you want. The library may have begun its subscription after the date you are looking for or cancelled its subscription before the date you require.

Practical exercise

Try to find the following articles either online or in the library:

1. C Walker, 'The governance of emergency arrangements' (2014) 18 International Journal of Human Rights 211.

2. C Piper, 'Neglect neglected in the Crime and Courts Act' (2013) 43 Family Law 722.

3. R Pattenden, 'Machinespeak: Section 129 of Criminal Justice Act 2003' [2010] Crim LR 623.

8.3 Finding official publications

Government departments and other official organizations conduct a great deal of research prior to recommending changes to the law and their findings may be an incredibly rich source of information. If you need to understand the priorities that shaped the content of the current law or the reason why an Act of Parliament covers certain issues but not others, it is likely that you will find the answer in an official publication. For example, the Sexual Offences Act 2003 was enacted after a prolonged period of consultation over a period of years and the final statute was very different to the original proposals. If you wanted to know what the earlier proposals were and how and why they were altered, you would need to find the consultation papers that were published and look at records of Parliamentary debates. For this reason, official publications can be excellent sources of information about the policy behind the law.

8.3.1 Making sense of Command Paper abbreviations

Every Command Paper is given a unique reference which is printed on the front cover of the report (in the bottom left-hand corner). However, there have been six series of Command Papers, which use different abbreviations as shown in Table 8.2.

It is important to look at the style of abbreviation. This will give you an indication of the date of the Command Paper—remember that there is a thirty-year gap between Cmnd. 1 and Cm. 1 for example.

8.3.2 Online

8.3.2.1 gov.uk publications

The gov.uk website contains an extensive search facility for official documents available at www.gov.uk/publications. It allows searching by topic, Government department, geographical location, and official document type as well as filtering by date range.

Table 8.2 Series of Command Papers

Series	Dates	Abbreviation
1	1833–69	[1]–[4222]
2	1870–99	[C. 1]–[C. 9550]
3	1900–18	[Cd. 1]–[Cd. 9329]
4	1919–56	[Cmd. 1]–Cmd. 9889 (the use of square brackets was discontinued in 1922)
5	1956–86	Cmnd. 1–Cmnd. 9927
6	1986–date	Cm. 1–(series 6 contains around 8480 Command Papers as at November 2012)

Publications

You can use the filters to show only results that match your interests

Contains

keywords

Publication type

All publication types

Topic

All topics

Department

All departments

Official document status

All documents

World locations

All locations

Published after

e.g. 01/01/2013

Published before

e.g. 30/02/2013

56,949 publications

Get updates to this list ✉ email 🔊 feed

Weekly rainfall and river flow summary: 30 July to 5 August 2014
7 August 2014   EA   Statistics   Part of a collection: Water situation reports for England

Defence logistics support chain manual (JSP 886): version and legacy records
7 August 2014   MOD   Guidance
Part of a collection: The defence logistics support chain manual (JSP 886) and Joint Service Publication (JSP)

Defence supportability engineering: volume 07 (JSP 886)
7 August 2014   MOD   Guidance
Part of a collection: The defence logistics support chain manual (JSP 886) and Joint Service Publication (JSP)

Commodity supply management: volume 06 (JSP 886)
7 August 2014   MOD   Guidance
Part of a collection: The defence logistics support chain manual (JSP 886) and Joint Service Publication (JSP)

Inventory management for defence: volume 02 (JSP 886)
7 August 2014   MOD   Guidance
Part of a collection: The defence logistics support chain manual (JSP 886) and Joint Service Publication (JSP)

Support chain management: volume 03 (JSP 886)
7 August 2014   MOD   Guidance
Part of a collection: The defence logistics support chain manual (JSP 886) and Joint Service Publication (JSP)

Figure 8.7 gov.uk publications
© Crown copyright

8.3.2.2 UKOP

UKOP (www.ukop.co.uk) is a subscription service provided by TSO (the Stationery Office). It is the official catalogue of UK official publications since 1980. It contains around 450,000 records from over 2,000 public bodies. It provides full search facilities and an alphabetical list of issuing bodies and departments. It provides the full text of over 30,000 documents. Where the full text is not available it provides details of where you can obtain a printed copy. It is updated daily.

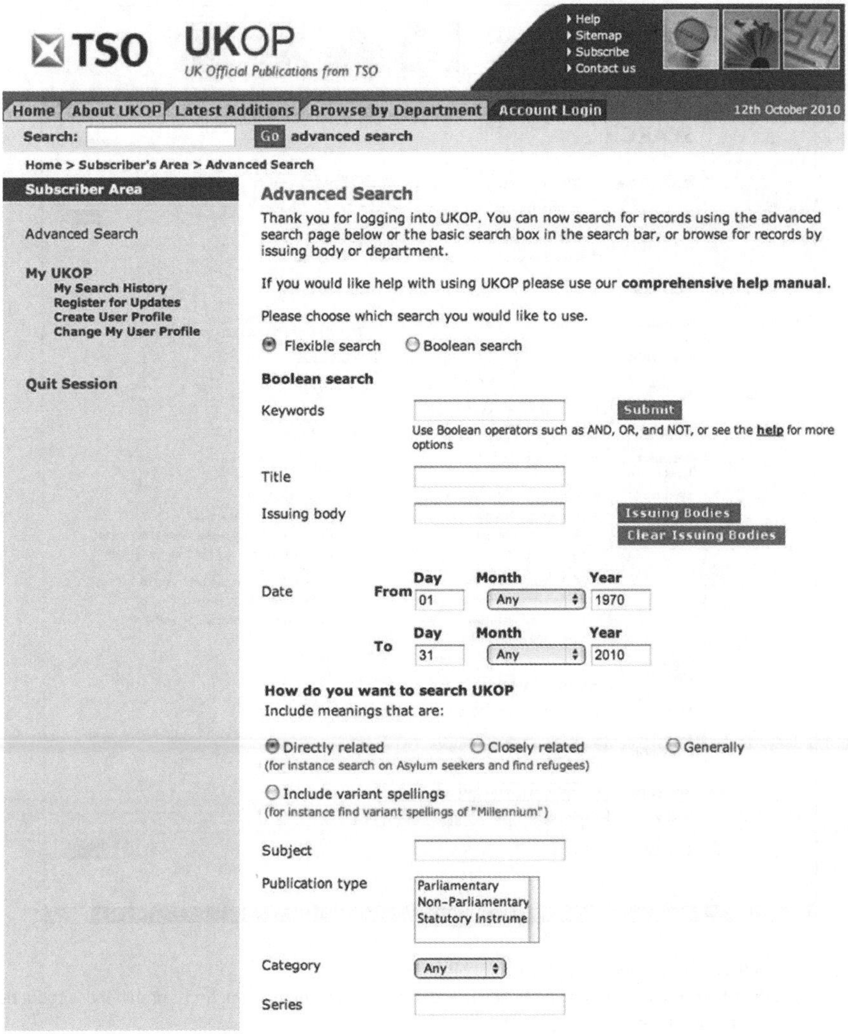

Figure 8.8 UKOP

8.3.2.3 *House of Commons Parliamentary Papers*

House of Commons Parliamentary Papers is a commercially-available service (parlipapers. chadwyck.co.uk/marketing/index.jsp). It provides a searchable full-text facility as well as a detailed index. It includes over 200,000 House of Commons Sessional Papers from 1715 to the present with supplementary materials from 1688.

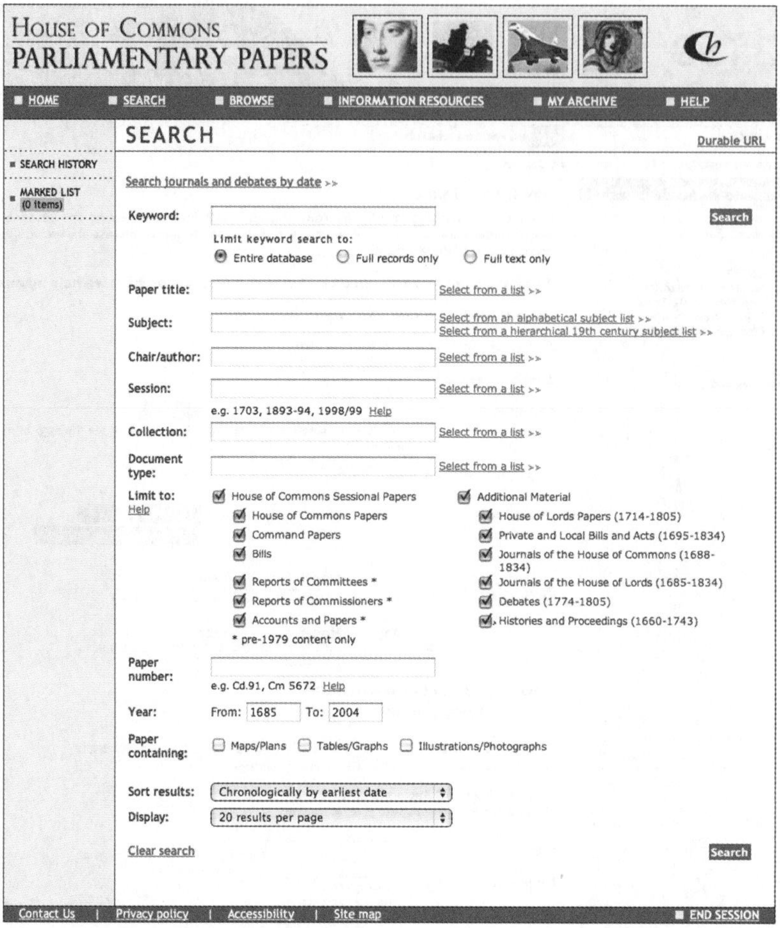

HOUSE OF COMMONS
PARLIAMENTARY PAPERS

■ HOME   ■ SEARCH   ■ BROWSE   ■ INFORMATION RESOURCES   ■ MY ARCHIVE   ■ HELP

SEARCH   Durable URL

■ SEARCH HISTORY
■ MARKED LIST
  (0 items)

Search journals and debates by date >>

Keyword: [   ]   [Search]

Limit keyword search to:
● Entire database   ○ Full records only   ○ Full text only

Paper title: [   ]   Select from a list >>

Subject: [   ]   Select from an alphabetical subject list >>
                                                       Select from a hierarchical 19th century subject list >>

Chair/author: [   ]   Select from a list >>

Session: [   ]   Select from a list >>
e.g. 1703, 1893-94, 1998/99 Help

Collection: [   ]   Select from a list >>

Document type: [   ]   Select from a list >>

Limit to: ☑ House of Commons Sessional Papers   ☑ Additional Material
Help   ☑ House of Commons Papers   ☑ House of Lords Papers (1714-1805)
                ☑ Command Papers   ☑ Private and Local Bills and Acts (1695-1834)
                ☑ Bills   ☑ Journals of the House of Commons (1688-1834)
                ☑ Reports of Committees *   ☑ Journals of the House of Lords (1685-1834)
                ☑ Reports of Commissioners *   ☑ Debates (1774-1805)
                ☑ Accounts and Papers *   ☑ Histories and Proceedings (1660-1743)
                * pre-1979 content only

Paper number: [   ]
e.g. Cd.91, Cm 5672 Help

Year: From: [1685]   To: [2004]

Paper containing: ☐ Maps/Plans   ☐ Tables/Graphs   ☐ Illustrations/Photographs

Sort results: [Chronologically by earliest date ▼]

Display: [20 results per page ▼]

Clear search   [Search]

Contact Us | Privacy policy | Accessibility | Site map   ■ END SESSION

Figure 8.9 House of Commons Parliamentary Papers
The screenshot is published with permission of ProQuest LL. Further reproduction is prohibited without permission. www.proquest.com

8.3.3 In a library

Most libraries will contain a collection of Command Papers. These may be arranged by series and number, in which case it is a very straightforward task to find the paper you want. However, some libraries organize their Parliamentary materials in *sessional sets*: in other words bound together in volumes for a particular session of Parliament. These will therefore be organized by year. If your library organizes its Command Papers in this way, you will need to have some idea of the year of the paper as well as its abbreviated reference.

8.4 Finding Bills

8.4.1 Making sense of Bill citations

The role of Bills in the Parliamentary process is covered in chapter 1.

Public Bills carry a serial number in the bottom left-hand corner of the first page of the Bill. For example, the 2014–15 Modern Slavery Bill is Bill 8.

A

BILL

TO

Make provision about slavery, servitude and forced or compulsory labour; to make provision about human trafficking; to make provision for an Antislavery Commissioner; and for connected purposes.

BE IT ENACTED by the Queen's most Excellent Majesty, by and with the advice and consent of the Lords Spiritual and Temporal, and Commons, in this present Parliament assembled, and by the authority of the same, as follows:—

PART 1

Offences

Offences

1   Slavery, servitude and forced or compulsory labour

(1) A person commits an offence if—

    (a) the person holds another person in slavery or servitude and the circumstances are such that the person knows or ought to know that the other person is held in slavery or servitude, or

    (b) the person requires another person to perform forced or compulsory labour and the circumstances are such that the person knows or ought to know that the other person is being required to perform forced or compulsory labour.

(2) In subsection (1) the references to holding a person in slavery or servitude or requiring a person to perform forced or compulsory labour are to be construed in accordance with Article 4 of the Human Rights Convention.

(3) In determining whether a person is being held in slavery or servitude or required to perform forced or compulsory labour regard may be had to all the circumstances.

(4) For example, regard may be had to any of the person's personal circumstances (such as their age, family relationships, and any mental or physical illness) which may make the person more vulnerable than other persons.

Bill 8

Extract 8.1 2014–15 Modern Slavery Bill

This Bill would be cited as shown in Figure 8.10.

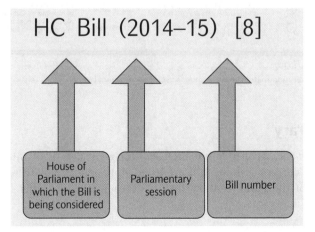

Figure 8.10 Bill citation

The convention for citing Bills therefore begins with HC (for House of Commons) or HL (for House of Lords). Since Bill numbering restarts at 1 with every new Parliamentary session, the dates of that session must be given to identify the Bill precisely. Finally, the citation provides the number of the Bill.

Traditionally, Bills in the House of Commons had a number in square brackets, and Bills in the House of Lords had a number in round brackets. You will still see this convention used in relation to Commons Bills, but Lords Bill numbers have now lost their brackets.

8.4.2 Online

Details of the Bills before Parliament in the current session can be found on the UK Parliament website: services.parliament.uk/bills.

Figure 8.11 Parliament Bills
Contains Parliamentary information licensed under the Open Parliament Licence v1.0

8.4.3 In a library

The *House of Commons Weekly Information Bulletin* gives details of Bills that are before Parliament in the current session. Bills are listed alphabetically by title. The *Bulletin* also provides details of the Parliamentary history of each Bill including the dates of each reading in the House of Commons and House of Lords and any proceedings in Standing Committee.

8.5 Finding Parliamentary debates

Remember that the Official Reports of Parliamentary Debates are generally referred to as Hansard. *See chapter 3.*

8.5.1 Online

Hansard is available free of charge online on the UK Parliament website at:

- www.parliament.uk/business/publications/hansard/commons (Commons)
- www.parliament.uk/business/publications/hansard/lords (Lords)

Figure 8.12 Hansard
Contains Parliamentary information licensed under the Open Parliament Licence v1.0

The format of the House of Lords pages is identical to that of the House of Commons.

Hansard online covers debates in the House of Commons since 1988–89 and the House of Lords since 1994–95. If you need to find earlier debates, then you will have to use the bound paper volumes, although there is much earlier *Hansard* information available online in the Parliamentary Archives.

Two other useful free websites that allow you to search *Hansard* can be found at:

- hansard.millbanksystems.com/
- www.theyworkforyou.com/debates/

8.5.2 In a library

Hansard is published daily and reprinted each week as *Weekly Hansard*. An index to the debates is also published every two weeks.

At the end of each parliamentary session *Hansard* is republished as a set of bound volumes with a corresponding index. These volumes are numbered sequentially—there are approaching 600 of them. *Hansard* is printed in a two-column format, and references to *Hansard* quote column numbers rather than page numbers. If you have a volume and column number, it is a simple task to find the extract you require in the printed volume.

 Practical exercise

Try to find the debates in both the House of Commons and the House of Lords leading to the enactment of the Computer Misuse Act 1990 and the Hunting Act 2004.

 Self-test questions

Having completed this chapter, use your research skills to attempt the following more challenging research questions involving books, journals, and official publications.

1. What is the Command Paper reference for the Annual Report by the Wales Office that was presented to Parliament in June 2005?

2. Who was the author of an article on the meaning of 'charity' under Bermuda's Charities Act 1978 that was published in *Trusts & Trustees*?

3. On what date did Sir Waldron Smithers ask in Parliament how many cases in the Metropolitan Police area there had been per week in that particular year of 'footpads in London causing grievous bodily harm to citizens'?

4. Who were the Parliamentary Agents responsible for the private Milford Haven Port Authority Bill which received Royal Assent on 7 November 2002?

5. Give the full citation of the article in which Kiron Reid and Clive Walker discussed s 27 of the Northern Ireland (Emergency Provisions) Act 1991.

Answers to the self-test questions can be found on the Online Resource Centre

CHAPTER SUMMARY

Books

- Your own library's catalogue is the first place to start looking for books
- Copac is a free consolidated online catalogue covering the libraries of twenty-seven institutions
- The *Current Law Monthly Digest* and *Current Law Year Book* provide lists of new books published during a specific month or year, although they can be difficult to use

Journals

- The *Cardiff Index to Legal Abbreviations* is a useful free online resource to help you decipher unfamiliar journal abbreviations
- Westlaw UK contains an up-to-date *Legal Journal Index* database
- Lawtel indexes across seventy-two different UK publications
- LexisLibrary indexes around eighty-five journals
- HeinOnline is an American database, with sporadic coverage of major UK journals. It has a good selection of historical material and provides page images of the journals. It also carries *Statutes of the Realm* and the *English Reports*

Official publications

- Most libraries carry a range of official publications in print
- gov.uk is the official free online reference facility for Command Papers containing all from 2005/06 and a selection from 1994 onwards
- UKOP is a commercial service from the Stationery Office. It is the official catalogue of UK official publications from 1980 onwards with the full text of over 30,000 documents
- *House of Commons Parliamentary Papers* is a commercial service with searchable full text and an index for papers since 1801

Bills

- Details of Bills can be found either in the *House of Commons Weekly Information Bulletin* or online via the UK Parliament website

Hansard

- *Hansard* provides a verbatim transcript of all Parliamentary debates
- It is freely available online on the UK Parliament website which also provides comprehensive search facilities
- The online service covers Commons debates from 1988–89 and Lords debates since 1994–95.
- Historic *Hansard* debates can be found at hansard.millbanksystems.com

PART II

Academic legal skills

This part of the book covers the skills that you will need to get to grips with the academic requirements of legal study. It begins by covering some general skills in the first two chapters on study and writing skills. It will then turn to introduce the idea of legal reasoning: that is, it will give you the skills you need to analyze the ways in which judges decide cases. The remaining chapters build on these general skills, focusing on addressing essay questions, tackling dissertations, and handling problem questions. Each of these chapters will demonstrate various ways by which you will be able to strengthen your technique. This part of the book also contains an important chapter which will build your referencing skills and help you to avoid plagiarism. The chapters in this part of the book contain specific research-focused material to give you help with the particular research requirements of essays, dissertations, and problems, whilst recognizing and demonstrating that the research process must always be tailored to the task in hand. Finally this part closes with a chapter covering the skills required to revise effectively and to translate that revision into success in examinations.

9 Study skills

INTRODUCTION

This part of the book, then, starts with a focus on study skills. 'Study skills' is an umbrella term that includes a range of disparate skills that will make the business of being a student and studying law generally easier and more manageable. This chapter covers some of the obvious study skills such as note-taking and time management but it also picks up upon some other less obvious areas where students encounter difficulty, such as getting help from your tutor and forming a supportive study group with other students. Some of these topics could be seen as personal skills rather than study skills but the approach taken in this chapter is to outline ways in which these personal skills contribute to more effective and productive study techniques. Many study skills provide a foundation upon which other, more focused skills, are built. As such, this chapter will make frequent reference to other chapters in this section as it explains, for example, how strong time-management skills can contribute towards the development of an organized revision strategy (chapter 16).

Resist any temptation to dismiss study skills as unimportant or to assume that they are something that you must already possess as you have enjoyed sufficient success in your studies to take you to university. Study skills are important as they underpin the whole process of learning a new subject and acquiring knowledge. If you think that you are already good at this, perhaps you are but why would you not want to improve and to find ways to make study an even smoother process? Moreover, study at degree level is bound to be different and require more from you than your previous studies so it is important to adapt and develop your existing skills to ensure that you are able to work successfully at this higher level. Finally, study skills should be seen as something that evolves and matures all the time that you study. Hopefully, you will complete your degree not only with a comprehensive mastery of the law but also with an increased confidence in your ability to engage in self-supported independent study.

LEARNING OUTCOMES

After studying this chapter, you will be able to:

- Appreciate the contribution made by personal skills of communication and organization to the evolution of effective study habits and practices
- Recognize the value of lectures and seminars and find ways to gain maximum benefit from these activities
- Develop an efficient and effective method of recording and organizing your notes

- Reflect upon your ability to manage your time and adopt some useful strategies to help you to organize your studies more effectively

- Deal with lecturers in a polite and professional manner and recognize the potential for making study more effective and enjoyable by working with other students

9.1 Studying the law

The first issue to address before focusing on the various skills that you will need to study the law is how the law degree is structured and what sorts of activities you are likely to encounter as part of that degree. Obviously, each university is different and has its own way of delivering the law degree but there are some common factors that can be outlined in this section of the book that will help you to picture the situations in which you will need the various skills covered in this chapter.

9.1.1 Structure of the law degree

One of the difficulties in explaining the structure of the law degree is that this tends to vary between institutions and each university tends to use different terminology to describe the way that the degree is structured.

For example, the question 'what course are you taking?' seems straightforward but in some universities this will mean 'what degree are you taking?' so that the answer would be 'law' whilst in others, a course is one of the components of the law degree so your answer might be 'criminal law'.

In essence, you will be taking a degree (or course or programme) that is made up of smaller units of study (likely to be called modules, units, courses, or subjects) some of which are compulsory and others of which you will select yourself from a range of options available. It is usual for the subjects that you take in the first year to be compulsory and for you to have some level of choice in the second and third years of the degree.

Part of the reason that certain subjects are compulsory is because the Law Society requires that all students taking a qualifying law degree (that is, a law degree that qualifies you to go on to the next stage in becoming a solicitor or barrister) must be competent in certain subjects. These are called core subjects or the foundations of legal knowledge. The seven core subjects are:

- Constitutional and Administrative Law (sometimes called Public Law)
- Contract Law
- Criminal Law
- Equity and Trusts
- European Union Law
- Land Law (sometimes called Property Law)
- Tort Law

These core subjects will be a compulsory part of your law degree. In addition, there may be other subjects that your own university has decided should be a compulsory part of your studies. For example, many law degrees include a compulsory subject that is studied in the first year which covers how the law operates that may be called something like English Legal Systems, English Legal Institutions and Methods or Foundations of Legal Study. Other subjects may also be made compulsory.

There is no single approach to allocating the teaching of these seven subjects across the three (or sometimes four) years of degree study. You might find that your first year is spent learning Criminal Law, Tort Law, Contract Law, and Foundations of English Law whilst your friend who is studying law at a different university has EU Law, Public Law, Contract Law, and Property Law in their first year.

9.1.2 Structure of teaching

Most subjects are taught using a combination of lectures and small group teaching methods. A lecture is a large group session in which all students taking that subject attend together to listen to a lecturer outline principles of that subject. You will have a series of lectures in each subject usually at the rate of one or two each week.

Small group sessions tend to be called either tutorials or seminars (although the term workshops or supervision may also be used). These can range in size from fewer than four up to forty students. The frequency of these sessions will vary according to the practices adopted in each university but it is usual to expect to have a seminar/tutorial every week or every fortnight. Most lecturers will set work that is to be completed in advance of the seminar/tutorial that will be discussed during the session. You will be expected to contribute to this discussion.

In addition to lectures and seminars/tutorials, you will be expected to do a significant amount of private study. Some universities may have other (compulsory or optional) activities which are used to teach the law such as mooting (see chapter 18) or group work projects.

9.1.3 Approaches to assessment

Just as the way that the degree is organized and the way that teaching is structured varies between different universities, you will find that each university also has its own approach to assessment. In some universities, all assessment is by way of an examination (although this is becoming increasingly less common) whilst others use a combination of coursework and examination. Some universities might also use group project work as a means of assessment or a moot (see chapter 18) or an oral presentation (see chapter 17).

The coursework and exam combination is the most usual method of assessment but this still involves a number of variables:

• How many pieces of coursework are required in each subject?

• Do these all count towards your grade for the subject (summative assessment) or are they to allow you to practise and develop your skills (formative assessment)?

• What is the word limit for each piece of coursework?

• How long is the examination?

• How many questions are on the paper and how many do you have to answer?

Different combinations of these variables mean that two students taking contract law in their first year at different universities could face vastly different approaches to assessment. For example, one student could have two pieces of 2,000 word coursework and a three-hour exam with a choice of three questions from six whilst the other could have one piece of 1,500 word coursework with a two-hour exam with a choice of two from ten questions.

Table 9.1 Assessment objectives

	Criminal Law	Contract	English Legal System	Constitutional and Administrative Law
Deadline	(1) 12 December (2) 7 February	9 January	(1) 31 October (2) 23 January (3) 13 March	27 March
Details	(1) 1,500 word essay (2) 1,500 word problem question	2,000 word essay	(1) 500 word case commentary (2) 500 word project summary (3) 2,500 word group project	2,500 word essay
Exam dates	4 May	12 May	1 May	22 May
Details	Four essays or problem questions from a choice of eight. Three hour exam.	One compulsory essay and two problem questions from a choice of four. Two hour exam.	Ten short answer questions and one essay from a choice of three. Two hour exam.	Three essays or problem questions from a choice of eight. Three hour exam.

This demonstrates how difficult it is to make generalizations about what any student is likely to encounter as there is so much scope for variation between different universities. The main point to remember is that you should find out at the start of the year what form of assessment you will be facing in all of your subjects so that you are clear about what you need to achieve and when it has to be done. This is a crucial part of planning your workload and managing your time. It is a good idea to record key information about assessment on a grid and keep it somewhere visible to remind you of your objectives (see Table 9.1).

Once you have an idea of the way that the law degree is structured in your own institution and have some knowledge of the methods of teaching that you will encounter and the timing and requirements of assessment, you will be able to think about what skills are needed to negotiate the requirements of the degree successfully.

9.2 Lectures

Students tend to like lectures. Lectures involve the unidirectional communication of information from lecturer to student, they usually involve the circulation of a handout with the key points noted upon it and/or some form of PowerPoint presentation and, unlike seminars or tutorials, lectures involve minimal risk that participation from the student will be required (unless your lecturer favours the Socratic method in which questions are directed at students during the lecture but this is not a popular method of lecturing in this country). Some lecturers use electronic response systems as a means of stimulating some student interaction in large group teaching. In essence, students tend to view lectures as a relatively effortless method of learning as little more seems to be required than attending, listening,

1. At the lecture
Listen, think and note what seems to be the main points made by the lecturer. Check the handout and supplement this with your own notes rather than rewriting what is provided. Highlight anything that the lecturer identifies as a particularly important point.

2. After the lecture
Read through your notes to ensure that they make sense and that they are complete. Make a list of key cases that you need to read, key commentators whose views you need to discover and note anything that puzzles you as an issue to follow up in your own reading.

3. Before the next lecture
Find the relevant chapter in your textbook that covers the material covered in the previous lecture and use this to supplement and expand your lecture notes. Read cases and articles to gain a greater depth of understanding. If possible, glance over the subject matter of the next lecture so that you have a chance to think about how this links to the material that you have already covered.

Figure 9.1 Three-stage learning process

and writing notes. Is this view correct or is there more benefit to be gained from a lecture by taking a different approach?

This passive approach to lectures tends to limit their potential value. You may leave with a set of notes that summarizes the topic covered but a more active approach that involves some prior reading and more work after the lecture would enable you to make the most of the information contained in the lecture by situating it within the broad subject of study and improving your depth of knowledge of the topic. One way of doing this is to view the actual lecture as the middle slice of a three-stage learning process as Figure 9.1 demonstrates.

By adopting an approach that uses the content of the lecture as the foundation of more detailed study, you will gain a more complete and comprehensive understanding of the topic than if you rely on lecture notes as the only source of information. This is particularly important as lecturers tend to view lectures as an opportunity to present partial rather than complete information about a topic. There are three dominant schools of thought amongst lecturers regarding the purpose of a lecture and the level of detail that should be provided:

1. To outline the basic aspects of a topic in order to provide students with a foundation of knowledge upon which to build by undertaking tutorial preparation and independent reading

2. To cover an aspect of the topic in an engaging manner in order to capture the interest of the students and encourage them to carry out thorough reading on the topic

3. To build upon basic knowledge acquired through private study undertaken prior to the lecture and to explain complex concepts that the students will have encountered in their reading as the basis for more advanced private study

These three views have one thing in common which is that all share an assumption that students will supplement the information communicated in the lecture with their own reading.

Each of the three approaches is based on the provision of incomplete information in the lecture:

1. This approach provides a complete overview of the topic but at a very basic level so the lecturer expects that you will add depth and detail with your own reading

2. This approach covers only one or two aspects of the topic in depth in the expectation that students will cover the other issues in the same level of depth as private study

3. This approach is predicated on the assumption that students have covered the basic aspects of the topic in their own reading and will go on to read about the topic in more depth after the lecture

As no lecturer is trying to give you complete information, it would be foolish to view your lecture notes as all you need to know about a topic.

Another common theme is that all three approaches see the lecture as based on the communication of information to the audience. Whichever of the views listed earlier are held by your lecturer, they are agreed that they are telling you something in the lecture that they think that you need to know. If the job of the lecturer is to give out information, it must be the task of the student to receive it but what does this suggest about the most effective approach to lectures for students in terms of recording the information provided by the lecturer?

9.2.1 Methods of recording information

The majority of students attend lectures intending to make notes. This raises two questions: what method of recording information is most effective and what points from the lecture should be recorded?

For most students, handwritten notes seem to be the preferred method of recording information although the number of students who type directly into their laptop or tablet computer in lectures is increasing. Taking notes by hand offers a great deal of flexibility. You can draw diagrams, use arrows to show linking concepts and even scribble a picture down if it helps you to capture the essential points being made (students often find that simple pictures help them to remember the facts of cases: you will find more on this in relation to revision techniques in chapter 16).

Different note-taking strategies work for different people. Many students adopt a traditional linear approach to note-taking that records the information in words and sentences as it is presented, sometimes using headings and subheadings to identify particular topics. However, consider alternative techniques such as flow diagrams and arrows (excellent for those who like to see the logical relationships between different points) or mind maps (suited to students who have strong visualization skills). You will find examples of each of these methods in the section on note-taking later in the chapter. Whichever approach you take, remember that not every word spoken by the lecturer should be recorded in your notes.

 Practical exercise

 Watch the video clip of the lecture on the Online Resource Centre and take notes.

Compare your notes to the three examples of notes taken from the lecture that are also on the Online Resource Centre and see whether you feel that they are more or less useful than those that you took. Which of the three sets of notes do you prefer? Think about why this is the case and consider whether there are any techniques that you could use to improve your own approach to note-taking during lectures.

Using a laptop or tablet to make notes offers advantages in terms of speed, as most people can type faster than they can write by hand, and also ensures that your notes are legible. There is less scope for the use of visual note-taking strategies, however, so notes taken electronically tend to use words rather than images and you might want to bear this in mind if your lecturer uses diagrams or charts.

Some students like to make a recording of the lectures. This, they reason, means that they do not have to write any notes at all as they can simply take notes from the recording at a later date. However, you need to bear in mind that some lecturers do not like having their lectures recorded and that some institutions have a 'no recording without prior permission' policy that is relaxed only for students with a specific learning need that makes recording a necessity. If you would like to record the lecture, investigate the policy at your institution and always approach each individual lecturer and seek permission.

You should also question whether recording is actually very useful. Most students who record lectures transcribe the recording into a set of written notes. This will produce a set of notes that are more detailed than those that would have been taken at the time but that does not necessarily mean that they are more useful, particularly given the level of repetition often involved in lectures as the lecturer rewords and repeats the same point to ensure that it is understood. Students who record lectures tend to sit without writing in the lecture itself and then, when students who took written notes during the lecture are following up on key points and engaging in further reading, the student who recorded the lecture is still producing their first set of notes: a process which tends to take far longer than the duration of the lecture itself. Obviously, making a recording of the lecture is a matter of choice for the individual (within the constraints of the university's policy and lecturer's preferences) but most students who start by doing this tend to realize quite quickly that it is not the most effective approach and abandon it in favour of scribbling away in the lecture.

9.2.2 Asking questions in lectures

Lecturers will vary in terms of how receptive they are to being asked questions about the substance of the topic during lectures. It is usual for the lecturer to have a clear plan of the information that is to be covered in that session so dealing with questions can interfere with that plan and lead to insufficient time to deal with the material that needs to be covered. Some lecturers, however, are perfectly amenable to being asked questions in lectures and will usually tell you this at the start of the course.

However, as the main aim of the lecture is to transmit information, it is essential that the audience are able to hear and understand, so it is perfectly acceptable to ask questions that relate to these sorts of issues even if the lecturer has made it clear that they do not usually welcome questions:

- I'm afraid I didn't catch that last point, could you repeat it?
- Could you please speak more slowly; I'm finding it difficult to keep up?
- Could you please speak up a bit; it's hard to hear at the back?
- I didn't understand that point, could you explain it again?
- I'm struggling to understand this. Do you have an example that might make it clearer?

These suggestions demonstrate an effective way to phrase the question by combining the request with the explanation for its existence; this is generally viewed as a softer approach than a request on its own. If the request is for elaboration rather than repetition or a change of speed/volume, you may find that the lecturer responds by telling you to bring up the

Table 9.2 Tips for getting value from lectures

DO	DON'T
Listen and think about what the lecturer is saying. It is more important to understand what is said than it is to capture every word in note form.	Write everything that is said without thought. Try to be selective and note only key points. This will make your notes more manageable.
Review your notes after the lecture. Make a note of anything that you do not understand and follow up any points that are not clear to you by using a good text book and supplement your notes with independent reading.	Rely on the lecture to give you all the information that you need about a subject. A lecture gives you a framework of information and you should supplement this with your own reading to build a more complete picture of the subject.
Develop a system of abbreviations to speed up the process of taking notes. Develop a structured approach to note-taking (see section 9.4) to ensure that your notes are organized and easy to use for reference.	Talk to other students during the lecture. It is discourteous (to other students and to the lecturer), it will disrupt the concentration of those around you who are trying to listen and it may even result in your being asked to leave the lecture.
Take paper. It is a mistake to think that there will be enough room for your notes on the handout.	Arrive late, leave early, eat food, read a newspaper, tweet, check Facebook, or text your friends.

question in the seminar, in which case you should make a note of your question so that you remember to do so. Table 9.2 gives some tips for getting value from lectures.

9.3 Seminars and tutorials

Seminars and tutorials are terms used to describe a method of small-group teaching. It is usual for students to be given work to do in advance of the tutorial. This may involve reading a particular case or a section of a textbook and either making notes or answering particular questions. This will often relate to an issue covered in the lecture, thus giving the students an opportunity to explore that issue in greater depth and ask questions or offer opinions about that issue in order to improve their understanding. Unlike lectures, which tend to involve a one-way process of communication from lecturer to student, seminars and tutorials are based upon group communication so that each member of the group should try to make a contribution to the discussion. It is useful to view a small-group session as an opportunity to voice your thoughts about the topic rather than expecting to receive information from the lecturer. Some lecturers allocate a topic to a student and require them to prepare a short presentation on it to be given in the next seminar.

9.3.1 Preparation

You will derive far more benefit from seminars and tutorials if you undertake the required preparation. The background reading will help to familiarize you with the topic and make it more likely that you will understand and be able to contribute to the group discussion whilst answering any questions that have been set will enable you to check your understanding by comparing your answers with those suggested by others in the seminar group.

When you are carrying out the required reading prior to the seminar, make sure that you make a note of any issues that you find difficult. This will enable you to compile a list of questions that you would like answered by the seminar. This does not mean that you need to ask all these questions yourself; it is likely that the answers will emerge as the seminar discussion progresses and other students make comments or ask questions. It can be a useful technique to make a list of numbered questions on a separate sheet of paper and leave a sufficient gap in between each question so that you can make a note of the answer when it comes up in the discussion. This will give you a clear method for recording information so that your seminar notes do not get confused with the problem areas that you have identified and it will also enable you to see at a glance whether all your questions have been answered during the session. If you feel that you lack confidence to contribute to the group discussion by answering a question, you can ask one of the questions that you have noted. Not only will this clarify your understanding, it will help you to feel more involved with the group discussion and this should help you build up your confidence to make more frequent contributions to the debate. This issue is explored in greater detail in the next section.

Preparation for a seminar usually involves a combination of reading and some other activity whether this is answering a series of questions about the reading or writing an answer to a problem question. It is important to actually do the activities as well as the reading. Some students are particularly reluctant to attempt to answer a problem question on the basis that they are not sure about the correct answer. That does not matter; the value of the activity will not be negated by some errors of law and it is only by attempting to tackle the problem that you will be able to identify whether or not you understand the law in question.

One technique that can be useful is to prepare an answer by dividing your paper in half down the middle, noting the points that you are confident about on the left-hand side and those of which you are unsure on the right-hand side. As the answer builds up in the seminar, mark off each correct point and make a note of the correct answer in relation to points where you were not correct. By using this technique, you will have tackled everything and you will be able to see at a glance which points you had answered correctly. It can be very encouraging to see a line of ticks against points that you felt may have been wrong.

9.3.2 Participation

Many students are reluctant to participate in seminar discussion. Students give a range of explanations for this but several of these have a common theme relating to their lack of confidence, either to speak out or about the accuracy of their legal knowledge (see Table 9.3).

These concerns are perfectly natural, particularly at the earlier stages of your studies. Most people are reluctant to put themselves in a position where there is a risk of being wrong in public. One of the most effective ways of bolstering your confidence is with thorough preparation so that the chance of you actually giving an incorrect answer is minimized. It can be useful to volunteer an answer to an easy question at an early stage in the seminar as the initial questions tend to be more straightforward. Not only will it boost your confidence to give a correct answer but it reduces the risk that the lecturer will direct a question towards you when the voluntary contributions start to dwindle as the seminar progresses and the questions get harder.

Table 9.3 Common fears concerning participation in seminars

I'm not confident that I know the right answer.	Many of the other students in the group may feel the same way so at least if you get the wrong answer out of the way, the group as a whole will be closer to finding the correct answer. Anyway, you may be right and, even if you are not, at least you tried.
I don't understand the question so how can I give an answer?	You can't answer a question if you don't understand what it is asking but you can (and should) tell the lecturer that you don't understand the question so that he can explain it to you in a different way. Once you do understand the question, you may realize that you know the answer after all.
I don't like speaking out in front of others in the group.	This is generally linked to a fear of giving the wrong answer but it can be a more general anxiety about speaking in front of others. This is something that you really should try to overcome, particularly if you aim to practise law as this tends to require the ability to express yourself orally as well as on paper. Try volunteering an answer to one of the easier questions that you feel confident to answer. This should help you find your voice.
I've got a question but I don't want to ask it in case I look stupid.	If you don't ask your question, you will never know the answer. In any case, it is extremely likely that other students in the group are stuck on exactly the same point but won't ask for exactly the same reason. Try to be supportive; if someone else asks a question, say 'yes, I was wondering that too' and even that will help you to feel that you've played an active part in the tutorial.
There are some really talkative people in my group and I'm not sure how to involve myself in the discussion.	It can be a problem that a couple of confident students make a great deal of voluntary contribution to discussion which causes less confident students to feel as if they cannot chip in too. Try not to let that stop you making a comment or asking/answering a question because it is your seminar too and you need to make sure that it serves its purpose of strengthening your grasp of the topic. It can be useful to wait for a gap in the discussion to interject or to raise your hand slightly and make eye contact with your lecturer, who will then spot this and draw you into the discussion. If you feel that it is a major problem, raise this with your lecturer, in person or by email, so that they are aware that you want to speak but are a little shy; once they are aware of this, they will be able to ensure that you have a chance to contribute.

Overall, the message with seminars and tutorials is that the more effort that you put into them in terms of preparation and participation, the more value you will derive from attendance. There are always some students who are enthusiastic about making contributions to group discussion and these are the people who are deriving the best value out of the tutorials. Remember, that is it your tutorial too but that you can only claim your share of the value by taking part.

 Practical exercise

Think about your feelings about seminar participation. Do you take part enough (or at all)? What would help you to play a more active role in seminars? Are you more active in some seminars than others? If so, try to identify what factor it is that makes you feel more or less able to speak out: is it the lecturer, the subject, your grasp of the subject, or even the room layout? Reflect upon these questions and try and list three things that (a) encourage and (b) deter your participation. This can be the basis upon which you build to strengthen your level of participation in seminars.

9.3.3 Tips for making the most of seminars and tutorials

- Find out what is expected from you by way of preparation and make sure that you do it to the best of your ability. Students are often deterred because they do not know the answer to the questions that have been set. If you are not sure, at least have a go at answering the questions because it is by trying and getting feedback that we really learn

- Take the materials that you need with you. This should include, as a bare minimum, the questions that you have been set and your own answers to them. You might also want to take your textbook and copies of any additional reading that was set or that you have found. It should go without saying that you take a pen and paper

- Try to participate in the discussion. Although speaking out in seminars might seem daunting, it gets easier and easier the more you do it. Try to answer questions that the tutor asks early on in the seminar if you are nervous as these tend to be easier questions. If there are small group activities set by the lecture as part of the seminar, make sure you try to take part rather than leaving the others in the group to do all the work

- Do not be discouraged if the lecturer appears to disagree with your contribution to the discussion. Lecturers often play devil's advocate to get a discussion going and are simply trying to get someone else in the group to present an opposing view

- Do remember that seminars are an opportunity to engage in discussion with the lecturer and other students in order to strengthen your understanding of the topic. As such, you should go along expecting to speak and listen rather than to write notes. Of course, there will be points that you want to note during the discussion but try not to scribble all the time or you will miss valuable discussion

9.4 Note-taking

Reading and taking notes is a significant part of studying the law. You will take notes in lectures and as part of your preparation for seminars, coursework, and revision as well as in the course of your own private study and reading. In fact, it is likely that a great deal of your time will be spent making notes so it is important that you are able to do so in an effective manner that enables you to make use of your notes when you come to consult them. Some points about note-taking in lectures were covered in section 9.2.1. The sections that follow outline some of the approaches to note-taking that you can use either in lectures or when taking notes from written material. However, before we consider approaches to note-taking, we will spend a few moments considering a crucial question: 'why are you taking notes?'.

9.4.1 Why are you taking notes?

The most important point to remember about note-taking is that you should consider before you write a single word what it is that you are trying to achieve: what is your goal in taking notes? It may sound as if the answer is obvious—'to record the important pieces of information in this lecture, book, article, or case'—but many students report that they find themselves unthinkingly copying large chunks of material out of books without any real thought of why they are doing it. If you give yourself a specific goal then you will be taking notes with a purpose and this should mean that you are able to work more quickly and effectively.

Consider, for example, the common situation in which you are set a chapter of a book to read for a seminar with some questions to answer. Of course, you would want to read the entire chapter but do you make notes on all of it or only sufficient notes to answer the question? Some students prefer to take notes on the whole chapter on the basis that it is only by writing things down that it sticks in their minds whereas others read the entire chapter but only take notes of points that are relevant to the questions asked. The latter approach is an example of focused note-taking as it involves reading the chapter in its entirety but with the purpose of extracting particular pieces of information.

Focused note-taking can work particularly well when reading articles and cases. Many students have said that when they take notes on an article, the end result is a slightly condensed hand-written version of the article. Try to think about what you want from the article:

- Are you interested in new developments in the law?
- Are you looking for arguments to use in an essay?
- Do you want to find out the author's key points for seminar reading?

If you are clear about what it is that you want from the article, it will be easier to find it as you will be reading with a purpose. This will allow you to make focused notes that are more useful to you.

 Practical exercise

Have a look at the article about criminal liability for injuries caused during sports that you will find on the Online Resource Centre. Read through it and make notes imagining that you have one of the following aims in reading the article:

1. To identify key cases for an essay about criminal liability for injuries sustained in the course of sports.

2. To find out the author's views about the relationship between criminal and civil law in relation to sporting injuries for your dissertation.

3. To prepare for a seminar question that asks 'Professor Davies was playing in a staff-against-students football game. James, a final year student, was mocking Professor Davies' performance, calling out "come on grandpa, try and get the ball". Professor Davies tries to tackle James but by the time he made contact the ball had been passed to another player. James fell awkwardly and broke his leg. Professor Davies wants to know whether he may be criminally liable for causing the injury to James'.

 Once you have prepared your notes, have a look at the commentary on the Online Resource Centre.

9.4.2 Recording information

The following examples demonstrate the variation in methods of recording the same information. It is worth experimenting with different approaches to recording your notes to find one that is most effective for the way that you think and organize your ideas.

9.4.2.1 Linear notes

This is the traditional approach to note-taking using blocks of text, often separated by headings or bullet points. Key points can be emphasized by highlighting or underlining.

Although this method is probably still the most widely-used note-taking technique, it does have pitfalls as students do tend to capture every word in lectures and to copy out large chunks from written sources. The imperative to write everything can transform the process into an exercise in hand-writing that results in reams of notes that have very little value. It would be more useful to spend time reading a chapter or article with a view to listing its five or six main points rather than mindlessly copying out every point. If you are taking notes in a lecture, it may be that you cannot distinguish what are the key points at the time (although you should listen out for any clues from your lecturer: 'the leading case in the area' or 'the most important thing to remember'). This is why it is important to review your notes after the lecture (see section 9.4.4).

9.4.2.2 Flow diagram

This approach to recording information seeks to include an indication of the relationship that different points have to each other. You might find it a particularly useful way of noting the elements of an offence. These are generally easier to produce once you have all the information in front of you so might be better suited to note-taking from a text source rather than in a lecture. Of course, you could always produce a flow chart from your lecture notes as part of the review process (see Figure 9.2).

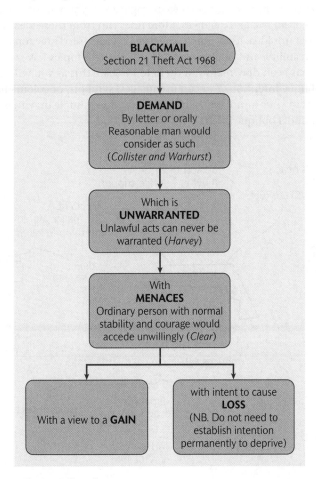

Figure 9.2 Flow diagram

9.4.2.3 Mind maps

Mind maps (also called concept maps and spider diagrams) are a way of recording not just the key words, ideas, and concepts but also the links between them. This reflects the way that memory operates: your mind automatically makes associations between the different pieces of information stored in your memory and mind maps provide a way to depict information that shows these links and associations. Many students report that they find it easier to recall information from mind maps than they do from linear notes because of the visual image involved: in other words, they can picture the shape of the map and then recollect the information that it contains. The ease with which they can be recalled make mind maps an excellent revision tool (see chapter 16) as well as a quick and concise way of recording lecture notes. Mind maps are also useful for planning purposes so can be really helpful when brainstorming ideas to include in an essay (see chapter 13).

There is software available that will help you to produce mind maps but it is very simple to do using a pen and paper. Simply draw a shape in the centre of a piece of paper and write the name of the topic in it. Many students use a rectangle or circle as their central shape but some students like to use shapes that reflect the nature of the topic: in the example in Figure 9.3, you will see that a gun has been used as the topic is murder. As each major theme emerges, draw a line that runs from the central shape and write the name of the theme at the end of the line. Repeat this for other major themes: in Figure 9.3, you will see that the three 'big' ideas are *actus reus*, *mens rea*, and defences. More lines run from these ideas to create links to particular aspects of this idea: for example, defences divides into three topics: loss of control, diminished responsibility, and suicide pacts. If any of these topics have their own separate mind map, a box has been drawn around them to indicate this as you will see in relation to causation, and oblique intention. You can use images, symbols, or colours to help points to stand out and stick in your mind. For example, you will see simple drawings accompany the case names listed under oblique intention.

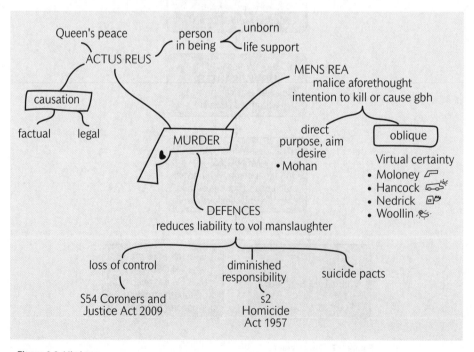

Figure 9.3 Mind map

9.4.3 Making useful notes

Whatever approach to note-taking you adopt, the most important thing to remember is that they should be useful to you. The main purpose of making notes is to give you a record of important information so that you can refer to it in the future. This means that you need to be able to understand what you have written.

Many students think that this means that their notes need to be tidy. A significant number of students spend time after the lectures rewriting their notes so that they are neat. This is not really a good use of time, especially as students report that rewriting their notes tends to take longer than the one hour of the original lecture. The time spent copying out notes that are already perfectly legible if a little untidy could be used in looking up some of the references from the lecture or preparing for a seminar.

Students often think that they need to write everything down in the lecture but this is not really the case. Lecturers tend to repeat the same point more than once as this helps to ensure that everyone understands what has been said so if you write everything your notes could be quite repetitive.

Have a look at the two examples of note-taking in Figure 9.4 and Figure 9.5. They are notes of the same evidence lecture which discussed s 80 of the Police and Criminal Evidence Act 1984 (PACE) and both use a linear approach to note-taking but they are very different.

Can you see that the first set of notes contains far more words but that both contain largely the same information? Which set do you find easier to use? Looking at both sets of notes, try and find the exceptions to s 80. It is likely that you found the information more quickly in the second set of notes because the information was not hidden in amongst a mass of words. It is not just the spacing of words that makes the second example a better set of notes: have a look for some of these features and think about how you can use them to improve your approach to note-taking.

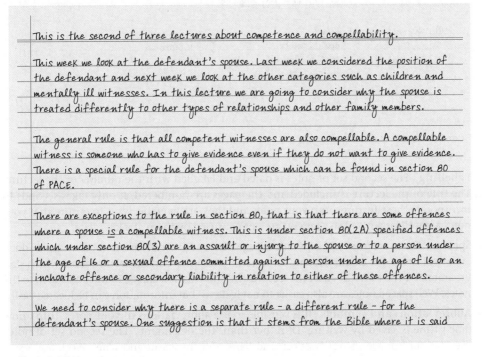

This is the second of three lectures about competence and compellability.

This week we look at the defendant's spouse. Last week we considered the position of the defendant and next week we look at the other categories such as children and mentally ill witnesses. In this lecture we are going to consider why the spouse is treated differently to other types of relationships and other family members.

The general rule is that all competent witnesses are also compellable. A compellable witness is someone who has to give evidence even if they do not want to give evidence. There is a special rule for the defendant's spouse which can be found in section 80 of PACE.

There are exceptions to the rule in section 80, that is that there are some offences where a spouse is a compellable witness. This is under section 80(2A) specified offences which under section 80(3) are an assault or injury to the spouse or to a person under the age of 16 or a sexual offence committed against a person under the age of 16 or an inchoate offence or secondary liability in relation to either of these offences.

We need to consider why there is a separate rule - a different rule - for the defendant's spouse. One suggestion is that it stems from the Bible where it is said

Figure 9.4 Evidence lecture notes

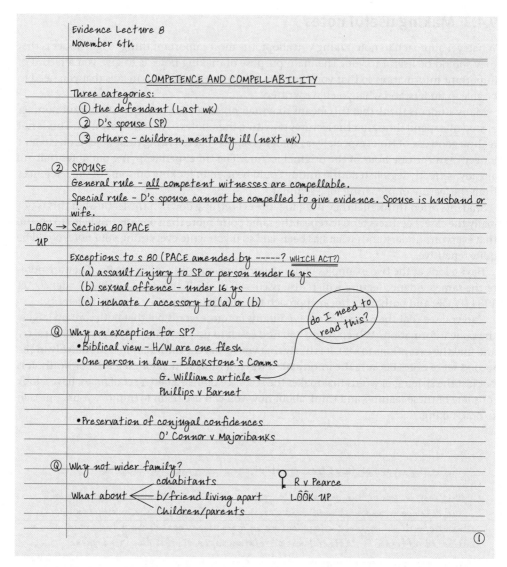

Figure 9.5 Alternative evidence lecture notes

- **Labelling**. The second set of notes is dated and labelled with the number of the lecture. The title of the lecture is included and the pages are numbered. It only takes seconds to incorporate these features into your notes and they are valuable ways to ensure that your notes are well-organized so that you are not confused by them at a later date.

- **Spacing**. There are plenty of gaps on the page where additional information could be added after the lecture. For example, some information was missed in the lecture about which statute amended s 80 of PACE. After the lecture, this information can be found and added to the notes. Well spaced notes are also easier to navigate so that information can be located easily.

- **Abbreviations and symbols**. It is sensible to use abbreviations in your notes: think how much time is saved by writing 'D' rather than 'the defendant'. The second set of notes uses 'SP' for 'spouse', 's' for 'section' and 'H/W' for 'husband and wife'. Work out a system of abbreviations to use in your notes, making sure that you can remember what each abbreviation means and never use the same letter or symbol to mean more than one thing. Can you imagine the confusion caused by a student who used the letter 'T' to stand for trust, trustee, and testator in a single set of notes? You can use symbols as well as letters: see how the second set of notes uses an outline of a key to symbolize an important (key) case.

- **Annotation**. It can be a good idea to add notes to remind yourself of points that occurred to you when you were writing your notes. This might be a reminder to look up the wording of a statutory provision or to read a case that seemed to be particularly important. You might want to highlight any points that you did not understand so that you can remember to pay particular attention to these when reading your textbook to supplement your lecture notes. Questions might occur to you that you want to remember to follow up in seminars or you might notice points that seem particularly relevant to coursework. Equally, the lecturer might say something like 'this is just the sort of issue that might come up in the exam' in which case this is certainly something that you would want to remember. Some students use colour coding rather than annotation which can also be effective but make sure that you can remember what each colour represents as it would be unfortunate if you were reading your notes after the lecture and could not remember whether purple highlighting meant 'important point for coursework essay' or 'don't understand this point'.

9.4.4 Reviewing your notes

The best time to review your lecture notes is immediately following the lecture. However, this may not always be possible. You should try, therefore, to review your notes as soon as possible after the lecture so that the material is still relatively fresh in your mind. It is very hard trying to make sense of a set of notes a few days after they have been written.

Many students think that reviewing their notes simply involves copying them out again neatly. This is not the case: remember, your notes should be useful rather than tidy. You should try to take an active approach to reviewing your notes and there are a number of practical steps you can take to maximize the value that you get from them.

 Practical exercise

After a lecture, swap your set of lecture notes with a friend. Check the accuracy of each other's notes and your understanding of the key points of the lecture. Look to see if your friend uses any note-taking techniques that might be useful to you in future lectures. If there are certain points that were uncertain during the lecture, or if you think that you missed an important point, case, or statute so that your notes are incomplete, follow this up by asking your lecturer or seminar tutor, or by doing your own independent reading.

You could also try reworking your lecture notes using a different method, such as a flow chart or mind map. This can sometimes make their content clearer in your mind. It is also good practice to highlight key points which can later be used to produce summaries for revision purposes. Finally, you should think whether this particular topic relates to previous study topics, or to other courses that you are studying, and begin to recognize themes and relationships.

9.4.5 Organizing your notes

A well-organized set of notes is one in which you can find the information that you want with ease. This means that you will need a system of organization to ensure that you are not left with an ever-increasing pile of disorganized papers which costs you valuable searching time even if you 'know it's in there somewhere'. Spending a little time organizing your notes just after you have finished making them will make life much easier when you come to refer back to your notes for revision.

You should devise a system that works for you. It is a good idea to number your pages. While this may seem unnecessary, remember that files have a tendency to spring open at the most inopportune times, depositing all your work in a random heap. If your pages are numbered, it will make reordering them much simpler. You may like to try using different colours of paper for different subjects, making a contents page for each of your files or using dividers in your files. These are all methods that can be used to greatly improve the accessibility of your notes.

9.5 Working with others

It is important to your success as a student that you are able to interact effectively with others. Communication and other interpersonal skills are extremely attractive to employers so you should take advantage of the opportunities available during your time at university to develop this set of skills. More than this, the ability to work with others could be viewed as a study skill, as proficiency in this area will make a significant contribution to the ease with which you are able to work through difficult areas of your studies.

9.5.1 Lecturers

This section might seem like an unusual topic to include in this chapter as it seems to be tackling an issue of personal communication rather than study skills but the ability to interact effectively with your lecturers can play an important role in your studies. It is also something that many students find difficult. The student/lecturer relationship is not like any other relationship that you will have encountered because the lecturer does not view you in the same way that you were viewed by your teachers at school. It is a difficult relationship in some respects because you are simultaneously an adult who is attending university by choice and a student who is subject to the rules of the institution. As such, you are dealing with your lecturer as an adult which suggests that the relationship is one of equals but you are nonetheless subject to their authority as they are obliged to enforce certain rules and to follow university procedures. To this extent, the relationship is not equal and, in any case, it is not quite the same as any relationship you will have encountered previously and that can create difficulties for the student. This difficulty is exacerbated by the fact that there is a lack of uniformity of approach amongst lecturers, so it is no easy matter to work out the best approach to dealing with them.

9.5.1.1 Form of address

One area where this is immediately apparent is in the tricky issue of what mode of address to adopt with your lecturer. Do they like to be addressed by their title and surname (Professor Macdonald) or by their first name (Elizabeth)? Many lecturers adopt the 'equals/adults' approach and encourage students to address them by their first name whilst other lecturers prefer a more formal approach and like to be addressed by their title and surname. Some institutions have a policy on this whilst others leave it to the individual (the lecturer, not the student) as a matter of personal choice. A good rule of thumb is to err on the side of formality initially using the lecturer's title and surname; if your lecturer prefers to be addressed by their first name, they will soon let you know.

9.5.1.2 Email etiquette

It does not matter how informal your language when emailing your friends, your email to your lecturer should be constructed in a more formal manner. This should go without saying but it is surprising how many students send incomprehensible or inappropriate emails to their lecturers. One of the authors once received an email which read:

> Hello. I want a place on the minibus. Anyway, cheers.

This is not good practice.

- **Salutation:** do not just start writing but preface your email with a salutation such as Dear Professor Jones or by their first name if that is how you would address them in person. Students often start their emails without a salutation when they do not know what to call the lecturer, but this is no reason to be impolite so use their title and surname if you are uncertain (not title, first name and surname). Make sure that you use the correct title; this will not be difficult for you to find out—look on the University website if you are not sure—and it is only courteous to take the trouble to use the correct form of address.

- **Identify yourself:** do not assume that they know who you are just because you know them. Lecturers see a large number of students and it is difficult to keep up with names and faces, so explaining who you are will smooth your communications along. Something like 'I am one of your personal tutees' or 'I am in your tort law seminar on Thursday morning' will suffice.

- **Use clear and concise language:** the lecturer has to understand your communication so using abbreviations or text-speak may hamper this. Equally, rambling on in excess detail may blur the content of your email. Think about what it is you want to achieve—an appointment, advice on course content, an extension for an essay, to participate in an extra-curricular activity—and make sure that this is made clear in the email.

- **Be polite:** again, this should go without saying but you should not send an email that is offensive or abrasive even if you are very upset.

- **End with your name:** many students, having logged in using their university user name, think that this will suffice to identify them but the lecturer is likely to have no idea who you are if they see W8381325 under sender details and is unlikely to have the means of finding out easily so it makes sense to add your name at the end of the email.

If you followed this advice, the earlier email would read:

> Dear Professor Smith, I was in the lecture today when you said that there were still places available on the minibus to attend the Law Fair. I would be grateful if you could please reserve a place for me. Thank you, Lucy (Harris)—from your Friday 5 p.m. contract tutorial.

9.5.1.3 Office hours

Institutional practice on office hours various enormously but it is usual for lecturers to set aside a period of time each week to see students. This may be by appointment, in which case you will have to sign up using the list provided on the door or email to book a time (giving the lecturer some indication of the nature of your problem so that they can work out how long to allocate to you) or on a 'drop in' or 'open door' basis which means that students can turn up without an appointment. The open door system is less formal but it does mean that you may have to wait if another student is already inside with the lecturer. If this is the case, wait patiently; it is extremely rude to keep banging on the door when you are aware that people are inside having a meeting. Equally, if you make an appointment, it would be rude and selfish (other people might have wanted it) not to keep it. If you are delayed or cannot attend, you should contact the lecturer to explain and apologize.

Do make use of office hours to go and see your lecturers. Most lecturers spend the entire time waiting for someone to turn up so do not feel that you are being a nuisance or taking up their time. Office hours are allocated so that students can go and ask questions, so do take advantage of this. However, you should not assume that lecturers will be free to see you outside the allocated hours and it is also not reasonable to assume that they have to see you because they are in their office and you want to see them.

9.5.2 Students

It is likely that you will need to work collaboratively with other students at some point during your studies. This may be a voluntary decision based upon a shared enthusiasm for mooting or a desire to share the work involved in revision or it may be imposed upon you by a require-ment that you produce a presentation or an essay as a group. The ability to work effectively with other people is also important, owing to the value placed upon it by prospective employ-ers, so it is worth devoting some time to the development of team-work skills, both in a work and leisure context.

9.5.2.1 Compulsory group work

Many institutions, conscious of the emphasis placed upon the ability to work as part of a team by employers, create group activities that form a compulsory, sometimes assessed, part of the syllabus of a particular module. It is also becoming increasingly common for one of the first-year subjects to involve a compulsory moot. It is also not unusual for compulsory group activities to allocate students to a group rather than allowing the groups to be self-selecting. Students tend to dislike the latter situation as it involves working with a different group of people who they may not know or may dislike. However, the ability to work effectively alongside a whole range of people is an important one, hence the popularity of this strategy.

If you have free choice and agree to work with your friends, it can be useful to establish boundaries for their tasks. In other words, try not to let your working arrangement interfere with your social relationships, otherwise there is a risk that acrimony will arise on a personal level if the working relationship does not run smoothly. It can be very difficult to work with your friends as resolving disputes and dealing with unequal contributions to the task can be challenging. These issues, of course, can arise when working with strangers but at least there is no existing friendship at stake if all does not go according to plan.

A first meeting that establishes ground rules can be a valuable way to avoid conflict. There is not usually any need to elect a group leader; in fact, doing so tends to create more problems than it resolves. The sorts of ground rules that will be useful involve the frequency and dura-tion of meetings, the need for each person to complete any task that they undertake, and the importance of good communication between group members.

Ensure that everybody is clear about what the group's goal is and when it needs to be achieved. The task can then be sliced into segments, allocated to individual group members, and agreement reached about what should be achieved by the next meeting.

9.5.2.2 Study groups

Working with others can be a fantastic way to strengthen your own performance so it is worth-while to consider forming a study group with other students. A group with between four and six members seems to be the most effective but smaller or larger groups can also work; a great deal depends on the personality of the group members and their contribution to the group.

Discussions with others can really help to clarify your own ideas and understanding. The most effective way to test whether you truly understand a particular concept is to explain it to someone else and ask them to report back to you what they have grasped as a result of your explanation. It can be a useful way of generating ideas or sharing the workload; for example, each group member undertakes to find one article of relevance to a forthcoming essay and summarize it for the group. Discussion can also help to fix information in your mind, making group work of particular value at revision time.

You will find a range of suggestions for group activities that will aid revision in chapter 16.

Many students report difficulties in getting started in writing coursework because they have done some research but they are not sure if they have understood the material that they have read or interpreted the requirements of the question correctly. This can be a real problem, particularly if it causes you to delay the start of writing so long that you end up having to rush the work and submit it in a less than satisfactory state. Group work can help here. A brainstorming session that analyzes an essay title or unpicks the facts of a problem question can give you confidence to tackle the question. Be sure that you do not take collaboration too far though; preliminary discussion is fine but you must produce your answer independently or there is a risk that you will be vulnerable to accusations of plagiarism.

You will find more detailed discussion of plagiarism in chapter 12.

9.6 Time management

For those of you that have come to university directly from school, you will quickly discover that university life is very different from school life: there is a great deal more freedom. Therefore, although this freedom might seem liberating at first, you now have to take responsibility for your learning. You must self-manage your studies and research the topics yourself. Such autonomous learning requires good time management and self-discipline, both to meet deadlines and to make sure you do not become overloaded or stressed in the process.

9.6.1 Planning

There are a range of planning techniques that you can use in order to manage your time more effectively. This section will outline one simple method of planning, but you should feel free to adapt it to your own particular way of learning. Effective planning requires some knowledge of the way in which you work—this is a very personal thing. It should also be an iterative process. The first time you work through the planning cycle, you may not know how long certain things will take. However, it is still better to have some sort of plan based on best guesses rather than no plan at all.

At the beginning of the academic year, consider what is expected from you. Draw up a list of the 'big goals' for the year (see Figure 9.6).

GOALS FOR THIS YEAR

Pass Legal Foundations
Pass Criminal Law
Pass Land Law

Figure 9.6 'Big goals'

GOALS FOR THIS YEAR		
Pass Legal Foundations		
Pass Criminal Law		
Pass Land Law		
PASS LEGAL FOUNDATIONS	**PASS CRIMINAL LAW**	**PASS LAND LAW**
1. Coursework essay due 1 December	1. Coursework problem questions due 7 December	1. Coursework essay due 1 December
2. Coursework library exercise due 31 January	2. Coursework essay due 15 January	2. Coursework problem questions due 15 January
3. Exam sometime in May	3. Exam sometime in May	3. Exam sometime in late May

Figure 9.7 Sub-goals

Once you have established the 'big picture' you will now be able to cascade these goals into a series of smaller goals. In our example, the big goals are passing the courses in Legal Foundations, Criminal Law, and Contract Law. To break these down to the next level, you must become familiar as quickly as possible at the start of each course with any handbooks or guides that are provided for that course. These will give you the requirements of each course, without which you will not be able to plan properly. The next-level goals will most likely be the various assessment components for these courses. Write these down (see Figure 9.7).

You should now draw up a good timetable that shows all your lectures, seminars, free periods for extra study, and basic time out for having a life for yourself beyond study. This will give you an indication of how much spare time you have available week by week to allocate to these particular goals.

Now that you have the individual deadlines set out, and the number of hours you have available, give some thought to the amount of time that you think each of them might take. You should think in terms of actual time spent towards each task rather than in elapsed time: in other words 'I think my criminal law problem questions will take about 15 hours' work' rather than 'I think my criminal law problems will take me a month to get done'. Armed with an idea of the number of hours each task might take and the number of hours you have available per week, you can start to work backwards and decide when you are going to start working towards each goal: whether it is starting a piece of assessed work, or starting revision towards an examinable component. You will probably find that you need to start sooner than you thought—particularly if, as in this example, you find that you have concurrent deadlines!

Finally, you should embed your plan into your weekly timetable so that you can see, for any given week, not only the lectures and seminars you have to attend but what and when you need to do so in furtherance of your goals.

Proper planning will mean that you stand less chance of ending up with a mass of work at the end of the semester. Leaving things until the last minute will make the entire process more stressful and unpleasant. If you, like many students, tend to do most of your work in marathon sessions near deadlines you will also have lost the opportunity to make appropriate use of various study aids and support that might have been available earlier in the semester. Make sure you use all the facilities that are available to you.

You should also ensure that you have allowed time in your plans for each task to do some reading and thinking. Every assignment will always require you to read some material—and if you want to do well, you must not take shortcuts with the recommended reading—so always incorporate reading time into your overall plan. You should plan to go to the library as soon as you can, particularly if the books needed have limited availability. This will give you a better chance of accessing a good selection of books rather than running the risk of important resources being unavailable. You should also build in time for breaks. You will work much more effectively if you allow yourself time to rest—even for a short period—and you will be able to derive the maximum benefit from your non-work time in the knowledge that you have planned to take it and that not working should not affect your ability to complete your task.

By planning so that you finish a little earlier—before the deadline—you can look back at your work and correct any problems. You will also have some flexibility to deal with unforeseen last-minute catastrophes, such as computer crashes and network errors (if you are required to submit your work electronically) or printer failures and empty ink cartridges (for work on paper).

9.6.2 Dealing with procrastination

Research suggests that up to 40 per cent of university students experience procrastination—that is, the constant postponing of work till another day—as a problem.[1] Therefore, if you suffer from procrastination, you are not unusual. The tendency for procrastination in the world of study is hardly surprising. Students are required to meet deadlines for assignments and examinations in an environment which is full of events and activities competing for time and attention, many of which are less stressful than actually getting on with the work. Therefore, procrastination can be a result of the natural inclination to avoid stressful activities: students often spend more time on tasks which they themselves consider to be easy rather than on those that they think will be difficult. Many students struggle with procrastination owing to a lack of time-management or study skills, stress, or being overwhelmed with the volume of work.

However, prolonged procrastination can lead to even more stress since delaying tasks will only allow them to mount up. Proper planning is therefore very important. Dealing with the underlying stressful aspects of the activities can assist in reducing the extent of procrastination.

 Practical exercise

If you are feeling overwhelmed by the amount of work that you have on your 'to do' list, then try making a 'one item' list. In other words, write the one item from your long list on a blank sheet of paper and work on that one item until you are done. This will help you to focus on the one task at hand without being distracted by easier or more enjoyable items on your list.

Even when you have only one task on your 'to do' list, it can still be difficult to start working. Most of the time, not starting seems to be related to fear of poor results or other negative feelings rather than to the actual difficulty of the work. Taking the plunge is the important thing. If you start work when your ideas are fresh, you will keep your sense of purpose, and

1. WK O'Brien, 'Applying the transtheoretical model to academic procrastination' (2002) 62(11-B) Dissertation Abstracts International. Section B: The Sciences and Engineering 5359.

your piece of work will begin to take some shape. This shape will allow you to identify the points you need to work on and—since you started early—you will still have time left to plan your work on these points.

    Practical exercise

Subdivide your single task into smaller steps that you think will take no more than, say, ten minutes to do. Start on one of these ten minute steps. You will often find that once the ten minutes have passed you will have engaged with the bigger task and will be able to continue productively.

9.6.3 Plan, plan, and plan again

As has already been mentioned, time management is meant to be an iterative process; that is, one which needs to be repeated, ideally taking the results of the previous cycle into account. Do not be discouraged if your first plans proved to be wildly over-optimistic. Every time you plan afresh, you will be basing your new plan on your increased experience—you will grow more accurate at estimating how long certain things take and how much rest time you need in order to work effectively. Therefore, as you repeat the planning cycle, your awareness of the particular ways in which you study and use time will improve and so will your ability to make a workable and realistic plan.

This will lead to increased confidence in your planning ability, particularly if you are able to meet the goals that you set for yourself. You must however remain flexible to replanning as you face the day-to-day realities of student life. You will have to learn from your experiences and tweak and adjust your plans.

Time management is not only a study skill; indeed, time management and self-management are transferable skills that may be applied in all aspects of life.

9.7 Personal development planning (PDP)

Personal development planning (which is usually referred to as 'PDP') serves two important purposes. First, it enables you to reflect upon and build your 'employability skills'; that is the set of skills that potential employers are seeking. This will be useful if you are looking for work placements or mini-pupillages, or if you wish to continue your academic studies further by pursuing a postgraduate course of study. Secondly, it will also enable you to improve your academic skills while you are at university. Improved academic skills should help you to study more effectively and achieve improved results.

9.7.1 What is PDP?

In 1997, the Dearing Report[2] recommended that there should be 'a means by which students can monitor, build and reflect upon their personal development'. This

2. The Dearing Report is actually a series of reports commissioned by the UK government into Higher Education in the UK. It is available online at <https://bei.leeds.ac.uk/Partners/NCIHE/>.

recognized the views of some employers that they needed more information to differentiate between growing numbers of graduates over and above basic degree classification and transcript information. PDP was defined by the Quality Assurance Agency for Higher Education (QAA)[3] as: 'a structured and supported process undertaken by an individual to reflect upon their own learning and to plan for their personal, educational and career development'.[4]

The key points within this definition are those of **planning**, **structure**, and **support**.

9.7.2 Planning, action, review, and reflection: the PDP cycle

Effective PDP will involve you in a continuous cycle of activity, which can be depicted as shown in Figure 9.8.

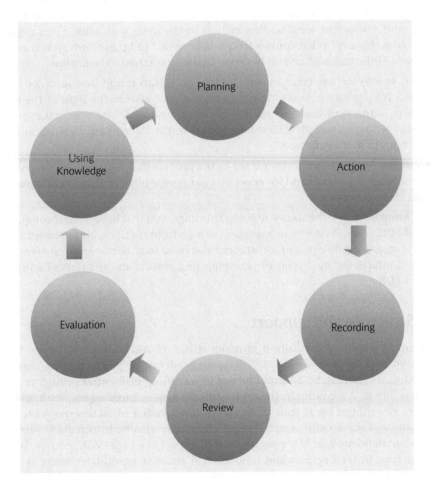

Figure 9.8 The PDP cycle

3.   The body which checks standards in UK higher education institutions.

4.   QAA, *Personal Development Planning: guidance for institutional policy and practice in higher education* (QAA 2009) <http://www.qaa.ac.uk/Publications/InformationAndGuidance/Documents/PDPguide.pdf>

As you can see, there are several stages in the process:

- **Planning**. Planning for PDP purposes requires you to set a list of targets and to work out how you can best achieve them. While this might sound straightforward, you will need to consider your skills and abilities and think about which facets of your legal studies that you are good at, why you are good at them, and whether there are any particular areas that you need to develop. Once you have identified areas for development, think about how you can go about improving them. Do you need more feedback? Are there any training opportunities that your university offers that could be of use to you?

- **Action.** Having identified areas for development, you now need to engage in the process necessary to reach the planned targets. Start taking the steps that you considered useful in the planning stage.

- **Recording.** You should start compiling a set of evidence of the achievements that you have made while putting your plans into action. What are your marks? Are they going up? Is your assessment feedback less critical in the areas with which you might have struggled previously? What courses have you been on? In other words, you should compile a set of information that will help you in the next stage of the process.

- **Review.** So far you have come up with a plan, put it into action, and recorded evidence of how it is progressing. You should now review your plan in the light of the recorded evidence. Is the plan making the difference you wanted? Are you making progress towards the targets you identified for yourself in the light of your own evaluation of your strengths and weaknesses?

- **Evaluation.** This is an important stage in the process that requires you to pass critical judgement upon yourself and to reflect on your review of your plan to evaluate its overall success or otherwise.

- **Using knowledge.** By the time you get to this stage, you will have been through a whole cycle of PDP. You will now be in a position to plan future actions, and to identify if there are new areas for development, or whether you need to enhance existing areas further. This will inform the next stage of your planning process and the start of a brand new cycle of PDP.

9.7.3 Structure and support

The extent to which an institution provides structure and support will vary. You may be required to provide evidence of PDP by an academic or personal tutor throughout your studies. There may be a formal means of recording PDP either online, or in some sort of handbook. Alternatively, the arrangements may be more *ad hoc*, with less formal structure. You should see if your university has a member of staff responsible for PDP within law, and make contact with them. There may also be information provided in your student handbook, or PDP may be covered as part of a Legal Skills course. Whatever structure your university provides (and even if there is very little), there is nothing to stop you going through the PDP process yourself, or within a group of friends, or suggesting that a more formal arrangement might be of benefit to students. All that is required is a desire to improve, self-reliance to take action for your own learning, and the maturity to reflect critically on your own abilities. Practically speaking, evidence of PDP and the ability to describe your own PDP experience is something that may well be of use to you in moving on to the next stage of your legal career, be it vocational or academic.

 CHAPTER SUMMARY

Lectures

- Lectures give a framework of information which should be supplemented by your own reading
- Listen and think instead of writing down everything that is said
- Always seek permission before recording a lecture
- Find out your lecturer's view on responding to questions in lectures and respect it

Seminars and tutorials

- Prepare thoroughly for seminars and tutorials to maximize your benefit
- Make notes of any difficult topics before the seminar and draw up a list of questions
- Participate in seminar discussions as fully as you can

Note-taking

- Try different styles of note-taking—linear, flow diagrams, and mind maps—to see what works best for you
- Always review your notes as soon as you can after a lecture or seminar
- Devise a system of organizing your notes so that you can find them again quickly and easily whenever you need to

Working with others

- Find out how your lecturers prefer to be addressed
- Be polite in email correspondence
- Make the most of office hours but do abide by the system in use at your institution
- Try not to let work arrangements interfere with social arrangements
- Study groups help to clarify your ideas and understanding

Time management

- Establish clear goals
- Try to set a realistic plan to achieve those goals. Remember to include time for yourself, for research, and for unexpected emergencies
- If you are struggling to get started, work on smaller tasks first
- Adjust your plans continuously as you learn by experience

Personal development planning (PDP)

- PDP is a process of reflection, planning and action for personal, education, and career development

- Check whether there is a PDP scheme at your institution and, if so, follow it

- If there is no formal PDP scheme, there is nothing to stop you going through the process yourself or in a group with friends

Writing skills

10

INTRODUCTION

This chapter will outline the elements of good written English with particular emphasis on the way that language is used in academic legal writing. It does not aim to be a complete guide to English usage but a reflection of the issues that students tend to find difficult. You will find sections on language, grammar, and punctuation as well as practical guidance on matters such as selecting quotations and writing in a concise manner so as to keep within the word limit. The material covered in this chapter should be seen as the foundation upon which good essays are built and should be read in conjunction with the guidance provided on writing essays (chapter 13) and answering problem questions (chapter 15). Some of the issues covered will also be useful in terms of examinations but a more complete guide on writing answers in examinations can be found in chapter 16.

The ability to use language, orally and in writing, is one of the key 'tools of the trade' for a lawyer, so it is essential that you are able to use language correctly and prepare precise and accurate written documents. Many cases turn on the interpretation of a particular word or phrase so it is essential that you have the skills to appreciate the implications of the choice of particular words and that you are able to communicate the precise meaning of the law. On a more pragmatic level, you need good writing skills to demonstrate your understanding of the law to your lecturers in your coursework and examinations. This requires that you adopt the styles and conventions of language used in the law. It is a mistake to think that an essay that is accurate in terms of its legal content will succeed irrespective of the language used to express the arguments or the way in which the essay is structured. Content is important but the way that a piece of writing is organized and expressed can be equally fundamental to its success or failure. You would not like this book if it were written in ungrammatical language so that you could not readily make sense of it or if it were so poorly structured that you could not locate the information that you needed. This means that you recognize the value of good writing skills so you should strive to ensure that your own work reaches the standards that you expect in the work of others.

LEARNING OUTCOMES

After studying this chapter, you will be able to:

- Make reasoned choices about the language and written style that you use in the preparation of coursework

- Construct a grammatical sentence that uses words correctly and which communicates your meaning to the marker

- Produce a polished piece of work that is free of common grammatical errors and which uses punctuation correctly

- Create paragraphs that keep a strong focus on the question and which link to each other to produce a flowing line of argument

- Select appropriate quotations to support your argument and integrate these effectively into your essay

- Write within the word limit and produce a piece of work with flawless presentation

10.1 Why are writing skills important?

In August 2008, a judge criticized the CPS solicitor who produced an indictment in a criminal case that was 'littered with errors' including five misspellings of the word 'grievous' and a reference to an offensive weapon 'namely axe' (rather than 'namely an axe').[1] Judge David Paget threw the indictment down, saying:

> It's quite disgraceful. This is supposed to be a centre of excellence. To have an indictment drawn up by some illiterate idiot is just not good enough.

If you think about it, a piece of writing that does not comply with the expected standards and conventions of correct written English suggests one of only two possibilities:

1. The writer cannot use the rules of language, grammar, and punctuation correctly (in which case, they lack sufficient ability in something that is fundamental to the study and practice of the law), or

2. The writer cannot be bothered to correct the mistakes that they have made in their first draft (in which case, they lack the attention to detail and the awareness of the importance of language)

Neither of these is the impression that you want to give to lecturers who are marking your work, to potential employers considering your application, and to members of the profession if you enter into legal practice. As John Redwood MP commented on his blog:[2]

> Many of the [people who have sent CVs for a job] have degrees. They send in CVs which start with similar paragraphs that they have been taught to write. They usually claim to be . . . brilliant communicators . . . The rest of the CV sometimes belies the standard phrases of the opening. Some are unable to write a sentence. There are usually spelling and typing errors – understandable in the rush of everyday communication but glaring in a considered and formal document like a CV. One example produced the following second sentence to the application: 'I fill the experience I have gained in past employment will put me in good persian for this role'.

Unfortunately, some students seem to have gained the erroneous impression that it does not matter how language is used in their coursework (or applications for work placements and training contracts) provided the content is correct. This is not a position that is acceptable in

---

1. ' "Illiterate" worker angers judge' *BBC News Online* (12 August 2008) <http://news.bbc.co.uk/1/hi/england/london/7554857.stm>.
2. Statement by J Redwood MP (Personal blog entry 12 June 2010) <http://www.johnredwoodsdiary.com/?p=6410>.

the law because ability to use language correctly and to express shades of meaning is vitally important, as the following example demonstrates.

A contractual dispute in Canada hinged on the presence of a single comma in one of the clauses.[3] Rogers Communications entered into a contract with Aliant Inc involving the installation of cable onto utility poles across Canada. It was intended that the contract would run for an initial five year period and thereafter for renewable periods of five years. This meant that, at the very least, the contract would run for five years. However, the contract contained a clause which stipulated that the agreement:

> shall continue in force for a period of five years from the date it is made, and thereafter for successive five year terms, unless and until terminated by one year prior notice in writing by either party.

The problem lies in the positioning of the second comma (after the words 'successive five year terms') as this means that the entire contract can be cancelled with one year's notice. If you remove the comma and read the clause again, you will see that it then only gives the parties the right to cancel the contract with one year's notice *after* the original five years has expired. This error in punctuation cost Rogers Communications $2.13m.

As this example illustrates, precision in the use of language and the ability to use grammar and punctuation correctly is important as incorrect usage can alter the meaning of the words that you have used. Remember, it is not enough to write in a way that makes sense to you: what is more important is that your writing makes sense and communicates your precise meaning to the person reading it.

In pragmatic terms, during the course of your studies, you will find that students who can write in a way that fits with the expectations and requirements of the lecturers will achieve greater success in their coursework. This is because you are assessed not solely on your legal knowledge but on your ability to write in a way that is in keeping with the formality and precision of language use within the legal profession.

10.2 Language

Practical exercise

Look at the following two paragraphs which were written by the same student. Which one of these was (a) the introductory paragraph to an essay about the independence of the judiciary and (b) was a section from an email to his mother about his essay?

<table>
<tr><td>

EXAMPLE A

I have to write this essay about the judiciary – you know, judges and the courts and all that. Basically, it is about whether the judiciary is independent enough. Why is it important that they are independent? Yeah, I don't know but I guess that I will do by the end of the essay!

</td><td>

EXAMPLE B

Many commentators state that the independence of the judiciary is a fundamental safeguard against injustice within the legal system. The reasons given for the independence of the judiciary will be explored and a conclusion reached about whether the judiciary can be said to be truly independent.

</td></tr>
</table>

Figure 10.1 Comparison of writing styles

3. 'The case of the million-dollar comma' *OUT-LAW News* (26 October 2006) <http://www.out-law.com/page-7426>.

Hopefully, you will have identified that Example A is the email and Example B is the introduction to the essay. Consider, though, what it was about the way that language is used that enabled you to reach this conclusion: after all, neither of the examples makes explicit reference to an essay or an email and both make largely the same points. If your answer is, as it should be, that Example A uses the informal language of conversation or email whereas Example B uses the more formal legalistic style of writing that is characteristic of an essay then you are already recognizing a very important point: there is a style of writing that is appropriate to an essay and other styles of writing which have their own roles but which should not be used in an essay.

 Have a look at the Online Resource Centre where you will find two further samples of writing. Consider whether you think that they are written in a style that is appropriate for a piece of law coursework. If you think that there are problems, make some suggestions for amending the style so that it is more appropriate and compare your answers with those provided.

It is important that you adopt an appropriate level of formality in your written style. The best way to gauge the appropriate level is to read a good-quality textbook that is written in language that you understand and to emulate that style.

10.2.1 Too formal or too informal?

Some students err on the side of excessive formality, believing this to be appropriate to legal writing, peppering their writing with words such as 'hereinafter' and 'henceforth'. Whilst there is nothing wrong with this as such, there is an increasing move towards the use of plain English within the legal profession, so it can be preferable to use words which are more readily understood. Moreover, using unfamiliar words raises the possibility that they will be misused, which will detract from the polished and professional impression that you are striving to present with your writing.

More frequently, students adopt an informal approach that is conversational in nature and more suited to a diary or an email to friends than a piece of academic writing. For example, there is nothing wrong in grammatical terms with sentences such as '[h]aving talked about the meaning of *x*, we now need to take a look at *y*', but it is nonetheless rather chatty and informal for a piece of coursework.

In essence, the language that is appropriate in informal communications between friends is not the sort of language that should be used in legal writing.

10.2.2 Appropriate legal writing style

As the examples in Figure 10.1 make clear, there is not a constant 'correct' style that can be applied to all forms of written communication. In essence, 'correct' means 'appropriate' so you should strive to develop a written style that is appropriate for communication in academic law, one that is relatively formal and which uses language in an accurate and precise manner. There are a few other matters that require particular consideration before the discussion of language is concluded.

10.2.2.1 Use of the first person

The grammatical first person is a way of referring to the participant role of the speaker or the writer. Accordingly, when a person writes as 'I', they are writing in the first person. This is entirely appropriate in informal communications and in other situations in which it is necessary to express a personal viewpoint but it is not appropriate in objective academic writing and tends not to be welcomed by lecturers. Some students, lacking a grasp of the complexities of English grammar, try to get around this prohibition on writing in the first person by switching to 'we' (first person plural), 'you' (second person singular or plural), or 'one' (third person neutral), not realizing that they are equally unacceptable.

In addition to being an informal writing style, the first person also situates the writer as an authority within the piece of writing: in other words, it makes you the narrator of the essay so that you are expressing your own perspective and views when it would be more appropriate to present the views of writers, judges, and other experts. If you accept that it is never appropriate to write 'I think' or 'I would argue' in your essay, then you will never be tempted to express your own opinion on the state of the law and you will have to resort to repeating the views of more experienced writers and commentators.

If you are accustomed to writing in the first person and struggle to find a form of words to use, then Table 10.1 should give you some ideas for alternative phraseology to get you started.

 Practical exercise

This is an aspect of academic writing that a great many students find difficult, especially if they have an educational background where informal writing was encouraged. Have a look at the following sentences and think about how you would reword them to create a more formal style of writing:

1. We have seen that the postal rule has been criticized by many academic commentators and that there is little judicial support for its continued use. I think that this indicates that the rule has no value in modern contract law and should be dismissed as an anachronism.

2. As the defendant did not suffer a loss of control that came from one of the qualifying triggers, I would conclude that he cannot rely on the defence of loss of control in the Coroners and Justice Act.

3. You could argue that the law in this area is outdated and should not be applied but one must appreciate that an old law is not necessarily a bad law.

 You will find suggested answers on the Online Resource Centre together with an explanation of how the answers were reached.

10.2.2.2 Gender neutral language

It is accepted convention in legal writing to use the masculine word forms to encompass the feminine: Interpretation Act 1978 s 6. In other words, 'he' means 'he or she' and 'his' means

Table 10.1 First person writing and objective alternatives

First person	Objective alternative
In this essay, **I am going to outline** the elements necessary to establish that a defendant is liable for negligence.	**This essay will outline** the elements necessary to establish that a defendant is liable for negligence.
Alternatively, **one could argue** that . . .	Alternatively, **it could be argued** that . . .
In conclusion, **I do not see** any need for reform in this area.	In conclusion, **the majority of writers do not see** a need for reform in this area.

'his or hers'. Some academics frown upon this approach, believing that the prevalence of male-orientated references is exclusionary and inappropriate. This is a matter of personal preference but do be aware of the need not to cause offence in your choice of language. It would be worth checking if your institution, department, or lecturer has any strong views on the subject and adapting your use of language accordingly.

10.2.2.3 Latin

In recent years, there has been a move away from the use of Latin words and phrases within the legal profession. Certain Latin legal terms have been renamed, for example, an order of *certiorari* is now known as a quashing order whilst an *ex parte* application has been renamed an application without notice.

However, there are areas of law in which the continued use of Latin is accepted; the conduct element of a crime is still known as the *actus reus*, for example, whilst it is accepted that phrases such as *res ipsa loquitur* are terms of art with an express legal meaning.

Be aware of the decline in the use of Latin and be sure to check both your textbooks and course materials for the appropriate approach to terminology. If you do have cause to use Latin words or phrases, there is a school of thought that they should always be italicized. However, according to the OSCOLA referencing system (see chapter 12 for more details) words that are in common usage in legal English are not italicized. OSCOLA gives a list of examples, such as ultra vires, stare decisis, obiter dicta, ratio decidendi, a priori, and a fortiori. There is no single correct approach here; check with your lecturers to see if they have a particular preference.

10.2.2.4 Legal words

As you will become increasingly aware as your studies progress, many words in everyday usage also have particular legal meanings that differ significantly from their ordinary dictionary definitions: intention, consideration, assault, nuisance, appropriation, land, property, consent, and negligence, for example. As these words hold a particular legal significance, you should avoid using them in their ordinary sense within the subject area where they have a specialist meaning.

For example, if you write that 'the defendant's assault caused the victim's death', this could be confusing as it will not be clear to your lecturer whether you are using the word in the legal sense or whether you intend the word to have its everyday meaning (Figure 10.2).

To avoid any confusion, especially when it carries the risk that your lecturer will think that you misunderstand the law, it is advisable to find a synonym to use in place of any word that has a clear legal meaning.

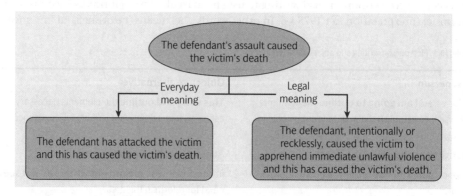

Figure 10.2 Everyday and legal meanings

10.2.2.5 Abbreviations

Some students are very keen to use abbreviations as a means of reducing the overall word count of their coursework but this can be a problem. Not only does the excessive use of abbreviations make a piece of work read more like a set of notes than an essay, it can also be confusing if non-standard abbreviations are used. Look at the following example:

Practical exercise

Read the following extract of text from an essay and see if you can decipher its meaning despite the overuse of abbreviations.

One of the main factors thought to contribute to the tendency of J to return NG verdicts in RTiC is that both D and V are presenting very similar versions of the facts to J. The evidence of D and V may differ only in the smallest details so it becomes difficult for J, even with the guidance of J, to determine which version of the facts is the truth. In such situations, the correct course of action is for J to return a NG verdict as they are not sure of D's guilt BRD but this nonetheless impedes the SOA from achieving its purpose of improving conviction rates in RTiC.

Were you able to work out the subject matter of this writing? Which, if any, abbreviations did you recognize as standard ones used in law? Did you think it was appropriate to use these abbreviations in an essay? The meaning of the abbreviations is noted in the discussion that follows, which will also explain which sorts of abbreviations it is acceptable to use in a piece of coursework.

Some of the abbreviations in the extract are commonly used in law. It is usual for lecturers to refer to the defendant as 'D' and the victim as 'V' in handouts and on lecture slides. However, while such abbreviations will save you time when you are making notes, this does not mean that they should be used in an essay. Remember that your coursework will generally require a more formal written style so it may be sensible to write these words out in full. There are other commonly used abbreviations that you might find useful when taking notes but which should not really find their way into your essay:

- G and NG = guilty and not guilty
- DC, CA, HL, and SC = Divisional Court, Court of Appeal, House of Lords, Supreme Court

You will also see that 'J' is used in the extract. If you found it difficult to work out its meaning, this is because it was used to represent three different things: the jury, the jurors, and the judge. When 'J' is used as an abbreviation in law, it is not used to represent any of these words but is instead a shortened way of referring to the title of a senior judge: 'J' is an abbreviation for 'Mr Justice' so Mummery J refers to Mr Justice Mummery. It is acceptable to use abbreviations in your work to denote the title of a judge:

- Denning J = Mr Justice Denning
- Denning LJ = Lord Justice Denning
- Denning CJ = Lord Chief Justice Denning
- Denning MR = Lord Denning, Master of the Rolls

It is also common practice to abbreviate the names of some statutes. In the extract, the Sexual Offences Act 2003 was written as 'SOA'. It is acceptable to abbreviate statute names in this way provided that the statute is written in full the first time it is mentioned and the abbreviation noted in brackets, e.g. the Police and Criminal Evidence Act 1984 (PACE). It is also acceptable to abbreviate certain other things in this way, for example:

- Crown Prosecution Service (CPS)
- Director of Public Prosecutions (DPP)
- Attorney-General (A-G)
- Anti-social Behaviour Orders (ASBOs)

The earlier extract also uses some non-standard abbreviations. These are essentially abbreviations that the writer has invented in order to reduce the word count of their essay rather than established acronyms used in law. In the example, 'RTiC' is used in place of 'rape trials involving consent' and 'BRD' replaces 'beyond reasonable doubt'. Inventing abbreviations in this way makes life more difficult for your marker, who has to puzzle out what you mean, and may lead to a deduction in marks for poor written style.

10.3 Grammar and punctuation

Good writing is about more than just words on paper: the words need to be arranged in such a way that they make proper sense to the reader. It is grammar and punctuation that transform a collection of words into meaningful sentences that can be understood by the reader. This is a particularly important factor in legal education as the ability to communicate precise and accurate meaning is crucial, and correct grammar and punctuation are central to this. Without grammatical expression and grammatical accuracy, the meaning of words can change as the following two sentences demonstrate:

> The panda eats, shoots and leaves (he has his dinner, kills another panda with his shotgun and moves on to a new territory); or,
> The panda eats shoots and leaves (the diet of the panda is shoots and leaves).[4]

If this seems like a trivial example, remember that the interpretation of statutory provisions can hinge on the meaning of one word or even on the positioning of punctuation; it is often said that Roger Casement was 'hanged on a comma', meaning that his execution was inevitable if he was convicted of the offence of which he was charged. His liability for this offence hinged upon the interpretation of the statute which was, in turn, contingent on the positioning of the comma. The importance of positioning of punctuation has already been seen in the Canadian contract example.

Unfortunately, not all students are able to construct a grammatical and well-punctuated essay by the time they arrive at university. This problem is compounded by the fact that many of these students will be unaware that there is any problem with their grammar and punctuation. You will find that the extent to which lecturers will (a) draw attention to grammatical deficiencies and (b) offer guidance on improvement varies enormously. Some lecturers will not mention problems at all, merely deducting marks for the lack of clarity of expression without giving any indication that there is a problem with grammar and/or punctuation. Some lecturers will comment that the grammar and/or punctuation in the essay was weak or could be strengthened but will not actually correct any inaccuracies. Finally, some lecturers

---

4.   L Truss, *Eats, Shoots and Leaves: the Zero Tolerance Approach to Punctuation* (Profile Books Ltd, London 2003).

will correct every inaccuracy and/or explain the correct approach on your essay so that you can understand the problem and how to rectify it. Although the first approach may seem very unhelpful, it is actually a throwback to the days when students that reached university were, in general, better able to construct a grammatical essay and there was little need for lecturers to comment on this aspect of a student's work.

This is not the place to engage in a discussion of the perceived decline in educational standards or the response of university lecturers to this problem. The aim of this chapter is to emphasize the importance of good written skills such as grammar and punctuation and to provide a practical guide to strengthening these skills.

10.3.1 Spotting the problem

As discussed earlier, not all lecturers will point out the problem so you will need to be alert for the signs that there may be a problem with your grammar and/or punctuation.

Poor grades provide a good indication that *something* is wrong. If you are receiving marks that are lower than you would hope or expect (remembering to be realistic), then it may be that you are not expressing yourself with sufficient clarity or precision. Poor grammar and punctuation frequently result in a lack of clarity as the words that you have written simply do not do the job that you want them to do.

If your marks are less than you hoped, have a close look at the feedback that has been provided, both on the feedback sheet and the script itself. Are there any comments, however vague, about the quality of your written style? Comments on the script such as 'lacks clarity', 'poorly expressed', 'what does this mean?', or 'vague' can also indicate that the problem is not with your understanding of the law but with the way that it is expressed. Some lecturers will simply underline phrases that they cannot understand and put a question mark in the margin whilst others will correct errors so do keep a look out for changes that have been made on your essay by your lecturer.

Some feedback sheets have categories of skills that the lecturers can tick to indicate your level of competence. The categories used will obviously vary between institutions but there will usually be some that refer to the technical aspects of the construction of the essay as well as to the use of the law itself. Have a look at the feedback form when you receive it. Do any of the categories refer to written style generally or to grammar or punctuation in particular? Anything less than 'good' could indicate a problem as 'satisfactory' is another way of saying 'could be improved'.

10.3.2 Getting help

Once you are aware that there is a problem, finding sources of assistance with strengthening your grammar and punctuation should be straightforward. Even if they cannot help you themselves, your lecturer or your personal tutor will be able to point you towards sources of assistance, whether this is a specialist skills adviser in your department or a study skills or student support service elsewhere in the university. You should not hesitate to seek help if you (or the person marking your work) feel that it is necessary; many writing problems result from a lack of understanding of the correct way to go about things and these can be corrected very easily with a little specialist assistance. Although the rules of grammar may seem complex and impenetrable, once they have been explained to you clearly and you have examples of correct usage, you will probably find that it is not difficult to adjust your written style to take these rules into account.

An alternative source of assistance is one of the many works on correct English usage. These can be found in the library and are increasingly available online. You could, of course, purchase a concise guide to English grammar and make reference to it as you write an essay.

A final, and frequently overlooked, source of guidance is the written work of others. Whether this is the work of your fellow students or the work of experienced academics in articles and textbooks, you should scrutinize the way that others write in order to gain experience of good writing practice. It is often the case that students who read a great deal have a better grasp of grammar and punctuation as they acquire an appreciation of the rules by virtue of encountering them more frequently in the writing of others. Ideally, you should aim to improve your written style on each piece of work that you submit and one really effective way of doing this is to evaluate the way that others write with a view to adopting examples of good practice that you encounter.

10.3.3 Varying approaches to grammar

One of the difficulties with choosing an appropriate approach to language is that there is a difference of opinion regarding the application of the rules. Some academics consider that particular rules of grammar are outdated or overly pedantic whilst others fear that failure to adhere to these rules is part of a larger picture of declining standards of literacy. This book does not intend to engage in that debate but rather to offer students advice on how to avoid falling foul of the debate.

It seems that those with a preference for traditional approaches to grammar are likely to take issue with its absence whereas it is unlikely that a lecturer with a more relaxed attitude is going to correct your work with a comment 'this is not incorrect but a little bit out-of-date'! For example, the paragraph below would offend a lecturer with traditional views about grammatical written English:

> There may be a difference of opinion as to the relevance of certain rules of grammar in today's society. But, in order to ensure that nobody is offended by your writing, it is a sensible idea to adhere to the correct approach wherever possible.

However, if this paragraph was presented as a single sentence (using 'but' in the traditionally correct manner), it is unlikely that anybody would object. Lecturers who take a more progressive approach to grammar tend to believe that certain of the rules of grammar are unnecessary but they do not tend to intervene if students use them. This is because the modern view is not that the traditional approach is incorrect, just that it is outdated. This is contrary to the traditional viewpoint, which holds that the modern stance is inaccurate, hence should be corrected.

It is for this reason that it is advisable to take a formal approach to grammar wherever possible in order to avoid any question of incorrect usage.

10.3.4 Foundations of grammatical writing

Although there is not scope to provide a detailed explanation of the rules of grammar in this book, the following is a summary of some of the basic principles that you need to be able to put into practice if you want to produce a competent piece of writing in law.

10.3.4.1 Basic word types

It is a good idea to ensure that you are familiar with the terminology used to describe the construction of a grammatical sentence and that you understand what each of the words and phrases that you have written contributes to the final sentence (see Table 10.2).

Table 10.2 Basic word types

Term	Explanation	Example
Noun	A word which names a person, thing, or object. It is usually preceded by 'a', 'an', or 'the'. Proper nouns describe actual names of people and places. Only proper nouns start with capital letters irrespective of where they appear in the sentence.	The **TRIAL** took place before a **JUDGE** and a **JURY.** The **APPEAL** was heard by **LORD JUSTICE BEARD** in the **HIGH COURT**.
Pronoun	A word that is used in place of a noun to avoid repetition: he, she, it, him, her, it, we, they, them.	The defendant entered a plea when **HE** appeared in court. The jury did not look at **HIM** when **THEY** entered the court.
Adjective	A word that describes a noun.	The **SERIOUS** case was heard by a **LENIENT** judge.
Verb	A word that describes an action (doing something) or a state (being something). It changes tense to indicate when things happened.	The jury **BELIEVED** the defendant's version of events. The judge **FROWNS** at the jury as he **THINKS** that the defendant **HAD LIED.**
Adverb	A word that describes how an action is done. It describes how the action (verb) is carried out. Adverbs also explain when or where something happened.	The client listened **CAREFULLY** to the solicitor's advice when they met **YESTERDAY**.
Conjunction	A word that joins two parts of a sentence together: because, and, but, so, or, when.	The solicitor hurried to court **BECAUSE** he was running late. The judge frowned at the solicitor **WHEN** he arrived.
Preposition	A word that links a noun, pronoun, or noun phrase to the rest of the sentence, usually in terms of space or time: to, with, in, through, by, under, at, for, from, of, under, over.	The defendant read a book **DURING** the trial. The jury searched **FOR** the truth **OF** the matter.
Article	A word that introduces the noun. It can be a definite article (*the* judge) or an indefinite article (*a* judge).	**THE** defendant wanted to hit **A** policeman (indefinite: he wants to hit any policeman) *or* **THE** defendant wanted to hit **THE** policeman after he was arrested (definite: he wants to hit a particular policeman).

Practical exercise

It will help you to construct more grammatical sentences if you become familiar with the types of words that comprise a sentence and how they relate to each other. Have a look at the following examples and use the explanations provided to identify what type of word has been emboldened in each sentence.

1. The **definition** of rape was expanded by the Sexual Offences Act 2003.

2. **Special** measures have been introduced to **protect** vulnerable witnesses.

3. **The** law was changed by statute in 1990 **but** these changes have not yet been implemented.

 You will find answers to these questions and many more exercises that will help you to test your ability to identify these different parts of a sentence on the Online Resource Centre.

10.3.4.2 Constructing a (grammatical) sentence

One lecturer recently told the story of how he wrote 'not a sentence' in several places on a student's essay to draw attention to the ungrammatical use of language. The student returned the essay to him with a request that he reconsider the grade as the criticisms were not justified because 'they were sentences. They started with capital letters and ended with full stops'. The lecturer amended his comments to read 'not a grammatical sentence' and returned the essay to the student with the grade unchanged.

This anecdote illustrates that there is much more to building a sentence than adhering to the conventions for starting (capital letter) and ending it (full stop): the words and punctuation that go in between are also vitally important.

A grammatical sentence can vary in length from a single word ('Guilty!' is a complete grammatical sentence) to thousands of words (there is a 4,391-word sentence in *Ulysses* by James Joyce).

Simple sentences have a subject (the defendant) and a verb (sobbed) or a subject (the defendant), a verb (sobbed), and an object (in court). An essay comprised solely of such short simple sentences has a rather bumpy and disjointed feel to it:

> Murder is a common law offence. It is the most serious form of homicide. It carries a mandatory life sentence. The judge has no discretion in sentencing. Loss of control and diminished responsibility are defences to murder. They reduce murder to voluntary manslaughter. Any sentence can be imposed for voluntary manslaughter. The penalties range from an absolute discharge to life imprisonment.

There are two ways to create longer sentences from these short sentences.

1. **Compound sentences** join two simple sentences together using a conjunction such as 'and' or 'but'. For example, 'It is the most serious form of homicide AND it carries a mandatory life sentence'.

2. **Complex sentences** formed of a independent and a subordinate clause. An independent clause is one that can stand alone as a simple sentence whilst a subordinate clause is one that does not make sense alone and needs to be joined to another sentence. The subordinate clause can precede the independent clause ('as the most serious form of homicide [subordinate clause], it carries a mandatory life sentence [independent clause]') or it can follow the independent clause (loss of control and diminished responsibility are defences to murder [independent clause]), which reduce liability to voluntary manslaughter [subordinate clause].

Using these techniques, you can reformulate the eight simple sentences into a combination of compound and complex sentences to create a more flowing and mature piece of writing:

> Murder is a common law offence. As the most serious form of homicide, it carries a mandatory life sentence thus the judge has no discretion in sentencing. Loss of control and diminished responsibility are defences to murder which reduce liability to voluntary manslaughter and can attract any sentence from an absolute discharge to life imprisonment.

You will notice that the rewritten form preserves the first simple sentence—'murder is a common law offence'. Simple sentences can have more impact than longer sentences simply because they are short and therefore sometimes seem to 'speak more loudly' to the reader. A combination of short and simple sentences with longer compound and complex sentences creates a more lively piece of writing that is more interesting for the reader.

10.3.4.3 Avoiding common errors

The following are common problems with sentence construction that can be easily resolved. They are a good place to start if you want to strengthen your written style.

- **Do not start a sentence with a conjunction.** The role of conjunctions such as 'and', 'but', and 'or' is to join two clauses together into a compound sentence. This means that these should never be used to start a sentence. A good way to avoid problems is to make a list of conjunctions and check your work to make sure that you never use one at the beginning of a sentence.

- **Do not end a sentence with a preposition.** Try to remember that good spoken English and good written English are two different species of the some language. When speaking, you might say 'I was told to find a case that I'd never heard of' but it is not something that you should write. Try correcting this by rephrasing the sentence: 'I had never heard of the case that I was told to find'.

- **Do not omit articles to defeat the word limit.** There are always some students who try to get around the word limit by taking every instance of 'the' out of their essay. This does reduce the word count but the ungrammatical essay that results will lose marks because it does not make sense. Never sacrifice the proper use of language in the interests of the word limit: rewrite sentences in a more concise manner.

- **Avoid illogical predication errors.** The word 'when' describes the time at which something happened and 'where' describes a location. However, students often use these words to introduce a definition or explanation: for example, 'a fixed trust is *where* the beneficiaries and their interests are stipulated by the settlor' or 'a fixed trust is *when* the trustee has no discretion as to the extent of the beneficial interest or the identity of the beneficiaries'. This is known as an illogical predication error or a faulty equation and it can be corrected by rewording the sentence: 'a fixed trust is *one in which* the beneficiaries and their interests are stipulated by the settlor'.

- **Avoid run-on sentences (also known as the comma splice).** This is a sentence made up of separate grammatical clauses that become ungrammatical due to the overuse of commas. For example, 'serious cases are sent to Crown Court for trial, they are heard by a jury, composed of twelve ordinary people, selected at random from the public, who do not have legal training'. Check any long sentences that contain commas to make sure that you avoid this problem. Correct it by rewording the sentence. This example uses italics to emphasize the changes that have been made: 'serious cases are sent to Crown Court for trial. They are

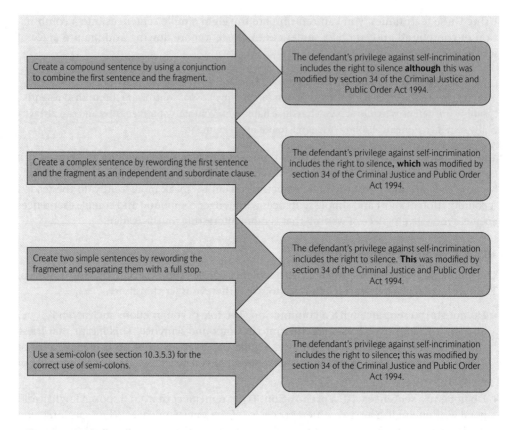

Figure 10.3 Sentence fragments

heard by a jury, *which is* composed of twelve ordinary people *who are* selected at random from the public *and* who do not have legal training'.

- **Be careful with 'who' and 'whom'.** 'Who' usually takes the place of a subject, and 'whom' generally replaces the direct object: 'the judge who delivered the verdict' and 'the defendant to whom the verdict was delivered'.

- **Look out for sentence fragments.** These are sentences that do not work as complete grammatical sentences because some essential component of the sentence is missing. They tend to start with words such as who, which, or where or with words ending in –ing. For example, 'the defendant's privilege against self-incrimination includes the right to silence. Which was modified by section 34 of the Criminal Justice and Public Order Act 1994'. This can be corrected in four ways as illustrated in Figure 10.3.

10.3.5 Punctuation

When people speak to each other, they use a range of devices to ensure that the intended meaning of the words is communicated to the listener. Think about the different meanings that you can convey in the single word 'hello': it can be spoken in a friendly tone as a greeting, shouted as a means of attracting attention, stated in a tone that conveys surprise or shock, or in a flat tone that indicates that the recipient is not liked or welcome, or it can carry an implied 'what do you want?' if it is said in a questioning tone of voice. In written language, it is not possible to convey different meanings by using tone, stress, or volume but punctuation, used correctly, can encode particular meaning into words to help the reader to extract the intended message.

Every written sentence is a combination of words and punctuation. The words and punctuation marks are selected by the writer as the best way to communicate the thoughts that are in the writer's head. In other words, when you write your coursework, you aim to capture your understanding of the law on paper using appropriate words and punctuation. If you want your meaning to be clear to the reader, you must use punctuation in the same way that they do or there is a risk that your meaning will be lost.

Even experienced writers struggle with the complexities of some rules of punctuation and there are areas of disagreement amongst experts about usage of punctuation in certain situations but this does not mean that you can disregard certain basic rules. Your lecturers will expect you to attain a certain level of communicative competence that includes the ability to use punctuation correctly.

10.3.5.1 Ending a sentence

Most people know that a sentence ends with a full stop (.). It can also end with a question mark (?) or an exclamation mark (!). There is no other correct way to end a sentence so one of these pieces of punctuation should be at the end of every sentence that you produce.

The majority of sentences that you write in your coursework will end with a full stop. This is not a difficult rule to understand but it does become more complicated in three situations if you need to incorporate any of the following into your essay:

- References
- Quotations
- Questions

When you incorporate references into a sentence, you need to make a decision about whether to position the full stop before or after the reference, irrespective of whether you are using footnotes or in-text referencing. Have a look at the following paragraph. Can you see a problem in relation to the positioning of footnote references and full stops?

> According to Dicey's traditional formulation of Parliamentary sovereignty, Parliament can make or unmake any law whatsoever and there is no competing body that can make law or set aside an Act of Parliament.[1] This principle, together with the rule of law and the separation of powers, is the cornerstone of the UK's unwritten constitution[2].

As you can see, the reference at the end of the first sentence follows the full stop but the reference is before the full stop at the end of the second sentence. This inconsistent approach is not good. The approach taken in the OSCOLA referencing system (chapter 12) is to place footnote markers outside punctuation (so in the example above, footnote 1 is correct and footnote 2 is incorrect according to OSCOLA).

The position regarding quotations and full stops is also not complicated if you stop to think about the sentence as a whole. If the quotation is incorporated into one of your own sentences (as in the following example) then the full stop must appear outside the quotation marks to denote that the sentence in its entirety is at an end.

> However, Ainsworth suggests that 'the traditional stance on sovereignty has not stood the test of time and the Dicean view cannot, in the face of the demands of Europe and the gentle erosion of the Human Rights Act 1998, be said to be correct in today's society'.[3]

If, however, the quotation is used alone without any of your words to introduce it then it is a complete sentence in its own right and the full stop should be inside the quotation marks as the example below demonstrates. You should, however, avoid using quotations as standalone sentences (as demonstrated in the following extract) unless you are using them as block quotations (see section 10.5.1) in which case you do not need quotation marks so the issue of positioning the full stop will not arise.

> However, some academic commentators believe that this view of sovereignty is no longer an accurate description of the position within the UK. 'The traditional stance on sovereignty has not stood the test of time and the Dicean view cannot, in the face of the demands of Europe and the gentle erosion of the Human Rights Act 1998, be said to be correct in today's society.'[3]

The key to success when asking a question and selecting the correct punctuation is to determine whether the question is a direct question or an indirect question:

- A direct question is one that is asked as if it were being spoken directly to someone: should the UK adopt the Euro as its currency? If a direct question is included in your essay, it does require a question mark at the end of the sentence
- An indirect question is a statement that a particular question needs to be asked: it is necessary to consider whether the UK should adopt the Euro as its currency. In this case, the sentence should end with a full stop, not a question mark. This is because you are not actually asking a question but merely identifying a question that needs to be asked

10.3.5.2 Commas

Of all the punctuation marks, the comma is probably the most frequently misused. The *Penguin Guide to Punctuation* suggests that this is because children are taught to use a comma in written language whenever they would pause when speaking, which is very misleading advice and tends to lead to commas being put into all sorts of unusual places in a sentence. There are actually only four uses for the comma (see Table 10.3):

Table 10.3 Uses for the comma

Use	Explanation	Example
Listing items.	The comma is used to separate words in a list so replaces the words 'and' or 'or' so that the sentence is less cumbersome.	**1.** 'The defendant was charged with theft and burglary and arson and resisting arrest' becomes 'the defendant was charged with theft, burglary, arson, and resisting arrest' **2.** 'The defendant could be charged under section 18 or section 20 or section 47 depending on the seriousness of the victim's injuries' becomes 'the defendant could be charged under section 18, section 20, or section 47 depending on the seriousness of the victim's injuries'.

(Continued)

Table 10.3 *(Cont.)*

Use	Explanation	Example
Joining two sentences together.	The comma links two separate sentences into a single sentence. It can only be used in this way if it is followed by a word that connects the two sentences together: but, and, or, while, yet. Other connecting words cannot be used after a comma so it is incorrect to join two sentences together with a comma if it is followed by any of these words: however, thus, therefore, hence, consequently, nevertheless.	Correct: 'The terms of the offer were unclear, and the claimant sought to argue that he was not bound by the contract.' Incorrect: 'The terms of the offer were unclear, therefore the claimant sought to argue that he was not bound by the contract'.
To allow words to be omitted from a sentence.	A comma can be used to show that words have been left out of a sentence if the missing words would be a direct repetition of words already used earlier in the sentence.	'Some members of the jury wanted to convict the defendant; others, to acquit him.' The use of the comma makes it unnecessary to repeat the words 'members of the jury wanted' a second time.
To mark the insertion of additional detail in a sentence that interrupts the main point.	The comma is used here to separate the additional comment from the main sentence. In this role, the comma is sometimes called a bracketing comma or an isolating comma to indicate its purpose in separating a minor part of the sentence from the major part. Check to see if you have used commas correctly for this purpose by removing the bracketed phrase: the sentence should still make grammatical sense without it. The minor part of the sentence can appear at the beginning, middle, or end of the sentence.	Beginning 'Having discussed the jury selection process, it is necessary to move to consider the role of the jury in a criminal trial.' Middle 'The jury, composed of twelve ordinary men and women, are not equipped to hear complex fraud trials.' End 'Complex fraud trials usually last at least eight months, which places a great burden on the jury.' *Do you see that the main sentence still makes sense without the words separated by the comma or commas?*

10.3.5.3 Colons and semi-colons

There is often great confusion between these two types of punctuation. Both colons and semi-colons appear in the middle of sentences and they are similar in appearance so many students tend to use them interchangeably. This is a mistake because they have different roles to play in a sentence as the following figures demonstrate.

It might help you to ensure that you have a good grasp of the difference between colons and semi-colons and the job that they do in a sentence if you compare their operation with that of the full-stop in three sentences which are identical except for the differences in punctuation. See Table 10.4.

The colon is used to divide a sentence into a statement followed by elaboration on that statement. The part of the sentence that precedes the colon should be a complete sentence but that part that follows the colon need not be a complete sentence: it could be a single word and often takes the form of a list.

FOR EXAMPLE

There are three key constitutional principles that underpin the unwritten constitution: Parliamentary sovereignty, the separation of powers, and the rule of law.

Can you see that the words after the colon elaborate on the statement prior to the colon by identifying the relevant principles?

Figure 10.4 Role of the colon

The semi-colon is used to divide a sentence into two separate statements, each of which is a complete sentence in its own right and which could be separated with a full-stop or joined with a conjunction. The reason that the two sentences are joined with a semi-colon is to demonstrate the close link between them.

FOR EXAMPLE

Most countries have a written constitution which outlines the rights and responsibilities of the State and its citizens; the constitution of the UK is unwritten.

Can you see that the sentence could be divided into two using a full-stop in place of the semi-colon or the two parts could be joined by inserting the word 'but' in place of the semi-colon?

Figure 10.5 Role of the semi-colon

Table 10.4 Full-stops, colons, and semi-colons

Punctuation	Example	Explanation
Full-stop	The judge directed the jury to find the defendant 'not guilty'. One of the jurors admitted to using a Ouija board in the jury room in an attempt to contact the dead victim during the murder trial to find out the identity of the murderer.	This is two separate sentences that make two separate statements of fact. By separating the sentences with a full-stop, you are suggesting that there is no relationship between them: they are just facts about the trial.
Semi-colon	The judge directed the jury to find the defendant 'not guilty'; one of the jurors admitted to using a Ouija board in the jury room in an attempt to contact the dead victim during the murder trial to find out the identity of the murderer.	The use of a semi-colon here suggests that the two statements are related in some way: perhaps the lack of evidence against the defendant caused the judge to direct to acquit and frustrated the juror so that he tried to find an alternative (spectral) source of evidence.
Colon	The judge directed the jury to find the defendant 'not guilty': one of the jurors admitted to using a Ouija board in the jury room in an attempt to contact the dead victim during the murder trial to find out the identity of the murderer.	The use of the colon indicates a causal relationship between the two sentences. Remember that the statement after the colon explains the statement that precedes the colon. Here, then, the judge has ordered that the defendant should be acquitted *because* of the use of the Ouija board by the juror.

10.3.5.4 Apostrophes

One of the problems with the apostrophe is that it is so widely misused that it is easy to see all sorts of examples of its incorrect use: menus offer 'free pizza's for the under 12's' (two instances of incorrect use), shops advertise 'ladie's shoe's' (another two examples of misuse), and even museums have signs that state that the exhibit 'was used in the 1920's'. With all this misuse of the apostrophe in evidence, it is hardly surprising that students struggle to master the correct usage of this form of punctuation.

There are two situations in which you are likely to want to use an apostrophe:

- **Contractions.** An apostrophe is used to indicate that a word or words have been shortened by the omission of letters: shouldn't (should not), can't (cannot), he'll (he will), I've (I have), o'clock (of the clock).
- **Possession.** The apostrophe is used to indicate possession: the victim's injury, the judge's summing-up, the UK's role in the European Union.

One very easy way to reduce the problems posed by apostrophe use in your coursework is to make sure that you do not use contractions at all. These are informal forms of expression so should never be used in academic writing. Do not make the mistake of thinking that contractions are an easy way to cut back on words and fit your essay into the word limit: the marks that you will lose for poor written style will be more than those you will gain in the few extra words that you save by using contractions.

Once you have ruled out the possibility of using contractions, the apostrophe should only make an appearance if you are using it to indicate possession. The secret of success here is to distinguish between possession and pluralization. Both of these involve the use of the letter 's' but only the former requires an apostrophe.

- **Possessive not plural:** the claimant's claim in negligence was dismissed by the court (there is one claimant and it is his claim so an apostrophe is needed).
- **Plural not possessive:** the claimants claimed damages in negligence (there are several claimants so the letter 's' is added to the word but the sentence refers to their actions rather than to possession so no apostrophe is needed).
- **Plural and possessive:** the claimants' claim was unsuccessful (there are several claimants so the 's' is added to change the word 'claimant' into its plural form. These claimants have a claim so an apostrophe is added after the plural 's' to indicate possession).

If you can get to grips with the distinction between plural and possessive word forms, you will be well on your way to mastering the use of the apostrophe. Take particular care when making reference to a period of years: many people write 'in the 1990's' as if it were possessive whereas it is actually a way of describing a collection of years so it is plural and should be expressed without the apostrophe as 'in the 1990s'.

One final problem concerns the word 'its' (in the possessive sense rather than as a contraction of 'it is'): the court delivered its judgment, Parliament determines its own procedural rules. Students often use an apostrophe here, writing 'its' as 'it's' to denote possession. However, this is not correct: 'its' is the abstract equivalent of 'his' or 'hers' and you would not consider using an apostrophe with those words. The simple way to avoid problems is to make sure that 'it's' (with an apostrophe) never appears in your academic writing: if you are using the apostrophe correctly then you are using the contraction for 'it is' and contractions are too informal for inclusion in academic writing but if you are using 'it's' as a possessive form then it is incorrect use of apostrophe so the word should be corrected so that it appears without punctuation.

Practical exercise

Have a look at the following passage of text and see if you can spot and correct the incorrect use of apostrophes.

In the 1980's, there was an increase of case law that examined the role of the trust in relation to domestic property ownership. It's role was of particular importance in relation to spouse's who had not made a direct contribution to the properties purchase price. This was criticised as unduly harsh on spouses who's financial contribution has facilitated the property's purchase as it's too generous to husband's and wife's who had not paid towards the price of the property. Many argue that it isn't fair to give a beneficial share in property to a non-contributing spouse.

 You will find the answers and an explanation of them on the Online Resource Centre where you will also find other examples for you to use to improve your understanding of the correct use of the apostrophe.

10.4 Paragraphs

Paragraphs exist for the convenience of the reader. It is far easier to follow your argument if it is broken up into a series of separate points using paragraphs. Each paragraph should contain a separate idea which should flow from the paragraph before it and lead into the paragraph that follows after it.

Unlike sentences, there are no hard and fast rules about paragraph construction but it can be useful to use the following technique in helping you construct useful paragraphs that flow into each other and which link back to the question.

- **Topic.** The topic sentence announces the main focus of the paragraph.
- **Expansion.** The sentences that follow should explain the topic or elaborate upon it. There should be at least one sentence that elaborates on the topic and there is no maximum number although it is important that paragraphs do not become long and unwieldy: for instance, 700 word paragraphs are undesirable (especially in an essay with a 1,500-word limit). You should aim to have at least two paragraphs on a single side of A4 if you are using double-line spacing. Paragraphs should also not be too short, otherwise you could end up with an essay that reads more like a set of notes or bullet points.
- **Illustration.** You will usually want to provide an example to support the point that you have made or to demonstrate how a particular principle operates. Case law will often be a source of illustrations but there are a range of alternatives including hypothetical examples and points taken from articles, government reports, or newspapers.
- **Link.** The paragraph should end either by leading into the paragraph that follows or by relating the content of the paragraph directly back to the question by, for example, explaining how the point made in the paragraph addresses the point raised by the question.

You will see in the example that there is an extra line space to separate the paragraphs. This makes it clear to the reader where one paragraph ends and the next paragraph begins. The alternative approach is to indent the first line of the new paragraph. Either approach is acceptable. Remember that the aim is to make the essay clear and easy for the marker to follow.

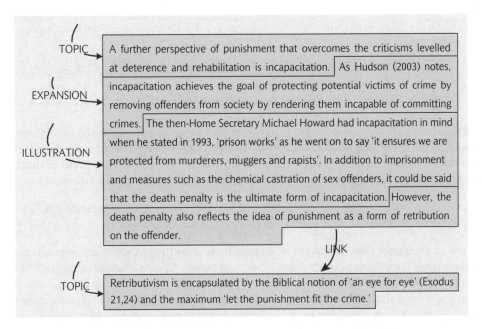

Figure 10.6 Paragraph construction

A final point to note is that there has been a recent proliferation of primary and secondary paragraphing to denote the strength of the relationship between a paragraph and the one that follows it by varying the size of the gap between the paragraphs. This is nonsense and not something that would be acceptable in writing at university level. There are sentences and there are paragraphs. If a sentence is closely related to the previous sentence, it belongs in the same paragraph; if it is not closely related, it belongs in the following paragraph.

 You will find further examples of these rules and their application on the Online Resource Centre.

10.5 Using quotations

Quotations can add authority to your work as you are, in effect, using the words of someone with far more legal expertise than yourself to support your argument. They can also give you a form of words to describe something in a way that is far better than you would be able to explain it yourself.

Although the judicious use of quotations can really strengthen your argument and provide evidence of the breadth of your research, they can have a negative impact on your work if they are not used with care. Have a look at the extract taken from an essay on the role of equitable maxims in trusts as it demonstrates two of the most common problems that arise in relation to quotations in student essays.

A maxim is defined in the Oxford English Dictionary as a 'general truth or a rule of conduct expressed in a sentence' thus an equitable maxim is 'a general truth or rule of conduct about the operation of equity'.[1] 'The maxims are not rules to be construed like statutes, but rather a general basis around which much of equity formed'[2] and they can be said to be 'an attempt to formulate in short pithy phrases the key principles which underline the exercise of equitable jurisdiction'.[3]

[1]   R Clements and A Abass, *Equity and Trusts: Text, Cases and Materials* (OUP 2008) 34.
[2]   S Wilson, *Textbook on Trusts* (OUP 2005) 9.
[3]   R Pearce and J Stevens, *The Law of Trusts and Equitable Obligations* (3rd edn, Butterworths 2002).

There is heavy reliance on quotations in the extract: sixty-two out of the eighty-five words (about 73 per cent) were not written by the student and the overall impression given is that this is an essay that is made up of a series of joined together quotations. The problem that this raises can be seen clearly if you read the same extract with the quotations taken out.

A maxim is defined in the Oxford English Dictionary as a . . . thus an equitable maxim is . . . and they can be said to be . . .

As you can see, once the quotations are omitted, there is nothing in the words remaining that demonstrates the student's knowledge of the subject matter. As such, it would be difficult for the marker to award marks for the student's understanding of equitable maxims. Remember that you should use your own words to explain key concepts to show the marker that you understand them or, alternatively, use a quotation and follow this with an explanation of your own.

The second problem with the extract is that it uses textbooks as a source of its quotations. Try to remember that textbook writers have gathered together all the relevant statutes, case law, academic commentary, and other source material and distilled it into a condensed and accessible explanation of the law to help students. As such, textbooks are explaining the law that can be found elsewhere or comments made about the law by experts. Ideally, you should use the textbook to give you an overview of the topic and then follow up the references or conduct your own research to find the law and comment upon it to use as the source material for your essays rather than relying on the explanations provided in textbooks. By quoting from cases and articles, you are demonstrating your research as well as supporting your work with authority so try to ensure you quote from these sources rather than textbooks wherever possible.

10.5.1 Presentation of quotations

The way to present a quotation within your work depends on the length of the quotation. Anything from a single word to a fragment of a sentence of about a line-and-a-half of text can be incorporated as part of your sentence whilst longer quotations and those that are complete sentences in their own right should be presented as block quotations.

An equitable maxim is a statement that sums up 'in short pithy phrases'[1] the principles and operation of equity.

In this example, a short quotation that captures part of the nature of an equitable maxim has been incorporated into the sentence. Note that the quotation appears within quotation marks and is accompanied by a reference that indicates the source of the material; both of these features are essential in order to ensure your work is referenced properly and to avoid any suspicion of plagiarism (see chapter 12 for more detail on these issues).

By contrast, a longer quotation is set apart from the main body of your essay and quotation marks should not be used: they are not needed as the indentation of the quotation separates it from your own work and indicates to the marker that it is a quotation. A reference must still be provided that acknowledges the source of the words.

An equitable maxim is a concise statement that captures one of the principles of equity. These maxims are not rules with the capacity to bind in future cases like principles of common law but are more like general guidelines that capture the central sentiments of equity. As Marshall explains:

> Equitable maxims do not bind or control but guide and inform. They are a gentle reminder of the principles of fairness that permeate the system of equity. If they were to be harsh and unyielding, they would not serve the purpose that equity exists to achieve.[1]

This reference to equitable maxims as a 'gentle reminder' highlights the relationship between equity and the 'harsh and unyielding' common law as equity originally operated as a separate system of law administered by different court in order to counteract any unfairness that arose due to the strict application of the common law.

Figure 10.7 Using quotations in an essay

This example also illustrates the practice of using single line spacing to present quotations as a further way of differentiating the words of others from the main text of the essay. This is a matter of preference: it is perfectly permissible to use the same spacing for quotations as you have used for the rest of the text.

See further section 10.7.1 on formatting.

10.5.2 Effective use of quotations

There is quite a skill to using quotations effectively. Too many students fail to realize this and, as a result, the quotations that are included in their essay serve to highlight this lack of skill so that the quotations actually weaken rather than strengthen their work. The following guidelines should help you to use quotations to good effect in your writing.

- **Introduce your quotations.** Irrespective of whether you are using a few words or several sentences of quoted material, you must blend it into your essay with words of introduction. This could be a simple identification of the author such as 'As Jones argues "the remedial constructive trust offers little of value to the modern law of trusts"' or a more detailed approach that introduces the topic as well as its source: for example, 'Jones argues that the constructive trust has little role to play in modern trust law, suggesting that "it is an exhausted anachronism that should be laid to rest and never revived"'. It is very poor practice to have a quotation as a stand-alone sentence with no words of your own to introduce it.

- **Use an appropriate verb to situate the quotation.** You could introduce every quotation with the words 'Keller says the postal rule is outdated' or 'Keller states the postal rule is outdated' but 'says' and 'states' are neutral verbs that do not give the reader any clues as to how the quotation that follows fits into the rest of your essay. Think about the difference that it would make to introduce a quotation with the words 'Keller alleges that the postal rule is outdated'. This implies that you will be disagreeing with this view in your essay; you would expect the quotation to be followed by 'but' and an argument in favour of the postal rule. Compare this with the impression given by the statement 'Keller notes that the postal rule is outdated'. Take time to think about the role of the quotation in your essay and select a verb that is appropriate to that role. The following are some of the verbs that you could use.

says	observes	alleges	argues	thinks
states	notes	claims	asserts	remarks
comments	explains	suggests	affirms	adds

- **Discuss the quotation.** Remember that the purpose of a quotation is to support your own words, not to replace them. This means that you should make the quotation work for you by explaining its meaning or relevance rather than leaving it to speak for itself. If you look back at Figure 10.7, you will see that a good example of how Marshall's quotation is discussed and key terms from it are used to develop the writer's own argument. Whether you are using a quotation to illustrate a point or support your argument, it will only do this if you make it clear to the reader what its purpose is and how the quotation is relevant to your essay.

- **Avoid lengthy quotations.** Quotations are not a substitute for your own words. You should look for short phrases or a few sentences that make a point that you could not make in your own words or that is better expressed in the words of the original author. Try to capture a particular idea with a quotation but to explain its detail, significance, or operation in your own words. Markers will not be impressed to read long quotations when what they want to read is your own explanation, interpretation, and evaluation of the law.

- **Incorporate quotations so that they make sense.** Used properly, quotations should blend in with your own words. This means that if you have a sentence that is part quotation and part your own words, the two should combine to make a complete grammatical sentence. You can take words out of a quotation to help with this provided you indicate that words are omitted by the use of ellipses (. . .) and you can add words that are not in the original quotation using square brackets. Square brackets can also be used to indicate a change from upper to lower case (or *vice versa*). For example, if you wish to take a fragment of a quotation and use it as a complete sentence, you will need to change the initial letter of the first word from lower to upper case as demonstrated in Figure 10.8.

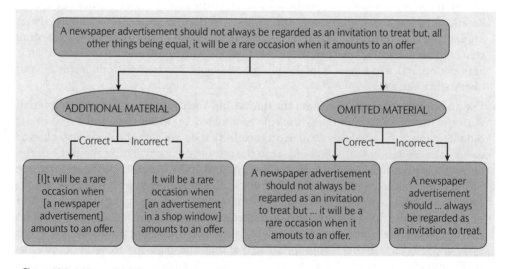

Figure 10.8 Adding and deleting words from quotations

10.6 Word limits

It is likely that most, if not all, of the coursework that you complete during your studies will have a word limit. Although students almost universally rail against word limits, protesting that they are too restrictive to enable them to answer questions properly or to enable them to say all that they want to say, essays and problem questions are carefully written to ensure that they will fit within the specified word limit. As such, it really is possible to write a good essay within the constraints of the word limit.

10.6.1 Why is the word limit a problem?

If you are struggling, consider whether any of the following are applicable:

- **Too much irrelevant information.** Check whether you have understood the question correctly and evaluate how relevant each point that you want to include in the essay is to the question. Have you gone off at a tangent? If you need to reduce your word count, look at every sentence and ask 'what does this add to my essay' in order to make sure that you are filtering out irrelevant material.

- **Too much descriptive detail.** Are you including lengthy explanations of the facts of cases when less, or even no, detail would suffice? One common problem is long descriptions of the facts of cases which add nothing to the answer and, in fact, interrupt the line of argument. Check each point for relevance and then experiment with the points remaining to see how you can reword them in fewer words.

- **Too long-winded in your written language.** Some people have an aptitude for concise expression whereas others use far more words than are necessary to express even the simplest of ideas. One of the most effective methods for reducing your word count without losing any material is to check every sentence to see if it can be reworded in fewer words; even one word taken out of each sentence will make a real difference to the overall word count. A common waste of words is saying 'in the case of X' rather than 'in X'. This uses three surplus words ('the case of') every time you refer to a case and these soon mount up throughout a piece of work.

Practical exercise

Bearing these points in mind, have a look at the paragraph below. It is the second paragraph in an essay that considers whether it is true that the law does not allow a trust to be established to benefit a purpose rather than an individual. Can you (1) remove any irrelevant material, (2) remove excessive descriptive detail, and (3) reword the paragraph so that it is more concise without losing its main points?

There are exceptions of situations that are exceptions to the rule against purpose trusts. Two situations in which a purpose trust can exist even though there are no identifiable human beneficiaries are the establishment of a purpose trust for the care of animals and a purpose trust that is dedicated to the erection and upkeep and maintenance of a monument. The use of a purpose trust to care for animals is illustrated in the case of *Pettingall* v. *Pettingall*.[1] In this case, the testator left the sum of £50 a year to the upkeep of his favourite black mare. This was held to be valid. In *Re Dean*,[2] a trust was upheld to maintain a horse and some hounds for fifty years provided that the animals lived that long. These cases demonstrate that purpose trusts can be valid if they are aimed at caring for particular animals. An illustration of a valid trust to maintain a monument can be seen in the case of *Mussett* v *Bingle*[3] where the testator left a sum of money to erect a monument in memory of his first wife. Also in the case of *Pirbright* v *Salway*,[4] the court upheld a trust to maintain a family burial enclosure and in *Re Hooper*[5] the court upheld a trust to ensure that a vault was maintained in good condition. However, in the case of *Re Endacott*,[6] the settlor left his residuary estate his local parish council for a particular purpose which was to provide a useful monument to him but this was held to be void because the court felt that the line of case law involving specific graves and monuments should not be extended. Although this case does demonstrate that not all trusts established to achieve a particular purpose will be valid, there is a fairly sizeable body of case law that does recognise that there can be a trust for a purpose if that purpose is to erect a specific monument or maintain a particular burial plot. These examples demonstrate that there are some exceptions to the more general rule that a trust cannot exist for purpose but only for the benefit of human beneficiaries.

 You will find a rewritten version of this paragraph on the Online Resource Centre with an explanation of the way that it was reduced from 361 to 120 words: cut by two-thirds!

Alternatively, you may find that you have said everything you want to say and have not yet reached the word limit. This may be because you have an admirable concise written style and that you have ensured that you have only included relevant material. Unfortunately, it is more likely to mean that you have:

- **Left out some relevant material.** If you are significantly short of the word limit, you have missed out something that should be included. Revisit the question and review your reading to see if there is something that you have overlooked.
- **Failed to provide sufficient detail.** This may arise because you have tried to keep description to a minimum and have gone too far and excluded some necessary explanation or because you have misjudged the complexity of a particular issue and provided only a simplistic explanation.

You will find more detailed advice on interpreting questions, selecting relevant material, and keeping a strong focus on the question in chapter 13.

10.6.2 Why stick to the word limit?

It is essential that you do adhere to the word limit, however challenging that may seem, as most institutions impose a penalty for failure to do so. This may be a deduction of marks or a refusal to read any words that go over the specified limit. Either type of penalty will reduce the mark that your work receives. In some institutions that have a cumulative deduction policy, i.e. a deduction of two marks for every ten words over the limit, an essay which was too far over the limit could end up with a mark that was lower than the pass mark once all the deductions have been taken into account.

Do not make the mistake of misstating the word limit—quoting that you have used 1,495 words in a 1,500 limit when you have really used 1,743—as this generally attracts an even more severe penalty, sometimes zero and a requirement that the coursework be repeated.

10.6.3 What counts towards the word limit?

Always check your department's regulations to determine how the word count is calculated. Some institutions exclude references to statute and case law from the word count, for example, so all statutory references and case citations can be deducted from the overall limit. This is likely to apply only to actual references rather than all discussion of case or statute law, so make sure that you make an accurate deduction. Equally, some departments will state that all references are included in the word count (which makes checking that you have made an accurate declaration of the word limit easier) whereas others exclude footnotes from the word count but specify that they must only be used to reference and not to introduce any additional text. There are many other potential policies on counting words that may arise at different institutions. This chapter does not aim to outline all the possibilities, rather just to orientate you to the existence of the different methods of counting words. It highlights the need to check the rules in order to ensure that you are adhering to the requirements of the word limit in force at your institution.

10.7 Presentation

Presentation of coursework, or how it looks on the page, is important. If you look at several pieces of work with identical content, you will probably find that you make instinctive evaluations about their quality on the basis of their visual appearance. A well-presented piece of work that complies with any institutional requirements with regard to font choice or formatting, for example, will create a good first impression with the marker. Whilst this may not necessarily contribute to the grade that the essay receives (unless your department awards marks for presentation), it cannot do any harm to ensure that the person marking your work feels favourably disposed towards it from the outset.

10.7.1 Formatting

If there is a house style with regard to presentation, use it even if you do not like the style chosen. Most people have a font style or pattern of layout that they favour but that is no reason not to adhere to the specifications that you have been given. Some departments even impose an automatic deduction of marks for failure to comply with the presentation requirements of assessed coursework, so it is always advisable to find out what the requirements are and follow them to the letter. In the absence of any specifications as to style, you may like to bear the following in mind when choosing how to present your work:

- **Font and font size:** choose a relatively straightforward font that is easy for the marker to read. It would generally be unnecessary to have a font size larger than 12-point in the main body of your text.
- **Line spacing:** double or one-and-a-half line spacing is advisable as it is easier to read in large quantities than single-spaced text. Moreover, wider line spacing ensures that your work covers more pages and gives the marker more space to write comments in the margin.
- **Margins:** as with line spacing, wide margins allow the marker space to write comments. The default settings should give sufficient space.
- **Paragraphing:** using a double space between paragraphs creates more 'white space' that makes the page easier on the marker's eye and gives additional space for comment.

Overall, these guidelines are aimed at ensuring that the page is not too crowded so that the words look squashed onto the page.

10.7.2 Statutes and cases

It is usual to use different formatting to ensure that statutory references and case names stand out from the bulk of the text. Your institution may have particular requirements in this respect but, if not, choose a style and stick to it throughout your essay. As with so many aspects of presentation, consistency is the key to success.

It is conventional to italicize case names but not the full citation.

For further information on referencing, see chapter 12.

10.7.3 Headings

This section addresses issues of the presentation of headings rather than their use in essays (which can be found in chapter 13). If you are using headings in your work, make sure that you use an appropriate and consistent approach to formatting them. For example, if you use two levels of heading (main headings and subheadings), make sure that the style you use for the main heading is more prominent than that of the subheading and that you use the same style throughout your work. Finally, do make sure that something follows the heading; leaving a heading 'hanging' as the final words on the bottom of the page whilst the text follows on the next is not an effective approach to the use of headings.

10.7.4 Page numbers

It is useful to ensure that the pages of your work are numbered. If your marker drops your essay, it might be difficult to reorder them if they are not numbered. Equally, if you staple the pages in the incorrect order (it happens!) and they are not numbered, your lecturer may not realize that the pages are not in order and merely assume that the flow of your argument is not logical.

10.7.5 Capital letters

There is an unfortunate tendency amongst students to capitalize every word that seems significant, such as Judge, Court, Case, and Law, or any phrases that seem sufficiently important, for example, Rule of Law, *Actus Reus*, or Invitation to Treat. This is incorrect and should be avoided. The use of capital letters should be reserved for the word at the start of a sentence and proper nouns only.

10.7.6 Checking for errors

Although the aim is to allow the marker plenty of space to write comments, you really want to attract feedback about the content of your legal argument rather than technicalities of presentation, so do ensure that the spelling, grammar, and punctuation are correct. There are few things more disheartening for a student than the return of an essay that is covered in corrections, so avoid this by ensuring that you do not give the marker a great deal to correct. It should go without saying that the work should be meticulously checked for basic errors prior to submission, but far too many students submit work that looks suspiciously like a first draft in that it is peppered with the sorts of error that should have been corrected prior to submission.

Check spelling and grammar	☐	Are footnotes on the right page?	☐
Check 'its' and 'it's'	☐	References: complete and correct?	☐
Does it look right on paper?	☐	Italics for case names	☐
Any hanging headings?	☐	Does it make sense?	☐
Check use of capitals	☐		

Figure 10.9 Checklist

The solution is to leave sufficient time prior to submission to check your essay thoroughly for accuracy. Use the spell check, making sure that it is set to UK English rather than US English (the spelling differs between the two) but remember that it cannot check for context. Accept that the spell check is not infallible (for instance, it will not catch errors such as statue/statute, trail/trial, electoral role/electoral roll) and proofread your essay yourself or, as it is often difficult to spot your own errors as you tend to read what you meant to write rather than what you have actually written, get a friend to check it for you.

One technique that can be particularly useful, even after you have strengthened your writing skills through years of study, is to compose a personalized checklist of potential problems. Everyone has some weakness in their writing style and it is easy to be blind to your own errors, so finding a way to remind yourself to take particular care over certain issues can be an excellent way of ensuring that you produce a polished and accurate piece of work. You could start with quite a general checklist in the early stages of your studies that reminds you to check such basics as spelling or the technicalities of presenting case names and citations correctly. As your written style strengthens, some of the basics will become second nature whilst other, more specific problems, will inevitably emerge. For example, perhaps you find the distinction between plural and possessive 'its' confusing or you are unclear about the difference between 'affect' and 'effect'. Irrespective of the nature of your problem, your checklist can evolve to reflect this as you progress.

One example of the sorts of points that you could include on your checklist is given in Figure 10.9.

 You will find some other suggested categories to get you started on the Online Resource Centre.

 CHAPTER SUMMARY

Language

- Strive for an appropriate level of formality in your written style; the approach used in good textbooks and articles will provide a useful example

- Avoid casual language such as text speak and the use of the first person

- Be alert for the conventions relating to gender-neutral language and the use of Latin

- Be aware that words that have legal and non-legal meanings, such as assault, can confuse the reader

Grammar and punctuation

- Take care to ensure that your work is grammatical as this contributes towards accuracy and precision

- Look for evidence that would suggest that there is a problem with your grammar and punctuation and ensure you seek appropriate assistance if it appears necessary

- Take note of the common problems that arise and strive to eliminate them from your writing

Quotations

- Incorporating quotations into your work can add strength to your arguments but you must ensure that you do not use a quotation out of context or misrepresent its meaning

- If you add or remove words or emphasis, this must be noted in the quotation or its reference as appropriate. Ensure that any changes do not alter the meaning of the quotation

- Do not overuse quotations. The bulk of your essay should be expressed in your words as opposed to merely joining together a string of quotations. Equally, do not use quotations, particularly from textbooks, to express concepts that could be expressed in your own words; your ability to explain legal concepts will attract more credit than your ability to select an appropriate quotation

Presentation

- Discover whether there are any mandatory requirements for the presentation of coursework and, if so, ensure that you adhere to them

- Ensure that you leave sufficient time prior to the deadline for submission to check your work thoroughly for presentational errors

 FURTHER READING

- If you require greater guidance on the essential matters of grammar, spelling, and punctuation than it has been possible to provide in this chapter, see J Peck and M Coyle, *The Student's Guide to Writing: Grammar, Punctuation and Spelling* (Palgrave 1999).

- A good source of grammar tips can be found online at grammar.quickanddirtytips.com

- Clear definitions and guidance of each type of punctuation are given in RL Trask, *The Penguin Guide to Punctuation* (Penguin 1997).

Legal reasoning

11

INTRODUCTION

This chapter provides an introduction to legal reasoning. In the first part of the book, you will have begun building the skills that you need to find and read the law and have also been introduced to the idea of judicial precedent and statutory interpretation. You will understand, then, that the law develops as a result of decisions made by the courts as well as new legislation that comes from Parliament or the European Union. This chapter will start giving you the skills to analyze the way in which judges decide cases. There are various points of view that judges can (and do) take in deciding the outcomes of cases, so this chapter will introduce some of the theory behind judicial reasoning before moving on to show how judges reason in practice. It should be read in conjunction with chapter 3, which focuses on using legislation and chapter 6, on using case law.

The ability to appreciate and understand legal reasoning is an important academic legal skill, although it also has some practical advantages. One of the keys to academic legal success is the ability to engage critically with the law and so it is important that you begin to build your skills in analysis by seeking out the reasons that underlie particular decisions. Students often make the mistake of thinking that applying the law is simple, but this is not the case: there are many other factors which can be taken into account when deciding what the outcome of a case should be. This context provides a backdrop for the historical development of the law, an appreciation of which will enable you to develop and demonstrate your critical thinking skills.

LEARNING OUTCOMES

After studying this chapter, you will be able to:

- understand the processes involved in logical legal reasoning

- explain how legal reasoning is more than just the mechanical application of law to facts

- distinguish between natural law, legal positivism, and legal realism

- be able to read a judgment and analyze the factors taken into account by judges

- appreciate the practical benefit of understanding legal reasoning

11.1 Reasoning

The *Oxford English Dictionary* defines the verb 'to reason' as:

> To think something through, work out in a logical manner

and 'reasoning' as:

> The action of reason; especially the process by which one judgement is deduced from another or others which are given.

You can see, then, that 'reasoning' (in the general sense) is working something out logically in a process of deduction. Before we move on to see what this means for legal reasoning, we must first take a brief look at some theory of logic.

11.1.1 Logic

One key form of logical argument is the *logical syllogism* which dates back to the time of the ancient Greeks (in particular Aristotle and Zeno of Citium in the third century BC). In syllogistic reasoning, one proposition is deduced from two or more others. The proposition that is deduced is the *conclusion* and the two or more statements from which it is inferred are called *premises*.

 Practical exercise

You have probably encountered syllogistic reasoning without actually having realized so. Many logic puzzles are based upon the syllogism. For instance:

- **Premise 1**: All horses are mammals
- **Premise 2**: All mammals are animals
- **Conclusion**: All horses are animals

Have a look at the following logic puzzles and decide whether or not the conclusion is valid or invalid: in other words, whether it follows logically from the two premises without the need for any further information.

1. If today is Tuesday, then I have a criminal law seminar. If I have a criminal law seminar, then I will pack Smith and Hogan in my bag. Therefore, if today is Tuesday, I will pack Smith and Hogan in my bag.

2. All gerbils in England eat sunflower seeds. Some rodents eat sunflower seeds. Therefore, some rodents are gerbils in England.

3. All lawyers are highly intelligent. Some lawyers are not polite. Therefore, no polite people are highly intelligent.

 You will find answers to these puzzles and an explanation of how they were reached on the Online Resource Centre.

So, a syllogism consists of two premises and a conclusion. For a syllogism to be valid, it must be logically impossible for its premises to be true and for its conclusion to be false. You will have seen from the practical exercise that it is not sufficient that both premises are true for the conclusion also to be true. Look at this example:

- All horses are mammals
- Some mammals can fly
- Therefore some horses can fly

The first two premises are certainly true: horses are mammals and some mammals (including bats and flying squirrels) can fly. However, outside the realms of mythology, there are no flying horses. The fact that horses are mammals and that some mammals can fly does not prove anything about the airborne capabilities of horses. So, in this example, since it is logically possible for the premises to be true *and* the conclusion to be false, then the argument is not logically valid.

In legal arguments, the parts of the local argument take certain forms. The first premise (known in logic as the *major premise*) is generally a statement of law. This is an abstract statement of a legal rule. The second premise (known as the *minor premise*) is usually a statement of fact; a statement which concerns a specific person, thing, or state of affairs. The conclusion draws together the general statement of law with the particular statement of fact and therefore explains how the general rule applies to the particular facts. In the legal context, this is *applying the law to the facts* and is the simplest form of legal analysis or reasoning.

11.1.2 Simple legal reasoning

The basic syllogistic framework is at the heart of legal reasoning, the steps in which can be broken down as shown in Figure 11.1.

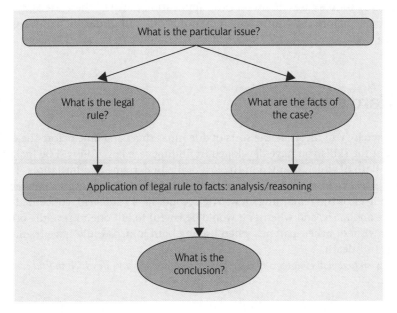

Figure 11.1 The process of legal reasoning

The steps in this process can be illustrated with a simple example:

- The **issue** in this particular case is whether Peter is criminally liable for the murder of John

- The **facts of the case** are that Peter knocked on John's front door. When John answered the door, Peter said 'I hate you and I want you to die'. He then shot John in the head, killing him instantly. Peter was not insane

- The **legal rule** is the definition of murder: where a person of sound mind and discretion unlawfully kills any reasonable creature in being (i.e. a human being) under the Queen's Peace (i.e. not in wartime) with intent to kill or cause grievous bodily harm

The **application of the law to the facts** is straightforward:

- **Sound mind?** We are told that Peter was not insane, so he was of sound mind at the time of the killing.

- **Unlawful killing.** There is nothing to suggest that Peter was acting in self-defence, was of diminished responsibility, had lost control, or was killing in pursuit of a suicide pact. Peter killed John by shooting him in the head. The killing is therefore unlawful.

- **Reasonable creature in being.** John is (was) a human being.

- **Queen's Peace.** There is nothing to suggest that this happened during wartime.

- **Intention to kill/cause GBH.** Peter's intention is demonstrated by his words and actions. At the very least shooting someone in the head would cause really serious harm.

Therefore, given that all the elements of the offence are made out, then Peter is criminally liable for the murder of John.

If only it was always that straightforward! Many law students—particularly those new to the study of law—assume that legal reasoning simply involves a mechanical application of the rules to the facts. This is not so. There are many other issues that courts take into account when deciding how the law should apply to particular cases. While it is true that many simple cases do involve the application of rules, there are also many hard cases that come before the courts which do not neatly fall under such a straightforward description.

11.2 Hard cases

The next exercise will illustrate the sorts of dilemmas that can come before the courts, and will also test the skills you have developed in finding case law. You will be looking at two hard cases, both of which resulted in the loss of life in extreme circumstances. The first *R v Dudley and Stephens*, involves the cannibalism of a cabin boy following a shipwreck in order to save the lives of the remaining crew. The second, *Re A (Children)*, concerned conjoined twins, Jodie and Mary, and whether it would be lawful to kill one to save the other, acting against the wishes of their parents, when leaving both joined would have resulted in their joint premature death.

You may wish to revisit chapter 5 to refresh your memory on ways in which to find case law.

Practical exercise

Using the database of your choice, find the following cases:

R v Dudley and Stephens (1884) 14 QBD 273
Re A (Children) [2001] Fam 147 (CA)
and answer the following questions for each case:

1. What was the legal issue in the case?
2. What was the legal rule that applied in this case?
3. What were the particular facts of this case?
4. What made this case a hard case?
5. Do you agree with the decision of the court?

You will find some comments on each of these questions on the Online Resource Centre.

You should have seen by studying the two cases *Re A (Children)* and *Dudley and Stephens* that the courts sometimes have to deal with very sensitive and delicate issues. More recently, you may have heard in the news about the continuing right-to-die cases: Tony Nicklinson, who had been paralyzed from the neck down since suffering a stroke in 2005, died in August 2012 after failing in a legal bid to end his life with the help of a doctor. This case ultimately ended in the Supreme Court which rejected the 'right-to-die' argument but the Supreme Court said that there is a 'real prospect' a future human rights challenge would succeed if Parliament did not reconsider the current ban. You can find the full judgment at *R (Nicklinson and another) v Ministry of Justice* [2014] UKSC 38, introduced by Lord Neuberger (President) who said::

> These appeals arise out of tragic facts and raise difficult and significant issues, namely whether the present state of the law of England and Wales relating to assisting suicide infringes the European Convention on Human Rights, and whether the code published by the Director of Public Prosecutions ('the DPP') relating to prosecutions of those who are alleged to have assisted a suicide is lawful.

So, judges have to deal with legal, ethical, and moral questions when making their decisions. Balancing these issues requires analysis of the relationship between law and morality and the role of the judiciary in making law and setting precedent. These are more abstract theoretical issues in law than you may have encountered so far on your legal studies, but it is worth persevering even if the immediate relevance of legal theory might not seem clear to you. The next section will introduce you to three different schools of legal thought before moving on to look at a classic example of different judicial approaches to the same difficult legal problem.

11.3 An introduction to legal theory

The philosophical consideration of law is commonly referred to as jurisprudence. While jurisprudence is not a compulsory topic in a qualifying law degree, some institutions require students to take a jurisprudence module at some stage in their legal studies as even a basic understanding of why the law is as it is assists in understanding the law in a deeper way and can have practical application in the real-world practice of law.

Within this section, we will introduce three key areas of legal theory:

- Natural law
- Legal positivism
- Legal realism

11.3.1 Natural law

Proponents of natural law consider it to be a system of law based on the laws of nature and which is, therefore, universal in application. It considers that law and morality are connected and that it is a higher system of law than any legal system constructed by man. It upholds certain rights or values that are inherent in human reason and human nature.

Natural law has been considered by philosophers over many centuries. Cicero commented in *De republica* ('on the commonwealth') that:

> True law is right reason in agreement with nature; it is of universal application, unchanging and everlasting; it summons to duty by its commands, and averts from wrongdoing by its prohibitions . . . We cannot be freed from its obligations by Senate or People, and we need not look outside ourselves for an expounder of interpreter of it. And there will not be different laws at Rome and at Athens, or different laws now and in the future, but one eternal and unchangeable law will be valid for all nations and for all times. . .

The basic principle of natural law is that, as a higher law, any law made by man must accord with its principles in order to be valid. If law is not moral, then it is not law and has no authority.

 Practical exercise

Consider your viewpoint on the following issues:

1. Is it natural to be homosexual?

2. Is it natural to be racially or religiously prejudiced?

3. Is it natural to die by suicide?

4. It is natural to be monogamous?

5. Is it natural to use contraception?

 There are no 'right' answers to these questions, although you will find some comments on each of them on the Online Resource Centre.

So, natural lawyers will always seek to reason for an outcome that upholds morality. St Thomas Aquinas (1225–1274), the Christian philosopher and theologian, called law without moral content a 'perversion' of law since 'good is to be done and promoted, and evil is to be avoided'.

The difficult question then becomes what is moral, or good, or evil and do the morals of the judiciary necessarily accord with the morals of the public?

A good example of a case that raised difficult moral issues was that of *Gillick v West Norfolk and Wisbech Area Health Authority* [1986] AC 112 (HL). This case followed the publication of guidance by the Department of Health and Social Security to area health authorities on family planning services which contained a section dealing with contraceptive advice and treatment for young people. It stated that clinic sessions should be available for people of all ages and that, in exceptional circumstances, a doctor could exercise his clinical judgement to prescribe contraception to children under 16 without parental consent. Mrs Gillick, a Roman Catholic, sought an assurance from her local health authority that no contraceptive advice would be given to any of her daughters while they were under 16 without their knowledge and consent. The conflicting arguments were:

- If parental consent was necessary, levels of teenage pregnancy would increase
- If parental consent was not necessary, the courts would be encouraging underage sex

 Practical exercise

Gillick was determined by a 3–2 majority in the House of Lords. Using your research skills, find the case and read the judgment. Then answer the following questions:

1. What was the outcome?
2. What were the arguments put forward by the majority?
3. What did the dissenting judgments say?
4. Do you agree with the outcome?

 You will find some commentary on these questions on the Online Resource Centre.

11.3.2 Legal positivism

In contrast to natural law, legal positivism holds law and morality to be separate issues. Man-made law is stated (or 'posited'; hence 'positivism') by the legislature, and, provided that it has been properly enacted, it is legally valid, regardless of its moral content (or lack thereof). Put another way, whereas natural law is considered valid by virtue of its content (and thus invalid due to a lack of moral content), positive law is considered valid by virtue of its source only (and thus would be valid despite a lack of moral content). Legal positivism considers that law is a human construct and does not recognize a higher natural law.

Thus, for the legal positivists, law is a clearly defined set of rules that is established by the state, for the benefit of the state as a whole. It has no moral purpose other than to ensure the survival of the state. The theory of natural law was put forward from the sixteenth century. Thomas Hobbes in *Leviathan* considered that without a man-made state, the natural law would result in a 'war of all against all' and, in the absence of a sovereign power controlling (amongst other things) executive, legislative, and judicial power:

> In such condition, there is no place for industry; because the fruit thereof is uncertain: and consequently no culture of the earth; no navigation, nor use of the commodities that may be imported by sea; no commodious building; no instruments of moving, and removing, such things as require much force; no knowledge of the face of the earth; no account of time; no arts;

> no letters; no society; and which is worst of all, continual fear, and danger of violent death; and the life of man, solitary, poor, nasty, brutish, and short.

Following on from Hobbes, Jeremy Bentham proposed the utilitarian principle of positive law, which evaluates actions based on their consequences: for Bentham, the law should create the greatest happiness for the greatest number. Bentham was not a fan of natural law, calling it 'nonsense upon stilts'. John Austin was greatly influenced by Bentham whose theory of law also separated moral concerns by saying that law is the command issued by a sovereign, backed by threat of sanction:

> The existence of law is one thing; its merit or demerit is another. Whether it be or be not is one enquiry; whether it be or be not conformable to an assumed standard, is a different enquiry. A law, which actually exists, is a law, though we happen to dislike it.

The focus of legal positivism shifted during the mid-twentieth century from the role of the legislative institutions to the role of the courts. Hans Kelsen proposed a pure theory of law which also rejected the necessity of a connection between law and morality, stating that laws derived their validity by reference to a basic 'grundnorm' and did not require additional moral content for their legitimacy. More recently, HLA Hart in *The Concept of Law* developed the theory of legal positivism which has been continued by Joseph Raz.

 Practical exercise

Look up the case of *Knuller v DPP* [1973] AC 435 (HL). This case involved a magazine which contained advertisements for readers to meet up and engage in homosexual practices. The appellants were convicted on counts of conspiracy to corrupt public morals and conspiracy to outrage public decency.

1. What was the outcome in the case?
2. Do you think that gay dating advertisements are immoral?
3. Do you think that attitudes to gay dating have changed since 1973?
4. Do you think this case would be decided differently today?

 You will find some commentary on these questions on the Online Resource Centre.

11.3.3 The Hart-Devlin debate

The contrast between the natural law and positivist positions was set out in a series of articles between Hart and Devlin following the consideration of the issue of legalizing homosexuality and prostitution by the Wolfenden Committee (1957). The Wolfenden Report claimed that it is not the duty of the law to concern itself with immorality.

Devlin's position on the function of morality within the law was as follows:

> Without shared ideas on politics, morals and ethics, no society can exist . . . If men and women try to create a society in which there is no fundamental agreement about good and evil, they will fail; if having based it on common agreement, the agreement goes, the society will disintegrate. For society is not something that is kept together physically; it is held by the invisible bonds of

common thought. If the bonds were too far relaxed, the members would drift apart. A common morality is part of the bondage. The bondage is the price of society; and mankind, which needs society must pay its price.[1]

So, Devlin considered that there is a common public morality that must be protected by the law and that to remove the regulation of morality by law would inevitably lead to the spread of immoral behaviour and the disintegration of society. It followed that conduct which was viewed as immoral by the majority at the time, such as homosexuality, needed to be suppressed in the interests of society.

Devlin's position was criticized by Hart.[2] Hart disagreed with Devlin over the existence of a common morality, preferring instead the idea of a 'number of mutually tolerant moralities'[3] and that the use of law to reflect a snapshot of the dominant morality of the time was potentially harmful. Hart believed that the prohibition of conduct on the basis of a moral consensus was an unjustifiable interference with the rights of the individual to do as they wished. Therefore, legislation designed to enforce moral standards could be flawed due to the difficulties of defining morality and deciding between what is immoral and what is not. However, Hart did concede a role for the law in the *maintenance* of morality, but only where necessary to protect those who would engage in such immoral activities. Hart's reluctance to treat law as a moral issue was later criticized by Dworkin who considered that law could never be entirely divorced from morality.[4]

11.3.4 Legal realism

Legal realism takes a different view to that of natural law or legal positivism. Legal realists are less concerned with what the law should be, or its precise wording in statute, instead holding the view that the law should be understood in the context of how it is used in practice. In other words, this position is more 'real-worldly' in that the law is reflected in the decisions of judges. Legal realists simply look to describe what the law *is*, rather than what it *ought* to be. The leading proponent of legal realism was an American jurist, Oliver Wendell Holmes, who considered that if law just required the mechanical application of rules, then there would be no need for adversarial proceedings: courts would just apply the law. However, realistically speaking, judges do have discretion in how they decide cases and their individual political views,[5] social class, temperaments, and philosophies will all have a bearing on their reasoning and the ultimate outcome of the case before them.

11.3.5 Summary

This section has set out to introduce some of the main areas of legal theory and its key commentators. It is necessarily brief, but should have led you to realize that there are different schools of thought that can be applied to complex legal issues. These are summarized in Table 11.1.

---

1. P Devlin, *The Enforcement of Morals* (OUP 1965) 26.
2. HLA Hart, *Law, Liberty and Morality* (OUP 1963).
3. HLA Hart, *Law, Liberty and Morality* (OUP 1963) 62–3.
4. R Dworkin, *Law's Empire* (Belknap Press 1986).
5. For more on this point, see JAG Griffith, *The Politics of the Judiciary* (Manchester University Press 1977).

Table 11.1 Key points in legal theory

Natural law	Legal positivism	Legal realism
Laws of nature are superior to any laws made by man	There is no superior 'higher law' than that made by man	Law is reflected in and explained by the decisions of the courts
Law and morality are inextricably linked	It is not necessary for law and morality to be linked	
Immoral laws are not valid	Laws lacking in moral content are still valid provided that they have been enacted in the proper way	

You may well be wondering what the real-world application of these theoretical perspectives are—after all, this is a book on legal skills and not on jurisprudence. However, an appreciation of the rudiments of legal theory can greatly assist you in understanding the principle and policy decisions behind judicial decision making and legal reasoning which can, in turn, enable you to demonstrate a greater level of critical engagement with case law when using it, particularly in essays or dissertations, in preparation for tutorials or in the exam room. The next section will look in detail at an example which will further emphasize the point that there is no single correct answer available in relation to legal reasoning.

11.4 One case, multiple approaches

This section is based around a famous hypothetical case known as 'the Case of the Speluncean Explorers' written by Lon Fuller and published in the Harvard Law Review in 1948. It is similar in some respects to the real case of *R v Dudley and Stephens* which you encountered earlier in the chapter. It is set in the fictional land of Newgarth and the case is being heard in its Supreme Court.

In summary, five cave explorers (spelunkers) were caught underground after a tunnel collapsed. They learned through radio contact that rescue was at least ten days away, and that they could not survive that long without food. They also learned that they could survive if they were to eat one of their number. They radioed to the outside to ask whether it would be legally and/or morally permissible to kill one among them to sustain the others, but no-one above ground would answer the question.

One of the explorers, Whetmore, suggested that they throw dice to determine who should be eaten, and they all agreed. Just before the dice were thrown, Whetmore suggested that they wait until they were closer to death before proceeding; but he was outvoted, and a die was cast on his behalf. Everyone, including Whetmore, agreed that the dice were thrown fairly. Whetmore lost. When the rescuers finally reached the explorers, they found that Whetmore had been killed and eaten.

The remaining explorers were put on trial for murder under the statute which stated 'Whoever shall willfully take the life of another shall be punished by death' to which there was no exception applicable to this case. They were found guilty and sentenced to be hanged.

The case is now on appeal to the Supreme Court comprising five Justices: Truepenny CJ, Foster J, Tatting J, Keen J, and Handy J.

Table 11.2 Verdicts of the Justices in the Case of the Speluncean Explorers

Justice	Opinion
Truepenny CJ	Affirmed conviction and sentence
Foster J	Reversed conviction
Tatting J	Withdrew from decision
Keen J	Affirmed conviction and sentence
Handy J	Reversed conviction

Practical exercise

Download the Case of the Speluncean Explorers which you will find on the Online Resource Centre. Read the full judgment carefully.

In order to analyze the reasoning of each Justice, we can start by listing whether or not they would have affirmed the conviction and sentence of the Court of General Instances as shown in Table 11.2.

Overall, with the Supreme Court being evenly divided, the conviction and sentence of the Court of General Instances was affirmed, and the Public Executioner was directed to hang each of the defendants by the neck until they were dead.

You should already be able to see that, even on one set of facts, the Justices came to divergent opinions—two to convict, two to acquit, and one abstention. The next part of the exercise involves a more detailed reading of each Justice's opinion in order to determine their reasoning. We will use the opinion of Truepenny CJ as an example. He states (at page 619):

> It seems to me that in dealing with this extraordinary case the jury and the trial judge followed a course that was not only fair and wise, but the only course that was open to them under the law. The language of our statute is well known: 'Whoever shall willfully take the life of another shall be punished by death.' N. C. S. A. (N. S.) § 12-A. This statute permits of no exception applicable to this case, however our sympathies may incline us to make allowance for the tragic situation in which these men found themselves.
>
> In a case like this the principle of executive clemency seems admirably suited to mitigate the rigors of the law, and I propose to my colleagues that we follow the example of the jury and the trial judge by joining in the communications they have addressed to the Chief Executive. There is every reason to believe that these requests for clemency will be heeded, coming as they do from those who have studied the case and had an opportunity to become thoroughly acquainted with all its circumstances. It is highly improbable that the Chief Executive would deny these requests unless he were himself to hold hearings at least as extensive as those involved in the trial below, which lasted for three months. The holding of such hearings (which would virtually amount to a retrial of the case) would scarcely be compatible with the function of the Executive as it is usually conceived. I think we may therefore assume that some form of clemency will be extended to these defendants. If this is done, then justice will be accomplished without impairing either the letter or spirit of our statutes and without offering any encouragement for the disregard of law.

Therefore, for Truepenny CJ, the law is clear. The statute clearly applies to the conduct of the defendants: they wilfully took the life of another by putting Whetmore to death before eating him. For Truepenny CJ, it is not open to the court to ignore the clearly drafted words of the legislature. He recognizes that the Executive may provide clemency (that is, moderate the severity of the punishment) and comments that it is not the role of the Executive to hold a hearing to judge the merits of the case: this would be encroaching too far on the role of the judiciary. Truepenny CJ concludes that justice would be done, with the defendants escaping death as the sanction for their actions via executive clemency, while leaving the integrity of the legal rule intact. Truepenny CJ does not use any arguments based on moral values in reaching his judicial decision. For him, the law is the law and the courts apply it. It is for the Executive to dispense justice in these particularly extreme circumstances. As his reasoning divorces law and morality, you should be able to see that he is approaching the issue from a legal positivist standpoint.

You may be interested to note that in the real-life case of *Dudley and Stephens* which you encountered earlier in the chapter, the court sentenced the defendants to the statutory death penalty with a recommendation for mercy. Their sentences were ultimately commuted to six months' imprisonment by the Home Secretary (exercising executive power).

 Practical exercise

Re-read the judgments of each of the other Justices in the Case of the Speluncean Explorers carefully. For each of the Justices, consider the following questions:

1. What were the facts or issues that concerned them most in reaching their decision?

2. What theoretical position do they most closely seem to represent?

3. What do they think their role as a judge demands?

4. What do they consider to be the correct outcome?

Once you have analyzed each opinion:

5. Which of the Justices do you agree with most closely, and why?

6. Which of the Justices (whose opinion you ultimately disagree with) do you find most persuasive, and why?

   You will find some commentary on these questions on the Online Resource Centre.

The purpose of this exercise is to demonstrate how the different theoretical perspectives introduced in section 11.3 are reflected in practice, and to underline the point that legal reasoning can be much more than the simple application of rules to a set of facts. Moreover, you should have grasped by now that, since the law of England and Wales is based on an adversarial system, that law is all about argument and, therefore, that there is no single 'right' answer in legal reasoning.

In practical terms, barristers get to 'know their judges' and understand the types of argument that will stand the strongest chances of being persuasive. For example, if you were defending the Speluncean Explorers in front of Truepenny CJ, and knew that he was, in essence, a positivist that holds to the letter of the law, you would not succeed if you ran a defence that said that the laws of society did not apply to the defendants once they were cut off from society, or that the purpose of the law of murder would not be fulfilled if it were applied to the men who acted in a way to provide the greatest chance of preserving the most life. However, if you used the same defence in front of Foster J, you would stand a much greater chance of winning your case.

CHAPTER SUMMARY

Logic and simple legal reasoning

- The logical syllogism involves forming a conclusion from two premises

- In legal reasoning, the major premise is a statement of law; the minor premise is the statement of fact. Forming the conclusion is referred to as applying the law to the facts

- There are many cases which come before the courts that do not neatly fall within the construct of simple legal reasoning

Hard cases

- Hard cases involve legal, ethical, and moral questions

- Determining hard cases requires an understanding of the relationship between law and morality and the constitutional role of the judiciary

Legal theory

- Natural law theory considers that the laws of nature are superior to the laws of man; that law and morality are inextricably linked; and that immoral laws lack legitimacy

- Legal positivism holds that there is no superior higher law than that made by man; that there is no link necessary between law and morality; and that 'immoral' laws are still valid provided that they have been enacted properly

- The relationship between law and morality was considered at length in the Hart-Devlin debate

- The legal realist position is that law is reflected in, and explained by, the decisions of the courts

Reasoning in practice

- The adversarial system in England and Wales is based upon argument and therefore there is no single 'right' answer in legal reasoning

- 'Knowing your judge' can assist in formulating arguments that stand a greater chance of success

12

Referencing and avoiding plagiarism

INTRODUCTION

This chapter deals with referencing and avoiding plagiarism. These skills are of critical importance to your studies since your academic work will inevitably require you to read, critically consider, and evaluate the work of others. However, you must ensure that you carefully and meticulously distinguish between your own work, ideas, and arguments and those of the authors or judges that you have encountered during your research. This is done by providing thorough references to the sources that you have used in your work. Failing to do so may leave you vulnerable to accusations that you have presented the work of others as your own—that is, plagiarism. This chapter will explain what is meant by plagiarism in more detail and introduce you to two widely-used systems of referencing which will help you to avoid inadvertent plagiarism: footnote (specifically, OSCOLA) referencing and in-text (or Harvard) referencing. Each system is then explored in greater depth and will show you how to reference the most commonly-encountered sources using footnote referencing (in section 12.3) or in-text referencing (in section 12.4). It should be read in conjunction with the chapters on writing essays (chapter 13), writing dissertations (chapter 14), and answering problem questions (chapter 15) which follow.

The ability to reference thoroughly, properly, and consistently should become second nature to you as you progress through your legal studies. Plagiarism is invariably treated very seriously by institutions and any suspected cases are investigated thoroughly. If a case of suspected plagiarism is upheld, then it is likely that some adverse penalty will be applied which could seriously limit your prospects of success in your course overall. Worse still, plagiarism could be considered to be evidence against good character by the Law Society and the Bar Standards Board which would mean that even if you successfully complete the academic stage of legal training, you may be unable to proceed to the Legal Practice Course or the Bar Professional Training Course. There is too much at stake to risk deliberate plagiarism or ignoring the requirements of good referencing needed to avoid inadvertent plagiarism.

LEARNING OUTCOMES

After studying this chapter, you will be able to:

- Define what is meant by plagiarism

- Know when to provide references and avoid inadvertent plagiarism

- Understand the risks associated with deliberate plagiarism

- Reference your sources consistently and thoroughly using footnote/OSCOLA or in-text/ Harvard referencing

12.1 Plagiarism

It is commonplace to think of plagiarism as a deliberate copying from an unacknowledged source with the intention to deceive, but this is not the case. Plagiarism covers *all* instances in which the work of another is used without sufficient acknowledgement.

Plagiarism The *Oxford English Dictionary* defines plagiarism as 'the action or practice of taking someone else's work, idea, etc., and passing it off as one's own; literary theft'.

Universities may have their own definitions within their regulations on academic conduct. For example, the University of Leeds defines plagiarism as follows:

> Plagiarism is defined as presenting someone else's work, in whole or in part, as your own. Work means any intellectual output and typically includes text, data, images, sound or performance.[1]

As you see from these definitions, the essence of plagiarism is the failure to give an indication of the source of material upon which reliance has been placed in a piece of work. This may be deliberate, such as in situations where a student copies material from the Internet (or a fellow student) and passes it off as their own or buys an essay from an Internet essay bank or essay-writing service, but it is more often inadvertent, arising as a consequence of poor or lazy referencing or from a lack of understanding about the need to provide a reference. Plagiarism does not require a deliberate attempt to cheat.

12.1.1 Inadvertent plagiarism

The most effective means of avoiding inadvertent plagiarism is to ensure that every piece of work that you produce is thoroughly and correctly referenced. This raises two issues: *when* to reference and *how* to reference. The latter issue will be addressed in the referencing section later in the chapter whilst the remainder of this section will deal with the question of when a reference must be provided.

12.1.1.1 When to reference

Certain situations are straightforward. Most students would appreciate that a reference to the source of the following should be provided:

- **Statements of law** should be attributed to the relevant case or statutory provision

- **Direct quotations** should be attributed to their source in a book, article, case, or other material

---

1. University of Leeds Office of Academic Appeals & Regulation, 'Cheating, plagiarism, fraudulent or fabricated coursework and malpractice in University examinations' <http://www.leeds.ac.uk/secretariat/documents/cpffm_procedure.pdf> accessed 5 January 2015.

- **Factual material** such as statistics or the findings of a research study should be attributed to their source, whether this is an official report or an academic or commercial study
- **Definitions** of legal concepts or any other matter should be attributed to the appropriate source in a dictionary, case law, statute, article, or other material

An essay is an accumulation of a number of different things. It is composed largely of the writer's own words and thoughts, which need no reference, but may be interspersed with other material from the four categories outlined above that add the weight of authority to these words and thoughts. Definitions and quotations are the direct use of another's words, and must therefore be acknowledged as such, whilst factual material and statements of law need to be referenced to their source in order to substantiate and evidence their authoritative status.

There are three main ways in which you might incorporate the work of another author in your legal writing:

- **Summarizing**—where the author's original words are rewritten in a shortened form but which captures the key points which the author made
- **Paraphrasing**—where the author's original words are rewritten, but the original meaning is retained
- **Direct quotation**—where the author's original words are reproduced exactly.

Take a look at the following piece of source material and the examples of each form of use which follow. Note that these examples use OSCOLA footnote referencing which is covered in more detail in section 12.3 later in this chapter:

Source:
The ability of networked technologies to disseminate, share, or trade informational (intellectual) property in the form of text, images, music, film and TV through information services has been one of the more significant developments of the internet. This property is informational, networked and also globalized, and its authors, or their licensees, have a right of ownership or control over it, including the right to receive payment for access to the content. Both the means of access to the services and also their informational property content have a market value which simultaneously creates opportunities and motivations for what has become known as cyber-piracy.
(DS Wall, *Cybercrime* (Polity Press 2007) 94)

Summarized version:
Cyber-piracy has arisen as a result of the Internet's capability to deliver content (for which the intellectual property owner may have a right to be paid) globally.[1]

[1] DS Wall, *Cybercrime* (Polity Press 2007) 94.

Paraphrased version:
Networked technologies have enabled intellectual property such as words, pictures, sound and video (TV or film) to be distributed, broadcast or dealt through online mechanisms. This is one of the most important advances that the Internet has made. The property in this information is available globally via the network and the owners or licensees of this property have the right to deal with this property in accordance with their own wishes. This includes the ability to charge for allowing the content to be viewed or downloaded. Therefore, the way in which the

information is accessed and the proprietary nature of the material has some economic worth which then gives rise to the prospects and incentives for so-called cyber-piracy.[1]

---
[1] DS Wall, *Cybercrime* (Polity Press 2007) 94.

Direct quotation:

Cyber-piracy has arisen because 'the means of access to the services and also their informational property content have a market value which simultaneously creates opportunities and motivations'.[1]

---
[1] DS Wall, *Cybercrime* (Polity Press 2007) 94.

While it might seem obvious that direct quotations need a reference, paraphrased and summarized sections of another's work must also be referenced in full. Paraphrasing someone else's work without reference is still using their work as your own even though very few of the words between the source and the paraphrase match. What you are doing here is putting together the same core idea in a different way and using different words to convey an identical meaning. As such, a paraphrase can *never* be the product of your own academic reasoning or argument. Similarly, a summary is a condensed version of another's work, not your own.

Another instance where inadvertent plagiarism may arise is in the case of an article, say, that gives a commentary or analysis of another piece of work:

Sources:

In this case [*Re A (Conjoined Twins)* [2001] 1 FLR 1 (CA)], one can say that the judges first reject, then accept, the existence of a contextual moral threshold concerning how intention is to be judged. They alternate their definition of intention to achieve the desired moral result, that the doctors can operate to save Jodie. The underlying problem is that the legal concept of intention is really out of phase with the intuited moral result. One might say here, rephrasing the old saw, that truly the road to legal hell is paved with good intentions.

(A Norrie, 'From Criminal to Legal Theory: The Mysterious Case of the Reasonable Glue Sniffer' (2002) 65 MLR 538)

As Norrie explains, the Court of Appeal's approach offers a good example of orthodox subjectivism being manipulated to satisfy the moral context of the case.

(N Lacey, C Wells and O Quick, *Reconstructing Criminal Law* (3rd edn, LexisNexis Butterworths 2003) 752)

Here, a student might have read the secondary source (Lacey, Wells, and Quick), but not the primary source (Norrie). In this instance it would be plagiarism to include material from the secondary source while only providing a reference to the primary source:

For Norrie, the Court of Appeal in *Re A (Conjoined Twins)*[1] exemplified the manipulation of orthodox subjectivism to satisfy the moral circumstances of the case.[2]

---
[1] [2001] 1 FLR 1 (CA).
[2] A Norrie, 'From Criminal to Legal Theory: The Mysterious Case of the Reasonable Glue Sniffer' (2002) 65 MLR 538.

This would be plagiarism as it relies heavily on the analysis of Norrie's article by Lacey, Wells, and Quick, but does not acknowledge the source of that analysis. In essence, it is passing off the work of Lacey, Wells, and Quick as the student's own without attribution, while also conveying the (false) impression that the student has read the primary source (Norrie's article in the Modern Law Review). This could be avoided by providing a full reference as follows:

> For Norrie, the Court of Appeal in Re A (Conjoined Twins)[1] exemplified the manipulation of orthodox subjectivism to satisfy the moral circumstances of the case.[2]
>
> ---
>
> [1] [2001] 1 FLR 1 (CA).
> [2] A Norrie, 'From Criminal to Legal Theory: The Mysterious Case of the Reasonable Glue Sniffer' (2002) 65 MLR 538 in N Lacey, C Wells, and O Quick, *Reconstructing Criminal Law* (3rd edn, LexisNexis Butterworths 2003) 752.

A more difficult situation exists in relation to material that has been read during the production of an essay but which is not referred to specifically within the text. This includes materials such as books and articles that have influenced your thinking about the topic or which have shaped the points that you have raised in your essay. It is in relation to this that greatest uncertainty about whether to reference exists. There are two general rules that can be used as guidance:

1. If you are using your own words to express an idea that is specific to a particular writer, for example something that a judge has stated in a case or the views of the author of an article, then a reference to the source of the idea should be provided even though you have used your own words to explain that idea. If, however, you have read several textbooks to gain an overview of a topic and the same issue is expressed in each book, then you are free to use your own words without providing a reference. This is because the mention of the idea in several places demonstrates that it is a general issue of common knowledge, so it does not need to be attributed to a particular source

2. If in doubt, reference. It is preferable to provide too many references in your essay rather than to face an accusation of plagiarism or receive a deduction of marks for providing insufficient references. If you receive a comment from a lecturer that a piece of work contained too many unnecessary references, you should make a point of asking them to point out to you which references were unnecessary and why this was the case so that you can make adjustments in subsequent pieces of work

12.1.1.2 Common knowledge

Material that is 'common knowledge' generally does not need to be referenced. While this might seem obvious and straightforward, it is unfortunately complicated by the fact that there is no consensus as to what falls within common knowledge. Experts on plagiarism and academic malpractice disagree on what counts as common knowledge. Some only consider factual material such as current and historical events potentially to be common knowledge (for instance, 'Adolf Hitler was the leader of the German Nazi Party during the Second World War while Winston Churchill was Prime Minister of Great Britain throughout most of the conflict'). Others consider common knowledge to be that which is commonly known within the particular broad subject area (for instance, 'the UK has an unwritten constitution').

To complicate matters further, as you become more expert in your study of the law, what counts as common knowledge becomes even harder to define. Should common knowledge be defined in terms of reasonably educated people in general or reasonable law students? Within law (as with every other discipline) there is a body of common knowledge which even an educated outsider might not know.

Two tests which are often used in helping to decide whether or not a piece of information is common knowledge are:

- **Quantity**—can the information be found in numerous places?
- **Ubiquity**—is the information known by many people?

Of course, the problem with this is how many places are needed to consider that the information can be found in 'numerous' places. As a rough rule of thumb, many guidelines consider 'numerous' to mean 'five or more', but again, you must remember that this is not a hard and fast rule. If the information crops up in all your textbooks on the subject without further attribution, it is likely to be ubiquitous enough to be 'common knowledge'. If you are still in doubt, you could seek guidance from your lecturer. Otherwise, point 2 made earlier still applies—if in doubt, reference.

You should always keep the notes you have made in preparation for your work (see chapter 9 on note-taking). You may be asked to provide your notes and draft work to your institution. By doing this, you will at least be able to provide some evidence that you have done the necessary research and read the materials—and therefore that your plagiarism might actually be as a result of poor referencing rather than a deliberate attempt to cheat.

 You will find more examples and guidance relating to inadvertent plagiarism on the Online Resource Centre.

12.1.2 Deliberate plagiarism

If inadvertent plagiarism arises from lack of clarity about referencing requirements, deliberate plagiarism arises when students make a deliberate decision to try and pass off the work of others as their own. Deliberate plagiarism is almost never successful, so why do students try to plagiarize and what are the reasons that such behaviour is unwise?

12.1.2.1 Why do students plagiarize?

There are many reasons why students may make a conscious decision to take words from a source and seek to pass it off as their own work. Plagiarism can arise from a failure to understand what the coursework requires, a desperate desire to obtain a good mark, an unwillingness to interfere with the way that an idea has been expressed, or simply from the pressure of time as a deadline is looming. Ultimately, these are all manifestations of a lack of confidence in one's own ability to provide an answer to the question. Alternatively, students may resort to plagiarism because they cannot be bothered to produce their own work or because they feel that their course was badly taught and therefore does not deserve the effort that it would take to write an original piece of work.

Another reason often given by students is that they believe that everyone else is doing it and that they will not get caught. It was reported in October 2008 that almost half of students admitted to plagiarism in a poll carried out by a students' newspaper at the University of Cambridge and that only one in twenty students had been caught.[2] In October 2009, *The Times* reported that 300 students per year are caught cheating.[3] Many students who plagiarize often think that because they have not been caught then they have 'got away with it'.

2.   M Stothard, ' "1 in 2" admit to plagiarism' *Varsity* (Cambridge 30 October 2008) <http://www.varsity.co.uk/news/1058> accessed 27 November 2012.

3.   G Slapper, 'Plagiarism can have serious consequences for law students' *The Times* (London 15 October 2009).

However, this is not always the case. For some lecturers, the additional effort required to research and prosecute a potential case of plagiarism might be too great. Instead, they may penalize the student heavily for producing a piece of work which is overly derivative or poorly referenced.

In any event, there is no justification for plagiarism and, certainly, none of the possible 'excuses' given here will provide a defence when plagiarism is detected and you are called to account by your institution.

12.1.2.2 Turnitin

Turnitin (available online at www.submit.ac.uk) is a web-based plagiarism detection system which is in use in most UK universities. It is accessed either through the university's own online learning environment or directly via Turnitin's own website at www.submit.ac.uk. Students upload their work to the system which is then analyzed and compared against multiple sources, including websites, books, journals, and other student assignments that have previously been submitted to Turnitin—not just from your university, but from all universities accessing the Turnitin databases. Once work is submitted to Turnitin, it is usually stored within the Turnitin student assignment database so that it can be cross-checked against future submissions from other UK universities.[4] According to Turnitin's own website, it uses three databases for content matching: 45 billion web pages, 337 million student assignments and 130 million articles from 110,000 journals, periodicals, and books!

Turnitin provides the following for each piece of submitted work:

- **Similarity index.** This indicates (as a percentage score) the proportion of the submitted work that Turnitin identifies as matching other sources in its database
- **Originality report.** This report shows each of the matches in more detail, including the precise location of the duplicate content within each source.

While this might sound alarming, you should remember that Turnitin does not directly identify plagiarism: it provides information that shows where plagiarism *may* have occurred. An accusation of potential academic misconduct could only be made once the Turnitin report has been reviewed by your lecturer in detail and in the light of their academic experience, expertise, and judgment. For example, a 20 per cent match could comprise a number of short phrases, case names, or statute names spread throughout the work, which should not be an issue. However, the 20 per cent could equally represent a few whole paragraphs that are copied.

Turnitin does not replace academic judgement: however, it can reduce the time spent by lecturers investigating possible cases of plagiarism and it does reduce the prevalence of plagiarism in institutions where it is used.

12.1.2.3 Reasons to avoid plagiarism

As well as the automated plagiarism detection provided by Turnitin, many experienced lecturers have also developed an instinctive 'nose' for suspected plagiarism which often proves to be correct. Overall, it is virtually impossible to copy from a source of material that cannot be detected, therefore resorting to plagiarism in an attempt to acquire a good mark will ultimately be unsuccessful. Such is the battle against plagiarism that many institutions annotate

---

4.   A common concern raised by students is that of copyright: students retain the copyright and all other intellectual property rights in the work they submit. The developers of Turnitin work closely with the UK Information Commissioner's Office to ensure that student work is used fairly and legally.

degree transcripts to include an explanation that a mark in the relevant subject was amended following a finding of plagiarism; something which is hardly going to impress future employers. Moreover, the Law Society and the Bar Standards Board require universities to notify them of proven cases of plagiarism: since plagiarism involves dishonest academic practice, a proven finding against a student suggests that they are not of good character for the purposes of a career in the legal profession. This is particularly so if, as is increasingly common, you are required to sign some sort of statement that all due credit has been given to the work of others as part of your submission rules. Dishonestly signing a false declaration would not be received well by your university or the professional bodies.

More than this, plagiarism is actually counter-productive as it deprives the student of the opportunity to test what they do know and how well they are able to express this. In other words, the learning opportunity provided by the coursework is wholly negated and the student learns nothing as a result. You will never improve your legal skills if you are not prepared to try and receive feedback on your ability. There is nowhere else in the progression of becoming a lawyer that you will be able to learn these skills and the later stages of qualification as a lawyer will expect that you are able to identify, explain, and analyze the law, so you need to acquire these skills now by a process of trial and error.

Finally, there is no guarantee that the source that you plagiarize will be good. This is particularly true of material taken from the Internet. Anyone can post anything on the Internet; there is no quality control or mechanism of checking, amending, or removing inaccurate material. Essay banks are equally unreliable and cost vast sums of money. Think about the rationale behind it. Students sell essays that they have written to an essay bank who may have no expertise in the subject at all. Essays with higher marks sell for a higher price, so students are likely to exaggerate the mark in order to gain maximum profit, so there is nothing to say that the essay that you buy as a first did not actually receive a lower second-class mark. Irrespective of this, that essay may be on the same subject matter but it does not answer the same question as that set as your coursework, so there is no point in submitting it. All you are doing is paying a vast amount of money for a piece of work of questionable quality that does not answer the question that you have been set and which is likely to be detected. Essays from essay writing services often contain extensive material from online sources as well as content from essay banks that have been recycled many times over. If you buy a 'custom-written' essay, it is still likely to be flagged by Turnitin.

Ultimately, plagiarism achieves nothing and will cause you untold grief when it is detected. Do not do it.

12.2 Referencing styles

On a practical point, it is essential that your written work is fully and correctly referenced otherwise you will lose marks. Not only are these relatively simple marks to gain, but poor referencing also detracts from the overall quality of your work and can leave a negative impression in the mind of your marker. In the worst case scenario, failure to reference your sources may leave you vulnerable to accusations of plagiarism and all the consequences that follow on from this. The previous section discussed the situations in which referencing should be provided whilst this section gives an overview of two common referencing systems which we will go on to cover in more detail later in this chapter. Before introducing those systems, though, we must first consider 'house style'.

12.2.1 House style

'House style' is the official guidance that you have been given by your institution about how to provide references within your work. It should therefore be the starting point for deciding how to reference. If you have not yet found any guidance, make sure that you investigate further as you will need to consult it in order to ensure that your work is correctly referenced. The level of guidance varies enormously between institutions so you may find that you are provided with detailed instructions with examples, given direction to use one of the standard referencing schemes or, merely told that 'footnotes must be used' or 'your work must be fully referenced'. You may also find that the preferred referencing style varies between modules, so you must check carefully. You may even find that there is no house style at all.

If you have been given instructions as to what style to use, it is imperative that you use this and not some other style of your own making or that you have used previously. Even if you are being given some examples as guidance rather than as part of a mandatory policy, you would be wise to follow the house style because it is likely to be correct and complete, whereas any approach to referencing that you have used previously was (presumably) not one that was specifically tailored to undergraduate law.

If you have not been given any detailed guidelines, the remainder of this chapter looks at two commonly-encountered systems which you may find useful: footnotes (specifically, OSCOLA) referencing, and in-text (or Harvard) referencing. Remember, however, that there is more than one way to reference the same material, so there are likely to be other equally valid approaches. The key to good referencing is completeness and consistency so keep these principles in mind when deciding which style of referencing to use. Finally, while the detailed guidance covers the most common materials that you will need to reference, it is impossible to cover all the possible sources within the scope of this book. There are some excellent online resources, which are highlighted in the Further Reading section at the end of this chapter. Remember that if there is a particular source which you are unsure how to reference, check your house style first (if you have one) or, failing that, ask your lecturer who should be willing to help.

12.2.2 Footnotes and OSCOLA

Most legal writing uses footnotes (sometimes called Roman, Oxford, or numerical referencing). This is the system of referencing used in this book whereby the reference details are provided at the bottom of the same page and their position in the text is denoted by a small raised (superscript) number. A bibliography is then provided at the end of the work, which details all the materials that you have used in its preparation, regardless of whether you have made specific reference to them in your answer. In other words, the bibliography contains everything that you have referenced in your footnotes *plus* anything that you read or consulted but did not mention specifically in your text, for example books that you used for background reading.

A **bibliography** is a list of *all* materials that have been consulted during the preparation of your work.

OSCOLA stands for the 'Oxford Standard for Citation Of Legal Authorities' and is a footnote-based system that is becoming widely adopted as standard in other universities. The most recent (fourth) edition of OSCOLA was released in November 2010.

12.2.3 Harvard referencing

An alternative method of referencing that you may encounter is called Harvard referencing. This is sometimes referred to as 'in text' or 'alphabetical/name-date' referencing. Harvard referencing requires abbreviated references to be given in the text itself with either a bibliography *or* a list of references provided at the end of the work. Within the Harvard system, a **list of references** is distinct from a bibliography as a list of references only provides the details of materials that have been referenced in the text but does *not* include preparatory or background materials that have not been specifically cited. As such, a bibliography is a fuller record.

A **list of references** is a list of all materials that have been specifically referenced within your work.

Footnotes are never used in the Harvard system.

12.2.4 Never mix different referencing styles

As a final word of caution, you must *never* mix different referencing styles together in the same piece of work. This means that there must be no in-text references if you use footnotes and no footnotes if you use Harvard referencing. Equally, if you are using footnotes, you *must* provide the complete reference in the footnote rather than the shortened 'name, date' approach used in Harvard referencing. Here is an example of an incorrect use of mixed referencing styles:

> Fafinski (2005) discussed the implications of *R v Barnes*[1] in relation to the role of consent in establishing criminal liability for sporting injuries.
>
> [1] [2004] EWCA Crim 3246; [2005] 1 WLR 910.

In this example there is an in-text reference to the article by Fafinski published in 2005 and a footnote reference giving the citation for *Barnes*. This could be corrected by consistent use of footnotes, like this:

> Fafinski[1] discussed the implications of *R v Barnes*[2] in relation to the role of consent in establishing criminal liability for sporting injuries.
>
> [1] S Fafinski, 'Consent and the rules of the game: the interplay of criminal and civil liability for sporting injuries' (2005) 69 JCL 414.
> [2] [2004] EWCA Crim 3246.

Alternatively, it could be corrected by consistent use of in-text referencing, without any footnotes, like this:

> Fafinski (2005) discussed the implications of *R v Barnes* [2004] EWCA Crim 3246 in relation to the role of consent in establishing criminal liability for sporting injuries.

This mixing of styles can sometimes happen accidentally especially if you copy directly from source material that uses different styles. Be careful to ensure that you are consistent in your use of referencing styles and reformat references accordingly to suit your chosen style. In other words: pick a system and stick to it.

12.2.5 Conventions used in this chapter

The remainder of this chapter will show how to reference the most common sources using footnotes/OSCOLA and in-text/Harvard referencing. The discussion of each source begins with a schematic showing the elements of the citation. Using OSCOLA cases by way of example, a typical schematic will look like this:

> *First party* | *v* | *Second party* | (year)/[year] | report abbreviation | page number | (court)

The conventions used in all these schematics are as follows:

- **Vertical lines** (|) are used to delineate elements of the citation. These are simply used to assist clarity and are *not* used in the actual reference itself.

- **Bold type** is used to denote text or punctuation that appears in the final reference: in the above example, the *v* between the parties, the round or square brackets around the year of the case report and the round brackets around the court are always provided. It is shown in bold for emphasis only: it is not bold in the actual reference.

- **Italic type** is used to denote elements of the reference that appear in italics in the final reference itself. Here, names of the parties to the case are shown in italics.

- **Regular type** is used to describe each element of the citation.

- **Slashes** are used to denote alternatives: here the year of report would either be in round or square brackets depending on the numbering of the particular report series being referenced.

12.3 How to reference using footnotes/OSCOLA

Referencing with footnotes is a three-stage process:

- Positioning the footnote marker in the text
- Providing the content of the footnote itself at the foot of the page; the precise way in which this is done will depend on the nature of the source itself (case, book, article, etc.)
- Compiling a bibliography/list of references

This section will walk through each of those stages in turn.

12.3.1 Positioning the footnote marker in the text

Footnote markers appear *outside* any punctuation (that is, *after* a punctuation mark and not before):

> The positioning of footnotes is discussed by Finch and Fafinski in Legal Skills.[1] Note that the footnote marker (superscript number 1) appears after the closing full stop in the last sentence.

[1] E Finch and S Fafinski, *Legal Skills* (5th edn, OUP 2015) 266.

The footnote marker usually appears at the end of a sentence, although it is perfectly permissible to include a footnote marker within a sentence at the point where the material to which the reference refers appears for the sake of clarity, as these two examples illustrate:

> As Finch and Fafinski note, it is common practice to provide a footnote reference to material at the end of the sentence in which it is mentioned.[1]
>
> ---
> [1] E Finch and S Fafinski, *Legal Skills* (5th edn, OUP 2015) 267.

> As Finch and Fafinski[1] explain, it is perfectly permissible for the sake of clarity to provide a reference for a particular book or journal at the point at which the name of the author or the title of the work is mentioned.
>
> ---
> [1] E Finch and S Fafinski, *Legal Skills* (5th edn, OUP 2015) 267.

Providing footnote markers within a sentence can also be useful if more than one source needs referencing in the same sentence. For example:

> As Fafinski comments,[1] the Court of Appeal's judgment in *Barnes*[2] meant that conduct in sport that was outside the rules of the game and led to injury still might not result in criminal liability.
>
> ---
> [1] S Fafinski, 'Consent and the rules of the game: the interplay of criminal and civil liability for sporting injuries' (2005) 69 JCL 414.
> [2] *R v Barnes* [2004] EWCA Crim 3246.

12.3.2 Providing the content of the footnote

The sections that follow demonstrate how to reference different sources using OSCOLA. Before getting into the details, it is important to cover some general points on content that apply to all footnotes and to explain the conventions used in the remainder of this section.

12.3.2.1 Additional material in footnotes

As well as the basic references themselves, it is sometimes acceptable to include a *short* note in a footnote if this relates to something explanatory that would interest the reader or assist their understanding but which would break the flow of the argument if included in the main body of the text.

For example, if your essay discusses a particular line of authority, you may want to add some interesting information about it or draw attention to an article that takes a critical approach to the law that you are outlining. This draws the reader's attention to it at the appropriate point of the essay but ensures that the flow of your argument is not broken. In many respects, notes provided in footnotes can be regarded as interesting asides:

> The House of Lords affirmed the current 'virtual certainty' test for oblique intention in *R v Woollin*.[1]
>
> ---
> [1] [1999] 1 AC 82 (HL). The line of authority that led to this point is complex: *Hyam v DPP* [1975] AC 55 (HL); *R v Moloney* [1985] AC 905 (HL); *R v Hancock and Shankland* [1986] AC 455 (HL); *R v Nedrick* [1986] 1 WLR 1025 (CA).

You should, however, exercise caution when including anything other than a reference in your footnotes (particularly if your word limit *excludes* words that are in footnotes) as this is sometimes viewed with suspicion by lecturers, who recognize that it is an attempt to circumvent the word limit by including material in the footnotes that should rightly be in the body of the essay:

> The House of Lords affirmed the current test for oblique intention in *R v Woollin*.[1]
>
> ----------
>
> [1] [1999] 1 AC 82 (HL). The facts of *Woollin* are as follows: The defendant violently shook his 3-month-old baby and then threw him across the room. The baby died. The defendant accepted that there was a risk of injury and admitted that the baby had hit the floor hard, but he did not think that it would kill him. The trial judge told the jury that they might infer intention if the defendant appreciated a 'substantial risk' of serious harm. The Court of Appeal held that although the words 'virtually certain' as in *Nedrick* were preferable, the jury was not misdirected if it was clear that the decision was theirs. The House of Lords held that the judge had confused the jury and since it was impossible to know which of the two statements the jury had followed this must be a material misdirection. The 'virtual certainty' test from *Nedrick* was affirmed with the modification that the jury may 'find' rather than 'infer' the requisite intention.

Do avoid doing this; not only is it poor academic practice, it may result in losing marks for poor referencing. As always, it is advisable to check the rules of your institution to determine whether there are any rules as to what can and cannot be included in a footnote.

12.3.2.2 Punctuation in footnotes

As you will see in the examples that follow, OSCOLA referencing uses minimal punctuation. Each section will explain precisely what is required, but, you will note that footnote text in OSCOLA is always closed with a full stop, question mark, or exclamation mark and is never left 'hanging'.

12.3.2.3 Abbreviations in footnotes

Students sometimes resort to abbreviated references in footnotes to avoid having to type the full reference to a particular source on each occasion. Not only is this a lazy (and unacceptable) approach to referencing, it can be readily avoided by using the following Latin referencing abbreviations for referring to material that has already been referenced elsewhere. You should note that these referencing conventions are sometimes misused, so you should be careful to select the correct one (see Table 12.1).

Of the phrases listed in Table 12.1, only 'ibid' and 'cf' are used within OSCOLA, where they are written in regular type with no punctuation and capitalized if at the start of the footnote text. However, as abbreviations of Latin phrases, you may see these written in lower case (with no initial capital letter) and italicized.

12.3.3 Referencing cases using footnotes/OSCOLA

12.3.3.1 UK cases (non-judicial review)

The elements of a typical case citation in OSCOLA are as follows. First where there is a neutral citation:

> *First party* | *v* | *Second party* | [year] | court | number | (year)/[year] | report abbreviation | first page

and secondly where there is no neutral citation:

> *First party* | *v* | *Second party* | (year)/[year] | report abbreviation | first page | (court)

Table 12.1 Latin referencing conventions

Abbreviation	Meaning
ibid	Short for *ibidem* which means 'in the same place'. This is used to refer to the immediately preceding footnote provided that it is identical in every respect, that is 'in the *very* same place'. If you want to refer to a different page in the work cited in the immediately preceding footnote, you could say 'Ibid 123' which means 'in the same work referred to in the previous footnote, but at page 123'.
Cf	This is an abbreviation for the Latin *confer*, which means 'compare' or 'consult'. You could therefore say 'Cf. Finch and Fafinski (n 12)' which means 'Compare this with whatever Finch and Fafinski say in whatever is referred to by footnote 12'.
op cit	This is short for *opus citatum*: 'the work previously cited'. It is used to refer to a book, article, or case that has already been referenced in the essay. *It is not used within OSCOLA.*
loc cit	This is short for *loco citato* meaning 'in the place cited'. In essence it refers to 'the page previously cited in the book previously cited' so it is a more specific reference than *op cit* and should only be used to refer to a particular page that has previously been referenced. *Like* op cit, it *is not used within OSCOLA.*

The party names are given in italics. OSCOLA separates them with a lower case unpunctuated italic *v*. This departs from an alternative established legal convention that shows only the party names in italics and the separator being 'v' in regular type, often punctuated by a full stop. Although the OSCOLA convention makes it quicker to format case names by highlighting both parties and the 'v' separator, there is a school of thought that says that strictly only the names of the parties themselves should be italicized. Therefore you might see, for example:

- *Entores v Miles Far East Corporation* [1955] 2 QB 327 (CA)
- *Entores v. Miles Far East Corporation* [1955] 2 QB 327 (CA)
- *Entores* v. *Miles Far East Corporation* [1955] 2 QB 327 (CA)

Only the first of these is OSCOLA-compliant. The year of the report is put in [square] brackets when the volume of the report series in question is identified by the year itself. For report series in which the volume numbers run sequentially, then the year that the case was heard is given in (round) brackets.

For more information on case citations including the use of neutral citations, see chapter 5.

OSCOLA also uses no punctuation in abbreviations for law reports—so, in the earlier examples you will see 'QB' for the Queen's Bench report rather than 'Q.B.'. For cases after 1865 (when the Incorporated Council of Law Reporting was founded) and where there is no neutral citation, the court is also given in brackets at the end of the citation. If a case has a neutral citation, this should be given before any reference to a report of the case and separated from it by a semi-colon. There is no need to identify the court at the end of the citation in these instances, since it is apparent from the neutral citation itself. Here is a House of Lords case which has both a neutral citation and a reference to the Appeal Cases reports:

- *R v G* [2003] UKHL 50; [2004] 1 AC 1034

When referring to a case in the main body of the text, the case citation is given in the footnote and not in the text. The text itself only contains the names of the parties to the case, like this:

> Astill J's dicta were disapproved by the House of Lords in *R v Bow Street Metropolitan Stipendiary Magistrate and Allison, ex p Government of the United States of America*.[1] This case involved the attempted extradition from England to the United States of an individual who had allegedly obtained 189 sets of credit card account information.
>
> [1] [2000] 2 AC 216 (HL).

OSCOLA referencing does not require the case name to be repeated in the footnote, (although some people like to do so) unless the text itself does not mention the parties by name, in which instance the full citation (including the parties) *must* be given in the footnote, as shown:

> The offence created by section 3 of the Computer Misuse Act 1990 was designed to encompass activities involving computer viruses, 'Trojan horses' and worms as well as interference with websites[1] or accessing subscription cable television channels without paying the subscription.[2]
>
> [1] *R v Lindesay* [2002] 1 Cr App R (S) 370 (CA).
> [2] *R v Parr-Moore* [2003] 1 Cr App R (S) 425 (CA).

12.3.3.2 Pinpoint referencing of cases

The page number given in a case citation denotes the page in the law report on which the case report begins. If a case is used as an authority for a specific point of law or to demonstrate the application of the law in a particular factual scenario, then a general reference to the case using just this opening page number will suffice:

> Outside the established duty situations, the existence of a duty of care between claimant and defendant is determined on the basis of individual circumstances.[1]
>
> [1] *Donoghue v Stevenson* [1932] AC 562 (HL).

However, case reports can be very lengthy and often cover a considerable number of pages. If you need to refer the reader to a particular page in the case report, then you need to provide a **pinpoint reference**. This is usually required when you want to draw attention to a particular argument or if you provide a quotation from the case. You should include a page reference/paragraph number and state the name of the judge concerned at the end of the citation in the footnote.

> The existence of a duty of care between claimant and defendant is determined on the basis of the 'neighbour principle' formulated by Lord Atkin in *Donoghue v Stevenson* who stated:
>
> > You must take reasonable care to avoid acts or omissions which you can reasonably foresee would be likely to injure your neighbour . . . persons who are so closely and directly affected by my act that I ought reasonably to have them in my contemplation as being so affected when I am directing my mind to the acts or omissions which are called in question.[1]
>
> [1] [1932] AC 562 (HL) 580 (Lord Atkin).

If the reference is to be attributed to a specific judge, then the judge's name is added in round brackets at the end of the citation. Sometimes judge's names are shown as '*per* Lord Atkin', but this Latin attribution is not used in OSCOLA.

Any pinpoint reference to a particular page is given *after* the designation of the court except when a case has both neutral citation and a law report citation. As the court is not identified at the end of the citation any pinpoint page references to the law report are delineated by a comma, like this:

• *R v G* [2003] UKHL 50; [2004] 1 AC 1034, 1037

If the judgment uses paragraph numbers, as is often the case with neutrally-cited cases, it is perfectly acceptable to use a paragraph number as a pinpoint. OSCOLA uses square brackets to denote paragraph numbers and to differentiate them from page numbers:

> The House of Lords held that it was 'not addressing the meaning of "reckless" in any other statutory or common law context'.[1]
>
> [1] *R v G* [2003] UKHL 50 [28] (Lord Bingham).

In this example, Lord Bingham's quote can be found in paragraph 28 of the judgment.

Note that the conventions on pinpoint referencing explained here apply equally to the other types of case report covered in the remainder of this section.

12.3.3.3 Judicial review cases post-2001

Judicial review cases are cited differently. In judicial review, the courts supervise the exercise of public power on the application of an individual, and there are therefore three parties involved:

• The public authority called in question (the respondent)

• The applicant

• The Crown (notionally representing the interests of the applicant against the public authority)

Judicial review cases post-2001 are cited in OSCOLA as follows:

> ***R*** | (*Applicant*) | *v* | *Respondent* | (year)/[year] | report abbreviation | first page | (court)

For example:

• *R (Lichniak) v Secretary of State for the Home Department* [2003] 1 AC 903 (HL)

You may also see such cases cited using the phrase 'on the application of' which may make it clearer that it involves judicial review, although this is not-OSCOLA compliant:

• *R (on the application of Lichniak) v Secretary of State for the Home Department* [2003] 1 AC 903

Neutral citations must precede the law report citation where available.

12.3.3.4 Judicial review cases prior to 2001

Judicial review cases prior to 2001 (when Order 53 of the Rules of the Supreme Court, which contained the rules of procedure for judicial review, was replaced by Part 54 of the Civil Procedure Rules) are cited slightly differently again:

> ***R*** | *v* | *Respondent* | *ex p* | Applicant | (year)/[year] | report abbreviation | first page | (court)

For example:

- *R v Secretary of State for Transport ex p Factortame Ltd (No. 2)* [1991] 1 AC 603 (HL)
- *R v Secretary of State for the Home Department ex p Bentley* [1994] QB 349 (DC)

Here *ex p* is short for *ex parte* which means 'by or for one party'. You may also see judicial review cases cited using *ex parte* in full in place of the abbreviated *ex p* used within OSCOLA, like this:

- *R v Secretary of State for Transport ex parte Factortame Ltd (No. 2)* [1991] 1 AC 603 (HL)

The meaning is the same and the use of *ex parte* in full is equally valid, although not OSCOLA-compliant.

Neutral citations must precede the law report citation where available.

12.3.3.5 Court of Justice of the European Union/General Court cases

Cases in the Court of Justice of the EU and the General Court also require the case number:

> Case case number | *First party* | *v* | *Second party* | [year] | report abbreviation | first page

Where possible, you should cite the reference from the official report: that is, the European Court Reports (ECR). CJEU cases are reported in volume 'ECR I' and General Court cases are reported in volume 'ECR II'. Note here that the volume numbers are given in Roman numerals using the letters 'I'/'II' and *not* the numbers '1'/'11'. The volume number and page number are joined with a dash. Since 1989 case numbers in the ECJ have been prefixed with 'C-' and cases in the Court of First Instance with 'T-'.

For example:

- Case C-176/03 *Commission v Council* [2005] ECR I-7879
- Case T-201/04 *Microsoft v Commission* [2004] ECR II-4463

Case numbers before 1989 carry no prefix:

- Case 203/80 *Re Casati* (Case 203/80) [1981] ECR 2595

If there is no official report available, you should cite the Common Market Law Reports (CMLR) report in the same way as for any other series of law reports, such as:

- Case C-440/05 *Commission v Council* [2008] 1 CMLR 22

If there is no report available, you should just provide the case number and party names with the court and date in round brackets like this:

- Case C-444/02 *Fixtures Marketing Ltd v OPAP* (ECJ 9 November 2004)

12.3.3.6 European Court of Human Rights cases

Decisions of the European Court of Human Rights up to 1 November 1998 are cited in the following way:

> *First party* | *v* | *Second party* | (App no | application number) | (year) | Series A | no | case number

For example:

- *Golder v UK* (App no 4451/70) (1975) Series A no 19

From 1 November 1998 the official reports were renamed Reports of Judgments and Decisions and are cited as 'ECHR' with the appropriate case number as follows:

> *First party* | v | *Second party* | (App no | application number) | [year] | ECHR | case number

For instance:

- *Janowski v Poland* (App no 25716/94) [1999] ECHR 3
- *Spyropoulos v Greece* (App no 5081/03) [2005] ECHR 569

12.3.4 Referencing legislation using footnotes/OSCOLA

12.3.4.1 UK legislation

Acts of Parliament are referenced by their short title and year (in that order). There is no comma before the year. For instance:

- Theft Act 1968
- Gender Recognition Act 2004
- Education Act 1996

Note that when you are mentioning an Act of Parliament within a piece of work, you should *never* capitalize 'the' before the short title like this:

> The law of theft was greatly simplified by The Theft Act 1968.

Parts of an Act are cited differently depending on their position in the sentence. If you are starting a sentence with a reference to a statutory provision, you should spell out 'section' in full:

> Section 3 of the Theft Act 1968 defines appropriation.

However, if you are referring to a particular provision later in the sentence, you may (if you wish) use an abbreviated form, like this:

> Appropriation is defined in s 3 of the Theft Act 1968.

Note that there is no full stop after the 's'.

However, when referring to a statutory provision in a footnote, the name of the Act comes first, followed by the provision number with no other punctuation other than the closing full stop:

> The *actus reus* of theft is comprised of three elements each of which is further defined in statute, namely, the appropriation[1] of property[2] belonging to another.[3]

---

[1] Theft Act 1968 s 3.
[2] Theft Act 1968 s 4.
[3] Theft Act 1968 s 5.

Statutory instruments are cited by name, year and serial number, where available.
For example:

- Data Protection Act 1998 (Commencement No. 2) Order 2008 SI 2007/1592
- Equality Act (Sexual Orientation) Regulations 2007 SI 2007/1063

12.3.4.2 European legislation

European legislation (Regulations and Directives) are cited as follows:

> Legislation type | Legislation number | Full title | [year] | OJ L | Issue number | / | Page number

The full title is found in the Official Journal of the European Communities. For instance:

- Council Directive (EC) 80/181/EEC of 20 December 1979 on the approximation of the laws of the Member States relating to units of measurement and on the repeal of Directive 71/354/EEC [1980] OJ L39/40
- Council Regulation (EC) 460/2004 of 10 March 2004 establishing the European Network and Information Security Agency [2004] OJ L 77/1

12.3.5 Referencing books and edited collections using footnotes/OSCOLA

12.3.5.1 Books

The basic elements of a book reference within a footnote are as follows:

> Author | *Title* | (series title | edition |publisher | date) | pinpoint page reference

Author's names are given with initial first in the footnote, but with surname first in the bibliography (see section 12.3.9).

If a book has up to three authors, then all are listed. If a book has more than three authors, then give the name of the first author only followed by 'and others'. You may also see *et al* used in some books. This is short for *et alii* meaning 'and others' in Latin but this is not OSCOLA-compliant. The author's name (or authors' names) are followed by a comma. There is no comma before the 'and' at the end of the list.

The title of the book is then given in *italics*. It is not enclosed in any form of single or double quotation marks.

After the title of the book, publication information is provided in round brackets. First, if the book is in a series, then the series title is provided and followed by a comma, otherwise this part of the reference is omitted. Similarly, if the book is not a first edition, the edition number is given, followed by 'edn' with a trailing comma. The name of the publisher is always given followed by the year of publication.

Here are some examples:

- D Ormerod, *Smith and Hogan Criminal Law* (13th edn, OUP 2011)
- S Fafinski, *Computer Misuse: Response, Regulation and the Law* (Willan 2009)
- L Zedner, *Criminal Justice* (Clarendon Law Series, OUP 2004)
- Y Akdeniz, C Walker and D Wall, *The Internet, Law and Society* (Pearson 2000)
- R Goode and others, *Transnational Commercial Law: International Instruments and Commentary* (OUP 2004)

12.3.5.2 Edited collections

If the book is an edited collection, then the same rules apply as for books above, except that (ed) is put after the editor's name (or (eds) if there are multiple editors). Note that no full stops are used in these abbreviations:

- Y Jewkes (ed), *Crime Online* (Willan 2007)
- C Hale and others (eds), *Criminology* (OUP 2005)
- R Brownsword and K Yeung (eds), *Regulating Technologies* (Hart Publishing 2008)
- M Maguire, R Morgan and R Reiner (eds), *The Oxford Handbook of Criminology* (3rd edn, OUP 2002)

12.3.5.3 Pinpoint referencing of books

When using footnotes, you should always provide a complete reference. This should include pinpoint references:

- For a direct quotation from a certain page of a book (or article—see section 12.3.6)
- If the reference is for an idea that is located on a particular page (or pages) rather than in the book (or article) in general

Here is an example of a general reference where the sentence in the text refers to the overall theme of the book rather than a particular page or section. In this case, the footnote reference need not specify a chapter or page number:

> Finch and Fafinski emphasize the importance of the ability to identify, locate and understand the law as well as the ability to use this effectively within an essay.[1]
>
> [1] E Finch and S Fafinski, *Legal Skills* (5th edn, OUP 2015).

Where the sentence in the text concerns a specific issue, reference is needed to the particular page (or pages) of the book that address that issue:

> It is essential that precise and detailed references are provided for all materials that are used in the construction of an essay.[1]
>
> [1] E Finch and S Fafinski, *Legal Skills* (5th edn, OUP 2015) 299.

Any pinpoint page references are always given after the closing bracket in the reference.

12.3.6 Referencing journal articles and chapters in edited collections using footnotes/OSCOLA

12.3.6.1 Journal articles

The basic form of an article reference within a footnote is as follows:

> Author | 'Title' | date | volume number | journal title | start page | pinpoint page reference

Author name(s) are provided in the same style as for books. The title of the article is then given in Roman (regular) type (rather than *italics* as used for book titles) and is enclosed in single inverted commas.

The year of publication is provided next. The same convention here is used as in case reporting where the publication year is given in square brackets if it identifies the volume, and in round brackets where the journal volumes are numbered consecutively (and thus the year of publication is not required in order to locate the volume).

Any volume number is given next, followed by the title of the journal (or abbreviated title of the journal—a list of common journal abbreviations is given in Table 8.1 in Chapter 8) in Roman (regular) type and the number of the page on which the article starts. If you need to add a pinpoint reference to a particular page (see section 12.3.5.3) then add a comma after the reference to the start page, followed by the particular page you wish to reference.

Here are some examples of journal articles correctly referenced using OSCOLA:

- R Baldwin, 'The New Punitive Regulation' (2004) 67 MLR 351
- S Cretney and G Davis, 'Prosecuting "domestic" assault' [1996] Crim LR 162

12.3.6.2 Edited collections

Another source commonly encountered is a chapter in an edited collection: that is, a contribution by a particular author to a book edited by someone else. The format of this reference is as shown here:

> Author of chapter | 'Chapter Title' | in Editor (ed/eds) | *Title of Edited Collection* | (series title | edition | publisher | date)

It is not necessary to give the page number of the contribution.

Here are some examples of chapters from edited collections:

- E Finch, 'The Problem of Stolen Identity and the Internet' in Y Jewkes (ed), *Crime Online* (Willan 2006)
- M Levi and A Pithouse, 'Victims of Fraud' in D Downes (ed), *Unravelling Criminal Justice* (Macmillan 1992)

12.3.7 Referencing Internet sources using footnotes/OSCOLA

A high proportion of plagiarism cases seem to involve material taken from the Internet that is not acknowledged as such. It is possible that at least some of these cases arise from a lack of understanding as to how to reference such material or, indeed, a lack of awareness that material derived from the Internet requires a reference.

A distinction can be made between material that is published solely on the Internet and that which is available in hard copy elsewhere and has simply been accessed online in the interests of convenience. In the case of the former, as it is only available on the Internet, it is essential that adequate information is provided to enable the reader to locate the same material.

As such, websites are generally referenced like this:

> Author | 'Title' | (Type of resource | date) | | accessed date of access

For web resources where the author is not known, you should use two conjoined 'em-dashes'. These are dashes which are longer than the hyphens commonly produced in word processing software and look like this: —. The precise way in which you insert them will depend on your word processing software. In Microsoft Word (Windows and Mac), they are found under Insert > Symbol > Special characters.

The title of the document is given in single inverted commas, followed by the type and/ or date of the document in round brackets if this information is available. This is followed by the URL, or web address, in angled brackets < >. It is essential that you are accurate in recording the URL as this enables the reader to find the material. You can increase accuracy by using the 'cut and paste' option from the address bar of your browser to your document. This will eliminate the possibility of typing errors and can be particularly useful in relation to long and complex URLs. It is important to remember, however, to ensure that the pasted URL matches the format of the rest of your text: coloured hyper-links (usually either blue or purple) in the midst of your essay give a very poor impression of the care you have taken with presentation, particularly if you print your work on a colour printer before handing it in. If you right-click on a hyperlink in Microsoft Word, you should see a 'Remove Hyperlink' option (on Windows) or a 'Hyperlink . . .' menu (on Mac).

Finally the date of access should be provided. It is important to include the date that the material was accessed as Internet content is frequently changed and updated, so there may be no permanent record of the material that you have referenced, unlike the situation in relation to printed material. It is for this reason that it can be useful to print out material found online that is not available elsewhere to ensure that you do have a permanent record that you can produce if the integrity or accuracy of your research is ever questioned.

For example:

- Council of Europe, 'Countries worldwide turn to Council of Europe Cybercrime Convention' (Press Release 413(2007) Strasbourg 13 June 2007) <https://wcd.coe.int/ViewDoc.jsp?id=1150107>accessed 2 June 2010

- RA Duff, 'Theories of Criminal Law' (Stanford Encyclopaedia of Philosophy, 2002) <http://plato.stanford.edu/entries/criminal-law/>accessed 2 June 2010

- ——, 'Avoiding plagiarism' <https://ilrb.cf.ac.uk/plagiarism/tutorial/index.html> accessed 2 June 2010

In relation to material that is accessed online but is available elsewhere, such as a Home Office report, some might say that there is no need to include any mention of the Internet as the report can be referenced without it in a way that enables the reader to identify the source material and locate it themselves should they wish to do so. From this perspective, the fact that the report was found online is irrelevant, so to include the URL upon which the report can be found would be the equivalent of adding 'as read in the Bodleian library on 20 January 2011' in the footnote in relation to a hard copy.

Whilst there is some sense in this view, it can never hurt to note the use of the Internet in relation to such material just to indicate that you have not actually read the report in the printed original. Strictly speaking, you should only do this if you have used an online version because the hard copy was not available to you.

One exception here is that you do *not* need to give details of websites on which you found cases or statutes. This is quite a common error. It is not necessary to give URLs to LexisLibrary, Westlaw UK, or the Statute Law Database if you have been looking up cases or legislation: your references should never look like this:

The interpretation of s 192 of the Road Traffic Act 1988[1] was considered in *Cutter v Eagle Star Insurance Co Ltd.*[2]

---

[1] <https://login.WestlawUK.co.uk/maf/wluk/app/document?src=doc&linktype=ref&&context=5&crumb-action=replace&docguid=I78960A30E44B11DA8D70A0E70A78ED65> accessed 2 June 2010.

> ² [1997] 1 WLR 1082 (CA) <https://login.WestlawUK.co.uk/maf/wluk/app/document?&src=rl&suppsrguid=
> ia744cc6400000129695d7b2d2ad4b23b&docguid=I9374E520E42711DA8FC2A0F0355337E9&hitguid=
> I9374BE10E42711DA8FC2A0F0355337E9&spos=3&epos=3&td=3&crumb-action= append&context=4>
> accessed 2 June 2010.

The following, also commonly encountered, is also incorrect:

> The interpretation of s 192 of the Road Traffic Act 1988[1] was considered in *Cutter v Eagle Star Insurance Co Ltd*.[2]
>
> ....
> ¹ Accessed on Statute Law database on 2 June 2010.
> ² [1997] 1 WLR 1082 (CA) accessed on Westlaw UK on 2 June 2010.

It should simply look like this, regardless of where you found the information:

> The interpretation of s 192 of the Road Traffic Act 1988 was considered in *Cutter v Eagle Star Insurance Co Ltd*.[1]
>
> ....
> ¹ [1997] 1 WLR 1082 (CA).

12.3.8 Referencing other sources using footnotes/OSCOLA

12.3.8.1 Law Commission reports

Law Commission reports should be referenced as follows:

> **Law Commission** | 'Title of Report' | (Law Com number | Command Paper number | year) | pin-point page/paragraph reference

For example:

- Law Commission, 'Criminal Law – Computer Misuse' (Law Com No 186 Cm 819, 1989)
- Law Commission, 'Intoxication and Criminal Liability' (Law Com No 314 Cm 7526, 2009)

See section 8.3.1 for information on Command Paper abbreviations.

12.3.8.2 Command papers

Command papers should be referenced as follows:

> Author | 'Title of Command Paper' | (Command Paper number | year)

For example:

- HM Treasury, 'Investing in Britain's Potential: Building our Long-term Future' (Cm 6984, 2006)
- Secretary of State for Work and Pensions, 'Ready for Work: Full Employment in our Generation' (Cm 7290, 2007)

See section 8.3.1 for information on Command Paper abbreviations.

12.3.8.3 Parliamentary reports

Parliamentary reports should be referenced as follows:

Committee Name | 'Title of Report' | **HL/HC** | (year of Parliamentary session) | report serial number | pinpoint page/paragraph reference

HL is used for House of Lords reports and HC for House of Commons. The report serial number can generally be found on the bottom of the report's title page. Joint Committee reports will have both a HL and a HC serial number, separated by a semi-colon. For example:

- European Union Committee, 'The Criminal Law Competence of the European Community: Report with Evidence' HL (2005–06) 227
- Joint Committee on Human Rights, 'The Council of Europe Convention on the Prevention of Terrorism' HL (2006–07) 26; HC (2006–07) 247

12.3.8.4 Parliamentary debates (*Hansard* or the Official Report)

Hansard debates are generally referenced as follows:

Hansard | HL/HC | volume number | column number(s) | (date)

For instance:

- Hansard HC vol 166 col 1135 (9 February 1990)
- Hansard HL vol 684 cols 604–606 (11 July 2006)

There have been five series of *Hansard*:

- Series 1 1803–20
- Series 2 1820–30
- Series 3 1830–91
- Series 4 1892–1908
- Series 5 1909–

The first four series have reports from the House of Lords and House of Commons bound together and are known as Parliamentary Debates. In the fifth series the reports of the two Houses are bound into separate volumes (HL and HC). Reports prior to 1909 are referenced like this:

Hansard Parl Debs | (series number) | volume number | column number(s) | (date)

For instance:

- Hansard Parl Debs (series 3) vol 33 cols 121–2 (22 April 1836)

However, there are a couple of complications in respect of written answers to questions. For written answers after 2001, you should put 'WA' *before* the column number for House of Lords Hansard, and put 'W' *after* the column number for House of Commons Hansard, like this:

- Hansard HL vol 673 col WA261 (21 July 2005)
- Hansard HC vol 449 col 1199W (25 July 2006)

For written answers before 2001 put 'WA' in parentheses after the date, regardless of whether you are considering the House of Lords or the House of Commons, like this:

• Hansard HC vol 357 cols 234–45 (7 February 1940 WA)

12.3.8.5 Newspapers

Articles from newspapers are referenced like this:

Author | 'Title' | *Newspaper* | (Place of publication | full date) | page

Articles from online newspapers are referenced similarly, but with the URL and date of access also provided:

Author | 'Title' | *Newspaper* | (Place of publication | full date) | | **accessed** date of access

As with websites (see section 12.3.7), if the author is unknown, use two conjoined em-dashes (——), unless the source is an unnamed editorial piece, in which case you should cite the author as 'Editorial'. URLs should be given in angled brackets as for general Internet sources. For example:

• ——, 'Ombudsman denies Law Society bias' *The Times* (London, 9 January 1984) 2

• Editorial, 'The cost of free speech: England's libel laws are still rotten' *The Guardian* (London, 13 April 2000) 23

• J Kirkup, 'Nine million face "green" road tax increases' *The Telegraph* (9 July 2008) <http://www.telegraph.co.uk/earth/earthnews/3346778/Nine-million-face-green-road-tax-increases.html> accessed 2 June 2010

12.3.9 Compiling a bibliography/list of references using footnotes/OSCOLA

The final stage in footnote referencing is compiling your bibliography. You may also be required to list a table of cases and a table of legislation at the end of your work. This is good practice in any event. Remember that a bibliography contains all the material you have read in preparation and may include sources that have not been explicitly referenced in footnotes. You may wish to compile your bibliography as you go, rather than doing it all at the end. If you do not, remember to allow enough time to do this thoroughly, particularly if you are working to a tight deadline.

The bibliography should list all sources, in alphabetical order by author surname. It should not contain any pinpoint references or full stops at the end of each item. The key difference, however, between bibliography entries and footnote entries is that in bibliographies, the surname comes *first* followed by initials. There should be no comma between surname and initials, but there should be a comma after the final initial. For example:

Akers R, 'Rational choice, deterrence and social learning theory in criminology: the path not taken' (1990) 81 Journal of Criminal Law and Criminology 653.

Baker T and Simon J (eds), *Embracing Risk: The Changing Culture of Insurance and Responsibility* (University of Chicago Press 2002)

Ceruzzi P, *A History of Modern Computing* (2nd edn, MIT Press 2003)

Denby K, 'Dissident websites crippled by Burma on anniversary of revolt' *The Times* (London, 22 September 2008) 4

12.4 How to reference using the Harvard system

Harvard, or in-text, referencing does not use footnotes. Instead, an abbreviated citation (based on author name and date) is incorporated into the text with either a list of references or a bibliography at the end that provides full details of the publications referred to in the text and allows them to be found. Harvard referencing is a two-stage process:

- Citing references in the text
- Compiling a bibliography/list of references

This section will walk through each of those stages in turn.

12.4.1 Citing references in the text

The way in which sources are cited in Harvard referencing depends on the number of authors and whether or not they are named directly in the text.

If the author is named directly in the text, their name should be followed by the year of publication of the source and a page number if a pinpoint reference is required. Page numbers should be preceded by 'p.' for a single page and 'pp.' where the citation spans multiple pages.

Here is an example of a citation for a direct quotation for a single named author:

> Ormerod (2008, p. 1013) considers that 'the impact of computer technology on society has been profound'.

This format is also used for indirect reference to the source where the author's name is still part of the text itself:

> It is generally accepted that computer technology has had a great impact on society. This view has been supported by Ormerod (2008, p. 1013).

Note that some variants of Harvard referencing may use a colon instead of 'p.' or 'pp.':

> It is generally accepted that computer technology has had a great impact on society. This view has been supported by Ormerod (2008: 1013).

If the author's name is not cited directly in the text, it is still provided in the reference, either at the relevant part of the sentence, or at the end of the sentence in brackets:

> It is generally accepted that computer technology has had a great impact on society. (Ormerod, 2008, p. 1013).

This reference is given to a particular page in a book. However, if the citation is to a book, article, or chapter that discusses a particular area, as opposed to pinpointing a particular passage, then just author and year are given, without a pinpoint:

> It has been postulated that the misuse of computer technology cannot adequately be governed by the use of the criminal law alone (Fafinski, 2009).

The situation becomes more complex when the work of more than one author is cited in a single sentence. If they are named directly in the text, then each is cited as before:

> Room (2004) and Walden (2004) have both noted that pressure for reform of the law also came from the UK's international treaty obligations.

However, if they are not named directly in the text, then they are listed in brackets with name and date of publication, separated by a semi-colon:

> Pressure for reform of the law also came from the UK's international treaty obligations (Room, 2004; Walden 2004).

When directly citing a work by two authors in the text, both surnames should be given, separated by 'and':

> Finch and Fafinski (2015, pp. 281–288) explain how to reference various legal sources using the Harvard system.

When the authors are not named directly, they are listed in brackets at the appropriate point in the sentence or at the end of the sentence (as with a single author). In this case their names are separated by an ampersand (&) rather than 'and':

> Various legal sources may be referenced accurately using the Harvard system (Finch & Fafinski, 2015, pp. 281–288).

For sources that have three authors, the same convention is used:

> Beyleveld, Kirkham and Townend (2002) comment on the House of Lords reasoning on retrospectivity and the Human Rights Act.

> There has been much criticism of the House of Lords reasoning on retrospectivity and the Human Rights Act (Beyleveld, Kirkham & Townend, 2002).

For sources with four authors or more, then only the name of the first author is used, followed by 'et al.'. Here *et al.* is short for the Latin term *et alii* meaning 'and others'. It is usually given in regular type, but may also be seen in italics in acknowledgement of its Latin origin:

> Bailey et al. (2002) provide a comprehensive discussion of the importance of context in statutory interpretation.

> The Sunday Observance Act 1677 is an interesting example of the use of the *ejusdem generis* rule of statutory interpretation (Bailey et al. 2002, 435)

If an author makes or reinforces a point in more than one publication, both should be cited in chronological order (that is, with the earliest publication listed first):

> Finch (2000, 2002) argues that section 2 of the Protection from Harassment Act 1997 is so broadly drawn that it covers innocuous as well as undesirable behaviour.

> Section 2 of the Protection from Harassment Act 1997 is broadly drafted: as such, it may cover innocuous as well as undesirable behaviour (Finch 2000, 2002).

If your piece of work contains references to several works published by the same author in the same year, these are differentiated by adding a lower case letter after the year for each work, starting with 'a' and moving through the alphabet:

> Finch and Munro (2005a) reviewed the law on intoxicated sexual consent in Scotland and England before embarking on a study (2005b) to investigate juror blame attribution in such cases.

If these sources are cited at the same point, then the lower case letters should both appear in the brackets:

> Finch and Munro (2005a, b) have conducted extensive research into the law on intoxicated sexual consent in Scotland and England and the way in which jurors attribute blame in such cases.

> Juror blame attribution under the law of Scotland and England has been the subject of extensive research (Finch & Munro 2005a, b).

Contributions to edited collections should cite the name of the author of the chapter, rather than the name of the editor:

> Finch (2006) has considered the issue of stolen identity which has been facilitated by the Internet.

There is nothing in the text that suggests that this is a chapter from an edited collection. However, in the reference list, you must give the details of both the chapter author *and* the editor of the collection (see section 12.3.6.2) so that both can be found if desired.

Secondary references (that is, reference to another's work contained in an original work) are denoted by the words 'cited in'. Look back at the example from section 12.1.1.1 which would be referenced in the Harvard system like this:

> For Norrie (2002 cited in Lacey, Wells & Quick, 2003, p. 752) the Court of Appeal in Re A (Conjoined Twins) [2001] 1 FLR 1 (CA) exemplified the manipulation of orthodox subjectivism to satisfy the moral circumstances of the case.

Or, indirectly:

> The Court of Appeal in Re A (Conjoined Twins) [2001] 1 FLR 1 (CA) exemplified the manipulation of orthodox subjectivism to satisfy the moral circumstances of the case (Norrie, 2002 cited in Lacey, Wells & Quick, 2003, p. 752).

In this instance, your list of references must only contain the works that you have read in the original (Lacey, Wells & Quick) and not the works to which they refer (Norrie).

12.4.2 Compiling a bibliography/list of references

The detail provided in the list of references should enable the reader to find the sources that have been cited in the text itself. If you are providing a bibliography instead, you should ensure that you also list the sources which you consulted in the preparation of your work, even if you did not cite them directly.

There are some variations in layout that are acceptable. In particular, punctuation can vary when using Harvard. Some references may have full stops after each part of the reference and some may not. Equally, the use of commas may vary. Remember to check first to see if there is a house style to which you should adhere and, most importantly, make sure that you are consistent with your style and use of punctuation throughout your work.

All sources should be listed alphabetically by author. The sections that follow will demonstrate the way in which most common sources should be referenced in your bibliography. Remember that tables of cases and legislation are normally listed separately.

12.4.3 Referencing cases using Harvard

Harvard referencing does not seem to have any hard-and-fast rules regarding the referencing of cases within the text of an essay. This is probably because the Harvard referencing emerged in the social sciences and did not require a standard for citing legal authorities as these were not commonly encountered in those disciplines. There are two options; first, include only the case name and year in the text (with the year in round brackets) but ensure that a list of cases with full citations is provided at the end of your essay, or, secondly, include the full case citation in the text of your essay. If you take the latter approach, remember that you should only provide the full citation the first time that the case is mentioned; after that, the case name alone (or its shortened form) will suffice. With this in mind, either of the two approaches shown here is acceptable. First, with just case years provided in-text:

> Recently, the Court of Appeal declined to follow the House of Lords decision in *R* v. *Smith (Morgan)* (2001), preferring the reasoning of the Privy Council in *Attorney-General* for *Jersey* v. *Holley* (2005). Of course, this is problematic in terms of the doctrine of precedent as, strictly speaking, *Smith* was binding upon the Court of Appeal and should have been applied in preference to *Holley*.
> **Table of cases:**
> *Attorney-General for Jersey* v. *Holley* [2005] 2 AC 580 (PC)
> *R* v. *Smith (Morgan)* [2001] AC 146 (HL)

Alternatively, with full citations provided in-text:

> Recently, the Court of Appeal declined to follow the House of Lords decision in *R* v. *Smith (Morgan)* [2001] AC 146, preferring the reasoning of the Privy Council in *Attorney-General for Jersey* v. *Holley* [2005] 2 AC 580. Of course, this is problematic in terms of the doctrine of precedent as, strictly speaking, *Smith* was binding upon the Court of Appeal and should have been applied in preference to *Holley*.
> **Table of cases:**
> *Attorney-General for Jersey* v. *Holley* [2005] 2 AC 580 (PC)
> *R* v. *Smith (Morgan)* [2001] AC 146 (HL)

There is no Harvard standard for citing European cases; you may wish to use the guidance given in section 12.3.3.5.

12.4.4 Referencing legislation using Harvard

Again, there is no Harvard standard for citing Acts of Parliament. However, there seems to be a general consensus that at least the following information is given for Acts post-1963:

> *Short Title of Act (including year).* | (c. chapter number)

The short title of the Act is given in italics. For example:

- Computer Misuse Act 1990 (c.18)
- Anti-Slavery Day Act 2010 (c.14)

For Acts prior to 1963 (when the Acts of Parliament Numbering and Citation Act 1962 came into force) the regnal year citation is given (see section 3.1.2):

> *Short Title of Act (including year).* | (Regnal year, c. chapter number).

For example:

- Charitable Uses Act 1601. (43 Eliz I, c.4).
- Caravan Sites and Control of Development Act 1960. (8 & 9 Eliz. II, Ch. 62)

Some styles also include the name the place of publication and publisher and/or the country of origin:

- *Charitable Uses Act 1601*. (43 Eliz I, c.4) London: HMSO
- Great Britain. *Caravan Sites and Control of Development Act 1960*. (8 & 9 Eliz. II, Ch. 62). London: HMSO

Opinion seems to be divided as to whether or not statutes in-text should be italicized. You should see if your lecturer has a particular preference.

Statutory instruments are cited in a similar way, with the year of publication and SI number also provided:

- Data Protection Act 1998 (Commencement No. 2) Order 2008 SI 2007/1592
- Equality Act (Sexual Orientation) Regulations 2007 SI 2007/1063
- Heavy Goods Vehicle (Drivers' Licences) Regulations 1977 SI 1977/1309

Finally, there is no Harvard standard for citing European legislation. Again, you may wish to use the guidance given in section 12.3.4.

12.4.5 Referencing books and edited collections using Harvard

12.4.5.1 Books

The basic elements of a book reference in the Harvard system are:

Author | (date) | *Title*. | Series title. | Edition. | Place of publication: | Publisher

Author names are given with surname first, followed by a comma and initials (with full stops after each initial). Books with two or three authors should list all authors with the last two being joined by an ampersand (&). For four authors or more, list the first, followed by 'et al.'.

The title is provided in italics followed by a full stop. Then come the series title (if any) and edition number (if not the first) in regular type. Finally the place of publication and publisher are given, separated by a colon and terminated with a full stop. For example:

- Ormerod, D. (2007) *Smith and Hogan Criminal Law*. 12th Ed. Oxford: OUP.
- Fafinski, S. (2009) *Computer Misuse: Response, Regulation and the Law*. Cullompton: Willan.
- Zedner, L. (2004) *Criminal Justice*. Clarendon Law Series. Oxford: OUP.
- Akdeniz, Y., Walker, C. & Wall, D. (2000) *The Internet, Law and Society*. Harlow: Pearson.
- Goode, R., et al. (2004) *Transnational Commercial Law: International Instruments and Commentary*. Oxford: OUP.

12.4.5.2 Edited collections

For books with an editor, then (ed.) or (eds.) are added after the author's name(s). Note that, unlike OSCOLA, both abbreviations are terminated with a full stop:

- Jewkes, Y. (ed.) (2007) *Crime Online*. Cullompton: Willan
- Hale, C. et al. (eds.) (2005) *Criminology*. Oxford: OUP
- Brownsword, R. & Yeung, C. (eds.) (2008) *Regulating Technologies*. Oxford: Hart Publishing
- Maguire, M., Morgan, R. & Reiner, R. (eds.) (2002) *The Oxford Handbook of Criminology*. 3rd Ed. Oxford: OUP

12.4.6 Referencing journal articles and chapters in edited collections using Harvard

12.4.6.1 Journals

For journals, the order of the bibliography entry is as follows:

> Author | (date) | Title of article. | *Full title of journal*, |Volume number | (issue number), | Page range

The author details are given in the same format as for books. Article titles are in regular type, terminated by a full stop and not enclosed in inverted commas. Journal titles are given in full (no abbreviations) and in italics. Any volume number is also given, followed by any issue information (usually an issue number or date) in round brackets, a comma and the range of page numbers in the article (preceded by pp.). This is different to OSCOLA which only requires the first page number to be cited.

For example:

- Baldwin, R. (2004) The New Punitive Regulation. *Modern Law Review,* 67(3), pp. 351–383
- Charlesworth, A. (1993) Addiction and Hacking. *New Law Journal*, 143(6596), pp. 540–541
- Cretney, S. & Davis, G. (1996) Prosecuting "domestic" assault. *Criminal Law Review* (March) pp. 162–174

12.4.6.2 Chapters in edited collections

Chapters in edited collections are referenced like this:

> Author of chapter | (date) | Title of chapter. | **In:** Editor **(ed./eds.)** | *Title of Edited Collection.* | Place of publication: | Publisher, | Page range/Chapter number

The elements of the citation follow the conventions for books and edited collections as before. Unlike OSCOLA, this form of citation requires either the chapter number or page range of the contribution to be provided:

- Finch, E. (2006) The Problem of Stolen Identity and the Internet. In: Jewkes, Y. (ed.) (2006) *Crime Online.* Cullompton: Willan, Ch. 3
- Johnson, D. & Post, D. (1997) And how shall the net be governed? A meditation on the relative values of decentralised, emergent law. In: Kahlin, B. & Keller, J. (eds.) (1997) *Co-ordinating the Internet.* Cambridge: MIT Press, pp. 62–91
- Levi, M. & Pithouse, A. (1992) Victims of Fraud. In: Downes, D. (ed.) (1992) *Unravelling Criminal Justice.* London: Macmillan, pp. 229–246

12.4.7 Referencing Internet sources using Harvard

Internet sources are generally referenced like this:

> Author | Year | *Title.* | Type of resource | **[Online]** | **Available at**: URL. | **[Accessed** | date]

You might see some variation in Harvard referencing of online resources: remember the guiding principles that you should provide enough information so that the reader can find the source and that you should be consistent in your approach to citation.

If there is no author name, then use the name of the website instead. The year of the material is given in round brackets as usual. However, you may find that online resources are undated, in which case you should put 'n.d.' (short for 'no date') in the year brackets. After the title of the source (in italics) you should then state [Online] in square brackets, followed by the URL (which is underlined) and the date of access in square brackets.

For example:

- Council of Europe (2007) *Countries worldwide turn to Council of Europe Cybercrime Convention.* (Press release 413(2007)) [Online] Available at: <u>https://wcd.coe.int/ViewDoc.jspid=1150107</u>. [Accessed 2 June 2010]
- Duff, R.A. (2002) *Theories of Criminal Law.* (Stanford Encyclopaedia of Philosophy) [Online] Available at: <u>http://plato.stanford.edu/entries/criminal-law/</u>. [Accessed 2 June 2010]
- University of Cardiff (n.d.) 'Avoiding plagiarism' [Online] Available at: <u>https://ilrb.cf.ac.uk/plagiarism/tutorial/index.html</u>.[Accessed 2 June 2010]

12.4.8 Referencing other sources using Harvard

12.4.8.1 Law Commission reports

Law Commission reports are referenced as follows:

Law Commission | (year) | *Title of Report.* | (Law Com number, | Command Paper number) | Place of publication: | Publisher

For example:

- Law Commission (1989) *Criminal Law—Computer Misuse.* (Law Com No. 186, Cm 819) London: HMSO
- Law Commission (2009) *Intoxication and Criminal Liability.* (Law Com No. 314, Cm 7256) London: HMSO

12.4.8.2 Command papers

Command papers should be referenced as follows:

Author | (year) | *Title of Command Paper.* | (Command Paper number) | Place of publication: | Publisher

For example:

- HM Treasury (2006) Investing in Britain's Potential: Building our Long-term Future. (Cm 6984) London: HMSO
- Secretary of State for Work and Pensions (2007) *Ready for Work: Full Employment in our Generation.* (Cm 7290) London: HMSO

See section 8.3.1 for information on Command Paper abbreviations.

12.4.8.3 Parliamentary papers

Parliamentary papers should be referenced like this:

Committee Name | (year) | *Title of Report.* | (**HL/HC** | report serial number | of | year of Parliamentary session) | Place of publication: | Publisher

For example:

- European Union Committee (2005–06) *The Criminal Law Competence of the European Community: Report with Evidence.* (HL 227 of 2005–06) London: HMSO

- Joint Committee on Human Rights (2006–07) *The Council of Europe Convention on the Prevention of Terrorism.* (HL 26 of 2006–07; HC 247 of 2006–07) London: HMSO

12.4.9 Parliamentary debates (*Hansard* or the Official Report)

Hansard debates are generally referenced as follows:

> **Hansard,** | **HL/HC/Parl. Debs.** | (series number) | Volume number, | Column number(s) | (date)

Remember that the first four series of *Hansard* contain reports from both the House of Lords and House of Commons bound together. They are referred to collectively as Parliamentary Debates. In the fifth series (from 1909 to date) the reports of the two houses are bound into separate volumes (H.L. Deb and H.C. Deb).

For more information on *Hansard* see section 7.3.4.

For example:

- *Hansard*, HC (series 5) vol. 166, col. 1135 (9 February 1990)

- *Hansard*, HL (series 5) vol. 684, cols. 604–606 (11 July 2006)

- *Hansard*, Parl. Debs. (series 4) vol. 21, col. 849 (20 February 1894)

12.4.10 Newspapers

Newspaper articles are generally referenced like this:

> Author | Year | Title. | *Newspaper* | Day and month | Page

Online newspaper articles also need the additional information required to find the source:

> Author |Year | Title. | *Newspaper* | **[Online]** | Day and month | **Available** at: URL | **[Accessed** | date]

If there is no author identified, or the article is an editorial piece, you should use the title of the newspaper in italics to begin your reference instead:

> *Newspaper* | Year | Title. | Day and month | Page

For example:

- *The Times* (1984) Ombudsman denies Law Society bias. 9 January, p. 2

- *The Guardian* (2000) The cost of free speech: England's libel laws are still rotten. 13 April, p. 23

- Kirkup, J. (2008) Nine million face 'green' road tax increases. *The Telegraph* [Online] 9 July. Available at: http://www.telegraph.co.uk/earth/earthnews/3346778/Nine-million-face-green-road-tax-increases.html. [Accessed 2 June 2010]

CHAPTER SUMMARY

- Plagiarism is a form of academic dishonesty that is readily detected and attracts negative consequences both within your institution and in the professional world

- Bear in mind that a thorough and precise approach to references will avoid accusations of inadvertent plagiarism. If in doubt, reference

- Note the situations outlined in this chapter in which a reference should be provided, taking particular care to ensure that ideas are attributed to their source

- Find out whether your institution or department has a 'house style' and, if so, ensure that you follow it

- Never combine footnotes and in-text references

- Familiarize yourself with the conventions for referencing and cross-referencing

- Take particular care with Internet sources

- Always provide a complete bibliography/list of references

FURTHER READING

- Staffordshire University has developed a very comprehensive guide to the Harvard referencing system which can be found at www.staffs.ac.uk/support_depts/infoservices/learning_support/refzone/harvard/index.jsp.

- The OSCOLA website at www.law.ox.ac.uk/publications/oscola.php contains the full OSCOLA referencing guide.

13 Essay writing

INTRODUCTION

The focus of this chapter is essay writing. Earlier sections of this book have outlined techniques for locating and understanding primary and secondary legal sources. This chapter builds on those skills by exploring the ways that this source material can be used in your coursework. It will also guide you through the stages of planning, research, and construction of an essay with practical advice on interpreting the question and producing a structured response that demonstrates the required skills and knowledge. It should be read in conjunction with Chapter 10, which focuses on writing skills and Chapter 12, for information on referencing. Doing so will ensure that you produce a polished piece of work that is well-expressed and fully referenced in an appropriate style.

The essay is a popular method tool of assessment in law, and essay questions make frequent appearances on exam papers across a range of modules as well as featuring heavily in coursework assessment. Given the prevalence of this method of assessment, it is important that you ensure that your essay-writing craftsmanship is of the highest level. Students often make the mistake of thinking that an essay is marked on its content alone but this is not the case: a good essay is a combination of knowledge and skills. In fact, there are a whole package of skills involved in essay writing, all of which need to be demonstrated if your work is to achieve good marks. This chapter will introduce these skills and explain what you need to do to demonstrate them to the person marking your essay.

LEARNING OUTCOMES

After studying this chapter, you will be able to:

- Appreciate the combination of knowledge and skills required to produce a successful piece of written work

- Be able to 'unpick' the question to ensure that you have a clear grasp of its requirements

- Conduct effective research and extract relevant information to enable you to produce a focused and well-supported essay

- Create an effective introduction and conclusion to your essay and structure a cohesive line of argument

- Evaluate the essay that you have written to ensure that it demonstrates the relevant skills and knowledge and that it adheres to the necessary style and referencing requirements

- Recognize and overcome the common barriers between grade boundaries/classifications to improve your performance

13.1 What makes a good essay?

This is an important question as you cannot be expected to produce a good essay until you know what features combine together to create a good essay. In essence, a good essay is one that answers the question and, in doing so, demonstrates a range of written and analytical skills. It is important to emphasize that a good essay requires as much thought to be given to the way that the essay is constructed as is given to its content. In other words, it is not enough that you know the relevant law and commentary; you must also know what to do with it in order to write an effective essay. A good essay should demonstrate the following:

- A foundation of accurate and relevant knowledge about the legal topic that is the subject of the question

- Wide-ranging research that identifies a variety of relevant source material appropriate to the subject matter

- Effective use of source material so that it is integrated into the essay and used to strengthen your arguments in a way that demonstrates your understanding of the material and its role in your work

- The ability to filter out irrelevant or peripheral points and to maintain a firm and consistent focus on the central issue raised by the question

- A flowing line of argument set in a clear structure with an effective introduction and conclusion

- An appropriate balance between description and analysis

- Good written communication skills in producing a coherent and eloquent piece of work

- A thorough approach to referencing that ensures that all source material is acknowledged in a complete and appropriate style

This mix of knowledge and skills can be further illustrated if the process of creating an essay is broken down into stages as illustrated in Figure 13.1.

This chapter will provide a detailed account of the requirements of each of these stages in order to assist you with the production of an essay that answers the question set, demonstrates appropriate skills, and which meets with the approval of your marker. Remember, though, that it may be necessary to move backwards and forwards through the stages: you may, for example, find that you need to do more research once you have moved into the writing stage or that you need to reconsider what the essay means during the research stage, but that is not a problem. This chapter does not intend to suggest that there is a rigid progression through the stages but to ensure that each stage is given adequate attention to help you with the production of your essays.

13.2 Analyzing the question

It is important to take time to analyze the question in order to work out what it requires. This is a fundamental first step although it may have to be combined with some initial research to help you understand the precise requirements of the question. For example, you may be able to identify the subject matter of the question on the basis of its wording and your existing knowledge but a little preliminary investigation in your textbook might be necessary to help you understand the question more fully. However, try to pinpoint the precise requirements of the question as early as possible as this will add focus to your research and enable you to identify relevant material more effectively.

13.2.1 What does the question ask?

It is essential to the effectiveness of every stage of the essay-writing process as well as to the overall success of the essay, in terms of the mark that it is awarded, that you focus on what the essay *asks* rather than the broader issue of what the essay is *about*. This distinction can be described in terms of the particular question (what the essay *asks*) as opposed to a more general topic (what the essay is *about*).

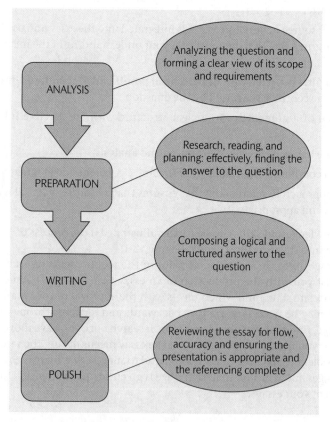

Figure 13.1 The four stages of essay writing

For example, if you asked someone how to make pizza, you would be annoyed if they respond by telling you where to buy pizza or how many calories there are in the average pizza or if they embark on an account of the history of pizza making. This is because they have not answered your question even though they are talking about the same general topic.

The same principle applies to essay questions in law. Take a look at the following question and decide (a) what it is about and (b) what it asks:

> *Critically assess whether the Sexual Offences Act 2003 has achieved its objectives of simplifying the law and affording greater protection to victims of rape.*

The answer to the first question is straightforward: the question is about sexual offences legislation and the offence of rape. However, there are any number of different questions that could be asked about this topic so it would be important that your answer focused on the specific question asked here which is whether this legislation achieved the two stated objectives.

Far too many students limit their prospects of success by responding to what the essay is about rather than narrowing their focus and providing a response to the specific question. This leads to the inclusion of irrelevant material as there is a vast range of points that could be made about the general topic (sexual offences) that have nothing to do with the specific question (the effectiveness of the legislation). For example, a discussion on grooming—an offence introduced by the Sexual Offences Act 2003 to deal with those who lure children into sexual activity—has little relevance to the question even though it is covered by the Act mentioned in the question. In other words, you do not have to take too many steps away from the specific question asked in order to stray into the realms of irrelevancy, even if your discussion is still within the same broad topic.

It is essential that you identify what the question asks and keep this to the forefront of your mind at every stage of the research, planning, and writing process to ensure that your essay does not lose its focus:

- Make sure that you isolate the specific question asked about the topic and write this in a prominent place so that it acts as a reminder whilst you are working on your essay

- Check every point that you find during your research for its relevance to the question (not the topic). You might want to develop a simple ranking system to help you with this

- Points that do not have immediate relevance can be made relevant if you slant them towards the question. For example, you could include a discussion of grooming in the earlier example if you used it to illustrate how it criminalizes conduct that might precede a rape

- When you are drafting your essay, make sure that each paragraph touches base with the specific question. You can use signposting to do this (this is discussed in section 13.4.4 later in this chapter)

13.2.2 Rewording the question

One of the most effective ways to work out what the question asks is to rewrite it in your own words with the aim of discovering one or two clear questions that you understand. For example, the following two questions simplify the sexual offences question and make it far easier to keep its core issues in mind when researching and writing the essay:

- Is the offence of rape easier to understand than it was prior to the introduction of the Sexual Offences Act 2003?

- Has the Sexual Offences Act 2003 improved the protection available for victims of rape?

This approach will enable you to establish and retain a focus on the question posed by the essay and it also offers a starting point for structuring the essay as it is clear that there are two separate issues that need to be addressed.

It can also be helpful to reword an essay question if it is phrased in a way that does not give you much by way of clues as to what is expected. A question that is made up of a quotation followed by the instruction to 'discuss' is an example of this as it puts the onus on the student to work out what it is that needs to be discussed. The way to deal with this is to reword the question yourself using alternative words so that you make a distinction from the start about what aspect of the question needs to be described and what it is that needs to be analyzed.

You will find an explanation of how so-called 'process words'—such as 'discuss'—are used in the construction of essay questions and how these can help you to understand what the question requires of you in section 13.4.5 later in this chapter.

Practical exercise

It is a good idea to practise analyzing essay titles by rewording them as this will give you the confidence to do it with your own coursework questions. There is an example below followed by some questions for you to try yourself:

The problems concerning the separation of powers have been resolved by the Constitutional Reform Act 2005. Discuss.

This can be reworded using process words to indicate what needs to be described in the question and what part of it should be the focus of analysis:

Outline the changes made to the separation of powers that were introduced by the Constitutional Reform Act 2005. Assess whether these changes have resolved all the problems associated with the separation of powers.

This can be made clearer still by breaking this down into a series of questions that need to be answered:

- *What is meant by the separation of powers?*
- *What was the position prior to 2005?*
- *What changes were introduced by the Constitutional Reform Act 2005?*
- *Why were these changes made? What problems were they trying to address?*
- *What is the current situation?*
- *Do the previously identified problems still remain?*
- *Are there new problems?*

So—have the problems concerning the separation of powers been resolved by the Constitutional Reform Act 2005?

Try to identify the questions that are asked by the following essay titles. You should be able to make an attempt at this even if you have little prior knowledge of the subject matter.

1. The postal rule is outdated and has little place in modern contract law. Discuss.
2. If the United Kingdom has a constitution at all, its central pillar is parliamentary sovereignty. Evaluate this statement with particular reference to the European Union.
3. Outline the approaches that a judge may take to statutory interpretation and consider their relevance following the enactment of the Human Rights Act 1998.

You will find answers to these questions and an explanation of how they were reached on the Online Resource Centre.

Remember that you are rewording the question to enhance your understanding of what it requires. You must take the utmost care to ensure that you are not rewording it in a way that changes its sense or meaning. When your essay is marked, it will only attract credit for material that is relevant to the question that was asked and not for other points, however interesting or clever, that are not pertinent.

13.3 Preparation: research and planning

The preparatory stages of research and planning should take at least as much time as the actual writing of the essay. During this stage you will find different points of interest leading towards a draft conclusion, select material for inclusion in your essay, and engage in some preliminary planning of the structure of your argument. Taking care with these preparatory stages does make the writing of the essay less troublesome, as many of the difficult issues will have already been resolved.

13.3.1 Focus on the question(s)

The aim of the last section was to emphasize the importance of working out the requirements of the question before starting the process of research, planning, and writing that will produce

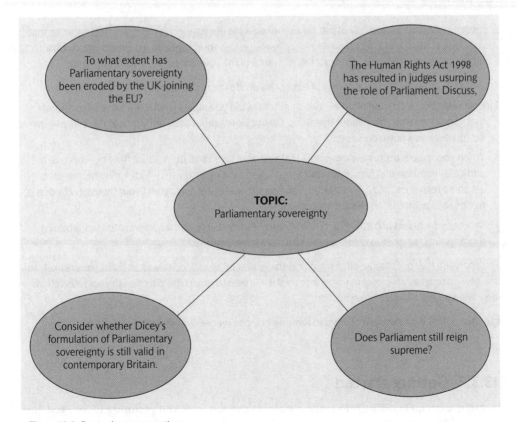

Figure 13.2 One topic, many questions.

the essay. This is because you cannot answer a question effectively unless you know what it is asking. Students sometimes think that research is the first stage, but you will be so much more effective in your research if you start with a clear idea of what you are trying to find out.

Try to remember that you do not need to know the answer in order to conduct research: after all, that is what research is all about—finding answers. Of course, you are likely to discover information during your research that assists you to reach a more closely informed understanding of the question.

You should be able to identify the general topic from the wording of the question itself and this will enable you to start your research. Remember that each topic has a number of different questions that can be asked about it (see Figure 13.2) and your initial job is to sift through the information on the topic and identify material that is pertinent to the particular question that you have been asked.

13.3.2 Brainstorming

One method of exploring what you already know about a topic is brainstorming. This involves writing down everything that you can think of about a topic in the order it comes into your mind. This technique is useful in essay writing as a way to establish a list of potential topics for inclusion in your essay so that you can make some preliminary decisions about relevance and thus direct the focus of your research and reading.

Practical exercise

Brainstorming can be a good way of getting all your possible points about a topic down on paper so that you can look at them and assess their relevance to your essay. You might find it useful to work with a friend as you can share ideas and discuss the relevance of the different points that you generate.

1. Write the topic at the top of a piece of paper and divide the paper into two columns.

2. Give yourself a set period of time—two minutes should be ample—to make a list of all the points that spring into your mind about that topic. Do not worry about their relevance at this stage—just get all your ideas down on paper.

3. When your time is up, review the points that you have listed and think about their relevance to the particular question that is asked in your essay. Use a ranking system in which 1 = highly relevant, 2 = some relevance, and 3 = irrelevant. You can also add notes that reflect your thoughts about the role of each point that is relevant in your essay.

4. Reorder your points according to their relevance. Alternatively, you might want to start grouping similar points together to create a draft structure for your essay.

This approach may not capture all of the points that you want to include in your essay as you are likely to find new material as your research progresses but it will help to give some direction to your research by identifying potential lines of investigation.

    You will find an example of a brainstorming exercise on the Online Resource Centre.

13.3.3 Getting started

It can be extremely difficult to make a start on the research and planning of an essay just because it all seems such an immense task, particularly if you feel that you are overwhelmed from the start because you are faced with a topic that you do not understand. This section outlines some of the early steps that can be taken that will help you to make a start on your preparation.

Earlier chapters in this book have provided in-depth coverage of a range of sources, how to find them, and how to make effective use of them. This chapter will not repeat that information but will merely highlight a few key points of particular relevance to conducting research for an essay. You will probably find that you need to make reference to earlier chapters to help you with the research process.

The most sensible starting point for your research is the relevant chapter(s) in a textbook. This is because textbooks are designed to provide exactly what you need at this point in time: a clear and relatively comprehensive explanation of areas of law. It is important that you use textbooks in an appropriate way when conducting research for your coursework. This means that you must use them in a way that is (a) useful to you and (b) acceptable to your lecturers.

- **Start with the set textbook.** Even if you do not like the book and have found an alternative, it would be a mistake not to read it in case you miss out on information that the lecturer expects you to know and that other students on your module will have read.

- **Make sure that you understand the basics of the topic.** If the set textbook does not give you a clear understanding of the important points, make a note of them and find a simpler explanation in an alternative book. You may need to try several textbooks before you find one that explains the issues in a way that makes sense to you but you must persevere with this as it is crucial that you have a grasp of the basics from a source aimed at students before you start to explore the issues in greater depth.

- **Use a range of textbooks.** Each author will explain the key points in the legal subject matter in their own way and will use different examples to illustrate their points so you can gain a broader perspective on the topic by using several different textbooks.

- **Do not make too many notes at this stage.** You are reading textbooks to gain an overview of the topic and to identify useful source material and lines of investigation relevant to your essay. It is not a good use of your time to copy large chunks out of the textbook so try to use a condensed approach to note-taking in which you describe the points that you want to find again and note the page on which it occurs. For example, you might write 'p. 174 talks about the 'red hand' rule and p. 178 refers to a useful article by Macdonald in *Legal Studies*'.

- **Move on to consult a wide range of sources.** Remember that textbooks are written for students. They do all the hard work for you by summarizing the information that you need to understand legal topics. You are expected to use this as a starting point to enable you to identify source material such as case law, relevant journal articles, and official reports that you will then read yourself and use as authority in your essay.

13.3.4 Gathering supporting materials

Once you have an idea of the basic points that you want to raise in your essay, you will need to turn your attention to the selection of supporting material. In other words, you will want to provide authority to substantiate your arguments. In particular, you should ensure that all statements of law are attributed to a particular source, whether this is case law or statute. It also adds strength to your arguments about the interpretation or application of the law if you can make reference to material which backs up your position.

13.3.4.1 Textbooks

As a general rule, you should only use textbooks to support your argument if you have quoted directly from them and you should only quote directly from them if there is no other source available and you feel that you cannot express the idea in your own words. Textbooks exist to give you an accessible summary of the law and the central debates surrounding the law; basically, they are the starting point upon which you should build your legal understanding. As such, you will be expected to demonstrate that you have read a variety of sources in the preparation of your essay rather than simply relying on textbooks.

Of course, some textbooks have an excellent reputation for their analysis of the law, in which case you may find that there are ideas expressed in there that you would like to incorporate into your essay. If this is the case, it may be a good idea to find out if the author of the textbook has elaborated on this point in an article or monograph and, if so, to rely on this to support your argument instead. Overall, it is advisable to be sparing in your reliance on textbooks in your essay.

13.3.4.2 Statutory provisions

The position regarding statutory provisions is straightforward. If you are referring to a particular piece of legislation, you should always indicate the name of the statute and, if appropriate, the section or subsection number. This does not necessarily mean that you should quote the full wording of the section itself; it will often be more appropriate to paraphrase the statutory provision or to select a segment of the section.

13.3.4.3 Case law

There are four main ways in which you might want to use case law in your essay to support your answer.

- **The source of a legal principle.** If a legal rule, definition, or test has evolved in case law, you should attribute it to its source in the same way that you would if the area of law was governed by statute. For example, in criminal law, the test for oblique intention was formulated by the House of Lords in *R v Woollin* [1999] 1 AC 82 (HL).

- **An elaboration on the meaning of a word or phrase.** Case law is a major source of interpretation of the meaning and application of words and phrases used in law. For example, the phrase 'ethnic origin' as found in the Race Relations Act 1976 was subjected to in-depth interpretation in *Mandla v Lee* [1983] 2 AC 548 (HL).

- **The operation of the law.** If you want to ascertain the scope of the law and how it applies in particular situations, you can look at how it has taken effect in case law. For example, if you were addressing the tort of defamation in relation to media coverage of the private lives of celebrities, you could use the cases involving the right to freedom of expression to determine the scope of the law. You can also use case law to demonstrate the impact of changes in the law as you can show how the outcome of a decided case would differ; this can be an especially powerful way to support your arguments for or against a particular interpretation of the law. For example, in relation to the sample essay, you could use cases decided under the old law and, in order to demonstrate its impact, explain how they would have a different outcome under the new law.

- **Judicial consideration of issues relevant to your essay.** Case law contains some fascinating in-depth evaluations of how the law is and how it could be as well as the implications of different interpretations of the law. Do not overlook dissenting judgments as these are often a great source of inspiration for opposing arguments.

13.3.4.4 Academic commentary

Sources such as journal articles and monographs can provide valuable support for the arguments made in your essay. It is suggested that you should also strive to include at the very least two, preferably opposing or contradictory, academic viewpoints within your essay to demonstrate the different perspectives that exist in relation to the issue under consideration.

This approach is much stronger than merely asserting your own opinion of the law, although it is perfectly permissible to produce academic arguments that concur with your own preferences. Remember, though, that there is a need for balance and objectivity; whatever your preferred view, you should ensure that an alternative stance is at least acknowledged in your essay. From a pragmatic point of view, identifying two different standpoints is likely to attract greater credit from the marker than reliance on a single view, plus you are also demonstrating your research skills in identifying more than one opinion on the same issue, thus showing evidence of wide reading.

13.3.4.5 Internet sources

Students tend to like the Internet as a research tool because it is a quick and easy source of information: type in a word or phrase and you will be presented with a whole host of results within a split second. However, traditional legal resources are reliable and accurate whereas the quality of material found on the Internet cannot be guaranteed. It is acceptable to use the Internet to access official publications, such as those found on the Ministry of Justice website, but you should use material of uncertain origin with great caution.

In particular, you should avoid Internet websites that provide a potted summary of the law, especially those aimed at A level students (the reason for this should be obvious). There is a great temptation to rely on Internet sources that make the law sound so straightforward but it is not a good idea: it is the online equivalent of relying on the simplest textbook on the topic. You do not demonstrate understanding of your topic if you rely on these sorts of web sources as the message that it gives to your marker is 'I used Google to find some websites that make the law really easy and here is my rewording of their analysis of the law'. This is not the message you want to give as it conveys a poor impression of (a) your research skills and (b) your level of comprehension of the topic.

If you need any further persuasion that many Internet sources are not the most suitable authority to cite in an essay, look no further than Wikipedia itself. Wikipedia reminds users that encyclopedias (hard copy or online) are not viewed as good academic sources:

> Most educators and professionals do not consider it appropriate to use tertiary sources such as encyclopedias as a sole source for any information—citing an encyclopedia as an important reference in footnotes or bibliographies may result in censure or a failing grade. Wikipedia articles should be used for background information, as a reference for correct terminology and search terms, and as a starting point for further research.
>
> As with any community-built reference, there is a possibility for error in Wikipedia's content—please check your facts against multiple sources and read our disclaimers for more information.[1]

If even Wikipedia itself suggests that you should not rely upon its content without checking it thoroughly, this should give you a very good reason indeed to avoid using it as a source.

---

1.   <http://en.wikipedia.org/w/index.php?title=Special:Cite&page=Law&id=387799726>.

When selecting supporting material, bear in mind the following guidelines:

- Statements of law need to be supported by reference to their source in either statute or case law
- Factual statements should be attributed to their source, for example a statement that 'over 5000 women are killed by their partners each year in England and Wales' must provide a reference to the source of the statistic
- Analysis, discussion, and speculation about the law are strengthened by reference to supporting material so look for articles, official reports, and commentary in good textbooks
- A balanced argument is more effective than a one-sided stance, so select supporting material that takes into account a range of perspectives on the issue under consideration
- Be cautious in your use of textbooks, using them only if you can find no other supporting material for a particular argument, example, or opinion and never as a reference point for a statement of law that is contained in a case or statute

Remember that all supporting material must be fully and appropriately referenced in your essay. Failure to do so carries a risk that you will be accused of plagiarism. You will find detailed information on correct approaches to referencing in chapter 12.

13.3.5 Assessing the quality of source material

There are various means of evaluating the relevance and value of source material. One that you may find useful was developed by the Open Library (the library service of the Open University) that uses the mnemonic PROMPT as shown in Figure 13.3.

Each of the parts of this mnemonic will be explained in the sections that follow. Remember that you should carry out a PROMPT analysis in the context of a particular piece of work or a specific topic, as an assessment of relevance needs a point of reference: a meaningful PROMPT analysis cannot really be done in the abstract.

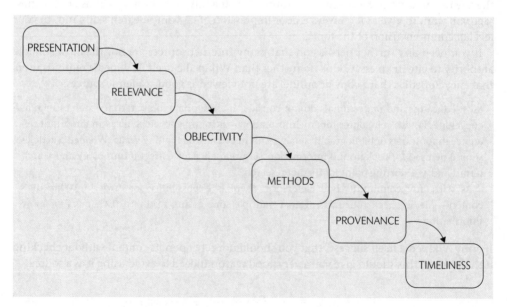

Figure 13.3   The PROMPT criteria

13.3.5.1 Presentation

Presentation refers to the appearance of the source material. For example, an academic article is characterized by dense text, mature use of language, and the inclusion of specialist terminology thus indicating that it is aimed at an expert audience, whereas a newspaper article will use more straightforward language and a more accessible layout to suit the general reader. Remember that the level of information aimed at the general reader might be too simplistic for your purposes (see the discussion on relevance in section 13.3.5.2).

The balance between text and illustrations can also give insight into the intended readership. Websites tend to vary in their presentation according to their target reader/user. Other aspects of presentation may be related to the credibility of the source: academic articles include institutional affiliations whilst websites might contain the logo of reputable organizations to add weight to their content.

Questions you might wish to consider when evaluating *presentation* are:

- Is the information communicated clearly?
- Are there errors of spelling, grammar, or presentation?
- What does the writing style suggest about the author or the audience?

13.3.5.2 Relevance

Relevance is closely associated with the purpose for which the source will be used. For example, a newspaper article covering proposed anti-terrorism legislation would be relevant to an essay that considered legal responses to extremism, but it would be less relevant to an essay on the use of the Royal prerogative[2] and of no relevance to an essay on easements. Relevance covers both the content of the source material and its nature: books and journal articles tend to be regarded as more relevant sources for academic writing, as they are aimed at the academic audience and tend to be in more depth and detailed than newspaper coverage or material found on websites. Of course, there will be circumstances in which newspaper articles are relevant to academic writing: they are produced more quickly (see the discussion on timeliness in section 13.3.5.6) than academic articles so may be the only source available for current legal developments, and some editorial pieces and articles produced by expert columnists, particularly in broadsheets, may offer a similar level of depth and detail to a short academic article. It is important to remember that a source does not have to be a perfect match with the topic under investigation in order to have some relevance. In order to stand the best chance of finding relevant material, you should be clear on your search strategy—what is it that you are looking for and why are you looking for it?

Questions you might wish to consider when evaluating *relevance* are:

- Does it contain the sort of information that is specifically required to illustrate or support the particular point being made?
- Is the level of this source suitable? Is it too detailed or too simple?
- Does it relate to a country or jurisdiction that is not under consideration?

13.3.5.3 Objectivity

Objectivity refers to the extent to which the source material takes a neutral stance or presents a balanced argument rather than arguing from one particular perspective. Journal articles

---

2. Although there is a power under the Royal prerogative to refuse or withdraw passports from British nationals who 'may seek to harm the UK' by travelling on a British passport to take part in terrorist-related activity.

tend to be more objective than media or online sources although this varies according to the nature of the source material. Academic writers tend to explore issues rather than to seek to promote a specific viewpoint, and even those which seek to persuade the reader that a particular approach is preferable tend to include and dissect contrary viewpoints. Newspaper articles may promote a single viewpoint or present more than one view but give primacy to one over the others; a good way to check for balance is to count the number of words that a newspaper article gives to each stance and to consider the relative positioning in the article of the viewpoints (early viewpoints tend to be more dominant). Web sources often have a single viewpoint to promote so care needs to be taken when relying upon them and consideration given to the interests of the individual writer or the organization in control of the publication. You will need to develop the skill of recognizing the perspective put forward by an author—biased opinion is fine, as long as you are able to recognize it as such.

Questions you might wish to consider when evaluating objectivity are:

- Do the writers state their position on the issue?

- Does the source use an emotive, sensational, or journalistic tone?

- Are there any hidden or vested commercial, political, or media interests? (see discussion on provenance in section 13.3.5.5)

- Is the source a mask for advertising a particular product, service, or organization?

- Is the information fact or opinion?

- Is the source complete, or does it just consider one point of view?

- What are the goals or objectives of the source?

13.3.5.4 Methods

Searching for an understanding of the methods used to produce the information within the source may be a useful indicator of its quality. While the idea of methods applies most commonly to socio-legal empirical research, you should consider where the information contained in the source document came from and whether or not it is reliable. For instance, an article might carry a review of the available literature together with some indication as to how that literature was selected for comment.

Questions you might wish to consider when evaluating *method* are:

- Are clear details provided within the document about its sources?

- Is the material simply an opinion or does it carry supporting evidence (documentary, case law, legislation, or otherwise)?

- Are vague terms such as 'sources/commentators suggest' used?

- If a newspaper article has used quotations, are these from experts?

13.3.5.5 Provenance

Provenance concerns the origins of the material—who produced it and where it came from—and can also give useful insight into its quality. However, each source should be judged on its merits. Some academic work is considered to be of great importance just because it is published in a prestigious journal, yet equally valuable work can readily be found in journals that are considered 'lesser' in some way. That said, provenance is an indirect indicator of quality and reliability—but remember that you should also consider the other areas of enquiry in the PROMPT criteria as well. In the context of your coursework, provenance is also important for your marker to be confident that you are using appropriate sources.

Knowledge of the author is helpful, as it enables you to see if they are acknowledged as an expert in a particular area (although remember that everyone has a first article—so the absence of a body of literature from the same person does not necessarily devalue their early work). It also helps you to see if their work has been referenced in other literature on the topic, or to see if they are well known for espousing a particular viewpoint or court controversy. Similarly, if the material was sponsored by a particular association, you will want to consider the purpose of that organization, to determine whether it is likely to have a particular agenda that would lead to a subjective viewpoint being expressed. For example, Stonewall—a campaigning and lobbying organization promoting lesbian, gay, and bisexual rights—published the Gay British Crime Survey 2013 which concluded that police forces should do much more to tackle homophobic hate crimes: this may cause you to question the objectivity of the report in interpreting the results.

With regard to articles in newspapers, you should remember that the purpose of these articles is to sell newspapers—this can lead to the omission of detail or the sensationalism of the facts, or reporting the story in such a way as to suit the political leanings of the newspaper (see the discussion on objectivity in section 13.3.5.3). Consider also the distinction between broadsheets and tabloid newspapers.

Finally, as you have already seen in this chapter, remember that anyone can publish on the web or post to a discussion forum: this is where the author's credentials are a useful indicator of quality. There is, however, a distinction between material that is *published* on the web and that which is *available* on the web: an article from the *Criminal Law Review*, for example, that is viewed online will be identical to that which first appeared in print and will have been subject to the same review processes. Most (but not all) academic journals are peer-reviewed: articles that are submitted will be evaluated by at least two independent experts and revisions may well be required before an article is accepted for publication. By contrast, not all electronic journals operate a peer review process—check to see if there are any statements on editorial policy.

Questions you might wish to consider when evaluating *provenance* are:

- Who wrote the material? Is there an institutional affiliation? Have they provided a contact email address?

- Is the author a well-known authority in the field? Are they trustworthy?

- If the material is supported by an organization, what are their interests? Who is paying for the material?

- Where is the information published? Has it been edited or reviewed prior to publication?

13.3.5.6 Timeliness

Timeliness relates to the currency of the information contained in the source material. This is particularly important in law where material—especially case law—can date very rapidly. That is not to say that there is no value in older source material: for example, in *De l'esprit des lois* (1748), Montesquieu described the separation of powers between the legislature, the executive, and the judiciary. Just because this view is over 250 years old does not make it invalid today. Older material can be informative in setting out the evolution of a certain theory or society's view of a particular issue at a certain point in time, or it may simply relate to a relatively static area of law. That said, you must remember to take the date of publication into account when assessing the source, but also remember that whether or not material is out of date depends on the purpose for which you want that material. Consider whether new research has been published since the source material that supersedes it or casts new light onto its findings.

Questions you might wish to consider when evaluating *timeliness* are:

- Do you know when the material was produced?
- Does the date of the material fit your needs?
- Is the information obsolete or superseded?

Finally, remember that the PROMPT criteria may not contain all of the factors that you want to take into account when assessing the value of a piece of source material. Any analysis undertaken using these criteria may also quite validly contain a critique of PROMPT as a method of assessing the usefulness of sources.

13.3.6 Organizing your research

During the course of your research, you will use a variety of sources and you will want to keep a record of the relevant information that you have found. There are two aspects to this: first, recording the points from the sources that you want to include in your essay and, secondly, ensuring that you keep a full record of the bibliographic details of each source so that you can reference it appropriately in your work.

The most popular method of recording information is, unfortunately, the least effective as it involves rewriting every textbook, article, and case in a more condensed form. This is labour-intensive and does not produce a very useful set of notes. A less time-consuming alternative is described earlier in this chapter. This involves making a note of the value of the point that you have found rather than writing out the point itself.

Although this method is quicker than writing full notes, it still results in a set of notes that is organized on a source-by-source basis. In other words, you have a set of condensed notes of each article as you read them. There is an alternative approach to organization that will make your notes easier to use when it comes to working out how they fit into your essay which is issue-by-issue.

This approach uses the points that you identified during your analysis of the question and your brainstorming as the basis for arranging your notes.

- Identify key words and phrases from your analysis of the question and brainstorming session and write each of these at the top of a separate sheet of paper (or create a document for each if working on a computer)
- Select a piece of source material and read it carefully, looking out for any points that are relevant to the issues that you have identified. If you are working from a copy, you could highlight these points or annotate the page to indicate that they are important points
- Make a descriptive note of the point such as 'discusses the validity of consent procured by fraud' under the relevant heading. Be sure to include something that identifies the source such as the name of the author or the article and the page on which the point appears
- Review your headings from time-to-time. It may be that certain issues need to be amalgamated or a discrete issue may emerge under one of your headings that you decide to treat separately. You may find material during your research that identifies a new issue that you had not originally thought of but which you discover has a place in your essay

These points will be the building blocks of your essay so it will be useful to have your notes arranged in this way. You will see an example of notes organized by issue in Figure 13.4. It shows sub-divisions within the page of notes on the left-hand side which have allocated space to note questions that have arisen during the research process and further avenues of investigation to be pursued. These separate sections within each page or document

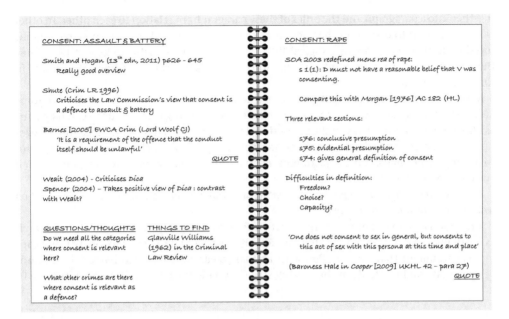

Figure 13.4 Notes organized by issue.

will serve as a useful reminder of thoughts that occurred to you as you were reading and will act as a prompt when you are deciding what further research needs to be undertaken.

You may also have noticed that some points in the example are written in full and that the word QUOTE appears in capital letters beside them. You might think that this is unnecessary as the words appear inside quotation marks but it very good practice to do everything possible to draw your attention to the fact that these words are not yours and must be attributed to their source if used in your essay. It is very easy to forget to add quotation marks or overlook them when reading your notes some time after they were written and think 'what a good point. I've expressed that really well' and include it in your essay without realizing that it was a quotation. As you will see from the discussion in chapter 12, even unintentional replication of the work of others without acknowledgement will contravene the plagiarism/unfair practice rules at your university so it is worth taking extra effort to ensure that you do not make a mistake when using your notes to create your essay.

Whichever approach you use to record and organize your material, it is important to remember that you must ensure that you keep full bibliographic details of all your source material. There is nothing more frustrating than having the feeling of success and relief that accompanies finishing your essay replaced by the realization that you still need to track down references for your source material. One useful approach is to start a separate document entitled 'references' as soon as you start working on your essay and add each source to it as you read it. You might also find it useful to keep a separate list of literature that you want to read but have not yet found, just as a reminder.

You will find some information on effective note-taking techniques in chapter 9.

13.3.7 Planning a structure

The structure of the essay is important as it is this that determines the coherence of your argument. Determining the best structure involves deciding which points should be grouped together into a paragraph and the order of these paragraphs in relation to each other. In other words, you need to decide on the content of each paragraph and then fit these paragraphs together so that they present a logical line of argument. It is useful to give at least some thought to this during the research stage so that you have an idea of how your points fit together before you start to write.

As your research progresses and you gather a detailed set of notes, you should develop some idea of the points that you want to make in your essay. If you organized your research by issue as illustrated in Figure 13.4, you should find that your notes are already arranged into categories that can help you to determine the content of each paragraph. This is just a starting point so be prepared to make some adjustments when dividing your points into paragraphs when you come to write your essay.

There is a more detailed discussion on creating structure within a paragraph in section 13.4 on writing an essay later in this chapter.

It is a good idea to create a working structure for your essay as you are conducting research as it will give you an idea of how all your ideas fit together and help you to identify any gaps in your argument that can be filled with further research. It will also reduce the amount of work that you have to do at the writing stage as you will have a preliminary structure in

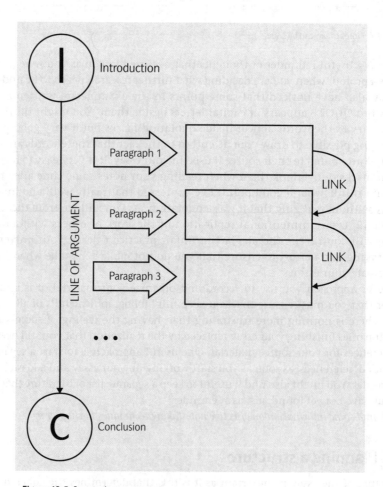

Figure 13.5 Structuring an essay

mind from the outset. Of course, it is often the case that your structure will change as you write but it is still a good idea to have a tentative idea of the shape of your essay before you start to write. One way to do this is to create a structure using the ideas for each paragraph as illustrated in Figure 13.5.

This structure reminds you that your essay must have an introduction, a conclusion, and a line of argument that runs through it whilst giving you space to label each paragraph according to its content or purpose. You can then use each label as a heading on a separate sheet of paper and make a list of the points that you plan to include in that paragraph. Alternatively, you might want to start by making a list of all the points that you want to include in your essay and then group them into paragraphs before deciding on a label for the paragraph and putting the paragraphs in order. The presence of the arrows acts as a reminder that each paragraph must be linked to the next and/or back to the question. You might find it helpful to add a few words to your plan to capture the nature of the link.

There is a discussion on the use of signposting words and phrases to create links between paragraphs and between your essay and the question in section 13.4.4.

13.3.8 Planning and drafting

Activities that you undertake during the preparation stage should make the writing a draft of your essay much easier as you will have your source material to hand and a good idea of how your points will be organized in your essay. However, this does not mean that you should treat preparation and writing as separate activities to be undertaken consecutively—it is actually a good idea to start drafting parts of your essay as soon as you feel able even if you are still following up some lines of research for other parts. Not only will the process of writing help to develop your ideas, it may enable you to identify gaps in your research or even new lines of investigation. Moreover, the sooner you start writing, the more time you will have to redraft your essay and refine your arguments.

Some students delay the start of the writing process and, as a consequence, are left with insufficient time to produce a polished piece of work. There is nothing worse than having to submit work that you know is something less than your best effort because you have run out of time.

There is a discussion of techniques that you can use to get started with writing in section 13.4.2.

13.4 Writing the essay

Once you have researched the topic, gathered your material, and put together a preliminary plan of your essay, it is time to start writing. This section will discuss the factors that contribute to the construction of a successful essay. It will start by outlining the key components of an effective introduction and set out some strategies for constructing paragraphs before moving to consider the need to achieve an appropriate balance between description and analysis. It will then address techniques for creating a focused and flowing essay before ending with an exploration of the characteristics of a strong conclusion.

13.4.1 Writing an introduction

It should go without saying that the first paragraph of your essay should be an introduction that unpicks the question and explains how it will be tackled but a great many undergraduate essays simply launch straight into the first substantive point without any attempt at an introduction. This may be an accidental omission by students who do not understand how to create an introduction and who believe that their first paragraph is actually fulfilling the role of an introduction. Alternatively, it may be a deliberate omission by students who have sacrificed the introduction in order to meet the word limit in the belief that it makes no difference to the essay whether or not it has an introduction. This is a mistake. The introduction has a number of functions to fulfil, all of which are important to the overall success of the essay:

- It identifies the central subject matter of the essay
- It unpicks the question thus demonstrating to the marker that you have understood the requirements of the essay
- It sets out the issues that will be addressed in the essay in order to answer the question which gives the marker an idea of what to expect in the essay
- It may give an indication as to the conclusion that is reached in the essay (although opinion is divided on this point)

In essence, then, the introduction gives the marker an instant impression of whether you have understood what the question requires and an indication of the points that you have included in your essay. This is why, from a pragmatic point of view, it is important for you to provide an introduction and to make sure that it is a good one: first impressions count so make sure that the first impression that your marker has of your essay is one that shows you are going to discuss appropriate subject matter in an organized manner. You will find an explanation of how to do this in Table 13.1 in response to the question: 'Discuss the extent to which the legitimacy of judicial review depends more on advancing constitutional values than accountability to the political process'.

Table 13.1 Structuring an introduction

Line	Role	Example
Your first sentence should grab the marker's attention.	Your marker has to read your essay but you should strive to make him want to do so by making your first sentence one that identifies the theme of the question in an interesting way or that shows you are engaging directly with the question. Under no circumstances should your essay start with the words 'this essay': it is very dull!	The legitimacy of judicial review depends more on advancing fundamental and enduring constitutional values than in accountability to the political process.
The next sentence establishes the specific focus of the essay question.	This sentence *can* start with 'this essay' as its role is to explain to the marker the objective of your essay.	This essay will consider this position and question how the courts in judicial review cases give effect to the constitutional values on which it is based.

(Continued)

Table 13.1 *(Cont.)*

Line	Role	Example
The next sentences should set out how the objective of the essay will be established.	This gives the marker an indication of the content of your essay and the structure that it will take. In essence, this aspect of the introduction tells the marker what to expect in your essay.	In order to do so, it will first analyze the constitutional values of doctrine of separation of powers, the rule of law, and parliamentary sovereignty as they are effected by judicial review. It will examine the nature of judicial review in the context of political accountability and the relationship between Parliament, the executive, and the judiciary. Finally, the relative strengths of these sources of legitimacy will be considered in the light of the proposition along with any arguments to the contrary.
Some lecturers like the final sentence of the introduction to give an indication of the conclusion. Be aware that some lecturers really dislike this, believing that the conclusion belongs at the end of the essay only. It would be worth checking with each lecturer to see if they have any strong preferences.	This ensures that the introduction provides a complete snapshot of the essay by giving the marker an insight into your conclusion right from the start.	Although there are contrary perspectives, it will be argued that judicial review upholds the rule of law, the separation of powers, and parliamentary sovereignty protecting, in turn, the fundamental values of legitimacy, justice, and fairness which are the primary sources of the legitimacy of judicial review.

Many students prefer to write the introduction to the essay at the end of the writing process so that they can reflect what is actually in it. This can be a useful approach because the eventual content of your essay may be different to your planned essay as your ideas evolve once you start writing. However, there is no harm in writing a draft of an introduction at the beginning so that it is always taken into account in the overall word limit. You can always amend it once the essay is finished.

13.4.2 Start writing

It is very frustrating to be in a situation in which you know that your essay deadline is approaching but you feel unable to start writing. There can be a number of reasons for this:

- **I don't know enough about the subject matter to start writing.** Be realistic. If you have done a lot of research, you should have sufficient source material to start to write even if there are still a few elusive sources that you have not been able to track down. You cannot expect to find everything that has been written on the subject matter so you may have to start writing on the basis of what you have been able to find. Of course, if you have only read a couple of sources, it is likely that you are right and you are not yet ready to start writing so keep going with your research until you feel better prepared.

- **I don't know where to start.** This is quite common and can be very frustrating. You have done all your research, it is organized into issues and you have broken it down into paragraphs but still the words will not come. One way around this is to write something that you know will have a place in your essay: it might be a definition of a key concept, a summary of the views of a particular theorist, or an outline of a relevant criminal offence. In other words, write content without context, i.e. without knowing where your words will fit in the essay, just so that you get over the block of staring at a blank sheet of paper or empty computer screen.

- **I can't write because I don't understand it.** Obviously it is not a good idea to start writing an essay if you have not yet understood the subject matter. Try to find a really simple explanation in a basic textbook, perhaps even using one that is not intended to be used at degree level. Once you have got the basic idea, you can revisit the section in your set textbook and see if it makes sense. Alternatively, you may have to ask a lecturer for help but remember that this may not be forthcoming in relation to assessed coursework. You could also try to write the parts of the essay that you do understand—it is sometimes the case that this will make things click in your mind and it will all become clear.

- **I just can't write.** Sometimes, the requirement to write in quite formal language can be off-putting so try writing in a way that is easier for you just to get your ideas flowing. One way of doing this is with free-flow writing.

You may find the following suggested approach to be useful in overcoming writer's block.

- Get a blank sheet of paper or open a fresh document on your computer.

- Write a trigger word or phrase at the top of the paper or document. This can either be a key term relevant to the essay or some idea that you want to put in it such as:

  - The aim of my essay is to. . .

  - In the first paragraph, I am going to explain. . .

  - The main argument that I want to make is. . .

  - What is it that I'm trying to say?

- Set yourself a short period of time—one or two minutes is plenty—and start writing. Do not worry about how you express your ideas or the order in which you make them. Just get your thoughts down on paper so you can see them.

- Make sure that you keep writing for at least the period of time that you have set yourself even if you feel as if you are writing nonsense. However, if you find that you still have points to make when the time is up then be sure to keep writing until you have exhausted your ideas.

- When you are finished, review what you have written. You should have produced something that captures your ideas in ordinary language but you can easily reword them into a more appropriate written style. You will probably need to reorganize your ideas too. This is fine. At least you are writing and getting your ideas down on the page.

13.4.3 Creating paragraphs

Paragraphs are the building blocks of your essay. They divide your essay into smaller, easily-digestible chunks with each one containing a separate idea or argument. Each paragraph should follow on logically from its predecessor and lead into the paragraph that follows it. In other words, there should be a sense of logical progression to your essay as your paragraphs are organized in such a way that each one contributes to the construction of a flowing line of argument.

This idea that each paragraph should contain a separate idea or argument does not really give a clear idea of how much detail should be in each paragraph. In fact, one of the commonest questions asked by students on this topic concerns the ideal length of a paragraph. This is a difficult question to answer. On the one hand, a paragraph should be as long as it needs to be in order to explain its argument but, on the other hand, it can be really hard work for the marker to read paragraphs that are pages long so many markers would say that there should be at least two paragraphs on every page of your essay. One technique that is quite widely used to determine the content of a paragraph is the PEE technique (point, elaboration, example) which has been modified here by the addition of a fourth characteristic (link) to create the PEEL technique:

- **Point.** A paragraph should start by outlining its central point
- **Elaboration.** The sentences that follow should expand on this point to explain it in greater detail
- **Example.** This provides support for the argument that you are presenting to make it more convincing
- **Link.** The final sentence should either relate to the point made, back to the question, or provide a link to the next paragraph.

You will find a more detailed discussion of paragraphing in chapter 10.

13.4.4 Signposting

Signposting is the process of making your essay clear to the reader. It refers to the words and phrases in your essay that explain the significance of your points. In essence, signposting words and phrases create focus (by linking your points to the question) and flow (by explaining how each paragraph relates to the next).

One way in which signposting is useful to the reader is in indicating the big ideas and themes in your essay. This is the equivalent of this book stating 'this chapter will deal with coursework' or 'this section explores issues associated with planning your essay'. This sort of signposting involves phrases that give the reader an insight into the overall focus of the whole essay or the next significant section of your essay and creates a strong structure for your work:

- The central focus of this essay is. . .
- The main theoretical perspectives examined in this essay are. . .
- The first section of this essay will be a review of the literature that examines. . .
- Having discussed [insert topic], it is now necessary to consider . . .
- The main argument that emerges from the case law is. . .

Signposting is also commonly used to communicate the relationship between different points and ideas to the reader. You might think that this is unnecessary and that the links are obvious but remember that you see your own work with full knowledge of the thinking behind it which gives you an advantage over your reader who has only the words on paper to rely upon. What seems obvious to you is therefore far less obvious to the reader so it is a good idea to add signposting to your essay so that your meaning is clear to the reader. The importance of signposting to indicate the relationship between points raised in your essay is demonstrated in the following example:

- Croall[3] states that technological change affects opportunities for crime, the forms of crime that are prevalent, and patterns of crime. Heidensohn comments that criminality takes novel forms from time to time

What is the relationship between these sentences? Do Croall and Heidensohn agree or disagree with each other? Is the essay presenting two opposing views or is it using two viewpoints in conjunction with each other to strengthen the argument? These questions can be answered without difficulty with the insertion of a single word.

- Croall states that technological change affects opportunities for crime, the forms of crime that are prevalent, and patterns of crime. Moreover, Heidensohn comments that criminality takes novel forms from time to time

- Croall states that technological change affects opportunities for crime, the forms of crime that are prevalent, and patterns of crime. However, Heidensohn comments that criminality takes novel forms from time to time[4]

The use of the word 'moreover' indicates that the points are to be read in conjunction with each other with Heidensohn's point adding support to Croall's view whereas the use of the word 'however' indicates that the two views are incompatible with each other.

As this example illustrates, a single word can add a great deal of clarity to your writing. Table 13.2 sets out the different roles played by signposting words and phrases in signalling the relationship between the points made in your essay.

Table 13.2 Signposting words and phrases

Agreement or similarity	moreover, also, similarly, in addition, furthermore, additionally, as well as, what is more, in the same way, likewise
Disagreement or contrast	however, nevertheless, on the other hand, conversely, by contrast, but, yet, by comparison, although, alternatively
Providing exemplification or explanation.	because, due to, as a result, owing to, by virtue of, as a consequence of, therefore, thus, particularly, hence, by way of illustration, including, especially
Reformulating or reiterating an idea	in other words, in essence, that is, in simple terms, to clarify, rather, to paraphrase, to reiterate
Enumerating and sequencing.	there are a number of considerations, firstly, secondly, finally, subsequently, consequently, before, eventually, first and foremost
Providing examples	to illustrate this point, for example, for instance, this can be demonstrated, such as
Summarizing	in conclusion, in summary, finally, hence, as an overview

3. H Croall, *Crime and Society in Britain* (Longman 1998).
4. F Heidensohn, *Crime and Society* (Macmillan 1989).

13.4.5 Description versus analysis

Earlier in this chapter, it was said that a successful essay is one that answers the specific question asked rather than discussing the topic in general terms. In order to answer the question, your essay must be analytical rather than merely descriptive. A descriptive essay is one that explains the key concepts whereas an analytical essay moves beyond this to investigate how those concepts operate or relate to each other, depending on the requirements of the question. For instance, if you were answering the question about judicial review that was used as an example in Table 13.1, a descriptive approach would explain what is meant by judicial review, Parliamentary sovereignty, the rule of law, and the separation of powers, but would not do enough to discuss how judicial review gains its legitimacy from furthering those constitutional values.

It is understandable that students often produce very descriptive essays, especially in the early stages of their legal studies, because it is far easier to describe than it is to analyze. Every textbook in law will provide its own descriptions of core concepts so all that is required is that these descriptions are read and reworded in your essay. Textbooks are far less likely to provide inspiration for the analysis part of an essay because the question will have been set by your lecturer to test your powers of reasoning and your ability to criticize and appraise issues in law. Many students lack the confidence to do this, particularly if they cannot find any source material to rely upon, and so fill their essay with description, often only trying to explain how this answers the question in the final paragraph.

Descriptive essays are limited in the success that they will achieve. It is essential that you create an essay that is a combination of description and analysis. You will be better able to do this once you have a good understanding of the clues provided by the wording of the question that will indicate what concepts need to be described and what direction the analysis should take. You can do this by using the 'do what to what?' technique. This asks 'what does this essay require me to do (skill) with what concept in law (description)?' as is illustrated in Figure 13.6.

This will give you a clear idea as to what needs to be described and what needs to be analyzed:

- Do what? Outline
- To what? Approaches to statutory interpretation in England and Wales
- Do what? Comment
- To what? The extent to which they allow judicial law-making

Of course, the success of this method rests on your ability to recognize what the words used in the question require you to do in your essay. The words which give you instructions are called process words and these are best understood by considering the work of educational psychologist, Benjamin Bloom. He conducted research into the skills demonstrated by students in their essays, divided them into six categories and arranged them in a hierarchy to demonstrate their importance and complexity as illustrated in Figure 13.7.

Outline the approaches to statutory interpretation taken by the courts in England and Wales and comment on the extent to which they allow the judiciary to make law.

Figure 13.6 'Do what to what'?

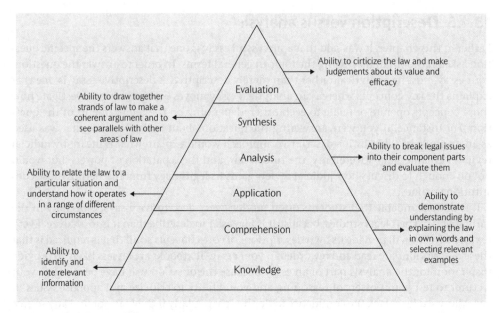

Figure 13.7 Bloom's taxonomy

Bloom described knowledge and comprehension—the two categories of skills at the bottom of the hierarchy—as lower-order skills because they are easier to demonstrate. By contrast, the higher-order skills of application, analysis, synthesis, and evaluation are harder to master and provide evidence that the student is able to *use* knowledge rather than simply to acquire and repeat it.

To take a very basic example, if you needed to drive to a new area that you had not visited before, you would be able to demonstrate *knowledge* by finding a map of the area and *understanding* by explaining the route to another person, but application would be demonstrated by actually reaching your destination. Once there, you might want to *analyze* how useful the route was and, ultimately, decide whether to use it again or to find an alternative.

You can identify the skills that are important within an essay by the process words that are used in the question. Table 13.3 identifies some of the process words commonly associated with each of the categories of skills and provides some elaboration on what each of these requires from the writer of the essay.

Bloom's taxonomy demonstrates the point that a successful essay rests upon more than mere identification and explanation of the relevant theory or literature relating to a particular topic. The lower-order skills are considered to be more straightforward and easier to demonstrate, so an essay which moves beyond knowledge and comprehension to demonstrate higher-order skills is likely to be more successful. That does not mean that the lower-order skills are unimportant or should be omitted, merely that they should be considered the foundation upon which a demonstration of higher-order skills is based. In other words, you need to be able to describe the state of the law in order to analyze it.

It is essential that you remember that a successful essay requires an appropriate balance between description and analysis. An essay that is heavily descriptive does not demonstrate sufficient higher-order skills to achieve a high mark whilst an essay which contains insufficient description will also struggle because analysis needs to be based upon a foundation of description in order to make sense. For example, you could not comment on the accuracy of measurement of recorded crime without first describing the methods by which crimes are recorded.

Table 13.3 Skills and process words

Skill	Indicated by . . .	Example
Knowledge	Words that invite a factual or descriptive response or a straightforward statement	describe, define, outline, state, identify, list, what, how, when, which
Comprehension	Words that require an explanation, interpretation, or the ability to extrapolate key information	explain, use examples, summarize, paraphrase, interpret
Application	Words that suggest the need to apply theory to different circumstances or to predict how such theories would react to a new situation	apply, demonstrate, advise, predict
Analysis	Words that indicate that a legal principle should be broken down into its component parts and subjected to close scrutiny	analyze, assess, consider, measure, quantify, how far
Synthesis	Words that indicate the ability to draw together strands of an argument and to identify similarities and differences	justify, compare, contrast, distinguish
Evaluation	Words that indicate that whether a response to a particular issue is effective, consistent, moral, desirable, better than before, or a useful solution to a particular problem	appraise, criticize, evaluate, comment, reflect, discuss, how effective

Achieving the right balance between the two is a difficult task as there is no magic formula that sets out the appropriate contribution of each to an essay as this will vary according to the question. The most effective rule to apply is to include sufficient description to support the analysis; in other words, describe things that need to be understood so that the discussion will make sense to the reader.

13.4.6 Writing a conclusion

As with the introduction, the conclusion plays a crucial role in your essay and yet it is often absent thus leaving the marker with the distinct feeling that the student just stopped writing when they ran out of time, inspiration, or words.

Remember, the conclusion is the last thing that your marker reads before he starts deciding what grade to award. Make sure that they are left with a good impression of your work by ensuring that it has a strong conclusion that ties together the strands of the argument that you have outlined in your essay to create a direct response to the question. This should include the following:

- A statement of the aim of the essay
- A brief reminder of the arguments that you have presented
- An evaluation of which of any opposing views is to be preferred
- A direct answer to the question

Your conclusion should not, as a general rule, introduce any new material that has not been discussed in the body of your essay, although it can make reference to a point that has not been discussed if it is simply there to emphasize your conclusion.

13.4.7 Remember your assessment criteria

Assessment criteria have an obvious importance to your essay as they are the criteria against which it will be marked. You should therefore make sure that you understand how essays are marked at your institution and what is expected of you. Assessment criteria tend to be agreed on a department-wide basis and identify the factors that your marker will be looking for in your essay. You may find these on an assessment feedback form that may be attached to your work when it is returned to you. It is often the case that the relevant criteria are listed and accompanied by a series of tick boxes in which the marker can indicate your level of achievement in each area (see Figure 13.8).

By looking at the categories that are listed on the form, you can identify what skills are being evaluated in your work and try to ensure that these are demonstrated. Another approach that is used to communicate the assessment criteria to students is to categorize the level of skills that are expected in work that falls within a particular classification. This is demonstrated in the example shown in Figure 13.9.

	Weak	Below Average	Satisfactory	Good	Excellent
Critical analysis	☐	☐	☐	☐	☐
Research	☐	☐	☐	☐	☐
Referencing	☐	☐	☐	☐	☐
Written style, grammar and punctuation	☐	☐	☐	☐	☐

Figure 13.8 Sample assessment criteria

FAIL: Less than 40%
A weak answer that fails to address the question posed and which shows inadequate understanding of the subject area. Little or no evidence of reading or research and reference to irrelevant materials. Significant weakness in presentation and organization as well as numerous errors of grammar and punctuation.

PASS, THIRD CLASS: 40–49%
A fair answer that provides some material of relevance to the question posed and which shows some limited understanding of the subject area. There may be some reference to supporting materials but little, if any, attempt at analysis; a highly descriptive answer with some errors and omissions. Presentation and organization are likely to be poor and there may be significant errors of grammar and punctuation.

LOWER SECOND CLASS: 50–59%
A satisfactory answer that covers a fair degree of the material of relevance to the question albeit in largely descriptive detail. There may be an attempt at analysis that is either ineffective or fails to get to grips with the issue at the heart of the question. There should be evidence of a reasonable level of understanding and an ability to incorporate some supporting materials into the answer. There may be some grammatical and presentational errors but these should not be widespread.

Figure 13.9 Example assessment criteria by classification

There are, therefore, various methods that can be used to ascertain what skills and competences you need to demonstrate to impress your lecturers with the quality of your essay. For some reason, students often fail to take these matters into account and continue to produce essays that comply with their own personal view of a good essay. This can be extremely costly in terms of lost marks if their view does not coincide with what the lecturer considers to be a good essay. Lecturers are looking for a combination of legal knowledge and an ability to use it and thus are likely to consider the following factors to be important:

- The relevance of the material included and the arguments put forward to the question
- Evidence of comprehension and an ability to analyze the law
- A strong structure and clear and logical organization of material
- Evidence of research and incorporation of wider reading into the essay
- An appropriate written style with good grammar and punctuation
- Full and accurate referencing including a bibliography
- Good presentation

13.5 Polish

It is a mistake to think that your essay is finished as soon as you have written the final word: this is just a first draft and there is still work to do to ensure that the work is ready for submission. This section covers a range of activities that should be done at the final stage of the essay-writing process to ensure that you produce a piece of work that is expressed with clarity, that develops a logical line of argument, and that has had sufficient attention paid to all aspects of its presentation. You should allow yourself plenty of time to do these things so do not leave it until an hour before the submission deadline.

13.5.1 Meeting the word limit

It is usual for each piece of coursework to have a maximum word limit that must not be exceeded. Many universities have a policy of imposing a penalty, usually a deduction of marks, on work that exceeds the word limit. Students often struggle with word limits, viewing them as an annoying restriction that stops them making all the points that they want to make in their essay but it is important that you ensure that your work does fit within the word limit.

So, what should you do to ensure that your work adheres to the word limit? The first step to take is to ensure that you know what the word limit is and what content counts toward it. The bibliography is usually excluded from the word count but what about the footnotes? You must find out what the regulations are on word count in your university because an inadvertent contravention of the rules will still attract a penalty.

There is some difference of opinion amongst lecturers and students about whether you should try and work to the word limit as you write or whether it is preferable to get all your ideas down as you want them to be and then redraft your work to fit the word limit. This is a matter of personal preference but each approach has advantages and disadvantages as you will see from Table 13.4.

Table 13.4 Condensing text

	Advantages	Disadvantages
Condense as you write	The process of condensing your work as you write it may help you to develop a more concise and precise written style. It may also encourage you to experiment with language to find new words that express the same ideas in fewer words. It will make you really concentrate on what is essential to your essay and conscious of using words wisely.	It can be time-consuming if you find you are constantly redrafting sentences to save words and it may ultimately not be necessary. You may stifle your flow of ideas or even discard whole lines of argument that would have been useful to your essay because you are concentrating on keeping your word count low.
Condense at the end	If you write everything that you want to write as you want to say it, your ideas will all be down on paper just as you wanted to express them. It may be that you find that you do not have a problem with the word limit.	You might end up with a piece of work that is double the word limit. You have to work through it from start to finish to reduce the word count which is almost the equivalent of writing the essay again.

If you do find that you are over the word limit, you are going to need to find a way to reduce the number of words that you have used. There are two ways to do this: you can either cut whole sentences or paragraphs out of your essay or you can keep all of your content but try to find a way to express it in fewer words. The best approach is a combination of the two methods. First, read your essay to ensure that you have not included any unnecessary points. Perhaps you have used two examples to support your argument when one would have done or maybe you have included a point because it was an interesting aside rather than being strictly relevant to the question. Once you have cut out the unnecessary material, you will have to find a more concise method of expressing the points that remain if you are still over the word limit. Look at each sentence and see if you can reword it using fewer words: even if you only reduce each sentence by a single word, that will be a significant reduction to the overall word count of the essay.

13.5.2 Structure, flow, and focus

Remember that your essay must present a flowing argument that develops in a logical way and which answers the question. This means that you need a strong structure, clear links to be made between each paragraph, and frequent references back to the question. Check that your essay has structure, flow, and focus using the following steps:

- **Structure.** Read each paragraph and describe its content in a few words. Look at the list that this produces and see if it tells a story in a logical order. Compare your list with the plan of your essay that you created before you started writing (see Figure 13.5). Departure from this plan is not necessarily a problem as your essay may not have fitted together as you expected before you started writing but it will be a useful reference point if you find that your essay does not seem to have a logical structure.
- **Flow.** Check that the relationship between the end of one chapter and the beginning of the next is clear. If not, add signposting words and phrases to clarify the connections between your ideas as this will ensure that there is a logical development to your essay. If you find a point or a paragraph that cannot be linked to the ideas around it using signposting then

it does not belong in that part of your essay and must be moved. If you cannot find a new place where it fits then it is likely that it does not belong in your essay at all.

- **Focus.** Does every paragraph make a contribution to the development of an argument that actually answers the question rather than simply being about the relevant topic? You might find that you need to 'touch base' with the question explicitly to strengthen your focus. You can do this by repeating key words from the question or by relating the point that you have made in your paragraph back to the question.

13.5.3 Proof reading

It is tempting to heave a sigh of relief when the final word of your essay is written and think 'that's it done' but you should really not assume that you got everything right in your essay in the first draft. Neither should you rely on the spelling and grammar checking tools on your computer to pick up all your mistakes—there are plenty of common typing errors that the computer will miss.

Practical exercise

Proof reading is an essential part of the process of ensuring that your work is fit for submission. Careless errors suggest lack of care and this is not the impression that you want your marker to have of your work. Many lecturers will deduct marks from work that is strewn with errors so it is worth taking great care to ensure that this does not happen to your essay.

1. Print a copy of your essay. It is much easier to read what you have actually written on paper than it is to spot errors on a computer screen.
2. Read it very carefully and slowly. Remember, you are not reading to find out what you have written but to spot mistakes and that requires you to pay close attention to every word. Some people find that reading out loud helps with this.
3. Circle every error and make a note in the margin as to what is wrong. You might also like to note how you intend to correct the error.
4. Pay particular attention to punctuation. If you are unsure as to whether you have used, say, a semi-colon correctly, reword your sentence so that it does not need one.
5. Use a thesaurus to check the meaning of any words if you are not confident that you have used them correctly.
6. Once you have been through the entire document, make all the necessary changes. Cross each circle made on your printed version so that you have a record of which problems have been addressed.

Ideally, you should carry out this process once again after the errors have been corrected just to be sure that no mistakes remain. Leave it overnight if possible or at least have a break of a few hours and start again with a clean printed copy of your work.

 There is an essay on the Online Resource Centre for you to proof read.

It is often easier to spot mistakes in the work of others because you will read it with fresher eyes. When you read your own work, there is a tendency to skim it because you are so familiar with its content whereas proof reading requires far more detailed attention. As such, you might find it useful to see if someone else will proof read your essay for you. Remember, though, that you must correct any errors that they spot yourself.

13.5.4 Referencing

You should have been adding references to your work as you wrote it so use this final stage of the essay writing process to check that all the necessary references are present, both in the text and in the bibliography. You should also ensure that your references are complete. This means that the reference in the text to specific points and quotations should include a page reference and that you should ensure that you provide full bibliographic information in your list of references.

You will find detailed guidance on when and how to reference in chapter 12.

13.6 Improving your performance

As you have seen from the earlier sections of this chapter, there are many techniques that you can use to strengthen your essay-writing skills. However, it is not unusual to find that students' marks consistently fall just short of a classification boundary, say 58 or 68. Being able to find a way of picking up just a couple of extra marks can make a tremendous difference to the overall final result of your law degree. In this final section, we will summarize some of the points that you can address that will raise your standard across the grade boundaries. Each of these points has been covered either in this chapter or elsewhere in the book, so this section also gives (in Tables 13.5 and 13.6) a cross-reference to the section or sections where you can find out more. It might be helpful for you to find a copy of your course grade descriptors or assessment criteria to have to hand as you work through this part (see section 13.4.7 for more detail). If you do find yourself 'on the boundary', consider speaking to your academic advisor, course leader or study support service to see if you can review a piece of work that you have already had marked. This should help you to identify

Table 13.5 Finding out more: 2.2 to 2.1

Issue	Where to look
Poor technical execution	Referencing—section 12.3
	Use of language—section 10.2
	Grammar and punctuation—section 10.3
	Paragraphs—section 10.4
	Using quotations—section 10.5
	Word limits—section 10.6
	Presentation—section 10.7
Too much description	Description versus analysis—section 13.4.5
Not answering the question	Focus on the question—section 13.3.1
Insufficient research	Preparation: research and planning—section 13.3
Inclusion of irrelevant content	Organizing your research—section 13.3.6
	Relevance—section 13.3.5.2

Table 13.6 Finding out more: 2.1 to First

Issue	Where to look
Perfect referencing	Referencing—section 12.3
Sophisticated use of language	Use of language—section 10.2
Engagement with theory	Legal reasoning—chapter 11
Wide ranging research	Preparation: research and planning—section 13.3
Finding a different angle	Academic commentary—section 13.3.4.4

possible ways in which you might be able to find those crucial few extra marks in your next assignment.

13.6.1 Moving from a 2.2 to a 2.1

The most common characteristics of a lower second class essay are:

- **Poor technical execution.** Technical issues can make a difference to the overall impression of your essay. In particular a lack of care with typos and incomplete or inconsistent referencing can hold back an otherwise reasonable piece of work.

- **Too much descriptive detail.** Weaker essays tend to contain far too much description. This, in turn, takes up words that would have been much better used in analysis.

- **Not answering the question.** Many weaker essays talk about the subject matter in general terms but do not do enough to actually answer the question in the sense of providing a specific answer to the particular question asked. This weakens the focus of the essay and limits its success.

- **Insufficient research.** Markers are looking for evidence that students have gone beyond (a) the textbook and (b) the cases and articles that have been discussed in lectures and tutorials.

- **Inclusion of irrelevant content.** This is another way in which the focus of the essay can be weakened. Make sure that every point serves a purpose in the essay and has direct relevance to the question that has been asked.

13.6.2 Moving from a 2.1 to a First

Some of the characteristics of a first class essay are:

- **Perfect referencing.** Your technical execution must be flawless so be sure that references are provided wherever needed, that they are complete and in the correct format including pinpoint references wherever necessary.

- **Sophisticated use of language.** Take great care to express your ideas with precision and accuracy but also aim to try and develop eloquence in your written expression that makes your essay pleasing to read. Think carefully about every word and try to develop your vocabulary.

- **Engagement with theoretical concepts.** Remember that your essay should not just consider *what* the law is, it should also engage—where appropriate—with *why* it is as it is. Thoughtful discussion of theoretical legal concepts and reasoning demonstrates a more sophisticated level of understanding than might be expected of an upper second class essay.

- **Wide ranging research.** Strong essays will contain a great breadth and depth of research. You should incorporate your findings and commentary in your essay, but remember that research should be used to support, and not to displace, analysis.

- **A different angle.** If you are looking for ways in which to set your essay apart, then see if you can find a different angle for discussion, such as proposals for legal reform, or a comparative slant drawing on treatments of the legal issue in other jurisdictions (but choose your comparators wisely).

CHAPTER SUMMARY

Preliminary analysis

- Make sure that you take time at the outset to analyze the essay rather than starting research or, worse still, writing without having identified the focus of the essay

- Rewrite the question(s) at the heart of the essay in your own words to make sure that you have a simple and clear grasp of what is required, taking care not to change the meaning of the essay

Research and planning

- Start by consulting a textbook to ensure that you have a clear understanding of the topic area but make sure that you move on to consider other materials such as monographs and articles; an essay written solely on the basis of textbook research will probably lack depth of analysis and certainly will not demonstrate impressive research skills or width of reading

- Keep careful note of the sources used in your research but try to avoid excessive note-taking that can degenerate into compulsive writing that is not accompanied by sufficient thought. Remember, you are looking for answers to a particular question, not producing a summary of all the material that you locate

- Plan a working structure for your essay that can be used as a framework for your writing. Make sure that you think about the way that your arguments will flow and never forget the importance of keeping a firm focus on the central issue of the question

- Give careful consideration to the selection of supporting materials, remembering that it is important to present a balanced argument that acknowledges different perspectives on the issue at hand

Writing the essay

- Make sure that you give yourself sufficient time to write the essay and bear in mind that the structure you have planned may not work in practice, in which case you may need to start from scratch and reorganize your arguments

- Take care to ensure that every paragraph does something to further your argument and give thought to the balance between description and analysis in your essay

- Keep a firm focus on the question; if you cannot see how a point relates to the question, it may be that it has no place in your essay. Remember, you are answering a specific question rather than merely writing about a particular topic

- The purpose of an essay is to test knowledge and understanding of the topic but also to assess the level of skill that you have in using your sources appropriately. Ensure that your essay strikes an appropriate balance between description and analysis

- Write an effective introduction and conclusion. The introduction is the first impression that your marker receives of the quality of your work whilst the conclusion is the last thing that they read, so may stick in their mind as indicative of the overall quality of your essay whilst they are marking

Polish and presentation

- Allow plenty of time to check your essay for coherence, accuracy, and consistency.

- Find out what the requirements are for the presentation of essays and ensure that you adhere to these requirements to the letter. Easy marks can be lost for failing to do so and it gives the marker a poor impression of your essay if you have not troubled to follow the rules regarding the submission of coursework.

- Check the presentation of your essay and, in particular, check that the referencing and bibliography are immaculate

14 Dissertations

INTRODUCTION

The focus of this chapter is the range of different skills involved in the production of a dissertation. Some of these skills are specific to the dissertation. For example, you will find sections on choosing a dissertation topic and formulating a research question as well as guidance on the sometimes tricky business of developing an effective relationship with your dissertation supervisor. There are also sections aimed at helping you to manage and organize a larger-scale research project and suggestions on how to make decisions about structuring the dissertation. However, many of the skills needed to produce a dissertation are covered elsewhere in this book so you will need to look back at chapters on research (chapter 2, chapter 5, and chapter 8), writing skills (chapter 10), and referencing (chapter 12) and use them to supplement the points made in this chapter.

Some students think of a dissertation as a long essay. Although it is true that dissertations do have some characteristics in common with an essay, to describe a dissertation as a long essay overlooks some of the key factors that set it apart from an essay. In particular, a dissertation gives control to the student: you select your own topic and decide how to approach it which allows you to determine the level of difficulty of the dissertation. The longer length of the dissertation makes it far more challenging to structure and there is greater emphasis on independent research. Due to the greater demands it makes, the dissertation is viewed as a real measure of the ability of the student and the range of skills involved in its production means that the dissertation is a real showpiece of your aptitude for the law that can be used to impress potential employers.

LEARNING OUTCOMES

After studying this chapter, you will be able to:

- Make reasoned choices about whether to undertake a dissertation, how to select a topic, and how to convert this into a research question

- Construct a proposal that outlines the scope of your planned dissertation, its importance as a topic, and how you plan to carry out your research

- Break down the production of the dissertation into manageable stages and organize your time so that work involved is spread over the time available

- Identify and locate relevant literature

- Structure the dissertation in an appropriate way and produce a piece of work that is well written, well presented, and thoroughly referenced

14.1 Why write a dissertation?

Some students write a dissertation because they have no choice: it is a compulsory component of the law degree at their university. For other students, the dissertation is one of a selection of optional modules that can be taken in the final year of undergraduate study. If it is a matter of choice, why might you opt to write a dissertation?

- **To pursue an interesting topic.** The dissertation gives you the ability to choose your own subject matter so it is an opportunity to focus on something that you find really interesting. Some students choose to write a dissertation on a topic that was touched upon in one of the subjects that they studied because they would have liked it to have been covered in more detail. Equally, sometimes students are disappointed that a particular option that they wanted to take was not offered or was over-subscribed so they use the dissertation as an opportunity to explore a particular aspect of that subject. A few students select an aspect of law that fascinates them but which is not covered at all on the undergraduate syllabus as the subject of their dissertation.

- **To develop research skills.** Research is the foundation of a good dissertation. You have a longer period of time to hunt for literature than is generally the case in relation to ordinary coursework so the dissertation offers an excellent opportunity to improve your research skills.

- **To avoid exams.** Some students opt for a dissertation simply because it replaces one or, in some institutions, two options that are assessed by examination. If you always perform far better in coursework than you do in exams, it might be that writing a dissertation is a good choice as it plays to your strengths.

- **To impress potential employers.** If you intend to practise law, you should consider writing a dissertation as it enables you to demonstrate that you possess skills that are relevant to legal practice. You can demonstrate to potential employers that you are capable of working independently with only skeletal supervision and that are you able to select, locate, and use the law effectively. It also demonstrates your ability to structure a larger piece of writing. You might find that there are questions on training contract application forms that can be answered by making reference to the experience of writing a dissertation and it is quite common for questions to be asked about your dissertation at interview stage.

- **To gain an additional referee.** You will work closely with your dissertation supervisor so they will be in an excellent position to write a detailed reference about you in support of your application for work placements, training contracts, or postgraduate study.

14.2 Dissertation topic and research question

Once a decision has been made to write a dissertation, the next important question that needs to be answered concerns the choice of general topic, the isolation of a particular topic and then, ultimately, the formulation of a research question; see Figure 14.1. This is a process that involves incremental narrowing of focus until there is a single question that needs to be answered which is at the heart of the dissertation.

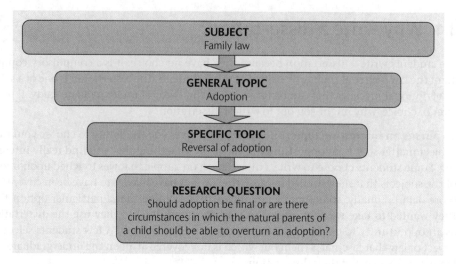

Figure 14.1 Moving from subject to research question

14.2.1 Choosing a topic

There are a number of factors to take into account when choosing a dissertation topic. Some of these are practical considerations: there must be enough relevant literature accessible to you to enable you to carry out your research, it must be a topic that someone in your department is willing and able to supervise, and the topic must be one that is capable of giving rise to a research question that can be explored in sufficient depth in the time available and within the constraints of the dissertation word limit.

In addition to these factors, it is important that the topic is one that invites analysis rather than merely description and that gives rise to a research question which raises sufficient complexities to allow you to present some 'clever' points in your dissertation.

A final factor which is often overlooked is that the topic must be one that you find interesting. Remember that it is a long-term project spanning the entirety of the academic year and that you will find it easier to maintain your enthusiasm for your dissertation if the topic is one that you think is interesting. Students who select a topic that is of no interest to them but which they think will present an intellectual challenge and result in a good dissertation tend to struggle to maintain their interest far more than students who were motivated by interest.

Students often find the process of identifying a dissertation topic to be difficult. Have a look at the five stages suggested in Figure 14.2 to help to identify a topic for your dissertation.

You might also find it useful to think about the answers to some of the questions that students are often asked about the choice of dissertation topic.

- **Can my dissertation topic be something that has been covered in lectures and seminars?** There is no reason not to select a topic that was covered in lectures and/or seminars and many students like to base their dissertations on such topics because they like the fact that they have already got a grasp of the subject matter which gives them a foundation of knowledge upon which to build. The other advantages of choosing topics that have been taught are that there will be at least one lecturer, more if the topic was taught as part of a core subject, who has sufficient expertise to supervise your dissertation and there is likely to be a good range of source materials available in the library. The disadvantage of choosing

1. Make a list of all the subjects that you have studied so far on your degree and cross out those that you disliked, found difficult/dull or that you simply do not want to revisit for a dissertation topic.	SUBJECTS STUDIED ~~English Legal Systems~~ ~~Land Law~~ ~~Constitutional Law~~ ~~Contract~~ Criminal Law Family Law Tort ~~European Law~~ Child Law ~~Land Law~~
2. List the subjects that remain in order of preference.	PREFERENCE 1. Family Law 2. Criminal Law 3. Child Law 4. Tort

3. Take the top three subjects and use them as headings. List up to four topics that you can remember enjoying from those subjects.	FAMILY	CRIMINAL	CHILD
	1 Domestic violence 2 Adoption 3 Cohabitants 4 Void marriages	1 Loss of control 2 Insanity 3 Necessity	1 Abortion 2 Right to know one's parents 3 Adoption

4. Create three columns: keep, consider and discard. Allocate each of the topics that you have listed to one of these columns.	KEEP	CONSIDER	DISCARD
	1 Adoption 2 Right to know one's parents 3 Loss of control	1 Necessity 2 Abortion 3 Cohabitants	1 Void marriages 2 Insanity 3 Domestic violence

5. Take each of the topics listed under 'keep' and conduct some preliminary searches to identify issues that could be the focus for your dissertation.	POSSIBLE DISSERTATION TOPICS 1. Reversal of adoption: see current case in news. 2. Assessing suitability of adoptive parents: FLR article. 3. Children of rapists – too harmful to know? 4. Knowing parents after adoption – links with adoption case. 5. Battered women who kill. 6. Loss of control and sexual infidelity

Figure 14.2 Stages in selecting a dissertation topic

such a topic is that you will need to move quite a way beyond the points covered on the syllabus in order to demonstrate your research skills. The best way forward is to put some sort of slant on the topic that takes you beyond the issues that were covered on your course. For example, if you are interested in adoption, have a look at the literature on the topic to see if you can find an interesting issue about adoption that was not covered in the syllabus.

- **Several other students want to write their dissertations on my topic—does that mean that I can't do it?** There are certain topics that are so popular that several students each year want to focus upon them. This does not mean that you cannot be one of them but you have to be aware that you are in competition for resources and that there is a certain extent to which you will be measured to see which of you produces the best dissertation (wider research, more depth of analysis, better written style). Try to avoid a direct comparison by adapting your chosen topic in some way that will make it different to the other dissertations: for example, domestic violence is always a popular choice so try a variant of this such as (1) male victims of domestic violence, (2) domestic violence in same-sex relationships, or (3) the impact of domestic violence on children.

- **I want to do something totally different that isn't covered on the law syllabus at my university—is this going to be a problem?** There are always one or two students each year who have a really original idea for a dissertation topic. Some universities place restrictions on novel dissertation topics, recognizing that students can come to grief if there is no supervisor available who can provide guidance on the subject matter, whilst other universities take the view that the supervisor's role is to guide the process of the dissertation rather than to check the accuracy of its content so it is immaterial whether or not they have expertise in the topic. If you want to research something a bit different, try approaching a few lecturers to seek their views on whether it is a good idea and whether they would be able to supervise you. You might find that your topic is a different slant to one of their existing areas of expertise or that you have provoked their interest so much that they are prepared to supervise outside their immediate area of expertise. For example, one of the most interesting dissertations supervised by one of the authors was on the topic of the legal regulation of spiritualist mediums: an original topic that made a fascinating dissertation.

14.2.2 Formulating a research question

In chapter 13, it was suggested that you will produce an essay with a stronger focus if you concentrate on what the essay question *asks* rather than the broader issue of what the essay is *about*. That same distinction can be made in relation to dissertations: your dissertation is *about* whatever the topic is that you have chosen but you should also *ask* a question that your dissertation sets out to answer.

It might help you to appreciate the importance of the 'asks/about' distinction if you view your dissertation in the same way that it is viewed in the more science-based disciplines. Scientific research is based on a two-stage process: (1) an experiment that tests a hypothesis and (2) the writing up of the findings of that experimental process (the dissertation). Whilst law students tend not to conduct experiments, you do carry out an investigation when you carry out your research and this investigation does aim (or, at least, should be aimed) at answering a question:

- Does the law on a particular topic achieve its purpose?
- Should the law regulate a particular situation?
- Is the law in operation fair to all those to whom it applies?

If you ask a question, finding the answer to that question becomes the focus of your investigation (the research stage of the dissertation). It should also make the writing stage easier as your introduction will outline the question and your conclusion will answer the question. Most students find that it is much easier to select material for inclusion and to sift out irrelevant or peripheral material if they are answering a question rather than thinking of their dissertation in terms of its general topic.

Students often find it difficult to formulate a research question but it is really just a matter of rewording your topic into a question: for example, if you were interested in male victims of domestic violence, you might want to ask 'does the law protect male victims of domestic violence as effectively as it protects female victims?' or 'does the law on domestic violence offer equal protection to male and female victims?'.

 Practical exercise

Imagine that the following statements have been made by students about their dissertation topics. How could they be reformulated as research questions?

1. I want to look at the spread of CCTV and relate that to the right to privacy.

2. I'm interested in the changes that were made in the law concerning the defendant's right to silence and how this impacts on his right to a fair trial.

3. My dissertation is about sexual infidelity and the defence of loss of control that came in with the Coroners and Justice Act 2009

 Look at the Online Resource Centre to find ways in which these statements could be rephrased as research questions.

14.3 Writing a dissertation proposal

Not all universities require that students submit a full dissertation proposal as part of the procedure of signing up to undertake a dissertation: some institutions require nothing more than students stating that they wish to write a dissertation and giving a broad indication of the proposed focus of the dissertation. However, in some institutions, places to undertake a dissertation are limited and the selection process involves the students submitting a dissertation proposal.

A detailed proposal will require a fair amount of thought, planning, and research. It is possible that your university will have particular requirements in terms of the points to be covered in the dissertation proposal. Make sure you find out whether this is the case and, if so, ensure that you adhere to the requirements of your particular institution.

If no guidance is provided on the content of the dissertation proposal, you might expect that it covers the following points:

- Identify the focus of the dissertation and state the research question

- Explain why the topic selected is interesting or why it raises an important question that is worthy of research. This is your justification for wanting to write the dissertation so it is important that you provide some sound rationalization for your choice of topic

- Outline the literature that has been identified so far or the steps that will be taken to identify relevant literature. This should include reference to the law that governs the dissertation topic so any relevant statute or important case law should be identified. Provide details of any books that you have found, any authors who seem to be specialists on the topic, and any journals that are likely to carry relevant articles. State any steps that you have taken or will take to conduct searches of databases such as Westlaw UK or LexisLibrary (see chapter 2, chapter 5, and chapter 8). Have you considered looking for literature produced by relevant interest groups or specialist government departments? Are there any websites that seem particularly useful? Remember that you are being asked not just whether useful literature exists but whether you will be able to get hold of it. State whether the material is held in your own university library or, if not, whether you can travel to another university to access it or order it on inter-library loan. If you are planning to access electronic journals, make sure that they are ones to which your university subscribes otherwise you will only be able to access the abstract and not the full article

- Provide a preliminary indication of how the dissertation might be organized in terms of the number and content of chapters. This is only an indication of a possible structure to establish that you have thought about how your material could be organized; you will not be expected to stick to this precise structure in the final version of your dissertation. It is usually the case that a planned structure changes once your research discovers points that you had not initially realized would be in your dissertation or once the writing is under way and you start to think about how the various strands of your argument fit together

You will find an example of a dissertation proposal that deals with these points at Figure 14.3. This is only an illustration: remember, it is important to find out what points your own institution expects to be covered in the proposal and what its requirements are in terms of factors such as the length of the proposal and level of detail to be provided about source material.

14.4 Planning and organization

Think, for a moment, of your studies as a series of activities with deadlines. You have some deadlines every week (seminar preparation) and others a couple of times a term (coursework submission) with one event occurring a fair time after everything else has finished (exams). This gives you a working pattern of constant seminar preparation with intermittent bursts of activity when coursework is due and a final push at the end when exams are looming. Consider how the process of researching and writing your dissertation will fit into this pattern of work.

Some students decide that the distant deadline of the dissertation means that it can be put aside and not given any thought at all until a couple of weeks before the submission date. This can be a dangerous strategy: you might be ill, your supervisor might be ill or otherwise absent from university, you may not be able to obtain the source materials that you need and, most importantly, you are likely to find that you have not left yourself enough time to think about the dissertation and develop your ideas. You should also be conscious that the later you leave your dissertation, the more likely it is that you will be writing it at a time when you should be starting to revise for your exams.

A far more effective approach is to work steadily at the dissertation throughout the time available. This research project is the largest task that you will have to complete during your

DISSERTATION PROPOSAL

'A final decision? Should a child's biological parents be able to apply for the reversal of an adoption order?'

Research Question

It is a well-established principle of family law that an adoption order creates a new and final family relationship that places the adoptive parents in the same legal position as the biological parents of a child. This could cause problems if there was some flaw in the adoption process. This dissertation will consider whether there are, or should be, circumstances in which the biological parents of a child who has been made the subject of an adoption order can seek to reverse that order thus restoring the rights of the biological parents. The question that will be addressed at the heart of this dissertation is 'should an adoption order always be final?'.

The Importantance of the Research

This dissertation poses a question that, until recently, has not been one that has troubled the family courts as the answer has always been a resounding 'yes'. However, there is a current case that seeks to challenge the established position. The crux of the case is that the initial adoption orders were unsound as they were based on allegations against the biological parents which were without foundation. This dissertation will outline the current law on adoption, examining the procedures which have to be followed in order to assess the extent to which they offer scope for incorrect decisions to be made and for children to be adopted against the wishes of their biological parents. It will highlight the policy concerns in relation to the desirability of placing children in a safe, appropriate and permanent family setting but also of ensuring that children are not irretrievably removed from their biological parents without cause. In doing so, this research will address important issues that go to the heart of the law on adoption.

The Literature

The foundation of the law is to be found in statute (Adoption and Children Act 2002) but has been interpreted in case law. The leading case law governing adoption will be identified and examined to extrapolate key principles. Particular attention will be given to the case currently being heard in which the parents are seeking to reverse the adoption order that removed three of their children from their family. Recourse will be had to authoritative works on family law and adoption including *Child Care and Adoption Law* (2006) and *Children, Family Responsibilities and the State* (2008). A literature search will be made to identify articles of relevance. It is anticipated that these are likely to appear in journals such as the *Family Law Review* and the *Journal of Family and Child Law* which are available in the library.

Proposed Structure

Introduction
Chapter 1: the evolution of the law governing the adoption of children.
Chapter 2: adoption procedures and the potential for problems to arise.
Chapter 3: case study: the application for the reversal of an adoption order.
Chapter 4: an evaluation of the law taking into account competing policy considerations.
Conclusion

Figure 14.3 Example of a dissertation proposal

studies so it makes sense to slice it up into smaller, more manageable chunks and to spread the workload across several months. There are various different ways that you can divide up with the work of researching and writing the dissertation that are outlined in the sections that follow. You might also find it useful to revisit the section on managing your time in chapter 9.

14.4.1 Allocate time

One way to ensure that you work steadily is to incorporate your dissertation into your timetable by allocating a certain amount of time to work on it: this might be one hour a week, one day a fortnight or one weekend a month depending on your other commitments and whether you prefer working in frequent short bursts or less frequent concerted chunks.

Try to be disciplined in sticking to the time that you have allocated. It might help actually to write in your dissertation study periods on your timetable and regard them as immovable obligations in the same way that you would view tutorials. Of course, you can build in some flexibility as there may be weeks when you find you are too ill to concentrate or that you are overburdened with coursework preparation so that your dissertation has to take a back seat. If this happens, try to make up the missed time so that you do not start to fall behind your schedule.

14.4.2 Establish milestones

Some people find it difficult to commit to a particular time slot on a regular basis and prefer to be more flexible in their working arrangements. If this sounds familiar, try to set yourself milestones to achieve at staged intervals so that you can be sure that you are making steady progress with your dissertation.

It can be useful to have a goal in mind that you plan to achieve each month. Think about the various stages of the dissertation and work out what it is reasonable for you to achieve in a month. This will allow you to take into account that some months will be busier with seminars and coursework than others so you can adjust your dissertation milestones accordingly. You should be specific when creating milestones so that you are clear about what it is that you are trying to achieve. Compare the two examples in Figure 14.4 to see how much more useful a detailed and specific list of milestones will be at helping you to keep on track with your dissertation.

Your university may have a structure of meetings and milestones that have to be met by certain dates; for example:

1. Attend dissertation lecture in Week 2
2. First meeting with supervisor to discuss purpose, aims, and timeframe of dissertation (Week 3)
3. Second meeting with supervisor to review progress (Week 10)
4. Third meeting with supervisor to review detailed chapter outline and at least one completed draft chapter (Week 16)
5. Final meeting with supervisor (Week 20)
6. Submission deadline—3 May (Week 24)

You should make sure that your plan fits in with the specific requirements of your university's dissertation programme. Check your student handbook to see if there are particular milestones and deliverables that you are expected to meet.

DISSERTATION MILESTONES	DISSERTATION MILESTONES
October: research November: research December: research January: plan out chapters February: start writing March: finish writing	October: search databases, Internet and textbooks to create a list of literature. Locate and acquire the literature. Write a preliminary list of chapters. November: Create a plan for each chapter. Continue identifying and acquiring literature. Write a summary of the current law for Chapter 1. December: Two pieces of coursework due but try to make progress with Chapter 1. Go to British Library to find any missing literature. January: Complete Chapter 1 and make a start on Chapter 2. February: Complete Chapter 2 and Chapter 3. March: Chapter 4 and introduction and conclusion. Check references and bibliography. Proof read. Submit by 30th March.

Figure 14.4 General and detailed dissertation milestones

14.4.3 Create a 'to do' list

The problem with allocating time or creating milestones is that they give you things to do at or by a particular time so you might feel despondent if you fail to meet your target. Nothing is more dispiriting than feeling as if you are already falling behind because you missed your second allocated study slot for your dissertation or you failed to meet your first milestone. For this reason, some students prefer to create a 'to do' list that details all the tasks that need to be done towards the completion of the dissertation.

It can be particularly useful to have a master list that details everything and then separate lists that break this down into smaller sections either task-by-task (so you would have a 'to do' list for each chapter) or month-by-month (or week-by-week if you prefer; it would give you a shorter list that might feel less daunting). The advantage of having separate lists for each month or chapter is that you can be very specific about the tasks that need to be done which will ensure that you are very clear about what it is that you need to achieve: see Figure 14.5. It is also very satisfying to see tasks crossed off the list or to put a tick by the tasks that have been completed: this is a real visible measure of your progress.

The flexibility that the 'to do' list gives you can be immensely valuable in ensuring steady progress. If your milestone for the month is 'write Chapter 1' then you put pressure on yourself to achieve this goal. This will make you feel as if you have failed if you find yourself sitting at your computer with a new document and a blank mind. However, if you have a 'to do' list that breaks down your chapter into a series of smaller tasks or a list for the month then you will be able to see that you have a whole range of other things that you can do that contribute towards your dissertation. As you can see that you are achieving tasks on your list, you will feel that you are making progress. This is important as students who feel positive about their dissertation tend to enjoy working on it even during the tricky stages whereas students who feel that they are making no progress develop a negative view of their dissertation and start trying to avoid it which can lead to a real crisis situation.

DISSERTATION: THINGS TO DO	THINGS TO DO: OCTOBER
~~Find the statute law on non-fatal offences.~~	Find a copy of the Offences against the Person Act 1861 (online or in a statute book).
Identify case law that contains important legal principles in general.	
Identify case law that deals with (a) psychology injury (Chapter 2) and (b) transmission of HIV (Chapter 3).	Search on Westlaw and LexisLibrary for cases decided under section 47, section 20 and section 18.
Find any proposals for reform of non-fatal offences:	Make a list of cases involving
Law Commission, Home Office	(a) psychology injury and
~~Read leading criminal law textbooks.~~	(b) transmission of HIV.
Search for relevant articles.	Print the cases and file them according to section.
Create a plan of each chapter with anticipated content.	
Create a bibliography file and keep it up to date.	Get the leading criminal law textbooks from the library and copy/make notes on their chapters on non-fatal offences.
Look for newspaper articles on the issues.	
Draft each chapter.	Note any articles or other materials mentioned in the footnote references of the textbooks.
Write each chapter.	
Polish each chapter.	
Write introduction	Write case summaries for the important cases.
Write conclusion.	
Check bibliography and references.	Email supervisor to arrange a meeting.
Check the chapters flow into each other.	
Proof read.	
Submit by 30th March	

Figure 14.5 Examples of 'to do' lists

 Practical exercise

Consider the different approaches adopted by three students to organizing their time. Who do you think is most likely to complete their dissertation on time by following their planned approach? What problems might you expect each of them to encounter? What advice would you give each student?

1. Andrew wants to finish his dissertation in good time so he decides to work on it for two hours every week. He looks at his timetable and sees that Friday afternoon is always free so he decides that Friday between 1 pm and 3 pm will be his dissertation time. He sticks to this and feels that he is making steady progress.

2. Bettina decides that the best way to ensure that her dissertation is completed on time is to set herself a deadline each month:

   October: general research, identify and acquire source material
   November: write chapter 1
   December: write chapter 2
   January: write chapter 3
   February: write chapter 4
   March: write introduction/conclusion, proof read ready for submission

3. Carole makes a 'to do' list of everything involved in the completion of her dissertation with an estimate of how long it will take her to complete:

   Literature search to identify source material: 3 days
   Acquiring copies of all material: 2 days

Planning structure of each chapter: 1 day (total 4 days)

Reading material and making notes: 10 days

Writing each draft chapter: 7 days (total 28 days)

Redrafting and polishing each chapter: 2 days (total 8 days)

Writing introduction: 1 day

Writing conclusion: 2 days

Checking referencing and bibliography: 1 day

Proof reading and checking for coherence: 1 day

 Go to the Online Resource Centre to find out whether the strategies outlined were successful for each of these students and to discover what, if anything, they would have done differently if they were starting a dissertation again.

14.5 Researching for a dissertation

One of the factors that will determine the success (or otherwise) of your dissertation is the quality of your research and your ability to identify and locate relevant source material. You will find information on searching in electronic databases in chapter 2, chapter 5, and chapter 8 so you might find it useful to refer back to these parts of the book.

It is essential that you find a wide range of source material to use in your dissertation because you are expected to demonstrate research skills. The person marking your dissertation is not going to be impressed by a 12,000 word dissertation that refers to three textbooks, an article, and two cases! Try to think beyond the 'usual' sources (textbooks, cases, articles, and official reports); for example, consider whether any of the following sources could contribute to your dissertation:

- **Case commentary.** Many journals have a commentary section in which experts in the field outline and analyze recent developments in case law. Commentaries can be really valuable in helping you to understand case law and its implications as well as providing inspiration that will allow you to engage in critical analysis of the case. If you are researching recent developments in the law, case commentaries may be particularly useful as they are published more quickly than articles and books.

- **Monographs and edited collections**. Monographs are more detailed books devoted to a specialist subject whereas edited collections are books that deal with a particular area of law but which are composed of different contributions from a range of authors. They provide a good source of material for a dissertation as they take a much closer look at a topic than a textbook. It can be difficult to find chapters in edited collections because catalogues tend to use the main title of the book rather than list the individual contributions but footnotes in textbooks or articles might help you to find relevant chapters or you could try searching Google Books.

- **Newspaper articles.** You might want to include a section in your dissertation about public perceptions of the topic in which case newspaper articles, which can be found online by using the Nexis newspaper database, will be useful. Newspapers are also a good source of information about court cases that are unreported, including first instance decisions. If, for example, you wanted to find out how diminished responsibility has been used in mercy-killing cases, a newspaper search will provide coverage of first instance cases where this was an issue. Of course, a newspaper article will only provide a summary and will probably not include the detail of the legal argument but it can still be a way to find information that is not available elsewhere.

- **Interest group websites and reports.** Specialist groups often carry out their own research and produce their own literature which can give detailed information about a topic, albeit from a particular perspective. It is important to remember that interest groups are advocating a particular position so their literature may not be objective but it may still play a valuable role in your dissertation; just remember to try and find other material that balances the argument. Some interest groups into sensitive topics provide material that you would just not find anywhere else: for example, the NAMBLA (North American Man-Boy Love Association) website makes available a range of literature supporting their stance in favour of sexual relations between adults and children that could provide an interesting perspective to a dissertation concerned with the legal regulation of paedophilia.

14.6 The writing process

You might find it useful to look at the chapters on writing skills (chapter 10), referencing (chapter 12), and essay writing (chapter 13) as these deal with many of the issues that are important to writing a dissertation.

There are some issues that are specific to dissertation writing and these are dealt with below by identifying some of the common problems experienced by students. You will find suggestions on how to overcome or, better still, prevent these problems arising in the first place.

- **I've done masses of research but I haven't started writing yet.** Some students get really immersed in the research process and are determined to track down every piece of information on their topic before they start writing. Thorough research is important but it is counterproductive if you do not leave yourself sufficient time to dedicate to the writing process. Avoid this problem by starting to write at an early stage of your dissertation so that you combine the research and writing processes.

- **I don't know when to start writing.** Start writing as soon as possible: the longer you delay, the harder it is to start writing. You do not have to complete your research for the first chapter in order to start writing it. Select something that you know is going to appear in your dissertation at some point—a summary of the current law is always a good choice—and write it. You will feel better once you have made a start on writing and it is something that you can show to your supervisor so that they can check whether your written style and approach to referencing are appropriate.

- **I don't know how to break my dissertation down into chapters.** This is something that puzzles many students. They have a clear picture of the material that needs to be in their dissertation but find it difficult to divide this into chapters. This is often something that you need to discuss with your supervisor because each dissertation topic would break down in a different way so generic advice could be misleading. However, one technique that you can use is to look at your research question and try to break it down into three or four smaller questions. For example, if you look at Figure 14.5, you will see the 'to do' lists for a dissertation that asks the question 'is the Offences against the Person Act 1861 able to deal with modern manifestations of harm or is the law in need of reform?'. This could be broken down by asking three questions: 'what is the law?', 'what situations have given rise to problems with the law?' and 'how could the law be reformed to overcome the problems?'. This then breaks down into chapters as follows: (1) an outline of the law and identification of three problem areas, (2) first problem area: consensual harm caused for the purposes of sexual gratification, (3) second problem area: psychological injury, (4) third problem area: transmission of HIV, and (5) proposals for reform.

- **I don't know what order the chapters should come in.** This is usually less of a problem once you have worked out what content goes in each chapter (as discussed in the previous bullet point). Once the content is decided, sum up the purpose of the chapter in one sentence and then look at these sentences to see what order you would put them in if you were putting together a paragraph to describe your dissertation.

- **I have to write an abstract but I don't know what it is or how to do it.** An abstract is a short summary of your dissertation that identifies the research question, why it is important, and how you set about addressing it. It is the part of the dissertation that somebody would read to see if your work was interesting or relevant to them. It is a good idea to make it sound interesting so start with an attention-grabbing sentence. For example, you could start by saying 'this dissertation will explore some of the problem areas that suggest that the Offences against the Person Act 1861 is not able to deal with modern instances of harm' but that is rather bland compared to 'Anthony Burstow harassed a female work colleague for seven years, causing her to develop a serious psychological disorder, before the House of Lords finally concluded his conduct was a contravention of the criminal law'.

- **I've found so much literature that I can't keep track of it.** This is a serious problem because you will be expected to provide references for all your literature and a comprehensive bibliography. The best way to deal with this is start a document called 'bibliography' on the very first day that you start your dissertation and make sure that you enter every book, article, website, and other source material into it (with full details including the date of access if you are referring to web materials) as soon as you find it. This will help you to keep track of your material and will mean that your bibliography is being constructed as you go which will save you the last-minute panic of trying to find all your references.

- **I don't know whether or not to use sub-headings in my chapters.** With a piece of work of this length, it is permissible to use headings and sub-headings *provided the rules relating to dissertations at your university do not prohibit this*. Remember, though, headings are no substitute for structure and do not relieve you of the need to signpost your argument so use headings with care.

- **My supervisor won't help me with my structure/writing/content.** Problems arise in the supervisor-student relationship if there is a misunderstanding between the parties about what sort of assistance can be expected. If your supervisor has refused to help you with some aspect of your dissertation, this might be because what you have asked for is something that goes beyond the help that supervisors are allowed to provide at your university. Have a look at the regulations for supervision that should be available in your student handbook to make sure that you are not making unrealistic demands on your supervisor. Try to remember that they are there to provide help and advice as to how to go about researching and writing a dissertation; they are not there to give you step-by-step instructions or to oversee your work to ensure that it is correct. This dissertation is a piece of independent research so it would not be proper for your supervisor to have too much involvement in its production. If you are really unhappy, try emailing your supervisor (politely) and explaining how confused you are about a particular aspect of the dissertation and asking if they can help or, as an alternative, if they can suggest an additional source of advice. For example, if your supervisor is not permitted by the rules of your university to comment on your writing style in your dissertation, perhaps a study skills adviser or your personal tutor would be able to do this.

- **I'm worried that there will be mistakes in my dissertation.** If there are mistakes regarding the law, this could be a serious problem that affects the mark that your dissertation receives. Avoid problems here by checking that your law is up-to-date and make sure that you puzzle out issues that are unclear rather than simply ignoring them and hoping that the marker will not notice. Mistakes in writing and referencing can also affect your mark. Make sure that you leave yourself time to proof read your dissertation, preferably a few days before the deadline so that you have time to correct any problems that you spot. It can be hard to notice your own errors so you might find it useful to offer to swap with another student and proof read for each other. Careless errors suggest lack of care so it is worth taking the time to make sure that your work is perfect before it is submitted.

CHAPTER SUMMARY

Dissertation topic and research question

- Select several alternative topics that you would like to research and conduct some preliminary research to identify what could form the basis of your dissertation

- Make sure that you select a topic that you find interesting as you will be working on it for a significant period of time

- Once you have decided on a topic, formulate a question that needs to be answered that can form the basis of your dissertation

Writing a dissertation proposal

- If you have to write a dissertation proposal, find out if your university stipulates how long this must be, what level of detail is required, and whether there are any particular issues that need to be addressed within the proposal

- If there are no guidelines on writing a proposal, it would be sensible to cover (1) the research question, (2) the importance of the research, (3) what literature you have found or where you plan to look for literature, and (4) a preliminary indication of how the dissertation will break down into chapters

Planning and organization

- Plan to work on your dissertation steadily in the time available rather than leaving it until a few weeks before the submission deadline to make a start

- Consider different ways to divide up the work of researching and writing the dissertation and adopt one (or adapt one) to suit your own study preferences

- Try to combine researching and writing as much as possible rather than seeing them as two separate stages of the dissertation process

Research

- Thorough research is the backbone of your dissertation. Remember that you are trying to impress your marker with the breadth and depth of your research

- Treat the research process as an investigation and do not be afraid to move beyond the sources of information that you would normally use in an essay. The dissertation gives you the scope to take a broader view of your topic so ensure that you make the most of this by using a wide range of resources

- Make sure that you know how to reference the materials that you are finding and keep a complete and accurate record of all sources to ensure that you can compile a comprehensive bibliography

Writing

- Refer to the chapters on writing skills, referencing, and essay writing to ensure that you have a thorough understanding of the requirements of good academic writing

- Start writing towards the beginning of the dissertation. It gets harder to start the longer you leave it

- Do not panic if you cannot think of how to start a chapter. If writing a whole chapter at once seems daunting, carve a section out of it that you know will be there and write that instead. A summary of the current law or an important case is a good starting point

- Leave yourself time to proof read your dissertation to ensure that your work is free of errors

15 Answering problem questions

INTRODUCTION

This chapter builds on the earlier sections in the book that outlined how to locate and understand the law by explaining how to use your legal knowledge. Chapter 13 provided guidance on how to use this knowledge to construct a focused and analytical essay and chapter 14 considered dissertations. This chapter will concentrate on the very different set of skills that are needed to use the law to answer a problem question. It will guide you through the process of analyzing a scenario in order to identify the relevant issues to ensure that your answer is comprehensive and does not miss any important points. It will outline strategies to use to ensure that the law is applied effectively and that good use is made of supporting authorities. This chapter should be read in conjunction with chapter 10 which covers writing skills, and chapter 12 on referencing as this will ensure that your problem answer is well-written, presented in an appropriate manner, and is thoroughly referenced.

The ability to use the law to determine the outcome of a dispute is one of the most important skills that a lawyer must develop. An abstract understanding of the law based upon how it has been used in decided cases is not enough; you must be able to apply the principles of the law to new and unusual factual situations. Remember, a client who comes to you for advice does not want an explanation of how the law has been used in other cases; he wants to know how it applies to his situation. It is also an important skill because problem questions are a popular means of assessing knowledge and skills in both coursework and examinations but, unfortunately, many students limit their success because they have not developed an effective problem-solving technique. This step-by-step guide to problem solving aims to help with this by explaining how to tackle problem questions and by demonstrating the steps with examples to ensure that you have a clear picture of what is required.

LEARNING OUTCOMES

After studying this chapter, you will be able to:

- Differentiate between the skills needed to answer a problem question and those required for the construction of an effective essay

- Analyze a problem question in order to identify the legal issues that need to be resolved

- Prepare to answer the question by engaging in effective research and planning

- Structure the answer in a logical and organized manner

- Provide concise and well-supported statements of law that are applied to the facts of the question in an effective manner

- Evaluate the answer that you have written to ensure that it demonstrates the relevant skills and knowledge and that it adheres to the necessary style and referencing requirements

15.1 All about problem questions

Before launching into an explanation of how to deal with problem questions, it seems sensible to take a little time to describe what problem questions are and what they seek to achieve. If you appreciate what it is that they aim to assess, this will help you to understand how to set about dealing with them in a way that is likely to meet with the approval of your lecturers.

15.1.1 What is a problem question?

A problem question involves a set of hypothetical facts that raises at least one question, usually more, that needs to be answered by reference to the law.

In other words, it is a short story about events that give rise to potential legal responsibility about which you are expected to offer advice to one or more of the parties or otherwise to comment on the legal position that arises from the facts. This is sometimes called a fact pattern or scenario question.

Problem questions tend to end with a question or instruction so that you are clear about the task:

- Does Chris have a claim in negligence?
- Can the contract be enforced?
- Advise Dawn as to the extent of her liability for property offences.
- Do Ashley's actions amount to a breach of Article 11 of the European Convention on Human Rights?

The facts of the problem will be constructed with care so that the answer to the question is not clear but needs to be puzzled out. You are unlikely to encounter a problem question (other than the example in Chapter 11) that begins:

> Peter hates Tony so he shoots him in the head at point-blank range shouting "I want you to die".

This is because there is no complexity to the issue: both elements of the offence of murder are so readily established that the question could be answered in a few lines.

This demonstrates a major characteristic of problem questions: they are designed to raise issues that do not have an obvious and straightforward answer so that you have to explore the intricacies of the law and speculate a little in order to reach a conclusion.

You will find an example of a problem question in section 15.3. This will be used in this chapter to demonstrate the process of building an answer that demonstrates both a good grasp of the relevant law and of the legal skills that are being assessed.

15.1.2 It is not an essay!

It is essential that you appreciate that the distinction between an essay and a problem question is not solely one of presentation; they require something qualitatively different from the student in terms of the skills used and the nature of the answer produced.

In general terms, an essay involves an exploration and analysis of a particular topic whilst a problem question requires the student to apply the law to a set of facts and reach a conclusion about the legal responsibility of the parties involved.

If you take the same approach to answering a problem question that you do to writing an essay, your problem answers will be weak and will not achieve high marks.

15.1.3 What skills are required?

There are a range of skills involved in dissecting and answering a problem question. As you will see, although legal knowledge is important, you will need to be able to do more than merely outline the relevant law; you must also be able to use it to reach a conclusion about the legal liability of the parties. This involves:

- The ability to sift through the mass of facts to identify those that are relevant, those that set the scene, and to oust any potential red herrings
- Sufficient knowledge of the area of law to be able to identify a potential basis for legal action, to establish a starting point for research, and to be able to understand the law that is uncovered during the research process
- Research skills that enable you to investigate the area of law and to locate statutory provisions and cases that are relevant to the facts of the problem
- Writing skills that enable you to structure an answer, to organize its content in a clear and logical manner, and to incorporate authority into your answer
- The ability to apply the law to the facts of the question in order to determine the extent of the parties' legal liability

Although all of these skills are important and play a role in constructing an effective answer to a problem question, it is the last of these—application of the law to the facts—that is crucial to the success of your answer.

In chapter 13, you will find a section which examines Bloom's taxonomy of skills and discusses these in the context of legal writing (see section 13.4.5). The higher-order skills of application and analysis are particularly important to problem solving.

15.2 Problem-solving technique

The key to success in problem solving is to develop an effective technique. This is something that will be invaluable in both coursework and examinations and which is transferable between the different topics that you study; in other words, a good problem-solving technique is equally applicable to criminal law, equity, and trusts, employment law or any of the other subjects on the law curriculum that use problem solving as a means of assessment.

Your own institution may provide guidelines on problem solving. If this is the case, you should study these carefully and take note of the information provided. Alternatively, there

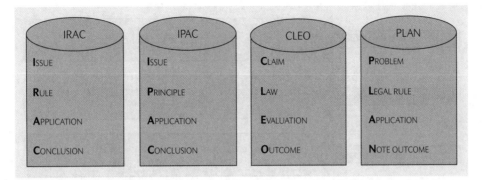

Figure 15.1 Some mnemonics for problem solving

are well-publicized techniques that you may find useful; these have different names but share a common basis in their approach to breaking down the tasks involved in problem solving (see Figure 15.1).

Despite the difference of terminology, each of the four stages used in each method is the same:

1. Identify the question that needs to be answered
2. State the law that enables the question to be answered
3. Work out how the law would operate in relation to the question identified
4. Reach a conclusion that answers the question

You might find it easier to understand this process in relation to a non-law example.

> Imagine that your university has a policy regarding the late submission of coursework that states that the penalty for submission up to one day after the deadline without good cause or prior permission attracts a deduction of 10 marks. Furthermore, work that is submitted more than one day late but within a week of the deadline attracts a deduction of 25 marks and work that is submitted more than one week late receives a mark of zero. The essays are stamped with the time and date of submission upon receipt in the general office. The submission deadline for your essay is 4 p.m. on Friday. Your essay is submitted at 4.02 p.m.

This is a very simple example but it demonstrates the process that is involved in problem solving (see Figure 15.2).

It is ironic that the method involved in problem solving causes so many headaches for students but, in reality and stripped of its legal content, the process of identifying a question to be answered, the applicable rule, and combining the two to reach a conclusion is one that we all do, all of the time, as part of everyday life: eligibility for a discount, complying with a shop's refund policy, nightclub opening hours, and even reading a train timetable all involve a similar process of the identification and application of a general rule to a particular factual situation.

Of course, your concern is to take this technique and apply it to legal problems. There are also other factors to take into account such as the level of detail needed, the correct approach to incorporating case law, and the difficulties of a factual situation that does not have a determinative answer, and all of these points will be addressed in the course of this chapter. However, quite apart from these complexities that are particular to law, it is

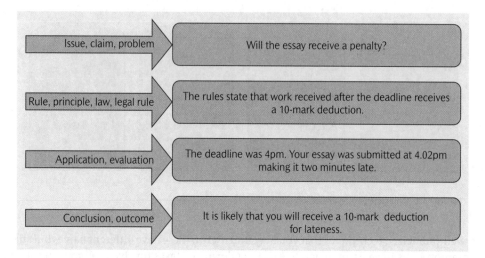

Figure 15.2 The problem-solving process

reassuring to know that the technique that is the cornerstone of effective problem solving is one that is familiar.

With this in mind, why not try the technique outlined earlier in relation to the following non-law examples:

 Practical exercise

These examples are designed to help you develop a methodical approach to problem solving. As such, they are very simple so you could reach a conclusion without going through the steps outlined earlier but that would defeat the purpose of the exercise. Try to follow the four-stage procedure with these simple facts to build up your confidence and expertise ready for solving more complex problems as the chapter progresses.

1. The Post Office has introduced a system of calculating the cost of postage based upon weight and size. A letter is one which weighs less than 100g, has maximum dimensions of 240mm x 165mm, and is no thicker than 5mm. This costs 60p postage. A large letter can have maximum dimensions of 353mm x 250mm, weigh up to 750g, and be up to 25mm in thickness and costs 90p postage if it weighs 100g or less, £1.20 between 101g and 250g, £1.60 between 251g and 500g or £2.30 between 501g and 750g. You wish to post a package that weighs 90g and is 4mm thick, 240mm long, and 170mm wide. How much will this cost?

2. Your grandmother offers you a cash incentive to encourage you to study for your exams. She agrees to pay you £10 for every exam that you pass and £50 extra if you pass all five exams. You pass four exams. How much money can you expect to receive?

3. You notice an advertisement for an essay-writing competition on the law school noticeboard. The first prize is £500 so you would like to enter. The competition rules state that the essay must be written by an undergraduate student under the age of 21 at the closing date (next 31 March) who has not yet studied tort law. Do you qualify to enter the competition (based on your own circumstances)?

You will find suggested answers to these questions on the Online Resource Centre where there is also an explanation of how the answers were reached.

You probably found it easy to work through these exercises and you should take heart from this because it means that you have already grasped the essential skills that you need to succeed in answering problem questions in law. These skills will need to be honed and developed and you will find help and guidance on this in the remainder of this chapter. The following sections explore each aspect of problem solving in greater depth in order to help you develop your understanding of what is required.

15.2.1 Warning

It is of fundamental importance that you separate the question into a series of issues and deal with each of these separately. The IRAC, IPAC, CLEO, and PLAN techniques will not work if you try and apply them to the question as a whole. It is a common mistake for students who first encounter this technique to use it as a means of dividing their answer into four sections and dividing the content as follows:

1. Issues: all the issues from the question as a whole are identified and listed
2. Rules: an abstract discussion of all the law that is raised by the issues, all amalgamated together
3. Application: a short section that is usually extremely weak because it is detached from the law and it does not break the question down into sufficiently small issues
4. Conclusion: a short factual paragraph that summarizes the findings

If you make the mistake of dividing the whole answer into sections as explained earlier, rather than slicing it up into a series of issues and subissues as explained in the following section, it is extremely likely that your answer will fail as you will not have demonstrated an effective problem-solving technique to the marker.

15.3 Issues, claims, and problems

The first stage in the problem-solving process is to identify the question that needs to be answered. In the earlier example about late submission of coursework, this was quite simple: will the essay receive a penalty? However, it is not always a straightforward matter to identify the issue within a problem question; indeed, it is likely that there will be multiple issues within a single question that need to be extrapolated from the mass of detail. This is an important stage in the process as if you do not isolate the correct question to ask, you cannot hope to reach the right conclusion.

This is an example of a typical problem question that you might encounter. As you see, it involves a series of events that involve several different parties. This tort problem about injuries sustained by visitors to a farmyard activity centre will be used throughout this chapter to demonstrate the process of building up an answer to a problem question.

> Brian runs a small farm yard activity centre in West Yorkshire. Gladys and her granddaughter, Camilla (7) visit the centre. They go into the stable yard where there are large signs that read 'horses may bite, so mind your fingers' and 'please do not feed the horses—they may think you're offering them an apple and gnaw your hand instead'. Gladys sees the signs but has left her glasses in the car so cannot read what they say. She feeds slices of apple that she has brought with her to several horses and receives a nasty bite from Clopper, the centre's temperamental stallion.

There used to be a sign on his door that warned that stallions can behave unpredictably but it had fallen off the previous day and not yet been replaced. Upset by her experience, Gladys goes into the cafeteria. She tells Camilla not to wander off but Camilla ignores Gladys and goes into Brian's exhibition of farm equipment. Two of the rarest machines are roped off to protect them from the public (and the public from them). Camilla climbs over the ropes and starts to climb on one of the machines but receives a deep laceration from one of the exposed cutting blades. In the cafeteria, employee Betty is making a pot of tea for Gladys. The cafeteria is newly refurbished. The work was done by local handyman, Andy, who is an excellent carpenter but who lacks expertise in electrical fitting. As a result, some of the wiring is incorrect and this causes a massive power surge during which the tea urn explodes, showering Betty with boiling water and causing her to suffer serious burns.

Advise Brian as to the extent of his liability, considering occupiers' liability only and not considering any potential claims in negligence.

15.3.1 Analyzing the question

The most effective means of identifying the issues in a problem question is to analyze the facts that you have been given and take a note of relevant facts relating to the two key variables: parties and events. This will help you to address the key question: who has done what to whom?

15.3.1.1 Parties

There will be at least one party in the problem, probably more in many subject areas. You may encounter a single party in problem questions on public law topics, such as constitutional and administrative law and criminal law, as these areas of law involve the liability of an individual in relation to the state. Of course, it is possible for public law topics nonetheless to involve other parties; there may be multiple applicants in a judicial review problem, for example, or several defendants or a range of victims in a criminal law problem. Problem questions in areas of private law, such as contract and tort, will involve at least one party making a claim against another, so it is important that you identify both the claimant(s) and the defendant(s) (see Table 15.1).

Make a list of the people in the question and determine whether they are parties who have a claim or parties who face liability. It may be that there are other people in the question who fall into neither of these categories. If this is the case, do not simply ignore them but consider why they have been included. It is likely that they are there for a reason.

The instructions that accompany the problem facts are often an excellent source of information that will assist you in the identification of the roles of the various parties. In the example given in this chapter, you are told to advise Brian about the strength of the claims against him, so it is a straightforward matter to identity him as the defendant.

Table 15.1 Parties in the problem question

Claimant	Defendant	Other parties
Gladys	Brian	
Camilla	Brian	Gladys (child's grandmother)
Betty	Brian	Andy (the handyman)

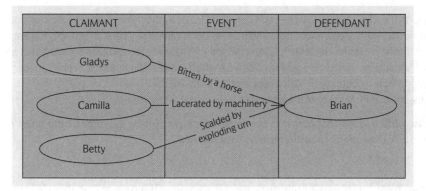

Figure 15.3 Claimants, events, and defendants

15.3.1.2 Events

It is also important to work out what has happened to the parties as this provides the necessary information to ascertain what area of law is relevant to the topic. It is extremely useful to establish these facts at the outset as this will act as a reminder that precise reference needs to be made to them at some point in your answer. As you will see in the discussion of application later in the chapter, one of the more common weaknesses in a problem answer is the failure to make reference to precise facts, therefore having a list to hand from the outset may help to overcome this problem (see Figure 15.3).

This diagram depicts the answer to the 'who did what to whom' question in the sample question and this gives three potential situations in which Brian may be liable. In a question involving several parties, the obvious structure for your answer is to consider each party in turn, particularly if the basis for liability is the same for each of them as it is here (the issue is occupiers' liability in each case).

It is important to be methodical and thorough. Start at the beginning of the question and work through each sentence in turn, making a note of potentially relevant information. It may not be clear at this stage how each piece of information is relevant but this should become apparent as you become more familiar with the legal issues raised by the question during the course of your research.

It is important to devote time and attention to this early stage of the problem solving process as it is the cornerstone of the success of your answer. If you fail to identify issues at this stage or omit relevant facts, it is inevitable that the remainder of your answer will have gaps. You should bear in mind that it is not always straightforward to identify the issues in a problem question.

Practical exercise

Use the techniques outlined earlier to identify the issues in this problem question. Do not worry if you cannot make an exact identification of the relevant offences; focus on framing the issues at this stage. It is perfectly permissible to identify a range of potential offences, i.e. burglary/theft, or to go for a general topic, i.e. one of the non-fatal offences against the person, at this stage as the research that you go on to conduct will help you to narrow down the possibilities.

Matt is short of money and hopes to borrow £500 from his brother, Luke. In order to get into Luke's good books, Matt decides to take him a bottle of whisky that he plans to steal from the local supermarket.

Once inside the supermarket, Matt loses his nerve and leaves without going near the alcohol aisle. Instead, he goes into a department store and uses his credit card to buy Luke an expensive sweater, knowing that he is over his credit limit. Luke is thrilled with the sweater but refuses to lend Matt any money. Matt punches Luke in the face causing a cut which requires stitches. Luke sets fire to the sweater and leaves it burning on Matt's doorstep the following day.

Discuss the criminal liability of the parties.

 You will find suggested answers to these questions on the Online Resource Centre where there is also an explanation of how the answers were reached.

Once you have completed a preliminary analysis, you will have a reasonably clear picture of the questions that need to be asked. Although it is important to identify and frame the 'big' issues that raise questions about the liability of the parties, this may not be the most effective way for you to structure your answer. It is important that you are able to break down the topic into smaller and more manageable subissues.

15.3.2 Finding the subissues

At this stage of the analysis of the sample problem, we have three 'big' issues which were identified by concentrating on the parties and the events:

1. Can Gladys hold Brian liable for her injuries after she was bitten by a horse?

2. Can Camilla hold Brian liable for the lacerations caused by his machinery?

3. Can Betty hold Brian liable for the burns she received when the urn exploded?

In order to break this down into more manageable subissues, more information is needed about the basis upon which Brian may be liable. In this particular example, the instructions that accompany the facts make it clear that the relevant area of law is occupiers' liability. This makes it an extremely straightforward matter to break each of the big issues down into subissues on the basis of the elements that have to be established in order to establish occupiers' liability (see Figure 15.4).

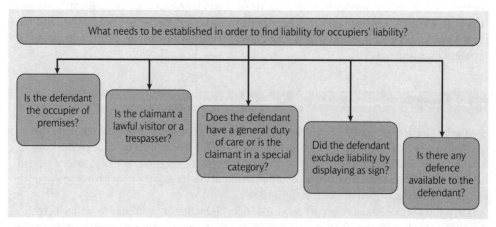

Figure 15.4 Subissues

By exploring the subissues within the big issue, you are effectively breaking the answer down into a series of mini problem questions, so the techniques outlined earlier can be used in relation to each subissue. As such, it will be a succession of IRAC's (or whichever of the acronyms you prefer).

By taking each subissue in turn and subjecting it to a methodical analysis, you will give the answer a strong structure and it should help to ensure that you are thorough and do not omit any important points from consideration.

ISSUE 1: Is Brian liable under Occupiers' Liability for the injury sustained by Gladys when she is bitten by his horse?

- **Subissue 1.1** Is Brian an occupier of premises?
  - State the law
  - Apply it to the facts
  - Conclusion
- **Subissue 1.2** Is Gladys a lawful visitor or a trespasser?
  - State the law
  - Apply it to the facts
  - Conclusion
- **Subissue 1.3** Is there a general duty of care or does Gladys fall into a special category?
  - State the law
  - Apply it to the facts
  - Conclusion
- **Subissue 1.4** Has Brian excluded his liability by displaying a sign?
  - State the law
  - Apply it to the facts
  - Conclusion
- **Subissue 1.5** Is there any defence available to Brian?
  - State the law
  - Apply it to the facts
  - Conclusion

Conclusion on the big issue by drawing together the strands of argument presented in the subissues.

You would then repeat this technique with the next two big issues and this would provide a structure for your answer.

15.3.2.1 Identifying the correct area of law

However, if the problem question does not specify the particular basis of liability, you will have to identify this from the nature of the question. Imagine that the sample question merely asked 'Advise Brian of the extent of his tortious liability'. This would require you to identify the relevant basis of liability and this makes the problem question more challenging as inaccuracy here can put the entire answer off course.

There are various steps that you can take to help you identify the relevant topic(s):

1. Look at your syllabus and eliminate all topics that you will not have covered by the time that the coursework is due for submission

2. Make a list of topics covered on your course so far and summarize them in a few words that capture their essential nature. If you do that with topics which are likely to be found

on a tort course, you will see that some of the topics covered have no relevance at all to the sample problem. For example, if you used this technique on the sample question, you would soon conclude that only negligence, occupiers' liability, and employers' liability (in relation to Betty) could possibly have any relevance to the question:

- Negligence: breach of duty of care leading to harm
- Special duties: particular type of negligence
- Nuisance: interference with quiet enjoyment of one's property
- Employers' liability: duty towards employees
- Occupiers' liability: duty of landowner to visitors and trespassers
- Defamation: harm to person's reputation

3. If all else fails, ask for guidance. You can share information with other students (remembering not to take this too far for fear of contravening plagiarism regulations: see chapter 12) but you could also check with your lecturer. They will not be prepared to give you too much specific guidance but a quick (and polite: see chapter 9 for guidance on how to get help from lecturers) email saying 'I was planning to cover negligence, employers' liability, and occupiers' liability, in my answer but am concerned that this may be too broad and perhaps I should focus exclusively on occupiers' liability' could elicit a helpful response

15.3.2.2 Multiple areas of law

Many problem questions will involve several different legal topics within a problem question. One of the reasons for this is that it enables the lecturer to assess your knowledge of more than one topic but, more importantly, it tests your ability to differentiate between different topics.

This is an important facet of learning a topic. It is a relatively straightforward matter to look up the relevant law and apply it to the facts if you are told what topic needs to be considered, but it is far more difficult to work out from the facts what the relevant topic is in the first place. Imagine how much harder the question about Brian and his farmyard activity centre would have been if it had not been specified that the relevant area of law was occupiers' liability and not negligence.

If you are confident that a particular issue raises potential liability in more than one area of law, you will need to discuss both and this will require some careful thought in terms of the structure of the answer. You will, however, be able to gain additional credit by evaluating which area is the most suitable basis for liability.

15.4 Rules, principles, and law

The first stage of the problem-solving process is to identify the question that needs to be answered. Once that is identified, the next stage is to provide a statement of law that will enable that question to be answered.

15.4.1 Researching the law

In order to identify and state the law as part of your answer to the problem question, you will need to undertake research to ensure that you have a good understanding of the relevant law. The following suggestions should help you to carry out effective research:

- Start with a textbook and read the entire chapter or section of the chapter that is relevant to your legal issue. This will give you a solid overview of the topic

- Once you have a grasp of the topic, you should have a clearer appreciation of how accurate you have been in framing your issues and subissues. Review these now and make any changes that are necessary in light of your initial research

- Take each subissue individually, using a separate sheet of paper for each if this helps you to organize your thoughts. Make a note of any material in the textbook that seems pertinent to each issue, paying particular attention to statutory provisions and case law

- If you feel that you are struggling to understand the law, try consulting a different textbook to see if that makes the issues clearer. Different authors explain the same concepts in different ways so you may be more able to follow the explanations in an alternative textbook

- Make sure that you are precise in noting the wording of statutory provisions and in recording full case citations; you will need these when you come to write your answer

- Be prepared to follow up references contained in the footnotes of your textbook. For example, if a case is cited in the footnote in relation to the definition of an occupier but there is nothing in the text that elaborates upon this, you will need to find the case to discover whether it says anything that is relevant to your question

- Remember that a problem question is concerned with the current law and its interpretation. Concentrate on finding this and do not be distracted by discussion of how the law used to be or how it came to be as it is today. This sort of historical background is relevant to an essay question and to your broader understanding of the topic but it has no place in an answer to a problem question

- Bear in mind that problem questions are designed to assess your ability to apply the law to new and novel situations, so do not expect to find an exact answer to all the issues raised in your question in the textbook. It is likely that some of the issues are framed so that you have to look at what law there is and speculate upon how that might apply. With this in mind, try to find cases that state general principles that can be applied to your issue or which deal with similar, although not identical, situations

Taking these points into account, you should aim to have a series of notes that gives you the basis to make statements of law in relation to each of the issues raised on the facts of the problem. You might want to note your thoughts about the way that the issue is likely to be decided as you go, as this will make the job of applying the law to the facts much easier (see Figure 15.5).

DEFINITION OF OCCUPIER

No statutory definition although Occupiers' Liabilty Acts 1957 (visitors) and 1984 (trespassers) deal with liability in general.

Defined in *Wheat v E.Lacon & Co Ltd* [1966] AC 552 (seems to be leading case) as person who exercises an element of control over premises.

This includes physical control of premises and legal control of premises—*Harris v Birkenhead Corporation* [1976] 1 WLR 279

THOUGHTS: seems straightforward as Q says that Brian runs the farmyard activity centre so presumably has physical control of the centre even if he is not the legal owner.

Figure 15.5 Thoughtful research with notes organized by issue

15.4.2 Stating the law

This is a crucial part of the problem-solving process and what is required is an initial abstract statement of a legal principle (from statute or case law) and, if necessary in relation to the issue at hand, some further elaboration on aspects of that principle.

This can be quite difficult to understand so the first subissue from the sample question will be used to demonstrate this technique in practice:

ISSUE 1: Is Brian liable under Occupiers' Liability for the injury sustained by Gladys when she is bitten by his horse?

- Subissue 1.1 Is Brian an occupier of premises?
  - **State the law:** There is no statutory definition of 'occupier' under the Occupiers' Liability Acts 1957 and 1984 but an occupier is defined in *Wheat v E Lacon & Co Ltd* [1966] AC 552 (HL) as a person who exercises an element of control over premises.
  - **Apply it to the facts**
  - Conclusion

This demonstrates an initial statement of a relevant legal principle which could be applied to the facts as they stand. However, it might be useful to elaborate on this by reference to case law that provides further clarification of the meaning of this definition, as this will facilitate more precise application:

- Subissue 1.1 Is Brian an occupier of premises?
  - **State the law:** There is no statutory definition of 'occupier' under the Occupiers' Liability Acts 1957 and 1984 but an occupier is defined in *Wheat v E Lacon & Co Ltd* [1966] AC 552 (HL) as a person who exercises an element of control over premises. In *Harris v Birkenhead Corporation* [1976] 1 WLR 279 (CA), it was held that this meant physical control over the premises as well as legal control.
  - **Apply it to the facts:** As Brian is described as the person who runs the farmyard activity centre, this implies that he has physical control over the premises even if he is not the legal owner of the centre.
  - Conclusion

It is always a question of judgement as to how much law to state in relation to any particular point. In the sample problem, the issue of occupier of premises is not particularly complicated but needs to be established with sufficient clarity because it is the foundation of Brian's liability in this area of tort law. There are other issues in the problem that will require more detailed exploration with reference being made to different statements of law.

As a general rule, the more uncertain the area of law and the more complicated the issue, the more legal principles you will need to include within your answer.

15.4.3 Common problems

This stage of the problem-solving process is relatively straightforward and does not pose as great a challenge for the student as breaking the problem question down into appropriate issues and the application of the law. However, there are problems that do arise with a fair degree of frequency in relation to this stage of the process that are worthy of mention.

15.4.3.1 Law in large chunks

Success in problem solving is dependent on breaking the law down into small chunks and dealing with each chunk individually. Therefore, an answer which deals with a clump of legal issues together is going to be weaker than one that separates them out for individual attention. It is essential to remember that once you have sliced up each issue into a series of subissues, each one of these should have some statement of law, however brief.

> Three certainties are required for the existence of a valid trust. There must be certainty of intention, certainty of subject matter and certainty of objects. Certainty of intention requires . . . Certainty of subject matter requires . . . Certainty of objects requires . . . The first of these is satisfied by . . .

This example starts well by identifying the main issue and breaking it down into three sub-issues, but then it provides a statement of law for each of these without any application. This provides a block of legal statements pertaining to three separate subissues. A preferable approach would be to complete the discussion of each subissue by providing a statement of law, applying it to the facts, and reaching a conclusion before moving on to state the law relevant to the next subissue, as the following example illustrates:

> Three certainties are required for the existence of a valid trust. There must be certainty of intention, certainty of subject matter and certainty of objects. Certainty of intention requires that there is evidence that the testator intended to create a trust rather than disposing of his property as an outright gift. The testator has (application and conclusion). Certainty of subject matter requires . . . This is established by . . .

15.4.3.2 No abstract statement of the law

This stage of the problem-solving process is concerned with providing an accurate and concise statement of the current law. It does not require that this law is explained in the context of the particular facts of the problem; that is an issue of application which is important at the next stage of the process.

If you combine the statement of law and its application, you are failing to demonstrate an appropriate problem-solving technique *and* omitting to demonstrate your knowledge of the law. However, it is common for students to provide an explanation of the law in the context of the facts. If you do not understand what is meant by this, the examples shown in Table 15.2 should demonstrate the point:

Table 15.2 Examples of abstract statements of law

Explanation of law in context of the facts	Abstract statement of the law
The *actus reus* of theft is putting the cuff-links in his pocket.	The *actus reus* of theft is the appropriation of property belonging to another.
The relevant standard of care is that of a qualified and experienced doctor.	The relevant standard of care is that of the reasonably competent professional.
The applicant will have standing to bring a claim for judicial review because the grant of planning permission will have an effect on his everyday life.	The applicant will have standing to bring a claim for judicial review if he has sufficient interest in the issue.

The statements in the first column are *not* accurate statements of the law; they are explanations of how the requirements of the law are satisfied in relation to a particular set of facts. As such, they are *applying* the law rather than *stating* it.

Students sometimes take the combined approach as a deliberate ploy to conserve words. This is a mistake: it may save words but it loses marks.

15.4.3.3 Too much detail

A further factor that can weaken a problem answer is the inclusion of an excessive level of detail when providing a statement of law. This tends to take two forms:

- Too much descriptive detail, for example the detailed facts of a case
- Inclusion of irrelevant material, for example issues not raised by the facts

Both of these problems can be addressed by use of the 'so what?' test. This involves asking 'so what does this contribute to my answer?' in relation to each sentence included in your answer. If the answer is 'nothing', the sentence should be removed. It is seeking to identify material that is not directly relevant to the issue at hand.

 Practical exercise

Use the 'so what?' technique to eliminate the unnecessary material from these sample answers based upon examples used earlier in the chapter.

1. Sheena has submitted her essay at 9.15 a.m. the day after the deadline for submission. The rules state that there is a 10-mark penalty for submission up to one day after the deadline. An essay which is more than one day late will receive a 25-mark penalty if it is within one week of the deadline but after that it will receive zero. It is likely that Sheena will receive a 10-mark penalty unless she can establish that she had good cause for late submission.

2. Steve has punched Adam in the face causing a cut which required stitches so may be liable under s 20 of the Offences against the Person Act 1861. The *actus reus* requires a wound or the infliction of grievous bodily harm. Grievous bodily harm is defined as 'really serious harm' and according to the CPS Charging Standards includes serious injuries such as broken limbs. Moreover, it has been held by the House of Lords that psychological injury can amount to grievous bodily harm if it is sufficiently serious and is established as a matter of expert evidence. It does not include mere emotions such as distress or fear but requires an established psychiatric injury. A wound is defined as a break in the continuity of the skin and will be satisfied as a cut that requires stitches must have broken Adam's skin.

 These are quite straightforward examples to demonstrate the point, but you will find an additional exercise on the Online Resource Centre that you may find useful in helping you to eliminate irrelevant details from your answers.

15.5 Application and evaluation

It is this stage of the process that is at the heart of problem solving. The first stage enabled you to identify the questions that needed to be answered; the second stage involved identification of the law needed to answer these questions, but it is this third stage that involves combining the issue and the law and actually answering the question.

This is the aspect of problem solving with which students struggle the most and yet it is quite straightforward, as the following example demonstrates:

- Subissue 1.1 Is Brian an occupier of premises?
- State the law: There is no statutory definition of 'occupier' under the Occupiers' Liability Acts 1957 and 1984 but an occupier is defined in *Wheat v E Lacon & Co Ltd* [1966] AC 552 (HL) as a person who exercises an element of control over premises. In *Harris v Birkenhead Corporation* [1976] 1 WLR 279 (CA), it was held that this meant physical control over the premises as well as legal control.
- **Apply it to the facts:** As Brian is described as the person who runs the farmyard activity centre, this implies that he has physical control over the premises even if he is not the legal owner of the centre.
- Conclusion

As you see in this example, the essence of application/evaluation is to draw upon the facts provided to demonstrate how the requirements of law are satisfied.

Here, the law defines an occupier as a person who exercises a degree of control over the property so the application/evaluation stage of problem solving picks up on evidence from the scenario which demonstrates that Brian exercises control over the farmyard activity centre.

The application stage is sometimes said to require the greatest level of skill and understanding of the law as it requires the student to look at the facts and select the ones that fulfil the requirements of the law. This is not something that can be cribbed from a textbook, remembered from a lecture, or looked up on the Internet; it requires actual understanding of the requirements of the law and an ability to recognize them amongst a mass of facts.

Practical exercise

It is a good idea to practise with some simple examples to gain confidence in identifying the relevant facts. Have a look back at the farmyard activity centre scenario and pick out the facts that satisfy the following requirements:

1. If the definition of 'premises' includes land and buildings, what facts suggest that the injuries sustained by Gladys, Camilla, and Betty occurred on the premises?

2. To fall within the provisions of the Occupiers' Liability Act 1957, the person who is harmed must be a lawful visitor to the premises, i.e. someone with express or implied permission from the occupier to be on the premises or whose presence is known to the occupier. What facts suggest that Gladys, Camilla, and Betty are visitors?

3. An occupier will not be liable for a visitor's injury if he has given sufficient warning to enable the visitor to be reasonably safe. Are there any facts that suggest that any of those who have been injured have been given a warning and, if so, was it sufficient to enable them to be reasonably safe?

4. An occupier may have to take additional measures to protect children from harm, especially if there are allurements on the premises, but the law strives to seek a balance between the duty of an occupier and the responsibility of parents for the safety of their children. In this scenario, what might act as an allurement to a child, what measures has Brian taken to protect against this, and what factors might suggest some element of parental responsibility?

You will find answers to these questions on the Online Resource Centre along with an explanation of how the answers were reached. You will also find a further example which will test your ability to identify relevant facts from the question that will demonstrate that the requirements of law are satisfied. This is an important area, so it will be worth taking some time to ensure that you are able to apply the law effectively to the facts.

15.5.1 Common problems

This stage of application/evaluation does hold a range of pitfalls that can lead students astray. The following is an outline of some of the problems that seem to arise frequently, with some suggestions for their avoidance.

15.5.1.1 Lazy application

This is a phrase that can be used to describe situations when students have made some mention of the facts but in such a general way that it is not really application at all as it does nothing to resolve the issue at hand. Phrases such as 'this requirement is satisfied on the facts' or 'it is clear from the facts that this is satisfied'. This may well be so, but there is no credit available for application that does not refer to *specific* facts from the problem to establish that the requirements of the law are satisfied.

It also describes the situation when the student abdicates responsibility for application by delegating it to someone else, usually 'the court' or 'the jury'. Here, the student is acknowledging that a decision will have to be made about whether the requirements of the law are satisfied but strives to find a way to avoid doing this themselves. To be clear, even if the issue is one of fact that will be decided in court by the jury, that is not a useful stance to take in a problem question. Imagine if a client says to you 'am I going to be convicted of murder?'. He will not be in the least impressed if your advice is that this will be a question of fact for the jury! Accordingly, you must extrapolate evidence from the facts that give an indication of how the issue is likely to be decided. You might find that speculative application (see section 15.5.2.1) helps to overcome this problem.

The following example demonstrates both of these flawed approaches to application as well as some illustrations of a more effective approach to application (see Figure 15.6).

15.5.1.2 Essays in disguise

Another weakness which limits the success of many answers is a greater resemblance to an essay than to a problem question. This arises when students engage in detailed discussion of the law raised by the question that strays further and further away from the issue at hand.

Try to remember that essays and problem questions have very different requirements. A problem question requires a concise and focused statement of the relevant law. Exploration of how the law used to be, how it might be in the future, or what it is in other jurisdictions are only rarely relevant in a problem question.

Students also have a tendency to include far too much descriptive detail of the law and this gives their answer the feel of an essay (see section 15.4.3.3). Try not to test relevance by asking 'is this point relevant?' as this question will be answered in relation to the topic in general. 'Is this point necessary to establish this part of the law?' is a far better question and one that will keep your answer focused and prevent it from turning into an essay on the general issue.

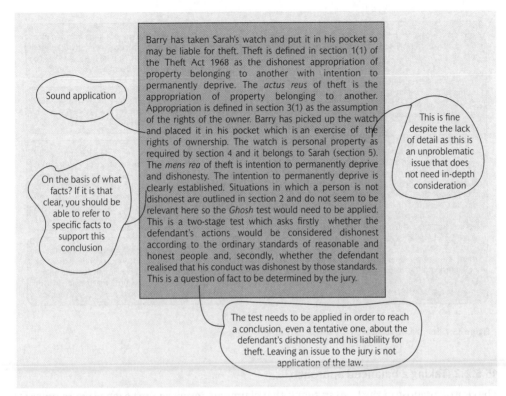

Figure 15.6 Lazy and effective application

Another useful way of keeping the answer to the point is to ensure that every paragraph includes a mention of the name of one of the parties and at least some mention of specific facts from the problem. By doing this, you will force yourself to link up with the question and this should stop you from straying too far into abstract discussion.

15.5.2 Strengthening application

In addition to avoiding these common problems, there are a variety of techniques that can be used to improve the quality of your answer by strengthening the application of the law to the facts.

15.5.2.1 Speculative application

As you have doubtless realized by now, problem questions do not provide all the facts that you need to reach a determinative answer to all the issues raised. You will often encounter a situation in which you have worked through the subissues and need to establish just one more point to reach a conclusion about liability, only to find that the information you need in order to do so is simply not included in the question.

When this situation arises, it is perfectly permissible to engage in a little speculative application. This means that you can explore some hypothetical situations in order to engage in some conjecture: if *X* then *Y*. This is demonstrated in the following example (see Figure 15.7).

Huw has submitted his essay after the 4pm deadline. The rules state that essays submitted after the deadline that are up to one day late will receive a 10-mark penalty.	Application of the general rule could be followed by a conclusion that Huw will receive a penalty but there are exceptions to the rule so it is reasonable to speculate about whether Huw might fall within them.
There are some exceptions to this noted in the rules. For example, if Huw had been granted an extension by a lecturer, there would be no penalty. There is nothing in the facts to suggest that this is the case.	This is straightforward situation to discuss as Huw either has an extension or he does not so there is little more to be said on this point.
Equally, the rule states that a person who has good cause for late submission will not be penalised. If Huw was late because his printer broke, this is unlikely to be regarded as a good reason as it is such a commonplace occurrence that he should have contemplated that it could happen and have planned for it. However, if Huw was late because he was knocked off his bicycle on the way to submit his essay and delayed by the need to seek medical treatment, this is likely to be regarded as a good cause for lateness.	This situation can involve more detailed speculation as it revolves around interpretation of 'good cause'. Inclusion of hypothetical possibilities to illustrate understanding of the scope of the exception add further strength to the answer. This approach can be used when case law has considered the interpretation of a particular word or phrase.
There is no evidence to suggest that Huw has received an extension or has good cause to submit his essay late thus, in the absence of such circumstances, it seems that Huw will receive a 10-mark deduction for late submission.	The conclusion that follows speculative application should always draw reference to its contingent nature by noting that it is the best conclusion possible on the known facts but may alter if further facts come to light or a particular interpretation is preferred and applied.

Figure 15.7 Speculative application

15.5.2.2 Taking a balanced approach

The central premise of the legal system is that claims are tested against each other in order to establish which of the opposing arguments between private parties (in civil cases) or between the state and an individual (in criminal law) is the stronger. As such, it is important that you demonstrate this objectivity in your answers by considering both sides to the argument when exploring liability. Moreover, from a pragmatic perspective, if you present one argument, you will get credit for that but if you provide a second argument to counter that initial point, there is additional credit available.

Therefore, it is important to scrutinize every issue to determine whether there is a viable counter-argument that needs to be considered. There will not always be a counter-argument; in the scenario involving theft of Sarah's watch, it is a straightforward matter to determine that the watch is personal property, so there is no counter-argument to consider. However, moving on to consider the issue of intention to deprive permanently, although it is reasonable to assume that this is Barry's intention as he has surreptitiously placed the watch in his pocket, it may be that he only wants to borrow it because, moving to consider the issue of dishonesty, he wants to have it cleaned and repaired as a surprise for Sarah. If the facts are silent on an issue, it may be necessary to engage in speculative application in order to explore both sides of the argument (see section 15.5.2.1).

Equally, if the issue involves interpretation of a particular word or phrase, do not be content with finding one case on the issue and assuming that this provides the answer. You should research the issue and see if there is any conflicting authority that suggests an alternative outcome is possible.

15.5.2.3 Supporting authority

The inclusion of authority to support your application of the law is a real strength but it is also something that is not always done very effectively by students. All too often, an argument is raised that requires support which is either not provided at all, or the relevant case is added on in brackets at the end of the sentence or in a footnote reference with no indication of how it supports the proposition asserted.

> Although Camilla is a lawful visitor to the farmyard activity centre, she may have become a trespasser by climbing on the roped-off machinery (*The Calgarth* [1927] P 93).
>
> Although Camilla is a lawful visitor to the farmyard activity centre, she may have become a trespasser by climbing on the machinery as it was roped off to prevent the public approaching it. This issue was discussed in *The Calgarth* [1927] P 93.

Neither of these examples makes effective use of the authority; in fact, the second is misleading as it could be read as meaning that the issue of moving into a roped-off area was discussed in *The Calgarth*. A better approach is one that explains the principle from the case:

> Although Camilla is a lawful visitor to the centre, she may have become a trespasser by entering the roped-off area. It was said in *The Calgarth* [1927] P 93 that a person who is given permission to enter a house is not necessarily given permission to slide down the banisters, so it may be that Camilla has exceeded the permission given to her by entering the roped-off area.

One way to ensure that you use authority effectively is to make sure that you have linked the case to the facts in some way. This requires you to explain how it is relevant and consider how it might impact on the outcome of the case.

15.6 Conclusion and outcome

The final stage of the process involves reaching a conclusion on the basis of the preceding application of the law as is demonstrated by reference to the sample question:

- Subissue 1.1 Is Brian an occupier of premises?
- State the law: There is no statutory definition of 'occupier' under the Occupiers' Liability Acts 1957 and 1984 but an occupier is defined in *Wheat v E Lacon & Co Ltd* [1966] AC 552 (HL) as a person who exercises an element of control over premises. In *Harris v Birkenhead Corporation* [1976] 1 WLR 279 (CA), it was held that this meant physical control over the premises as well as legal control.
- Apply it to the facts: as Brian is described as the person who runs the farmyard activity centre, this implies that he has physical control over the premises even if he is not the legal owner of the centre.
- **Conclusion:** Therefore, Brian will be regarded as the occupier of the farmyard activity centre for the purposes of establishing occupiers' liability.

You will need to reach a conclusion for each subissue and then draw these together to reach a conclusion for the main issue. If you consider the issue of Brian's liability for the injury sustained by Gladys, you will see that it contained a series of subissues that combine to provide an answer to that main issue. Each of these—whether Brian is an occupier, whether the stable yard is premises, whether Gladys is a visitor, and so on—will be considered and a conclusion reached and these can then be considered cumulatively to reach a conclusion on liability.

Of course, it may be that it is not possible to reach a definite conclusion. It is a mistake to think that there is always an answer in law: it is not usually a case of right and wrong but of strong and weak arguments, so you should remember that you are not looking for the 'right' answer but for the conclusion that is likely to be reached based upon which argument is the strongest.

Take the following factors into account when reaching a conclusion:

- **There are three different levels of conclusion**: (a) a conclusion for each subissue; (b) a cumulative conclusion that draws upon each of these to reach a conclusion for each issue; and (c) an overall conclusion to the problem question. This should outline the liability of the party or parties for each issue that was raised by the question. In essence, the end conclusion is a summary of your findings.

- **Make sure that your final conclusion is consistent with your earlier discussion**. It would be unfortunate if, in the early stages of the essay, you concluded that Brian had given sufficient warning of the dangers posed by feeding the horses only to state in your final conclusion that he was liable for the injury sustained by Gladys. Thorough checking once the answer is complete should help you to spot any inconsistencies.

- **Do not be afraid to reach an 'it depends' conclusion.** As stated earlier, it is not always a case of finding the right answer but of exploring the possibility of liability, so it is perfectly acceptable to reach a conclusion that says 'it seems that Brian may be liable for the injury sustained by Gladys but this depends upon whether his notices are regarded as adequate warning of the dangers inherent in feeding the horses'. Making a note of the contingencies will strengthen your answer.

- **Do provide an overall conclusion.** Given the constraints of the word limit, students are sometimes tempted to stop writing after dealing with the final issue and leave the marker to pick out the conclusions for each issue that are distributed throughout the answer. This is poor practice and will weaken your answer. The question will require that you discuss someone's liability and your conclusion should always provide a concise and focused answer to the question posed, so it is important that you draw together all the strands of your argument here.

15.7 Tips for success in problem questions

There are a range of points to bear in mind that will help you to strengthen your problem-solving technique.

15.7.1 Follow the instructions

This is an obvious but frequently overlooked point. If the instructions tell you to discuss the liability of a particular party and to consider liability in a particular area of law, this is all that you should cover in your answer. There is no credit available for discussing other issues that are raised on the facts but which are excluded by the instructions.

For example, if a problem stated that Tom had smashed his way into David's house and injected him forcibly with a lethal dose of heroin and you were asked to discuss Tom's liability for homicide offences, there would be no point whatsoever in establishing that Tom is liable for criminal damage to David's door, or considering whether the injection constituted a battery or assault occasioning actual bodily harm—David is dead, so there is no point in discussing non-fatal offences against the person!

Consideration of irrelevant issues will not give you any marks and it will weaken the quality of your answer because it will either cost you words that could be used to discuss a relevant issue (in a piece of coursework) or time that could be devoted to a relevant issue (in an examination).

Students sometimes think that discussing points that are outside the scope of the instructions will attract additional credit from the marker, particularly if this means covering an area of law that is not covered on the course syllabus, because this will demonstrate their research skills. This is generally not the case, so avoid the temptation to do this and concentrate on the instructions that you have been given and the areas of law covered on your syllabus.

Similarly, if a question is broken down into parts and subparts such as (a), (b)(i), (b)(ii), etc., then you must make sure that you answer the question in the same order and label the parts of your answer accordingly. Do not make up and impose your own structure. This will make your marker's life difficult, since marking schemes may give a total number of marks for each part answer and presume that the structure set out in the question will be followed. Your aim is to make your marker's task as easy as possible, so, quite simply, if there is a structure in the question, then you must follow it.

15.7.2 Get to the point

Be careful not to write lengthy introductions to problem questions that simply restate the facts given. For instance, look at the following introduction:

> The following is an essay that uses three statutes: the Offences against the Person Act 1861, the Theft Act 1968 and the Criminal Attempts Act 1981, to interpret criminal liability for the fictional characters involved in a hypothetical scenario. The scenario involves a young man (Adrian) taking his Uncle Ben's sports car to drive to his mother in the hospital, and having a road accident on the way. The accident is witnessed by a bystander—Claire—who invites Adrian into her cottage, where he attempts to steal two of her Japanese miniatures. Meanwhile, a local gang-member—Den—attempts to break into Ben's house . . .

As you can see, this sets out some relevant law and then recites the facts of the question. It also uses 102 words. There is very little credit to be gained in restating material from the scenario without application of the relevant law: it is also a waste of words which could be better used in application and analysis.

15.7.3 Methodical approach

If you follow the guidance given in this chapter, you should be able to work through each of the issues in turn in a methodical manner. This should ensure that you do not miss any important issues and that your answer is thorough and systematic. These are essential features of a strong answer. Students are often tempted to 'jump in' and deal with the most obvious issue first—usually something that they can recall discussing in a seminar or which bears a strong resemblance to a decided case—but this makes the answer weak because you are failing to deal with the other issues that are also raised by the question but may be less obvious, and you are also not demonstrating a thorough and methodical approach to problem solving.

15.7.4 Check and polish the final answer

You should never submit the first draft of your answer. It is important that you take the time to check every aspect of the answer prior to submission: the formatting, spelling, and grammar, the referencing and, of course, the accuracy of the content. Try to leave sufficient time before submission to have a break from the answer and come back to read it with fresh eyes otherwise it is all too easy to read what you think you have written rather than what you have actually written, so mistakes could be overlooked. It might help to read your answer on paper rather than on the computer screen as mistakes can seem more visible in print.

You will find more detailed guidance on writing skills in chapter 10 and referencing in chapter 12 that will help you to ensure that you submit a well-written and thoroughly referenced piece of work.

 Practical exercise

 Reflect upon the guidance provided in this chapter and use it to evaluate an answer to a problem question that you have written either as part of your coursework or in preparation for a seminar. Make a list of its strengths and weaknesses to identify areas where improvement can be made in subsequent pieces of work. As the chapter on study skills suggests, reflecting on your own work can be an excellent way to improve your performance. However, if you would like to use the points raised in this chapter to evaluate answers written by others, have a look at the Online Resource Centre where there is a practical evaluation and marking exercise that you might find useful.

 CHAPTER SUMMARY

Finding the issues

- Take time to analyze the facts of the problem question in terms of the parties and events so that you know 'who has done what to whom' as this provides a good basis for structuring your answer

- Break an issue down into a series of subissues so that each can be considered in turn. It is essential that the issues are sliced up into manageable chunks, so that the law can be stated and applied to the facts

Stating the law

- Start by consulting a textbook to ensure that you have a clear understanding of the area of law but make sure that you move on to consider case law as this will ensure that your answer has sufficient depth of understanding

- Provide concise and abstract statements of the law that can be applied to the facts. Avoid reams of descriptive detail such as lengthy explanations of the facts of cases

- Make sure that there is some supporting authority—either statute or case law—for each statement of law that is made

- Remember to look at both sides of the argument for complicated issues. It may be necessary to search for cases that give alternative outcomes or different definitions of key words or phrases

- Keep careful notes to record your research. It is very frustrating to arrive at the writing stage and not be able to find details of a case you need because you thought you would remember. A systematic approach to note-keeping is a real asset and can save a great deal of time

Application of the law

- Look at the facts and extrapolate specific information that demonstrates that the requirements of the law are satisfied

- Never rely on lazy application such as 'this is clearly established on the facts'. If the facts are that clear, it should be easy for you to identify them and include them in your answer! Equally, never abdicate responsibility for application of the law to the fictitious jury

- Speculative application that considers hypothetical situations can be a useful way of increasing the depth of analysis in your answer and demonstrating your understanding of the law, but do not stray too far away from the facts provided in the answer

- Support your application with case law wherever possible but make sure that this is done effectively by stating the principle and incorporating it into your answer. Case names tacked onto the end of a sentence add nothing to the quality of your answer

- Present a balanced and objective answer by looking at both sides of the argument

Conclusion

- Reach a conclusion on each subissue, issue, and the overall liability of the parties and make sure that there is consistency between these different levels of conclusion

- Do not be afraid to reach a conclusion that is not determinative. Problem questions are written to raise difficult issues, so it may be that the best answer is one that says 'it depends' and then notes the contingent factor(s)

- Make sure that the final conclusion draws together all the strands of your answer and provides a concise summary of your findings as to the liability of the parties

- Do not be tempted to omit the final conclusion in the interests of the word limit

16

Revision and examination skills

INTRODUCTION

The earlier chapters in this part of the book have been aimed at helping you to develop the skills that you need to succeed as your course progresses. Chapter 9 outlined a range of study skills whilst chapter 10 provided a detailed examination of writing skills and chapters 13 and 15 contained detailed guidelines on writing essays and answering problem questions. This chapter focuses on the skills needed to ensure that your revision is effective in preparing you for the examinations that you will need to pass at the end of each year (or twice-yearly, depending upon how your course is structured). This chapter will not only guide you though the revision process but also through to the examination itself by outlining various strategies that can be used to ensure that your knowledge is used to good effect in the examination room.

Revision and examination skills are important and yet they are not always covered by lecturers or in study skills resources. Perhaps this omission is due to an assumption that students who have worked steadily throughout the course will have all that they need to succeed in the exams without any additional advice on revision and exam preparation. This is a misconception and one that can leave students ill-equipped for success in the exams, particularly as the approach to revision that is favoured by students—rereading and rewriting notes—is not particularly effective. This chapter provides a selection of practical tips on formulating an effective revision strategy from planning and organization through to a series of practical tasks that can be undertaken alone or in groups. The overall aim of the chapter is to provide some insight into the variety of ways that revision can be made more variable, engaging, and effective.

LEARNING OUTCOMES

After studying this chapter, you will be able to:

- Formulate a realistic plan of revision appropriate to your circumstances

- Review your syllabus to identify appropriate topics for revision

- Use a range of different strategies to engage in active revision

- Acknowledge the value of practice answers and incorporate these into your revision strategy

- Recognize the different requirements of essays and problem questions and take account of these in your revision and in the exam

- Plan and produce focused and successful answers to exam questions

- Avoid some of the common problems that limit exam success

16.1 Preparing to revise

Planning and preparation are the keys to successful revision. Too many students dive straight into the revision process without any clear idea of what they are trying to achieve. It is worth taking time to organize your thoughts at the outset and devise a workable and effective revision strategy, taking the factors outlined in the following sections into account.

16.1.1 Timing and structure of the exams

In order to plan your revision, it is essential that you have a clear picture of the task ahead of you. A vague knowledge that you have to sit five papers in five weeks' time is not sufficient information upon which to base an effective revision strategy. Try to ensure that you can answer the following questions as your first step in the revision process.

16.1.1.1 When do your examinations take place?

This question is of immediate importance because it defines how long you have available for revision. The time available for revision varies enormously between institutions. Count how many days, including weekends, there are from the first day of your revision to the first day of the exam period. If you divide each day into two study periods, you can also give yourself half-day breaks that will give you some relief from studying. Once you have a clear idea of how many days of revision there are, you can start to plan how to break those days down into study periods for the various subjects.

16.1.1.2 How much time is there between papers?

Again, this varies enormously, not only between institutions but from year-to-year within the same institution. You may be fortunate and have exams evenly spaced out over a period of two weeks or you could be unlucky and face four papers in two days. Irrespective of the time between papers, it is not a good idea to take these gap days into account when calculating the number of revision days available for the following reasons:

- You could be tempted to use all the pre-exam revision time for the first subject and then slot the remaining revision into the gap days which will give disproportionate attention to the subject of the first exam and leave you short of time to deal with the other subjects

- If you are reliant on gap days to revise a particular subject, you will be in difficulties if something interferes with that plan such as illness or some unexpected setback

It is a much better strategy to count only the days before the first exam as full revision days and then to use gap days generally to refresh your memory, confident in the knowledge that the bulk of the work is already done.

16.1.1.3 How many papers will you be sitting?

With a wide range of optional subjects on offer and a more diverse range of methods of assessment, it is impossible to make generalizations about the 'usual' number of papers that any student will sit. Some students prefer to opt for subjects that are assessed exclusively by coursework, so may be facing few (or no) examinations whilst others, particularly students taking 'half credit' subjects, will have more examinations.

Your revision time should be spread fairly evenly across the number of subjects that you are studying. It is one of the unfortunate facts of student life that half-credit subjects carry less weight towards your degree than full-credit subjects but tend to involve just as much work in terms of revision. As such, it is probably not a good idea to differentiate between full and half-credit subjects when allocating revision time.

With these details in mind, you can get a good general idea of the number of days available to revise each subject. If you have forty-two days until the first examination, this gives you potentially eighty-four half-day study periods to allocate to five subjects. Rather than dividing seventy-five half-days (remember to factor in rest days) by five to allocate fifteen study periods to each subject, you may want to take other factors into account in the allocation process; for example, you may have found some subjects particularly difficult or they may be assessed solely by examination so that more is at stake (see Table 16.1).

It is a good idea to draw up a revision calendar and mark the subjects on it so that you have an immediate visual reminder of where you are in the revision process (it is also very satisfying to be able to cross out completed tasks, giving a real feeling of progress). There are two ways in which you could allocate time by subject in your revision timetable:

1. Clustered: consecutive study periods are allocated to the same subject. This allows a concentrated focus on each subject but does mean that the first revision topic is rather distant by the time that the exam period starts. Some people who use this method start their revision with the final exam subject and work towards their first subject so that this is revised immediately prior to the start of the exam period. In this way, the gap days can be used to work back through the revision topics

2. Dispersed: this method allocates days on a revolving basis so that there are no concentrated periods of study and no subject becomes stale. It can make the revision process more interesting, particularly if some of the options were not as enjoyable as you had hoped, but there is a lack of continuity of thought, especially if you have chosen a diverse range of options (see Figure 16.1)

Table 16.1 Allocating revision time

Subject	Percentage of exam	Difficulty	Number of sessions
Family	50	4	10
Medical	50	3	17
Company	100	1	22
International	60	2	18
Criminology	25	5	8

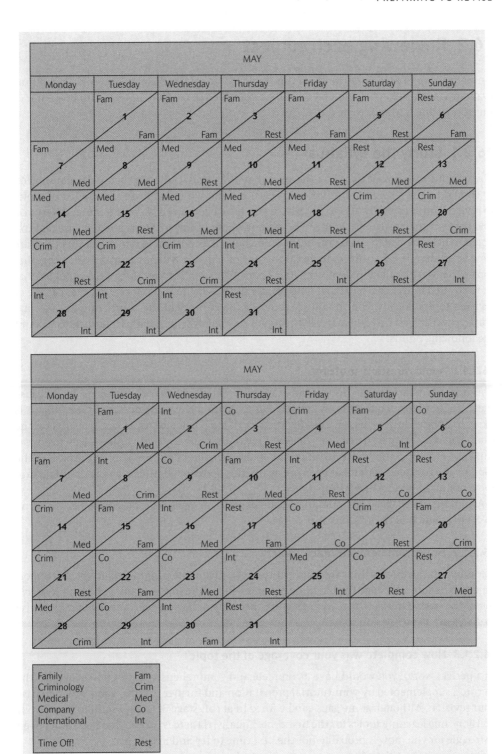

Figure 16.1 Clustered and dispersed revision timetables

16.2 Reviewing each subject

Once you have worked out how much time to devote to each subject, you need to spend time evaluating each subject on which you will be examined so that you have a plain understanding of how much work is to be done.

16.2.1 Study the syllabus

The syllabus will provide details of the areas that have been studied in that particular subject, so should be the starting point for your revision from which you can make a list of topics to revise. Think carefully about any advice you have been given by your lecturers: were you told that any topics were not going to be examined, for example? Many students use revision books to help them at this stage of their studies, but it is important to remember that these are generic guides, so may contain material that is not on your syllabus or may omit altogether topics that were studied in depth on your course. The aim is to produce a list of topics that were covered in the course so that you can use this to ensure you select a sufficient range of revision topics. Ideally, you should try to revise the entirety of the course but, failing that, aim to cover at least three-quarters of the topics covered by your syllabus, taking into account the following points.

16.2.1.1 Avoid question spotting

This involves making predictions about exam content on the basis of past papers. Just because there has not been a question on a particular topic for a few years does not mean that it is likely to appear on your paper. Equally, the fact that a particular topic has appeared on the exam paper for the past three years does not mean that it is any more or less likely to appear this year. Finally, do not make assumptions about the content of the exam on the basis of the topic of any coursework that has been set; again, this does not eliminate it as a potential exam topic nor make it more likely to appear.

Avoid this unreliable (but popular) method of selecting revision topics in favour of aiming to cover as much of the syllabus as possible.

16.2.1.2 How prominent was each topic?

The emphasis given to a topic by your lecturers can give some insight into its overall importance to the subject, hence the likelihood that it will feature in the exam. For example, if five out of the twelve weeks in tort were given to the study of negligence, it does not make sense to disregard it as a revision topic.

16.2.1.3 How complete was your coverage of the topic?

In a perfect world, you would have a complete and comprehensive set of notes taken at the lectures, supplemented by your tutorial preparation and further reading upon which to base your revision. Although some gaps can be filled in at this stage, it is not useful to spend your revision time learning topics for the first time. Equally, if there is a topic that has always been a struggle for you, now is probably not the best time to try and master it.

Once you have a list of topics to revise in each subject, you can start to slot these into your revision timetable. Do bear in mind that you will need to be realistic in allocating time to any particular topic; it would be unrealistic to expect to cover all of negligence in a single half-day session. Setting yourself unrealistic goals means that you will struggle to meet them, which can lead you to lose motivation and to feel overwhelmed by the whole revision and examination process. It is better to overestimate the amount of time that it will take to revise a particular topic and then give yourself a reward when you finish with time to spare.

16.2.2 What is the format of the exam in each subject?

Some institutions have a single universal format for examination papers which means that they are always the same length and involve the same number of questions. If your institution does not adopt this approach, make sure that you find out the length and format of the exam in each subject you are sitting. This is essential information to have during the revision period because it can give an indication of the level of detail that is expected in each answer and the breadth of revision of the subject as a whole that is needed.

Make sure you know the answers to the following questions in relation to each subject that you are sitting.

16.2.2.1 How long is the exam?

This can be a good indicator of the depth of analysis expected in each answer when considered in conjunction with the number of questions that must be answered. For example, if there is a requirement to answer two questions in a two-hour exam paper, more detail will be needed to answer the questions than would be the case if there was a requirement to answer four questions in the same time period. It is also useful to know how much time to allocate to each question so that you use your time in the exam room effectively and can practise writing answers within the relevant timeframe as part of the revision process (see section 16.3.4).

16.2.2.2 How many questions are there?

It is also important to know how much choice there is in terms of questions: a paper that requires you to answer four questions out of six is likely to be far more challenging than one that requires you to answer four out of ten. It is also the case that a smaller choice of questions implies either that the entirety of the syllabus will not be examined or that a range of topics will be combined in a single question. You can obtain a good idea of the approach taken at your institution by looking at a range of past papers.

16.2.2.3 Are there any compulsory questions?

Compulsory questions can be a gift or a curse. Some institutions include compulsory questions on important issues within a subject but advise students in advance what this will be, so that they know to include it in their revision. Other institutions include compulsory questions but give no guidance as to the subject matter, which means that thorough revision of the entire syllabus is essential.

16.2.2.4 What type of paper is it?

Closed-book examinations are traditional but many institutions are moving towards alternative methods such as open-book exams (where certain textbooks or other materials such as statute books may be taken into the examination room) or seen papers (where some or all of the questions are released to the students in advance).

Each type of paper requires a slightly different approach to revision. In general, it is advisable to revise open-book exams as if they were closed-book but with the additional requirement that you are familiar with the layout of the book, as you do not want to waste valuable exam time fumbling around the index.

16.2.2.5 What is the format of the paper?

Some exam papers give the student a free choice, for example answer any four questions from eight, whereas others are divided into sections with a requirement that at least one question is answered from each section. This latter approach needs to be taken into account in the revision process, so it is important that you determine the basis upon which the two sections are categorized. It might be that one half of the paper is essays whilst the other half is problem questions (quite a common practice). If so, you will have to ensure that your revision of each topic is sufficient to enable you to deal with both types of question (the revision process is different for essays and problems as will be discussed in section 16.3.6). Alternatively, the paper may be divided into sections on the basis of subject matter. For example, some tort courses have a two-part examination paper with one part dealing with negligence and the other with the remainder of the torts. In such a case, a student who was unaware of this fact may give insufficient attention to negligence as a revision topic and be significantly disadvantaged as a result.

16.2.2.6 What can you take into the exam room?

This is an issue at the planning stages of revision because you will need to make sure that you have the appropriate materials. For example, many institutions allow students to take a statute book into the exam room but place restrictions either upon which series of statute book may be used or require that the book be free from annotation.

Find out what the regulations are and ensure that you adhere to them (it is very off-putting for students to have their material removed in the exam room because of non-compliance). If you can take materials into the exam room, make sure that you familiarize yourself with them as part of the revision process to avoid any waste of time fumbling around the book in the examination.

All this information should be readily available to you. If you are not sure, it is worth asking your lecturer, tutor, or course leader to ensure that you have clear and accurate information.

16.2.3 Your strengths and weaknesses

It is a good idea to tailor your revision plan to suit your own ability and preferences. On a basic level, some people work well in the morning whilst others find it difficult to get started. Just before the exam is not the time to try and force new study habits upon yourself, so ensure that you devise a revision plan that fits within your usual working preferences provided, of course, that this gives you an appropriate timeframe within which to work.

You should also be aware of your strengths and weaknesses, both in terms of the topics that you study and your preparation for essays and problem questions. Some students have a strong preference for essays whilst others favour problem questions but all students will need to answer a mix of both in the examinations, so do give thought to strengthening your technique if you are weak in one or other answer style. Honing the quality of your answers should be an integral part of the revision process; remember, success in exams is not attributable exclusively to what you know/can remember but also to how you use it.

16.3 Revision strategies

It is not only the organization of revision into manageable chunks that can cause difficulties; once the structure for revision is established, it can often be hard for students to know what to do in that structure.

In other words, whilst everyone knows that they must revise, not everyone is clear on what exactly this involves. This lack of certainty leads many students to read and reread their notes in the hope that the information contained therein will stick in their minds whilst other students take this further and write and rewrite their notes. These strategies may lead to a greater familiarity with the relevant information, but it is not nearly as effective as some other revision techniques that involve more active engagement with the material.

Rather than viewing the purpose of revision as fixing information in the mind, it is preferable to see it as a process that prepares you for the exam. This involves recollection of information and the ability to use it in an effective manner. Simply rereading or rewriting notes in isolation is not sufficient to achieve the first aim and does nothing whatsoever towards the second. An active approach to revision is far more effective in achieving both of these aims.

16.3.1 Consolidating notes

Although note-making alone is not an effective revision strategy, a good set of notes is the foundation of successful revision. Ideally, these will have been produced incrementally as the course has progressed; it is not useful to start the revision process with a blank sheet of paper and nothing to revise. You should aim to take the notes that you have made during lectures, in preparation for seminars, and as part of your private study and condense them into a more concise and memorable set of key points.

Condensing your notes is an important part of the revision process. Not only does it produce a set of concise points that can be committed to memory, the actual process of filtering and recording information will contribute to your understanding of the material as you make decisions about the significance of different points and the relationship between them.

16.3.2 Recalling information

It is essential that you find a way to make the material memorable.

The first point to note is that it is much easier to recall things you have understood. This is why it is useful to review the syllabus and weed out topics that have never made any sense to you. If you have not grasped them by the time the revision period starts, it will probably require far too great an investment in time to get to grips with them now. In fact, you should only really try to incorporate topics that have always mystified you into your revision if it is absolutely necessary, for example the topic is the subject of a compulsory question or you have been puzzled by so much of the course that dealing with some difficult topics is essential.

Memory is triggered by association so it can really help the revision process if you vary your strategies so that each topic is somehow associated with something in particular. If you sit in the same place, doing the same thing for all the topics that you revise, there is nothing for your memory to latch onto in order to differentiate it from all the other legal information milling around inside your head. Try varying the following factors to create an association.

16.3.2.1 What you do to revise

If you vary the activity in which you engage when revising, this can aid recollection by linking a particular topic to a particular activity. For example, you might decide to use a topic map to revise theft, a quiz for homicide offences, and flashcards for defences. Remember that many people remember images more readily than words which could be another reason to incorporate diagrams into your revision.

16.3.2.2 Where you revise

If you vary the location where you revise, you may be able to picture the place where you were and use this to link to the information. For example, you could revise negligence in your room, damages sitting in the park, and remedies in the library. This is an effective aid to recollection, particularly if you can link this to other senses such as a particular type of music or the smell of flowers if you revised a particular topic in the park. You can also use visualization of the location to take you back to a particular lecture or tutorial where a specific topic was discussed.

16.3.2.3 Others involved in your revision

If you get other people involved in your revision, not only will you be engaging in more active revision, but you may be able to make links between the topic and the person concerned that will facilitate recollection. For example, a family member could quiz you on offer and acceptance, you could engage in collaborative revision of exclusion clauses with a friend, and explain the finer points of misrepresentation to your partner.

16.3.2.4 Use numbers, rhymes, and pictures

Make use of numbers, rhymes, and pictures to help you remember.

- For example, the elements of theft are defined in the sections which follow in the order that the words appear in the definition of theft:
- Section 1 defines theft as the dishonest (section 2) appropriation (section 3) of property (section 4) belonging to another (section 5) with the intention of permanently depriving the other of it (section 6) so if you learn the definition in section 1, this will help you to remember the section numbers of its elements
- Rhyming techniques are also useful: burglary is fine (section 9) but robbery is great (section 8)
- Pictorial techniques are particularly good in relation to case law (see Figure 16.2)

16.3.3 Active revision

Reading notes can become monotonous and even the best attempts at concentration can end with the eye gliding over the paper without taking in anything, whilst copying out reams of notes can end up as nothing more than an exercise in handwriting. One of the most effective ways to activate the brain is to ask it to do something so try to devise strategies that are more engaging.

16.3.3.1 Revision flashcards

These are small cards that have a question or piece of information to be recalled on the front and the answer on the back. Preparing these can be useful revision in itself as it requires you to identify and note key issues. They are particularly popular as a means of revising cases, but remember that you are concerned with the facts *and* the legal principle from the case.

These cards limit the amount of information that can be recorded so should help you to keep your points brief, which will make them easier to remember (see Figure 16.3). They are portable so you can carry them with you to revise in spare moments and they contain the answers, so make it easy for others to help you with your revision by testing you even if they know nothing about the law.

16.3.3.2 Templates and quizzes

Activities which test your recollection are a particularly valuable part of revision as they enable you to assess how much you do know and how much work you still have to do. These are both activities that you can do as part of your revision and are particularly useful for

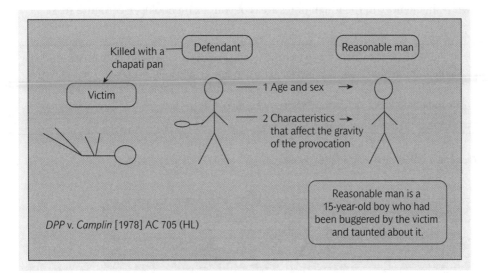

Figure 16.2 Using pictures to remember case law

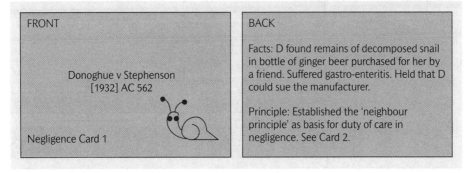

Figure 16.3 A revision flashcard

testing how much you can remember from one session to the next if you use the first session to prepare a template or quiz that you will complete in the session that follows.

A template is a paragraph that explains a particular case, principle, or concept but which leaves out certain key words and phrases (see Figure 16.4).

The preparation of a template is as much a part of the revision process as the test of recollection that it offers once it is completed, as preparation requires the student to consider what information is essential about a topic and to omit appropriate key words. Equally, the preparation of a quiz requires that you give thought to the construction of sensible questions. You might find quizzes a useful way to engage in collaborative revision with other students.

16.3.3.3 Diagrams and flow charts

Visual representations of information can be a great asset during revision in terms of enabling you to see the entirety of a large topic at a glance. This can be useful in helping you to understand and remember the relationships between the elements of an offence or a set of offences. The preparation of a flow chart or diagram will make you really think about these relationships and, once in the exam room, you should be able to visualize the diagram which is an excellent way of jogging your memory as to its contents. You could scribble the diagram down from memory in the rough notes areas of your exam booklet (see Figure 16.5).

> JUDICAL REVIEW is a process by which the…court exercises its…jurisdiction to review the decisions of…In order to bring an action for judicial review, an applicant must have…, meaning that he must have a…interest in the case, and bring the claim…and at least within…months. There are three grounds for judicial review which were identifi ed by Lord…in the…case: these grounds are (1)…(2)…and (3)…

Figure 16.4 A template for judicial review revision

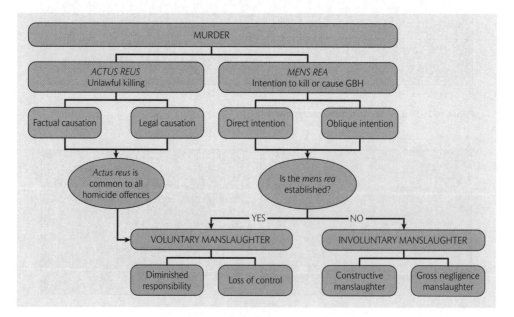

Figure 16.5 A murder flow chart

16.3.3.4 Recorded notes

Making a recording of your notes that you can play back can be a good way of adding variety to the way in which your mind receives information and can help you to make effective use of spare periods of time, such as when travelling by car or train, sitting in the bath, or lying in bed at night (although the merits of playing recordings through the night are hotly debated—do make sure that you have proper rest during the busy revision period).

A variation upon this theme is to record a group of friends discussing a revision topic and listen to this, bearing in mind that you have less control over the accuracy of the content.

16.3.3.5 Free-flow writing

Free-flow writing is a fantastic way to generate ideas and you will often be surprised by how much you do actually know. You make a note of a word or phrase at the top of a blank sheet of paper or fresh document and allow yourself a set period of time in which to write absolutely everything that comes to mind about this topic without any concern for structure, order, or grammatical sense. Any period of time from one to five minutes will work well for revision and it might be an idea to start short and build up to longer periods of time as your knowledge increases. It can be a useful starting point for revision, so that you can identify what you know and, more importantly, what you do not know by comparing your free-flowing writing with your notes.

Remember that although free-flow writing can be a useful way of unlocking information stored in the brain, it is not necessarily a useful technique to use if you become stuck in the exam itself as this could encourage you to spill all sorts of unrelated information onto the page when what is required is that you provide a focused answer to the question. It is a good technique to use for revision and could help if your mind goes blank during the exam, provided that you do this as part of your rough work and extrapolate relevant points to use in your actual answer.

16.3.4 Practice answers

Writing practice answers is *the* most important part of revision. This involves finding questions from past papers or from tutorials, for example, and writing an answer in the same constraints as would apply during the exam:

- Hand-written
- Within a set time
- Without notes

Students are often disinclined to write practice answers and give two main explanations for this reluctance.

16.3.4.1 Cannot see the value of the exercise

It is sometimes said that there is no point in using revision time to write practice answers to past questions because those questions will not come up on the paper. This is true but the value of the exercise lies not in finding a perfect answer to a question that is likely to appear on the paper but in strengthening your ability to tackle any question that appears on the paper.

As stated earlier in this chapter, exams do not just test *what* you know, they also test *how* you use that knowledge. Therefore, a good level of legal knowledge and the ability to recall it is not desperately useful unless you can use it to construct a coherent essay or produce a balanced answer to a problem question. These are inherently practical skills which require practice to get them right. You would not expect to be able to drive a car after having read a book about how to do so; you need to practise actual driving on the road. The same applies to essays and problem questions; you cannot expect to be able to produce effective answers in the exam without practice.

Even if you have written essays and answered problem questions as part of your coursework, this is not the same as doing so in the exam room without notes and within tight time-constraints. Writing practice answers, in conditions that are as close as possible to those that you will encounter in the exam, enables you to test, review, and refine your technique and is the key to producing effective and successful exams in the exam room.

16.3.4.2 No feedback on the accuracy of the answer

Some students question the value of the exercise if there is no means of determining whether the content is correct or of receiving comment on the quality of the answer and what needs to be improved. In other words, it does not seem to be a useful exercise unless the end result is marked.

This is a misguided standpoint. Part of the value of the exercise lies in familiarizing yourself with the amount that you can write within the given timeframe and it gets you used to the requirement to engage with a question and formulate a focused answer under pressure. Unlike coursework, you do not have time in the exam to think about what the question means, to ask lecturers for guidance, or to talk it through with your friends, so writing an exam answer is an unfamiliar skill and one that needs practice.

Moreover, it is not true that there is no feedback available on the content and quality of your answers. If you ask, you may find that your lecturers are prepared to offer comment on at least one practice answer and, of course, there is nothing to stop you evaluating your own answer. In fact, the ability to engage in critical evaluation of one's own work is a key skill that you should be striving to develop and this is a perfect opportunity to put it into practice. You can compare the content with your notes to spot any material that you have left out and reflect upon aspects of the answer such as structure, clarity, language, and detail.

This exercise may be more effective if you enlist some other students to take part. Several students could attempt the same question and then exchange answers in order to comment on each other's work. This will be particularly useful if it generates some discussion of the legal issues that are relevant to the answer, for example it could lead to a debate about whether or not a particular point should have been included in the answer or which of the range of cases used was the most effective. Never underestimate the contribution to improving your own essay writing or problem-solving skills that is made by engaging in constructive criticism of the work of others.

Overall, then, the benefits of writing practice answers are:

- Getting the 'feel' of how much can be written within the amount of time available per question in your examination
- Testing how much information you are able to recall about a particular topic
- Practising the skills that are necessary to use the information effectively: essays require analytical skills whilst problem questions need application of the law to the facts
- Enhancing your knowledge and understanding of a topic by reviewing your own answers or those written by others

16.3.5 Collaborative revision

One of the best ways to make revision more effective and more enjoyable is to work with others. There are a range of ways that have already been mentioned earlier in this chapter in which you can involve others in your revision, but the following are a few more suggestions of things that other students have found particularly useful.

16.3.5.1 Study groups

If you form a study group with other students, you will be able to share the workload of revision amongst the members of the group. You could:

- Agree that each person will prepare a set of revision notes on a particular topic and distribute these amongst the group. With four people in a group, you would have notes on eight topics even though you had only prepared two sets of notes yourself. Obviously, you are dependent on the work of others, so it is useful to choose students that you trust to do the work and to do it to a reasonable quality

- Select a topic for discussion or a task to complete as a group and either record the activity or nominate someone to take notes, so that you have a record of what was said and done. For example, you could agree to spend an hour working out what the key elements of negligence are and what cases should be used to support the main principles

- Prepare templates and quizzes to share with the group or write practice answers and compare them with the rest of the group. One group once spent a great deal of time making a version of Trivial Pursuit that replaced the usual categories with the six subjects that they were studying in their second year which they then played at every opportunity. It was so good that other students offered to pay to take part! This shows that you can make revision into an enjoyable activity but do be wary of devising activities that take too much time to set up and organize. These students came up with the idea at Christmas and spread the writing of questions across several months

Not only do these activities split the workload of revision, they all encourage you to talk to others about the law and this can be one of the more effective methods of gaining an understanding of the material.

16.3.5.2 Talking to others

Some people say that you can only be sure that you understand something fully if you are able to explain it to someone else in a way that they understand. As such, this can be a useful factor to take into account with your revision. Take a concept and explain it to a friend or family member who does not have any background in the law. Try and make it as clear as possible but without unnecessary detail. Give them an opportunity to ask questions to clarify any points that are unclear and then ask them to explain the concept back to you. If they are able to give you a relatively clear and detailed account, then your explanation to them was a good one.

16.3.6 Essays and problem questions

A key factor to take into account as part of your revision strategy is whether you are revising a particular topic in preparation to answer an essay or a problem question. Many students fail to take this into account and just tackle each topic of their revision in the same way. However, as essays and problem questions have different requirements, both in terms of the nature of the content and the type of skills involved in their production, it stands to reason that the approach to revision in preparation for each type of question would be qualitatively different.

16.3.6.1 Problem questions

These assess your ability to disentangle a mass of interwoven facts in order to make a determination about the legal liability of the parties by applying the current law to the factual situation. As such, it requires knowledge of the current law and an awareness of the variety of ways in which it could be applied as demonstrated in case law.

16.3.6.2 Essays

Essays involve a greater depth of knowledge about the topic which might include historical information about the evolution of the law and the ability to comment on future developments by way of evaluation of proposals for reform. The emphasis here is on the ability to consider the law in depth, to address policy considerations, and to engage in critical evaluation of the efficacy of the law. Figure 16.6 illustrates the differences between essays and problem questions in relation to oblique intention in homicide offences.

You will find a more detailed consideration of the requirements of essays and problem questions in chapter 13 and chapter 15. There will also be some discussion of factors that are important in tackling each of these types of question in the sections that follow.

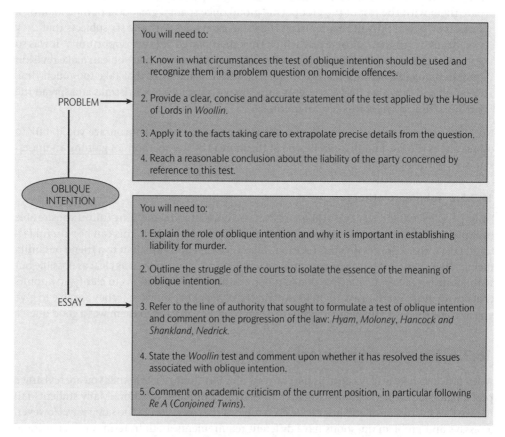

PROBLEM →

You will need to:

1. Know in what circumstances the test of oblique intention should be used and recognize them in a problem question on homicide offences.

2. Provide a clear, concise and accurate statement of the test applied by the House of Lords in *Woollin*.

3. Apply it to the facts taking care to extrapolate precise details from the question.

4. Reach a reasonable conclusion about the liability of the party concerned by reference to this test.

OBLIQUE INTENTION

You will need to:

1. Explain the role of oblique intention and why it is important in establishing liability for murder.

2. Outline the struggle of the courts to isolate the essence of the meaning of oblique intention.

ESSAY →

3. Refer to the line of authority that sought to formulate a test of oblique intention and comment on the progression of the law: *Hyam, Moloney, Hancock and Shankland, Nedrick*.

4. State the *Woollin* test and comment upon whether it has resolved the issues associated with oblique intention.

5. Comment on academic criticism of the currrent position, in particular following *Re A (Conjoined Twins)*.

Figure 16.6 The different requirements of essays and problem questions

16.4 The exam

It is probably true to say that however much revision you have done and however diligently you have followed the advice in the earlier section of this chapter, you will probably still quail at the thought of the exam itself. Most people dislike exams and suffer from varying degrees of nerves. The following sections are designed to address a range of issues related to the exam with a view to ensuring that you are able to put in a good performance that makes the most of your hard work during the revision period and throughout the year.

It is important that you realize there is not an expectation that you will produce coursework quality answers during exam conditions. Naturally, you will be able to produce less detailed answers during the exam but that does not mean that there should be any sacrifice of the other elements that contribute towards the final answer. Although the primary purpose of the exam is to test knowledge and understanding, it also assesses your ability to use the law to produce structured and discursive essays and methodical answers to problem questions, so it is important to use the exam as an opportunity to demonstrate your legal skills as well as your legal knowledge.

16.4.1 Be prepared

It is important that you have everything with you that you will need during the examination. Many students feel quite stressed on the day of the exam, so it might help you to feel less flustered if you gather your things together the day before. Work out what you are likely to need (pens, pencil for rough work, ruler for underlining case names, highlighter to mark key points on the question paper) and ensure that you have spares as back-up in case anything breaks or runs out of ink during the exam. It would also be worth checking to see if your institution has a list of prohibited items such as correction fluid.

Give some advance thought to any materials you are permitted to take into the examination room. For example, if you are allowed to use a statute book, does your institution specify that it is from any particular series or require that it is free from annotation? If the latter applies, check through your statute book to make sure it is free from any markings, as you may have made notes earlier in the course that you have since forgotten. Checks are made in the exam room and materials that do not comply with the rules will be removed.

16.4.2 Follow the rubric

The rubric is the explanatory notes or instructions that accompany the exam and are generally found on the front of the paper giving instructions about the format of the paper, the number of questions that must be answered, and the timing of the exam.

Once in the exam room, it will be important to take a few moments to check the rubric on the exam paper to ensure that you are clear about what is expected from you in the exam. Do not assume that the requirements of this exam will be the same as any other that you have sat previously unless you are absolutely certain that there is a uniform format for all exams in your department or institution. It is important to check the rubric as it will draw your attention to any compulsory questions or any requirements to answer questions for a particular part of the paper.

16.4.3 Read the paper

Some institutions give you a short period of reading time at the beginning of the exam, during which you can read the paper but you cannot start writing your answers. If your institution does not have this policy, make sure you take a few minutes to read the paper carefully; it does not matter if everyone else has started writing straight away. A few minutes spent analyzing the paper and thinking about the requirements of each question and whether or not you would be able to answer it will save you time overall.

It can be useful to make notes about the questions, either on the paper itself (if this is permitted), or on rough paper (if it is provided) or at the back of your answer booklet, to ensure that you have a clear idea of the scope of the questions. This will enable you to make an informed decision about which question to answer. You may find this technique useful for analyzing the paper:

1. Write the question numbers on a sheet of paper, leaving a gap of a few lines between each number and note the main topic of the question and whether it is an essay or problem question

2. On the basis of this information, eliminate any questions that you feel you would prefer not to answer. For example, if there is an essay on misrepresentation and you have a preference for problem questions and did not revise misrepresentation, you can probably rule out the possibility of answering that question from the outset

3. For the remaining possibilities, look at the questions again and note a few more details about them that might help you to appreciate what they require and whether you might want to tackle them. Bear in mind that it is not enough to know a lot about the topic, you have to be able to answer that particular question

4. If you are not sure whether or not you would be able to answer a particular question, try making a quick list of the issues you think are raised by the question to see how much information you can generate

5. Make a note of the questions you feel you could definitely answer. Hopefully this will be sufficient to tackle the paper. If you have ticked more questions than are needed, you will have to make a judgement about which of these to tackle based upon your preferences for the subject matter. If you have not ticked sufficient questions to complete the paper, you will have to revisit some of those that you have crossed off and reconsider whether you could attempt an answer (see Figure 16.7)

16.4.4 Plan each answer

It does not take a great deal of time out of the overall time available to write an answer plan and this investment of time tends to pay immense dividends as it leads to a stronger and more focused answer. It is important that you realize it is not just knowledge that attracts marks in the exams, but the way this knowledge is deployed in response to the question. As any form of assessment, exams assess not just what you know but what you do with that knowledge, so it is crucial to your success that your answers reflect a range of legal skills, including the construction of a structured essay and a methodical answer to a problem question, as well as your legal knowledge.

16.4.4.1 Structure

Students who start writing straight away without making a plan often produce a poorly structured essay that is peppered with asterisks and arrows denoting paragraphs that need to be inserted. Unplanned answers also tend to lack logical progression as the student raises different points as they come to mind and this impedes clarity of expression, limits the possibility

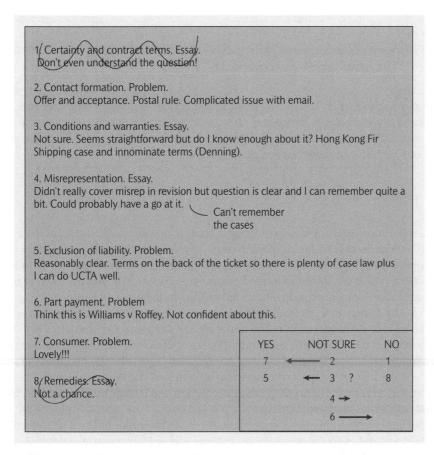

1. Certainty and contract terms. Essay.
Don't even understand the question!

2. Contact formation. Problem.
Offer and acceptance. Postal rule. Complicated issue with email.

3. Conditions and warranties. Essay.
Not sure. Seems straightforward but do I know enough about it? Hong Kong Fir
Shipping case and innominate terms (Denning).

4. Misrepresentation. Essay.
Didn't really cover misrep in revision but question is clear and I can remember quite a
bit. Could probably have a go at it.   Can't remember
                                                the cases

5. Exclusion of liability. Problem.
Reasonably clear. Terms on the back of the ticket so there is plenty of case law plus
I can do UCTA well.

6. Part payment. Problem
Think this is Williams v Roffey. Not confident about this.

7. Consumer. Problem.
Lovely!!!

8. Remedies. Essay.
Not a chance.

YES	NOT SURE	NO
7 ←	2	1
5	← 3 ?	8
	4 →	
	6 ——→	

Figure 16.7 Analyzing the question paper

for depth of analysis (in an essay), and carries a real risk that important material will be omitted (a particular issue with answers to problem questions).

Another major issue with answers to problem questions is that students tend to 'jump in' and deal with the most obvious issue raised by the question. This is usually something that reminds them of the facts of a case or they can remember the issue being discussed in a seminar. By tackling the obvious point first, this weakens the structure of the answer and carries a real possibility that the issues that were raised by earlier sections of the question are never addressed.

16.4.4.2 Focus

It is imperative that you answer the question that has been asked and not the question that you had hoped would be asked. It is all too easy to focus on the overall topic of an essay question and to include all sorts of points that are relevant to the topic but have no bearing whatsoever on the specific question.

As there is no credit available for material that is included in the answer that does not answer the question, a failure to filter out information that is relevant to the topic but not the question can have a detrimental impact on the success of the answer (see Figure 16.8).

> Question
> Critically assess how developments in the past twenty years have impacted on the traditional notion of Parliamentary sovereignty expounded by Dicey.
>
> Introduction
> The development which has had the most dramatic effect on Dicey's traditional notion of Parliamentary sovereignty is membership of the European Union. This essay will outline the elements of Dicey's traditional view of sovereignty and move on to consider how this has been eroded by the provision of the European Communities Act 1972.

Figure 16.8 Focus on the question

As should be immediately obvious, this essay is going to encounter difficulties as the question specifies a focus on developments in the past twenty years, such as the coming into force of the Human Rights Act 1998 in October 2000, devolution, and the proposals for an independent Scotland, whilst the introduction to the answer makes it clear that the focus is going to be on earlier developments concerning membership of the European Union.

This may be a result of a misreading of the question; it is common for questions on sovereignty to involve a consideration of the impact of the European Communities Act 1972, so it is possible that the student has not paid sufficient attention to the actual question but has made assumptions about its requirements. Alternatively, it may be the case that the student has only revised sovereignty in relation to membership of the European Union, so cannot comment on the Human Rights Act 1998 or devolution and is adapting the question to cover material with which they are familiar.

Although these situations are common, they are both the result of bad exam practice and will result in a weak mark for this question as there will be little relevant material.

Such problems can be avoided if care is taken at the planning stage. Write the key words from the question in capitals at the top of your planning page or highlight them on the exam paper so that they are to the forefront of your mind and make a list of points for inclusion that are relevant only to this particular topic within the broader topic.

16.4.5 Writing the answer

This section will address a range of factors that you need to take into account when writing your exam answers and will lead in to a list of five of our 'top tips' for success in exams.

16.4.5.1 Timing

It is relatively common for students to run out of time and fail to complete the requisite number of questions. Avoid this by dividing the time available by the number of questions to determine how much time is available to answer each question. Factor into this the five minutes that is needed to plan each answer and make yourself a time plan for the exam. Write this down and note the time at which you need to start a fresh question and make sure that you stick to it. In a three-hour paper that requires that you answer four questions, your time plan might look something like Table 16.2.

It can also help to write the starting time alongside the relevant question on the exam paper as this might help you to keep to it. It is important that you allocate equal amounts of time for each question (unless there is not an equal weighting between them). There is

Table 16.2 Planning your time

Question	Plan	Answer	Finish
7	2pm	2.05	2.45
5	2.45	2.50	3.30
2	3.30	3.35	4.15
3	4.15	4.20	5pm

always a temptation to devote more time to the questions that you feel you can answer more proficiently but this is not a good practice.

In this example, there are four questions to be answered in three hours. Each carries equal marks, so it would be a mistake to spend the first hour-and-a-half answering your first question, the next hour answering the second, twenty minutes on the third and then having a frantic scribble for the last ten minutes to try to put something down for the final question, and yet this is exactly how many students end up allocating their time. Some students try to avoid doing this by answering the question they feel will be their weakest first on the basis that it will probably not take up so much of their time. This can be a useful strategy but it can also be dispiriting if you are disappointed with the quality of your answer. It is preferable to start with a presumption that each question will take the same amount of time and move on as soon as your chunk of time for a question has finished, irrespective of whether or not your answer is complete. You can always go back and complete the answer if you have time spare at the end.

16.4.5.2 Stick to the plan

If you have taken the time to write a plan, you should try to stick to it. If a fresh idea occurs to you whilst you are writing, rather than putting it straight into your answer, make a note of it in your rough work area and then take a moment to consider where this additional point fits within your plan, what that will do to the structure of your essay, and how it will impact on the other points that you had planned to raise. There is nothing wrong with finding fresh points to include as your answer progresses—sometimes writing out one point jogs your memory about another—but do bear in mind the need for an organized and flowing answer.

16.4.5.3 Incorporate authority

The use of authority in the exam is an issue that tends to trouble students. It is true that your answer will appear more polished and knowledgeable if you are able to incorporate some reference to authority into your answer but it is important that the use of authority demonstrates understanding rather than appearing as if a random selection of case names have been sprinkled over your exam paper.

It may seem as if there is an immense amount of case law to learn and remember but try to identify a few key cases in relation to each topic, with particular emphasis on those that demonstrate essential principles. Remember that it is more important that you know the legal principle from the case rather than the facts but that the facts might help you to demonstrate the operation of the law. Equally, do not trouble your memory with lists of case citations: the name and, if possible, the year will suffice. If you cannot call the case name to mind, draw reference to it by the use of key facts:

In a reported case in which a tramp dropped his cigarette and failed to deal with the smouldering mattress, it was held that. . .

16.4.5.4 Essays and problem questions

It is important to remember your essay writing and problem-solving skills. It is unfortunate that many students concentrate on putting words on paper in the exam and give insufficient attention to the construction of effective essays and methodical problem answers.

You may like to consult the chapters on essays (chapter 13), problem questions (chapter 15), and writing skills (chapter 10) to remind yourself of the core characteristics that should be presented in a good answer.

The following list draws attention to points that are of particular relevance in an exam context:

- Your essay should have an introduction that identifies the central issue and sets out the structure and content of the essay. This is important as it is the first impression the marker receives of the quality of your answer, so it is worth taking trouble to ensure that the impression conveyed is good

- Although there is not a requirement of the same level of detail in an essay in an exam as there would be if the same essay were set as coursework, there is still a need for analysis. A wholly descriptive answer will meet with limited success, so remember the need to present an objective and analytical discussion as part of your essay

- The key to success in problem questions lies with a methodical approach to untangling the facts and identifying the issues that need to be resolved

- Remember that the key task when answering a problem question is to reach conclusions, even tentative or contingent conclusions, about the liability of the parties. Keep your focus on this and do not become distracted into a lengthy abstract discussion of the law. If you turn the problem question into an essay, you will get very little credit

- Do not include lengthy outlines of the facts of cases in either an essay or a problem question. It may be appropriate to include some discussion of the facts but make sure this is done in a way that supports, rather than detracts from, the main thrust of your essay or your analysis of a party's liability

16.4.6 Top tips for exam success

The chapter concludes with some general pointers that should help to strengthen your exam performance.

1. Answer the correct number of questions. Some students tackle an extra question if they have done the required number and there is time remaining but you would be better advised to use that time to improve one of your existing answers as you cannot have credit for five questions if the exam requires that you answer four. Equally, some students find that they are struggling to find a question to answer and give up without completing the required number of questions. Always try a last question, even if you feel that your answer will be weak. You will know *something* of relevance to the question—perhaps more than you realize—and it will at least attract some marks whereas making no attempt will attract no marks at all

2. Make sure that your script is legible. You cannot be credited for work that cannot be deciphered. There are various policies on illegibility, so it is impossible to make a generalization about what will happen if your writing cannot be read by the examiners, but options include discounting illegible material altogether, or requiring the student to pay for the script to be typed out so that it can be read

3. Stay until the end of the exam. If you think that you have finished but there is an hour of the exam remaining, it is likely that you have not written enough, so it is important to revisit each of your answers and read them through carefully to see if anything can be added to improve their quality. Have you missed out an important issue in a problem question or omitted a key point in an essay? If you can spend that hour adding material to your answers that increases the grade of each question by two marks, that will give your paper an additional eight marks, which is almost a whole classification

4. Follow the instructions. There is no credit available for material that is outside the scope of the question, so it is essential you read the question carefully and do exactly what is asked. For example, if a problem question in criminal law sets out a series of events involving Kate and Dave and then instructs you to 'discuss Dave's liability for homicide offences', you will receive no marks whatsoever for discussing Kate's liability for murder, or Dave's liability for theft or non-fatal offences. Irrelevant material attracts no credit and takes up time that could be spent writing material that would gain marks

5. Keep calm. Many students find exams stressful and get into such a keyed-up state that they are not functioning properly in the exam. This is counter-productive as it interferes with their performance and this leads to a self-perpetuating cycle as they receive poor exam results, so become even more anxious in the next set of exams. If you are aware that you suffer in this way, take steps to deal with this prior to the exam. There are some excellent courses on dealing with exam nerves and it may be that some are on offer at your institution. Investigate what help is available and take advantage of it

 Self-test questions

 Unlike the other chapters in this book, this chapter has not included any practical exercises or self-test questions. There are, however, practical activities on the Online Resource Centre that are relevant to the material covered in this chapter, including an exercise in marking exam answers written by other students to help you to identify the good and to learn from their mistakes! You will also find further examples of revision flashcards and revision templates that you may find useful in helping you put together your own revision materials.

CHAPTER SUMMARY

Preparing to revise

- Take time to reflect on the requirements of the exams and the content of each subject to be examined in order to prepare an effective revision timetable

- Tailor your programme of revision to your own strengths and weaknesses as a student

Revision strategies

- Try to avoid exclusive reliance on reading and rewriting notes as a revision strategy as this is a passive approach which does not test your ability to use the material effectively

- Vary the activities that you use as part of your revision. This is to help you to remain engaged and interested in the process and it will aid recollection in the exam

- Consider using a range of methods to record information: written notes, diagrams, pictures, and tape-recordings all engage the brain in a different way

- Involving others in your revision distributes the workload and enriches the revision process

- Writing sample answers is the most effective revision activity as it orientates you to the amount of writing that can be done in the timeframe and enables you to make your mistakes prior to the exam and learn from them in order to strengthen your exam performance

Exam technique

- Make sure you are fully equipped for the exam with writing equipment, any materials that you are entitled to take into the exam room, and a clear knowledge of where and when the exam will take place

- Read the question paper carefully, including the rubric, and analyze each question to determine its requirements so that you can make decisions about which questions to answer at the outset

- Allocate your time equally between the questions and remember to include a five-minute period of planning and, preferably, time at the end to read through your answers, making any necessary amendments

- Do not forget that the ordinary requirements of structure, language, analysis, and application that are applicable to essays and problem questions are still needed in the exam. Answers that demonstrate legal skills as well as legal knowledge tend to be more successful

- Remember to include reference to authority to support your answer

- Answer the required number of questions—no more and no less—in legible handwriting using all of the time available. Pay particular attention to any instructions that accompany the question as there are no marks available for moving outside the requirements of the question

PART III
Practical legal skills

This final part of the book covers some practical legal skills: namely presentations, mooting, and negotiation. These will help you move beyond online and written study to give you a broader range of real-life legal skills. The first chapter in this part will give you the skills you need in order to prepare and deliver an effective oral presentation, covering the issues of content as well as those relating to timing, combating nerves, and engaging the interest of your audience. The second chapter moves on to discuss mooting, which offers unparalleled opportunities for the development of the skills associated with the delivery of a comprehensive and persuasive oral argument as well as providing an opportunity to develop your research skills and enhance your ability to construct and organize a coherent legal argument. Finally, this part will conclude with an introduction to negotiation, which will give you an opportunity to develop a feel for how the law operates in practice and how it affects the lives of real people.

Presentation skills

17

INTRODUCTION

This chapter will draw upon some of the material covered in previous sections of the book that focused upon helping you to locate and understand the law (Part 1) in order to prepare and deliver an effective oral presentation. This will start by outlining some guidelines on preparing a presentation, including selecting an appropriate topic and making decisions about the use of supplementary materials such as handouts or PowerPoint slides. The chapter will then move to consider issues relating to the delivery of the presentation, including matters such as timing, combating nerves, and engaging the interest of the audience.

Many students are reluctant to give an oral presentation. For some students, this aversion is so extreme that they will avoid taking optional subjects that include a compulsory presentation element, even if the subject is otherwise one that they would like to study. These feelings are entirely natural; an oral presentation focuses the attention of many people on a single person which makes it a very nerve-wracking situation even for otherwise confident students. However, the ability to present information orally is a core skill for most professionals, not just those working within the law, so it is essential that you overcome any qualms about addressing others. Like anything else, the prospect of giving a presentation is daunting only until you know that you can do it proficiently. Many people are not natural speakers and will always quail at the thought of addressing even a small audience, but the fear does recede with practice so it would be extremely valuable if part of your university development included some attempts to overcome your anxiety about public speaking. This is particularly important given the growing tendency amongst prospective employers to require a presentation from applicants for work placements and training contracts. This chapter aims to equip you to prepare and deliver an easy-to-follow and engaging presentation.

LEARNING OUTCOMES

After studying this chapter, you will be able to:

- Select an appropriate topic that fits within the constraints of your course

- Conduct effective research into your presentation topic

- Construct an organized and flowing presentation

- Prepare some appropriate visual aids and use them effectively

- Understand the importance of practising the presentation

- Deal with common problems associated with nerves

- Deliver a comprehensive and engaging presentation

- Take questions from the audience with confidence

- Reflect upon your performance in order to strengthen future presentations

17.1 The presentation process

For most people faced with the need to deliver a presentation, the focus is on the actual delivery of the material. It is usual to think of 'the presentation' as the time-slot in which the material is communicated to the audience. Whilst this is clearly an important time, most of the work required for an effective presentation will be complete before you get to your feet in front of your audience. Planning and preparation are essential prerequisites of a good presentation and yet this 'behind the scenes' activity tends to receive very little attention.

Most students accept that they have to do *something* before standing up and speaking, but there seems to be general uncertainty as to what form this preparation might take and how exactly it prepares you to speak for the required amount of time.

One of the problems seems to be that students omit an essential stage of presentation preparation, treating it as a two-stage process (see Figure 17.1).

Although this approach does serve the purpose of transmitting the information to the audience, this is not necessarily packaged in a particularly palatable form. In fact, many student presentations are extremely boring because of the way in which the material is delivered: listening to someone read their notes for ten minutes is not in the least engaging for the audience and it can be very off-putting for the presenter to look around and see a distracted and bored audience.

To overcome these problems, it is valuable to insert a further stage in between research and delivery (see Figure 17.2).

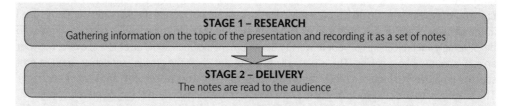

Figure 17.1 Two-stage presentation process

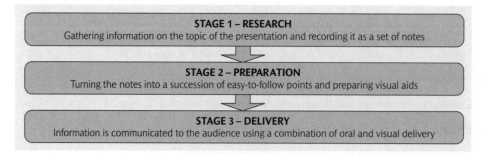

Figure 17.2 Three-stage presentation process

As you will see, by inserting a middle step in the process, the end stage is also different and as a result the presentation is far more engaging for the audience.

It is important to consider a fourth stage that takes place after the presentation is complete. This stage involves a period of review in which the presenter takes stock of the way in which the presentation was received and seeks to identify examples of good and bad practice. The reflection stage maximizes the learning impact of the presentation and should enable you to strengthen future performances (see Figure 17.3).

Each of these stages will now be considered in turn to guide you through the process of preparing, constructing, and delivering a presentation as well as providing comment on the reflection stage.

17.2 Research stage

It is always tempting to see the delivery of the presentation itself—the end product—as being of primary importance. After all, it is this that determines the success (or otherwise) of the presentation, irrespective of whether success is measured in terms of the response of the audience or, in the case of an assessed presentation, the mark awarded. However, an effective end product is only possible if the groundwork has been done properly; it is for this reason that the 'five Ps' are often used to emphasize the importance of the pre-delivery stages of a presentation (see Figure 17.4).

17.2.1 Choosing a topic

In some instances, particularly if the presentation is part of assessed coursework or is a compulsory non-assessed part of a course, the topic of the presentation will be allocated to you. Although this gives you no scope to choose your subject matter, it does ensure that you have a workable presentation topic that gives you a clear direction for your research. This means the topic 'fits' within the time allocated (or is capable of 'fitting' within it), that there is sufficient material available for you to research the topic, and that it is sufficiently linked to the relevant course material.

In the absence of a predetermined topic, you will have to choose an area of law upon which to base your presentation. This can be a tricky business as the success or otherwise of your presentation may depend upon the choice of subject matter, so give it some serious thought and take the following factors into account.

STAGE 4 – REFLECTION
Critical evaluation of the performance in order to improve future presentations

Figure 17.3 The reflection stage

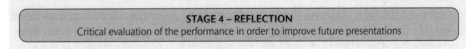

Proper **P**lanning **P**revents **P**oor **P**erformance!

Figure 17.4 The 'five Ps'

17.2.1.1 Time frame

Choosing an appropriate topic will depend upon the time frame available for your presentation: obviously, a greater level of detail is expected in a forty-five-minute presentation than would be the case in a ten-minute slot at the start of a tutorial. Never try to cram too much information into the time available. Content overload is a major weakness in a presentation as it tends to leave the audience reeling; it is better to leave material out than to overload your audience with too much information delivered at high speed.

For example, if you have to deliver a thirty-five-minute presentation on employment law, your initial decision might be to focus on sex discrimination. After some preliminary research, you are likely to discover that this is too broad to cover in this time frame. You will therefore need to select a smaller issue such as pregnancy-related dismissals or discrimination on the basis of sexual orientation. It may help to phrase your presentation title as a question—for example, 'how effective has the English law been in protecting postoperative transsexual people from discrimination?' and ask your lecturer if they feel that the topic will fit within the time frame of the presentation. If your lecturer offers an opinion on the breadth of your topic, do take this into account; they have a clearer idea of the material available and the amount of detail that is appropriate for the time frame of the presentation. Setting the boundaries of your presentation too wide or too narrow can have adverse consequences on its overall success.

- **Too wide**: you will struggle to fit all the information into the time available, so will end up either rushing your delivery, leaving out relevant material, or taking too superficial an approach

- **Too narrow**: you will run out of things to say or fill up time by repeating points or including superfluous material that weakens the focus of the presentation

17.2.1.2 Assessment criteria

If the presentation is assessed, students should check the assessment criteria to determine what attributes are regarded as important and what weight is given to them. Is there an equal emphasis on both content and presentation style, for example, and is there any credit available for the use of visual aids?

This can be useful in helping you to select a topic. For example, if credit is available for demonstrating independent research skills, selecting a topic that is covered in detail in the textbook is not going to enable you to demonstrate this skill, so your presentation will not attract a great deal of credit for this element. It may help to make a list of the desirable characteristics of a successful presentation from the assessment criteria and note how your topic will satisfy these characteristics.

It is essential that you know what you are aiming to do and even if it feels as if the answer is to 'survive the presentation', the ultimate answer will probably be to 'get a good mark in the presentation'; the latter is more likely if you have the assessment criteria in mind from the outset.

17.2.1.3 Aim

Make sure that you are clear about what you are trying to achieve in your presentation. If you have been given a title, what does it suggest about the aim of your presentation? Is it to introduce the topic, to give an overview, or to deal with a particular issue in depth? If you are unclear, seek clarification from your course materials or by asking your lecturer.

If you have free rein to select your own topic, it will add focus to your presentation and make the preparation process easier if you identify a clear aim to be achieved by your presentation. Keep this to the forefront of your mind when researching and planning your presentation. When delivering it, remember to tell your audience what your aim is from the outset as this will give them clear guidance on what to expect from your presentation.

17.2.1.4 Audience

Although you may have subjective aims in mind when delivering a presentation, such as obtaining a good mark, not looking foolish in front of your friends, or impressing a prospective employer, the predominant aim of any presentation is to communicate something of value to the audience. To be able to do this, you need to have some idea of what the audience wants, needs, or expects from your presentation. In other words, in order to choose an appropriate topic and select content at a suitable level, you need to understand how much your audience already knows about the subject matter.

If you are presenting to your peer group as part of an assessment, you have the advantage of knowing exactly what level of prior knowledge they have about your topic and this will help you to select an appropriate level of depth. Equally, your assessment may specify the level of expertise of your audience by providing instructions such as 'imagine you have been asked to deliver a thirty-minute presentation to senior partners at your law firm that updates them on a recent development in employment law' which will help you to determine what sort of depth is required and this in turn will be useful in selecting an appropriate topic.

17.2.1.5 Available material

You will need to make sure that there is sufficient source material available to enable you to research your presentation topic thoroughly. This means that you need to be able to identify a range of source books, articles, reports, and cases on your chosen topic and be able to obtain them in good time to prepare for your presentation. The increasing availability of online resources may help here, but remember the importance of ensuring that material that you encounter online comes from a reputable academic or professional source.

You will find some valuable guidance on evaluating the source of online materials contained in chapter 7. Remember that anyone can post anything on the Internet, so you should not rely on material for academic purposes unless it comes from a reputable source.

17.2.1.6 Interest and popularity

If you have free choice, it is also useful to take into account any interests of your own within the subject as it is always easier to research something that interests you and your enthusiasm for the topic will communicate to the audience, making your presentation more engaging.

It can also be sensible to take into account any information you have about the choice of topic made by other students. This can be significant if there is an entirely free choice of topic for an assessed presentation as it will be difficult to make your treatment of a topic seem original and interesting if it covers the same material as ten other students have already presented. In short, overlap with topics chosen by others will make your presentation seem uninspired even if it is the result of a great deal of hard work and independent research. If you are committed to presenting on a popular topic, try to find an unusual slant on the material.

17.2.2 Researching the topic

Once you have a clear idea of the topic of the presentation, you can start with the research.

17.2.2.1 Start early

Try to leave as much time as possible to do this before the presentation date in case it is difficult to acquire some of the material that you need. That said, it is also important to know when to stop the research and start the construction of the presentation as both take time and both make an important contribution to the finished product. Aim for a roughly equal division of the time available between research and construction; you can always go back to research if you find you have overlooked something once you start to put the presentation together.

17.2.2.2 Be focused yet flexible

Achieve a good balance between keeping your focus and being receptive to new material. If your topic was allocated to you, there is far less flexibility to pursue different avenues of research but if you have some element of choice, take some time to follow up potentially interesting side-issues as they may change for the better the slant of your presentation. Remember, however, that if you change the focus of your presentation, you will need to change the title to reflect this. If you were required to submit a title in advance, you should check to find out whether changes are permissible.

17.2.2.3 Be effective in your note-taking

Remember, there is little to be gained by copying reams of material from books and journals, but do ensure that you have a clear and complete record of the sources you have used. Although you are presenting your material orally, you may still be required to produce a bibliography or a research journal and, of course, you may wish to include quotations or extracts from these sources on any handout that you produce to accompany your presentation, in which case you will need to be able to provide full bibliographic details.

   In particular, you should take care to keep a note of any ideas you have during the research process about how the material could be used in the presentation. Try to devise a note-taking strategy that allows you to differentiate between factual material and your ideas, for example by dividing your page into two columns or by using different coloured ink to highlight your thoughts.

   You will find more information on note-taking in chapter 9 that deals with study skills.

17.3 Preparation stage

Once you have conducted your research into your presentation topic, you will probably feel somewhat overwhelmed (a) by the volume of material that you have gathered, and (b) by the prospect of turning it into a presentation. These feelings are not unusual, but can lead to two of the key issues that limit the effectiveness of student presentations:

1. Trying to cover too much information in the time available
2. Reading from a set of notes that are not suited to oral delivery

Both of these problems can be resolved by judicious selection of material and by planning a structured presentation that is not exclusively reliant upon oral delivery but which makes use of visual aids.

17.3.1 Selection of material

It is always tempting, having devoted time and effort to conducting research, to try to make use of all the interesting facts that you have discovered. However, it is important to ensure that you do not exceed the time allocated for your presentation: in fact, if the presentation is assessed, you may actually lose marks for failing to work within the time frame stipulated. Equally, a hurried presentation that skims over a great deal of material is very difficult for the audience to follow and is likely to be a negative factor if your presentation is assessed.

Formulating a question that you will answer in your presentation is a good way to identify your focus and select relevant material as it tends to identify the 'job' that the presentation is trying to do. Once you are clear about what you are trying to achieve, you can sift through all the material you have gathered in order to eliminate that which is not relevant. As with essay writing, remember to judge the relevance of material in relation to the issue, not the topic: in other words, try not to think 'is this about provocation?' or even 'is this about the reasonable man in provocation?' but rather 'does this help me to explain the policy of the law towards the characteristics attributable to the reasonable man in provocation?'. The more specific you are in framing your issue, the easier you will find it to decide whether material is relevant.

Practical exercise

The following exercise can be used to help you determine the relevance of the material to your presentation.

1. Write your title at the top of a blank sheet of paper (or at the start of a new document).
2. Make a bullet point list of all the points that you could include.
3. Review the list, grouping similar points together and eliminating any repetition or overlap.
4. Draw three columns headed: essential, peripheral, and irrelevant and allocate each of your points to one of the columns, remembering that the question of relevance is determined by reference to the specific details of your presentation title and not to the general topic of the presentation.
5. Use this as guidance when determining the content of your presentation, starting with material that you have categorized as essential. If you still feel that you have too much information, you should repeat the exercise, this time using the three columns to divide up the points that you initially categorized as essential.

A worked example of this technique can be found on the Online Resource Centre. You might find it useful to take a few moments to look at this example and read the accompanying notes to ensure that you have a good insight into the prioritization of the material.

17.3.2 Organization of material

Once you have made a preliminary selection of the material you want to include in the presentation, you need to consider the order in which your points will be made. Bear in mind that your presentation should follow a logical progression, it should 'tell a story' and, like all

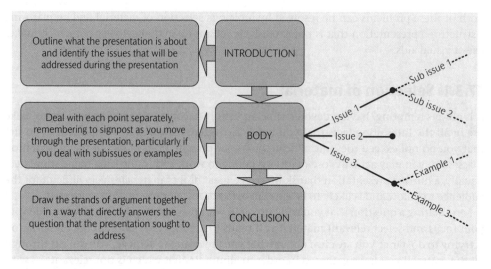

Figure 17.5 Organizing the material

good essays, it should have a beginning (introduction), middle (the bulk of the presentation, divided into a series of issues), and an end (conclusion) (see Figure 17.5).

17.3.2.1 Introduction

The introduction and conclusion should be succinct, clear, and straightforward. The introduction should outline the topic to be discussed, explain the structure and duration of the presentation (including any time allocated for questions at the end), and tell the audience why the topic is important and/or interesting. In essence, the introduction should give the audience an understanding of what is to follow and give a clear and concise account of the question that the presentation will address and the reason that this is important.

17.3.2.2 Main body

The body of the presentation can be more complicated to organize, so keep in mind the argument that you are going to advance and break this down into a series of issues and subissues. Bear in mind that one point should lead into another and that you should take care to select examples that demonstrate the point you are making and do not distract from the flow of your presentation. You may want to experiment with more than one potential structure to ensure that you find the most effective way to organize your material.

For the audience listening to the presentation, there are two tasks that need to be carried out simultaneously. First, the listeners have to digest the point you are making and, secondly, they have to slot this into the bigger picture of the topic as a whole. This can be difficult, so it is essential that you help your audience to follow the structure of the presentation with clear signposting; phrases such as 'there are three points of importance here and I shall discuss each in turn' or 'this is a powerful argument but there is an equally compelling counterargument that we must now consider'. Signposting explains to the audience how each piece of information relates to that which precedes and follows it and how it fits into the broader topic, so it is an important consideration and one which can contribute to the success of your presentation.

17.3.2.3 Conclusion

The conclusion should provide a brief summary of the material covered and a direct answer to the question addressed in the presentation. Try to think of a way to make the central message of the presentation stick in the mind of the audience by identifying a maximum of three points that you want them to remember and highlighting these.

> *You will find some examples of possible wording for introductions and conclusions on the Online Resource Centre where there is also advice on using signposting phrases that can help to guide the audience through the main body of the presentation.*

17.3.3 Using visual aids

Research into the psychology of effective communication has indicated that people take in more information from visual images than they do from listening. Therefore, it is a good idea to ensure that your presentation engages the eyes as well as the ears of the audience by using visual aids, whether in the form of a handout, use of an overhead projector or a PowerPoint presentation, or by writing/drawing on a whiteboard or flipchart as the presentation progresses.

Effective use of visual aids can achieve the following four objectives (see Figure 17.6).

1. **Aid clarity:** a successful presentation is one which can be followed by the audience with ease. Visual aids can add clarity to a presentation by helping the audience to follow the line of argument and see links between the different topics. Look at Figure 17.6 which outlines the benefits of visual aids. It has immediate impact in communicating that there are four factors to be taken into account whilst Figure 17.5 on the structure of the presentation makes it apparent that there are three stages but that the second of these is the more complex and detailed. Diagrams, graphs, illustrations, flow charts, and other devices add clarity, so visual aids can have a positive impact on the comprehensibility of your presentation.

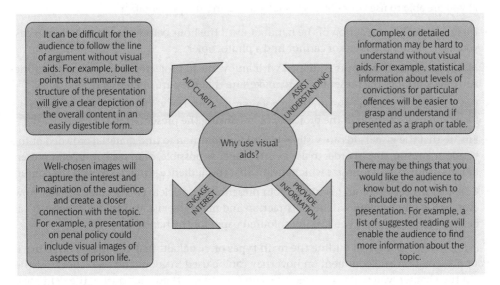

Figure 17.6 Effective use of visual aids

2. **Assist understanding**: an oral presentation is a series of spoken words that are constantly replaced by others. The audience has to listen, understand, and keep pace with what you are saying and this may be a struggle, particularly if your presentation is dealing with complex issues. Visual aids will provide a written or pictorial source of reference that the audience can use to help them make sense of what you are saying and to remind themselves of the key points. Equally, it is often said that 'a picture paints a thousand words', so you may find that your audience is more able to understand if you complement your words with illustrations.

3. **Engage interest:** giving the audience something to look at whilst you are speaking can be an excellent way of engaging their interest and, if the images are well-chosen, of capturing their imagination. Most people tend to take in information more readily by observation than they do by listening, so using visual images can really enhance the impact of your presentation. That said, a presentation that is littered with gratuitous illustrations that have only a tenuous link with the material in question will act as a distraction as the audience ponder the connection between the content of the presentation and the seemingly irrelevant illustration.

4. **Provide additional information:** in a limited time frame, you may not be able to cover all the information that the audience needs about a topic or you may have additional points of interest that were not directly relevant to the content of the presentation that you would nonetheless like to communicate to the audience (perhaps the issues that were in the third column when you categorized your material) that could be listed on a handout as 'further thinking'. Be sure to give careful thought to including additional information on a handout, however; visual aids are supposed to supplement the spoken word and your presentation is supposed to be a self-contained exposition of a topic, so it is not good practice to use the handout as the repository for all the material that you did not have time to include.

Although there are clear benefits to using visual aids, you should do so only if you are prepared to devote effort to their preparation, as shoddy and ill-prepared visual aids will give a wholly negative impression to the audience. You must also take responsibility for ensuring that you are able to use your chosen visual aids during the presentation:

- Do not leave the production of the handout until the hour before the presentation in case you have printer problems or cannot find a photocopier

- Make sure that the room is equipped with an overhead projector or PowerPoint facilities and check prior to the presentation to make sure that they are operational

- Have a back-up plan in case anything goes wrong with the visual aids. What will you do, for example, if the bulb in the projector blows during the presentation?

- Ensure that the visual aids are visible! It is all too common to find material crowded onto a handout, presumably in order to use as little paper as possible, or to see PowerPoint presentations using a small font size which means that the audience struggles to read the content

- Consider the use of colour to enliven your presentation. Stick to two or three colours, however, as too much colour will be a distraction and make the visual aids look chaotic. It can be very effective even if you just use coloured paper for the handout

The following section will outline the main types of visual aid that you may wish to use in your presentation and comment on how they can be used to good (and bad) effect. Further on in the chapter, you will find suggestions on how to use these aids during the delivery of the presentation (see section 17.4).

17.3.3.1 Handouts

You should always prepare a handout to accompany your presentation unless you are told not to do so by your lecturer. Even if you are using one of the other visual aids such as PowerPoint, it is still a good idea to provide a handout. A good handout should enable the audience to follow the structure of your presentation and should give a snapshot of the content that they can supplement with notes if they choose to do so. Moreover, you can include information on the handout that needs to be communicated accurately but that the audience may not be able to note down during the presentation, such as definitions, quotations, statutory references, and case citations.

As such, a handout is a guide and a source of essential information. It should not be overloaded with detail and it should never be a word-for-word copy of your presentation—why would the audience bother to listen if they have been given a transcript of the presentation? A room full of people who are clearly paying no attention when you speak is very off-putting for a presenter, so make sure that you use your visual aids to increase engagement with the audience rather than to distract them or give them an excuse not to listen. Remember, visual aids supplement, rather than replace, the spoken word.

Part of the skill in putting together a handout is thinking about how the information looks on the page. This requires that careful thought is given to the appearance and size of the font used and how the information is spaced out on the page. Think about your own views, positive and negative, of the handouts given to you by lecturers by way of guidance.

Practical exercise

The following exercise can be used to help you to appreciate the qualities that characterize a good handout and the factors that render a handout less useful to the audience.

1. Take a few minutes to read through the handout shown in Figure 17.7.

2. Make a note of the things that you consider to be the strengths and the weaknesses of the handout. You will see that three of the weaknesses have been noted already to give you a start but there are many more points to note remaining.

3. Is there anything lacking that you would want to see included?

4. How useful do you find the handout?

5. Draw out your own version of the handout with a view to making it more user-friendly.

 You will find an improved version of the handout on the Online Resource Centre with some commentary on its merits that you may like to compare with your own thoughts.

17.3.3.2 PowerPoint

PowerPoint (or its Mac equivalent, Keynote) is an excellent visual aid and one that you should certainly try to use if it is at all possible. Not only does it have a range of features, such as the opportunity to incorporate sound and video clips, that are not available with other visual aids, it has the added advantage of improving your computer literacy skills by giving you experience of a new, and increasingly widely-used, package. If you are not familiar with PowerPoint, most institutions run courses on its use and, besides, it is very easy to pick up by experimentation as it is based on a template into which you insert text, images, and other features.

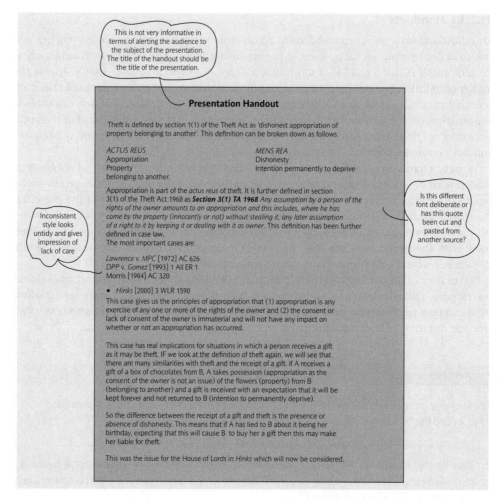

Figure 17.7 An example of a handout concerning theft

If you decide to use PowerPoint, you should ask your lecturer if the room in which you are due to present is suitable for you to do so; if not, it may be possible to arrange a change of venue if you give sufficient warning of your intentions.

There is some disagreement about how many PowerPoint slides should accompany a presentation with some suggesting an approach based on slides per minute of presentation, for example one slide every two minutes. Not only is this rather onerous in long presentations, it is also rather unrealistic; you should use as many slides as you need to communicate your point to the audience. The following points may help you to plan the slides you need to accompany your presentation:

- **Title slide:** this tells the audience who you are and what you are going to talk about.

- **Presentation outline:** this should be used during your introduction as you explain to the audience what points you are going to cover and in what order. See Figure 17.8 for an example of an outline slide.

- **Content slides:** the general rule is that there should be one slide for each major concept or idea that you introduce to the audience. You should be relatively sparing with the amount

> **Overview**
> • Role of appropriation in theft
> • Outline of leading cases:
>   – *Lawrence v MPC* [1972] AC 626
>   – *DPP v Gomez* [1993] 1 All ER 1
>   – *R v Morris* [1984] AC 320
>   – *R v Hinks* [2000] 3 WLR 1590
> • When is the recipient of a gift guilty of theft?
> • Implications for the law of theft

Figure 17.8 An example outline slide

of words used on each slide and remember to keep the font size large: visual aids are not useful if they cannot be read by the audience.

- **Summary slide:** this corresponds with your conclusion and lists the points that you have covered to demonstrate the way that your ideas fit together. It may be spread over several slides if you want to include an 'implications' or 'future directions' section in your presentation.

- **Any questions?:** however much you hope that nobody will ask any questions, most presentations require you to allow time for questions and it is certain that your lecturer will ask something even if nobody else does.

You will find two sample PowerPoint presentations on the Online Resource Centre with some comments of the choice and layout of the material.

17.3.3.3 Overhead projectors (OHPs)

Until the recent growth in popularity of PowerPoint, OHPs were the main visual aid used during presentations. Most lecture and seminar rooms will have an OHP whereas the facilities to use PowerPoint may not be available in the room in which your presentation is due to take place. If you do plan to use an OHP, it is advisable to visit the room before the presentation and make sure the equipment works, as blown bulbs are a common hazard. It is also a good idea to familiarize yourself with the operation of the OHP prior to the presentation. Make sure you have enough acetate sheets and the correct pens and plan out the spacing of the content carefully: the general rule is no more than seven points of seven words on each sheet. If you are going to print the content, make sure you use a sufficiently large font (no less than 18 point) and one that is relatively plain, such as Arial, as this is easier for the audience to read. If you want to include diagrams or graphs that are copies from books or other sources, make sure that these can be reproduced at an appropriate size and that any change of size does not blur the content.

17.3.3.4 Whiteboards and flipcharts

If there is a whiteboard in the room, you may like to use this to note information as the presentation progresses, because this can give quite a dynamic feel to the presentation. It can be particularly useful if you want to show the links between points, such as the overlap between the branches of state in relation to the separation of powers, or if you want to provide a visual depiction of the development of a topic such as noting a chronology, for example.

There are, however, a number of pitfalls for the unwary or inexperienced user of a whiteboard. You need to ensure that your writing is sufficiently clear to ensure that it can be read by all of the audience and you must remember that writing takes longer than speaking, so you may feel ill-at-ease with the silence whilst you are using the whiteboard. Of course, you can speak whilst writing but this means that you are facing away from your audience and you might find it hard to do two different things at once, particularly if you are finding the delivery of the presentation stressful.

Flipcharts are not used very often during student presentations, possibly because they are rarely available, but they can be very effective. Unlike a whiteboard presentation, your materials can be prepared in advance, although there is also the flexibility to write/draw as your presentation progresses. Make sure that your writing is sufficiently large and clear and do not go overboard on the use of colour: one main colour and one accent colour should be sufficient. As with handouts, do not try to crowd too much material on a single sheet of paper—it can be a good idea to plan out the content of each sheet in pencil first to see how it looks before using marker pens. One of their key advantages is that the paper can be annotated lightly in pencil to give you reminders of things to do and say that cannot be seen by the audience during the presentation.

As you can see, there are a range of visual aids available to support your presentation. Although the preparation of visual material can be quite time-consuming, the positive impact that it has on the presentation generally makes it a worthwhile exercise. Many students find that preparing a thoughtful and polished selection of visual aids makes them feel more confident about their presentation; if nothing else, it gives the audience something else to look at, so diverting attention away from the speaker.

Although there is much to be said in their favour, do not feel pressured into using visual aids if you do not feel comfortable in doing so. Some students feel that having to use an OHP, for example, makes them very self-conscious during the presentation whilst others find that worries about whether PowerPoint will work properly add to the overall anxiety that accompanies the presentation. Overall, it is preferable not to use visual aids, other than a handout, if they are going to be more of a hindrance than a help.

17.3.4 Practice

The most important element of preparation is practice. Most people are not used to speaking in public, so it is inevitably something that is going to need a little bit of practice.

17.3.4.1 Why practise?

You must practise your presentation several times over to ensure that:

- The presentation fits within the time allocated to it
- The order of the material is appropriate and one point runs smoothly into another
- There are no tricky words or phrases that trip up your tongue
- You familiarize yourself with the appropriate pace at which to speak
- You become accustomed to hearing your own voice
- You know how and when to use any visual aids
- You identify and eliminate any distracting habits

Many of these points will be more readily addressed if you practise in front of an audience. For example, you may think that your pace of delivery is appropriate but only someone who is listening can tell you whether that is the case. Equally, if you have any odd habits, such as fiddling with a pen or flicking your hair, you are likely to be unaware of this unless it is pointed out to you. Finally, a third party can give you feedback on the most important element of all: whether your presentation makes sense to the audience.

17.3.4.2 What to practise?

Although the obvious answer to this question would seem to be 'the presentation', it is not necessarily useful to devote too much practice time to the actual presentation. There are two separate facets to a good presentation: (1) the subject matter, and (2) the presentation style.

Although you will want to practise the actual presentation for the reasons noted in the preceding section, you should not neglect to practise in order to strengthen your presentation style. Until you are a seasoned public speaker, it might be an idea to practise the two separately, particularly if you are asking an audience of your peers to comment on your presentation as they may be tied up with commenting on the content rather than style.

Practical exercise

The following exercise can be used to help you to practise your presentation style. You will find that it will also help you to work on issues such as the organization of the content of the presentation and incorporating signposting.

1. Choose something that you know extremely well as the topic for a five-minute presentation. There is no need for it to have any academic merit as the essence of a good presentation is the communication of information, irrespective of the nature of that information. Suitable topics could be (a) good pubs in your home town; (b) favourite sporting activities; or (c) your first term as an undergraduate student.

2. Prepare a presentation on the topic. The idea of the exercise is to evaluate your presentation style, but this will not work if you treat it as a freeflow speaking activity in which you spill forth thoughts without structure. Use some of the techniques suggested in this chapter to help you to structure and organize your presentation.

3. Ask a couple of friends to observe your presentation and comment upon your style. Try to emphasize to them that you want honest and constructive feedback: it is much easier for your friends to say 'that was great' as they do not want to upset you, so you may need to convince them that you want to hear an objective review of the strengths and weaknesses of your technique. It can help to give them a feedback table and ask them to write comments as they may find this easier than voicing any negative views to you in person.

4. Make a list of the strengths and weaknesses that your audience noted. Ask them for suggestions as to what they think would improve on areas of weakness. Reflect upon your own experience as a presenter: how did it feel when you were delivering the material? What things would you change in future presentations?

5. Rework the presentation taking these observations on board and ask your friends to watch it again or present to a different group of friends. The aim is to determine whether you have improved on your previous performance.

 You will find video clips of students presenting on the Online Resource Centre.

Have a look at these and note your own comments of the strengths and weaknesses of their presentation styles.

Once you have some general insight into your presentation style, it would be useful to practise the actual presentation to work on issues associated with the content. Remember to practise with the visual aids that you plan to use to make sure that you can use these without interrupting the flow of your presentation.

Having considered the mechanics of putting together a presentation, all that remains is to consider how to deliver it to the audience with clarity and confidence.

17.4 Delivery stage

This is the stage of the process that you probably think of as *the* presentation. Having followed the steps outlined in relation to preparation, you should have a presentation in a clear and accessible form, supplemented by carefully constructed visual aids. This section will go through some of the factors that will influence the success of the actual delivery of the presentation.

17.4.1 Delivery style

Your main objective in giving a presentation is to communicate an idea to the audience. This means that they need to be able to understand you. It is your job to make sure that you deliver your presentation in such a way that it is capable of being understood and, more than that, that it is packaged so that the audience *wants* to listen. As such, you will need to take the following points into account.

17.4.1.1 Engage with the audience

One of the worst ways to deliver a presentation is to read it to the audience from a prepared script. It leads to a flat and uninteresting delivery, which is very boring for the audience and it often causes the presenter to speak far too quickly. Reading a script also means that you have little or no eye contact with the audience as you have to focus your attention on the page.

The best way to avoid reading a script is not to write one in the first place. There really is no need as you will be familiar with your subject matter and you can ensure that you remind yourself of the order in which the points need to be raised by using cue cards. This frees you to look at the audience (collectively rather than any particular individual) and your delivery will be more natural as a result. Cue cards should be numbered (in case you drop them) and contain short reminders of each key point. Do not be tempted to divide your script into chunks and write these on cue cards as you will find that you merely read from those instead.

It is important also to remember that good written language and good spoken language differ dramatically. Speech tends to involve shorter sentences and more readily understood language than written communication, so if you write a script, the chances are that it will not be in language that is suited to oral delivery.

It is also easier to engage the audience if you replicate the variations in pace and tone that occur in natural speech. Try to make sure that you sound as much like yourself as possible in ordinary conversation, taking into account the need to pace your delivery. It can help to include instructions to remind yourself of these points on the cue cards. Write appropriate phrases such as 'pause', 'slow down', and 'look at the audience' on the cue cards but make sure that you do so in a different colour so that you do not confuse it for the text of your presentation. Nobody wants to engage the audience by making them laugh when you read out 'change the slide' from the cue cards!

Hopefully, you will have gained an awareness of these issues from your practice sessions.

17.4.1.2 Timing, pace, and volume

During the planning stages, you should have taken steps to ensure that your presentation fits within the time allocated to it. Remember that the audience will find it difficult to digest complicated material, so you will need to reduce your speed of delivery so that it is slower than ordinary speech. This can feel strange and it is not uncommon for speakers to start at a measured pace but to pick up speed as the presentation progresses until they are going too fast for the audience.

You will also probably find that you need to speak at a slightly louder volume than you would in ordinary conversation. Your voice will project better to those at the back of the room if you remember to face the audience. This is particularly important when using visual aids: even experienced speakers tend to look at their materials rather than the audience and this can really muffle the voice, so should be avoided.

17.4.1.3 Signpost your presentation

Telling the audience what you are doing makes it so much easier for them to follow the development of your argument. It is good practice to ensure that you start each fresh point with an explanation of how it relates to the rest of your material. If you think about it, there are only three options:

1. **It picks up on something said earlier in the presentation.** Try using phrases such as 'you may remember that I explained this at the start of the presentation' or 'referring back to the definition that I outlined earlier'.

2. **It is one of a series of points.** You can remind the audience of this by using a phrase such as 'the second point to consider here is . . .' or simply 'secondly'.

3. **It is a move to an entirely new issue or perspective.** Advise the audience of the change by using phrases such as 'having outlined the position under English law, we now need to consider how this has been altered by membership of the European Union' or 'that concludes the discussion of dishonesty so I'll move on to consider issues relating to appropriation'.

It also helps your audience to follow your presentation if you signpost your use of visual aids with simple phrases such as 'this slide lists the four characteristics of an easement' or 'you will find the definition set out in full halfway down the first page of the handout'. Although this may seem like stating the obvious, you must realize that what is obvious to you—who is so familiar with the content and structure of your presentation—is not obvious to the audience. Moreover, it is important to remember that the audience will regard your presentation favourably if you have made life easy for them, so giving frequent clues as to the location of key information or the relevance of a particular point to the overall topic will always create a good impression.

17.4.1.4 Using visual aids

Visual aids are there to support your presentation but they can only do so if you use them effectively.

- Make sure that your handout, slides, or other materials follow the order of your presentation; if you have made last-minute changes to your content, you should check to see whether this necessitates alterations in your materials

- Practise using any equipment so that you are confident you will be able to operate it during the presentation

- Think about where you are going to stand in relation to the equipment. You do not want to block the screen or to have to keep walking across the room to change your slides

- Do not use visual aids as a substitute for speaking, by, for example, telling the audience to read a PowerPoint slide or section of a handout. One of the worst comments that could be made about your performance would be 'lousy presenter but a competent projectionist'

- Talk to the audience and not to the visual aids. Even the most experienced speakers make this mistake, as they look at their own PowerPoint slides or the material they have written on the whiteboard when they are explaining the points, rather than looking at the audience

17.4.2 Combating nerves

Nerves are a problem for many students who are faced with the prospect of making a presentation. Even students who are confident of speaking out during group discussion in tutorials tend to find the prospect of standing in front of the group and speaking somewhat daunting. One of the best ways of overcoming nerves is to try and isolate what it is that is causing anxiety—knowing what the problem is takes you halfway towards overcoming it. Common fears include the following:

17.4.2.1 Presenting inaccurate material

This is such a common worry and yet it is one that should really not trouble you. If your research and preparation has been thorough, the content of your presentation should be accurate, so there should be no cause for anxiety on that front. Even if it is dreadfully inaccurate, it is extremely unlikely that other students will notice and even less likely that they will point it out. Your lecturer should not interrupt during the presentation, particularly if it is an assessed component of the course, although they may speak to you afterwards if they feel that you have missed the point or made mistakes regarding the law.

If you are particularly worried about inaccuracy—for example, if you feel that you may have misinterpreted the law or missed a vital point—it would be perfectly acceptable to approach your lecturer, explain your worries, and ask them to look at your planned content to ensure that there are no dreadful errors or omissions. If the presentation is assessed, your lecturer may not be able to do this, in which case you could cooperate with other students in the group, asking them to check your work for accuracy and agreeing to do the same for them in return.

17.4.2.2 Forgetting what to say

Thorough research and preparation will have made you extremely familiar with the subject matter, so, provided you have a note of the order in which you want to make points, it is extremely unlikely that you will forget what to say. You should be able to explain all the key concepts in your presentation without relying on any particular form of words. However, this fear tends to lead students to write a full script, which they intend to follow to the last word. As discussed earlier, reading a script (or reciting a memorized script) is not effective as it leads to stilted delivery, a fast delivery pace, and lack of engagement with the audience. Try making a numbered list of the points that you want to make and explaining each of them out loud without any further notes or prompts. The more you practise doing this, the more fluent you will become and this should help your fear of 'drying up' during the presentation recede.

Rather then merely forgetting what to say, you may fear that you will be incapable of speaking; that you will open your mouth but no words will come out. This is a common fear but an exceptionally rare occurrence. If you have never been incapable of speech at any time previously in your life, there is no reason to think that it will happen during your presentation. Of course, the stress of the situation may make your mouth dry—that is an entirely explicable physical response to fear—so make sure that you have some water with you to sip during the presentation. You should practise your opening sentence as often as possible—write it out on cards and pin them up at different places around your room so that you see them all the time; once the first sentence is out, the rest will follow on naturally.

17.4.2.3 Being visible and/or being judged

Probably the most frequently expressed concern arises from the visibility attached to the delivery of a presentation. Most student discussion takes part within a group where there is far less emphasis on any particular group member and where any lack of knowledge is readily concealed. A presentation removes these safety features and focuses uninterrupted attention on one person for a protracted period of time. This visibility and focus renders the speaker vulnerable to the criticism of their peers and it is probably this factor that induces the most anxiety: in fact, you could say that the three points listed earlier are merely specific examples of the overriding fear of looking foolish in front of others.

There are a couple of points to note here. First, do not imagine for one moment that every member of the audience is actually paying attention. The only person that you can guarantee is actually listening to what you say is the lecturer—even your friends are probably letting their minds drift whilst maintaining expressions of encouragement or polite attention. Secondly, even if people are paying attention, they are doing so out of interest in what you are saying, not because they want to criticize you. In fact, most people will be willing you on to succeed, knowing that they have either survived the experience or have their own presentation to give later that term, so it is really a mistake to assume that there is any negative judgement being directed towards you.

Overall, then, most presentation anxiety arises from a concern about looking foolish in front of others. Most of the reasons that you might feel foolish, such as inaccurate material or forgetting what to say, can be overcome with careful preparation and by practising the presentation several times beforehand. Other factors that might cause concern, such as inability to operate the equipment, can also be addressed by practice. Ultimately, most people do not have to speak in front of others very often, so a presentation is unknown territory and it is human nature to fear the unknown.

You can take various steps to minimize this prior to the presentation, such as ensuring that you become used to speaking out in front of other students by contributing to tutorial discussion. Some students find that the best way to appear confident is to pretend to be confident.

They watch those who they consider to be confident presenters and emulate their behaviour. Other students take a contrasting approach by starting the presentation by confessing that they are feeling very nervous.

 Practical exercise

The following exercise can be used to help you to practise your presentation style. You will find that it will also help you to work on issues such as the organization of the content of the presentation and incorporating signposting.

1. Have a think about your fears about giving a presentation. Try to articulate these as precisely as possible and note them as a list of numbered points on a sheet of paper.

2. Deal with each numbered point in turn and ask yourself (a) why you think that this will happen, and (b) what the outcome will be if it does happen. For example, you might be afraid that you will run out of time and not be able to deliver all of your presentation. This could result in loss of marks in an assessed presentation.

3. Think of at least two ways that you could stop the problem from arising. For example, you could practise the presentation several times to make sure that it fits within the time allocated and you could review the content to consider which points could be omitted if you run short of time on the actual day.

4. Consider how you will deal with the outcome of your feared situation occurring. In other words, address not just the consequence but the consequence of the consequence! For example, if you run short of time you will lose some marks as a result but it is unlikely to make the difference between a pass and fail, besides which it is unlikely that the course is assessed 100 per cent on the presentation.

By tackling your fears directly, you will be able to think of ways to prevent them from occurring and also realize that the consequences of their occurrence are not actually as bad as you imagine.

17.4.3 Dealing with questions

Most presentations conclude with a period of time for the audience to ask questions. It is probably fair to say that even the most confident presenter has some qualms about dealing with questions. This is because it is actually the only part of the presentation that you cannot control. If the presentation is assessed, the ability to deal with questions assumes a particular importance because it gives the marker an indication of the depth of the speaker's background knowledge. Try to take into account the following points to help you deal with questions:

• Listen to the question. Concentrate on what the person asking the question is saying rather than worrying that you will not know the answer

• Ask them to repeat the question if you did not follow it or to reword it if you did not understand it

• Take time to think about the answer to ensure that you have something sensible to say rather than saying the first thing that pops into your head just to fill the silence

• Be honest. If you do not know the answer, say so

- Do not talk for too long in answer to any particular question. It will come across as if you are rambling which will detract from the overall impression of your oral presentation skills. Think about your answer and make a couple of succinct points

17.5 Post-presentation stage

You may think that your task is complete as soon as the final question has been answered and you have taken your seat with a sense of relief and achievement but there is another stage of the process which is frequently overlooked in its importance and that is the post-presentation reflection.

17.5.1 Why reflect?

You should reflect upon your performance in order to ensure that you gain something from the activity, so that you will be a more effective and confident presenter on the next occasion. You may think that once was enough and that you will never be called upon to present again but you cannot be sure of that, so it will maximize the learning potential of the activity if you set aside a little time to reflect upon how the presentation went and what, if anything, you would do differently if you were able to repeat the presentation the following day.

Try and formalize this process a little by making notes so that you have a record of your thoughts whilst they are still fresh in your mind. It will not help you improve in the future if, two years down the line when you need to give a presentation as part of an application for a training contract, you have difficulties calling to mind the topic of your presentation let alone your views on its strengths or weaknesses.

17.5.2 Seek feedback

The process need not take long and you can make use of any feedback that you have been given by your lecturer and by the audience. If the lecturer gave you feedback at the time, it might well have been based as much on content as it was on style and it may have been sanitized a little if there were negative aspects to the presentation, so that you did not feel embarrassed in front of the audience. It would be worth sending the lecturer in question an email to request more tailored feedback. Remember that you will receive a specific answer if you ask a specific question, so rather than saying 'could you give me some more feedback on my presentation?' try asking your lecturer to list three things that they liked about your presentation style and three things that they think that you should change. You may also receive written feedback at some point, particularly if the presentation was assessed.

It may be useful to consider in advance how to elicit the most useful feedback from your audience. Why not prepare a form to distribute at the beginning of the presentation and ask the audience to complete the forms and leave them behind at the end of the presentation? This could take a simple format that could be quite general, to give the audience the ability to note their own thoughts, or it could ask specific questions. Remember, however, not to ask too much of the audience as they are there to listen and learn rather than to provide you with a detailed commentary on your presentation technique. See Figure 17.9 for an example feedback form.

> **FEEDBACK FORM**
>
> Thank you for attending my presentation on 'The Evolution of Appropriation in the Offence of Theft'
>
> Please take a few moments to note your thoughts about this presentation:
>
> What were the good aspects of the presentation that you enjoyed or thought were useful?
>
> 1.
>
> 2.
>
> 3.
>
> What aspects of the presentation did you think were less good and which you found unhelpful?
>
> 1.
>
> 2.
>
> 3.

Figure 17.9 An example feedback form

CHAPTER SUMMARY

The research stage

- Take care to formulate a presentation topic that takes account of the time frame within which the presentation must be delivered, the availability of material, the aim of the presentation, and the requirements of the assessment criteria

- Start your research as early as possible to ensure you have time to identify and obtain relevant material and make sure that your note-making is effective

- Strive to find an original or interesting slant on the material to ensure that the presentation is interesting, particularly if you are aware that other students are covering the same topic

Preparing the presentation

- Content overload is a major problem for many presentations. Select your topic and the content of the presentation carefully to ensure that you do not try to cram too much material into the time available

- If you are having difficulties in making a decision about the content, try ranking each point on the basis of its relevance to the question that your presentation is seeking to answer

- Make sure that your presentation tells a story by giving it a clear introduction, a series of interrelated points within the body of the presentation, and a conclusion that draws together the issues raised and provides a succinct answer to the question posed by the presentation

- Always prepare a handout unless explicitly told not to do so. This should contain a skeleton of the presentation to give the audience an insight into its structure and content as well as noting any detailed information such as quotations that the audience could not be expected to note down during the presentation

- Give careful thought to the selection and presentation of visual aids to ensure that they complement, rather than replace or distract from, the presentation

- Practise, preferably in front of an audience. Present on everyday topics to practise your delivery style and then practise the actual presentation to ensure that it fits within the time frame and that everything flows smoothly

Delivering the presentation

- Try to adopt a style of delivery that is engaging for the audience to listen to and follow. Take particular care with the timing, pace, and volume of your presentation and remember that good spoken English differs enormously from good written English

- Never read from a prepared script. If to recollect the content of the presentation poses a problem, use numbered cue cards with key words and phrases noted that will jolt your memory

- Signposting is essential to enable your audience to follow the line of your argument and to understand how each point relates to others in the presentation. Use a signposting phrase in relation to each new point raised

- Anticipate issues that will cause you to feel nervous and try to formulate a means of pre-empting any problems that you fear may arise. Remember that most people suffer from presentation nerves

- Be prepared to answer questions from the audience. Listen carefully to what is being asked and take a moment to think about the answer before launching into a response

Review and reflection

- Presentations are increasingly required as part of the job application process, so take advantage of this opportunity to become a more accomplished presenter by reflecting upon your performance. Try to be honest with yourself about your limitations as a presenter and find ways to strengthen areas in which there is room for improvement

- Be active and precise in seeking feedback from others about your qualities as a presenter and remember that asking precise questions tends to elicit precise answers

- Circulating a feedback sheet and inviting the audience to complete it is a really valuable source of feedback, as written feedback tends to be more objective, hence more useful to your review of your performance, than face-to-face comment

18 Mooting skills

INTRODUCTION

The focus of this chapter is mooting. It will provide a step-by-step guide to assist students through the process of preparation and delivery of a moot argument with reference made to associated issues such as conducting legal research and production of a skeleton argument. Attention will be drawn, in particular, to aspects of mooting that students tend to find worrying or difficult, such as formulating a flowing argument, developing a confident oral presentation style, and dealing with judicial interventions. This chapter is a general guide that will be invaluable for preparation of any moot but a sample moot is used throughout as a source of specific explanation and illustration.

Participation in a moot will provide an insight into the way that the law is used in practice and also acts as an invaluable introduction to the skills that are required to present a case on appeal. Mooting offers unparalleled opportunities for the development of the skills associated with the delivery of a comprehensive and persuasive oral argument as well as providing an opportunity to develop your research skills and enhance your ability to construct and organize a coherent legal argument. It is this 'skills-richness' that makes mooting an excellent activity for demonstrating a commitment to a career in the legal profession; thus, your level of involvement with these activities should be emphasized on your curriculum vitae and in applications for a pupillage or training contract. Despite the clear benefits of taking part in these activities, many students are reluctant to do so. Although the explanation for this reluctance is usually said to be fear of standing up and presenting an argument, this fear often arises from a lack of understanding of what is required. This chapter seeks to demystify the mooting process and encourage more students to take part in this valuable and ultimately enjoyable activity.

LEARNING OUTCOMES

After studying this chapter, you will be able to:

- Analyze a moot problem and understand its requirements from the perspective of each of the mooters

- Appreciate the role of each of the mooters and be aware of the mechanics of mooting in terms of the timing and delivery of submission

- Engage in detailed and meticulous research and preparation including the production of a skeleton argument and a bundle

- Evaluate the strength of the opponent's argument and check to determine that the authorities relied upon are current and relevant

- Deliver a logical and organized moot speech with confidence and deal with judicial interventions

- Adhere to mooting conventions and the requirements of mooting etiquette including the use of appropriate terminology

18.1 The moot problem

Just as a moot point is one that could be argued either way, a moot revolves around an unsettled legal argument that could go either way depending on the skill of the mooter. It involves a fictitious factual scenario set in one of the appellate courts, generally the Court of Appeal or the Supreme Court. Two teams of two mooters present submissions for each party and seek to persuade the judge that theirs is the correct interpretation of the law. The example provided is a typical moot problem that demonstrates its characteristics. It is always worth devoting time to the analysis of the moot problem as it has a great deal of essential information to convey to the mooters, as you will see in the sections that follow (see Figure 18.1).

18.1.1 Level of the court (1)

There will always be an indication of the level of the court in which the moot will be heard. Take note of this and ensure that you keep it in mind when researching and constructing your legal argument. It will be influential in the way in which you use authorities and formulate your submissions owing to the doctrine of precedent.

Issues of precedent and the hierarchy of the courts are detailed in chapter 6, so you may like to revisit this and refresh your memory on the 1966 Practice Statement concerning the ability of the Supreme Court to depart from its own decisions and the rule in Young v Bristol Aeroplane *in relation to the status of Court of Appeal authority.*

18.1.2 The case name (2)

You will have been told by the organizer of the moot whether your team represents the appellant or the defendant. Armed with this information, you need to work out which of the parties that means you are representing. In this example, this is straightforward as the first-named party (Boyer) is the appellant and the second-named party (West) is the respondent. The case name does not necessarily indicate which party is the appellant and which is the respondent. It is essential to use the past history of the case and the way in which the grounds of appeal are stated to ascertain the roles of appellant and respondent. It is always painful when mistakes are made and a judge is confronted with two opposing teams who think they are representing the same party. Not only is this embarrassing for the team who made the mistake, it means elimination from the moot and a waste of all the time devoted to preparation.

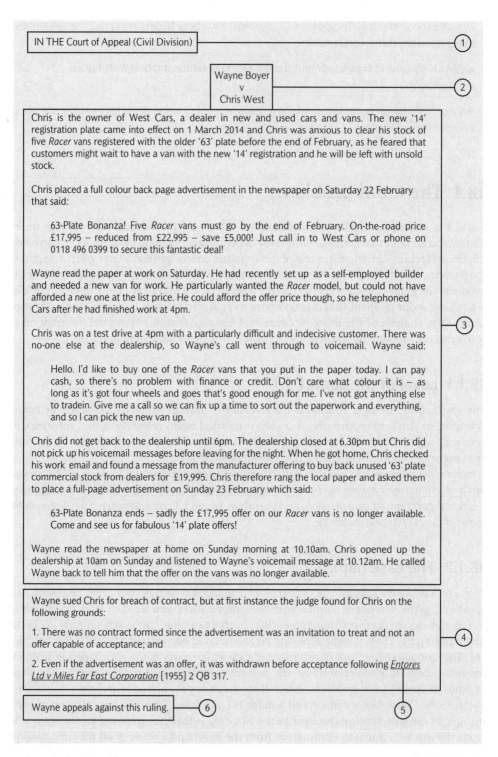

IN THE Court of Appeal (Civil Division) ——————————————————— ①

Wayne Boyer
v ——————————————————— ②
Chris West

Chris is the owner of West Cars, a dealer in new and used cars and vans. The new '14' registration plate came into effect on 1 March 2014 and Chris was anxious to clear his stock of five *Racer* vans registered with the older '63' plate before the end of February, as he feared that customers might wait to have a van with the new '14' registration and he will be left with unsold stock.

Chris placed a full colour back page advertisement in the newspaper on Saturday 22 February that said:

> 63-Plate Bonanza! Five *Racer* vans must go by the end of February. On-the-road price £17,995 – reduced from £22,995 – save £5,000! Just call in to West Cars or phone on 0118 496 0399 to secure this fantastic deal!

Wayne read the paper at work on Saturday. He had recently set up as a self-employed builder and needed a new van for work. He particularly wanted the *Racer* model, but could not have afforded a new one at the list price. He could afford the offer price though, so he telephoned Cars after he had finished work at 4pm.

Chris was on a test drive at 4pm with a particularly difficult and indecisive customer. There was no-one else at the dealership, so Wayne's call went through to voicemail. Wayne said:

> Hello. I'd like to buy one of the *Racer* vans that you put in the paper today. I can pay cash, so there's no problem with finance or credit. Don't care what colour it is – as long as it's got four wheels and goes that's good enough for me. I've not got anything else to tradein. Give me a call so we can fix up a time to sort out the paperwork and everything, and so I can pick the new van up.   ③

Chris did not get back to the dealership until 6pm. The dealership closed at 6.30pm but Chris did not pick up his voicemail messages before leaving for the night. When he got home, Chris checked his work email and found a message from the manufacturer offering to buy back unused '63' plate commercial stock from dealers for £19,995. Chris therefore rang the local paper and asked them to place a full-page advertisement on Sunday 23 February which said:

> 63-Plate Bonanza ends – sadly the £17,995 offer on our *Racer* vans is no longer available. Come and see us for fabulous '14' plate offers!

Wayne read the newspaper at home on Sunday morning at 10.10am. Chris opened up the dealership at 10am on Sunday and listened to Wayne's voicemail message at 10.12am. He called Wayne back to tell him that the offer on the vans was no longer available.

Wayne sued Chris for breach of contract, but at first instance the judge found for Chris on the following grounds:

1. There was no contract formed since the advertisement was an invitation to treat and not an offer capable of acceptance; and   ④

2. Even if the advertisement was an offer, it was withdrawn before acceptance following *Entores Ltd v Miles Far East Corporation* [1955] 2 QB 317.   ⑤

Wayne appeals against this ruling. ——⑥

Figure 18.1 Moot problem

18.1.2.1 Civil cases

In civil cases, the name of the case usually remains the same from inception to completion; a case that is listed as *Boyer v West* at first instance would be listed in the same way on appeal, irrespective of which party initiated the appeal. There are exceptions to this general rule. For example, *Nattrass v Tesco Supermarket* became *Tesco Supermarket v Nattrass*[1] upon appeal so it is advisable always to check carefully to ensure you are clear about which party you are representing in the moot.

18.1.2.2 Criminal cases

Criminal cases always list the Crown as the first party followed by the name of the defendant: *R v Smith*. If the defendant appeals against conviction, this will be listed as *R v Smith*. If the defendant is successful in the Court of Appeal and the prosecution appeal against this decision, the case will remain listed as *R v Smith*. The only exception to this occurs if the first appeal is initiated by the prosecution, i.e. the appeal is by the Crown against the defendant's acquittal, as this is listed as *DPP v Smith* (with DPP standing for 'Director of Public Prosecutions').

18.1.2.3 Judicial review

Judicial review cases involve a different style of case citation, appearing as either *R v Secretary of State for the Environment ex p Smith* or, if the case took place after 2001, as *R (Smith) v Secretary of State for the Environment*. Irrespective of the method of citation, the parties in a judicial review case are the aggrieved individual or group (Smith) and a public body (Secretary of State for the Environment); the Crown is never an actual party to the proceedings but is named in the citation as judicial review cases are public law matters in which the Crown is notionally representing the interests of the individual or group against the public body.

18.1.2.4 Unrepresented parties

The final style of citation that you might encounter is *Re Smith*. This indicates that the proceedings involve a party who is incapable of representing themselves. This is common in probate cases (dead person), family proceedings (child), or cases involving mental incapacity.

 Self-test questions

 Have a look at the sample moots on the Online Resource Centre and work out which party is the appellant and the respondent in each case. Compare your answers with those provided on the Online Resource Centre and make sure that you understand the explanations that are also provided.

18.1.3 The facts (3)

The bulk of the information provided in a moot problem is the factual background that led to the dispute.

---

1. [1972] 1 AC 153 (HL).

18.1.3.1 Issues of fact and law

It is important that you remember that these facts were (hypothetically) established at first instance so cannot be changed, reinterpreted, or supplemented in any way. A moot is an argument on a point of law, so there is no scope whatsoever for a re-evaluation of the facts; you must work with the information that is provided. This means that you cannot research (or, worse still, invent) supplementary facts that support your argument. For example, in *Boyer v West*, the respondent may want to establish 'normal business hours' for a car dealership but cannot refer to figures in *Car Dealer Magazine* that indicate that 98 per cent of independent car dealers open at 10 a.m. on a Sunday as this is a question of fact and not a question of law.

18.1.3.2 Make use of the facts

Pay careful attention to the facts. Some mooters present an abstract legal argument on their ground of appeal that is too detached from the particular facts of the appeal. Remember that your job is not only to argue the niceties of the distinction between an offer and an invitation to treat but to *use* this to persuade the judge that the notice in the newspaper was an offer (if you are representing Boyer) or an invitation to treat (for West). Reference to the particular facts of the moot will help you to ground your argument and, because abstraction from the facts is a common weakness, your ability to relate the law to the facts will impress the judge if it is done effectively.

18.1.4 Case history (4)

The past history of the case, i.e. how it was decided at first instance and in any previous appeals, can be useful, particularly if the problem includes details of the reasoning of the judge.

18.1.4.1 Respondent's perspective

For the respondent (who won at the earlier stage of the proceedings), it can be a powerful argument that the decision of the judge at first instance, who had all the facts before him and had the advantage of hearing oral evidence from the parties, should not be disturbed (or the jury decision if the issue involves criminal law). The respondent should pick up on the reasoning given by the judge as the starting point for their submissions.

18.1.4.2 Appellant's perspective

The reasoning of the judge can also assist the appellant as it provides insight into the sort of argument that the respondent is likely to advance, so a fair amount of effort should be devoted to refuting this argument.

Neither party should limit their submissions to the issues raised in the reasoning of the judge but should include this as only one factor to be taken into account when dealing with their point of appeal.

 Practical exercise

Boyer v West does not give detailed reasoning for the judge's decision at first instance other than to state that reliance was placed upon *Entores Ltd v Miles Far East Corporation*. Have a look at the other moots on the Online Resource Centre that include more detailed reasoning for the earlier decisions and try to determine:

1. How the arguments raised could be used to assist the respondent
2. How the arguments raised could be used to assist the appellant
3. What dangers exist if either party fails to take these reasons into account?

 You will find some comment on these questions on the Online Resource Centre.

18.1.5 Court authorities

If a moot problem includes reference to a particular case within the facts, this acts as a court authority. This means that it can be used by both the appellants and the respondents without counting towards their allowed number of authorities. Therefore, if *Boyer v West* was mooted and the rules stated that each mooter could rely on four cases, this means that each person may use four cases in addition to *Entores Ltd v Miles Far East Corporation*.

18.1.6 Grounds of appeal ⑥

In *Boyer v West*, the grounds of appeal are not specifically stated but can be taken from the two findings of the trial judge. Other moots will phrase this differently and will state 'Wayne appeals on the following grounds'.

 There are some examples that are differently worded on the Online Resource Centre.

 Self-test questions

It is essential to mooting success that you can identify which 'way round' the arguments go—in other words, what are the appellant and respondent respectively arguing? Have a look at *Boyer v West*. Senior counsel for the appellant is arguing that the advertisement is an offer but what are the other parties arguing?

1. Junior counsel for the appellant
2. Senior counsel for the respondent
3. Junior counsel for the respondent

 Answers to the self test questions can be found on the Online Resource Centre where you will find other sample moot problems. Make sure that you can identify the argument for each of the mooters in a couple of these and check your conclusions with the answers online.

It is worth noting that it is only a convention that the senior counsel deals with the first ground of appeal and that the junior counsel deals with the second. However, as it is such a well-established convention, if you intend to depart from this, it must be made clear to the judge in the opening submission of the senior counsel.

18.2 Participants

Mooting involves a simulation of an appellate hearing where the focus of the activity is the presentation of arguments on a particular point of law. This can be distinguished from a mock trial which is an enactment of a first instance trial where the focus is on the presentation of evidence and the examination of witnesses. Both activities are excellent vehicles for the development of advocacy skills but the latter is little used, largely owing to the complexities of its organization. Mooting, by contrast, is far easier to organize and can go ahead with just five people—four mooters and a judge—although it is relatively commonplace for the judge to be assisted by a clerk.

18.2.1 Layout and roles

This typical layout shows the relative positioning of the parties in the moot room. It is important to ensure that the judge can see each of the mooters clearly and that the clerk is positioned so that they can communicate easily with both the judge and the mooters (see Figure 18.2).

Each participant in the moot has a particular job to do (see Table 18.1).

In addition to the participants, the *Master of Moot*[2] also has a key role to play in organizing the moot, setting up the room, and overseeing the exchange of skeleton arguments and authorities as well as organizing any refreshments after the moot is complete (usually only if the moot is an internal final or part of a national competition involving teams from visiting institutions). As such, it is important that the role is held by someone reliable who is not

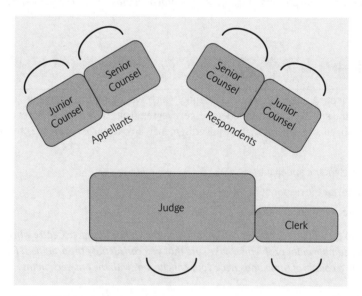

Figure 18.2 A typical moot room layout

---

2.   The title 'Master' in this context is gender neutral, although you may encounter the alternative 'Mistress' of Moot which has become popular among some female Masters of Moot.

Table 18.1 Moot participants and their roles

Participant	Role
Judge	Presides over the moot, hears arguments from counsel, asks questions during the moot, delivers a judgment on the law, and determines which team has won the moot
Clerk	Assists the judge by passing authorities and finding page references, keeps time and indicates how much time is remaining to the mooters
Senior counsel (appellant)	Opens the moot and introduces all the parties to the judge, presents the submissions concerning the first point of appeal on behalf of the appellant. In some instances, exercises a right to reply on behalf of himself and his junior
Junior counsel (appellant)	Addresses the second point of appeal on behalf of the appellant, ensures that the closing of his speech summarizes both points of appeal and invites the judge to overturn the ruling of the lower court and uphold the appeal
Senior counsel (respondent)	Opens the moot for the respondents, presents submissions on the first point of appeal on behalf of the respondent, taking care to address the points raised by senior counsel for the appellant
Junior counsel (respondent)	Deals with the second point of appeal, responds to and counters the arguments advanced by the junior counsel for the appellant and closes the submissions for the respondent

averse to putting time into doing the spadework without getting any of the glory attached to winning a moot.

18.2.2 Appellants and respondents

The two opposing teams are called the appellants and the respondents. Although the job of all the mooters has a strong common theme in terms of presentation of legal arguments with a view to persuading the judge that a particular outcome should be reached, there are distinctions between the job of appellant and respondent.

18.2.2.1 Appellants

The appellants are the team allocated the task of presenting the appeal, so will represent the party who was unsuccessful at the previous hearing. As the side that initiates the appeal, the appellants will set out the reasons why the previous ruling should be overturned. This means that the appellants set the agenda for the moot.

18.2.2.2 Respondents

The respondents, as the name suggests, must *respond* to the points raised by the appellants; in other words, they must tackle each of the submissions made by the appellants as to why the previous ruling should be set aside. Failure to address a submission advanced by the appellants is taken as conceding that point, i.e. accepting that the appellants are correct. Therefore, the respondents must negate the arguments of the appellants before advancing their own submissions.

18.2.2.3 How do the roles differ?

It seems from this that the respondents have a harder task before them than the appellant as they have to tackle the arguments raised by the appellant before they can present their own submissions.

This seeming advantage to the appellants is actually less beneficial than it appears at first glance. An appellant who sets out their own argument without a thought for what opposing counsel will say in response is demonstrating a narrower range of mooting skills than the respondent who has to take note of what the appellant is saying and tailor the response to address the points raised.

Stronger mooters will incorporate an anticipated response into their submissions when acting for the appellant. As Figure 18.3 illustrates, this involves the appellant speculating about the way in which the respondent will seek to counter the appellant's submission and then explaining why the respondent's argument is unsatisfactory. By doing this, the appellant makes the work of the respondent much harder as they now not only have to get around the appellant's submission, they also have to find a way to overcome the appellant's anticipated rebuttal of their submission that has not yet been made!

This approach can be extremely effective for the appellant. Of course, it is only speculation about what the respondent *might* argue and it is always galling when the respondent actually advances a wholly different line of argument, particularly if the respondent presents this with an air of incredulity. For example, the respondent may say:

> Senior counsel for the appellant has seen fit to entertain Your Lordship with fanciful arguments based upon a strange interpretation of *Carlill*. My Lord, I would not seek to waste Your Lordship's time with such frivolous arguments based upon a manifest misunderstanding of the law.

It would, of course, take a courageous respondent to make such a statement as the judge might respond by saying 'But I was quite convinced by senior counsel for the appellant's use of the authorities. Perhaps you could explain to me why you see them as erroneous.' In general, unless you are feeling exceptionally brave *and* very sure of your own interpretation of the law, it is preferable to take a less scathing approach to the submissions advanced by your opponent.

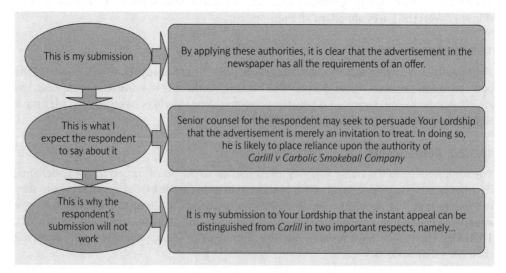

Figure 18.3 Anticipating responses

18.2.3 Senior and junior counsel

Just as it is a well-established mooting myth that it is easier to act as appellant than it is to take the role of respondent, it is also often said that it is easier to act as junior counsel.

So, how true is this?

The main advantage attached to the role of junior counsel is that senior counsel speaks first, so there is never any requirement to be the first person to stand up and speak. For this reason, it is usual that the most experienced of the pair of mooters should act as senior counsel. The allocation of the role of senior counsel to the more experienced (or less nervous) mooter is particularly advantageous to the appellants as senior counsel for the appellant utters the first words of the moot and a confident start has obvious advantages. Equally, it is senior counsel for the appellant who will exercise the right to reply if this is available and it makes sense for this role to be given to someone who is not too uncomfortable at voicing less practised submissions.

Having the more experienced mooter as senior counsel is less compelling for the respondents. Indeed, some teams of respondents allocate the role of junior counsel to their more experienced mooter for a number of reasons. First, the second ground of appeal is often (but not inevitably) more complex than the first, thus requiring a more adept presentation. Secondly, there is no particular need for experience attached to the role of senior counsel for the respondent. Finally, as junior counsel for the appellant will often be a less experienced or less skilful mooter than senior counsel for the appellant, it can be advantageous if the stronger respondent is pitched against the weaker appellant, particularly as senior counsel for the respondent is (in the absence of a right to reply) the last person that the judge will hear speak, leaving the judge with a favourable opinion of the advocacy skills of the respondents.

18.2.4 Timing and order of submissions

Each moot will have its own rules concerning the amount of time given to each of the parties to present their submissions, including rules relating to the way that this period of time is calculated. Some moots may also stipulate the order in which each of the parties must present their submissions.

18.2.4.1 How much time is available to each mooter?

Each of the mooters will have a particular amount of time allocated to them in which to present their submissions. This varies according to the rules of the particular moot, so it is essential that you check carefully to see how long you have to speak and what is included in this period of time.

For example, some moots may specify that each mooter has fifteen minutes to speak but that this does not include time taken in responding to judicial interventions. This approach makes life easier for the mooters because the amount of time available to deliver their submissions is clearly defined. It is much harder to prepare a speech when the rules state that the clock will not be stopped during questioning as it is impossible to predict how many or how few questions the judge will ask and how much of the allocated time will be taken up with judicial questioning.

18.2.4.2 Who speaks when?

The two main options are depicted in Figure 18.4. The first approach allows the judge to hear the entirety of the appeal case before hearing from the respondents whereas the second approach ensures that the first point of appeal is dealt with before the second is raised. The first option is more usual but some judges prefer the second approach, particularly if the points of appeal are complex, so it is worth checking before the moot starts. If neither the rules nor the judge specify an order of play, it is courteous for the opposing teams to reach agreement prior to the commencement of the moot and to ensure that this is communicated to the judge and the clerk.

18.2.4.3 Right to reply

The right to reply gives the appellants one final opportunity to rebut the submissions made by the respondents. This is a right given solely to the appellants (and generally exercised by senior counsel for the appellant on behalf of both senior and junior counsel) because the respondents have already had an opportunity to rebut the appellant's submissions.

Not all moots include a right to reply. This is because the aim is to ensure that each of the mooters have a task of equivalent difficulty before them, hence they all speak for the same amount of time (although some moots allocate more time to senior counsel than junior). As the right to reply is only an issue for senior counsel for the appellant, some competitions take the view that this imposes a greater burden on senior counsel for the appellant.

If there is an option to reply, senior counsel is well advised to exercise it. Judges are aware that it is one of the more difficult tasks in the moot, particularly as it requires the senior to deal with the junior's grounds, plus it means that the appellants have the last word and their submissions are fresh in the judge's mind as he retires to make a decision.

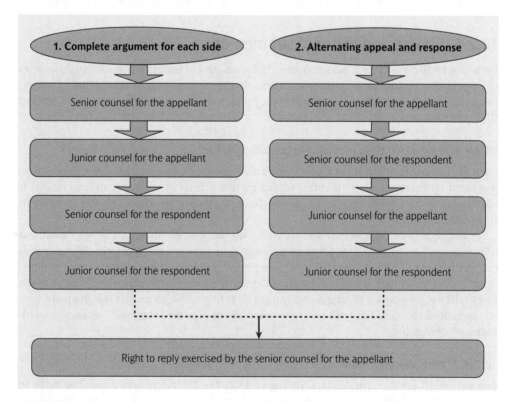

Figure 18.4 Who speaks when?

18.3 Researching the moot

Although mooting is associated with advocacy skills and the ability to 'think on one's feet', the contribution of detailed research and preparation to the quality of the speech that is delivered should not be underestimated. It is true that the best mooters are able to bluff their way past any gaps in their knowledge but the thought of being lost for words during the moot is one of the greatest concerns expressed by prospective (and more experienced) mooters and the best way to avoid it is to engage in thorough and meticulous preparation.

18.3.1 Analyze the facts

The starting point for preparation should be an analysis of the moot problem itself. It is a good idea to familiarize yourself with the facts and issues before researching the law. It is true that some mooters prefer to start by researching the legal issues on the basis that a moot concerns a point of law. However, it seems preferable to know what the problem is (the facts) before investigating the answer (the law). By familiarizing yourself with the point of appeal and the relevant facts, you will be able to undertake more purposeful and effective legal research.

18.3.2 Keep focused

Make sure that your point of appeal is at the forefront of your mind at all times to focus your research and your thinking. In the sample moot, the point of appeal for senior counsel for the appellant is simple: the advertisement is an offer. As you will see from the other examples on the Online Resource Centre, this is not always the case and some points of appeal can be several sentences long. If this is the case, then try to reword your point of appeal in the simplest terms (without losing the meaning) to avoid confusion. Some mooters like to write their issue at the top of each page of their notes to help them retain their focus whilst others note it prominently at the top of their copy of the moot problem.

18.3.3 Construct a time line

It is usually useful to construct a time line of events that led to the appeal. Some moot problems span months or even years whilst others, like the sample moot used in this chapter, involve events that occur over more condensed periods of time. Irrespective of the time frame involved, sifting through the facts of the moot and forming a chronology of significant events will help you to form a clear picture of how the situation developed and can be crucial in helping you to identify key issues (see Figure 18.5).

18.3.4 Search for relevance

Do not forget that each sentence holds information of relevance. You may not be able to work out why a particular fact is relevant at first reading. It may not become apparent until you have researched the law and given the facts further thought. If the relevance of a particular fact remains elusive, it can sometimes be illuminating to consider how the problem would be different if that fact was either altered or entirely absent.

For example, unless you had studied contract recently, you would probably not grasp the significance of the fact that Chris has only five *Racer* vans available at the discounted price.

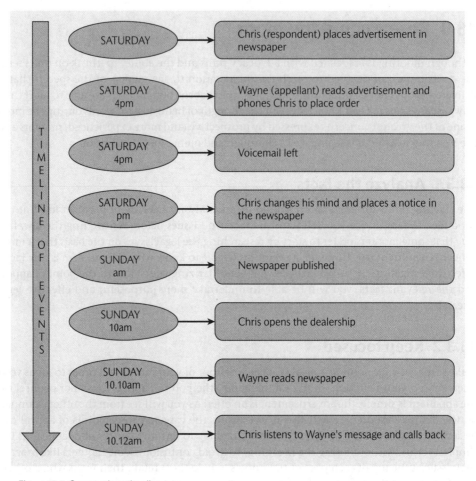

Figure 18.5 Constructing a time line

Nonetheless, you should note it as a point that you do not understand and search for its relevance when researching the law. Never ignore facts merely because you do not understand them as they may be crucial to your opponent's argument.

18.3.5 Two sides to the argument

Remember that the point of appeal has been chosen because it can be argued either way, so there are probably as many facts in the problem that support your opponent's argument as there are that support your own.

Never blind yourself to your opponent's argument. A good mooter knows the opposing argument as well as they know their own, as only if you have considered how your opponent will attack your submissions can you attempt to defend them against this. Scrutinize the facts carefully for information that supports your own stance and for facts which favour your opponent and make a note of these. For example, a preliminary evaluation of the sample moot from the stance of senior counsel for the appellant might elicit the information shown in Figure 18.6.

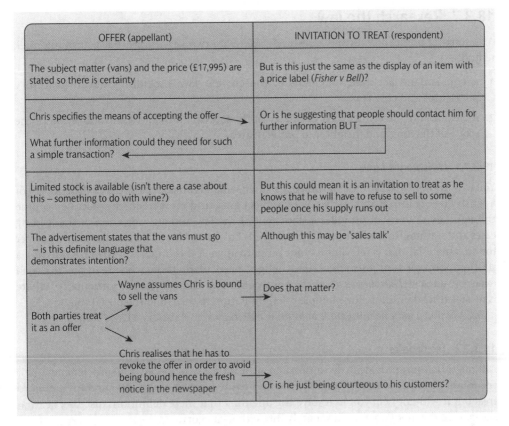

Figure 18.6 Evaluating both sides

18.3.6 Identify questions to be answered

Once you have a clear idea of the facts surrounding your point of appeal, you will probably find it relatively straightforward to make a list of questions that need to be answered. Of course, as you have not yet made a start with your research, your list of questions will probably be quite broad and general but it is still worth making a list, as this should identify the core issues and it is always much easier to research if you have a series of questions that need to be answered.

In relation to the sample moot, the following questions would probably appear on the list at this stage of the preparation process:

- What is the definition of an offer and what are its essential characteristics?
- What is the definition of an invitation to treat and what are its essential characteristics?
- Is there case law on advertisements in newspapers?
- What is the relevance of the finite quantity of items?
- If both parties behave as if the advertisement was an offer, does that help my argument?

Having analyzed the facts and formulated some questions that need to be addressed, it is time to move on to consider the research process.

18.3.7 Research the law

As a starting point for your moot research, there are two key things that you should seek to find:

1. A concise and accurate statement of the current law, including relevant statutory provisions and case law

2. A clear and relatively detailed summary of the law that provides some indication of the scope of the topic and insight into problem areas

18.3.7.1 *Halsbury's Laws*

You will find the first of these in *Halsbury's Laws*, which is an encyclopedia of the entirety of English law organized alphabetically by subject area, and most frequently accessed online through LexisLibrary. It provides a statement of the law and an indication of the leading cases and statutes from which the law is derived. This can give you an excellent early pointer towards material that is relevant to your point of appeal. It is important to make *Halsbury* a starting point for your research as many judges, particularly those who are in practice, will expect you to cite *Halsbury* as a source of any definition of key concepts, particularly if there is no statutory definition, for example offer, invitation to treat, and the postal rule.

You will find a more detailed guide to locating material using Halsbury's Laws *in chapter 8.*

18.3.7.2 Textbooks

Although *Halsbury* provides a definition and authority, it will not provide sufficient detail for the totality of the moot. For example, it will provide a definition of offer and invitation to treat but it will not help you to resolve the dilemma that these definitions disclose, i.e. that the facts of the moot do not fall squarely into either category.

Make sure that you identify and use a range of the leading 'heavyweight' textbooks; a moot judge will not be impressed if you quote from a revision guide as a source of law in the moot. Select a text which goes beyond straightforward description of the law to tackle some of its complexities—you may even find some discussion of the moot point but remember that if the textbook makes your point of appeal seem simple, you need to find a more detailed and analytical text.

Moots tend to require a great depth of knowledge about a relatively narrow aspect of the law, so it will not take you long to grasp the basics from textbooks and be ready to move on to deal with more detailed sources of information. You would also expect to find references to other pertinent materials in your textbook so you should ensure that you look at those texts that offer plentiful footnotes and references to articles and specialist works that deal with the more complex points.

You will find guidance on how to identify and locate books, journals, and official publications in chapter 8.

18.3.8 Using cases

Case law should form the bulk of your research for a moot. Starting with the core cases identified by *Halsbury* and your textbook research, you should read each case carefully, noting the points that support your point of appeal and the points that go against you. It is essential that you do not simply ignore the points that do not fit your argument, as it is likely that the judge will tackle you about this even if your opponent does not. It can be useful to use a two-column approach to organizing your notes that matches the points that favour your argument and the opposing points that favour your opponent.

There are a range of issues to take into account when dealing with case law.

18.3.8.1 Which court heard the case?

Remember the importance of the doctrine of precedent and the hierarchy of the courts. If you are in the Court of Appeal, you are likely to be bound by decisions of the Supreme Court or the House of Lords unless you are able to establish that the facts of the appeal are materially different to the case law. A decision of a lower court is of less assistance unless it is the only case that tackles the precise legal issue that is at the heart of your point of appeal.

18.3.8.2 What is the legal issue?

The legal issue is that question that needs to be resolved by application of the law. For example, in the sample moot, the legal issue is whether the advertisement is an offer or an invitation to treat. If you can find a case that deals with the same legal issue as your point of appeal, it is likely that it will be of some assistance to you in preparing your submissions, irrespective of whether the case supports or undermines your argument.

18.3.8.3 What was the *ratio* and what was merely *obiter*?

You should ensure that you have extrapolated the *ratio* from every case on which you seek to rely and on which your opponent places reliance as a routine part of your moot preparation. Remember that only the *ratio* of the case is binding whilst the remainder of the judgment—the *obiter dicta*—is merely persuasive. You should ensure that you can distinguish between the *ratio* and *obiter* statements. Part of your task as a mooter is to convince the judge that your submissions have more legal force than those of your opponent, so do not be afraid to draw the judge's attention to the fact that you are presenting a binding authority to the court (but do so respectfully).

This is something that students tend to find difficult. You will find more discussion on the distinction and tips on identifying the ratio *of a case in chapter 6, which should help you to deal with this issue.*

18.3.8.4 In what jurisdiction was the case heard?

This is important as only cases heard within your own jurisdiction—England and Wales—can be binding upon the court. This does include, however, certain decisions of the Court of Justice of the EU (see chapter 6). Cases heard in other jurisdictions, such as Scotland, Ireland, Commonwealth jurisdictions, and other Member States of the European Union, may be persuasive authority. Privy Council decisions are also persuasive as the Judicial Committee of the Privy Council is comprised of Justices of the Supreme Court.

Never overlook the value of persuasive authority in mooting. If the law in this jurisdiction seems to go against you, there is much to be gained by finding overseas authority that deals with the issue in a different way; you may be able to persuade the judge to rule in your favour, particularly if you are mooting in the Supreme Court. Be sure to draw the fact that you are relying on a persuasive authority to the attention of the judge rather than hoping that they will not notice and explain why it is useful to the appeal in hand. This will be addressed in more detail in the section later in the chapter on constructing a moot speech.

You will find a more detailed discussion of the nature of persuasive authorities in chapter 6.

18.3.8.5 Has the case been used in subsequent cases?

Not only can awareness of this alert you to additional authorities but the way in which a case is used in the future can affect its status as an authority.

You should make it a habit to check the status of each case that you encounter; it is very embarrassing (and ultimately fatal to your prospects of success in the moot) to present an argument based upon a case that has been overruled. You should, of course, extend this practice of checking to your opponent's authorities when these are revealed to you upon exchange of skeleton arguments (discussed in section 18.4.3).

This is a key part of your moot preparation so make sure that you are able to check the status of your cases effectively rather than leaving it to chance. The means by which you can find out how a case has been used since it was decided and the effect of this on its status as an authority are detailed in chapter 6.

Practical exercise

1. Use one of the methods outlined in chapter 6 to find out how *Entores* has been used in subsequent cases, for example has it been applied, distinguished, or overruled?

2. Look at the summaries of any cases that you have identified to determine whether any of those cases would be of assistance in resolving the issue at the heart of the second point of appeal in the sample moot—whether a voicemail message should be treated like a letter or a telex. It is worthwhile to get practice at checking cases in this way as it is a relatively quick and easy way of locating potentially useful resources to support your moot argument.

 Compare your findings to the answers provided on the Online Resource Centre.

18.3.8.6 Are the facts of the case similar to the facts of the moot?

The closer the factual match between the case and the moot, the more likely it is that you will be able to convince the judge that the case should be followed.

Even if the facts are not identical (and it is very unlikely that you will find an identical set of facts), look for parallels. Conversely, if the case is one that you want to avoid (because it favours your opponent's argument), you will need to point to how the cases differ in order to distinguish the case from the issue before the court.

In the sample moot, the issue is whether a message left on a voicemail system is more closely analogous to a letter (in which case the postal rule applies) or a telex[3] (the rule relating to instantaneous electronic communications displaces the postal rule). As such, you would need to think what characteristics a voicemail message shares with each of the other forms of communication.

18.3.8.7 Which series of reports should be used?

Remember to use the correct version of a case that is reported in more than one set of reports. You will find details of the hierarchy of law reports and the Practice Direction (in chapter 4) but you may find Figure 18.7 useful for ease of reference.

----

3.   The mode of communication used in *Entores*. The telex network is a switched network of printers similar to a telephone network, for the purposes of sending text-based messages. It was common at the time of *Entores* but has now mostly been superseded except in some maritime communications.

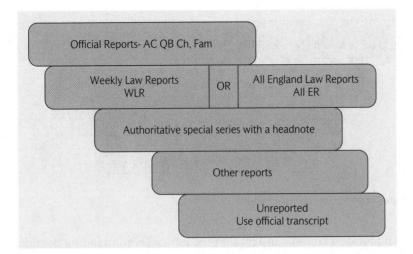

Figure 18.7 Hierarchy of law reports

It is frequently the case that mooters become so focused on the actual delivery of their speech that they forget that a whole range of other factors contribute to a thoroughly prepared and well-polished moot. Little details such as ensuring that you select the most appropriate series of reports for a particular case can go a long way to communicating an impression of professionalism and attention to detail to the judge. In the final decision as to who has won the moot, the judge can be swayed by small details like this if the parties are otherwise evenly matched: a moot can be won by a quarter of a point, so even the smallest detail can be crucial.

Practical exercise

Make sure that you are familiar with the hierarchy of law reports. It is a good idea to practise selecting the most appropriate authority so that it becomes second nature to do so.

For now, can you put these (fictitious) case citations in the correct order?

1. *R v Jones* [1999] 2 Cr App R 345

2. *R v Jones* [1999] Ch 345

3. *R v Jones* [1998] 3 WLR 1234

4. *R v Jones* [1999] 1 All ER 98

5. *R v Jones* [1998] Crim LR 42

You will find additional exercises on the Online Resource Centre which will give you further guidance on choosing the appropriate reports to use.

18.3.9 Articles

It can be useful to think of engaging in research for a moot as a staged process whereby you take a progressively deeper look at an increasingly narrow issue (see Figure 18.8).

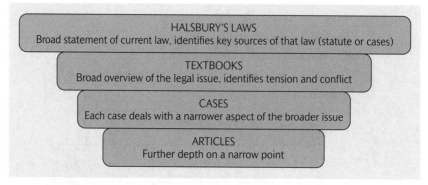

Figure 18.8 Researching a moot problem

Articles can provide a fantastic insight into the intricacies surrounding the interpretation of a particular issue or speculating on the implications of a particular case, so, in a way, can carry some of the weight of formulating your submissions for you. Articles may also provide a means to expand a particular legal principle into a new area in the absence of any case law that considers the issue. For example, the second point of appeal in the sample moot concerns whether a voicemail message should be likened to a letter or some other form of communication. It may be that you are able to find an article that looks at the law and considers how it applies to different forms of communication.

 Practical exercise

Review the methods outlined in chapter 8 for finding articles. Note that the first stage of searching concerns the selection of key words and phrases to use as search terms. What words and phrases would you use to locate articles that might provide insight into the second point of appeal in the sample moot? Using search techniques effectively is a skill that will improve with practice so have a go at finding articles on the following issues:

1. Offer and acceptance by voicemail

2. The *cy près* doctrine for charitable purposes concerning animals

3. Circumstances that render the recipient of a gift liable for theft

4. Liability for psychiatric injury caused to rescuers

 Compare your findings with the answers given on the Online Resource Centre. You will find an explanation of the search terms and methods used to locate the material. There are further practical exercises on the Online Resource Centre that will help you to become faster and more effective in locating relevant material.

18.3.9.1 Choosing an article

When relying on articles to support your submissions in a moot, you should bear in mind that the receptiveness of the judge to the article may depend either on the status of the journal in which it was published or the reputation of the author that wrote it. Obviously, you cannot predict the preferences of the judge with regard to articles and it is a sweeping generalization to say that practitioner judges (solicitors, barristers, judges) prefer practitioner publications such as the *New Law Journal* whilst academic judges (lecturers) favour 'heavy-weight' publications such as the *Modern Law Review* or the *Criminal Law Review*. Therefore, the best approach to take when choosing articles as authority is to use the one which best supports your argument. If the judge criticizes your choice of authority or asks if you are aware of a different article, try to have a reasoned explanation for your choice:

> I am aware of the shorter piece in the *New Law Journal* but the article to which I have referred Your Lordship is a more detailed analysis of the law.
>
> I have read the piece to which Your Lordship refers but the article on which I rely is a more recent consideration of the law that takes into account new case law.

Of course, it may be that there is only one publication on that particular issue, in which case you could advise the judge of this to circumvent any criticisms regarding your choice of authority:

> This is the only academic commentary on this issue, My Lord, and is therefore the only guidance on the interpretation of this case that is available.

Do try to find out something about the author of an article if you want to rely upon it to support your interpretation of the law. Clearly, an article written by a leading expert with twenty years' experience will be better received than a case note written by a PhD student (not that the latter has no value, far from it, but the former is more likely to carry weight with the judge). Nobody will expect you to have a detailed knowledge of the background of the author, but a general awareness of the level of expertise of the writer will help your case:

> This article was written by so-and-so who is a Professor in Contract Law at the University of *x* who specializes in *y* and is the author of the leading work in this area.

This is preferable to either of the following (both of which are real answers given by mooters in response to a question from the judge about the author of an article they had relied upon):

> I don't know, my lecturer told me to use it.
>
> She's my criminal law lecturer. She's sitting over there. Do you want a word with her?

18.4 Preparing to moot

Once you have conducted your research and made a note of material pertinent to your point of appeal, you will be ready to move onto the next stage of preparation which takes you from the research stage to the moment that you enter the moot room. Do not keep these stages too firmly delineated in your mind; it may be that you do not realize that there is a gap in your research until you are putting your submissions together, in which case you will have to do more investigation of the law. Equally, once you receive the skeleton argument from your opponents, you will need to conduct research to find out exactly what it is that you plan to argue.

18.4.1 Constructing submissions

A submission is a strand of argument used to advance your point of appeal. In essence, your moot speech will be comprised of a series of submissions, each one dealing with a separate legal issue. There is no 'right' number of submissions and the same point of appeal could be broken up in several different ways, all of which would be perfectly acceptable. The following examples use the first point of appeal from the sample moot by way of illustration.

18.4.1.1 A single submission

In essence, this approach takes the entirety of the point of appeal and presents it as a single point:

1. The advertisement in the newspaper was an offer

This has the merit of simplicity but it is not a particularly imaginative way to approach this point of appeal. It would be preferable if at least some information was added to substantiate this view and to make it read a little less like a straightforward 'cut' from the moot problem:

1. There is binding authority upon this court which provides that the advertisement in the newspaper must amount to an offer

This is a brave approach as it leaves the mooter with little space to manoeuvre if the judge does not accept that the authority to which he is directed is binding. A less cut-and-dried alternative might be preferable:

1. The preponderance of authority favours the construction of the advertisement in the newspaper as an offer

There is nothing wrong with making a single submission but it is worth considering whether your argument could be broken into more digestible chunks for the judge, particularly considering that the average time allocated to each mooter is around fifteen to twenty minutes.

18.4.1.2 Alternative submissions

This approach breaks your speech into chunks and avoids putting all your mooting eggs into a single basket as you are giving the judge two different ways of finding in your favour:

1. The preponderance of authority favours the construction of the advertisement in the newspaper as an offer

2. Alternatively, if this interpretation is not accepted by the courts, there are compelling policy arguments to support the construction of the advertisement as an offer

A policy argument is one which is not supported by authority (and which may actually go against authority) but which is nonetheless compelling on, for example, common sense or moral grounds. It may be the case that strict application of case law would lead to a result which seems absurd in the context of the particular facts of the moot, for example, in which case policy grounds may dictate that the letter of the law should not be followed. Policy arguments can be supported by reference to overseas authorities or academic writings as well as case law and statute.

18.4.1.3 Cumulative submissions

This approach also breaks the speech into chunks but by dividing the overall point of appeal into smaller and more manageable segments:

1. The advertisement in the newspaper was sufficiently certain in its terms to amount to an offer

2. The inclusion of a specified quantity of goods in the advertisement removed any possibility of the vendor being contracted to supply goods that were no longer in existence

3. The respondent's subsequent actions in placing notification in the newspaper that the goods were no longer available demonstrated that he intended the advertisement to be an offer which would be binding upon acceptance

It is important to remember that each submission should be a self-contained legal argument that is supported by authority as well as part of a larger legal question. For example, it is true to say that the 'big' legal question in the sample moot is whether the advertisement is an offer but this does break down into a series of subquestions that form the basis of the three submissions above, each of which has been judicially considered in its own right.

18.4.1.4 Combined submissions

As the heading suggests, this approach combines cumulative and alternative submissions:

1. The advertisement in the newspaper was sufficiently certain to amount to an offer

2. The conduct of the respondent indicated that he intended the advertisement to amount to an offer

3. Alternatively, even if the authorities do not support these submissions, there are compelling policy arguments that favour the construction of the advertisement as an offer

This approach is sometimes popular as a means of dividing the submissions that have some basis in legal authority into segments and then adding an alternative argument based upon policy as a 'back stop' if the earlier arguments are unsuccessful. This can be particularly useful if you feel that your arguments based upon legal principle are quite weak.

18.4.2 Preparing a speech

You will now be ready to turn your research and planning into a speech that can be delivered to the judge. Note from the outset that this section refers to the preparation of a speech rather than writing a speech. This is because writing out every word that you intend to address to the judge is one of the most counter-productive activities that you can do when preparing to moot.
    There are several reasons for this:

1. **Good written English and good spoken English are not the same.** If you write a speech, you will probably use the same sort of words and phrases that you do when writing an essay, but this is not the sort of language that is best used in oral presentation. Oral communication tends to make use of more straightforward words and you may find that much of a written speech does not flow easily off the tongue when spoken out loud. Take heed of the experience from the early mooting career of one of the authors[4] who wrote a speech that included the phrase 'these cases are clearly of distinguishable material facticity' to which the judge responded 'do you mean that the cases can be distinguished on the facts, counsel? If so, say so. And stop reading your essay and speak to me, preferably in words that I can understand.'

2. **If you write a speech, you will read it.** If you read your speech, it is highly likely that it will sound flat, stilted, and expressionless plus you will not be able to make eye-contact with the judge if you are reading from a sheet of paper. Moreover, if you read, you are likely to lose your place if you take your eyes away from your paper and this is likely to make you flustered and waste valuable time as you shuffle through your papers to find your place (plus, rustling papers tends to annoy most moot judges).

---

4. Emily.

3. **Your speed of delivery will be too fast.** Mooters who read from a prepared speech almost inevitably tend to do so far too quickly for their argument to be comprehensible to the listener. Remember that it takes more time to listen and to digest what you have heard, than it does to speak. Think about your lecturers. You would probably be really infuriated if any of them delivered their material at too fast a pace because it is difficult to take in what they are saying, let alone make a note of it. If you speak rather than read, you will have to think about your words and this is likely to slow your pace of delivery.

4. **Reading does not demonstrate oral presentation skills.** Reading a prepared speech precludes the mooter from exhibiting a whole section of skills that are being evaluated by the judge. Not only does reading reduce your marks in this particular moot, it deprives you of an opportunity to improve upon your oral presentation skills.

5. **A scripted presentation is inflexible.** The judge may ask you a question that raises an issue that you had planned to address later in your speech. If you are tied to your script, you will need to find that point of your speech (more paper rustling) or, if you answer the question without reference to your script, you may find that you actually repeat the same point when you encounter it later in your speech.

That is not to say that you should not take any written material into the moot. Nobody expects you to deliver a twenty-minute speech without any written notes whatsoever and you will find that most practitioners have some notes to aid their recollection of the points that they wish to make and the order in which they are to be made. The form of your notes is a matter of personal preference. Many mooters use a series of cards (always numbered in case you drop them) each of which has a key point whilst others work from a plan that contains a list of numbered points.

 You will find some examples of these approaches on the Online Resource Centre.

18.4.2.1 Remember the housekeeping

Your speech must include various issues of housekeeping such as:

- Introductions: senior counsel for the appellant introduces everyone, senior counsel for the respondent introduces himself and his junior, junior counsel introduce themselves

- Summary of the facts: senior counsel for the appellant summarizes the facts of the appeal and senior counsel for the respondent may do so if there is a discrepancy between the team's view of the facts

- Summary of submissions: all mooters must summarize their submissions at the end of their speech

- Handover to the next mooter: all mooters should pass over to the next mooter properly rather than merely stopping and sitting down

- Reminder of the desired outcome: both junior counsel should close by reminding the judge of what they would like him to do, for example 'I would invite Your Lordship to uphold the appeal and confirm the finding of the court at first instance'

18.4.2.2 Practise

It is always advisable to practise your moot speech out loud, preferably to an audience of at least one person, prior to the moot itself and to time your presentation. In the absence of an audience, you may have the means to record yourself delivering your speech; there is much to be learned from listening to an audio recording or watching a video recording of your performance. Try to overcome the natural reluctance to see yourself from a third-party perspective and instead take note of practical features: make sure that you are audible, that your pace of delivery is appropriate and that you do not fidget or wave your arms about, for example. Try really to evaluate your performance objectively. You could make a two-column list of good and bad points and then try and think of practical ways in which you could improve on the weaknesses; for example, pausing at the end of key points or looking up towards the judge more often. Then record your performance again and see if it has improved. Even if you have no means of recording yourself, practising will help you become accustomed to the sound of your own voice and make the whole experience of standing up alone and speaking a more familiar one.

18.4.3 Skeleton arguments

A skeleton argument is an outline of the submissions to be made in furtherance of the grounds of appeal that give the opposing team and the judge an indication of the nature of your case and the authorities that you intend to rely upon.

18.4.3.1 Exchange of skeletons

The rules of most competition moots require the exchange of skeleton arguments at least twenty-four hours prior to the moot whilst some national competitions will require exchange up to three days in advance. This means that you must construct a skeleton argument that outlines your submissions and authorities and provide a copy for the opposing team, usually via the Master of Moots (who will generally send a copy to the judge at this time). Even in internal competitions, an exchange of skeleton arguments or at least an exchange of authorities is usual the day before the moot.

IN THE Court of Appeal (Civil Division)

Wayne Boyer

-v-

Chris West

Senior counsel for the appellant:

The advertisement in the newspaper was an offer capable of immediate acceptance and not an invitation to treat as contended by the respondents.

1. The advertisement in the newspaper was sufficiently certain in its terms to amount to an offer capable of immediate acceptance.

Fisher v Bell [1961] 1 QB 394 (DC)
Partridge v Crittenden [1968] 1 WLR 1204 (DC)

2. The inclusion of a specified quantity of goods in the newspaper advertisement removed any possibility that vendor could be contracted to supply goods that were no longer in existence.

Grainger v Gough (Surveyor of Taxes) [1896] AC 325 (HL)

Junior counsel for the appellant:

The offer contained in the newspaper advertisement had been accepted thus a binding contract was formed prior to the purported revocation by the respondent.

1. A unilateral contract is capable of acceptance by performance. The appellant followed the stipulations of the newspaper advertisement thus a binding contract was formed between the parties.

Carlill v Carbolic Smoke Ball Company [1893] 1 QB 256 (CA)

2. Even if the contract was not formed by performance, the respondent's revocation was not effective as the principle in *Entores Ltd v Miles Far East Corporation* [1955] 2 QB 327 (CA) is not applicable to these facts.

Entores Ltd v Miles Far East Corporation [1955] 2 QB 327 (CA)

LJ Korbetis v Transgrain Shipping BV (The 'Alexia M') [2005] EWHC 1345 (QB)

Senior Counsel: Mr Dudley Smith

Junior Counsel: Miss Constance Compton

Extract 18.1 Sample skeleton argument

18.4.3.2 Dealing with the opponent's skeleton

Ideally, once you have received your opponent's skeleton argument, you will be able to spend time studying their submissions and reading their authorities in order to ensure familiarity with their argument. It is a grave mistake to neglect this stage of preparation but some mooters take the view that they will still present their own arguments irrespective of the plans of the opposition team. This is an extremely unfortunate attitude and one that can lead to difficulties. In mooting, you should aim to know the opposing arguments as well as you know your own as only then are you in a position to counter them, and studying the opposing team's skeleton should provide a real insight into their approach to the moot.

- Obtain a copy of the authorities upon which the opposing team intends to rely
- Read them carefully, noting the points that have the potential to support their argument and, more importantly, any points that are useful to your submissions
- Are the cases that they have selected good law or have they been doubted or overruled?
- Can the cases they have chosen be distinguished on their facts from the facts of the appeal?

Remember, you cannot alter the wording of your submissions as they appear on the skeleton that you have sent to your opponents, but you can modify the content of your submission to take into account any points that have arisen as a result of the exchange.

18.4.3.3 Ethical considerations

Finally, a word about ethical considerations in the preparation of the skeleton argument: ideally, it should contain:

1. A clear statement of the submissions that will be made

2. A corresponding list of the authorities that will be used to support these submissions

Some mooters are reluctant to 'give away' their arguments to the opposing team in advance and try to formulate opaque or, worse still, misleading submissions. The ultimate in unethical behaviour is to include a case, usually a long and complicated one, which the mooters have no intention of using but which is listed on the skeleton to distract and confuse the opposing team. These practices are unacceptable and will be noted by the moot judge. Remember, moots are won by meticulous preparation and persuasive delivery, not by springing surprises on the opposing team.

18.4.4 Bundles

The final point to consider in preparation to moot is the construction of a bundle. A bundle is a collection of material upon which you will be placing reliance during your submissions. In practice, this is generally:

- A copy of the moot problem
- A copy of the skeleton argument
- Copies of each of the cases used by you (if you have individual bundles) or yourself and your partner (if you have a team bundle) in the order that they appear on your skeleton argument for the first time. It is good practice to use the copies of the bound law reports that you will find in the library rather than online transcripts (this is largely because of the pagination)

18.4.4.1 Bundle or no bundle?

In most moots, the preparation of a bundle is left to the discretion of the mooters. Bear in mind that it can be quite costly to prepare a bundle as it requires a fair amount of additional photocopying, so it is only worthwhile doing this if it is going to be an advantage to you.

A good bundle that is used effectively by the mooters can be a real plus but a poorly prepared or ill-used bundle is worse than no bundle at all, so it is not advisable to prepare one unless you do it properly and remember to guide the judge around it.

18.4.4.2 Preparing the bundle

If you decide to produce a bundle, you must be prepared to make full copies of each authority that you intend to use. It is poor practice to include only segments of a case. There is no need to include copies of cases that your opponent intends to use unless you plan to refer to the case in detail yourself, for example by quoting from it, in which case it should be included in the bundle. Make sure that you remember to signpost your use of your opponent's authorities, otherwise the judge may think that you have exceeded the number of cases permitted by the rules of the moot.

You should number each page of the bundle and some mooters use numbered dividers to separate the cases so that negotiation of the bundle is easier for the judge. Although you should have the relevant passages of the authorities marked (see Practice Direction 52 as amended by the Practice Direction: Citation of Authorities (2012)) you are still expected to be able to guide the judge there, using appropriate words:

> I refer Your Lordship to the case of Fisher and Bell which was reported in the first volume of the Queen's Bench Reports in 1961 at page three hundred and ninety five. Your Lordship will find this case at Tab 3 of the bundle. I would like to direct Your Lordship to the words of Lord Chief Justice Parker on page three hundred and ninety seven of the judgment, which is at page 17 of the bundle, halfway down the page, paragraph C, sentence commencing 'In my opinion'.

Bundles should not include authorities for propositions that are not in dispute.

18.5 Delivering a moot speech

Although this can seem like the most daunting aspect of mooting, remember that you have a solid background of research and preparation to rely on. Moreover, the majority of students

SENIOR COUNSEL	JUNIOR COUNSEL
Introductions	Introductions
Senior counsel address the judge first on behalf of the appellant or respondent so are responsible for introducing the mooters and the issues to the judge.	As junior counsel follow on from their senior counsel, the main introduction will already have been made thus all that is needed is to remind the judge of your name.
Senior counsel for the appellant should introduce the appellants and the respondents whereas senior counsel for the respondents should simply introduce themselves and their junior.	Facts
	Whilst there is no need to outline the entirety of the facts of the appeal, it is always useful to remind the judge of the key issues that comprise the second point of appeal.
Facts	Conclusion
Senior counsel for the appellant should also offer the judge a summary of the facts of the appeal. Senior counsel for the respondent should only deal with the facts of the appeal if he feels that the senior counsel for the appellant has misrepresented them in some significant way.	As the last person that the judge will hear speak for either the appellant or the respondent, junior counsel must summarize the submissions of both senior and junior counsel to pull the two strands of the appeal or response together. Junior counsel should invite the judge to grant the appeal and reserve the finding of the trial judge or Court of Appeal (appellant) or dismiss the appeal and uphold the decision of the trial judge or Court of Appeal (respondent).
Conclusion	
Although the main responsibility for concluding for the appellant and respondent lies with junior counsel, senior counsel should summarize their submissions as they pass over to their junior.	

Figure 18.9 Structuring the speech

who do participate in mooting will tell you that their nerves disappear as soon as they rise to their feet and start speaking to the judge. It can help to concentrate on the first words that you will say to the judge, as you will usually find that the words flow relatively easily once you are started.

18.5.1 Introductions, submissions, and conclusion

The starting point and conclusion of your speech will differ slightly according to the role that you have taken or been allocated in the moot (see Figure 18.9).

It is also good practice for each mooter to outline their submissions to the judge at the start in order to give a clear overview of the structure and content of the speech that will follow. The following is suggested wording for the opening and closing of senior and junior counsel arguments. Remember, there is no magic to any particular form of words; these are merely examples of the approach that could be taken.

Senior counsel for the appellant has the most information to include in the opening:

If it pleases Your Lordship, my name is Mr Smith and I am senior counsel for Mr Wayne Boyer who is the appellant in this case. I am assisted by my junior counsel Miss Compton who will be addressing Your Lordship on the second point of appeal. My learned friends opposite Mr Simpson and Mr Burns appear for the respondent Mr West. Would Your Lordship benefit from hearing a summary of the facts of the case? [pause to await a response, provide a brief summary if required and move on] My Lord, I shall be addressing the first point of appeal, namely that the advertisement in the newspaper was an offer and not an invitation to treat as contended by the respondents. I shall be making three submissions in furtherance of this point of appeal, namely: [list them concisely—do not provide the same level of detail that is on the skeleton argument]. My Lord, might I proceed with my first submission?

Senior counsel's closing should be brief:

In conclusion My Lord, it is the submission of the appellant that the advertisement in the newspaper is sufficiently certain that it can amount to an offer which is capable of immediate acceptance. My learned junior will now address Your Lordship on the question as to the point in time at which the offer was accepted and a binding contract was formed. Unless I can be of further assistance to Your Lordship that concludes my submissions on the first point of appeal.

Junior counsel's opening may be equally concise:

My Lord, as you have heard, my name is Miss Compton and I shall be addressing the second point of appeal on behalf of the appellant, Mr Boyer, namely, that the offer was accepted and a binding contract formed prior to any purported revocation of the offer by Mr West. I have two submissions to make in furtherance of this argument: firstly [concise list]. May I proceed with my first submission?

The closing will be more detailed:

My Lord, you have heard from my learned senior that the authorities favour the construction of the advertisement in the newspaper as an offer and that reliance has been placed in particular on the attitude of the parties themselves towards the situation to support this conclusion. Your Lordship has also heard my submissions concerning the point in time at which the offer was accepted by Mr Boyer and irrespective of whether this is to be taken as the time that the email was sent, when it arrived or at the resumption of trading hours, all these events preceded the notification of revocation to Mr Boyer. Accordingly, I would invite Your Lordship to find in favour of the appellant by upholding the appeal and overturning the decision of the trial judge. Unless Your Lordship has any further questions, that concludes the case for the appellant.

18.5.2 Dealing with judicial interventions

It is almost inevitable that the judge will interrupt the delivery of your submissions to ask questions. This does not mean that your submissions are inaccurate or unclear; it is just part of the practice of mooting that enables the judge to test some of the core skills involved. For example, the judge will be able to ascertain how well you understand the issue at the heart of your point of appeal and the law that relates to it by asking questions and he will also be able to assess how you are able to depart from what you planned to say and then regain the flow of your argument after addressing the question. Keep in mind the following points.

18.5.2.1 Listen to the question

Too many mooters fail to listen to what the judge is asking as their mind is filled with thoughts along the lines of 'oh no, he's asking a question, I won't know the answer and then I'm going to look so stupid'. It is perfectly understandable that the prospect of answering questions might cause you to panic, particularly in the early days of your mooting career, but you cannot hope to give a good answer if you have not listened to the question.

18.5.2.2 Think before answering the question

Even if you have listened to and understood the question and know what to say, it is a good idea not to 'grab' at the question but to think carefully about how to present the answer to its best effect. Remember that it is better to pause and give a reasoned and coherent answer to the question rather than to gabble away with the first words that come into your head.

18.5.2.3 Ask for clarification

There is absolutely no point in trying to answer a question that you do not understand. Ask respectfully: 'I'm afraid that I didn't grasp Your Lordship's meaning' or 'My Lord, I would be obliged if Your Lordship could rephrase the question'. Alternatively, you could rephrase what you understand the question to be to check that this is correct before attempting to answer: 'Am I right in thinking that Your Lordship is asking whether . . .'.

18.5.2.4 Deal with the question when it is asked

The judge will sometimes ask a question about an issue or case that you are going to address at a later point in your submissions. It is not good practice to tell the judge that you will deal with this 'later' for several reasons:

- It is impolite to make the judge wait for an answer
- The question must be relevant at this point of your submission or the judge would not have asked it
- It suggests to the judge that you are wedded to a script and cannot depart from it to answer a question

If you are really convinced that answering the question now would ruin the structure of your argument, it is permissible to seek permission to deal with the question later: 'My Lord, I was planning to address this issue at a later point of my submission but, of course, if Your Lordship prefers I will deal with it now'.

18.5.2.5 Provide a clear, concise, and confident answer

Your response to questions should have the same ring of confidence as your submissions and should be relatively concise—it is poor form to keep rambling on in the hope that you will eventually hit on the answer to the question. Check that you have answered the question to the judge's satisfaction; 'Does that address Your Lordship's question?' (never 'Is that alright?'). If you are keen to avoid the possibility that the judge might ask more questions, try asking instead: 'My Lord, might I continue with my submissions?'.

18.5.2.6 Ask for assistance

Ask the judge if you need some time/assistance to answer the question. The judge may say 'no' but there is no harm in asking: 'My Lord, might I take a moment to consult my notes/

the authorities so that I am able to address your question fully?' or 'My Lord, may I consult my learned junior?' (as you may not speak to others in the moot room without seeking the permission of the judge).

18.5.2.7 Know when to give up

If you really cannot answer the question, communicate this politely to the judge, stating 'My Lord, with apologies I find that I am unable to assist you on the point, might I return to my submissions'. The judge will usually allow you to do so and will only keep you with the question if he feels that he can guide you to the answer.

 There are a series of video clips demonstrating these and other useful strategies and phrases on the Online Resource Centre.

18.5.3 Using cases

It is usual for a great deal of time to be spent during the moot on the use of cases. The general idea is that the mooter presents principles of law taken from cases and seeks to persuade the judge that they should be applied to the facts of the moot in a particular way. As such, the effective use of cases is an essential part of a polished moot performance.

18.5.3.1 Which cases can I use?

To a certain extent, this depends upon the way that the moot rules are worded. If the rules state that each team can use eight cases, then each mooter within that team can use all eight cases if they wish to do so. If, however, the rules state that each mooter may use four cases each, then you cannot rely upon the four cases used by your mooting partner. Remember that a case which is cited in the facts of the moot is a court authority which can be used in addition to the allocated number of cases. In addition to this, you may use any of the cases relied upon by your opposite number (so senior counsel for the respondent if you are senior counsel for the appellant). In addition to this, you may refer to any material whatsoever, irrespective of whether it has been included on the skeleton argument of any mooter, in response to a judicial question.

18.5.3.2 Correct citation

Just as it is important to use the appropriate series of case reports during the moot, it is also essential that you follow mooting convention when referring to a case. This is best demonstrated by way of example. You will be familiar with the way that a case citation looks on paper:

> *Fisher v Bell* [1961] 1 QB 394

If you read that citation out loud, you might say that it is Fisher versus Bell nineteen sixty-one one queue-bee three nine four. This is *not* the correct way to cite a case orally. The following rules apply:

- The '*v*' in the case name should be read as 'and' (in a civil case) or 'against' (in a criminal case) and never as 'versus' or 'vee'
- The name of the reports is said in full; they are never called by their abbreviation
- Page and volume numbers must be spoken as words and not as numbers, e.g. two hundred and fifty five rather than two five five

Following these conventions, you will be able to read the citation for *Fisher v Bell* correctly:

> I refer Your Lordship to the case of Fisher and Bell which is reported in the first volume of the Queen's Bench Reports for nineteen sixty one at page three hundred and ninety four.

You would only provide a citation for the case the first time that it is mentioned. On subsequent occasions, it is entirely proper to refer to the case as '*Fisher* and *Bell*'. If you are the respondent and the case has already been cited to the judge, you may refer to it as '*Fisher* and *Bell* as cited by my learned friend opposite'.

Just as the '*v*' in a case name is read as 'and' or 'against', the '*R*' in a criminal case is read as 'the Crown'. Therefore, a criminal case, such as *R v Caldwell* [1982] AC 341 would be read as 'the Crown against Caldwell which is reported in the Appeal Cases reports for nineteen eighty two at page three hundred and forty one'.

18.5.3.3 Summarize the facts

You should always offer the judge a summary of the facts of the case that you seek to rely upon after you have cited it to the court:

- Is Your Lordship familiar with the facts of this case?
- Would Your Lordship like to be reminded of the facts of this case?
- Would Your Lordship like a summary of the facts?

You should prepare a summary of the facts of each case that you intend to present to the court—your own authorities, any court authorities and, if you are the appellant, your opponent's authorities if it is possible that you will refer to them during your submissions as this will be the first time that they are presented to the court.

When you offer a summary of the facts to the judge, they may ask whether the facts are relevant. You need to know the answer to this question as it will become obvious if you are wrong in your answer. The judge is asking you whether you intend to draw parallels between the case cited and the appeal in order to persuade the court to reach the same conclusion or whether you intend to distinguish the facts in order to persuade the court not to follow the case. If so, then the facts are relevant. Alternatively, the facts may have no bearing whatsoever on the issue at stake in the moot but you are merely using the case as authority for a general legal principle. For example, you would cite *Ghosh* in a criminal law moot as authority for the test to be applied to establish dishonesty; you would have no interest in the facts of the case, only the legal principle.

18.5.3.4 Quoting from a case

It is usual to quote from sections of the case. In doing so, it is your job to ensure that the judge can find the passage from which you are quoting: 'I would like to draw Your Lordship's attention to the words of Lord Diplock at page 324 of the judgment [pause for the judge to find that page; watch him, he will look up or nod when he has it] at paragraph B, halfway through the paragraph, sentence beginning "there is no doubt" [again look at the judge and wait until he indicates that he has found that right place and then begin to quote]'. You would pause at the end of the quotation to denote to the judge that you have finished and then recommence your submissions, preferably by explaining how that quotation applies to the facts of the moot.

Never quote from the headnote (anything said in the headnote will also be in the main body of the judgment) or from the speeches of counsel.

CHAPTER SUMMARY

Getting started

- Make sure that you understand the roles of the different parties involved in a moot. It is a good idea to watch a moot or look at the clips in the Online Resource Centre to ensure you are clear about what happens when and how

- Analyze the moot problem carefully to ensure that you know what party you are representing, what ground of appeal you are addressing, and what the relevant facts are that make up the issue in hand

- Take care to ensure that you are familiar with the rules of the moot in relation to such matters as the number of cases that can be used and the time available for each mooter to present their submissions

Researching the moot

- Remember that you need to start with an accurate and authoritative statement of law so *Halsbury* might be a useful port of call

- Add depth to your understanding by reference to leading textbooks, articles, and cases

- Keep a strong focus on the central issue of the point of appeal and ensure that you take a balanced approach that notes rather than ignores opposing authority

- Be thoughtful in your selection of authorities and supporting material. Be prepared to justify your choice of cases to the judge if questioned

Preparing to moot

- Experiment with different structures and vary the content of your submissions until you find an approach that feels right. Your final choice of submissions should be the result of careful planning rather than being based on the first submissions that came to mind

- Prepare your submissions and note the main points on numbered cue cards. Never write a complete script or you will be tempted to read it and this is a cardinal mooting sin

- Leave yourself sufficient time to practise on several occasions before the moot, preferably in front of an audience of at least one person who will give you honest and constructive feedback on your performance. Alternatively, watching a recording of yourself can be a good way to gain insight into your performance

- Construct a clear and concise yet open and honest skeleton argument and ensure you meet the deadline for exchange

- If you decide to use a bundle, make sure that it is meticulously presented and that you are able to use it effectively, otherwise it will do you more harm than good

- Check each authority upon which you intend to place reliance to ensure that it is still good law and that you have the correct and appropriate series of law reports

Delivering the moot speech

- Try and make a confident start however nervous you may be feeling. Most people find that they forget about the presence of anyone else other than the judge once they have started to speak so it is effectively a two-person dialogue

- Take heed of courtroom etiquette at all times. In particular, make sure you address the judge appropriately as My Lord or Your Lordship and never Judge or Your Worship

- Do not stray too far from the facts of the moot. Abstract statements of law are all very well and good but your key task is to use that law to persuade the judge to find in your favour in the moot. The judge will not do this unless you explain how the law applies to the set of facts before them

- Deal with judicial interventions when asked to do so and in a confident manner. Do not be afraid to ask for clarification or time to think

- Make sure you give the judge time to find the right place in a case or in your bundle. Pause frequently and watch the judge to see if they are keeping pace with you. Do not carry on regardless and hope they catch up. There is nothing to fear in silence so stand quietly and wait until the judge looks at you as this is a sign that they are ready for you to speak

Negotiation skills

19

INTRODUCTION

The focus of this chapter is negotiation, which is a method of alternative dispute resolution that seeks to resolve the dispute without the need for litigation. This chapter will provide an introduction to the skills needed to prepare for and conduct an effective negotiation including the research process and different negotiation styles. It will also cover the sorts of problem that can arise during negotiation and outline a range of strategies that can be used to overcome them. In essence, it is a step-by-step introduction for those with no previous negotiation experience as well as a source of advice for the more experienced negotiator. The chapter will make use of a range of examples to demonstrate the skills involved in negotiation.

The role of alternative dispute resolution has increased dramatically in recent years with approximately 90 per cent of civil and family disputes settled by negotiation or mediation rather than in the courtroom. It plays a role in the lives of most legal professionals and the ability to conduct an effective negotiation that reaches a settlement which is acceptable to both parties is an important legal skill. It is increasingly common for negotiation to feature in the lives of undergraduate law students, as well as those on the LPC and BPTC, either as an extra-curricular activity or as part of the skills programme that is embedded within the curriculum. Participation in negotiation will give you a feel of how the law operates in practice as opposed to limiting your experience to 'law on paper' and it demonstrates a commitment to the development of legal skills that should strengthen your curriculum vitae.

LEARNING OUTCOMES

After studying this chapter, you will be able to:

- Appreciate the role of negotiation in professional practice and have some insight into skills necessary to conduct an effective negotiation

- Analyze a negotiation scenario and extrapolate information that provides insight into the aims and interests of the client

- Engage in preparation and planning for the negotiation which includes detailed research into the legal and factual issues

- Open the negotiation in a professional manner and establish a workable agenda of issues that need to be addressed during the negotiation

- Deal with each of the issues in an effective and ethical manner, eliciting information from the other team and asking questions to clarify areas of uncertainty

- Engage in critical reflection of the success of the negotiation and your performance in a way that enables you to use the experience as an opportunity for skills development

19.1 About negotiation

The courts are keen to encourage parties to a dispute to seek alternative means of resolution without using the ordinary civil court system wherever possible. In addition to the courts and tribunals system, there are a number of other less formal mechanisms that may be employed: arbitration, mediation, and conciliation.

In November 2008 the Master of the Rolls, Sir Anthony Clarke, commissioned a report to review the costs of civil litigation. Jackson LJ was appointed to lead the review and to examine in detail the rules and principles governing costs in civil litigation. The final report was published in January 2010 and contained a number of wide-ranging recommendations. Amongst these is the recommendation that a 'serious campaign' should be undertaken to ensure that both lawyers and judges fully understand how all forms of alternative dispute resolution (ADR) work and the benefits it can bring. Jackson suggests that a 'handbook for ADR' should be prepared for use by clients and as a training guide for lawyers and the judiciary, along with a simple and clear brochure to educate the public and small businesses about ADR. However, he does not go so far as to say that parties in dispute should be compelled to mediate.

At the heart of ADR is the desire to reach a negotiated settlement: negotiation, therefore, is the process by which (usually) two parties with an interest in the same issue seek to reach an agreement that is acceptable to both sides. This may be done directly but is frequently done via lawyers. It can take place by telephone, in writing, or by email but is usually conducted face-to-face. Distance negotiations give less opportunity to interpret and respond to visual cues but that distance can be preferable when dealing with complex or emotional issues. Many negotiations use combined methods; for example, an initial meeting at which the issues are introduced and explored, followed by an exchange of written communications and a final face-to-face negotiation to finalize the details of the agreement.

Agreement between the parties is the essence of negotiation. Without agreement, there is not settlement, unlike arbitration where a third party is able to impose an outcome on the parties, making it more akin to litigation. Mediation is more similar to negotiation except that, rather than the face-to-face oppositional process that characterizes negotiation, proceedings are controlled by a mediator who coordinates and facilitates the discussion. Although mediators are objective, they are able to introduce issues for discussion whereas parties to negotiation have direct control over which issues are discussed.

Negotiations can occur at any stage in the proceedings and can feature in most types of dispute. Even in criminal law, there is scope for negotiation prior to court proceedings as representatives of the defendant can explore the possibilities for withdrawing or altering the charges for the CPS.

In recognition of the importance of negotiation as a legal skill, there is a national negotiation competition each year which is open to teams of undergraduate and postgraduate students and is organized by the Centre for Effective Dispute Resolution.[1]

---

1. You can find out more about the negotiation competition and the work of CEDR more generally by visiting their website at <http://www.cedr.com>.

19.1.1 Types of negotiation

It is generally accepted that there are two main types of negotiation (although the terminology used to describe these categories varies) (see Figure 19.1).

19.1.1.1 Positional bargaining

This approach is best deployed in situations where the issue is purely financial, there are no other issues to take into account, and no need to preserve amicable relations between the parties.

For example:

> Mark damaged two panels of his neighbour's fence beyond repair and agrees to pay for replacements. Dawn, his neighbour, maintains that Mark should pay for the entire fence (ten panels) to be replaced as two new panels would stand out and spoil the look of the garden. She also demands top quality panels (£50 each) whilst Mark proposes to provide average quality panels (£30 each). Dawn can fit the panels herself and there are no delivery costs.

The sum payable could be calculated four different ways:

- Two panels of average quality £60
- Two panels of high quality £100
- Ten panels of average quality £300
- Ten panels of high quality £1000

This gives a range of possible negotiated outcomes as shown in Figure 19.2.

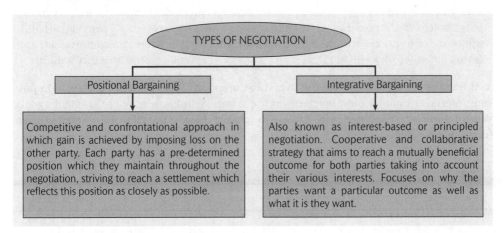

Figure 19.1 Positional and integrative bargaining

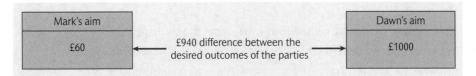

Figure 19.2 Positional bargaining

From a positional bargaining perspective, every pound gained for Dawn leaves Mark one pound worse off. This is described as a zero-sum game.

Zero-sum game describes a situation in which one party's gain is equivalent to the other party's loss. In the earlier example, if you calculate one party's gain and deduct the other party's loss, the total would be zero. It is useful to think of this in terms of sharing out a pie: the larger the slice taken by **A**, the smaller the piece remaining for **B**.

Positional bargaining is criticized for its inability to deal with non-pecuniary issues and its ineffectiveness in tackling complex negotiations involving multiple issues. Not everything can be reduced to monetary value: imagine using financial incentives to settle a dispute about access to children following marital breakdown.

It can be useful in negotiations involving a strong financial element or one in which there is a narrow issue to be resolved and where reference to broader issues would emphasize the differences between the parties.

19.1.1.2 Integrative bargaining

Integrative bargaining focuses on the interests of the parties. It focuses on the client's needs, fears, desires, and emotions in order to reach a negotiated outcome that is compatible with their goals. If you focus exclusively on *what* the client wants without any understanding of *why* they want it, you could reach an objectively reasonable settlement that wholly fails to satisfy your client's subjective interests, as this simple example illustrates:

> Tom and Jonathan are arguing over one remaining orange. Their mother, Jenny, cuts the orange in half and gives half to each child, seeing this as a perfect compromise. However, if she had asked *why* each child wanted the orange, Jenny would have discovered that each had a different assignment at school the following day that involved part of an orange: Tom needed the juice for home economics whilst Jonathan needed the peel for an art class. As such, Jenny's objectively fair solution failed to meet the subjective needs of either child whereas asking *why* they wanted the orange would have led to a different basis for division that would have given each child exactly what they wanted.

As this example shows, it is not useful to make assumptions about a client's goals or to impose your interpretation of a good outcome on the client. With knowledge of the client's goals, you will be able to negotiate more flexibly to achieve these in the face of unexpected offers from the other side.

(?) Self-test questions

Make a note of the sorts of interests that could be at stake in the following situations for each party. Remember, you need to move beyond an identification of *what* each party might want in order to discover *why* they want it.

1. A husband and wife engaged in negotiations for his access to their children following the breakdown of the marriage.

2. Negotiations for the sale of a house between the vendor and purchaser.

3. Contract negotiations undertaken on behalf of a professional golfer and a new sponsor.

4. The owner of a hotel and a carpet fitter concerning the supply and installation of new carpets.

Answers to the self-test questions can be found on the Online Resource Centre.

Even in cases which appear to be limited to negotiations of a financial nature, integrative bargaining can be a more effective approach to adopt than positional bargaining. A client whose instruction is to obtain the highest financial settlement possible may actually want money for a number of reasons. Asking *why* should provide insight into the issues motivating the client and therefore give you greater flexibility in achieving a favourable settlement.

Asking *why* may be useful even in situations that appear to be exclusively financial and may give greater flexibility and creativity in reaching a favourable settlement that fulfils the client's needs.

> David agreed to renovate Lydia's classic car by the end of March but fell behind schedule and is in breach of contract. David has completed most of the work and has purchased some expensive parts but Lydia wants her money refunded in full.

This seems straightforward but further insight is provided by enquiring into Lydia's goals. She needs the money to pay Shane who has agreed to fix the car within a week. Lydia needs the car within this time so that it can be used at her sister's wedding. Awareness of this goal gives more flexibility to negotiate with David on non-financial terms as David is able to offer Lydia a choice of three classic cars to use for her sister's wedding if she agrees to allow him to complete work on her car and keep the payment that has been made.

This should go some way to demonstrating the benefits of looking beyond the seemingly straightforward financial aspects of a dispute in order to find a more creative solution.

19.2 Negotiation skills

It is likely that you have a great many of the skills needed to negotiate already. Most people do as we learn how to make bargains from a very early age. Think of the sorts of deal that are struck between parents and children such as those shown in Figure 19.3.

Various factors will influence the success of the negotiation. For example, the child may think that a trip to the park does not justify the effort of tidying his room whilst the parent may feel that the responsibility of feeding and entertaining another child is too onerous to be repaid by washing-up.

Experience teaches us to deal with more complex negotiations in which more accurate predictions are made about factors that will act as an incentive to the other party (see Figure 19.4).

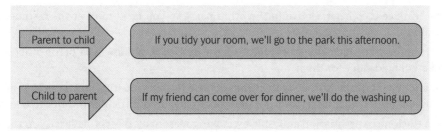

Figure 19.3 Deals between parent and child

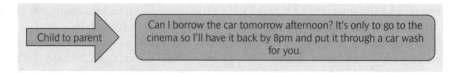

Figure 19.4 A more complex deal between parent and child

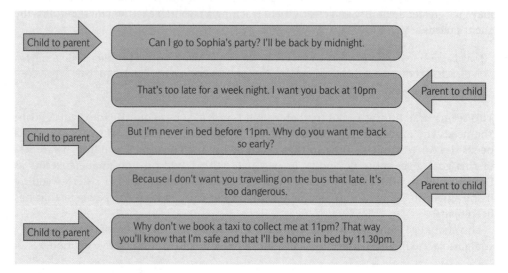

Figure 19.5 Room to manoeuvre

The child attempts to predict factors that might deter the parent from accepting the bargain and negate them in order to gain agreement (a venue not associated with alcohol consumption and an early return time). This is supported with an incentive (washing the car) that involves little effort or loss to the child but which is consistent with the notion of taking care of another's property.

We also learn the value of allowing room for manoeuvre and of asking questions to elicit information about the concerns of the other party (see Figure 19.5).

The child starts with a later return time so that she can be seen to make concessions but still stay until the desired time of 11 p.m. This gives room for movement and prevents an appearance of stubbornness. By asking questions about the parent's concerns, the child is able to make a suggestion that overcomes these fears and contributes to achieving her own objective.

From these simple examples of negotiation that have resonance with the everyday experience of many people, we can identify some key negotiation strategies:

- The deal needs to be attractive to the other party so you need to offer them something of value
- Find out (by asking questions) or predict (on the basis of your knowledge of the other party) what will hold value for them
- Enhance your offer by 'throwing in' things of little value to you (this illustrates the variable nature of 'value': what holds value for one person may be of little significance to another)
- Keep the tone of negotiation amicable by making reasonable offers that leave you room to manoeuvre

You may wonder why you need this chapter if negotiation skills are learned in childhood. The answer is that you need to be able to use the principles of negotiation in a structured and methodical way in relation to multifaceted and complex issues. Everyday negotiations between parents and children may give you some skills but do little to prepare you to negotiate access arrangements for children following divorce or multimillion pound commercial negotiations.

Overall, although it is fair to say that most individuals have some experience of the basic tools of negotiation, they are not sufficiently developed or sophisticated to deal with the complexities of conducting legal negotiations on behalf of a client. They do, however, provide a basis upon which we can build.

19.3 Preparing to negotiate

Simulated negotiations involve two teams (usually with two students in each team) who each represent one party to a legal dispute. It is usual for each team to be given a set of written facts that outline the facts of the dispute from the perspective of their client, although some negotiations may also involve a set of common facts which are distributed to both teams. In more sophisticated negotiations, the parties may have the opportunity to ask questions of their client, usually by email to a member of staff responsible for the negotiation who formulates an appropriate response. It is more usual for the facts to be limited to a written outline.

It is sometimes the case that students negotiate, having done nothing more than read though their instructions. This tends to lead to a weak performance as the team is not sufficiently familiar with the facts and has not undertaken the necessary research and preparation to reach a favourable settlement.

Rather than thinking of 'the negotiation' as solely concerned with the face-to-face discussion between the teams, it is preferable to think of it as a two-stage process (see Figure 19.6).

Although settlement is reached at the second stage, the preparatory process should be viewed as the essential foundation to conducting a negotiation and should be undertaken with diligence. The second stage simply cannot be completed with success if the first has not been undertaken thoroughly.

19.3.1 Analysis of the scenario

As the scenario is the only information that the team has as the basis of the negotiation (plus common facts if they are available), it is essential that it is subjected to careful analysis to

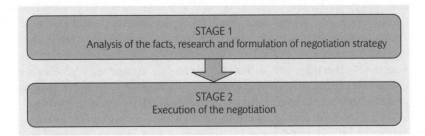

Figure 19.6 Negotiation as a two-stage process

identify the client's interests and priorities, whether explicit or implicit, and to determine what, if any, instructions limit the scope of the settlement.

Working as a team has advantages in terms of the execution of the negotiation but it is useful during the preparation too as two pairs of eyes minimize the risk that a key fact will be overlooked. It may also draw attention to ambiguities in the scenario if the team members have drawn different inferences from the same facts or reached divergent conclusions about the client's priorities.

When analyzing the scenario, make a note of the key points:

- What does the claim concern? In other words, identify the relevant area of law, e.g. contract, family law, negligence, personal injury

- What does the client want? Make a list of things that you need to achieve for your client during the negotiation, taking note of implied as well as express aims such as a quick resolution, a desire for an amicable resolution, or reluctance to litigate

- What are the client's interests? Again, these might be stated explicitly in the scenario or you may need to read between the lines. Exercise caution in doing this; remember the pitfalls of making false assumptions about the client's interest noted earlier. Identify the client's interests by working down the list of 'wants' and asking the question 'why'. For example, the client may want to avoid court action but do you know why? It may be because it is expensive or in order to avoid any negative publicity and maintain an undamaged reputation. The underlying issue is likely to have an impact on the way in which the negotiation is handled

- What, if any, limitations are there? For example, are you instructed to prioritize a particular aspect of the negotiation? Are you told that a particular outcome is unacceptable?

- What, if anything, does the scenario suggest about the issues that are important to the other party? Are there any clues that provide insight into their priorities?

- What are your strengths and weaknesses and how do you plan to deal with them in the negotiation?

> *This is an example of a scenario that might be given to one team. This negotiation will be used as the basis for many of the practical exercises in the remainder of this chapter. The facts that would be given to the opposing team can be found on the Online Resource Centre.*

Access Negotiation Scenario A:

Rhys has been married to Angharad for twelve years and they have three children: Tomas (ten), Gethin (seven) and Bethan (five). Rhys has felt that the marriage was unfulfilling for several years but stayed with Angharad because he had always had very strong Christian views and believed that marriage was a lifelong union of man and woman. Three months ago, he went on a 'Discover Yourself' course organized by his local church and, unfortunately, returned from this course with an insight into his own personality that has made it difficult for him to continue with his marriage as he realized that he would like to live life as a woman. He tried to discuss his views with Angharad but she refused to listen and Rhys became increasingly depressed. He feels that he will suffer irreparable harm if he remains married to Angharad but he wants to have an ongoing relationship with his children. Unfortunately, Angharad has told him that she will only tolerate him having any contact with the children if he 'behaves like a normal husband and father'. Rhys tried to carry on but became very depressed and was hospitalized after a suicide attempt. He realized that he cannot deny his true feelings and has investigated the possibility of gender reassignment surgery. In pursuit of this, he has started to dress as a woman and has changed his name to Rhiannon.

Rhys/Rhiannon has purchased a small house near to Angharad and the children. He says that he has been accepted by his friends and neighbours and that he has not encountered any hostility for his choice to live as a woman except from Angharad and her family. He wants this to stop. To make matters worse, Angharad has discussed matters with the children that Rhys/Rhiannon had assumed would remain personal between himself and his wife and now his older son, Tomas, has declared that he never wants to speak to his father again and his younger son, Gethin, is afraid to be in his company. Angharad says that Gethin has a panic attack if his father's name is mentioned and that she is afraid to allow him to see his father.

Rhys/Rhiannon wants regular access to his children that commences immediately. He would like them to stay with him in his new house every other weekend and for them to visit two afternoons a week after school. Rhys/Rhiannon is a freelance writer so he has no difficulty in being able to find time to care for his children. He is prepared to agree to any financial demands that Angharad makes provided he obtains an access agreement that gives him regular contact with his children. He wants Angharad to agree to stop turning the children against him and not to make any adverse comments about transgendered people in general in front of the children. Angharad has also started to attend a very traditional church that preaches that alternative lifestyles are wrong and that transgendered people will go straight to hell. He is afraid that this will alienate his children even further so he wants Angharad to stop going to this church and to return to the church that they attended together as it has more moderate views—the priest has already made it clear to Rhys/Rhiannon that he will be welcome to rejoin the congregation as a woman.

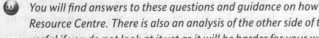

Self-test questions

Analyze the negotiation scenario provided, remembering to take into account the six points noted earlier:

1. What is the legal framework for the negotiation?
2. What does your client want?
3. What are your client's interests?
4. What boundaries are placed upon the negotiation?
5. What are the other side likely to want?
6. What are your strengths and weaknesses?

You will find answers to these questions and guidance on how they were reached on the Online Resource Centre. There is also an analysis of the other side of the negotiation but it might be useful if you do not look at it yet as it will be harder for your work on this side if you have already seen what the other party wants and how it plans to tackle the negotiation.

19.3.2 Research

Once you have a good grasp of the facts of the scenario and have identified the general area of law raised, you will be ready to engage in research.

19.3.2.1 Researching the law

Researching the legal issue should be straightforward as it should be apparent what area of law is raised by the scenario. The emphasis in negotiation is on use of the facts, so it should not be necessary to do any more than read the relevant sections in one or two textbooks to gain an appropriate grasp of the law.

It may be that your scenario raises issues that you have not covered in mainstream textbooks; for instance, there may be legal limitations on the rights of pre-operative transgendered people. If you do identify any uncommon legal issues, you will need to use some of the methods outlined in chapter 2 and chapter 5 for finding the relevant legal provision.

You must be focused in your legal research. Try to isolate particular questions that need to be answered. One of your key tasks should be to work out how the case would be decided if it went to court. This gives rise to two questions, the answers to which should help you to formulate a negotiation strategy:

1. **If this case was heard in court, would I win?** Unless the answer is an unequivocal 'yes', you have every incentive to work towards a negotiated settlement, even if this means achieving an outcome that is less than your client hoped; remember, part of something is better than all of nothing. Even if you are confident that your case would succeed in court, there are still incentives to negotiate. Litigation is costly and time-consuming and it may be that your client is unwilling to go to court. Moreover, there is more flexibility in negotiation for your client to determine the shape of the settlement that is reached to suit his or her requirements.

2. **If this case succeeded in court, what would I receive?** This should be your bottom line as there are few advantages to reaching a negotiated settlement that leaves your client with a worse outcome than that which would have been imposed by the court. You will need to take into account factors such as the cost of litigation and the likely time frame of events, so be sure to work this into your calculation. Where the dispute may involve a financial settlement, remember to take advantage of tables for calculating damages,[2] for example, in working out the likely position of your client following court action or looking for decided cases with analogous facts as a basis for comparison. You can refer to these in your negotiation, to give support to your arguments.

....

BATNA (best alternative to a negotiated agreement) is an acronym used to describe the best possible outcome that will result for your client if you do not negotiate or if the negotiation fails. This will be explored in more detail in relation to negotiation strategy but needs to be taken into account at this stage because you need to know whether your case would win or lose at court and what the outcome would be if you won in order to work out your BATNA.

....

These two questions may not be relevant if the scenario involves preliminary steps to enter into an agreement as illustrated by the example negotiation used in this chapter where the parties are hoping to seek resolution to a family dispute. If this is the case, you should research the relevant law on access to children to ensure that you cover all the necessary requirements to agree an access agreement during your negotiation.

Remember that negotiation is an agreed settlement and is not binding. This is important, whether the negotiation is aimed at resolving a dispute or if it is a facilitative negotiation, i.e. agreeing the terms of a contract. The lack of enforceability should give you cause to consider one further question that is pertinent to your legal research:

3. **What will happen if the agreement is breached?** If the negotiation is aimed at dispute resolution, the answer is usually that the injured party will either give up or the case will end up in court. Therefore, there is a real need to ensure that the settlement is genuinely

....

2.   W Norris and others, *Kemp & Kemp: Quantum of Damages* (Sweet & Maxwell 2014). Updated quarterly; also available online via Lawtel.

acceptable to both parties as this minimizes the chances of breach. If the negotiation is aimed at agreeing terms of a contract, for example, do not forget to consider the consequences of breach. Think about all the possible things that could go wrong and try to ensure that you find a way to write ways of dealing with these problems into the contract.

19.3.2.2 Researching the facts

Conducting research into other issues is less straightforward as the scenario will often involve factual issues about which you have no prior knowledge. This is a fair approximation of what will happen in legal practice. However, in simulated negotiations, unlike practice, you cannot simply ask the client for that information. In any case, you should never place too great a reliance on the facts presented by a client if they can be objectively ascertained. A client may be misguided or simply have chosen the facts that most suit their expected outcome. For example, imagine conducting a negotiation for the sale of a property based exclusively on the client's estimation of the value of the property! You would not place reliance on this and you should always ensure that facts which are objectively determinable are objectively determined. In other words, if it is possible for you to find something out for yourself, you should do so as only then will be you be confident that you are basing your negotiations on accurate and unbiased information.

It is impossible to cover all the sorts of questions that you would want to research given the infinite range of scenarios that you might encounter, so this aspect of research will be demonstrated in relation to the access negotiation.

Practical exercise

Think about the facts you would need to know in preparation for the access negotiation.

 You will find some suggestions on the Online Resource Centre along with explanations of the reasoning behind them.

It is important to research the facts as well as the law as this may disclose all manner of negotiation points that you would not have considered otherwise, particularly if you keep your client's interests in mind.

Take the facts at face value and research accordingly. For example, you know that Rhys wants Angharad to stop going to her traditional church and return to the church that they attended together before he started living as a woman. Could you suggest an alternative which proposed a different church for Angharad that she could attend without Rhys? This might temper her 'extreme' views without requiring her to be seen out with Rhys dressed as a woman. Try to be flexible and creative—what alternative ways could you suggest to achieve the client's goals without departing from the instructions given?

It is worth emphasizing that your research into factual issues must be conducted in an honest manner. For instance, please do not call a surgery and make enquiries about gender reassignment surgery; that would be simply unethical. The Internet is a wonderful repository of all sorts of information that is readily available to researchers prepared to exercise a little effort and ingenuity.[3]

---

3. See, for example, the Chartered Institute of Personnel and development introductory guidance on sex discrimination, sexual orientation, gender reassignment and employment at <http://www.cipd.co.uk/hr-resources/factsheets/sex-discrimination-sexual-orientation-gender-reassignment-employment.aspx>. This requires (free) registration to the CIPD website, which then enables access to a good range of further resources.

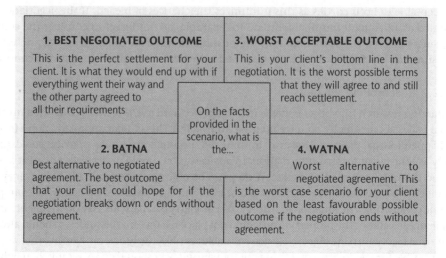

Figure 19.7 Identifying potential outcomes

19.3.3 Strategy

Formulating a research strategy is not a straightforward matter as there are a multitude of factors to take into account. Foremost amongst these is the need to evaluate the strength of your case and the various potential outcomes of the negotiation.

19.3.3.1 Identifying potential outcomes

In light of your analysis of the scenario and your research, you should be able to establish four things (see Figure 19.7).

It is essential that you establish each of these as this will enable you to calculate a strategy designed to achieve the most favourable outcome for your client.

? Self test questions

In relation to the access negotiation, calculate:

1. Best negotiated outcome.
2. BATNA.
3. Worst acceptable outcome.
4. WATNA.

Having done this, consider the strength of the client's position to negotiate? What do you consider to be the characteristics of a strong bargaining position?

 Answers to the self-test questions can be found on the Online Resource Centre.

19.3.3.2 Formulating the issues

Once you have identified the most beneficial negotiated outcome for your client, you can break this down into a series of issues that can be dealt with individually within the negotiation.

For example, in relation to the access negotiation, you may have decided that the best negotiated outcome for the client is:

- For Rhys to have immediate regular access to his children every other weekend and for two afternoons each week
- For Angharad to stop making derogatory comments about transgendered people in general and Rhys in particular
- For Angharad to stop attending her new church and return to the former marital church with Rhys

This can be broken down into three separate issues:

1. Access: how frequently and where will the access visits take place?
2. Comments: how can Rhys enforce the agreement even if Angharad concedes?
3. Church: which church will Angharad and Rhys attend?

Once you have identified the issues, you might want to decide in what order you would like to take them. There is no right or wrong answer to this but be prepared to justify your decision. For example, given that access to the children is at the heart of the negotiation, it could be beneficial to deal with it first as there is no point in agreeing the other issues if this point cannot be settled. Alternatively, given that the client needs to reach an agreement (because the BATNA is not particularly advantageous), it might be preferable to start with an issue such as financial arrangements (with which Rhys has no real issue), so the negotiation starts with the client offering something potentially advantageous to the other party.

 Practical exercise

1. Do you agree with the division of the negotiation into these three issues? Are there other issues that could be included? Could any of these issues be (a) combined or (b) divided and what are the advantages of taking this action?
2. What order would you take the points in and why? What other order did you consider and why did you reject it?

It is important that you reflect upon the reasons for your decisions. In a negotiation competition, the judge(s) will ask you why you chose a particular course of action and expect you to have a reasoned explanation for this, so it is useful to form the habit of scrutinizing your own decision-making process.

 Answers to these questions can be found on the Online Resource Centre.

19.3.3.3 Balancing the issues

Negotiations involving multiple issues can be difficult because you cannot expect to achieve your desired outcome on every issue. You need to be able to see the relationship between the issues so that you can exercise flexibility on one issue in order to gain ground on another.

There are two aspects to this process:

1. Establishing a top and bottom line of each of the issues
2. Ranking them in order of importance to the client

When you can see the boundaries of each issue and their relative importance to the client, you can start to think about trading them off against each other. You may have to make concessions on one issue in order to gain ground on another issue. This is an effective negotiation strategy, provided you always keep the 'big picture' of the client's goals in mind and you do not act contrary to any explicit instructions.

For example, the most pressing need for the client in the access negotiation is to gain regular access to his children. Therefore, although they might like to do this with twice weekly and alternate weekend visits to his home, provided a solution can be found that facilitates access, the client is likely to be satisfied. As such, you may be able to make concessions on the location of the access or the way in which Rhys dresses when he sees his children so long as Rhys actually manages to find a way to spend time with his children. This would not be a possibility if, for example, the instructions said that it was essential for the client always to be dressed as a woman when the children pay a visit.

 Self-test questions

1. Rank the issues in the access negotiation in order of importance to the client. Note that this may well differ from the order in which you decided to negotiate the issues.

2. Calculate the boundaries of each of the issues, i.e. work out the best and worst outcome on each issue to determine how much bargaining scope there is on each point.

3. Consider ways in which you could offer concessions on one issue in order to gain something beneficial for the client on one of the other issues.

 Answers to the self-test questions can be found on the Online Resource Centre.

19.3.3.4 Generating more options

The negotiation scenario does not provide detailed instructions of all the potential outcomes that are agreeable to your client. You are provided with some indication of their aims and also of their broader interests and you should have tried to anticipate what the other party will want from your client. Working within this framework, try to generate some creative ways in which the aims of both parties could be satisfied.

For example, if the issue of surgery becomes contentious, i.e. both parties are insistent that they want incompatible outcomes (Rhys wants to undergo gender reassignment surgery and Angharad wants him to remain as he is), it could be a useful way of breaking a potential deadlock to offer a delay in the date for surgery in return for supervised child access for your client, whilst agreeing that surgery can take place at a later date once the parties are more used to the unusual arrangements.

This is just one example of a creative use of the facts that could help you to reach an agreement. Remember that you are not permitted to make up facts that are not included in your scenario (and in competition will be heavily penalized for doing so) but you can make reasonable inferences from the facts provided that you are acting within the spirit of your instructions.

? Self-test questions

Go back to the access negotiation scenario and review your analysis of it. Can you think of any other creative ways in which the needs of the parties can be fulfilled that are not immediately obvious? Try to focus in particular on what your client has identified as a potential difficulty: regular contact with his children. Your client is prepared to agree to any financial demands to achieve this but will that be acceptable to the other party (remember that cutting the orange in half did not work in the example given earlier)? Assuming that both parties would ideally like incompatible outcomes, are there any other ways that this could be achieved? Think about the interests of your client and think of potential interests that could be motivating the other party; does this help to formulate creative solutions to this Solomon-esque dilemma?

 Answers to the self-test questions can be found on the Online Resource Centre.

19.3.3.5 Negotiation plan

Once all the analysis and planning is complete, you might find it useful to prepare yourself a schedule of negotiation that notes the issues that you need to discuss, the order in which you would like to address them and your best and worst outcome on each issue so that you can see quite clearly how much scope for negotiation there is on each point. This can serve as a particularly useful reminder not to move outside your instructions. This need be no more than one side of A4 and should be used as a reminder of your key issues rather than a strict schedule (you will be expected to demonstrate flexibility, so must be prepared to depart from your plan) or a crib sheet (good negotiations involve personal contact, not paper shuffling).

19.4 Conducting the negotiation

Negotiation is an inherently reflexive activity. The ability to listen and to ask appropriate questions are essential skills that contribute to a successful negotiation as they will help you to piece together a complete picture of events. A good negotiator will be able to elicit information from the other parties and incorporate this into their understanding of the situation in order to make appropriate proposals for resolution based upon the information received. It is essential that you do take the other party's interests into account as a negotiated settlement is one that suits both sides rather than one in which the stronger party forces an outcome on the weaker party.

This final section of the chapter covers some of the key components of an effective negotiation.

19.4.1 Preliminary matters

It will be tempting, particularly in a competition that involves completing the negotiation within a tight time frame, to jump straight into a discussion of the first issue but there are certain preliminary matters that will need to be completed before the negotiation proper commences. Not the least of these is reaching an agreement with the other parties as to what the first issue for consideration should be.

19.4.1.1 Introductions

It is a matter of good practice to introduce yourself and identify the party that you are representing. This need not be a lengthy business and involves little more than a handshake and a brief sentence. More important than the words themselves can be the manner in which the introductions are undertaken. First impressions are important, so think carefully about what image you want to present, both individually and as a team.

19.4.1.2 Establishing the framework for negotiation

It is useful to outline, in a couple of sentences, the factual basis of the negotiation. This should be a very basic statement of the facts that are likely to be agreed between both sides. For example:

> We have been instructed by Angharad Evans to seek to reach an agreement regarding access to her children.

In this negotiation, the name of one of the parties is actually a sensitive matter and should be treated as such in the introduction:

We have been instructed by Ms Rhiannon Evans, who you will know as Mr Rhys Evans, in order to make arrangements for child access.

19.4.1.3 Setting an agenda

As part of your preparation, you will have decided the order in which you want to negotiate the various issues. As outlined earlier in this chapter, there are various factors that might influence how you prioritize the order of your issues and decide what issue to deal with first:

- The issue that is of primary importance to the client as settlement may not be possible unless a core objective of the client is achieved
- The most complicated issue to get it out of the way, or
- The most straightforward issue so that the negotiation starts with an issue on which agreement is reached easily, as this sets a positive tone for the remainder of the negotiation

It is possible that the other side will disagree either about the issues for negotiation or about the order in which they should be addressed. This can lead to a 'negotiation within a negotiation' as the agenda itself becomes a contentious issue. This process might set the tone for the negotiation, so treat it with importance but do not fall into the trap of spending too much valuable time determining the agenda. Ultimately, provided all your issues are on the agenda, the order in which they are discussed should not make too much difference to the overall outcome. This stage can be important, however, in setting the tone of the negotiation, so it is important that you do not become too insistent about following your own agenda or allow the other party wholly to override your wishes.

The overall objective at this stage is to establish an agreed agenda.

19.4.2 Fact-finding

Eliciting information from the other team is an important aspect of negotiation. It should not be confined to the start of the negotiation but should take place throughout the discussions.

It can be a useful starting point if one of the parties commences by providing a brief summary of their client's position. Some students are reluctant to do this as they feel that it 'gives away' important information to the opposing team; try to remember that a negotiated outcome is one that suits both sides, so there is little to be gained by being reticent with information. However, that does not mean that you have to be wholly forthcoming at this stage, particularly with information that weakens your client's position.

If you decide to offer an outline, select your facts carefully. Do not overwhelm the opposing side with detail. Try to contain your outline to the material facts that provide the framework for the negotiation. If the opposing team offers an outline of their facts, try not to interrupt even if you disagree with them; after all, they are giving you information that you need to know in order to understand their position, so it is important to listen carefully and make notes of any key points.

Good negotiation involves interactive, not unidirectional, communication. This means that it is important that each side has the chance to ask questions, to seek clarification, and to add information. Ending the summary of the facts with an invitation to comment will facilitate interactive communication:

- Is there anything that you would like to add?
- Do you have any questions?

19.4.2.1 Ask questions

The most effective means of eliciting information is to ask questions. If you are unclear about something or are struggling to grasp the other party's position, you should ask questions to help you gain a better understanding. These fall into two general categories (see Figure 19.8).

Remember the importance of 'why' questions that provide insight into the motivation of the client and shed light on the 'big' aims that the client wishes to achieve. If you can elicit information about the overall objective of the other client, you will be better placed to make creative solutions which might achieve that objective.

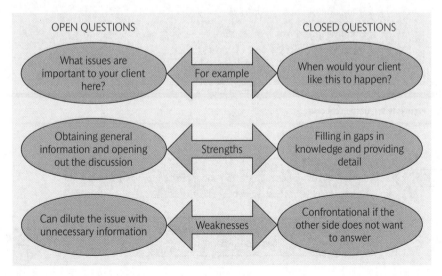

Figure 19.8 Open and closed questioning

It can be helpful if you prepare a list of information that you feel you need to know prior to the start of the negotiation and then think of the most effective types of question to ask to elicit this information. If you prepare this as a grid, you can tick off the questions that have been answered (to avoid repetition) and make a quick note of the answer as seen in Figure 19.9.

19.4.2.2 Give reasons

If you tell the other team that you do not understand or provide some other explanation of why you want to know a particular piece of information, it makes it harder for the other team to refuse to provide it.

- I don't understand why your client wants access to the children to commence immediately. Are there other factors that are important here that I need to take into account?

- You don't seem receptive to my suggestion of a significant financial payment in return for access. I thought this would be an attractive proposition so is there some reason why you feel this would not be welcomed by your client?

19.4.3　Breaking deadlock

Deadlock occurs when the parties cannot reach agreement on a particular issue and are no longer prepared to make any movement towards each other. This can occur all too easily. Imagine the following situation in Figure 19.10.

19.4.3.1　Avoiding deadlock

The most effective strategy is to avoid deadlock occurring in the first place. Try to avoid making 'make or break' demands in absolute terms. If you allow yourself no room for movement,

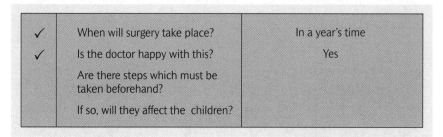

Figure 19.9 Question checklist

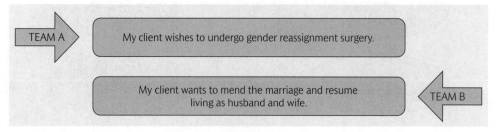

Figure 19.10 Deadlock

there is nowhere for you to go if the other side refuses to agree with your requirements. Moreover, backing the other side into a corner in which they either have to stand against you or give in entirely is confrontational and aggressive, so is viewed as bad negotiation practice. You are supposed to be reaching mutual agreement, not imposing your will on others.

19.4.3.2 Keep the negotiation moving

If you cannot settle a particular issue, it can be a good idea to move away from it and find an issue where agreement can be reached:

> It seems that we're struggling to find common ground in relation to the way in which my client dresses. Would it help to move on to consider the other arrangements for access to the children to see if this helps us to resolve the perceived gender issue?

Even if this does not resolve the disputed issue, at least it keeps the negotiation in progress and demonstrates your commitment to finding a way around deadlock.

19.4.3.3 Ask questions and offer solutions

As mentioned previously, if you can gain insight into why the other team is adopting a particular position, you may be able to find an alternative way to help them to achieve their objectives:

- Why is the choice of church so important to your client?

If the other team is not forthcoming with explanations, it might help to posit potential explanations:

- Is your client unwilling to return to the church she previously attended because she is concerned about being seen with her husband dressed as a woman? If so, perhaps we could agree that they both attend a different church in which they were not previously known?

The other team will either have to agree and confirm that your speculation was correct, in which case you can work towards resolving the problems or they will deny that this is the reason, in which case you can at least rule it out as a possibility. Whichever of these applies, you will have demonstrated your willingness to explore all the options and an inclination to reach agreement, both of which are key negotiation skills.

Be creative in the solutions that you offer but do ensure that they are within the overall spirit of your instructions. There is no point in finding a solution to the problem that your client finds unacceptable.

19.4.3.4 Highlight concessions

This is an assertive way of applying reasonable pressure to the other team to demonstrate flexibility. Although negotiation should not be aggressive, undue passivity could allow you to be pressured into accepting an agreement that is not on particularly favourable terms for your client, so do not be afraid to apply a little pressure if it seems appropriate. It is important that you do not seem unreasonable, so identifying areas where you have already made concessions can underline the fact that you have been reasonable and flexible whilst the opposing team has been inflexible:

- I understand that the issue of church attendance is important to your client but it would help us to reach agreement if you could be a little flexible here. After all, the issue of immediate access to the children was important to our client and yet we moved towards you considerably on this point by agreeing to a timetable of supervised visits

It is for this reason that it can be useful to move away from a contentious issue into more straightforward areas as settlement reached elsewhere can be a useful lever to prompt settlement once the difficult issue is revisited.

19.4.3.5 Take a break

There is provision within most negotiation competition rules for both teams to take a short break during the negotiation. This can be used effectively in a number of ways but can be a particularly useful strategy for breaking deadlock, especially if relations between the teams have become strained. It will give you the opportunity to have a private discussion with your team mate in which you can discuss how to deal with the situation. Remember to do your best to cast off any negative emotions during this period and come back into the negotiation room in an objective and professional frame of mind.

19.4.3.6 Walk away

There is no point in reaching an agreement that is unacceptable to your client, so if none of the other strategies succeeds in breaking the deadlock and the other team's requirements are outside your instructions, there is no option other than to end the negotiation without reaching agreement. If you contemplate doing this, you should cast your mind back to your BATNA and WATNA as these were the possible outcomes if no agreement could be reached. However, if you make it clear that you are contemplating ending the negotiation without agreement, the other team will also reflect about their BATNA and WATNA which might make them realize that there is room for movement after all.

19.4.4 Teamwork

One of the criteria upon which your negotiation will be judged is your ability to work effectively with the other member of your team. It would be useful to give this some thought during the planning period and consider how you are going to relate to each other in the most effective way. Factors that you might like to take into account are as follows:

- Your relative skills as communicators (assertive, conciliatory, patient, forceful, etc.) and how these can be used to best effect in the negotiation
- Distribution of workload such as allocation of issues, responsibility for note-taking, strategies for intervention if the other person is struggling, and dealing with opening and closing the negotiation
- Dealing with conflict within the negotiation. It can be useful to decide how you will respond if the other team introduces an option that you had not considered if you disagree about its value to your client. *Never* argue with each other

19.4.5 Ethical considerations

It is important that your negotiation is conducted within the parameters of professional practice, which means that you must act in an ethical manner. It is of the utmost importance that you do not misrepresent your position or otherwise mislead the other team. Not only must you not do this deliberately, you must be cautious in your choice of language to avoid any possibility that you will mislead the other team inadvertently.

It can be particularly tempting to misrepresent the upper and lower limits in relation to a financial issue, for example, in order to obtain a more favourable deal for your client. You must not do this.

Imagine that you are trying to negotiate a settlement for personal injury following an accident that the other team concedes was the fault of their client. Your client has instructed you to get 'as much as possible and certainly not less than £5,000'. If the other team suggests £6,500, you are not compelled to accept it but you cannot say 'my client would not agree to that, he would rather go to court' as this is simply not true. You need to find alternative ways of seeking to persuade the other team to increase their offer without making false representations of your instructions:

- That is towards the lower end of the usual award of damages for this type of injury. Let's not forget that your client was wholly responsible for the accident and my client has suffered a great deal of pain since this happened

19.4.6 Closing the negotiation

It is important to close the negotiation in an effective way so that everybody is clear about the terms of the agreement that has been reached. It can be useful to refer back to the agreed agenda and make a note of the outcome of each point that was listed, drawing particular reference to any issues that might require further consultation. Remember that the agreement that you have reached is subject to your client's agreement, so be sure to reflect this in your closing comments.

19.5 Post-negotiation reflection

Most negotiation competitions allocate a period of time at the end of the negotiation in which each team deliberates on their performance in the presence of the judges. This is not done in the presence of the opposing team. This stage of the negotiation gives the judges insight into the success of the negotiation from the perspective of the teams. This should include:

- Did the negotiation go according to plan? If not, what aspect of it was unexpected and could a different approach to planning and preparation prevent such an occurrence in subsequent negotiations?

- How well did the team work with each other and how well did they relate to the other team? If there were problems, what was the cause of these and were they resolved in an effective and professional manner?

- Was the outcome of the negotiation acceptable? Did the team gain a better deal for their client than they had anticipated or is the agreement that is reached disappointing? What factors might account for this?

- What were the strengths and weaknesses of the negotiation? Do not be afraid to identify weaknesses as this demonstrates to the judges that you are aware of the shortcomings of your own performance. If you are able to suggest ways that you would improve upon these areas in the future, this will satisfy the judge that you have gained something of value from participation in the negotiation

- If you conducted the negotiation again, what would you do differently and why?

It can be difficult to reach an understanding of such a practical activity from reading a chapter such as this, so you might find it useful to look at some of the examples of negotiation on the Online Resource Centre and think about the commentary that accompanies the clips.

CHAPTER SUMMARY

Planning and preparation

- Analyze the negotiation scenario to ensure that you have a clear grasp of the issues that need to be resolved

- Use the strategies outlined in this chapter to assess the strength of your position. Work out the scope of movement in relation to each issue and consider how the issues can be used in conjunction to strengthen your bargaining power

- Research the relevant law and the facts to ensure that you have a thorough grasp of the key information

- Take a holistic view of your client's aims and think of creative ways to achieve these objectives within the spirit of your instructions

Conducting the negotiation

- Make a firm professional start with clear introductions, a summary of the factual situation, and a suggested agenda. Be prepared to amend your proposed agenda to reflect the requirements of the other team

- Remember that you only know half the story, so take time to find out about the issues that concern the other team and fill in the gaps of your factual knowledge

- Elicit information by asking questions. Remember that 'why' questions give insight into the aims of the other team's client and this may enable you to propose creative solutions that facilitate agreement

- A skilled negotiator will try and work around obstacles rather than stopping when confronted with them to try to use a range of different strategies to avoid or break deadlock

- It is important to evolve a strategy that enables you to work as a team and to form an effective working relationship with the other team, irrespective of their approach to negotiation

- Ensure that you are always ethical in your dealings with the other team, taking care not to mislead them or misrepresent your position

- Conclude by outlining the proposed agreement to ensure that everyone is clear on its terms

- Critical reflection will help you to improve your negotiation skills and enable you to improve upon your performance